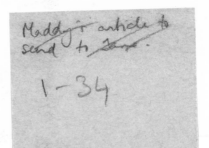

India's Islamic Traditions, 711–1750

THEMES IN INDIAN HISTORY

Oxford in India Readings

India's Islamic Traditions, 711–1750

edited by
Richard M. Eaton

OXFORD
UNIVERSITY PRESS

OXFORD
UNIVERSITY PRESS

YMCA Library Building, Jai Singh Road, New Delhi 110 001

Oxford University Press is a department of the University of Oxford. It furthers the University's objective of excellence in research, scholarship, and education by publishing worldwide in

Oxford New York

Auckland Bangkok Buenos Aires Cape Town Chennai
Dar es Salaam Delhi Hong Kong Istanbul Karachi Kolkata
Kuala Lumpur Madrid Melbourne Mexico City Mumbai Nairobi
São Paulo Shanghai Taipei Tokyo Toronto

Published in India
By Oxford University Press, New Delhi

First published 2003

ISBN 0 19 565974 0

Typeset by Inosoft Systems, New Delhi 110 092
Printed by Roopak Printers, Delhi 110 032
Published by Manzar Khan, Oxford University Press
YMCA Library Building, Jai Singh Road, New Delhi 110 001

Contents

Introduction

Richard M. Eaton

India was severely shaken in December 1992 when religious activists demolished the Babri Masjid of Ayodhya, Uttar Pradesh, built in 1528 by the first Mughal emperor. Unprecedented in recent history, this act dramatically brought late twentieth-century Indians face to face with their pre-colonial past. 'We all live today in a 1026–1528–1992 present,' wrote Shahid Amin four years after the incident, 'and not in the 1757–1885–1947 of the past.'[1] Many were stimulated to raise, or to rethink, long-dormant questions. How did South Asia become home to more Muslims than those who live in the entire Middle East? How were religion and state power related in pre-colonial times, and how did Muslims in political authority interact with non-Muslims? More fundamentally, is Islam best understood as a foreign intrusion in South Asia? Or, over the course of more than twelve centuries, had Muslims and Islamic traditions become indigenized as natural elements of India's cultural landscape? What, exactly, were those traditions, and how did they change over time, or vary from region to region within South Asia?

These are some of the questions addressed by contributors to the present volume. It is the aim of this introductory essay to assess the state of scholarship respecting Indian Islamic traditions that emerged between 711 and 1750; to chart the changing ways that scholars have thought about them, especially in the decades since 1947; and to locate the debates concerning these traditions within larger interpretive frameworks. For the study of history is a dynamic enterprise. Where pre-colonial Islamic traditions are concerned, as with any theme in India's history, historians are not only finding new ways of answering age-old questions; they are asking new ones. In the following pages of this Introduction, some of these questions are highlighted for extended discussion, namely:

a) What were 'Indian Islamic traditions', and how did they operate across time and space?
b) How and why has Islam been represented as a foreign intrusion in pre-colonial India?
c) How has the growth of Indo-Muslim communities been explained?
d) How can one explain variety and change in Indian Islamic traditions in the face of claims of a continuous tradition of 'orthodoxy'?

WHAT ARE ISLAMIC TRADITIONS?

Indian Islamic traditions in the pre-colonial period encompass an enormous range of thought, practice, artifacts, and performance. They include the letters and recorded conversations of Sufi shaikhs, the works of religious scholars (*'ulamā*), vernacular epics, romance tales, mosque inscriptions, visual arts, *qawwālī* music, commentaries on the Qur'an, historical chronicles, folk ballads, legal opinions, hymns, travel memoirs, dramatic performances, biographies of the Prophet, biographies of great shaikhs, and more. The great variety of traditions reflect in part the great variety of sects, linguistic communities, and social classes found among pre-colonial South Asian Muslims—land-holding or self-styled 'high-born' (*ashrāf*) classes claiming Arab, Turkish, or Afghan origins (Saiyids, Shaikhs, Mughals, Pathans); Sunni Muslims adhering to Hanafi and Shafi'i legal traditions; Shi'i Muslims belonging to the Twelver and Isma'ili sects; distinct ethnic communities such as the Mappilas of the Malabar coast or the Marakkayar long-distance trading community of the Coromandel coast; or in rural areas, a host of fragmented, caste-like endogamous groups (*qaum*, *barādarī*) of craftsmen, artisans, small traders, herdsmen, farmers, and service groups such as barbers, butchers, oil-pressers, or washermen. Contrary to popular belief, South Asian Muslims were far—very far—from constituting a homogeneous or monolithic community.

In spite of their variety, however, and despite the plethora of South Asian Muslim communities from which they sprang, the traditions mentioned above shared common elements. First, they were all discursive traditions, in the sense that they were rooted in written or oral genres that had sufficient historical depth to lend them the weight of authority. And they were Islamic traditions inasmuch as they all related themselves in some way to the Qur'an or the Traditions of the Prophet.[2] Thus, for example, when a writer of a compendium of Sufi biographies sat down to do his work, there would already have existed in his mind an established model of what such a work should be like, and that model would in turn have had its roots in formulations and explications of piety traceable to the foundational texts of the religion. The same was true of visual arts, such as miniature paintings or mosque architecture, inasmuch as their creators, too, had inherited models for their endeavours, though, of course, there was always room for innovation within the framework of those models.

The historical role played by pre-colonial Indian Islamic traditions becomes clear when seen in light of an apparent paradox—namely, how the Qur'an, which had been revealed to the Prophet Muhammad in Arabic, was mediated to South Asia, a non-Arabic-speaking region. In a recent study, Lamin Sanneh elaborated on what he considers a critical difference between Christianity and Islam. Christians, he argues, freely translated the Bible out of Hebrew and Greek into numerous languages, thereby allowing scripture to enter other cultures from within their own structures of language and thought. Muslims, on the other hand, prohibited the Qur'an from being translated and required that rituals like formal prayers (*ṣalāt*) be performed only in Arabic, which in Sanneh's view effectively conjoined the Islamic religion with Arab culture. As Sanneh puts it, the religion 'is implanted in other societies primarily as a matter of cultural identity', resulting in the displacement or rejection of prior cultural identity.[3]

What is striking about this position is its narrow, literal sense of 'translation'. Given that the Qur'an was never translated in its entirety into any of South Asia's vernacular languages in pre-colonial times, one might wonder how South Asians could have come to comprise a third of the world's Muslim population. Clearly, Islam was, and *had* to have been, 'translated' into India. To say this, however, requires a broader conception of translation than the sort of word-by-word rendering of Qur'anic scripture into non-Arabic languages that Sanneh has in mind. In fact, the non-translatability of the Qur'an may well have compelled Muslims to be creative—perhaps more so than they might otherwise have been—in devising ways to adapt the content of the Qur'an to Indian literary genres and modes of communication.

One finds considerable variation, for example, in the ways that scripts served as vehicles for the transmission of Islamic traditions in India. One way this was accomplished was by adapting the Arabic script, which is phonetic and hence easily portable across language barriers, to existing vernacular languages. By the tenth century this had already happened on the Iranian Plateau, where modern Persian emerged from the adaptation of the Arabic script to the base language of pre-Islamic Iran. This facilitated the influx of a vast amount of Arabic vocabulary into modern Persian, together with the direct transmission of Qur'anic ideas of prophethood, cosmology, divinity, and so forth. In India, too, from about the fourteenth century the Arabic script—by this time, the Perso-Arabic script—was gradually adapted to vernacular languages and dialects, ultimately producing Urdu literary traditions in both the Deccan and north India. As had occurred earlier in Iran, the use of the Perso-Arabic script greatly facilitated the direct transmission of Islamic terms and the ideas they carried into Indian vernacular traditions.

A second means by which concepts originally expressed in Arabic entered Indian thought streams was through the use of both Indian scripts and Indian vernacular languages. Whenever this happened, South Asians inevitably built upon, and even expanded—as in the case of the Bengali or Tamil traditions examined in this volume—notions of cosmology or divinity that were already embedded in the literary traditions of those scripts. That is, the production of 'Muslim Bengali' or 'Muslim Tamil' traditions necessarily involved a good deal of creative engagement with Hindu literary genres. Still other Indian Muslims neither adapted the Arabic script to a local vernacular nor used an existing script for their purposes, but created an altogether new script and adapted it to vernacular speech. This happened in the case of the Khojki script of Isma'ili communities of western India, also examined in this volume. In sum, South Asians of the pre-colonial period exhibited considerable ingenuity in integrating Qur'anic ideas into India's vernacular languages without actually translating the Qur'an into any one of them.

Each of these scripts served to carry, sustain, and stabilize a great variety of Islamic traditions in India. And here again, it appears that the non-translatability of the Qur'an stimulated forms of creativity that would not have been necessary—or even possible—had that text been translated directly into Indian vernaculars. Consider the tradition of interpreting scripture by writing commentaries (*tafsīr*) on the Qur'an. As Andrew Rippin writes:

> All commentaries are concerned with the process of analyzing the [Qur'an's] text in light of the 'external world', however that be defined for the individual author, with the aim of resolving any apparent conflict and making the text 'clear'.[4]

In other words, while all commentaries on the Qur'an spoke in principle to all time and to all Muslims, in practice they spoke to particular communities at particular moments, thereby helping to accommodate the Arabic Qur'an to a host of diverse human societies over time and space. This illustrates Islam's capacity to grow and evolve after the time of the Prophet, and far beyond the Arab world in which that text had been revealed.[5] Such a possibility was acknowledged by the great Spanish-Arab mystic and philosopher Ibn 'Arabi (d. 1240), who asserted that all the various meanings, or 'senses', that different commentators derived from particular Qur'anic verses were not only already known to God, but were in fact *intended* by Him.[6] Diverse interpretations of scripture were therefore more than permissible; they were inevitable.[7]

Much the same may be said of the writing of biographies of the Prophet. As in the case of commentaries, this tradition was already well-developed by the time Muslim Turks became politically dominant in India. And it, too, would be an important vehicle for the accommodation of Islamic ideals to South Asian socio-cultural realities. For example the *Nabī-Baṃśa*, composed by the sixteenth century Bengali poet Saiyid Sultan, consists of more than 22,000 rhymed couplets composed in the style of a Puranic epic, which effectively harmonized the world of Prophet Muhammad with the tropical, monsoon world of medieval Bengal. At the time of the work's composition, the Bengal delta was already saturated with literary traditions (e.g., *maṅgala-kāvya*) celebrating the region's many Śaiva, Vaishnava, and forest goddess cults, among others. Significantly, Saiyid Sultan's work sought not to displace or reject this complex religious universe, but to *connect* it with the historical, cosmological, and prophetic world of the Arabian Prophet. By commenting extensively on Vedic, Vaishnava, and Śaiva divinities, in addition to biblical figures, the *Nabī-Baṃśa* fostered the claim that Islam was the heir, not only to Judaism and Christianity, but also to the religious traditions of pre-Muslim Bengal.[8] A similar statement could be made of the *Cīṛāppurāṇam*, a seventeenth-century Tamil biography of the Prophet analysed in this volume by Vasudha Narayanan. Other kinds of Indo-Islamic traditions such as works of art and architecture, hymns, or shrine cults may be seen in the same light.

But the diversity of such traditions, not to mention the divergent interpretations found within any given tradition, does not imply disarray or religious anarchy. As suggested above, Indian Islamic traditions may be understood as discursive formations that, by possessing established and authoritative models, imposed a measure of uniformity over any individual work. Also serving to unite and hold together Islamic traditions, as William Graham argues, was a common 'sense of connectedness' that was achieved by symbolically or ritually linking believers with the revelation of the Qur'an and its historical context. Many Islamic traditions—prophetic biographies, scriptural exegesis, histories, legal discussions, craft guilds, Sufi orders—established chains of authority that linked believers across time and space to the point in human history when God revealed the

Qur'an to the Prophet Muhammad.[9] It is thus no coincidence that a common term for a Sufi order is *silsila*, meaning 'chain', in the sense of an unbroken series of intermediate links extending from the Prophet Muhammad forward in time and outward in space. Some years ago, the leader of a Sufi shrine in the Deccan presented me with a printed genealogical table (*shajara*) that named all the intermediaries, one for each generation, who had transmitted that order's spiritual authority from the Prophet Muhammad down to the present day. On the bottom of the list was a blank space to be filled in with the name of any new recruit to that order, thereby connecting that person both horizontally with a living spiritual community and vertically with previous 'links' in the chain, extending ultimately to the Prophet of Islam.[10]

In sum, the Indo-Islamic traditions that grew and flourished between 711 and 1750 served both to shape Islam to the regional cultures of South Asia and to connect Muslims in those cultures to a worldwide faith community. In this respect, of course, India was hardly unique. From the seventh century on, Muslims everywhere had been engaged in projects of cultural accommodation, appropriation, and assimilation, which had the effect of transforming what had begun as an Arab cult into what we call a world religion. In fact, the whole of Islamic history can be seen as a 'venture' consisting of the many ways that peoples living in different ages and cultures managed, without rejecting their local cultures, to incorporate into their lives a normative order as they understood it to have been revealed in the Qur'an.[11]

It is precisely this double-movement between the local cultures of South Asia and the universal norms of Islam that makes the study of Indian Islamic traditions so rewarding. Even within South Asia, one finds enormous variation of Islamic traditions not only across social class and over time, but also across space. Along South Asia's central Perso-Islamic cultural axis stretching from Lahore through Delhi to the Deccan, many Islamic traditions seem aligned with international, especially Persian, styles. In South Asian regions lying beyond that axis, on the other hand, accommodation with local styles appear more pronounced. Yet even in such regions, one repeatedly sees how traditions rooted in South Asia simultaneously connect local communities with the larger Islamic world. For example, from the outside, a mosque built in pre-colonial Malabar may not look at all like a mosque of the same period in Kashmir or Bengal; indeed, its vernacular style would have more in common with other structures in Malabar than with anything outside that region. And the same could be said of Kashmiri or Bengali mosques in terms of their rootedness in their respective regions. Yet, upon entering any of these mosques, one

Misqal Mosque, Calicut, Kerala (sixteenth century). Courtesy of Stephen F. Dale.

Atiya Mosque, Mymensingh District, Bangladesh (1609).

sees the structural similarities shared by all three regional variants: an alignment with Mecca, a niche indicating the direction of prayer, ample interior space for worshippers, a platform for the preacher, and so on. In different ways, chapters in the present volume explore such complex kinds of double-movement between the regional cultures of South Asia and the wider world of Islam.

THE QUESTION OF AN ISLAMIC INTRUSION IN INDIA

Many of the authors represented in this volume also challenge the image, found in many textbooks on pre-colonial India, of a monolithic and alien Islam colliding with an equally monolithic Hinduism, construed as indigenous, and after ca. 1000 AD, as politically suppressed. Consider the perspectives of the following recent studies. A 1995 text on religion depicts South Asian religious history as a sequence of distinct cultural 'layers', rather like the sedimentary strata successively deposited on the ocean floor. The earliest and deepest layers, building up from the 'Indus Valley' to the 'Indic (Hindu-Buddhist-Jain)', are seen as indigenous and authentically South Asian, whereas the more recent layers—the 'Indo-Islamic' and 'Indo-Anglian'—were alien and fundamentally unassimilable.[12] Indeed, from the late tenth century, remarks this writer, 'intrusions' by Muslims 'became serious threats to the independence of the subcontinent'.[13] A study of South Asian geopolitics, published in 2000, treats the period from the rise of the Islamic religion to the rise of the Mughals in subsections luridly entitled 'The Spreading Fire', 'The Submission of India', and 'Persecution and Resistance'.[14] The association of Islam with foreignness is also found in works by art historians. In a 1992 survey, we read:

> Rajput and Mughal can be equated with Hindu and Muslim, or even with indigenous and foreign: and the study of these paintings allows us to see how the two quite different cultural systems react to the same visual stimulus—to India—as well as to each other.[15]

Not only is Islam often portrayed as an alien intrusion in India; for many, religion emerged as the defining characteristic of north India's dominant ruling class from the thirteenth century on. Modern textbooks routinely characterize the advent of Persianized Turks in India as a 'Muslim conquest', and the entire period from the thirteenth to the eighteenth century as India's 'Muslim Era'. That is to say, the agent of conquest is not a people as defined by their ethnic heritage or place of origin, but rather, a religion, the Islamic religion. Moreover, the 'arrival' of this religion is repeatedly held to constitute the most cataclysmic rupture in South Asian history prior to the rise of British power in the eighteenth century. One sees how striking this formulation is by framing it against other, comparable historical encounters. For example, although sixteenth-century Spaniards justified their conquest of Mexico in religious terms, modern texts never speak of a 'Christian conquest' of America; nor is the post-1492 period ever called America's 'Christian Era'. Rather, one hears of a 'Spanish conquest' of Central and South America, and of 'European settlement' in North America. How, one might then ask, did the notion of an 'Islamic' conquest of India find such a secure hold in the historiography of South Asia?

The notion of a deep fault-line running between India's 'Islamic' and 'pre-Islamic' eras is traceable in good measure to the views of medieval Indo-Persian chroniclers, most of whom served Indo-Muslim rulers. With the significant exception of Akbar's courtier Abu'l-fazl (d. 1602), most chroniclers at least implicitly identified Islam with the fortunes of their royal patrons and assumed that India had entered history with the advent of Indo-Muslim rule.[16] Such an outlook dates from the beginning of Turkish rule in north India, owing in part to the coincidence that the Delhi Sultanate was consolidated at the very time—the early thirteenth century—that western Asia was subjected to devastating Mongol invasions. These invasions not only uprooted great numbers of Persianized Turks from their homelands in Iran and Central Asia, driving them to India where they found shelter, and often service, in the new sultanate. They also led, in 1258, to the razing of the Abbasid capital of Baghdad and the abolition of the office of the Caliphate. These acts effectively destroyed the central institutions of Islam and instilled a markedly conservative mentality among Delhi's refugee community. With the spectre of Mongol destruction vivid in their consciousness,[17] many of these traumatized refugees came to see their adopted homeland, India, as the *de facto* focus of the Islamic world.[18] Elite administrators, men of arms, and literati—non-elite or India-born Muslims would be another matter—thus habitually equated 'Muslim' sovereignty in India with Islam itself.

Contemporary Rajput, Brahman, and other Indian elites, however, saw things differently. From the eighth to the fourteenth centuries, as we know from contemporary Sanskrit sources, such elites referred to invaders or immigrants from the Iranian Plateau not by their religion, but by their linguistic identity—most typically, as Turks ('Turuṣka').[19] These findings permit dramatically new ways of conceptualizing the character of cultural encounters at the dawn of the appearance of Muslims in north India. They suggest above all that, whatever medieval Indo-Persian chroniclers might have thought, contemporary Indian elites did not regard the religious traditions of the newcomers as sufficiently alien to South Asia, or even as sufficiently remarkable, to warrant identifying those peoples as Muslims. Rather, they were conceptually accommodated as just one more ethnic group—like Gurjaras, Vangas, etc.—in an already ethnically diverse region. What impressed contemporary non-Muslim Indian sponsors of inscriptions and chronicles was not the religious identity of these 'Turuṣka' invaders or rulers, but their power and how they used it: they would be condemned as barbarian (*mleccha*) when they used their power to destroy social order, but praised and even imitated when they used it to preserve that order.[20]

If non-Muslim Indians, contemporary with the advent of Indo-Turkish rule, did not think in terms of an 'Islamic conquest', a 'Muslim era', or even of 'Muslims', how, then, did these categories become so compelling for historians in the colonial and post-colonial eras? For one thing, European Orientalist scholars in the colonial period privileged the use Indo-Persian chronicles over other kinds of pre-modern historical data, which naturally inclined them to view Islam in much the same terms as did the authors of those chronicles—as a 'foreign' intrusion in South Asia.[21] Further inclining scholars to locate 'Islam' in classical texts or chronicles was a tendency, found in much scholarly writing in Europe and America during the nineteenth and twentieth centuries, to collapse religion with culture, and to conflate both of these with civilization and even territory. In this way, human populations became understood as naturally divided into self-contained and mutually exclusive civilizational/territorial units. Reduced to checklists of enduring, ahistorical 'core' values, these civilizations were in turn construed as immutable structures, in a sense lying beyond the corrosive effects of historical process or change. Scholars invested considerable energy to classifying, demarcating, and thereby imparting substance to, the world's 'great civilizations', those to the east of Europe falling under the purview of self-styled 'Orientalists'. One need only think of the *Encyclopaedia of Islam*, a vast project which, directed from The Netherlands, sought to define, describe, and fix once and for all what its editors and authors have taken to be a bounded, self-contained entity—Islamic civilization.[22]

What is more, many theorists of the nineteenth and twentieth centuries assumed that each civilization's essential qualities were stamped on it at the moment of its birth and persisted throughout all time. Such a reductive and ahistorical approach attributed special significance to a civilization's place of origin, for only there could it be construed as truly indigenous and hence genuinely authentic.[23] Scholars accordingly focused on seventh-century Arabia to discover the 'essence' of Islam, characterized by Max Weber (d. 1920) as a 'national Arabic warrior religion'.[24] Stereotypes associating Islam conceptually with war and geographically with the Arab world would persist with remarkable tenacity, as would the quest for civilizational essences and origins.[25]

In the twentieth century, colonial efforts to dominate India by dividing its peoples into neat, religiously defined categories, and by projecting these into constitutionally distinct units, helped translate subjective schemes into objective political realities. In this atmosphere many Muslims, fearing political subordination as a minority community in an anticipated post-colonial democratic state, subscribed to M.A. Jinnah's 'two-nation theory'—that is, the notion that India's Muslims had 'always' formed a single, homogeneous socio-political community. As the ideological justification for a separate Islamic state in post-colonial South Asia, this theory represented the political incarnation of scholarly conceptions of Islam as an autonomous civilization, fundamentally separate from Indian civilizations. Finally, Muslim and Hindu reform movements launched in the late nineteenth and early twentieth centuries inclined many South Asians to read pre-colonial history through the purified filters of their own day, with some locating an idealized 'Golden Age' of Islam not in South Asia but in the Middle East between the seventh and thirteenth centuries, while others located a Hindu 'Golden Age' in ancient India.[26]

These developments would have consequences reaching far beyond 1947. During the first several decades following the Partition of British India, many nationalist-minded Indian and Pakistani historians, seeking to legitimize their new states by finding continuities with the past, consciously or subconsciously projected the 'two-nation' ideology backwards into South Asia's pre-colonial eras. In effect, they mapped onto earlier periods a vision of polarized Hindu-Muslim relations that mirrored the polarized political relations between these two new South Asian states. For example, in 1973 the Indian historian R.C. Majumdar wrote that Hindu and Muslim communities in medieval Bengal 'resembled two strong walled forts, standing side by side....'[27] And in 1962 the Pakistani historian I.H. Qureshi wrote that 'at all times the Muslims of the subcontinent were resolute in refusing to be assimilated to the local population and made conscious efforts to maintain their distinct character'.[28] True to the tradition of medieval Indo-Persian chroniclers, Qureshi's principal theme—one can even say his principal actor—was a homogenized Islam, and not a mosaic of different ethnic groups that happened to be Muslim. The first three chapters of his *The Muslim Community of the Indo-Pakistan Subcontinent (610–1947)* are entitled 'Islam Enters the

Subcontinent', 'Islam Gains a Foothold in the North-West', and 'Islam Spreads into Other Areas'.[29]

During the 1980s and 1990s, however, one notes a shift in how scholars treated Islam in pre-colonial South Asia. By this time, many had grown skeptical of the notion of bounded civilizational entities, which previous scholarly generations had taken for granted. Postmodernist schools of thought challenged the idea of all fixed and stable identities, whether political, religious, or civilizational. 'Decentredness' and 'contingency', rather than 'centredness' or 'authenticity,' became the watchwords of the 1980s and 1990s among scholars influenced by Euro-American 'cultural studies' or 'discourse analysis' movements.[30] Ironically, though, the very notions of cultural authenticity that those scholars had discarded were gaining currency among populations then reacting to the culturally corrosive aspects of globalization. Worldwide, the 1980s and 1990s saw the rise of atavistic social movements that powerfully reasserted what were considered primordial identities—e.g., the Taliban movement in Afghanistan, Serbian nationalism, Islamic fundamentalist movements in Egypt and Algeria, the Israeli settler movement in the occupied West Bank, and patriarchal, born-again Christian movements in the United States.

In India, too, a revised version of the 'two-nation theory', this time projecting a continuous and monolithic 'Hinduism' onto India's distant past, was invoked by those seeking the country's transition to a Hindu state. As this idea took hold among local elites and wider social classes, both urban and rural, the visible symbols of earlier Islamic presence in India became even more endangered. It was in this context, in 1992, that the most politically charged of such symbols, the Babri Masjid, was destroyed. As the growth of Hindu nationalism threatened the secularist foundations of the modern Indian state, many secular-minded scholars added their voices to those who had already questioned the fixity of bounded religious communities. Some, when referring to earlier periods of South Asia's cultural history, displayed a hypersensitivity to the use of the terms 'Hindu' and 'Muslim'—fraught as they are with today's communalist connotations—and explored alternative categories like 'Indic' and 'Islamicate'.[31] Coined in the 1960s by the historian Marshall Hodgson, the latter term was intended to capture a broader, more flexible, and less communal notion of culture than is conveyed by the more narrowly religious terms 'Muslim' or 'Islamic'.

But one may question the usefulness of any and all binary oppositions. What does one do, for example, with terms like 'Hammira' or 'Suratrana'? As used in Sanskrit inscriptions and vernacular literature of the thirteenth to fifteenth centuries, these terms referred respectively to powerful chieftains or sovereigns of any religion. Should one, then, consider them 'Islamicate' inasmuch as they are derived from the Arabic *amīr* ('commander', 'chieftain') and *sulṭān*? Or, are they rather 'Indic', in as much as they had become thoroughly naturalized in Indian political discourse? By resisting easy placement in any dichotomized scheme, such terms would seem to illustrate the commonplace fact that human societies are constantly taking something from 'out there' and making it their own, quite heedless of its historical origin.

That is to say, cultural processes of appropriation and assimilation seem so deeply ingrained in the human experience that they defy the attempts of later generations, when thinking about earlier eras, to make neat distinctions between foreign and indigenous, Muslim and Hindu, or, in this case, Islamicate and Indic. In recent times, Orientalist scholars, colonial administrators, religious reformers, and nationalist historians—each with their own agenda—have made strenuous efforts to establish such dichotomies and project them backwards in time. But the endeavour seems hazardous at the very least. Indeed, as noted above, early medieval evidence revealing Indians' indifference toward Muslims *as* Muslims would suggest that the question of whether Islam in India was or was not an unassimilated 'foreign intrusion' is fundamentally misplaced. Posing such a question might say more about contemporary anxieties or political agendas than about past realities.

THE QUESTION OF 'CONVERSION'

Contemporary understandings of Indo-Islamic history have been greatly influenced—and sometimes distorted—by attempts to explain the appearance of South Asia's substantial Muslim communities. Here, too, one sees how readily the past has been held hostage to contemporary agendas or conceptual categories. Let us explore three common theories of Islamic 'conversion' in India, and their underlying assumptions.[32]

The oldest theory stresses the role of military force in the diffusion of Islam in India and elsewhere. This idea attained special prominence in the late nineteenth and early twentieth centuries, during the high tide of European imperial domination over Muslims worldwide, when much Orientalist scholarship identified Islam with warfare and the warrior as Islam's 'ideal type'. But the theory is deeply flawed, as its proponents tended to confuse conversion to Islam with the extension of Turko-Iranian rule in north India after ca. 1200, a confusion originating at least in part in too literal a translation of Indo-Persian chronicles that narrated an 'Islamic' conquest of India. As Yohanan Friedmann has observed, in these accounts one frequently meets with ambiguous phrases like 'they submitted to Islam', or 'they came under submission to Islam', in which 'Islam' might mean either the religion, the state, or the army. But a contextual reading of such passages suggests that it was usually the Indo-Muslim state, and, more explicitly, its military arm, to which people were said to have submitted, not the Islamic faith.[33] Moreover, if Islamization had ever been a function of military or political force, one would expect that those areas exposed most intensively to rule by Muslim dynasties would in modern times contain the greatest number of Muslims. Yet the opposite is the case, as those regions where the most dramatic Islamization occurred, such as eastern Bengal or western Punjab, lay on the fringes of Indo-Muslim rule, where the means of coercion were necessarily weakest.

Others sought to explain Islamization in India in terms of political patronage, arguing that conversions followed the granting of non-religious favours from the ruling class, for example, relief from taxes, promotion in the bureaucracy, and so forth. It is true that, in the early fourteenth century, some Indians presented themselves as new converts to the Khalji sultans, who in turn rewarded them with robes of honour according to their rank.[34] According to nineteenth-century census reports, many landholding families of Upper India were remembered as having declared themselves Muslims in order to escape imprisonment for non-payment of revenue, or to keep ancestral lands in the family.[35] However, although this kind of explanation might help account for the relatively low incidence of Islamization in the heartland of Indo-Muslim rule—i.e., the upper Gangetic Plain and Delhi Doab—it cannot explain the massive growth that took place along the political fringe of that rule, as in Punjab or Bengal. Like the influence of the sword, political patronage would have decreased rather than increased as one moved away from the centres of that patronage.

By far the most widely-held theory of Islamization in South Asia—generated by British colonial ethnographers, elaborated by Pakistani and Bangladeshi nationals, and subscribed to by countless journalists and historians of South Asia[36]—links religious change with social improvement, and more specifically, with liberation from a Brahmanically defined social order. The theory postulates a Hindu caste system that is unchanging through time and rigidly discriminatory against its own lower orders. For centuries, it is said, members of the lower castes suffered under the crushing burden of oppressive and tyrannical high-caste Hindus, especially Brahmans. Then, when Islam 'arrived' in the Indian subcontinent, carrying its liberating message of social equality as preached (in most versions of the theory) by Sufi shaikhs, these same oppressed castes, seeking to escape the yoke of Brahmanic oppression and aware of a social equality hitherto denied them, 'converted' to Islam *en masse*.[37] By juxtaposing what is perceived as the inherent wickedness of Hindu society and the inherent justice of Islam, this theory identifies motives for conversion that are, from a Muslim (or indeed a Christian) perspective, eminently praiseworthy.

The problem, however, is that no contemporary evidence supports the theory. For example, there is no reason to believe that Islam in pre-colonial times was associated with ideas of social equality. In comparing their tradition to other Indian religions, pre-modern Muslim intellectuals wrote of Islamic monotheism as opposed to Hindu polytheism, and not of Islam's ideal of social equality as opposed to Indian notions of inequality.[38] Moreover, this theory of conversion, like the first two, is refuted by facts of geography. Owing to the uneven distribution of Brahmanic culture in ancient and early medieval India, the bulk of the indigenous peoples of eastern Bengal, western Punjab, the Northwestern Frontier region, and Baluchistan had not, at the time of their contact with Muslims, been fully integrated into a Brahman-ordered society. Yet it was precisely in these regions that the vast majority of South Asian Muslims ultimately emerged, as was indicated in the earliest reliable census returns. In short, having never been fully absorbed into a Brahman-ordered society in the first place, there was no logical way that peoples of these areas could have sought escape from an oppressive Hindu social order.

Most attempts to explain 'conversion' suffer from other, conceptual flaws. Two such flaws are found in the formulation of the seemingly simple question, 'Why did Hindus convert to Islam?' First, any notion of 'conversion' from religion 'X' to religion 'Y' presupposes a pre-existent society that is already 'X'—in the South Asian case, a society presumed already to have been Hindu. This in turn presupposes that at some time in the misty past all the peoples of 'India', however that word is construed, lay within some monolithic and seamless Hindu 'fold'. In such a formulation, conversion to Islam necessarily involved movement to a position 'outside the fold'.[39] But the problem here is that the areas that saw the most dramatic growth of Muslim populations—e.g., eastern Bengal, western Punjab, Kashmir—were economic and cultural frontier zones where Brahmanical notions of religious and social power had not yet become fully institutionalized, and where religious identity among indigenous peoples was highly diffuse, flexible, and pliable. Such regions proved ideal for the sort of religious creativity that *in retrospect* would be called 'conversion' to Islam. But from what? One could hardly speak of leaving a 'Hindu fold' when no contemporary evidence suggests that those indigenous peoples who ultimately adopted a Muslim identity were already fully Hindu before their contact with Islamic culture.

A second difficulty with the question, 'Why did Hindus convert to Islam?' is its implied assumption of an underlying *motive* for religious change. That is, as formulated in this manner, the question seems to seek a plausible reason why a potential 'convert' would choose to change his or her religion, on the assumption that such a change was necessarily a deliberate and conscious act. But the presumption of conscious intentionality on the part of such 'converts' seems rather to have been a backward projection of nineteenth- and twentieth-century notions of religious conversion, which in turn had been informed by models and terminology generated by the worldwide Protestant missionary movement. In the latter context, conversion was understood as not only conscious and deliberate, but sudden and thorough: darkness was replaced by light, error by truth. The following revivalist hymn, which comes straight out of this movement, captures the spirit of a willful, self-conscious religious actor:

> Amazing grace, how sweet the sound
> That saved a wretch like me.
> I once was lost but now am found;
> Was blind, but now can see.

In this deeply Protestant revivalist vision of religious action, the individual is construed as an autonomous and conscious actor, and therefore as someone who deliberately *chose* to convert and who had specific reasons or motives for making that choice. Even the word 'conversion', which connotes a sudden and complete rejection of one's former religious identity in exchange for a new one, has clear Protestant overtones.

Imbued with this model of religious change, early twentieth century scholars who studied the growth of Islam in South Asia perhaps unconsciously sought pre-modern Indian analogues for what nineteenth-century Christian missions had been doing in European colonies. In his influential study *The Preaching of Islam* (1896), T.W. Arnold explained the growth of Islam in India mainly in terms of the 'preaching' by Muslim 'missionaries'.[40] Not surprisingly, scholars writing in this tradition found motives for 'conversion' to Islam—e.g., a desire to escape Brahmanical oppression, or to achieve social equality—that reflected contemporary debates both within and beyond missionary circles over the dynamics of conversion to Christianity in colonial India. But the projection of this Protestant model backward into medieval or early modern eras did considerable violence to the contemporary data, which seldom indicate deliberateness or intentionality of any sort, much less specific motives for 'conversion' such as those just mentioned. Nothing in pre-colonial Indian sources suggests that there ever occurred among whole communities a conscious or dramatic 'turning-over' of religious identity. What the original evidence rather points to is a slow, almost glacial process of religious evolution that was so gradual in pace as to go largely unnoticed by either inside or outside observers.[41]

Yet another difficulty with most models of 'conversion' is that they share a vision of Islam as a monolithic and pure essence that somehow 'spread' to India, and of the Indian 'convert' as a passive recipient of a foreign creed carried to and within the subcontinent by some mediating agency. One of the principal metaphors used to capture this process, as Joya Chatterji has noted, is the botanical one of transplantation. 'Biological metaphors of insemination, implantation, and germination', Chatterji writes,

> abound in scholarly writing on conversion to Islam. Inevitably, the role of the host society is seen as passive, merely receiving the living seed which takes root, grows and struggles to survive. And where the cultural distance between the host society and Middle Eastern cultures is great, the 'soil' is deemed to be too poor to sustain a healthy tree: the Islam that grows in such soil will inevitably be a poor debased sort of faith.[42]

Reliance on such 'transplantation' metaphors also served to explain what many considered 'incomplete' Islamization among South Asian communities. For, if the young shoots arising from the transplanted seed of Islam had to struggle through India's thick religious foliage, the result would be either stunted growth or hybridization.[43] Problems associated with the notion of 'syncretism', or religious mixing, are discussed at length in this volume by Tony Stewart. Here it will suffice to note the term's generally negative connotations, which lie in the *a priori* assumption that any religion that is conceived in terms of pure essence will, if mixed with another religion, yield debased, diluted, or distorted offspring. This is perhaps why one often detects a note of disapproval in discussions of such traditions as pīr-veneration or tomb cults, as if the people practising such traditions did not understand 'true' Islam and, in their ignorance or confusion, had allowed these 'un-Islamic' influences to be carried into their devotions or beliefs.

Such condescending attitudes presume that the observer has a better understanding of the Islamic religion than the observed, an attitude adopted for example by Clifford Geertz in his classic study, *Islam Observed.* The Javanese peasantry, Geertz writes:

> absorbed Islamic concepts and practices, so far as it understood them, into the same general Southeast Asian folk religion into which it had previously

> absorbed Indian ones, locking ghosts, gods, jinns and prophets together into a strikingly contemplative, even philosophical, animism.

Geertz sees the product, which 'can properly be called syncretism', as constantly alternating between religiousness and religious-mindedness—that is, between Islam as it is and Islam as it should be—which in his view leaves Javanese Muslims 'rather thoroughly mixed up'.[44] In a similar way some observers of Islam in Bengal find contradictions between 'true Islam' and the 'Bengali reality'. Such thinking, notes Chatterji, 'has forced us for too long into the untenable position of regarding the Bengali Muslims as victims perpetually trapped in a dilemma of identity, forever torn between their (irreconcilable) Bengaliness and Muslimness.... So it is their lot to be either Muslims only in name, or else to be Bengalis only in name'.[45]

Believing that Islamization in pre-colonial South Asia had been 'incomplete', that Indian Islamic traditions were 'hybrids' and thus inevitably 'syncretic', or that South Asian Muslims were conflicted in their religious identity, many scholars would interpret colonial or post-colonial era reform movements as destined to correct, or at least try to correct, the 'distortions' of Islam in pre-colonial South Asia. That is, 'orthodoxy' would supplant 'syncretism'. But these two terms are probably the most over-used but under-theorized terms in the entire lexicon of religious studies. The idea of 'syncretism' presupposes two or more self-contained and static essences, when in fact religious systems can be neither self-contained nor static. As historical phenomena, they are necessarily porous, organic, and even chameleon-like. And 'orthodoxy', for its part, presupposes a fixed and privileged reference point within a faith community, from which position it presumes to judge others in that community. But one might wonder how it is possible to determine which of several competing segments within a given community is 'orthodox', when they all might claim to be so.

Many of these problems seem to have arisen from an earlier tradition of scholarship that viewed Indo-Muslim cultural history from the standpoint of the Arab 'heartland', understood as the natural home of an unadulterated, pure, 'orthodox' Islam. This perspective necessarily consigned India to the role of 'periphery', and hence its vast and diverse populations of Muslims as practising forms of religion that were to some degree debased or diluted. Recent scholarship, however, has adopted a more decentred perspective. Instead of viewing the Middle East as a net exporter of religious culture and South Asia as an importer—a perspective underlying the idea of the 'spread' or 'expansion' of Islam—scholars have begun exploring the ways that South Asians actively engaged with and creatively incorporated Islamic traditions into their lives and cultures, thereby making them their own. It is precisely here that one finds the historical significance of Indian Islamic traditions, which over time became indigenized as part of South Asia's cultural landscape, thereby harmonizing the truth-claims of a universal religion with the particularities of South Asian cultures.

Clearly, then, there can be no single explanation for the appearance of sizable Muslim communities across South Asia. Having emerged under very different historical circumstances, such communities, not surprisingly, exhibit great social and ethnic diversity. Nonetheless, one pattern does stand out. In the regions of the heaviest growth—e.g., eastern Bengal, western Punjab, and Kashmir—a deepening of Muslim identities in the pre-colonial period often coincided with the integration of non-agrarian communities into agrarian economies. That is, among previously non-cultivating non-Hindu groups, Islam gradually became identified as a religion of the axe and the plough, as well as a religion of 'the Book'. In this way it became perceived as a 'civilization-building' ideology. Such a connection between agrarian change and cultural change would explain why, for example, so many Muslim holymen (pīrs) of Bengal are remembered as having introduced to the delta both Islamic piety *and* the technology of rice-cultivation.[46] It also explains why biographies of local pīrs—one of several Islamic traditions that emerged in this dynamic environment—situate such men in two worlds simultaneously. On the one hand, they possess genealogies linking them with north Indian or Central Asian Sufi orders; on the other, they are invested with the charismatic authority of traditional Bengali folk-heroes, renowned for their capacity to tame the jungle and its wildlife.

THE QUESTION OF 'ORTHODOXY'

The term 'orthodoxy', mentioned in the preceding paragraphs, is found repeatedly in discussions of Indian Islamic traditions, as in the field of religious studies generally. Although no contemporary Arabic or Persian term exactly answers to the term, which is Greek for 'correct belief' (and is usually contrasted with 'heterodoxy', literally 'other belief'), many scholars have postulated the presence of an essentialized core of 'orthodox' Islamic beliefs and practices running through the whole of South Asian history. In his comprehensive *The Indian Muslims*, for example, M. Mujeeb included a chapter on 'orthodoxy and the orthodox' for each of the three historical periods in which the book is divided.[47] K.A. Nizami characterized the entire period from the thirteenth through eighteenth centuries in terms of an ongoing struggle between 'orthodoxy' and 'pantheism'. From age to age, in his view, neither position changed; only the men representing them did.[48] In as much as the notion of an essentialized core of Islamic 'orthodoxy' has greatly influenced our understanding of the historical and religious significance of all Indian Islamic traditions, where, we might ask, did it originate?

The idea of an unchanging Islamic 'orthodoxy' derives in part from Orientalist assumptions that by the close of the tenth century, Islamic beliefs and institutions had become fixed in the form of the *sharī'a*, Islamic Law.[49] By that time, in this view, the fluid, formative period of Islam had come to an end: the four schools of law acquired a definitive structure, the proper relationship between state and community was worked out, and the possibility of 'individual reasoning' (*ijtihād*) as a basis for scriptural interpretation ended. In the classic formulation, the 'gates of *ijtihād*' had swung shut. With correct belief and practice now encased in a theoretically self-contained and immutable body of law, Islamic 'orthodoxy' had, in this view, become a fixed pole-star in relation to which non-conformist belief was considered at best deviationist, and at worst heretical or subversive.[50] In short, 'orthodoxy', depending on one's perspective, was judged either negatively as slavish imitation of tradition (Ar. *taqlīd*), or positively as a God-given, universal, and unchangeable code for conduct. Either way, the idea of an unchanging orthodoxy after the tenth century induced scholars to suppose that India's Islamic traditions, which did not fully emerge until the eleventh century, were destined to uncreative repetition. As Mujeeb put it:

> We find no originality in Indian Muslim thought, except to some extent in the modern period; it began and fulfilled itself in the affirmation of the Muslim *sharī'ah* as the perfection of doctrine.[51]

More recent work, informed by greater sensitivity to forces of historical change and to the complex ways that religious institutions are embedded in socio-political structures, has questioned the notion of a static Islamic 'orthodoxy' running through South Asian history. In so doing, such work has exposed the inadequacies of entrenched scholarly dichotomies related to the orthodox/heterodox opposition, such as Great Tradition/Little Tradition, normative/popular, urban/rural, etc. For example, rather than assuming that an orthodox, normative, or urban-based Islam had simply 'spread' into medieval Kashmir, Mohammad Ishaq Khan—both in the essay reproduced in this volume and in a 1994 monograph—examines how Kashmiris wove the religion into their local traditions. This he does by focusing on indigenous mystics, the Rishis, who had retained their pre-Islamic traditions of vegetarianism, seclusion, celibacy, and ascetic rigour even after being transformed into a Sufi order in the fifteenth century. By using the Kashmiri form of the Sanskrit 'Bhagawān' to convey 'Allah', or by referring to the Prophet Muhammad as 'the first Rishi', Kashmir's most renowned Muslim mystic-poet, Shaikh Nur al-Din Rishi (d. 1442), assimilated Islamic notions of prophecy, divinity, and cosmology to 'the warm, earthy, mystic religion of the [Kashmir] Valley'.[52] By the end of the eighteenth century, the great majority of the Valley's non-Brahman population had become formally Muslim, their devotional life nourished by the cults that had formed around the tombs of departed Rishis.

But in no way did contemporary outsiders or Kashmiris themselves regard their Islamic traditions as heterodox or pantheistic. To the contrary, toward the end of the sixteenth century the Mughal court considered the Rishis, who then numbered some 2,000 persons, as Kashmir's most respectable class, as true worshippers of God, and as men devoted to social welfare.[53] Nor was Islamic piety in Kashmir split along an urban/rural dichotomy. By the eighteenth century there had appeared a body of hagiographic literature, the *Rishinamas*, which portrayed the Rishis as active farmers who conferred dignity on manual labour. Nur al-Din's own poetry had challenged the pretensions of 'high-born' castes and praised the dignity of such labour, especially agricultural labour.[54] Thus in pre-colonial Kashmir, as in Punjab and Bengal, Islam had become a powerful force in the rural landscape, an outcome quite opposed to stereotypes, common both to Orientalists and to traditional 'ulamā, characterizing proper Islam as an essentially urban phenomenon, in respect to which peasants were at best marginal.[55] For understanding Muslim society in much of rural South Asia, then, it has seemed less useful to identify 'orthodox' or 'heterodox' Islamic traditions than to explore how Islamic piety effectively merged with agrarian values in forging dynamic civilization-building ideologies.

It is often alleged that the sharī'a, being a fixed code, was for the most part never really applied, that it was too cumbersome or theoretical to be put into practice, or that it was merely the work of bookish clerics who spun elaborate theoretical models and were not centrally concerned with practice. This is the view of the sharī'a as monument rather than as a workable basis for judicial practice.[56] However, recent studies have challenged such a view, showing instead how the sharī'a at all levels was gradually reinterpreted to suit a changing world. Muzaffar Alam notes, for example, that the historian Zia al-Din Barani (d. ca. 1360), who served several sultans of Delhi, interpreted the sharī'a as requiring a king to manage the interests of Muslims only. On the other hand Nasir al-Din Tusi (d. 1274), who served a non-Muslim Mongol ruler in Iran, interpreted the sharīʻa as requiring a king to ensure the well-being of *all* the diverse groups in his kingdom, and not just the Muslims. Significantly, it was Tusi's more inclusivist vision that was inherited by the imperial Mughals. By the sixteenth century, terms for 'king' (e.g., *mālik, sulṭān, bādshāh)* had become thoroughly accommodated even in the theological literature of Mughal India, while the sharīʻa was interpreted as not only tolerating a world with kings in it, but as actually requiring such a world for the Law's proper functioning.[57]

Studies of how the sharīʻa was implemented by local qazis (judges) have found even less evidence of an immutable Law or fixed Islamic 'orthodoxy'. Prescriptions of legal handbooks were subject to considerable interpretation by local judges, so that application, which was often shaped by specific contexts or by a particular qazi's understanding of legal principles, was far from rigid or immutable.[58] The Mughal emperor Aurangzeb (r. 1658–1707), for example, ordered a comprehensive and authoritative codification of Hanafi law, the *Fatāwá-i ʻĀlamgīrī*—examined in this volume by Alan Guenther—to be used in judicial courts throughout Mughal India. But in a study of legal documents dating to Aurangzeb's reign, M.L. Bhatia found that although qazis were repeatedly directed to apply the sharīʻa in their judicial decisions, their cases were more likely decided according to local custom (*rusūm, qānūn-i ʻurfī*), while the sharīʻa pronouncements on matters such as wine-selling or usury were simply ignored.[59] Moreover, local qazis did not even hear cases in some areas theoretically covered by the sharīʻa, such as public order or land revenue. Cases in these areas were generally handled by local military or revenue officers respectively (*faujdār, ʻāmil*), and these, too, were generally settled by local custom, not Islamic law.[60]

Even more clearly than Persian or Arabic materials, pre-colonial vernacular sources suggest that religious institutions, including the office of village qazi, were implicated in local politics, thus further undermining the possibility of a monolithic Islamic 'orthodoxy' standing beyond state authority. Sumit Guha's analysis of seventeenth- and eighteenth-century Marathi records finds that in Maharashtra the office of the local qazi, together with religious institutions such as mosques, temples, and Hindu or Muslim shrines, could not operate independently of state authority. Enjoying effective monopolies over the flow of cash and/or local patronage, those who controlled such institutions would seek the local government's recognition of their status and protection from their rivals, which governing authorities would grant, generally in return for fees.[61] With qazis, mosque officials, and other religious functionaries so enmeshed in the webs of local politics, one may appreciate why it was that local custom was so likely to prevail in village courts, even though qazis might well have declared—and believed—such custom to have been in conformity with Islamic law.

What, then, if anything, remains of the notion of Islamic 'orthodoxy', and how could we relate such a notion to Indian Islamic traditions? In a thoughtful essay, Talal Asad has suggested that orthodoxy

> is not a mere body of opinion but a distinctive relationship—a relationship of power. Wherever Muslims have the power to regulate, uphold, require, or adjust *correct* practices, and to condemn, exclude, undermine, or replace *incorrect* ones, there is the domain of orthodoxy.[62]

It would be going too far, however, to suggest that orthodoxy is a function of power alone. While it had to have power on its side, it also had to appeal to aspects of the Islamic 'tradition'—that is, it had to claim and demonstrate the authority of scripture—even as that tradition was itself constantly modified in the process of being appealed to. One must also clarify what is meant by 'correct' or 'incorrect' practices. As an anthropologist concerned with how societies deal with normative ideologies, Asad argues that there is not and cannot be any fixed, essentialized orthodoxy. Being historically constituted, Islamic traditions are always subject to contestation and redefinition. That is, argument and conflict over the substance of Islamic traditions are intrinsic to, and constitutive of, those traditions. Asad therefore suggests that what scholars need to do is 'to understand the historical conditions that enable the production and maintenance of specific discursive traditions, or their transformation—and the efforts of practitioners to achieve coherence'.[63]

We need to know, in other words, why any given Islamic tradition assumed its particular form where and when it did, and why it might have taken another form in a different historical context. Why, for example, did a biography of the Prophet Muhammad, composed in sixteenth-century Bengal, adopt the format of a Bengali *maṅgala kāvya* poem, in contrast to its nineteenth-century successors? Why were Sufis of sixteenth-century Delhi, Jaunpur, and Bihar the first to pioneer a new genre of mystical romance literature in vernacular Hindavi? Why would a mosque built in one era have resembled other monuments of its region, whereas a mosque built in another era, or one built in the same era but in a different region, might have imitated foreign models? Why and how did the central teachings of Sufi shaikhs of the Naqshbandi order change as their most articulate leaders migrated from Central Asia to India? There are certainly many ways of approaching such questions. But if Islamic traditions were indeed historically constructed, then it follows that if they are to be properly understood, they cannot be detached from the specific social and historical contexts in which they are found. It would therefore be useful to identify the social classes or communities that produced and/or promoted particular Islamic traditions at particular points in Indian history, and to seek connections between changes in the traditions and the changing social groups that sustained them.

Much of the forward movement of Islamic history can be viewed in terms of the creative ferment that arose either from conflicts within Muslim communities over issues of doctrine or practice, or from encounters between Muslims and non-Muslims who lived along the frontiers of moving Muslim societies. It was in such unstable contexts that Islamic traditions were continuously defined, contested, redefined, and contested again, producing anything but the sort of static 'orthodoxy' often said to have characterized Islamic history. For example, in the eighth and ninth centuries, converts from older, Hellenized communities living in the multi-religious atmosphere of Baghdad brought Greek modes of argumentation into Muslim circles, leading to a 'rationalist' tradition in Islamic thought. The leaders of this 'Mu'tazila' movement advocated doctrines such as individual free will or the created (as opposed to eternal) Qur'an that for a while enjoyed the Caliph's support, and were hence 'orthodox'.[64] Although the movement was ultimately eclipsed by another Caliph and another 'orthodoxy', this historical and intellectual encounter would never be forgotten.[65] Later, with the decline of Caliphal authority, 'correct belief' was no longer defined by rulers or upheld in formal tribunals (as was the case in medieval Europe), but rather emerged from competitive struggles (Ar. sing. *fitna*) among socially prominent groups. Thus in thirteenth- and fourteenth-century Damascus, powerful households played out their mutual rivalries by backing the scholarly advocates of different schools of law who struggled over the correctness of such doctrinal issues as the created character of the Qur'an, the visitation of tombs, or the divine attributes. 'The contest over correct belief', writes Michael Chamberlain, 'was one of the premier forms of social combat in the city'.[66]

One sees evidence of such 'creative conflict' not only in early Islamic history, but more particularly as Muslims moved beyond the Arab world and encountered non-Muslims in Iran, Sind, or Malabar, or as Persian-speaking Muslims encountered non-Muslim Turks in Central Asia, or later, as Muslim Turks encountered non-Muslim peoples of Punjab and the Gangetic Plain. Most of these encounters led to the revision of earlier traditions in light of the new environments in which such revisions were produced, even though their authors typically considered them to be in perfect conformity with earlier traditions, and hence, with the Qur'an itself. In this way new 'orthodoxies' emerged, as the communities, classes, or households supporting such revised traditions rose and fell in relative socio-cultural power.

Consider, for example, the rise of the Safavi order of Sufis in late fifteenth-century northwestern Iran. At the time, this was a volatile frontier zone between Muslims and Christians, where military power rested with newly-converted, semi-literate Turkoman pastoral tribes under the leadership of charismatic Safavi shaikhs. In this fluid social context Shi'i Muslim doctrines, which had themselves evolved out of earlier conflicts within the Arab Muslim community, were considerably elaborated. Mobilizing their Turkoman followers for war against nearby Christian communities, and later against Ottoman Sunni armies, Safavi shaikhs presented themselves as living embodiments of the *imām*, that is, the quasi-divine leader of Shi'i Muslims. In poems composed in the dialect of his Turkoman followers, Shaikh Isma'il's Safavi (d. 1524) went still further and projected himself as a millennial saviour figure.[67] Such doctrinal claims were 'orthodox' so long as Isma'il's tribal followers formed the basis for the movement, which proved sufficiently powerful to launch one of Iran's most brilliant dynasties, the Safavids (1501–1722). But in the early sixteenth century, when the new dynasty settled into the everyday business of running a civilian government, learned and conservative Shi'i scholars were imported from Iraq and Lebanon to lend the regime their administrative expertise, which entirely altered the regime's social base, and hence, too, its understanding of religious 'orthodoxy'. In this new context, the more radical components of Isma'il's theology were softened and ultimately replaced by a conservative, less millennial ideology more suitable for purposes of maintaining imperial stability.

As the frontier of Muslim societies moved further east into South Asia, so too did the conditions for the rise of new dominant social classes, which in turn promoted newer revisions of earlier Islamic traditions. In much of thirteenth-century north India, for example, Islam was associated with the ruling ethos of Turkish conquerors, and the earliest Islamic traditions from this period, such as historical chronicles or Sufi literature of the Chishti order, reflect this ethos. But in the fifteenth and sixteenth centuries, when the authority of the Delhi Sultanate was resisted by local landed chiefs—as also occurred in the eighteenth century in an age of Mughal decline—imperial visions of Islam were replaced by more localized perceptions, which might explain the emergence in these periods of regionally based hagiographies pitting local Sufis against Hindu yogis in competitive 'spiritual combat'.[68]

With the assertion of imperial authority under the Mughals, immigrants from the Iranian Plateau styling themselves *ashrāf*, or 'high-born', acquired social prominence as administrators, soldiers, mystics, and scholars. For them, Islamic piety was mediated by the rich tradition of Persian art and literature that appeared in the sixteenth and seventeenth centuries. But the further Mughal authority extended from Delhi, the more Islamic piety was shaped by regional forces. Traditions from the Punjab, for example, bear the proud stamp of socially and politically powerful Jat clans. In Bengal, Kashmir, and much of the Punjab, the socially dominant carriers of Islam were peasant cultivators whose own traditions—hagiographies, genealogies, epic literatures—reveal such cultivators as the true vectors for social and ecological change in these regions. Further to the south, Islamic traditions in pre-colonial Malabar and Tamilnadu reflected the values of long-distance merchants linked to larger Indian Ocean commercial networks, or of 'warrior martyr pirs' who were rooted in a cultural landscape saturated with cults devoted to fierce goddesses and blood-stained warrior-heroes.[69]

The growth of such a diverse variety of Indian Islamic traditions across many centuries reflects both the dynamism of Islam and the fluidity of Indo-Islamic identities. In this way, these traditions refute arguments that Islam had largely ceased to evolve beyond its formative years in the Arab Middle East. They also challenge obsolete stereotypes of medieval Indo-Muslim actors—e.g., the peace-loving, liberal-minded Sufi; the temple-smashing sultan; the doctrinaire, rigid religious scholar; or the fanatic warrior. Perhaps most importantly, the traditions examined in this volume reflect a remarkable double-movement. On the one hand, one clearly sees their interaction with, and embeddedness within, particular sub-cultures of South Asia, such that by the end of our period Islam had become as Indian as any other religious tradition of the subcontinent. Yet at the same time one sees their connectedness with a worldwide religious community, such that Indo-Muslim culture emerged in this period as authentically Islamic as anything to be found in the Middle East.

NOTES

1. Shahid Amin, 'A Balding Nation-State', *Biblio* (March, 1996), p. 8. As William Faulkner observed, writing in a different context (in *Absalom, Absalom!*), 'the past isn't dead; it isn't even past'.

2. For a useful discussion of the matter, see Talal Asad, *The Idea of an Anthropology of Islam*, Occasional Papers Series (Washington, DC: Center for Contemporary Arab Studies, Georgetown University, 1986), pp. 14–17.

3. Lamin Sanneh, *Translating the Message: the Missionary Impact on Culture* (Maryknoll, NY: Orbis books, 1989), p. 29.

4. Andrew Rippin, 'Tafsir', *Encyclopaedia of Islam*, new edn., vol. 10, fasc. 163–4, p. 84.

5. Writes Imtiyaz Yusuf, who has studied the assimilation of Islam in East Africa's Swahili culture, '*Tafsīr* seeks to convey the meaning of the Qur'an to an Arabic or non-Arabic audience. The task entails not only explaining the Arabic meaning but also making an alien religion comprehensible to the local perspective with which it has no historical or doctrinal affinity'. Imtiyaz Yusuf, 'An Analysis of Swahili Exegesis of *Surat al-Shams* in Shaykh Abdullah Saleh al-Farsy's *Qurani Takatifu*', *Journal of Religion in Africa* 22, no. 4 (1992), p. 356.

6. 'We say concerning the senses of a verse that all are intended by God.... The verse of God's speech, of whatever sort it may be—Koran, revealed book, scripture, divine report—is a sign or a mark signifying what the words (*lafẓ*) support in all senses and intended by the One who sent down His Speech in those words.... Hence, when someone understands a sense from a verse, that sense is intended by God in this verse in the case of the person who finds it.' Ibn 'Arabi, *Futūḥāt al-makkiya* (Cairo, 1972), ch. 266: II 567.19, in William C. Chittick [tr.], *The Sufi Path of Knowledge: Ibn al-'Arabi's Metaphysics of Imagination* (Albany: State University of New York Press, 1989), p. 244.

7. 'The attempt to understand the Qur'an', notes Wilfred Cantwell Smith, 'is to understand how it has fired the imagination, and inspired the poetry, and formulated the inhibitions, and guided the ecstasies, and teased the intellects, and ordered the family relations and the legal chicaneries, and nurtured the piety, of hundreds of millions of people in widely diverse climes and over a series of radically divergent centuries.' Wilfred Cantwell Smith, 'The True Meaning of Scripture: an Empirical Historian's Nonreductionist Interpretation of the Qur'an', *International Journal of Middle East Studies* 11 (1980), p. 498.

8. Richard M. Eaton, *The Rise of Islam and the Bengal Frontier, 1204–1760* (Berkeley: University of California Press, 1993), pp. 285–90.

9. William A. Graham, 'Traditionalism in Islam: An Essay in Interpretation', *Journal of Interdisciplinary History* 23, no. 3 (Winter, 1993), pp. 501, 509–10.

10. See Richard M. Eaton, *Sufis of Bijapur, 1300–1700: Social Roles of Sufis in Medieval India* (Princeton: Princeton University Press, 1978), p. 306.

11. This was the perspective of Marshall Hodgson in his classic study, *The Venture of Islam: Conscience and History in a World Civilization*, 3 vols. (Chicago: University of Chicago Press, 1974).

12: Gerald J. Larson, *India's Agony over Religion* (Albany: State University of New York Press, 1995), p. 53.

13. Ibid., p. 103.

14. Graham P. Chapman, *The Geopolitics of South Asia: From Early Empires to India, Pakistan and Bangladesh* (Aldershot, UK: Ashgate Publishing Co., 2000).

15. Milo C. Beach, *New Cambridge History of India: I:3: Mughal and Rajput Painting* (Cambridge: Cambridge University Press, 1992), p. 2.

16. Harbans Mukhia, 'Medieval India': an Alien Conceptual Hegemony?' in *The Medieval History Journal* 1, no. 1 (1998), pp. 96–7.

17. The following remarks, recorded between 1308 and 1322 by Amir Hasan Sijzi of Delhi, refer to a century of nearly constant Mongol pressure on the peoples of Iran, Central Asia, and North India: 'The son of Khwaja Rukn al-din, the venerable Chishti saint...was taken captive during the onslaught of the infidel Mongols. He was taken before Chinghiz Khan' (99). 'During the Mongol onslaught, the infidels of Chinghiz Khan turned toward India. At that time, Qutb ad-din counseled his friends, "Flee, for these people will overpower you" ' (101). 'When the Mongols reached Nishapur, its ruler summoned Shaykh Farid ad-din 'Attar...and asked the Shaykh to petition God' (142). 'It was then that I heard the report from Ghazna: the Mongols had reached that city and martyred my mother, father, and all of my close relations' (165). 'As the Lahore traders were making their way home, they were informed en route that the Mongols had invaded their city and reduced it to rubble' (216). Bruce B. Lawrence, tr., *Morals for the Heart: Conversations of Shaykh Nizam ad-din Awliya, recorded by Amir Hasan Sijzi* (New York: Paulist Press, 1992).

18. Writing in 1260 from Delhi, just beyond the Mongols' reach, India's most prominent historian of the age, Minhaj Siraj Juzjani, noted bitterly that 'the accursed' Genghis Khan had just overrun the Islamic heartlands in Central Asia, Iran, and Iraq, and that 'the authority of the Muhammadan religion departed from those regions, which became the seat of paganism.' But, he added, 'the kingdom of Hindustan, by the grace of Almighty God, and ... the protection of the Iltutmishi dynasty [i.e., the Delhi sultans], became the focus of the people of Islam, and orbit of the possessors of religion.' Minhaj Siraj Juzjani, *Tabakat-i-Nasiri: A General History of the Muhammadan Dynasties of Asia, Including Hindustan*, tr. H.G. Raverty, 2 vols. (1881; repr., New Delhi: Oriental Books Reprint Corporation, 1970). 2:869–900.

19. Brajadulal Chattopadhyaya, *Representing the Other? Sanskrit Sources and the Muslims* (*Eighth to Fourteenth Century*) (New Delhi: Manohar, 1998), pp. 28–43, 92–7.

20. Ibid., pp. 79–91. Thus a 1276 Sanskrit inscription found in Palam, near Delhi, listed the sultans of Delhi from Muhammad Ghuri and Aibek through Balban as the legitimate successors to the Tomaras and the Cauhanas. It then portrayed the reigning monarch, Sultan Balban (whose kingdom was 'abounding in benign rule'), as so satisfactorily protecting India's social order that the serpent of eternity, 'Śeṣa, altogether forsaking his duty of supporting the weight of the globe, has betaken himself to the great bed of Viṣṇu; and Viṣṇu himself, for the sake of protection, taking Lakshmī on his breast, and relinquishing all worries, sleeps in peace on the ocean of milk.' Pushpa Prasad, *Sanskrit Inscriptions of Delhi Sultanate 1191–1526* (Delhi: Oxford University Press, 1990), pp. 12–13.

21. What is more, beginning in 1818 with the appearance of James Mill's *History of British India*, colonial historians projected a tripartite division of time onto India, transposing Europe's 'Ancient-Medieval-Modern' scheme into a 'Hindu-Muslim-British' scheme for the history of South Asia. In this model, one era of indigenous rule was followed by two of foreign rule, the first construed as Islamic and despotic, the second as European and benevolent. Ronald Inden,

Imagining India (Oxford, UK: Basil Blackwell, 1990), pp. 45–6; Mukhia, 'Medieval India,' pp. 100–01.

22. The 'overwhelming thrust of Orientalist thinking', writes Achin Vanaik, 'was to endorse the idea of different civilizations with different essences, each evolving in its allotted sphere.' Achin Vanaik, *The Furies of Indian Communalism: Religion, Modernity and Secularization* (London: Verso, 1997), p. 132.

23. W.C. Smith has called this the 'genetic' fallacy. According to this reasoning, as he notes, 'If one wishes to understand oak trees, one need only study acorns.' See Wilfred Cantwell Smith, "The True Meaning of Scripture: an Empirical Historian's Nonreductionist Interpretation of the Qur'an', *International Journal of Middle East Studies* 11 (1980), p. 499.

24. Max Weber, *The Sociology of Religion*, trans. Ephraim Fischoff (Boston: Beacon Press, 1964), p. 265.

25. Clifford Geertz, one of the late twentieth century's most influential anthropologists of Muslim societies, wrote, 'It is perhaps as true for civilizations as it is for men that, however much they may later change, the fundamental dimensions of their character, the structure of possibilities within which they will in some sense always move, are set in the plastic period when they first are forming.' Clifford Geertz, *Islam Observed: Religious Development in Morocco and Indonesia* (New Haven: Yale University Press, 1968), p. 11.

26. See, for example, Syed Ameer Ali, *The Spirit of Islam* (Calcutta: Lahiri, 1902).

27. R.C. Majumdar, *History of Medieval Bengal* (Calcutta: G. Bharadwaj & Co., 1973), pp. 196–7.

28. I.H. Qureshi, *The Muslim Community of the Indo-Pakistan Subcontinent (610–1947)* (Hague: Mouton & Co., 1962), p. 102.

29. Ibid.

30. '"Cultural" difference', wrote anthropologist James Clifford in 1988, 'is no longer a stable, exotic otherness; self-other relations are matters of power and rhetoric rather than of essence. A whole structure of expectations about authenticity in culture and in art is thrown in doubt.' James Clifford, *The Predicament of Culture* (Cambridge, MA: Harvard University Press, 1988), p. 14.

31. See, for example, the Introduction to David Gilmartin and Bruce B. Lawrence, eds., *Beyond Turk and Hindu: Rethinking Religious Identities in Islamicate South Asia* (Gainesville: University Press of Florida, 2000).

32. The following several paragraphs are drawn from my *The Rise of Islam and the Bengal Frontier, 1204–1760*.

33. See Yohanan Friedmann, 'A Contribution to the Early History of Islam in India', in *Studies in Memory of Gaston Wiet*, ed. Myrian Rosen-Ayalon (Jerusalem: Institute of Asian and African Studies, 1977), p. 322.

34. Ibn Battuta, *The Rehla of Ibn Battuta*, tr. Mahdi Hussain (Baroda: Oriental Institute, 1953), p. 46.

35. Peter Hardy, 'Modern European and Muslim Explanations of Conversion to Islam in South Asia: a Preliminary Survey of the Literature', in Nehemia Levtzion, ed., *Conversion to Islam* (New York: Holmes and Meier, 1979), pp. 80–1.

36. See, for example, H. Beverley, *Report on the Census of Bengal, 1872* (Calcutta: Secretariat Press, 1872), p. 132; James Wise, 'The Muhammadans of Eastern Bengal', *Journal of the Asiatic Society of Bengal* 63 (1894), p. 32.

37. For example, the historian K.A. Nizami writes, 'When the Muslims conquered these caste-cities they threw open their gates to everybody, with the result that the egalitarian principles of Islam attracted large number of non-caste Hindus and professional groups to the fold of Islam. It was this conversion of the lower caste population to Islam which swelled Muslim society in this country. The Muslim saints handled the problem of conversion with great sympathy, understanding and love.' K.A. Nizami, 'al-Hind: v.—Islam', *Encyclopaedia of Islam*, new edn. (Leiden: Brill, 1965), 3:429. 'To many', writes I.H. Qureshi of the early Islamization of Sind, 'Islam appeared as a deliverer from the tyranny of Hinduism and the example of tolerance set by the Arabs seems to have inclined many a Buddhist heart towards Islam.' Ishtiaq Husain Qureshi, *Muslim Community*, p. 42.

38. See Yohanan Friedmann, 'Medieval Muslim Views of Indian Religions', *Journal of the American Oriental Society* 95 (1975), pp. 214–21. In fact, the idea that Islam fosters social equality (as opposed to religious equality) seems to be of relatively recent origin, dating only from the period of the Enlightenment, and more particularly from the legacy of the French Revolution among nineteenth-century Muslim reformers. See Albert Hourani, *Arabic Thought in the Liberal Age, 1798–1939* (London: Oxford University Press, 1962), *passim.*; Bernard Lewis, 'The Impact of the French Revolution on Turkey: Some Notes on the Transmission of Ideas', *Journal of World History* 1, no. 1 (July 1953): pp. 105–25.

39. The idea of a 'Hindu fold' also implies that any group that had for any reason fallen outside were potential candidates for 'reconversion' to Hinduism, an argument that seems to be subtly advanced in Gauri Viswanathan, *Outside the Fold: Conversion, Modernity, and Belief* (Princeton: Princeton University Press, 1998).

40. T.W. Arnold, *The Preaching of Islam: A History of the Propagation of the Muslim Faith* (New York: Charles Scribner's Sons, 1913), pp. 254–93.

41. See the essays in this volume on Kashmir and Punjab, by Mohammad Ishaq Khan and Richard M. Eaton respectively. See also Eaton, *Rise of Islam*.

42. Joya Chatterji, 'The Bengali Muslim: A Contradiction in Terms? An Overview of the Debate on Bengali Muslim Identity', *Comparative Studies of South Asia, Africa, and the Middle East* 16, no. 2 (1996), p. 17. For example, Aziz Ahmad opens his article on 'Islamic Culture' in the *Encyclopaedia of Islam* with the words, 'The transplantation of Islamic culture on the Indian subcontinent....' Aziz Ahmad, 'Hind: vi—Islamic Culture,' in *Encyclopaedia of Islam*, new edn. (Leiden: Brill, 1965), 3: 438.

43. As K.A. Nizami writes, 'Since most [Indian Muslims] were converts from Hinduism, it was not possible for them to break away completely from their social background. In varying degrees and at different levels the Hindu traditions and customs were consequently continued among the Muslims. In certain rural areas, where conversion was not complete, many of the social customs, even some religious practices of Hinduism which had become a part of their social

life, were accepted.' K.A. Nizami, 'al-Hind: v.—Islam', *Encyclopaedia of Islam*, new edn. (Leiden: Brill, 1965), 3:436.

44. Geertz, *Islam Observed*, pp. 13, 18. For an alternative analysis of Islam in Java, which among other things critiques Geertz's work, see Mark R. Woodward, *Islam in Java: Normative Piety and Mysticism in the Sultanate of Yogyakarta* (Tucson: University of Arizona Press, 1989).

45. Chatterji, 'Bengali Muslim', p. 17.

46. See Eaton, *Rise of Islam*.

47. For Mujeeb, it was India's rich tradition of free-thinking Sufism that 'inevitably came into conflict with orthodoxy', and this because the latter enjoyed state support and was in theory and appearance based on the Qur'an and the Traditions of the Prophet—a formulation that precludes the possibility that Sufis based their own practices on the Qur'an and the Tradition. M. Mujeeb, *The Indian Muslims* (London: George Allen & Unwin, 1967), p. 120.

48. Thus in the thirteenth-century Middle East, orthodoxy was espoused by Ibn Taymiyya and pantheism by Ibn 'Arabi and Jalal al-Din Rumi. In the next century, Ibn Taymiyya's orthodox teachings reached India, where they were embraced by the Tughluq court and Shaikh Muhammad Husaini Gisudaraz, while Nasir al-Din Chiragh adopted the pantheistic perspective. In the sixteenth century, the Naqshbandi Sufi order spoke for the orthodox position, which was opposed by the pantheism of Shattari Sufis and the Rawshaniyya movement. In the sixteenth and seventeenth centuries, Shaikh Ahmad Sirhindi and Emperor Akbar represented the two respective positions, culminating dramatically in the 1658 War of Succession in which the armies of the brothers, Aurangzeb and Dara Shikuh, battled not only over the Peacock Throne, but also over orthodoxy and pantheism. For Nizami, the issue was closed in the eighteenth century when Shah Wali Allah declared that there never had been any fundamental difference between the ideas of Ibn 'Arabi and Ahmad Sirhindi. For other observers, however, some such struggle continued into the twentieth century, when orthodoxy finally triumphed with the creation of Pakistan. K.A. Nizami, 'Islam—Growth of Muslim Society', in *Encyclopaedia of Islam* (Leiden: Brill, 1965), new edn., 3:429–30.

49. For the dating of this phenomenon, see Christopher Melchert, *The Formation of the Sunni Schools of Law, 9th–10th Centuries, C.E.* (Leiden: Brill, 1997).

50. For a review of the literature on the 'closing of the gates' of *ijtihād*, see Wael B. Hallaq, 'Was the Gate of Ijtihad Closed', *International Journal of Middle Eastern Studies* 16 (1984), pp. 3–41; and idem., 'On the Origins of the Controversy about the Existence of Mujtahids and the Gate of Ijtihad', *Studia Islamica* 63 (1986), pp. 129–41. For a critique of Hallaq's argument, see Sherman A. Jackson, *Islamic Law and the State* (Leiden: Brill, 1996).

51. Mujeeb, *Indian Muslims*, p. 98.

52. M. Ishaq Khan, *Kashmir's Transition to Islam: the Role of Muslim Rishis* (New Delhi: Manohar, 1994), pp. 114, 167, 225.

53. Ibid., p. 41.

54. Ibid., pp. 125–30.

55. The texts studied by Orientalists were themselves typically products of urban literati, which is probably why Orientalists tended to identify Islam with city life. But the elision of peasants from studies of Muslim societies also derives from the work of Western anthropologists. As Talal Asad points out, for many such scholars the truly 'vivid' figures of Muslim societies are those who *act* in what such scholars construe as a theatre–like Islamic drama. 'Peasants, like women', he writes, 'are not depicted as *doing* anything. In accounts like [Ernest] Gellner's they have no dramatic role and no distinctive religious expression—in contrast, that is, to nomadic tribes and city-dwellers.' Asad, *Idea of an Anthropology of Islam*, p. 10.

56. See, for example, Joseph Schacht, *An Introduction to Islamic Law* (Oxford: Clarendon Press, 1964), ch. 10; Noel J. Coulson, *Conflicts and Tensions in Islamic Jurisprudence* (Chicago: University of Chicago Press, 1969), pp. 40–4.

57. A treatise compiled in the seventeenth-century Deccan even identified the sharī'a with *nāmūs*, a non-Islamic term associated with kingly dignity. Muzaffar Alam, *'Sharī'a* and Governance in the Indo-Islamic Context', in Lawrence and Gilmartin, eds., *Beyond Turk and Hindu*, p. 236.

58. For a study of the flexibility and creativity with which jurists adjudicated cases in the Ottoman Empire, see Judith E. Tucker, *In the House of the Law: Gender and Islamic Law in Ottoman Syria and Palestine* (Berkeley: University of California Press, 1998). For a similar assessment based on the decisions of Ottoman jurists in sixteenth-century Istanbul, seventeenth-century Palestine, and eighteenth-century Syria, see Haim Gerber, *Islamic Law and Culture, 1600–1840* (Leiden: Brill, 1999), especially chs. 4–6. See also *idem.*, *State, Society, and Law in Islam: Ottoman Law in Comparative Perspective* (Albany: State University of New York Press, 1994), especially chs. 3 and 6.

59. M.L. Bhatia, *Administrative History of Medieval India* (*A Study of Muslim Jurisprudence under Aurangzeb*) (New Delhi: Radha Publications, 1992), pp. 158–60.

60. Ibid., p. 136.

61. Thus, when one Qazi Qasim, son of Qazi Ibrahim, disputed the right of Saiyid Hisam to function as the qazi of Pune, an office that carried lands and considerable potential for fees, the matter was resolved by the Maratha sovereign Shivaji, whose earlier order in the matter was reconfirmed in 1673. In the same order, the king ordered one Hasan Tamboli and his ally Chandji, the headman of Phursinge, not to dispute the control of the village mosque with its hereditary custodian. The next year, Shivaji ordered both Brahmans and Shudras to pay a fee to the government secretary (*chitnis*) in order to gain readmission into their caste or to undergo purificatory penances for sins they had committed. Half a century later, in 1726, Mughal authorities in Maharashtra required Hindu pilgrims to obtain a permit from Aurangzeb's city chief (*kotwāl*) at Nasik, presumably for a fee, before they could proceed to the important centre of Tryambakeshwar. As Guha points out, the Mughals were following long-standing local custom in respect to the government's regulation of religious affairs. Sumit Guha, 'Religion, Authority, and Political Power in Medieval India', Association for Asian Studies annual meeting, Boston (March 11–14, 1999).

62. Asad, *Idea of an Anthropology of Islam*, p. 15.

63. Ibid., pp. 16–17.

64. See Josef van Ess, 'Mu'tazilah,' in *The Encyclopedia of Religion* (New York: MacMillan, 1987), 10:220–29.

65. Richard C. Martin and Mark R. Woodward, with Dwi S. Atmaja, *Defenders of Reason in Islam: Mu'tazilism from Medieval School to Modern Symbol* (Oxford: Oneworld, 1997).

66. Michael Chamberlain, *Knowledge and Social Practice in Medieval Damascus, 1190–1350* (Cambridge: Cambridge University Press, 1994), pp. 167–75.

67. See V. Minorsky, 'The Poetry of Shah Isma'il I', *Bulletin of the School of Oriental and African Studies* 10, no. 4 (1942), pp. 1006–53; *idem.*, 'Iran: Opposition, Martyrdom, and Revolt', in G.E. von Grunebaum, ed., *Unity and Variety in Muslim Civilization* (Chicago: University of Chicago Press, 1955), pp. 183–206.

68. Muzaffar Alam, 'Competition and Co-existence: Indo-Islamic Interaction in Medieval North India', *Itinerario* 13, no. 1 (1989), pp. 41–8, p. 57, f. 18.

69. Susan Bayly, *Saints, Goddesses, and Kings: Muslims and Christians in South Indian Society, 1700–1900* (Cambridge: Cambridge University Press, 1989).

PART ONE

Representing Self and Other

Most of the Islamic traditions examined in this volume developed in historical contexts in which Muslims comprised a demographic minority amidst larger populations of non-Muslims. Therefore, the issue of cultural representation—that is, the various ways in which Muslims and non-Muslims viewed and understood each other—constitutes an important backdrop for interpreting the meaning of those traditions. Four samples of the scholarship on this issue are presented chronologically here, with a view to suggesting how different scholarly generations have approached the subject between the 1960s and the 1990s.

Aziz Ahmad's 'Epic and Counter-Epic in Medieval India', published in 1963, proposes that Turkish and Rajput competition for power in north India during the decades and centuries after 1192 engendered two opposing literary genres sharply divided by language, religion, and readership. It was in the context of military confrontation, Ahmad argues, that writers like Baladhuri, Amir Khusrau, 'Isami, or Babur wrote their 'epic' narratives of conquest, or that writers patronized by Rajput houses composed 'counter-epics' of resistance. Postulating a mutual and enduring Hindu-Muslim opposition, of which this literary dichotomy is understood as emblematic, Ahmad's essay, published not long after Partition, likely reflected the hardened political and ideological positions that had crystallized with the creation of independent India and Pakistan.

By the 1980s most scholars had abandoned the idea of a single, monolithic Islamic perspective on Hindu India in pre-colonial times. In his 1986 essay reproduced here, Yohanan Friedmann explores the wide range of understanding that Indo-Muslim thinkers, writing between the eighth and eighteenth century, had of non-Muslim Indian culture. The essay constructs a typology of perspectives that range from the most hostile, represented by the historians Barani and Badayuni, to the most accommodating, represented by Abu'l-fazl and Dara Shukoh, the latter having held that a knowledge of Hindu scriptures was actually necessary for a full understanding of the Qur'an. Friedmann's survey is limited, however, inasmuch as most of the figures he examines were closely associated with Delhi's imperial establishment and wrote in Persian (or Arabic), the language of inter-regional Islamic cosmopolitanism. As subsequent essays in this volume show, a consideration of vernacular Indo-Islamic traditions greatly expands our knowledge of the range of Muslim perspectives on, and engagements with, Indian cultures.

Eleanor Zelliot's essay shifts the level of analysis from the macro to the most micro level possible—a contemporary, though hypothetical, dialogue between a single Hindu and a single Muslim over issues that are squarely religious in nature. Composed in the sixteenth century by the Marathi *bhakti* poet Eknath, the kind of text here translated and discussed by Zelliot is perhaps unique in the entire corpus of Indian literature. At once witty, profound, comic, and poignant, this short drama-poem, while having its own message and agenda, provides a rare glimpse into how unlettered villagers could have experienced religious alterity. Moreover, it is unlikely that Eknath could have imagined the dialogue, or that his village audience could have understood it, had not Indo-Muslim culture and society already attained a familiar presence in rural Maharashtra.

By the 1990s many scholars of pre-colonial India, seeking to move beyond normative visions of either Islamic or Hindu society as reflected in the mass of Arabo-Persian or Sanskrit textual materials, turned to sources that were less self-consciously prescriptive in nature, such as vernacular literature and architecture, numismatics, or epigraphy. Representing this tendency is Cynthia Talbot's 1995 study of Telugu inscriptions produced in Andhra between the fourteenth and seventeenth century. Talbot concludes that non-Muslim representations of Muslims in this region were not only historically constructed, but constantly in flux. Thus, for example, when upstart Telugu warriors attempted to mobilize support for their fledgling kingdoms in times of political instability, they typically drew upon ancient tropes in order to demonize 'Turks' as barbarians. In times of political stability, on the other hand, non-Muslims of Andhra not only respected these same 'Turks' as legitimate and powerful rulers, but rhetorically assimilated them as a natural part of India's cultural landscape.

1
Epic and Counter-Epic in Medieval India*

Aziz Ahmad

Muslim impact and rule in India generated two literary growths: a Muslim epic of conquest, and a Hindu epic of resistance and of psychological rejection. The two literary growths were planted in two different cultures; in two different languages, Persian and Hindi; in two mutually exclusive religious, cultural and historical attitudes, each confronting the other in aggressive hostility. Each of these two literary growths developed in mutual ignorance of the other; and with the rare exception of eclectic intellectuals like Abu'l-fazl in the sixteenth century, or the seventeenth century Urdu poets of the southern courts of Bijapur and Golkonda, their readership hardly ever converged. The Muslim and the Hindu epics of medieval India can therefore hardly be described as 'epic' and 'counter-epic' in the context of a direct relationship of challenge and response. Yet one of them was rooted in the challenge asserting the glory of Muslim presence, and the other in the response repudiating it. In this sense one may perhaps use the term 'counter-epic' for the Hindi heroic poetry of medieval India as I have done. Also, the contrast between these two literary growths is not confined to what is classified in Western literatures as full-blown epic, but to the epic material in general.

MUSLIM EPIC OF CONQUEST

The Muslim epic of the conquest of India grew out of the *qaṣīdas* (panegyrics) written on the occasions of Indian campaigns by the Ghazanavid poets at Ghazna and Lahore, and later by the poets of

* Reprinted from the *Journal of the American Oriental Society* 83 (1963), pp. 470–6.

the sultanate like Nāṣirī and Sangrīza in Delhi. Amir Khusrau's *Miftāḥ al-futūḥ*[1] is the first war-epic (*razmīya*) written in Muslim India. It celebrates four victories of Jalāl al-Dīn Khalji (1290–6), two of them against Hindu *rājās,* one against the Mongols and one against a rebel Muslim governor.

The next historical narrative of Amir Khusrau, *Khazā'in al-futūḥ*,[2] was written in prose, but the epic style and formulae were retained as well as the thematic emphasis on the glorification of the Turk against the Hindu. The concentration is on style in the tradition of Hasan Nizami's *Tāj al-ma'āthir* rather than on history;[3] and the stylist's effort to make use of the artifices of prose composition Khusrau had recommended in his treatise on rhetoric, *I'jāz-i Khusrawī*,[4] is manifest throughout the work as a continuous *tour de force*, unfolding itself in extended images, parallelisms, stylistic deductions, conceits and analogies. For instance:

> . . . the Rāi became *hot* at their words and thus disclosed the *fire* that *burnt* in his breast: 'Our old and respectable *fire-worshippers*, the *lamps* of whose minds *burnt bright*, have said clearly that never can the Hindu stay before the Turk, or *fire* before water.[5]

In the *Khazā'in al-futūḥ*, the glorification of the Khalji conquest of the Deccan exults in irrepressible bravado of iconoclasm:

> There were many capitals of the *devs* (meaning Hindu gods *or* demons) where Satanism had prospered from the earliest times, and where far from the pale of Islam, the Devil in the course of ages had hatched his eggs and made his worship compulsory on the followers of the idols; but now with a sincere motive the Emperor removed these symbols of infidelity ... to dispel the contamination of false belief from those places through the muezzin's call and the establishment of prayers.[6]

Read as epic all this makes sense as a historical attitude rather than as history. Historically, as the English translator of the epic points out, the 'Deccan expeditions had no clear object—the acquisition of horses, elephants, jewels, gold, and silver .... Of course the name of God was solemnly pronounced. The invaders built mosques wherever they went ... This was their habit. Of anything like an idealistic, even a fanatic religious mission, the Deccan invasions were completely innocent'.[7]

And yet as an unconscious rival of the Hammira epic, the *Khazā'in al-futūḥ* offers some interesting parallelisms. It boasts, perhaps as unhistorically as the Hammira cycle, of the massacre of thirty thousand Hindus at Chitor,[8] and describes the self-destruction of Rajput warriors and self-immolation of Hindu women with a gesture of heroic contempt: 'Everyone threw himself, with his wife and children, upon the flames and departed to hell'.[9]

Amir Khusrau's next epic *'Āshiqa*[10] was courtly (*bazmīya*) in theme, relating the romantic story of the love of 'Ala al-Din Khalji's son Khizr Khan for the Hindu princess of Gujarat, Dewal Rani, setting the pattern for a recognized type of Indian Muslim love story in which the hero is invariably a Muslim and the heroine a Hindu, asserting the conqueror's right not only to love but to be loved, in an attitude of romantic bravado which was antithetical to the more hysterical sexual jealousy in the medieval Hindu legend. The atmosphere and sensuous reactions in this beautiful epic of Khusrau are indigenous, quite unlike the imagic atmosphere and sensuous appraisal in the Persian *ghazal* written in India; but the glorification of India is there as a consequence of the Muslim supremacy. 'Happy Hindustan, the splendour of Religion, where the (Muslim holy) Law finds perfect honour and security . . . The strong men of Hind have been trodden under foot and are ready to pay tribute. Islam is triumphant and idolatry is subdued'.[11]

Amir Khusrau's *Nuh Sipihr*,[12] combining stylistic variations and elements of the war epic and the court epic, was a command performance, written to celebrate the victories of Qutb al-Din Mubarak Khalji and his general Khusrau Khan in the Deccan, before the latter murdered his master and turned apostate in 1320. The thematic emphasis is again on the Turk's destiny as conqueror who is decreed to hold the Hindu in subjugation, though the commander of the Turkish army in this case was a convert from Hinduism.

Amir Khusrau's last epic narrative, *Tughluq Nāma*, had a real epic scope—the re-establishment of Muslim power in India by his hero Ghiyath al-Din Tughluq, and the defeat he inflicted on the apostate Khusrau Khan. But though the poem is full of religio-political fervour, it lacks in epic magnitude. Amir Khusrau, now old and failing in genius, concentrates on the historical narrative and the equation of incident with image, but the opportunities of heroic emphasis are missed.

'Isami's *Futūḥ al-salāṭīn* is directly in the tradition of Amir Khusrau, though it claims inspiration from Nizami and Firdausi.[13] Its heroic emphasis is traditional, glorifying the role of Mahmud of Ghazna who made the Muslim conquest of India possible.[14] It emphasizes throughout the epical superiority of the Turk over the Hindu.[15] Essentially a historical narrative, told as a *razmīya* (war epic), it hardly ever misses a chance to weave in the *bazmīya* (court epic) elements of romance, such as the fanciful account of a Rajput princess's representation to Muhammad bin Sam Ghuri,[16] or the famous love story of Khizr Khan and Dewal Rani.[17]

Versified history, with epic elements fading out, continued to be written in Muslim India until the middle of the seventeenth century. Azuri, a poet who had earlier been connected with the court of Shah Rukh in Central Asia, took service under Ahmad Shah Bahmani (1422–36) and composed the *Bahman Nāma*, a history of the Bahmanids in verse. The last considerable effort in this genre was Muhammad Jan Qudsi's verse rendering of the *Bādshāh Nāma* of Lahori during the reign of Shah Jahan.[18]

The motif of a war waged to protect or avenge the honour of Muslim women, similar to the motif 'rape of Helen' in Greek epic and historiography, originally an epic theme, lends itself again and again to Muslim historiography in India. The official *casus belli* in the case of Hajjaj bin Yusuf's expedition against Sind (in 711 AD) reads in al-Baladhuri very much like the first few pages of Herodotus; the expedition was claimed to have been in response to the appeal of Muslim women captured by the pirates of Debal, and since their release could not be obtained by negotiation, it was accomplished by war and conquest.[19] One of the expeditions of Sultan Bahadur of Gujarat (1526–37) against a Hindu chieftain was to avenge the dishonour of two hundred and fifty Muslim women whom he had captured. Sher Shah Suri's expedition against Puran Mal, the Raja of Raisin, was undertaken on the complaint of some Muslim women: 'he has slain our husbands, and our daughters he has enslaved and made dancing girls of them.' Puran Mal was defeated and slain and his daughter was given away by Sher Shah to some wandering minstrels who might make her dance in the bazars.[20]

Outside the epic proper, the impressions of Central Asian Muslims freshly arrived in India and recorded by them in historical or autobiographical writing have something of that interesting raw material of antagonism on which epic generally draws. Kamal al-Din 'Abd al-Razzaq, the ambassador of Shah Rukh to the Hindu courts of the Deccan, regarded the Hindus at first sight as a curious tribe 'neither men nor demon', nightmarish in appearance, almost naked, incomprehensibly matriarchal and, of course, idolatrous.[21] It was only after he had lived for some time in the highly cultured atmosphere of Vijayanagara that he discovered the beauty and the symmetry of Hindu civilization and paid it glowing tribute.[22] More familiar is the damning tribute of Babur:

> Hindustan is a country that has few pleasures to recommend it. The people are not handsome. They have no idea of the charms of friendly society, of friendly mixing together, or of familiar intercourse. They have no genius, no comprehension of mind, no politeness of manners, no kindness or fellow-feeling, no ingenuity or mechanical invention in planning or executing their handicraft works, no skill or knowledge in design or architecture; they have no horses, no good flesh, no grapes or

musk-melons, no good fruits, no ice or cold water, no good food or bread in their bazaars, no baths or colleges, no candles, no torches, not a candlestick.[23]

HINDU EPIC OF RESISTANCE

The main intellectual resistance to the Muslim power did not come from the Brahmans. In the beginning they believed in Medhatithi's thesis: 'Aryavarta was so called because the Aryans sprang up in it again and again. Even if it was overrun by the *mlechchas*, they could never abide there for long'.[24] The faith in this thesis dwindled as the Muslim power came to be more and more firmly entrenched in the subcontinent. 'With the Yaminis, the successors of Mahmud,' continues K.M. Munshi, 'firmly established in the Punjab, the *Aryavarta-consciousness* lost whatever significance it had. The belief that *Chaturvarnya* was a divinely appointed universal order, characteristic of the land, was shaken; for now a ruling race in the country not only stood outside it, but held it in contempt and sought its destruction'.[25] Hindu reformers passed over the question of Muslim domination in silence as the fruit of *karma* without making suggestions for its overthrow.[26]

The literary reaction that echoed the psychology of Hindu resistance and reaction was popular rather than learned. It was mainly represented by the bardic tradition of Rajputana and in such works as *Prithvī Rāj Rāsō*, the epics of the Hammira cycle, and the history of Bundelkhand composed by Lal in the seventeenth century. This bardic literature embodies tales of Rajput struggle against the Muslims as well as internecine chivalric warfare among the Rajputs themselves, as specifically treated in the *Ālha Khand*.

Of these the *Prithvī Rāj Rāsō* is attributed to the authorship of Chand Bardai, Prithvi Raj's minister and poet-laureate, who is reported to have died fighting against the Muslim invaders in 1193. It might be assumed that the nucleus of the poem was composed soon after the events it narrates, but additions, interpolations, and polishing continued until well into the seventeenth century, as the epic has about ten per cent Persian vocabulary and mentions the use of artillery.[27] As such its anti-Muslim epic-content goes far beyond the tragic situation of a single historical event, and weaves around it an accumulated arena of heroic resistance spreading over several centuries. It anachronistically telescopes within the time and space of Ghurid invasions the eponymous representatives of later ethnic groups of Muslim invaders, as the names of Muslim generals in the epic like Tatar Khan, Khan Mongol Lalari, Khan Khurasani Babbar,

Uzbek Khan and Khildai (Khalji? Ghilzai?) suggest. The poem abounds in heroic similes of considerable emotion and sensitiveness:

> The warriors in columns are like a line of devotees of the Yoga... Abandoning error, illusion, passion, they run upon the gleaming edge (of the sword) as to a place of pilgrimage.[28]
>
> As the infidels with a rush greedily fall (upon the Hindus) they resemble pigeons, which, turning a circuit settle down.[29]
>
> The Hindus, catching the *mlechchas* by their hands, whirled them round, just as Bhima did to the elephants; (but) the comparison does not do justice (to the fight).[30]

Another epic of the Prithvi Raj cycle is *Prithvīrāja Vijaya*, probably composed by the Kashmiri Jayanaka between 1178 and 1200.[31] The poem accuses Muslims of confiscating charity lands and oppressing Brahmans. The *Turushka* (Turkish) women are condemned for bathing in the sacred lake while in their menses.[32] The epic seems to confuse Mahmud of Ghazna's invasion of Gujarat with the Ghurid invasion of Ajmer. The victory of a Hindu hero, Anorāja, is celebrated—a hero who compelled the defeated Turks to retreat, who in their plight in the desert had to drink the blood of their horses to survive,[33]—obviously an exaggerated echo of the plight of Mahmud's army in the desert of Sind after his sack of Somnath. Equally confused in historical perspective is the joyful news of the defeat of Ghuri at the hands of the 'Raja of Gujarat,'[34] while Prithvi Raj was planning to destroy Ghuri and the *mlechchas*, 'the fiends in the shape of men'.

The unhistorical epic legend[35] of Raja Hammir Dev's (c. 1300) gallant fight against 'Ala al-Din Khalji, and his heroic death, was celebrated in bardic literature of several Indian languages.[36] Chief among these are *Hammīr Rāysa*, and *Hammīr Kāvya* by Sarang Dhar, a bard of the mid-fourteenth century.

In the middle of the fifteenth century, Nayachandra Suri rewrote this legend in his *Hammir Mahākāviya*. Although a Jain, he invoked the blessings of Hindu gods on this epic, because of its Hindu chivalric theme and because of its anti-Muslim content.[37] The epic weaves in the heroic history of the Chauhans from Prithvi Raj to Hammira, and has a section of Prithvi Raj's exploits. Rajput rajas gather in gloom round Prithvi Raj to tell him of Ghuri, who is accused of burning Hindu cities and defiling Hindu women, and who is said to have been sent to this earth 'for the extirpation of warrior caste.'[38] Then follows the legend of Prithvi Raj taking Muhmamad bin Sam Ghuri a prisoner in Multan, presumbly after his victory at Tara'in, and later setting him free. Unable to defeat Prithvi Raj in open battle, the Ghuri invader has recourse to a ruse; he sends some

Muslim minstrels in disuise in the Rajput army, who enchant the Rajput hero's horse Natyarambha with their music, and Prithvi Raj is himself so enthralled with the dancing of his horse that he forgets to fight and is taken prisoner by the Muslims.[39]

Another anti-Muslim hero in Nayachandra Suri's epic is Vīranarāyana, who turns down Jalal al-Din Khalji's offer of alliance—alliance with the *mlechchas* would have been disgraceful betrayal of Rajput chivalry—as also does Vagbhata, who seizes the throne of Malwa, and whose son Jaitra Singh has a beautiful queen Hira Devi, who is at times 'possessed with a desire to bathe herself in the blood of Muslims' during her pregnancy, 'a desire which was often gratified by her husband.'[40] The child she gave birth to was the last great hero of the Rajput epic, Hammira.

The Hammira epic narrates the legendary story of 'Ala al-Din Khalji's expeditions against Hammira, the Raja of Ranthambore, who had ceased to pay tribute to the Muslim sultan. Bhoja, a formerly vanquished foe of Hammira, takes refuge in 'Ala al-Din's court. The first Khalji expedition led by the sultan's brother, Ulugh Khan, wins an inconclusive victory because of the treachery of a Rajput noble. The second is defeated by the Rajputs, who also capture some Muslim women who are forced 'to sell buttermilk in every town they pass through.'[41] Significantly, the Mongols are in alliance with Hammira against the Khalji sultan, though Hindu chiefs all over India ally themselves with him against Hammira.[42] 'Ala al-Din offers three alternative terms of peace to Hammira: to resume paying tribute, or to hand over the four Mongol chiefs who had taken refuge with him, or to give his daughter to 'Ala al-Din in marriage. As Hammira rejects all the three alternatives, 'Ala al-Din personally undertakes the siege of Ranthambore. One of 'Ala al-Din's (Hindu) archers kills by an arrow a Hindu courtesan, Radha Devi, who is defiantly dancing on the wall of the fort, but Hammira gallantly forbids his archers to shoot at 'Ala al-Din when they have a chance. Finally 'Ala al-Din wins over Hammira's minister, Ratipala, by permitting him to seduce his younger sister—humiliation of Muslim women being a recurring theme in the Hammira cycle of epics. Ratipala as well as Hammira's wives urge bestowing the hand of Hammira's daughter on 'Ala al-Din to put an end to the hostilities, and the girl herself requests her father to 'cast her away like a piece of broken glass,' but Hammira's regards giving his daughter away to an unclean *mlechcha* 'as loathsome as prolonging existence by living on his own flesh.' Hammira's womenfolk, including his daughter, throw themselves into flames to escape dishonour at the hands of the Muslims, and Hammira himself performing *jūhar* throws himself on the Muslim army, but 'disdaining to fall with anything like life into the enemy's hands, he severed, with one last effort, his head from his body with his own hands.'[43]

Neither this,[44] nor other legends about Hammira have any sound historical foundation. Another equally fantastic Rajput heroic legend describes Muhammad bin Tughluq's defeat and imprisonment at the hands of Hammira.[45]

On the other hand, the Rajput epic of internecine chivalry is generally neutral to the Muslims. An outstanding instance of this genre is *Ālha Khand*,[46] which belongs to the other Prithvi Raj cycle of Qannuj and Mahoba, and celebrates in Bundeli Hindi the exploits of Alha and Uden, heroes of Mahoba. Muslim characters in this epic are merely decorative. Prithvi Raj is confused with the Badshah in Delhi. Though the central theme of the epic, the rivalry between Prithvi Raj and Jay Chand, is based on a twelfth-century legend, additions seem to have been made by the reciting bards until as late as the middle of the eighteenth century, for there is a reference to the incursions of (Ahmad Shah) Durrani.[47] Towards Muslims the epic occasionally shows an attitude of reconciliation, which had its historical basis in the assimilation of Rajput chivalry in the composite machinery of the Mughal empire by Akbar.

The ninth century *Khumān Raysa* was recast in the sixteenth century, devoting a large section to 'Ala al-Din Khalji's sack of Chitor.[48] This and the Hammira cycle are the closet parallels and probably relative sources of Mālik Muhammad Jaisi's *Padmāvat* (1540). The case of Jaisi in the history of the anti-Muslim Hindu epic is a remarkable one. Himself a practising Muslim, saturated in the slightly heterodox rural version of the Chishti Sufi order as represented by his opium-eating preceptor Shah Mubarak Bodle, Jaisi seems to have had some familiarity with the *Vedanta*, though much less with the *Puranas*; shows strong influences of Kabir, and an interest, extraordinary even for a Muslim living among the Hindus in a village like Amethi, in Hindu lore.[49] His patron Jagat Dev was a Hindu ally of Sher Shah Suri. Among his friends was a Hindu musician, Gandharv Raj; and he had studied Sanskrit grammar and rhetoric under Hindu pandits.[50] Under all these influences and away from the Muslim-oriented atmosphere of cities, where the Muslim elite was developing an insular anti-Hindu literature, Jaisi accepted in all simplicity, at a non-sectarian level, the bardic legends of Rajput heroism against 'Ala al-Din at their face value, and moulded his Ratan Sen on Hammira.

The story of Jaisi's *Padmāvatī* falls in two parts. The first deals with the love-quest of Ratan Sen for Padmini (Padmavati), the princess of Ceylon, inspired by the pandering wisdom of Hiraman the parrot (allegorically the wise preceptor, the Hindu 'gurū,' the Sufi 'pīr'), and with the adventures that befall the hero on his return journey to his capital, Chitor. This part of the story is straightforward romance, without any epic element; and the legend of the wise parrot was popular in the oral tradition of Avadh,[51] as well as in Sanskrit anti-feminist literary history. This early part borrows elements from such earlier versions as Udayana's *Padmāvatī* and the *Ratnāvali*.[52]

The second part of Jaisi's poem assumes the form of an epic with an allegorical clue. Raghu Chitan Pandit (the devil), a minister of the court of Ratan Sen (epically sublimated Hammira, allegorically the human mind or soul) disgraced by his master for sorcery, tempts 'Ala al-Din (epically counter-hero, allegorically *māyā*, *majāz*, unreal of the Sufis, illusion) with jewelled bracelet (symbol) and description of the beauty of Padmavati (epically the Hindu heroine personifying honour, allegorically 'intelligence' or *firāsat*, regarded as a supreme merit for a monarch and his courtiers in Muslim political philosophy). 'Ala al-Din demands that Ratan Sen surrender Padmavati, and when the hero refuses indignantly, the counter-hero besieges the fort of Chitor (allegorically human body). Then, because of the Mongol pressure (an element also borrowed from the Hammira cycle), Ratan Sen (mind) negotiates for truce, and against the advice of his trusted generals Badal and Gora (heroic 'twin' as Alha and Uden in *Alha Khand*), he entertains 'Ala al-Din (illusion), who sees the reflection of Padmavati (intelligence) in a mirror, falls in love with her, and takes Ratan Sen prisoner by a trecherous ruse. Gora and Badal enter the imperial fort of Delhi by a counter-ruse (which is a parallel to the 'Trojan horse' motif) and rescue Ratan Sen (mind), who returns to Chitor and fights against Deopal (character and episode of unestablished allegorical significance, borrowed from the cycles of Rajput internecine chivalry), who had insulted Padmavati in his absence. Ratan Sen kills Deopal but himself receives a mortal wound. His (mind's) two consorts, Padmavati (intelligence) and Nagmati (world chore), burn themselves to ashes on his funeral pyre. 'Ala al-Din (illusion) arrives and storms Chitor (body), only to find Padmavati (intelligence) reduced to ashes with Ratan Sen (the mind). This allegorical epic of Rajput chivalry, written by a Muslim, ends with an anti-Islamic finale: 'and Chitor became Islam.'

As the author is a Muslim, the array and might of the Turks is not belittled, though his sympathy lies with the Rajputs. He makes an open reference to Hammira,[53] sees in the Rajput struggle something of the epic grandeur of *Mahābhārata*,[54] and quotes without contradiction Gora and Badal's version of the inherent treachery of the Turks.[55] Much more remarkable is his complete self-identification with the sense of tragic intent in a Rajput epic-theme, and its view of his own culture and religion;

for the outwardly simple phrase 'Chitor became Islam' signifies, in its allegorical equation, the unsubstantial victory of illusion.

Historically, the story of 'Ala al-Din Khalji's love and pursuit of Padmavati is not related by any Muslim historian before Abu'l- fazl, who has borrowed it from Jaisi[56] or from other cognate Rajput legends. None of the historians of the sultanate mentions it, not even 'Isami, who hardly ever misses a chance to introduce romantic material, or Khusrau, who might have found in the story a theme more interesting than that of Khizr Khan's love for Dewal Rani.

An examination of the historical material of Jaisi's allegorical epic yields interesting results.[57] Ratan Sen (1527–62), the Rana of Chitor, was a contemporary not of 'Ala al-Din Khalji, but of Jaisi himself and of Sher Shah Suri.[58] The ruse of warriors entering an enemy fort in women's palanquins, though a motif paralleled in epic and romance, had also some historical basis as it was used by Sher Shah to capture the fort of Rohtas.[59] In 1531, nine-years before the composition of *Padmāvat*, a case of mass *satī* by Rajput noblewomen had occurred in a Rajput fort sacked by Sultan Bahadur of Gujarat to avenge the dishonour of two hundred and fifty Muslim women held captive in that fort.[60] There might have been a conscious or unconscious confounding in Jaisi's mind of 'Ala al-Din Khalji with Ghiyath al-Din Khalji of Malwa (1469–1500), who had a roving eye and is reported to have undertaken the quest of Padmini, not a particular Rajput princess, but the ideal type of woman according to Hindu erotology.[61] Ghiyath al-Din Khalji, according to a Hindu inscription in the Udaipur area, was defeated in battle in 1488 by a Rajput chieftain Badal-Gora,[62] multiplied by Jaisi into twins. It therefore seems that Jaisi, or possibly the transmitters through whom the changed version of the Hammira legend reached him, incorporated several near-contemporary historical or quasi-historical episodes in the original legend. Jaisi himself confesses at the end: 'I have made up the story and related it.'

In Jaisi's legend 'Ala al-Din Khalji, the counterhero, is not exactly the villain of the piece; his imperial title is acknowledged, and though his unchaste love for Padmavati is condemned, much of the Muslim tradition favourable to him has been woven in and he is complimented as a righteous and noble sultan.[63] On the whole, the allegory is loose and the epic strain second-hand and subordinated to the didactic. Jaisi's real intention seems to be to tell a good story that would appeal to his fellow-villagers, the large majority of whom were Hindus.

Long before the composition of *Padmāvat* by a Muslim, the Hindu secondary epic occasionally adjusted itself to eclecticism, as in the case of Vidyapati Thakur's *Purusha Pariksha*, which tells of Hindu rajas coming to the aid of Muḥammad bin Tughluq against a fellow-Hindu raja and *kāfir*.[64]

The idealization of Hindu women who preferred death to the embraces, conjugal or otherwise, of Muslims passed on from Rajput epic to popular song in other areas such as Bihar.[65] Sexual hostility produced curious juxtapositions on the popular Hindu mind such as the one describing Akbar as the illegitimate son of the Hindu poet, Narhari Sahay, who was given, according to the legend, Choli Begum (The Lady Brassiere), a (non-existent) wife of Humayun, as a gift by Sher Shah.[66]

Anti-Muslim secondary epic burst into boiling fury in Maharashtra, after Aurangzeb's reversal of Akbar's tolerant policies, especially in the *Granthāvalī* of Kavi Bhushan, whose idealization of Shivaji as a hero has little in common with the tragic heroism of Rajput epic and is much more intensely religious.[67] It formulates the epic of revival, not resistance: 'The Muslims have destroyed all our temples; they are hoisting 'Ali's (Allāh's?) flag everywhere; rajas have fled; everywhere one sees (Muslim) *pīrs* (saints), and *payghambars* (prophets), nowhere Hindu *sants* and *sādhūs*; Kashi has lost its splendor and there are mosques in Mathura. If there were no Shivaji everyone would have been circumcised.'[68] According to Kavi Bhushan, Aurangzeb is the incarnation of Kumbhkaran (elder brother of *Rāmāyaṇa's* villain Ravana).[69] Shivaji is his antithesis. He is the arch-hunter, who chases Mughal generals who are like storks, Mughal amirs who are like peacocks, Bangash Pathans who are like herons, Baluchis who are like ducks, whereas the horses of the Maratha hunter are like hawks.[70] The epic continues with obvious self-satisfaction: 'The goddess Kali has become fat eating the heads of the pigtailless Muslims.'[71]

NOTES

1. In Amir Khusrau, *Ghurrat al-kamāl*, British Library, Add., 25, 807.
2. Amir Khusrau, *Khazā'in al-futūḥ*, Eng. tr. by M. Habib, Madras 1931.
3. Wahid Mirza, *The Life and Works of Amir Khusrau*, Calcutta 1935, p. 223.
4. Amir Khusrau, *I'jāz-i Khusrawī*, Lucknow 1876, *passim*.
5. Eng. tr. and italics of Wahid Mirza, *Life and Works*, p. 224.
6. *Khazā'in* (Habib), p. 49.
7. Habib, Introduction to ibid., p. xv; cf. N. Venkataramanayya, *Early Muslim Expansion in South India*, Madras 1942.
8. *Khazā'in*, p. 49.
9. Ibid., cf. M.L. Mathur, 'Chitor and 'Ala al-Din Khalji', *Indian Historical Quarterly*, Calcutta, XXVII (1951), pp. 52–69.
10. Amir Khusrau, *'Āshiqa*, British Library, Add., 25, 807.
11. Ibid., tr. Henry Elliot, *History of India as Told by its own Historians*, Allahabad, 1964, III, p. 546.

12. Amir Khusrau, *Nuh Siphir*, ed. Wahīd Mirza, Calcutta, 1950.
13. 'Isami, *Futūḥ al-salāṭīn*, ed. A.S. Usha, Madras 1943, pp. 17, 114.
14. Ibid., p. 29.
15. Ibid., pp. 230–6, and passim.
16. Ibid., pp. 81–4.
17. Ibid., pp. 322–33.
18. Ghulam 'Alī Āzād Bilgrāmī, *Sarv-i Āzād*, India Office Library, Pers. MS, 1852 (Ethé), p. 683, ff. 29b–30a.
19. al-Balādhurī, *Futūḥ al-buldān*, Cairo 1932, p. 423.
20. 'Abbās Khān Sarwānī, *Tārīkh-i Sher Shāhī*, relevant section tr. in Elliot, IV, pp. 402–3.
21. Kamal al-Dīn 'Abd al-Razzaq, *Maṭl'al-Sa'dayn*, British Library, Or. 1291, ff. 204b–205a.
22. Ibid., ff. 208a–210b.
23. Babur, *Tuzuk* (Leyden and Erskine), II, p. 241; cf. ibid., II, p. 201.
24. Medhatithi on Manu, II, p. 22, quoted by K.M. Munshi, Introduction to R.C. Majumdar (ed.) *The Struggle for Empire*, Bombay 1957, p. x.
25. Ibid., p. xiii.
26. K.M. Ashraf, 'Life and Conditions of the People of Hindūstān (1200–1550)', *Journal of the Royal Asiatic Society of Bengal*, Calcutta 1935, Third Series, I, p. 142.
27. Maḥmud Sherani, *Punjāb meñ Urdū*, Lahore 1930, pp. 122–3.
28. Chand Bardai, *Prithvirāj Rāsō*, Part II, vol. I, ed. and tr. A.F. Rudolf Hoernle, Calcutta 1886, p. 29.
29. Ibid., p. 23.
30. Ibid., p. 63.
31. Har Bilas Sarda, 'The Prithvīrāja Vijaya,' in *Journal of the Royal Asiatic Society* 1913, I, pp. 260–1.
32. Ibid., p. 262.
33. Ibid., p. 273.
34. Ibid., pp. 279–80.
35. Mathur, 'Chitor', pp. 52–7.
36. G.A. Grierson, *The Modern Vernacular Literature of Hindustan*, Calcutta 1889, p. 6.
37. Nayachandra Suri, *Hammīra Mahākāviya*, ed. N.J. Kirtane, Bombay 1879, p. 8.
38. Ibid., p. 17.
39. Ibid., pp. 17–20.
40. Ibid., p. 26.
41. Ibid., p. 34.
42. Ibid., pp. 35–6.
43. Ibid., pp. 29–47.
44. Mathur, 'Chitor'.
45. Mahdi Hasan, *Rise and Fall of Muhammad bin Tughlaq*, London 1938, pp. 97–100.

46. *Ālh-Khand*, Eng. tr. by W. Waterfield and G.A. Grierson (*The Lay of Ālha*), London 1923.
47. Ibid., p. 159.
48. Grierson, *Modern Vernacular*, pp. 1–2.
49. Malik Muhammad Jaisi, *Padmavati*, ed. G.A. Grierson and Sudharka Dvivedi, Intro. I; Jaisi, *Granthāvali, Padmāvat, Akhrāwat and Ākhrī Kalām*, ed. Ram Chandra Shukla, Allahabad 1935, p. 49; Kalb-i Mustafā, *Mālik Muhammad Jaisi*, Delhi 1941, pp. 29–30, 34–7.
50. Grierson, introduction to his edition of *Padmāvat*, p. 2.
51. Kalb-i Mustafā, *Jaisi*, p. 100.
52. Grierson, *The Modern Vernacular Literature of Hindustan*, p. 18.
53. Jaisi, *Padmavati*, Eng. tr. by A.G. Shirreff, Calcutta, 1944, p. 287.
54. Ibid., p. 361.
55. Ibid., p. 350.
56. Kalb-i Muṣtafā, *Jaisi*, p. 105.
57. For details see Iḥtishām al-Ḥaqq, *Afsāna-i Padmini*, Delhi 1939; K.S. Lal, 'The Myth of Rānī Padminī and 'Ala-ud-dīn Khaljī', *Annual Bulletin of the Nagpur Historical Society* I, 1946.
58. Kalb-i Muṣtafā, *Jaisi*, p. 111.
59. Ibid., pp. 112–3.
60. Ibid., p. 113.
61. Ibid., pp. 114–5.
62. Ibid., p. 116.
63. Shirreff, *Padmavati*, pp. 270–1.
64. Maheswar Prasad, *Purusha Pariksha of Vidyapati*, pp. 20 et seq.
65. G.A. Grierson, 'The Popular Literature of Northern India', *Bulletin of the School of Oriental Studies* I, no. 3 (1920), pp. 97–100.
66. Grierson, *The Modern Vernacular Literature of Hindustan*, pp. 38–9.
67. Kavi Bhushan, *Granthāvali*, Lahore, 1937, pp. 312–3.
68. Ibid., pp. 310–11.
69. Ibid., pp. 313–4.
70. Ibid., p. 347.
71. Ibid., p. 344.

2

Islamic Thought in Relation to the Indian Context*

Yohanan Friedmann

I

Among the 'further' Islamic lands, the Indian subcontinent is probably the area in which Islamic civilization attained its highest achievements. The Muslim population of India, Pakistan, and Bangladesh constitutes the largest concentration of Muslims anywhere. Islamic dynasties ruled substantial parts of the subcontinent since the thirteenth century. Muslim consciousness remained alive even after the disintegration of Muslim rule and the British takeover; it was intense enough to advance the demand for the establishment of an independent Muslim state after the termination of British rule. The establishment of Pakistan as an expression of separate Muslim nationhood is a unique event in modern Islamic history, bearing eloquent evidence to the vitality preserved by Indian Islam throughout the centuries.

In overall terms, Muslims have always been a minority in the subcontinent. Despite the fact that certain regions became in the course of time Muslim majority areas, the minority status of the Muslims in the subcontinent as a whole has always been an essential feature of their history and exercised its influence on various aspects of their thought. There was, on the one hand, the feeling that the Indian Muslims were constantly in danger of being overwhelmed by an environment that could only be described as an anathema to their cherished ideal of monotheism. This apprehension created an intense desire to preserve Islam in its pristine purity and to protect it assiduously from any encroachment of Indian customs and beliefs.

* Reprinted from Marc Gaborieau ed. *Islam et Société en Asie du Sud.* Paris: École des Hautes Études en Sciences Sociales (*Puruṣārtha* 9, 1986), pp. 79–91.

The development of strict orthodoxy was, however, only one result of the fact that the Indian Muslims lived in the midst of a non-Muslim, and, in their eyes, idolatrous and polytheistic population. Diametrically opposed to it was the attempt to find a common denominator for the two civilizations, to establish a mutually acceptable *modus vivendi* for their respective adherents, and to argue that all religions are essentially the same though their external and accidental features are diverse. This conciliatory trend was always weaker than the orthodox one. The few rulers who adopted it failed to inspire their successors, and the religious thinkers who developed it had few disciples who continued to walk on the path of inter-religious harmony and compromise.

The distinction between these trends in Indo-Muslim religious thought should not create the impression that all the thinkers can be classified under one of these two categories. On the contrary, many of them deal with subjects common to mediaeval Islamic thought everywhere and do not make many references to the particular conditions in which the Indian Muslims have lived since the beginning of their history. Islamic thought which emerged in India but carried few specifically Indo-Islamic features appears even to have been quantitatively preponderant. The significance of this observation for the overall assessment of Indian Islam must not be underestimated, but cannot be elaborated here. It is also clear that within the limited scope of this essay it will be possible only to present the general outline of the topic under discussion; the picture here created may have to be modified by further research and more detailed exposition.[1]

II

Religious law is undoubtedly one of the most important expressions of Islamic civilization. It is therefore fitting to start our discussion of Islamic thought in relation to the Indian context with a survey of legal issues that are specific to India. It is well known that Islamic law deals not only with questions that are religious according to modern Western classification, but also with matters that would be regarded in the West as part of constitutional or civil law. One of the more important questions of this kind treats the rights and obligations of non-Muslims who live in an Islamic state. These are known in Islamic law as *ahl al-dhimma*. In the central Islamic lands they normally were Jews or Christians. The Qur'an and other branches of early Islamic literature contain ample material on these two communities and define to a certain extent the relationship that the Muslim should evolve with them. With regard to India, the situation is different: the Qur'an contains no references to India or Indians, and the references in the *ḥadīth* lack any legal content (Friedmann 1977: 317–18). Muslim jurists had therefore to make their decisions without being able to base them on a religiously authoritative text. The possibility of treating the Indian population in accordance with the injunctions relative to the *mushrikūn* of the Arabian peninsula was out of the question due to the paucity of the early conquerors and to the precarious nature of their rule in the early period. The decision had therefore to be devised along lines similar to those adopted in the central Islamic lands: the inhabitants of India were treated as ahl al-dhimma, though classical Qur'anic exegesis did not regard them as ahl al-kitāb. This expansion of the concept entailed a compromise with idolatry that was not palatable to all schools of law. The Shafi'is and the Hanbalis insisted that only Jews, Christians, and Zoroastrians may be included in the category of ahl al-dhimma. The Malikis and the Hanafis, on the other hand, agreed to include among them all non-Muslims (even idolators) who were not Arabs or apostates. This view of the Hanafi *madhhab*, which became preponderant in India, enabled the Muslim rulers of the country to find legal justification for a policy that they had to adopt in any case. It is noteworthy that the decision to expand the concept of ahl al-dhimma in this way was attributed to the eighth century Arab conqueror of Sind, Muhammad bin Qasim, who is reported to have stated that 'the idol-temple is similar to the churches of the Christians, to (the synagogues) of the Jews and to the fire-temples of the Zoroastrians (*ma al-budd illā ka-kanā'is al-naṣārā wa al-yahūd wa buyūt nīrān al-majūs*) (Friedmann 1972: 180–2).

Being in Islamic legal terms non-Arab idolators, the Hindus were thus included in the category of ahl al-dhimma during the formative period of Islamic law. Strictly speaking, this should have settled the question of the relationship between them and the Muslims. From now on, they should have been treated according to the well-known rules concerning the non-Muslim inhabitants of a Muslim state: they should pay the jizya and abide by the discriminatory regulations specified by the *sharī'a.* The state should in exchange guarantee their safety and allow them limited religious freedom. The issue was, however, too complex for such a simple and straightforward solution, and it continued to exercise Indian Muslim minds throughout the centuries of their history. The realities of India, where Muslim dynasties ruled over a predominantly Hindu population, stood between the sharī'a and its implementation with regard to the Hindus. Practical considerations seem to have prevented the collection of the jizya in certain periods; there is evidence to suggest that the concept lost its specific legal sense during the Sultanate period and began to be used in the sense of tax in general (Hardy 1957: 566–7). The discrepancy between the legal requirements and the actual situation provoked angry reaction from some quarters. The devout historian Ziya al-Din Barani (Hardy 1959: 1036–7, idem. 1960: 20–39) not only advised the sultan to treat the Hindus with the utmost severity, but also recalled that not all schools of Islamic law agreed to include them in the category of ahl al-dhimma (Habib n.d.: 50). Barani also reported that certain 'ulama unsuccessfully tried to induce the sultan to declare that the Hindus must accept Islam or be put to the sword (Nizami 1961: 315–6). Beyond this, there was no attempt to deviate from the Hanafi ruling concerning the Hindus. The extent to which the Muslim rulers implemented the discriminate regulations against them varied (Ahmad 1964: 86–91), but their definition as ahl al-dhimma does not seem to have ever been questioned in a serious way.

III

The virtual consensus concerning the legal standing of the Hindus did not preclude the emergence of great variations in Muslim attitudes towards them in a more general sense. These attitudes range from utmost hostility to almost total acceptance of Hindu religious beliefs.

The first Muslim thinker who paid significant attention to Indian culture was also the most thorough and profound of all. Abu Raihan al-Biruni (973–1050), one of the great luminaries of mediaeval Islamic science, was born in Khwarazm. When his native place was overrun by Mahmud bin Sabuktigin in 1017, he was brought to Ghazna and later accompanied Mahmud on some of his military expeditions to India (Sachau 1964: I, vii ff). He studied with Indian sages and made great efforts to collect Indian books (al-Biruni 1958: 17–18; Sachau 1964: I, 23–4). In this way he acquired there a first-hand knowledge of Indian civilization (al-Biruni 1958: 18; Sachau 1964: I, 24), and subsequently wrote his outstanding account of India under the title: *Taḥqīq mā li-'l- Hind min maqūla maqbūla fī al-'aql aw mardhūla*. While al-Biruni cannot be considered an Indian Muslim in the full sense of the word, he visited the country and his importance is so substantial, that his views of India and of its civilization cannot be ignored in this context. He clearly writes as a Muslim, is in many places critical of Hindu beliefs, and the information provided by him may serve those who want to engage in polemics with the Hindus. Yet his basic approach is that of a scholar, and the *Taḥqīq* is avowedly informative, descriptive, and non-polemical (al-Bīrūnī 1958: 5; Sachau 1964: 1, 7). His critical attitude to idolatry is tempered by the statement that this type of worship is designed for the benefit of the uneducated, common people who are impressed only by the concrete (*maḥsūs*), and fail to appreciate the abstract (*ma'qūl*). In order to cater to the religious needs of their uneducated adherents, the Jews, the

Christians, and the Manicheans introduced 'pictorial representation' (*taṣwīr*) into their houses of prayer. Islam is different in this respect and did not make such concessions to the common people's predilection for concrete objects of worship; yet even a Muslim who does not belong to the educated part of his community would express his adoration should he be presented with a picture of the Prophet, of Mecca, or of the Ka'ba (al-Biruni 1958: 84; Sachau 1964: I, 111). Hinduism is therefore not substantially different from the other faiths: the Hindu idols were constructed only for the benefit of the common people whose understanding is limited (*inna hādhihi al-aṣnām manṣūba li-'l- 'awāmm alladhīna safilat marātibuhum wa qaṣurat ma'ārifuhum*) (al-Biruni 1958: 93; Sachau 1964: I, 122). The absurd beliefs (*khurāfāt*) which al-Biruni relates in his work belong also to the common people only, because

> those who march on the path of liberation, or those who study philosophy and theology, and those who desire abstract truth which they call *sārā*, are entirely free from worshipping anything but God alone, and would never dream of worshipping an image manufactured to represent him (*fa-amma man amma nahj al-khalāṣ aw ṭāla'a ṭuruq al-jadal wa al-kalām wa rāma al-taḥqīq alladhī yusammūnahu sārā fa-innahu yatanazzahu 'an 'ibādati aḥad dūn Allāh ta'ālā faḍlan 'an ṣūratihi al-ma'mūla*) (al-Biruni 1958: 85; Sachau 1964: I,113).

In this way al-Biruni reaches the conclusion that the elites of all communities, including the Hindus, worship Allah alone. On the other hand, all uneducated people, without regard to their religious affiliation, need concrete objects of worship, and their religious leadership frequently takes their susceptibilities into account (Friedmann 1975: 215).

The profundity and scholarly approach of al-Biruni to the Hindu tradition was not matched by any Muslim scholar or thinker in mediaeval times. There were, however, numerous Muslims who paid attention to Indian culture on other levels. The first among them was Amir Khusrau Dihlawi (1253–1325), who expressed his views of India and of Indian religion in his literary works. In his *Nuh Sipihr* (Amir Khusrau 1949), he pays glowing tribute to the land of India, describing it as Paradise on earth (*bihishtī bi-zamīn*) (Amir Khusrau 1949: 151–8). In this work he also pays tribute to the intellectual achievements of its inhabitants. The Hindus excel in logic, astronomy, and philosophy. The only science that is not to be found in India is Islamic jurisprudence, but Amir Khusrau is not unduly worried by its absence. As for the religious views of the Hindus, Amir Khusrau agrees that in this regard they went astray. Nevertheless, they hold some beliefs that are close to the Muslim ones: the existence and eternity of one God, His ability to create *ex nihilo*, and His ability to sustain all life. Religiously they are therefore better than some other groups, such as the dualists (*thanawiyya*), the Christians who attribute progeny to God, the star-worshippers (*akhtariyyān*) who acknowledge seven gods, and the *'unṣuriyyān* who believe in four gods. It is true that the Brahmans worship the sun, stones, and some animals; yet they do not consider these similar to God, but only a part of His creation. They worship them only because this is a part of the tradition transmitted to them by their ancestors, and they cannot dissociate themselves from it (Amir Khusrau 1949: 163–9)

This rather sympathetic approach to Hinduism is not evident in Amir Khusrau's other works. The *Khazā'in al-futūḥ*, for instance, is replete with hostile references to the Hindus and unreservedly condemns them as infidels. They are called 'Pharaohs of infidelity' (*farā'inat al-kufr*) and idol-worshippers (*hunūd-i but-parast*); the sultan 'washed the earth clean with a flood of these impure people's blood' (*az ṭūfān-i khūn-i ān nā-pākān khāk-i ān zamīn-rā pāk bi-shust*) and sent countless infidels to hell (Amir Khusrau 1953: 10, 45, 48, 49). Amir Khusrau's conciliatory remarks about the Hindus, made in the context of a patriotic description of his Indian fatherland, do not therefore have as much religious significance as might have been derived from them alone. One would, consequently, agree with Hardy's observation that Amir Khusrau 'never looked beyond Islamic revelation for an explanation of the meaning of life' (Hardy 1960: 93 and *passim*). Despite the sympathetic treatment of Hinduism in some of his works, Amir Khusrau remains convinced that religious truth is to be found in Islam alone. In this he does not differ from the consensus prevailing among the Muslims in his time and place.

Positive attitudes to India and favourable evaluations of its religious traditions received strong support during the reign of the Mughal emperor Akbar (1556–1605), whose well-known policies were exceedingly propitious for their development. Even if we treat Badayuni's hostile descriptions with the necessary circumspection, it is clear that Akbar's policies created an atmosphere in which the belief in the exclusive truth of Islam was substantially undermined. The willingness of Akbar to admit Hindu sages into his presence and to listen to their religious discourses implied that their views were worthy of consideration (Badayuni 1284 AH: 239 and *passim*). Abu'l-fazl's desire to discuss spiritual issues with sages who belong to religions other than Islam points in the same direction (Abu'l-fazl 1948: I: xxxv). The classical conviction that Islam is the only true religion (Qur'an, 3: 19, 85 and elsewhere) lost its axiomatic nature, and the way was opened for the development of conciliatory attitudes towards Hinduism. These attitudes are clearly in Abu'l-fazl's *Ā'īn-i Akbarī*. Like al-Biruni before him, Abu'l-fazl asserted that the Hindus 'one and all believe in the unity of God' and that the reverence that they pay to images of stone are only 'aids to fix the mind and keep the thoughts from wandering'. The intention of this exposition was to refute the equation between Hinduism and polytheism, hoping that the Muslim hostility towards the Hindus would thereby be reduced (Abu'l-fazl 1948: III, 2, 8). This revision of attitudes towards the Hindus resulted also in the reassessment of certain historical personalities: Maḥmūd of Ghazna, who was frequently considered an exemplary Muslim ruler and *mujāhid*, is depicted by Abu'l-fazl in a totally different light. He is said to have been incited to shed innocent blood by 'fanatical bigots representing India as a country of unbelievers at war with Islam' (Abu'l-fazl 1948: III: 377).

The most significant Muslim religious thinker representing the conciliatory trend towards Hinduism seems to have been the Mughal prince, Dara Shukoh (1615–59). In contradiction to Amir Khusrau, who only condescendingly admits that the Hindus maintain some correct beliefs, Dara Shukoh considers the Hindu tradition as an essential tool for understanding the religious truth and, indeed, for the real understanding of the Qur'an. Dara Shukoh's philosophy of religion is well explained in the introduction to his Persian translation of the Upanishads, entitled *Sirr-i-Akbar* ('The greatest secret'). His basic assumption is that religious truth is one. It is included in the Vedas, the Upanishads, the Taurat (Bible), the Injil (New Testament), the Zabur (Psalms), and the Qur'an. All these are heavenly books and contain the ultimate religious truth of monotheism (*tauḥīd*). Yet the degree of clarity and intelligibility with which this truth is expounded in them is not uniform. Turning first to the Qur'an, Dara Shukoh maintains that most of its contents is not formulated in an explicit manner. It is full of allegories (*akthar marmūz ast*) that are understood only by a few. The character of the Bible, of the New Testament, and of the Psalms is similar: the truth is not explained in them in a sufficiently detailed and full fashion (*bayān-i-tauḥīd dar ān-hā ham mujmal o marmūz būd*).

Being unable to attain his goal of full religious understanding with the help of these four books, Dara Shukoh turned to the religious thought of India. He noted that according to the Qur'an, no nation was left without prophetic mission (Sūra 35: 22), and India cannot be an exception to the universality of divine guidance. Indeed, the question of tauḥīd was extensively discussed in that country. Ancient Indian sages never rejected it and never condemned its upholders. Furthermore, the four Vedas, which are heavenly books, had been in India before all other books of the same kind. They were revealed to ancient prophets; the greatest among these was Brahma, who is, according to Dara Shukoh, identical with Adam. The quintessence of the Vedas are the Upanishads, which are a treasure of monotheism (*ganj-i tauḥīd*).

We are now ready to analyse Dara Shukoh's most significant statement concerning the relationship between Islam and the Indian religious tradition. Dara Shukoh creates an intimate connection between the Qur'an and the Upanishads by saying that they are hinted at in Sura 56: 77–80: 'Verily, it is a noble Qur'an in a protected book; none but the purified shall touch it, a revelation from the Lord of the world' (*innahu la-qur'ān karīm fī kitāb maknūn la yamassuhu illā al-muṭahharūn tanzīl min rabb al-'ālamīn*). The crucial question with regard to this verse is the interpretation of *kitāb maknūn*. Classical Islamic commentators normally prefer to consider this phrase as a reference to the 'preserved tablet' (*al-lauḥ al-maḥfūẓ*) in which the original text of the Qur'an was inscribed by Allah (Razi 1324 AH: VIII, 71; Ṭabari 1954: XXVII, 204–5; Ṭabari 1954: XVII, 132). Less frequently they take it to mean the actual copy of the book (*al-muṣḥaf alladhī fī aidīnā*), or the Taurāt and the Injīl (Rāzī 1324 AH: VIII, 72). Dara Shukoh does not accept any of these exegetical attempts. Without offering any substantiation of his view, he rejects the idea that *kitāb maknūn* refers to the Taurāt, the Injīl or the Zabūr. Subsequently he argues that the word *tanzīl* ('revelaton, sending down') used in the verse precludes the possibility that the phrase refers to the 'preserved tablet'. The reason implied here is that the 'preserved tablet' was never 'revealed' or 'sent down'. Having eliminated all other possibilities, Dara Shukoh concludes that kitāb maknūn refers to the Upanishads. In his view the Qur'an called the Upanishads 'hidden' or ' protected', because the Indian sages did their best to conceal them from the Muslims. The Upanishads, which undoubtedly are the earliest heavenly books and provided Dara Shukoh with answers to all his questions, are not only compatible with the Qur'an, but also serve as its commentary (*muwāfiq-i qur'ān-i majīd balkih tafsīr-i ān ast*). This is according to the principle that divine speech is its own exegesis: whatever is expressed concisely in one book is detailed in another. The concise formulation of one book can therefore be elucidated and understood by the detailed exposition found elsewhere (*kalām-i ilāhī kih khwud tafsīr-i khwud ast wa agar dar kitābī mujmal bāshad, dar kitāb-i dīgar mufaṣṣal yāfta shawad wa az ān tafṣīl ān ijmāl dānista shawad*) (Dara Shukoh 1957: introduction 3–6; Göbel-Gross 1962: 13–21; Hasrat 1953: 260–9; Friedmann 1975: 217).

In some of his works, Dara Shukoh also expressed high appreciation of the religious achievements of the Hindus. In the preface to the *Majma' al-baḥrain* he asserts that there is no fundamental difference between Islam and Hinduism (Hasrat 1953: 219). Elsewhere he ascribes to Hindu idolatry a positive, and even essential, role in the development of religious consciousness: the idols are necessary for those who are not yet aware of the inner (*bāṭin*) meaning of religion and therefore need a concrete representation of the deity; as soon as they come to know the bāṭin, they dispense with the idols (Huart-Massignon 1926: 290–1).

Dara Shukoh's view of the relationship between the Hindu religious literature and the Qur'an seems to be his most significant contribution to Islamic thought. The idea that one must use the Hindu scripture in order to attain the real meaning of the Qur'an is hitting at the very core of the conviction that Islam is a self-sufficient system that is in no need of ideas extraneous to it. It seems to have been deviant enough to put Dara Shukoh beyond the pale of mediaeval Indian Islam.

The eighteenth-century Naqshbandi Sufi Mirza Mazhar Jan-i Janan (died in 1781) also expressed relatively conciliatory views of the Hindus, but he did not go as far as Dara Shukoh in recognizing the legitimacy and validity of the Hindu religion after the emergence of Islam. Like Dara Shukoh, Jan-i Jahan accepted the antiquity and divine origin of the Vedas which, he thought, had been revealed at the beginning of creation. All Hindu sects agree that God is one, hold that the world is created, and believe in resurrection and retribution. Their idolatry does not involve association of partners with God; it rather resembles some *dhikr* ceremonies of the Sufis who meditate on the person of their pir in order to gain some spiritual benefits but refrain from carving out a concrete representation of him. The Hindus make representations of certain angels, concentrate their thought on them, thereby creating a link with the entities represented by them, and reaping some spiritual benefits. They even prostrate themselves in front of them, but this is only a prostration of greeting (*sajda-yi taḥiyyat*) and not a prostration of worship (*sajda-yi 'ubūdiyyat*). All this bears no resemblance to the idolatry of the pre-Islamic Arabs, who thought that the idols were powerful in themselves and not mere instruments of the divine power. Arab idolatry was, therefore, association of partners with God. Its Indian variety is different and serves only as a means that enables the worshippers to forge a spiritual link with the deity. This deity is totally different from its concrete representation.

Like Dara Shukoh before him, Jan-i Janan also thought that India was favoured with the divine gift of prophecy. Krishna and Rama Chandra fulfilled in his view prophetic tasks, and their title of *avatār* is to be understood as comparable—in Islamic terms—with messenger (*rasūl*), prophet (*nabī*), or saint (*walī*). This being so, the Hindu religion was in the past a true divine faith, and it was incumbent upon the Indians to follow the prophets who had been sent to their country. With the advent of Muhammad, however, a fundamental change took place in this regard:

all former religions were abrogated by Islam, and since that time nobody was justified in refraining from embracing it.

Thus, the crucial felure of Jan-i Janan's view of Hinduism is the distinction he made between the Hindus who lived prior to the mission of Muhammad and those of the Islamic era. Those who have lived since the coming of Islam without joining its fold are infidels even if their beliefs are different from those of the *jāhilī* Arabs and are not polytheistic. There is no contradiction between this and Jan-i Janan's statement, according to which all Hindu sects agree on the unity of God: even a monotheist who does not acknowledge the prophethood of Muhammad is an infidel.[2]

The thinkers whose attitudes have been discussed here are representatives of the conciliatory approach to Hinduism in Indo-Muslim thought. While there are valid reasons to characterize them in this way, we must also not lose sight of important differences between them. Al-Biruni differs from the rest by being first and foremost a scholar who speaks about the various religions, including Islam, with a considerable degree of detachment. As such, he is able to discern in the religions compared features that may easily escape a person whose starting point is his own personal faith. His analysis of religious attitudes characteristic of comparable social groups in various religious communities is a case in point. As for Amir Khusrau, he is mainly a historian and a poet, and the religious views expressed in his works seem to be of secondary importance. Thus, when he describes the land of India and expatiates on the virtues of its inhabitants, he has some positive things to say about their religious achievements; but when he deals with the military exploits of his regal patrons, he is not different from other court historians for whom Hindus were nothing but infidel enemies destined for hell.

On the other hand, both Dara Shukoh and Jan-i Janan are primarily religious thinkers, but they differ substantially from each other. While the relationship between Islam and Hinduism is for Dara Shukoh an all-pervasive concern, it is only one detail in Jan-i Janan's religious worldview. The nature of both thinkers' attitude to Hinduism is also not identical. Dara Shukoh ascribes to the Hindu scriptures a legitimacy not less than that of the Qur'an. In a certain sense the Upanishads are even superior to all other heavenly books, because the divine message is expressed in them in the most explicit fashion. They are therefore essential for understanding the less clear statements of the Qur'an. In saying this, Dara Shukoh abandons the cherished Islamic conviction that Islam is, in the eyes of Allah, the only true faith (Sūra 3: 19) and that the Qur'an is a clear, readily understandable book. It is precisely on this point that he differs from Jan-i Janan. While the tenor of Jan-i Janan's discourse about the Hindus is relatively moderate, and he speaks favourably about some ancient Hindu religious figures, he strongly believes that Hinduism was valid only in the pre-Islamic past. Islam abrogated all other faiths and has been the only true religion since its emergence. All people who are now not Muslims are therefore infidels. In contradistinction to Dara Shukoh and despite the conciliatory tone of his discourse, Jan-i Janan assiduously maintains the exclusive validity of Islam and does not deviate from the mediaeval *ijmā'* on this matter. His inclusion among the exponents of the conciliatory trends is due only to the fact that he displays some sympathy for the Hindu religion in its pre-Islamic past and that he expresses his views on Hinduism without the acrimony frequently encountered in mediaeval Indo-Muslim writings.

IV

We have said in our introductory section that the conciliatory trend described in the preceding pages was always weaker than its opposite counterpart. The idea that Islam is a self-sufficient system, that the religious truth is fully and exclusively contained in it, and that it must therefore enjoy the position of superiority over all other faiths, can be easily documented by copious quotations from the classical sources of Islam. The total incompatibility between Islam and the religious environment in which the Indian Muslims lived was favourable for the development of Islamic exclusiveness. In several Islamic traditions India was considered as the source of idolatry and as the first country in which this cult was observed (Friedmann 1975: 214). The possible analogies between Hindu India and pagan Arabia at the time of the Prophet encouraged the development of iconoclasm, which could easily be described as application of early Islamic ideas to the Indian context. Mahmud Ghaznawi's exploits in India, and particularly the destruction of Somnath in 1025–6 (Bosworth 1973: 78, 114), were praised as a sequel to Muhammad's obliteration of Arabian idolatry. The idol of Somnath was identified with the *jāhilī* idols Manāt or al-Lāt, which, so it seems, were brought to the safe haven of idolatrous India after the conquest of Mecca by the Muslims, but were apprehended and finally destroyed there by Mahmud bin Sabuktigin ('Aṭṭār 1962: 207–8); Bosworth 1966: 90; Habib n.d.: 5). Mahmud can thus be described as bringing the Prophet Muhammad's iconoclastic endeavour to its completion.

The historians of the Delhi Sultanate reflect the total rejection of Hinduism as an absolutely worthless and contemptible religion (Hardy 1960: 114 and *passim*). Ziya al-Din Barani declares that the sultan must not be content with taking jizya from the Hindus, who are 'worshippers of idols and of cow dung' (Habib n.d.: 46–7). He demands that the sultan should strive with all his courage to overthrow infidelity and to slaughter its leaders, who in India are the Brahmans'. (Habib n.d.: 46–7). A similar attitude is reflected in the writings of the Mughul historian 'Abd al-Qadir Badayuni, who bemoans throughout his *Muntakhab al-tawārīkh* the consideration shown by Akbar to Hindu beliefs and practices (Badayuni 1284 AH: 239 and *passim*).

An equally outspoken exponent of the uncompromising attitude to India and to its religious tradition was the celebrated Naqshbandi Sufi Shaikh Ahmad Sirhindi (1564–1624). On all issues relevant to this inquiry he adopted an attitude diametrically opposed to that of Dara Shukoh. In light of the Qur'anic view concerning the universality of prophethood, he had to admit that prophets were sent to India as to all other countries; but he is careful to follow this admission by saying that the mission of these prophets was a dismal failure and that none of them succeeded in establishing a community. The ruins scattered all over India are those of towns and villages that rejected the prophets and were consequently destroyed by divine wrath. Despite their failure, these prophets exercised some influence upon the spiritual life of India. Whatever the 'leaders of Indian infidelity' (*ru'asā'-i kufr-i Hind*) know about the necessary existence of God, they learned it from these unsuccessful apostles. The deficient intellects of the Brahmans would never have reached this awareness without prophetic guidance. Yet despite their indebtedness to the prophets, the Brahmans misuse the knowledge communicated to them, falsify the prophetic message, and induce people to bestow divine worship upon their own persons (Friedmann 1971: 71).

It is clear that in Sirhindi's view, absolutely no religious value can be ascribed to the Hindu tradition, which is the embodiment of infidelity. Islam and infidelity are two irreconcilable opposites, which can only thrive at the expense of each other. The honour of Islam requires the humiliation of infidels. The Hindus must therefore be oppressed, treated like dogs and mercilessly subjected to the jizya. The supremacy of Islam must fearlessly be demonstrated. A very effective way to do it is by cow-sacrifice, which is 'one of the most glorious commandments of Islam in India' (*min ajall sha'ā'ir al-islām fī al-hind*) (Sirhindi 1383 AH: 6; Friedmann 1971: 71). The utter disregard of Hindu sensitivities implied in this rite is taken as an indication of the extent to which Indian Islam preserved its pristine purity and refused to make any concessions to the pagan environment.

Sirhindi's son, Muhammad Ma'ṣum, thought along similar lines. In an evident allusion to the thought of Akbar and Abu'l-fazl, he rejected the attitude of 'universal tolerance' (*ṣulḥ-i kull*) and argued that those who supported it treated well all kinds of non-Muslims, but adopted an unreservedly hostile attitude to the followers of the *sunna* (Ma'ṣum n.d.: I,121). Indiscriminate tolerance is opposed to the injunctions of the Qur'an, which demanded the acceptance of Islam, called for *jihād*, and declared all religions except Islam as false. Sinners and infidels are enemies of God: Muslims must therefore dissociate themselves from them and fight them. 'Get close to Allah by hating the people of sin' (*taqarrabū ilā Allāh bi-bughḍ ahl al-ma'āṣī*), says a *ḥadīth* approvingly quoted by Muḥammad Ma'ṣum (Ma'ṣum n.d.: I, 113–6).

The relationship between Islam and Hinduism was not a very important issue in the thought of Ahmad Sirhindi or of his son. Both of them devoted the overwhelming portion of their works to Sufi theosophy, which does not relate to the Indian environment in any significant way. In the thought of the modern interpreters and admirers, however, Sirhindi's views of Hinduism acquired central importance (Friedmann 1971: 105–15). The development of Sirhindi's modern image is a clear reflection of the fact that the uncompromising attitude to Hinduism gained the upper hand, both politically and culturally. The execution of prince Dara in 1659 was not only the end of the struggle for succession to the Mughul throne: it also was a decisive event in the cultural history of Indian Islam.

NOTES

1. We include in our survey only views of Muslims who lived in India. Exposition of Indian tradition by Muslims who lived in the central Islamic lands are not dealt with here. For a substantial work on the latter subject, see Bruce B. Lawrence (1975), *Shahrastani on the Indian religions*. The Hague.

2. A more extensive treatment of Jan-i Janan's thought, with documentation and bibliography, can be found in Friedmann 1975: 217–21.

BIBLIOGRAPHY

Abu'l-fazl 'Allami (1948), *Ā'īn-i Akbarī*, trans. by H.S. Jarrett. Calcutta.

Ahmad, A. (1960), "Le movement des Mujāhidīn dans I'Inde au XIXe siècle", *Orient, 4 (3e trimestre)*, pp. 105–16.

Ahmad, A. (1964), *Studies in Islamic culture in the Indian environment*, London.

Amir Khusrau (1949), *The Nuh Sipihr of Amir Khusrau*, ed. by Muhammad Wahid Mirza, London.

Amir Khusrau (1953), *Khazā'in al-futūh*, ed. by Muhammad Wahid Mirza, Calcutta.

'Aṭṭār, Farīd al-Dīn (1962), *Mantiq al-ṭayr*, Tehran.

Badayuni, 'Abd al-Qādir (1284), *Muntakhab al-tawārīkh*, Lucknow 1284 AH; English trans. by W.H. Lowe, Calcutta 1924.

Al-Biruni (1958), *Taḥqīq mā li'l-Hind min maqūla maqbūla fī'l-'aql aw mardhūla*, Hyderabad (Deccan).

Bosworth, C.E. (1966), 'Mahmud of Ghazna in contemporary eyes and in later literature', *Iran*, 4, pp. 85–92.

Bosworth, C.E. (1973), *The Ghaznavids*, Beirut.

Dara Shukoh (1957), 'Abd al-Quddūs Gangōhi (1456–1573): the personality and attitudes of a medieval Indian Sufi', *Medieval India: a miscellany*, 3, pp. 1–66.

Friedmann, Y. (1971), *Shaikh Aḥmad Sirhindi*, Montreal/London.

Friedmann, Y. (1971a), 'The attitude of the *Jam'iyyat al-'ulamā'-i Hind* to the Indian national movement and to the establishment of Pakistan', *Asian and African Studies* 7, pp. 157–80.

Friedmann, Y. (1972), 'The temple of Multān. A note on early Muslim attitudes to idolatry', *Israel Oriental Studies*, 2, pp. 176–82.

Friedmann, Y. (1975), ' Medieval Muslim views of Indian religions,' *Journal of the American Oriental Society* 95, pp. 214–21.

Friedmann, Y. (1976), 'The *Jam'iyyat al- 'ulamā-i Hind* in the wake of partition', *Asian and African Studies*, 11, pp. 181–211.

Friedmann, Y. (1977), 'A contribution to the history of Islam in India', M. Rosen-Ayalon, *Studies in memory of Gaston Wiet*, Jerusalem.

Gobel-Gross, E. (1962), *Die persische Upanischaden-ubersetzung des Mogulprinzen Dara Sukkoh*, Marburg.

Habib, M. and Salim Khan, A.U. (n.d.), *The political theory of the Delhi Sultanate*, New Delhi.

Hardy, P. (1957), 'Djizya', *Encyclopedia of Islam*, 2nd edn., vol. 2, pp. 566–7.

Hardy, P. (1959), 'Barani', *Encyclopedia of Islam*, 2nd edn., vol. 1, pp. 1037–8.

Hardy, P. (1960), *Historians of mediaeval India: Studies in Indo-Muslim historical writing*, London.

Hardy, P. (1971), *Partners in freedom and true Muslims. The political thought of some Muslim scholars in British India 1912–1947*, Lund.

Hasrat, B.J. *Dārā Shikoh*, Calcutta, 1953.

Huart, C. and Massignon, L. (1926), "Les entretiens de Lahore entre le prince imperial Dārā Shikūh et l'ascète Hindu Baba La'l Dās", *Journal Asiatique*, 209, pp. 285–334.

Jamil-ud-Din Ahmad (1960), *Speeches and writings of Mr. Jinnah*, Lahore.

Lelyveld, D. (1978), *Aligarh's first generation: Muslim solidarity in British India*, Princeton.

Moin-ud-Din Ahmad Khan (1963), 'Hājī Sharī'at Allah: the founder of the Farā'iḍī movement (1781–1840)', *Journal of the Pakistan Historical Society*, 11, pp. 105–26.

Moin-ud-Din Ahmad Khan (1964), 'Religious doctrines of the Farā'iḍīs', *Journal of the Pakistan Historical Society*, 13, pp. 31–59.

Muḥammad Ma'ṣum (n.d.), *Maktūbāt-i Ma'sūmiyya*, Karachi.

Nizami, K.A. (1961), *Some aspects of religion and politics in India in the thirteenth century*, Bombay.

Qureshi, I.H. (1962), *The Muslim community of the Indo-Pakistan subcontinent (610–1947)*, The Hague.

Al-Rāzī (1324), *Mafātiḥ al-ghayb*, n.p. 1324 AH.

Sachau, E.C. (1964), *Al-Beruni's India* (reprint), New Delhi.

Sirhindi, Ahmad (1383 AH), *Ithbāt al-nubuwwa*, Haydarabad (Sind), 1383 AH.

Al-Tabari (1954), *Jāmi' al-bayān 'an ta'wīl āy al-qur'ān*, Cairo.

Al-Tabarsi (1954), *Majma' al-bayān fi tafsīr al-Qur'ān*, Beyruth.

Troll, C.W. (1978), *Sayyid Aḥmad Khān: a reinterpretation of Muslim theology*, New Delhi.

3

A Medieval Encounter Between Hindu and Muslim: Eknath's Drama-Poem *Hindu-Turk Saṃvād*[*]

Eleanor Zelliot

The goal is one; the ways of worship are different.
Listen to the dialogue between these two:
The Turk calls the Hindu 'Kafir!'
The Hindu answers, 'I will be polluted—get away!'
A quarrel broke out between the two;
A great controversy began...

The beginning lines of Eknath's sixteenth-century *bhāruḍ*, the *Hinḍu-Turk Saṃvād*,[1] set the stage for a long, hard-hitting, humorous argument between a Hindu and a Muslim. Composed in the heydey of Hindu-Muslim cultural interaction, it offers an interesting view of the way in which a Brahman viewed a Muslim and his religion. It may also offer some reality about the views of the Muslim, since Eknath's style in his drama-poems, or *bhāruḍs*, was to speak as accurately as he could through the voice of another person. It is an unusual source through which to approach the problem of the nature of the encounter between Hindu and Muslim in medieval times.

Recent studies of *saṇts* and poets in the bhakti, or devotional religion, schools of North India and of their Sufi counterparts in Islam have begun to shed considerable light on the ways in which Sufis and bhaktas may have influenced each other.[2] The actual encounter between Hindu and Muslim is another matter, and one for which there is little source material available in English. Leaving aside the all-important figure of Guru Nanak as the most radical synthesizer of Hindu and Muslim ideology and

* Reprinted from Fred W. Clothey, ed., *Images of Man: Religion and Historical Process in South Asia* (Madras, New Era Publications, 1982), pp. 171–95.

practice, one might point out three ways in which other Hindu bhaktas dealt with the presence of Muslims. Dadu of Rajasthan (1544–1603) dwelt on the 'majestic and absolute but benevolent God/Guru' much like the contemporary concept of Akbar, the Mughal emperor.[3] Kabir (fifteenth century) has recently been called the 'apostle of Hindu-Muslim unity,'[4] but often scorned the outward signs and symbols of both Hinduism and Islam and clung to his own tough poetic vision of reality. Chaitanya in Bengal (1486–1533) converted Muslims to his Vaishnava faith by showing them that the Qur'an told of a personal God much like Krishna, but that his way was the better way to approach that God.[5]

Eknath in Maharashtra (1533–99) had a rather different approach from any of these, as well as a very different way of presenting his (or his characters') attitudes toward Islam and Hinduism. Like Kabir, he was critical of much in Hindu and Muslim practice that seemed hypocritical, but he seems even more interested in finding similar practices and similar beliefs in both religions that can be incorporated into some higher truth. Like Chaitanya, Eknath believed that the God of the Qur'an was the God of the Hindus, but his theme is that God made both Hindu and Muslim in His full wisdom, and there need be no conversion. Eknath's purpose in writing the Hindu-Muslim dialogue was both to entertain his hearers with the ridiculousness of human behaviour and to instruct them in the very nature of religion.

Eknath's Hindu-Turk dialogue is one of some three hundred bhāruḍs, a bhakti poetry genre which has no strict rhyme or meter pattern but always involves the poet's speaking through the voice of some other person, animal, or bird, or through the metaphor of a game, a government document, or some other aspect of the work-a-day world. Eknath's other bhāruḍs include such things as a dialogue between a Brahman and a Mahar[6] and one between a Brahman and a dog; messages in the mouths of fortune-tellers, tumblers, untouchables, a hen-pecked man, a prostitute, a devotee of the god Khandoba, a snake-charmer, and a madman; and calls to devotion through the metaphor of a drum, a dance-game called *phugaḍī*, and an offical government letter of warning. Several bhāruḍs are in corrupt Hindustani and ten others are spoken as if by Muslims: a *darwīsh*, a faqir, and a Habshi or Ethiopian migrant to Maharashtra who ends each second line in his accounting of the ten incarnations of Vishnu with the word Muhammad!

As can be guessed from the listing above, Eknath's bhāruḍs are often dramatic and also humorous. Those that I have heard sung by *bhajan* groups today are acted out vigorously, often in costume, not sung reverently or ecstatically. Although the voices of the bhāruḍs are those of the non-orthodox, Eknath does not scorn or deride them. Rather, each character, from untouchable Mahar to heterodox Mahanubhav to Hindi-speaking Muslim, is allowed to be the voice of some aspect of the bhakti religion. The messages that Eknath expresses through the bhāruḍ form are most often these: the necessity for a moral life and for devotion to the sanṭs; the need to understand God as both *nirguṇa* (without qualities) and *saguṇa* (with qualities, a personal God); and the fact that underneath all the trappings of caste and sect is one reality. However, the trappings, the outward signs, symbols, and practices, are fully and often accurately delineated for each character. It is as if Eknath not only observed all the life around him with a keen eye but had a capacity for empathy with all living beings, however low, strange, or foreign.[7]

Eknath seems at first an unlikely author of such a popular, wide-ranging and occasionally vulgar set of poems. He was a scholarly Brahman who lived in the orthodox centre of Paithan, an ancient capital on the Godavari river in the heartland of the Marathi-speaking country. His vast amount of writing includes translation of and commentary upon a number of Sanskrit philosophical works, several thousand of the traditional bhakti songs called *abhaṇgs* in Marathi, a Marathi version of the *Rāmāyaṇa*, a narrative of the marriage of Rukmini to Krishna, and his masterpiece, a commentary on the eleventh *skanda* of the *Bhāgavata Purāṇa* known as the *Eknāthī Bhāgavata.*[8] In all his work, however, he tried to bring the highest of philosophical thought down to the level of understanding of the common man. The bhāruḍs seem especially shaped to appeal to the unlearned, to interest those who might not otherwise listen to the bhakti message.

Although Eknath's town of Paithan was considered so holy it was called the Banaras of Maharashtra, it was also a market city that produced a luxurious silk cloth called *paithāṇī*; it was on the trade route from the north of India to the sea; and it was forty miles south of Daulatabad, a former Muslim capital and an important city in the Ahmadnagar Sultanate. Eknath was not a Brahman recluse, but was a householder as well as scholar. The material in the bhāruḍs is drawn from all the bustling life, the variety of passers-by, the day-to-day sights and sounds that surrounded Eknath. Both the bhāruḍs and the legends of Eknath's life tell us that Muslims were an important part of the life in that area of Maharashtra.

There are five instances in the eighteenth-century biography of Eknath compiled by Mahipati[9] in which Eknath encounters some facet of Islam. First, Eknath's beloved guru was Janardan, who was not only a swami but also some sort of military commander in the army of Daulatabad, a town and fort within the Sultanate of Ahmadnagar. The legend goes that Eknath himself once led the Muslim armies of that town in a counter-attack rather than wake his guru from deep meditation. A little later, when Eknath is ready for initiation, the god Datta[10] appears as a bearded Muslim faqir, only revealing himself as the supreme being when Eknath drinks water from the pot the faqir has sent to be washed. Together with his guru Janardan, Eknath then meets Chandrabhat or Chand Bodhale, a distinguished Vaishnava. When Chand Bodhale wishes to be entombed alive, Eknath and Janardan build a Muslim tomb 'lest the Mahomedans should cause trouble,' and so that 'both Hindus and Muslims were satisfied.'[11] Recent scholarship has added to the legend the supposition that Chand Bodhale was both a bhakta and a Sufi of the unorthodox Malaṇg order.[12]

In the fourth instance, Brahma, Vishnu and Siva appear as Muslim faqirs to test Eknath's 'conviction of God being in every creature, and his love for them."[13] Eknath serves them food in his house, and is saved from excommunication by Paithan's orthodox Brahmans only by a timely miracle. The last story is the only one that indicates real friction between Hindu and Muslim. A Muslim who hates Brahmans spits on Eknath, who forgives him with saintly restraint.

There seem to be no references to Muslim government or to Muslim officials in Mahipati's story of Eknath, even though the area had been under Muslim control since 1296. Eknath's bhāruḍs in the metaphor of government documents, such as letter of assurance, letter of petition, injunction, etc., are heavily Persianized, and certainly indicate familiarity with officialdom. Modern Marathi hagiography usually casts Eknath in the role of saving Hinduism in Maharashtra from the hated Muslim tide, but a number of contemporary historians, both Hindu and Muslim, see the medieval period generally as one of tolerance, participation of Hindus in government, and cultural exchange.[14]

It is probable that there were Sufis in the Marathi-speaking area before the political presence of Muslims. The first recorded name, however, is that of Muntakhab al-Din of the Chishti order, who evidently came to Devagiri just before 'Ala al-Din Khalji stormed that Yadava capital in 1296. Muntakhab al-Din died in Devagiri in 1296 and was buried in Khuldabad just outside the city.[15] His tomb, now known locally as that of Muntajab al-Din Zar Zari Bakhsh Dulahen, is the site of one of the four largest religious festivals in Aurangabad district.[16] Chishti Sufis continued to come to Devagiri throughout the political upheavals of the next half century. Formal control by the Delhi Sultanate was established in Devagiri in 1310 after the death of the compliant, tribute-paying king of the Yadavas. In 1327, Muhammad bin Tughluq's curious effort to compel the population of Delhi to migrate to his new capital in Devagiri resulted in turmoil, and in the renaming of the city as Daulatabad.

As part of Tughluq's disastrous migration, a disciple of Nizam al-Din Auliya, the chief Chishti saint in India, was sent to Devagiri-Daulatabad. Mir Hasan 'Ala'i Sanjari lived in Daulatabad until his death in 1336, and, according to Subhan, spread Nizam al-Din's ideas there through a collection of his sayings, the *Fawā'id al-fu'ād* (Beneficent to the Heart).[17] Nizami credits Shaikh Burhan al-Din Gharib, 'one of the senior most disciples of Shaikh Nizam al-Din Auliya,' with making the great saints of the Chishti order 'household words in the mystic circles of the South.'[18] It is clear that for at least forty years, Daulatabad was one of the great Chishti centres in India.

With the loss of control of the Delhi Sultanate over provinces in the South, the Bahmani kingdom came into being, and shortly after its establishment in 1347, the Bahmanis shifted their capital from Daulatabad to Gulbarga, outside the Marathi-speaking area. During the hundred and fifty years of Bahmani rule, there seems to be a decline both in the importance of the Chishtis in Daulatabad, and in the creativity of Hindi *saṇts* and poets who had begun the Marathi literary tradition toward the end of Yadava rule. Dnyaneshwar wrote his great commentary on the *Bhagavad Gitā* shortly before his death in 1296, the very year of Khalji's raid into the Deccan. The devotional religious movement that stemmed from Dnyaneshwar, however, flourished through a great circle of sants and poets in the generation following chiefly through Namdev. After 1350, the year of Namdev's death, 'no literary work worth the name comes to hand till we reach the age of Eknatha.'[19] Curiously enough, the same thing could be said for Sufi writing during those two hundred years in the Maharashtra area.

The Bahmani kingdom began to break up toward the end of the fifteenth century, and out of its ruin came five sultanates, among them the Nizam Shahi government under Malik Ahmad. A new Muslim capital was established in the Marathi-speaking area, the city of Ahmadnagar, begun in 1494 some fifty miles south and west of Paithan. There was an influx of Marathi speakers into the new government, and although no great cultural synthesizer such as Ibrahim II in Bijapur arose, the Ahmadnagar centre saw a rich mixture of Persians, Turks, Hindus, and Abyssinians, including the famous Malik Ambar. There seems not to have been a Sufi revival,[20] but in the century following the establishment of the Ahmadnagar kingdom, the bhakti tradition was revived and invigorated. The key figure in this revival was Eknath, who forged links with the past through his editing of the initial text of the bhakti movement, the *Dnyāneshwāri*, written three hundred years before, and his biographies in poetic form of all the early saṇts. So well was the bhakti tradition nourished that it produced its greatest saṇt, Tukaram, in the next century.[21]

The vigor of the bhakti movement after Eknath's dedicated work can be judged by the fact that a number of Muslims became bhakti poets. Best known is Shaikh Muhammad of Shrigonde in the district of Ahmadnagar, whose guru was the same Chand Bodhale who inspired Janardan, the guru of Eknath.[22]

It was in this world, then, that the Hindu-Turk dialogue was written: a somewhat distant, always warring, reasonably tolerant Ahmadnagar kingdom; a memory of Sufi saints from the great and popular Chishti order; a Marathi literary renaissance so strong that even Muslims wrote bhakti poetry in Marathi. Exactly who the Muslim in Eknath's dialogue might have been and why Eknath cast his message in this form will be discussed at the end of the poem. Meanwhile the reader should note that there is no critical edition of this bhāruḍ. Mistakes and changes have undoubtedly crept in over the years, particularly as the use of Persian words has lessened. The typographical errors alone make accurate translation difficult, and Eknath's penchant for puns and word play adds to the difficulty. In addition, some lines are so spare that only an intelligent guess is possible. The Hindu speaks Marathi, using some Hindi words. The Muslim speaks a Marathi-ized Hindustani. In some cases I have simply romanized the script and let it stand; in these cases either the meaning has been totally lost, or Eknath was using meaningless words to carry his poem along, or to give it a little Arabic or Persian flavour. In spite of the difficulties, I am reasonably certain that the translation is fairly faithful to Eknath's spirit.[23]

Hindu-Turk Dialogue

Eknath: 1. The goal is one; the ways of worship are different,
Listen to the dialogue between these two!

2. The Turk calls the Hindu 'Kafir!'
The Hindu answers, 'I will be polluted—get away!'
A quarrel broke out between the two;
A great controversy began.

Muslim 3. 'O Brahman, listen to what I have to say:
Your scripture is a mystery to everyone.
God has hands and feet, you say—
This is really impossible!

Hindu 4. Listen, you great fool of a Turk!
See God in all living things.

You haven't grasped this point
And so you have become a nihilist.

Muslim 5. Listen, Brahman dipper-in-water,
You leap in the water like water ducks.
Whoever studies your scripture
Is a great big fool!

6. You have a *kamākhaloko* scripture.
It says God goes out to beg.
Bali caught him and made him a door-keeper!
This sort of story deceives people.

7. All your scripture is just ridiculous.
You make Allah a servant!
What a *bhāravalavillā*!
This talk is for dim-witted men.

Hindu 8. You don't remember your own book,
It can be read in the *Sulkhan*
pratham abdullā allā huve
[Allah] said begging is the sweets of heaven.
This begging is your God's counsel!

9. Faqir Abdulla was loved by God.
He went to Heaven by giving and taking alms.
Begging is ultimately holy—
God himself showed us this.

Muslim–or 10. I, the Faqir, speak straight out.
new character Faqir Fajtāri is praised by God.
of Faqir? The Faqir serves God.
The Faqir loves God.
Faqir—God
The Faqir says, 'There is no god'
The Faqir says, 'But God.'[24]
The Faqir is a servant of God.

11. Truth is duality.
Hājrat is the giver of life.
Make a joyful noise at the saint's tomb.
Salvation is in heaven;
The unwary go to sorrow.
Thig is Allah's creation;
The negligent go to hell.
I, the Faqir, ask alms.
Allah takes away sin.
Allā valkalatātil tū allā

O Allah, you exist everywhere.
Allah, you exist in the Caliph.
Allah, you are the seeing and the seen.
Allah, you are the knower and the known.
Allah, you are life and the giver of life.
Allah, you are the alms that fill the stomach
and take away sin.
Bring oil and bread, you who have ears!
Allah, give me milk and rice,
Allah, give me gravy, bread, wheat cakes,
Allah, give me lentil cakes,
Allah, give me sweets and sugar!

Hindu: (Sanskrit) I, the Brahman, recite a verse:
One who lives on alms lives on nothing;
Bhikshus reject only their homes.
One who is discontent is the real sinner.
The contented one is described as drinking soma.
Bali was a special devotee of God.
God loved his way of devotion.
So God always stands near him.
Why do you revile this?

Muslim: 12. Your Brahma laid his daughter.
The Vedas he preaches are all false.
Your Śāstras, your Vedas, your 'OM'
Are all evil tricks.
13. How many falsehoods, how much nonsense all
that is.
Thieves took away God's wife,
So monkeys came to help him!
You've read and read the scripture and died!
Admit your mistakes and shut up!

Hindu: 14. She you call your teacher's wife
You treat as your own wife!
Look at the 'faithfulness' of the Turk!
And he censures the Brahman!
15. Father Adam and Eve made a pair.
You have read this book.
You don't know your scriptures, you fool.
Why do you quarrel with us?
16. Adam and Eve enjoyed each other:
From that came the world of men!

You give your name as Adam.
You speak, and make a fool of yourself!

17. Baba Adam's Eve went away.
You say she was taken by Satan.
Well, Sita was stolen by Ravana.
Why do you deride our story?

18. Then the angels took counsel:
Gabriel
Israfael
mankāīl
naskāīl
Michael[25]
Victorious, they returned with wife Eve.
Rama called forth great warriors
To search for Sita.
(What's the difference?)

Muslim: 19. Listen, Brahman, you are clever as an ass!
Your answer is nonsense; your answer is stupid.
Whoever reads your scripture
Is greatly unenlightened!

20. Fool! Your God was imprisoned;
Kansasur came to kill him.
Devaki concealed your God.
What a stupid scripture for the ignorant!

21. What was hidden, closed in, was made open.
From this sort of thing comes knowledge?
yā hilā yā sālim!

22. You deceive yourself with your own mouth.
You call God a keeper of cows.
When you hear these stories you weep!
You call God a cattleman!

23. The *kāfir* has lost his sense.
You have destroyed the greatness of God!
Shall I give you a blow?
And still you argue!

Hindu: 24. Look how your mouth babbles on.
God is present in every place—
Why not in prison?
You take this as a contradiction in vain!

25. One who has greatness of mind
Knows God is not fixed in one place.

God is hidden in the secret, brother!
Read the Qur'an and see!

26. It is difficult for the mind to grasp God
But God can fill one's mind
And open the secret of the secret.
Your Prophet so spoke!

27. Holy man, holy man Shahmodin Ali
The great one said:
Cow, elephant, monkey—
God protects every one.
This is stated in your books.
Why don't you honour it?

28. Dogs, crows, rats, birds—
God protects these too.
You don't know your own scripture, dumbbell!
Why do you pick a fight with me?

Muslim: 29. You go on talking, talking, Brahman.
What sorts of pretexts are you giving me?
You bow before God,
But has God shaved your head and beard?

30. You Hindus are really wicked.
A stone statue rules over you.
You give it the name of God.
You wake it with an *ek tārī*!

31. In its presence you read the *Purāṇa*.
Men and women all stand together.
You bow and scrape in front of it.
Isn't that so, you great fool?

32. You smear ochre on a stone
And your women stand before it!
Naked sadhus, clad in lemon leaves,
Are followed by young maidens!

33. Your *Vedas* and all are impotent!
Without exception, your verses are unworthy.
You make such a hubbub when you worship
You must think God is unheeding, neglectful!

Hindu: 34. God is in water, in places, in wood, in stone.
That is the chief meaning of your book.
Look, you yourselves don't know it!
The Turk's ignorance is total!

35. The ghee, liquid or solid, is one substance.
So, see, the absolute and the image are one.
But you hate the images!
You are a great undiscriminating fool!
36. Whatever desire the devotee has,
That desire is fulfilled by God.
That is the theory of your book!
Why don't you realize this?
37. I have revealed your lack of faith to you!
You shout from afar at the God close at hand!
One time, 'Allah!' One time, 'Allah!'
The rest of your day is wasted,
And He has not met you so far.
38. For the distant, one gives a great shout!
For the near, one whispers.
You ought to meet Him who is close.
By shouting you only wake the children!
39. You think God is in the West.
Are all other directions barren?
You say God is in all four corners,
But you don't understand this, you fool.
40. Five times a day belong to God.
Are other times taken by thieves?
You have deceived yourself about your scriptures.
You have made a one-direction God!
41. You tell us we worship stones?
Why do you place blocks of stone over the dead?
You worship a *hājī* of stone.
You believe it to be the true *pīr*!
42. Why do you preserve the bones
Of those who are only corpses?
You cover the stone with flowers and silk cloth;
You burn incense before it!

Muslim: 43. You can bathe in the Ganga and become pure;
Then why do you maintain distinctions?
Even separate cooking and eating?
You call out 'Pollution, pollution!'
All is impure, sinful, to you.
44. You say God exists in all living beings.
Tell me, who of you eats all together?
One man doesn't touch another.
Each lives apart from the other.

45. If so much as a grain of his food falls on yours,
You catch him by the throat!
Don't leave your religion half-done.
What about this opposition between every two groups?

46. A woman must eat in her own home.
But sometimes you expel her!
You go to her at night, you sleep with her;
Then you don't call her impure!

47. That girl you have taken as mistress—
You don't eat in the house of her people!
You like the daughter but not the food!
O what a great book of the Brahmans!

48. 'Our food is very holy;
His food is completely bad.'
This is the relation between relations!
Your scriptures are false!

49. The daughter is pure, the father is impure!
Let your scripture become ash;
Let *karma. dharma*, be reduced to ashes!
To hell with the Brahman for his hypocrisy!

Hindu 50. You Muslims are complete fools.
You don't know what is faulty, or faultless.
When one creature gives pain to another,
How can he go to heaven?

51. If God kills an animal, look, it is carrion.
If you kill one—that is holy and pure!
You have become more pure than God!
The Muslim is deceitful and sinful.

52. When you sacrifice an animal, you throw it aside.
It suffers in front of you.
What the hell do you gain from this?
The learned one is mad, Maulana *sālīm*.

53. When sacrificed, the goat goes to heaven.
Then why do you fast and feast?
Why not kill yourself
To get to Heaven's home?

54. The Maulana may do a thousand killings,
But can the good Maulana bring one being back to life?
This is fruitless toil for heaven,
This immediately becomes a sin.

55. Hindu and Muslim both
Are created by God, brother.
But look at the belief of the Turk:
He is supposed to catch a Hindu and make him a Muslim!

56. Did God make a mistake in making the Hindu?
Is your wisdom greater than His?
You make the Hindu a Muslim
And assign the crime to God.

Muslim: 57. He who kills has committed a sin—
Look, the Turk says that is right!
Listen, he has committed a crime!
Let's not quarrel over nothing.

58. While killing, the Maulana recites from the Book,
But his tongue cannot move to restore life.
No one can do that but God.
What the Brahman says is true.

59. It is the hand of heaven that cuts the throat;
That hand really creates its own ways.
If trouble comes in the future
God will rule.

Hindu: 60. The Brahman says, O yes, swami.
As a matter of fact, you and I are one.
This controversy grew over caste and *dharma*.
When we go to God, there are no such things.

Muslim: 61. The Turk says, that is the truth.
For God, there is no caste.
There is no separation between devotee and God
Even though the Prophet has said God is hidden.

Eknath: 62. The Turk whose *dharma* had subsided
Listened to his inner heart.
He became filled with joy.
Instead of a *mantra*, instruction was given.

63. At that moment, they saluted each other.
With great respect, they embraced.
Both became content, happy,
Quiet, calm.

64. 'You and I quarrelled
To open up the knowledge of the high truth,
In order to enlighten the very ignorant.
In place of *karma*—awakening!

65. 'In place of words we have established the
word's meaning.'
The highest truth pierced them both.
Enlightenment was the purpose of this quarrel.
Both have been satisfied.
66. The argument was about oneness.
The argument became agreement.
Eka Janardan says, 'Self-knowledge
And great bliss came to both.'

What sort of a Muslim appears in this Hind-Turk dialogue? The 'Turk' can mean either an ethnic Turk or simply a Muslim.[26] Certainly no order of Sufis is clearly indicated, although verses 10 and 11 indicate a mendicant faqir is involved in the conversation, either as a new voice or as a facet of the character of the Turk. The terms the Hindu uses for the Turk are many, and only a few indicate Sufism. He addresses the Turk chiefly as Turk, but also calls him brother, using the Hindi word *bhāī*, and in verse 60, *swāmī*! When speaking of Muslims, the Hindu uses the terms *avaliya*[27] (Sufi saint or holy man), *maulānā* (in connection with the killing of animals), pir (in its proper usage regarding the *dargāh* or saint's tomb) and once *yavan* (stranger or foreigner). Only in verses 55 and 56 when the Hindu speaks about the crime of conversion does Eknath use the Persian (and Marathi) word *musalman*. Both call each other 'fools' in a rich variety of Hindi and Marathi ways which English cannot match!

Sufi technical terms do not appear in the bhāruḍ, although the faqir and the Turk both express Sufi ideas. The idea of *wahdatu'l-wujūd*, the unity of all beings, divine and human, is certainly behind the faqir's hymn to Allah in verse 11. 'Allah, you exist everywhere ... you are the seeing and the seen ..... the knower and the known.' Toward the end of the poem, the Turk says 'There is no separation between devotee and God even though the Prophet has said God is hidden' (verse 61). This is not orthodox Islamic thought, but it is a common theme in Indian Sufism.[28]

It seems to me from the content of the poem that Eknath certainly knew something of Sufism, perhaps even some remnant of Chishti thought. It is probable, however, that the Sufis he himself met were not of any established order, but members of the Malaṇg order, which was *be-shar'* (without the law).[29] The begging patter which follows the Sufistic statement in the faqir's speech and the seven faqir bhāruḍs which Eknath also wrote point to this sort of sufi order. One faqir bhāruḍ introduces a Malaṇg faqir, who speaks in the intoxication of *bhang*. There has been no study of the Malaṇgs in Maharashtra; but the current physical evidence seems to point to their importance. The *'urs* (commemoration of a saint's death day) of Haji Malaṇg in Kalyan, near Bombay, is a very important occasion, attracting several hundred thousand Hindus and Muslims. Local people say the tomb was built 750 years ago and that it is the dargah of Haji 'Abd al-Rahman, an Arab missionary. The dargah as it is today, however, was re-constructed in 1900, and is presided over by a Brahman with hereditary rights.[30]

There are a large number of pirs' tombs in the district of Aurangabad in which Paithan is located, some of which bear the term malaṇg. *Fairs and Festivals in Maharashtra* notes 104 'urs festivals, including ten in Paithan taluka. There are nineteen celebrations of Muslim saints' death days in the two talukas in Ahmadnagar district that border Paithan.[31] The percentage of Muslims in the Aurangabad district also testifies to considerable conversion activity: that area counts seven per cent of its population as Muslims, a higher per cent than in the Ahmadnagar district, which was the seat of the Nizam Shahi government, or in the other districts in Marathwada, which were under the Nizam's government in Hyderabad until very recent times.[32] Whether these conversions came in the great days of the Chishti centre at Daulatabad, or after Aurangzeb founded the city of Aurangabad, very near Daulatabad, in 1640, or during Eknath's period in which Muslim saints wrote Marathi poetry and unorthodox faqirs roamed the countryside, is anyone's guess!

My own supposition is that Islam was an important presence in Eknath's sixteenth-century world. Just as Eknath uses the ubiquitous untouchable Mahar as a voice in forty bhāruḍs to speak a tough bhakti message, he uses the familiar presence of the Muslim not only to speak about the basic unity of all religions, but also to get across some home truths about the hypocrisy of the Hindus. Most of the accusations of the Turk about the ridiculousness of Hindu concepts, such as the image which is god, the stories of Krishna and Bali which 'destroy the greatness of God', or the incestuousness of Brahma, are countered by the Hindu with jibes about similar Islamic practices and stories. The accusation the Hindu cannot answer comes in the taunts of the Muslim about caste divisions and pollution observances. All the Hindu can say is that 'when we go to God, there are no such things.' All of Eknath's writing points to this belief that the true bhakta may observe the inherent authority of the Brahman, but in spiritual matters he honours true bhaktas of any caste or creed.[33]

On the other hand, Eknath is very clear about the wrongness of conversion to Islam. 'Hindu and Muslim both are created by God, brother. Did God make a mistake in making the Hindu? Is your wisdom greater than His?' Eknath also hangs the turning-point of the Turk's attitude on a curious matter. The Muslim comes around to admitting the basic truth that God is in all living things when the Hindu accuses him of believing that killing an animal is a holy matter. This may be a reference to the very popular *bakrid* festival, a time of feasting when not only goats (*bakrā*) but cows and other animals were shared by the Muslim community. Hindus did sacrifice goats and buffalos in certain *devi* festivals, and the Muslim was often the butcher at these times, but Eknath disapproves heartily of this non-Brahman practice. His dwelling on this point may be a way of discouraging animal sacrifice among both Hindus and Muslims—or it may simply be a reinforcement of his basic idea that God dwells in all living beings and life should not be taken because it cannot be restored.

The ultimate message of the dialogue may be the simple statement found in verse 26, one which both Hindus and Muslims would understand:

It is difficult for the mind to grasp God.
But God can fill one's mind.

NOTES

1. The edition I have used is *Śrī Eknāth Mahārāj yāṇca abhangaṇcī gāthā*, edited by Brahmibhut Srinanamaharaj Sakhare (Poona: Indira Prakashan, 1952). *Saṃvād* means dialogue, talk, conversation.

2. See Charles S.J. White, 'Sufism in Medieval Hindi Literature,' *History of Religions* V: 1 (1965), pp. 214–21; Yohanan Friedmann, 'Medieval Muslim Views of Indian Religions,' *Journal of the American Oriental Society* 95: 2 (1975), pp. 214–21; and the chapter on 'Sufism in Indo-Pakistan' in *Mystical Dimensions of Islam* by Annemarie Schimmel (Chapel Hill: University of North Carolina Press, 1975). The bibliographies of these works as well as the references for Kabir, Dadu, and Chaitanya listed below contain references to older works on Hindu-Muslim interaction.

3. Harbans Mukhia, 'The Ideology of the Bhakti Movement: The Case of Dadu Dayal,' in *History and Society: Essays in Honour of Professor Niharranjan Ray*, edited by Debiprasad Chattopadhyaya (Calcutta: K.P. Bagchi, 1978), pp. 445–54.

4. Muhammed Hedayetullah, *Kabir: The Apostle of Hindu-Muslim Unity: Interaction of Hindu-Muslim Ideas in the Formation of the Bhakti Movement with Special Reference to Kabir, the Bhakta*, (Delhi: Motilal Banarsidass, 1977). For Kabir, also see David Carlyle Scott, *Kabir: Maverick and Mystic: The Religious Perceptions, Doctrines and Practices of a Medieval Indian Saint* (University of Wisconsin, Ph. D. dissertation, 1976) and Charlotte Vaudeville, *Kabir*, vol. I (Oxford at the Clarendon Press, 1974). The Kabir poetry translated in Baidyanath Saraswati's 'Notes on Kabir: A Non-Literate Intellectual', in *Dissent, Protest and Reform in Indian Civilization*, edited M.S. Malik (Simla: Indian Institute of Advance Study, 1977) bears an almost uncanny resemblance to some of Eknath's Turk's lines.

5. A long story about Chaitanya and the conversion of Muslims which offers an interesting comparison to Eknath's story is *Śri Chaitanya Caritāmṛta of Kṛṣṇadāsa Kavirāja Gosvāmi. Madhya-lilā* vol. 7, translated by A.C. Bhaktivedanta Swami Prabhupada (New York: Bhaktivedanta Book Trust, 1975), chapter 18: 162–212. See Edward C. Dimock, 'Hinduism and Islam in Medieval Bengal' in *Aspects of Bengali History and Society*, edited by Rachel Van M. Baumer (Honolulu: University of Hawaii, 1975), for a perceptive interpretation of medieval Bengali attitudes.

6. Translated in Eleanor Zelliot, 'Eknath's *Bhāruḍs:* the *Sant* as Link between Cultures,' in *The Sants: Studies in a Devotional Tradition of India*, edited by Karine Schomer and Hugh McLeod (Delhi: Motilal Banarsidass, 1987).

7. I have discussed Eknath's extraordinary empathy in 'Chokha-mela and Eknath: Two *Bhakti* Modes of Legitimacy for Modern Change,' *Journal of Asian and African Studies* 14: 3–4 (1980), Special Number on Tradition and Modernity in *Bhakti* Movements, edited by Jayant Lele.

8. Part of the *Eknāthī Bhāgavata* has been translated by Justin E. Abbott as *Bhikshugita, Poet Saints of Maharashtra* 3 (Poona, 1928). For Eknath's total work, see R.D. Ranade, *Pathway to God in Marathi Literature* (Bombay: Bharatiya Vidya Bhavan, 1961) and Shankar Gopal Tulpule, *Classical Marāthī Literature*, Volume 9, Fasc. 4 of *A History of Indian Literature*, edited by Jan Gonda. (Wiesbaden: Otto Harrassowitz, 1979).

9. Mahipati, *Eknath*, a translation from the *Bhaktālīlāmṛita* by Justin E. Abbott. *Poet Saints of Maharashtra* 2 (Poona, 1927.) Motilal Banarsidass in Delhi has reprinted this translation.

10. There are Muslim influences in the Dattatreya sect in Maharashtra and also in the Nath or Yogi tradition which Eknath bears in his very name. Speculation on Muslim influence on Eknath through these traditions is difficult since he seems to have abandoned them in favor of the bhakti movement, or *Vārkarī saṃpradāyā*. See S.A.A. Rizvi, 'Sufis and Natha Yogis in Medieval Northern India,' *Journal of the Oriental Society of Australia* 7: 1–2 (1970), pp. 119–33 and Simon Digby, 'Encounters with Jogis in Indian Sufi Hagiography,' a paper given at the Seminar on Aspects of Religion in South Asia, School of Oriental and African Studies, 1970, for interesting material on these encounters in the North.

11. Mahipati, *Eknath*, pp. 35–41. Janardan's place of *samādhi* and Chand Bodhale's tomb can still be seen at Daulatabad.

12. A.R. Kulkarni, *Social Relations in the Maratha Country* (*Medieval Period*), Presidential Address, Medieval India Section (32rd Session of the Indian History Congress, Jabalpur, 1970), pp. 8–9. See also Tulpule, *Classical Marathi*, p. 353, who adds that Chand Bodhale's Muslim name was Said Cāndasāheb Kādri, which may indicate the Qadiri order of Sufis.

13. Mahipati, *Eknath*, pp. 88–91.

14. See Kulkarni, *Social Relations*, various articles by P.M. Joshi in *History of Medieval Deccan*, vols. 1 and 2 (Hyderabad: Government of Andhra Pradesh, 1973, 1974), edited by H.K. Sherwani with P.M. Joshi as joint editor; and an earlier article by Moulvi Abdul Haq, 'The Influence of Persian on Marathi,' *Islamic Culture* 10 (1936), pp. 553–609.

15. John A. Subhan, *Sufism—Its Saints and Shrines* (New York: Samuel Weiser, 1970), p. 333. I have followed Subhan's spelling and dates in preference to more authoritative sources since his material seems to be corroborated best by local history.

16. *Fairs and Festivals in Maharashtra*, Part VII-B of the *Census of India 1961* Vol. 10 (Bombay: Maharashtra Census Office, 1969), pp. 175–6.

17. Subhan, *Sufism*, p. 335. For content, see Bruce B. Lawrence, *Notes from a Distant Flute: Sufi Literature in Pre-Mughal India* (Tehran: Imperial Iranian Academy of Philosophy, 1978.) Lawrence notes this Sufi's name as Amir Hasan. K.A. Nizami, 'Sufi Movement in the Deccan,' in H.K. Sherwani ed., *History*, pp. 174–199 of vol. 2, states that 'Amir Hasan Sijzi' went in the armies of Khalji to find 'a new field for mystic activity.'

18. K.A. Nizami, ibid., 179–80. The brief articles and the notes in larger studies on Indian Sufism make one yearn for a study on the Chishtis of Daulatabad and the later Sufis as rich as Richard Maxwell Eaton's *Sufis of Bijapur, 1300–1700: Social Roles of Sufis in Medieval India* (Princeton: Princeton University Press, 1978.) His notes on Sufis as warriors and as social reformers may have relevance in the Maharashtrian situation.

19. Tulpule, *Classical Marathi*, p. 344. It should be noted that the two great famines still remembered in Marathi folklore took place during this period, the Durgadevi famine beginning in 1396 and the Damojipant famine in 1460. See Mohd. Abdul Aziz, 'The Deccan in the 'Fifteenth Century,' *Journal of the Asiatic Society of Bengal*, New Series 21 (1925), pp. 549–91.

20. See Radhey Shyam, *The Kingdom of Ahmadnagar* (Delhi: Motilal Banarsidass, 1966), pp 378–90, for the court literature of Ahmadnagar (1490–1636). Patronage does not seem to have been extended to Sufis, except for land given to maintain the shrine of Hazrat 'Abd ur-Rahman Chishti in the reign of Ahmad Nizam Shah in the late sixteenth century, according to B.G. Kunte, *Maharashtra State Gazetteers History*, Part 2: *Medieval Period* (Bombay: Maharashtra State, 1972), p. 402.

21. The best introduction to the whole bhakti tradition is G.A. Deleury's *The Cult of Vithoba* (Poona: Deccan College Post-graduate and Research Institute, 1960.)

22. The Muslim contribution to bhakti literature has been described in R.C. Dhere's *Musalman marāthī saṇtkavi* (Poona: A.M. Joshi, 1967.)

23. For translating assistance, I am indebted to Mrs. Sumati Vasant Dhadphale of Pune and Jayant Karve of Minneapolis. Richard Eaton, and his associate Jaganath, gave invaluable assistance in interpretation, Maxine Berntsen greatly aided me in boldly interpreting some very difficult lines and correcting some errors, and John M. Stanley encouraged some further speculation on meanings. The faults of the final version are my own.

24. A song by Shah Hashim Khudawand Hadi sung by women at the grind stone, which uses this construction, may be found in Eaton, *op. cit.*, pp. 161–2.

25. See A.S. Jayakar, 'Angelology of Arabs,' *Journal of the Anthropological Society of Bombay*, VI: 6 (1901–1903), pp. 304–28.

26. See Annemarie Schimmel, 'Turk and Hindu: a poetical image and its application to historical fact,' in *Islam and Cultural Change in the Middle Ages*, edited by S. Vryonis (Wiesbaden: Otto Harrasowitz, 1975.)

27. I am tempted to think that line 27: 1 in the *Hindu-Turk Samvād, āvalīya āvaliyā śahāmodīn ālī*, which is followed by what 'the great one' said, may be a reference to Nizam al-Din Auliya, the greatest of the Chishti saints, whose sayings were circulated in the Deccan. The Nizam Shahi government in the area was replaced by that of the Nizam of Hyderabad, and a possible confusion of the two terms would allow for a corruption of the name in the text. *Shāhi* is still used in villages as a term relating to any government.

28. I am grateful to two former students, Jeff Coryell and Colleen Raske, whose interest and study led me into some of the by-ways of Sufi thought and Sufi orders in India.

29. Murray T. Titus in *Islam in India and Pakistan* (Calcutta: Y.M.C.A. Publishing House, 1956) offers a brief note on Malangs and other be-shar' 'orders of independent origin,' pp. 134–6. Eaton, *Sufis*, devotes a chapter to the *majdhūbs* of Bijapur and other darvishes who may be a similar group of faqirs, although their time period is the seventeenth century.

30. *Fairs and Festivals*, pp. 81–4.

31. Ibid., pp. 419–32, 313–17.

32. *Census of India*, Paper No. 1 of 1963. 1961 Census–Religion (Delhi: Manager of Publications, 1963), p. 25

33. G.B. Sardar discusses the depth and the limitations of the egalitarian spirit of Eknath and other *sanṭs* in *The Saint-Poets of Maharashtra* (*Their Impact on Society*), translated by Kumud Mehta (New Delhi: Orient Longman, 1969).

4

Inscribing the Other, Inscribing the Self: Hindu–Muslim Identities in Pre-colonial India*

Cynthia Talbot

The nature of medieval Hindu-Muslim relations is an issue of great relevance in contemporary India. Prior to the 200 years of colonial subjection to the British that ended in 1947, large portions of the Indian subcontinent were under Muslim political control. An upsurge of Hindu nationalism over the past decade has led to demands that the state rectify past wrongs on behalf of India's majority religion.[1] In the nationalist view, Hindu beliefs were continually suppressed and its institutions repeatedly violated during the many centuries of Muslim rule from 1200 AD onward. The focal point of nationalist sentiment is the most visible symbol of Hinduism, its temples. As many as 60,000 Hindu temples are said to have been torn down by Muslim rulers, and mosques built on 3,000 of those temples' foundations.[2] The most famous of these alleged former temple sites is at Ayodhya in north India, long considered the birthplace of the Hindu god, Rama. The movement to liberate this sacred spot, supposedly defiled in the sixteenth century when the Babri Masjid was erected on the ruins of a Rama temple, was one of the hottest political issues of the late 1980s and early 1990s. Tensions reached a peak in December 1992, when Hindu militants succeeded in demolishing the mosque.[3]

* Reprinted from *Comparative Studies in Society and History* 37, no. 4 (October 1995), pp. 692–722. Earlier versions of this article were presented at the 1993 Western Conference of the Association for Asian Studies meeting in Mexico City and the 1994 national meeting of the Association for Asian Studies in Boston. I am deeply indebted to Richard M. Eaton and Phillip B. Wagoner, my fellow panelists on both occasions, whose ideas have so heavily influenced my own. Their editorial assistance is also gratefully acknowledged, as is the help of Susan M. Deeds.

Today, Indian Hindus and Muslims see themselves as distinct religious communities, essentially two separate nations occupying the same ground. Hindu nationalist historians have projected this vision of separateness into the past, stating that Indian Muslims of the middle ages were a community totally different from, and implacably opposed to, the Hindu majority on religious grounds.[4] Moreover, Indian Muslims are defined as a social group that is not indigenous, but of foreign origin to the subcontinent. This implies that Muslims do not belong in India and have no real rights there. Secular Indian historians have decried this interpretation as a misrepresentation, a reading of the past that modern communal biases distort.[5] Since most Indian Muslims have descended from converts and not from immigrants, how can they be cast as an alien group whose way of life differed radically from that of their erstwhile Hindu brethren? At least at the village level, secular historians argue that Hindus and Muslims shared a wide spectrum of customs and beliefs, at times even jointly worshipping the same saint or holy spot.

The dominant scholarly trend of the past ten years has emphasized colonialism's impact on identity formation. Because large-scale conflicts between Hindus and Muslims began under colonial rule, the emergence of broadly based community identities during the nineteenth century has been closely investigated.[6] Communal violence was itself a British construct in some analyses because many other kinds of social strife were labelled as religious, due to the Orientalist assumption that religion was the fundamental division in Indian society.[7] There is a general consensus that it is questionable whether a Hindu or Muslim identity existed prior to the nineteenth century in any meaningful sense.[8] Paradoxically, given the current criticism of the colonial sociology of knowledge and its emphasis on caste, most scholars of the colonial period feel that pre-colonial society was too fragmented by subcaste and local loyalties to have allowed larger allegiances to emerge.[9] The primacy attributed to colonialism in forming contemporary Indian identities reflects the central role of modernity in current theories of nationalism and the emergence of nation-states. The work of Benedict Anderson, with its stress on the role of print-capitalism, has been particularly influential in promoting the belief that identities uniting large numbers of people could arise only after a certain technological level had been attained.[10]

No one would deny that modernization has led to the sharper articulation of identities encompassing broad communities, or that such identities have been 'imagined' and 'invented' to a large extent. Nor can we uncritically accept the primordialist view that postulates the inherent and natural roots of national and ethnic identity. However, modern identities do not spring fully fashioned out of nowhere. They commonly employ the myths and symbols of earlier forms of identity, which may be less clearly formulated and more restricted in circulation but are nonetheless incipient cores of ethnicity.[11] Thus, this essay joins a mere handful of other works on India, both in its insistence that supra-local identities did indeed exist in pre-colonial India and that these identities themselves were historically constructed and hence constantly in flux.[12]

Understanding earlier forms of Hindu-Muslim identities may help us grasp the impulses leading to modern communal conflict. It even offers us the dim hope of defusing present-day tensions by demonstrating that the communities of the past were not identical to those of the present. For, as Sheldon Pollock states in reference to the present Indian situation, 'the symbolic meaning system of a political culture is constructed, and perhaps knowing the processes of construction is a way to control it'.[13] Particularly critical is the recognition that Hindu and Muslim identities were not formed in isolation. The reflexive impact of the Other's presence moulded the self-definition of both groups—indeed, the label 'Hindu' was coined by Muslims to describe the people and culture of the Indian subcontinent. Only after prolonged contact with Muslims did the earlier inhabitants of India adopt the term. Although it may not be possible to reconstruct a detailed picture of Hindu–Muslim interactions in medieval India in terms of actual practice and behaviour, we can and must recover the history of their mutual- and self-perceptions.

In asking what it meant to be a Hindu or a Muslim in middle-period India, I focus on one particular region, Andhra Pradesh in the southeastern peninsula, from 1323 to 1650. This period commences with the collapse of Andhra's indigenous Kakatiya dynasty under repeated military pressures from the Delhi Sultanate and ends at the point in time when the last major Hindu dynasty in Andhra was extinguished. In essence, the years examined span the period from the early stages of Muslim military presence in Andhra to ultimate Muslim dominance. The primary sources utilized consist of approximately 100 records inscribed in the Sanskrit or Telugu languages.[14] The majority are situated within Hindu temple complexes, on stone slabs, pillars, or walls. Because the vast majority of inscriptions document the endowment of land and other valuables to religious institutions, they are by nature the products of the propertied class. The perspective on medieval south India that we can obtain from these sources is strictly a privileged one, limited chiefly to the religious and political elites; yet it is from this strata of society that pre-modern ethnicity typically arose. By utilizing inscriptions, we can get some idea of how the powerful and influential segments of medieval Hindu society viewed Muslims and, conversely, how they viewed themselves.

THE MUSLIM AS DEMONIC BARBARIAN

The early centuries of Islamic expansionism left South Asia largely untouched. Although the lower Indus valley region of Sind in modern Pakistan was conquered by Arabs in the early eighth century, the effects of the Arab presence were restricted to the western portions of the subcontinent. From approximately AD 1000 onward, however, major centres of power in northwestern India came under intermittent attack by armies of Turkic Muslims who were based in what is now Afghanistan. These raids into Indian territory culminated in the seizure of the Delhi region c. 1200 and in the establishment of a series of Islamic dynasties, collectively known as the Delhi Sultanate, that survived into the early sixteenth century. Much of north India came under the hegemony of the Delhi Sultanate in the early thirteenth century, while sultanate expeditions began penetrating south India at the very end of the thirteenth century. The most momentous era of contact between Islamic and earlier peoples of the Indian subcontinent thus occurred between the eleventh and fourteenth centuries.

The threat felt by Hindu society in the face of superior Muslim force during these initial centuries of interaction led to the political valorization of the ancient Ramayana epic, according to Sheldon Pollock's recent argument. Although the story of the hero-god Rama's conflict with the demonic king Ravana of distant Lanka had circulated widely throughout the subcontinent and beyond in the previous millennium, there are few signs of a temple cult of Rama worship prior to the eleventh century. Nor was Rama imagery often employed in the literature produced at royal courts. After approximately 1000, the situation changed dramatically with the spread of Rama temples and the frequent appropriation of Rama as a model for royal behaviour. Pollock believes that this is because Rama's legendary battle against (and victory over) the forces of evil represented by Ravana's demon hordes provided a profound symbol for Indian kings beleaguered by Central Asian Muslim warriors entering the subcontinent in growing numbers. Unlike earlier conquerors or immigrants who had been gradually absorbed into Indian civilization, Indo-Muslims retained the distinctive religious and linguistic practices derived from the high culture of Islamic civilization. Because they were 'largely unassimilating', Muslims were the Other *par excellence*, and their presence heightened Indian society's sense of self. Since the Ramayana epic was 'profoundly and fundamentally a text of "othering"', in Pollock's words, it was the perfect vehicle for demonizing these alien and dangerous newcomers.[15]

Inscriptions from Andhra provide little support for Pollock's thesis, as far as the Ramayana itself is concerned, for there are few direct references to the epic story. The demonization of Muslims that he argues constituted the medieval meaning of the epic can be perceived, however, even in the absence of explicit allusions to Rama. The most negative representations of Muslims in Andhra records appear in the immediate aftermath of the cataclysmic events of 1323, when armed forces of the Delhi Sultanate swept through the Andhra region and caused the collapse of the indigenous Kakatiya royal dynasty. Andhra warriors united under the Kakatiya banner had repeatedly fought the Turkic armies of Delhi during the previous twenty years. This was part of a larger conflict between the Delhi Sultanate and several kingdoms of peninsular India that began in 1296 with the sultanate's attack on Devagiri, the capital of the Yadava dynasty in modern Maharashtra. Within a roughly quarter-century span, the four regional kingdoms of peninsular India—those of the Yadavas, Kakatiyas, Pandyas (of southern Tamil Nadu), and Hoysalas (of southern Karnataka)—disintegrated under the sultanate's onslaught. By 1325, virtually all of southern India had been subdued by Muslim military force, and existing political networks were thoroughly disrupted.

The magnitude of the socio-political upheavals that the early fourteenth century Muslim conquests induced in peninsular India is reflected in the tone of Andhra inscriptions issued soon thereafter. Particularly striking is the Vilasa Grant of Prolaya Nayaka, a long copper-plate grant written in Sanskrit and issued sometime after 1325 but before 1350.[16] The beginning portion of the inscription praises the greatness of Andhra's previous Kakatiya dynasty and its last king, Prataparudra. The record then goes on to describe the hostilities between Prataparudra and the lord of the Turks, Sultan Muhammad bin Tughluq. After successfully fighting off the sultan's army seven times, Prataparudra was eventually captured and died on the banks of the Narmada river in central India while being taken to Delhi as a captive.[17] With the death of the righteous king, Kakatiya Prataparudra, the forces of evil became ascendant. In the words of the inscription, 'when the sun who was Prataparudra thus set, the pitch darkness of the Turks enveloped the world.'[18] Various proofs of the wicked character of Muslim rule are next adduced—Brahmans were forced to abandon their sacrificial rites; Hindu temple images were overturned and broken; tax-exempt Brahman villages confiscated; and cultivators deprived of their produce. Moreover, the vile Muslims were incessant in drinking wine, eating beef, and slaying Brahmans. And so, 'tortured in this way by the demon-like

Yavana soldiers, the land of Tilinga [Andhra] suffered terribly without hope of relief, as if it were a forest engulfed by a rampaging fire.[19]

Although some Hindu historians of Andhra have accepted the charges contained in the Vilasa grant as evidence of actual Muslim atrocities, the supposed depravity of the Muslims conforms too closely to a popular literary convention to be accepted as actual fact. The way that this inscription represents Muslims echoes the gloomy predictions of a body of Sanskrit literature known as the *purāṇas*, composed during the first millennium AD. Among the contents of the major *purāṇas* is the history of India, narrated in the form of royal genealogies that end in the fourth century AD with the dynasties of the Kali age, the fourth and last era in the cycle of time. In the ancient Indian conception, truth and morality declined in each successive era, and one of the main symptoms of the Kali age's degeneracy was the growing strength of foreign dynasties. Because political power would increasingly pass into the hands of foreigners and non-royal Indians, the *purāṇas* prophesied a terrible future. People would no longer have respect for the Vedas, the central ritual texts of Brahmanical tradition, in a world in which the hierarchical order of caste society was inverted through the ascendance of low-ranking castes over the ritually pre-eminent Brahmans.[20]

The historical memories embedded in the *purāṇas* reflect the anxieties of their Brahman composers and preservers in the period between the second century BC and the third century AD—a time when numerous peoples entered India from the northwest and, simultaneously, an era when the non-Brahmanical religion, Buddhism, achieved its greatest popularity. Similar fears of a loss of status resurfaced in the much later Vilasa grant of fourteenth-century Andhra, during another time of turbulence, when Brahmanical privilege was threatened. The Turks who invaded medieval Andhra are said to have oppressed Brahmans and suppressed religious practice, just as the earlier foreign invaders of the ancient period supposedly had done. It is notable that most of the evil acts attributed to Muslims in the Vilasa grant—confiscating villages endowed to Brahmans, destroying Brahman-controlled temples, and ending ritual sacrifices performed by Brahmans—directly affected the Brahman segment of the Andhra population. The majority of the people, the cultivators, are said to have suffered because their crops were confiscated, but this accusation is appended almost as an afterthought. The depiction of Muslim behaviour in the Vilasa grant is formulaic, in other words, and follows a pattern expected of foreign groups in the Brahmanical tradition.

In the Sanskrit literature of ancient and medieval India, foreigners were frequently described as *mleccha*. The best English translation of mleccha is 'barbarian', for the word clearly connotes a lack of culture and civilization. By the end the first millennium BC, mleccha was applied not only to aliens but also to indigenous tribes—communities who were not part of the agrarian caste society of Indic civilization.[21] As Romila Thapar has pointed out, mleccha was hence primarily 'a signal of social and cultural difference'.[22] It was a generic category into which all social groups lacking an adherence to Brahmanical norms were thrust. Among the early barbarians of foreign origin often mentioned in the *purāṇas* were the Yavanas and Shakas. Yavana, derived from Ionian, originally referred to the Hellenistic dynasties that controlled large areas of northwestern India and Afghanistan in the second century BC. These Indo-Greeks or Yavanas were displaced by another invading group, the Shakas of Central Asia, in the first century BC. The Shakas soon lost their hegemony over the entire northwest but remained entrenched in the Gujarat region of western India until the fourth century AD.

The names Yavana and Shaka were revived in medieval India to designate Muslims, along with the characterization of 'barbarian'.[23] As with earlier Others, whether foreign invaders or indigenous tribal peoples, those following the Brahmanical tradition were not concerned with the specifics of Islamic belief. What was significant was their common failure to uphold the hierarchical order of caste or, in short, Brahmanical privilege. This is why Muslims could be called by the same names as barbarian peoples of the ancient period, such as the Yavanas or Shakas. In another transposition, the Muslim barbarian could be equated with all beings hostile to the Brahmanical order. And, thus, Muslims were demonized, that is, represented as being like the demons of ancient myth who engaged in endless battle against the forces of good. Assimilating Muslims to the mythological category of demons and substituting the names of various other foreign groups for them erased the distinctiveness of Muslims. All that matters in this perspective is their Otherness.

The very fact that Muslims could be incorporated into a generic category of barbarians presupposes an existing sense of identity, at least among the Brahman composers of Sanskrit literary texts and inscriptions. A Brahman, if not Hindu, consciousness clearly pre-dated the Muslim entry into the Indian subcontinent. Upholding Brahman pre-eminence in a hierarchical society was the critical feature of this orthodox identity. In this respect, I take my stance with scholars like Anthony D. Smith, who believe that there are shared elements that unify members of an ethnic group, and that the attribution of alienness derives from a pre-existing sense of shared experience.[24] Others put more stress on the importance of boundaries in the formation of ethnicity, rather than on any commonly held content. For example, John A. Armstrong, following the Norwegian anthropologist Fredrik Barth, thinks that groups define themselves primarily by exclusion. This explains how ethnic identities can persist for so long, even when the composition of the group changes.[25] Identity formation in praxis always involves both processes—the articulation of group boundaries that excludes others, and the development of internal criteria for solidarity. These complementary aspects of ethnicity have been aptly described as 'us-hood' and 'we-hood' respectively, by Thomas Hylland Eriksen.[26] In the case of pre-modern India, it is clear that a persistent core of Brahman identity—a definite 'we-hood'—had existed since ancient times.[27]

ETHNOGENESIS IN A FRONTIER SETTING

Although the emergence of a sense of Hindu unity cannot be attributed solely to the stimulus of an opposing Muslim community, it is widely recognized that prolonged confrontation between different groups intensifies self-identities. While I believe that the Brahmanical tradition had a degree of self-awareness before the presence of Muslims, it seems that a broader, more inclusive, Indic identity began to develop after the Muslim polities were founded in South Asia. One sign of this is the non-Muslim writers' adoption of the designation 'Hindu', which begins to figure in Andhra inscriptions from 1352 onward, in the title 'Sultan among Hindu kings' (*Hindu-rāya-suratrāṇa*) assumed by several kings of the Vijayanagara empire.[28] To the best of my knowledge, this is the earliest dated usage of the term 'Hindu' in any Indian language source. Hindu was originally the Persian name for the Indus river of modern Pakistan, but the Arabs first included the entire Indian subcontinent under the rubric, 'the land of the Hind' (*al-Hind*). By the eleventh century, 'Hindu' had come to mean 'the inhabitants of India' in Persian, the literary language patronized by the Turkish warriors of the Delhi Sultanate.[29] When the early Vijayanagara kings of mid-fourteenth-century south India invented the title 'Sultan among Hindu Kings', they were borrowing both a phrase and a conception of being Indian that had originated in Muslim society.[30]

The fact that some non-Muslims called themselves Hindu in fourteenth-century south India does not imply that a unified religious consciousness developed in this period, however, contrary to the current Hindu nationalist view. Even among Muslims, the term 'Hindu' initially meant a resident of India rather than a person holding certain non-Islamic religious beliefs. Not until the late thirteenth century did Persian literature written in India routinely use Hindu as a religious designation.[31] When the Vijayanagara kings said that they were the sultans among Hindu kings, they were most probably declaring their paramount status among the non-Turkish polities of the peninsula. That is, to them Hindu meant Indic as opposed to Turkish, not 'of the Hindu religion' as opposed to 'of the Islamic religion'. In this interpretation, the definition of the self as Hindu can be seen as a sign of an incipient Indic ethnicity—incorporating territorial associations, language, a common past and customs, as well as religious affiliation—for ethnicity is composed of numerous elements, unlike linguistic or religious identity. Which of the several aspects of commonality is most emphasized in any particular ethnic group can vary considerably.[32] But the perception of sharing a whole set of traditions that differentiates one group from another is crucial to ethnic identity.

Support for my assertion that the fourteenth-century epigraphical meaning of Hindu was not primarily a religious one comes from the negative evidence that the terms Islam and Muslim (in its Persian variant, Musalman) never figure in Andhra inscriptions of the fourteenth through mid-seventeenth centuries. The Vilasa grant of Prolaya Nayaka instead uses the ethnic labels Turk (Turushka), Persian (Parasika), and Greek (Yavana) for Muslims. Nor do we get any allusion to Islamic religious beliefs or doctrine, other than the prohibition against eating pork. Inscriptions from other areas of the Indian subcontinent during the first centuries of contact are similarly silent about Islamic religion and the Islamic affiliation of the Turks.[33] The Turkic intruders were certainly considered to be a people other than the earlier inhabitants, but the sense of difference was not grounded primarily on a religious base.[34]

If religion was not the central feature of a budding Hindu self-identity, how do we explain the demonic representations of Muslims in early fourteenth-century Andhra inscriptions? To answer this question, we must first recognize that these records arose in the context of an advancing zone of military conflict. In frontier conditions such as these, large-scale destruction of existing socio-political networks is common, resulting in widespread uncertainty and feelings of crisis. At the same time, because of the rapid change occurring in a frontier setting, new socio-political groups are coalescing. Hence, frontiers are prime settings for ethnogenesis—the formation of new ethnic identities.[35] With war almost endemic along an active frontier, people were often brought together through some type of military association. The Franks of the late Roman empire, for instance, were basically a confederation of warriors assembled around kings claiming descent from the war god, Odin.[36]

In the case of fourteenth-century Andhra, the armed incursions of the Delhi Sultanate toppled the upper level of the political system when the Kakatiya dynasty was extinguished. But since the Kakatiya polity was a loosely knit organization of warrior bands, the loss of the capital did not mean the elimination of all armed resistance.[37] Prolaya Nayaka and other warriors who were entrenched in the localities continued to fight the Delhi Sultanate, which was also beset with internal strife. As quickly as the tide of conflict had washed over Andhra, it receded. By the 1340s, Muslim control in Andhra extended only over its extreme western sector. What was left behind, in this frontier borderland, was a power vacuum.

Presumably, the principal Kakatiya military leaders either died or were captured in the last days of the kingdom's defence, for none of them appear in inscriptions issued after the demise of the Kakatiyas. Instead, a totally different group of warriors figure in Andhra inscriptions of the 1330s and later. Prolaya Nayaka, who had the Vilasa grant composed, was the first member of the Musunuri lineage to leave behind historical traces. Rising from what must have been a humble background, he carved out a sizable domain for himself in the chaos following the Delhi Sultanate's incursions. A second man, Vema Reddi, is likewise the first historic figure in the Kondavidu Reddi lineage. Unlike Prolaya Nayaka's lineage, which waned rapidly, the Reddi lineage dominated coastal Andhra for nearly a century. Both of these men alleged prior association with the Kakatiya dynasty, and their descendants proudly publicized this connection. While it is possible that they may have held minor positions under some Kakatiya subordinate, there is no independent testimony to corroborate this assertion. It is more likely that the claim to have served the Kakatiyas stemmed from a desire to bolster their own tenuous positions.

Additionally, both Prolaya Nayaka and Vema Reddi emulated a classically royal style of behaviour by making generous benefactions to Brahmans. The explicit purpose of Prolaya Nayaka's Vilasa grant was to document a village endowment to a learned Brahman in Kona-sima, a small area in the delta of the Godavari river that even today is the heartland of Brahman scholasticism and ritualism in Andhra. Among Vema Reddi's Madras Museum Plates of 1345 AD was also a copper-plate grant recording the transfer of a village to a Brahman recipient.[38] Several other upwardly mobile warriors of fourteenth-century Andhra similarly boasted that they restored tax-free villages confiscated by the Turks to their rightful Brahman proprietors. Generally, these endowments were recorded in Sanskrit on copper-plates, a traditionally kingly type of gift and inscriptional medium.[39]

In their quest for acceptance as legitimate kings, chiefs like Prolaya Nayaka and Vema Reddi sought the most prestigious support possible. That included not only the use of the all-India literary language of Sanskrit, the patronage of Brahmans, and the memory of the previous

Kakatiya dynasty, but also the rich symbolism of the age-old fight against demons and disorder. This is the context for the Vilasa grant's demonization of the Turks. As previously described, this document bemoans the unfortunate state of Andhra after the Turks conquered the Kakatiyas. But all was not lost. The grant goes on to inform us that the depredations of the evil Muslims were halted by a savior, Prolaya Nayaka, who appeared almost miraculously, like an incarnation of the god Vishnu descending from heaven out of pity for the peoples' suffering. Prolaya Nayaka resurrected righteousness (*dharma*) by re-establishing Brahman villages, reviving Vedic sacrifices, and restricting himself to the lawful portion of the peasants' crops in revenue. He thereby 'purified the lands of the Andhras which were contaminated by sin because the Turks had passed through them.'[40] By granting a village to a learned Brahman, Prolaya Nayaka could thus represent himself in the Vilasa grant as restoring order to a world that the Muslim incursions had disordered. Vema Reddi also sought to portray himself in the Madras Museum Plates as a protector of Brahmans when he boasted that he had 'recovered all the Brahman villages that had been appropriated by the wicked barbarian kings since the time of Prataparudra, who was the jewel in the crown of the Kakatiya clan.[41]

The use of tropes drawn from the Brahman tradition does not indicate that the upstart warriors of fourteenth-century Andhra were religiously motivated in their actions. Nor can we assume that the pejorative language of these inscriptions reflects a deep hatred of the Muslim, much less proof of Muslim atrocities. But in a turbulent situation, where earlier sources of authority had been destroyed, the newly risen warrior leaders were attempting to mobilize public opinion and gain allegiance. One of the easiest ways of doing this was by resorting to older Brahmanical conceptions of barbarians and their demonic behaviour. Elsewhere outside of India, pre-modern political elites similarly employed religious myths and symbols because they were the most resonant images in a collective social memory transmitted largely by religious institutions and specialists.[42] By accentuating the threat from Muslims and their strange alien ways, aspiring kings in fourteenth-century Andhra could successfully cast themselves in the role of defenders of the Indic social order, the most essential justification for kingly status. The representations of Muslims as demons may therefore have been instrumental (that is, secondary) to the primary goal of providing Andhra warrior lineages with a secure notion of self and legitimate authority. In other words, the self-identity of an emerging warrior elite in Andhra was strengthened through recourse to traditional notions of the enemy Other.

COLLABORATION AND ACCOMMODATION ON THE OPEN FRONTIER

For the past several decades, historians have extended the frontier paradigm to many societies outside of the United States.[43] Yet, unlike its western counterpart, the Christian–Islamic frontier in medieval Europe, the Muslim–Hindu frontier in medieval India has been virtually overlooked. One exception is Richard M. Eaton's work on Bengal.[44] He differentiates the political frontier of Islam, which moved eastward most rapidly, from the religious frontier of allegiance to Islam. A further frontier was an agrarian one in which forest land was brought under settled agriculture. Where the agrarian and religious frontiers coincided for the most part, groups only recently introduced to settled agriculture identified Islam as a civilization-building ideology, a religion of the plough. As a result, the majority of the rice-cultivating population in eastern Bengal (modern Bangladesh) eventually became adherents of Islam. Islam never attained such religious dominance in south India, however, where the number of Muslims remained fairly low. Nonetheless, Muslim regimes were embedded in the peninsula's geo-political landscape after the early fourteenth century. The continuing south Indian political frontier between Muslim and Hindu can be characterized as 'open' since neither side had complete hegemony.[45]

From the early fifteenth through mid-sixteenth centuries, a relatively stable balance of power was maintained between three major power centres in the peninsula. A Muslim polity of some sort occupied the northwestern portion of the peninsula in what is today Maharashtra and northern Karnataka. The first to be established was the Bahmani Sultanate, which broke off from the Delhi Sultanate in 1347. Subsequently, several other sultanates were formed out of portions of the Bahmani realm. Of these, the 'Adil Shahi kingdom of Bijapur and the Qutb Shahi kingdom of Golkonda had the biggest impact on Andhra. Opposed to the sultanates of the peninsula's northwestern corner was the Vijayanagara empire. Under its first three dynasties, Vijayanagara controlled most of the southern portion of the peninsula, the area south of the Krishna river encompassing much of modern southern Karnataka, southern Andhra, and the Tamil country. Two successive Hindu dynasties—the Eastern Gangas and Gajapatis—held sway over the northeastern portion of the peninsula along the Orissa–Andhra border. The areas in between were hotly contested and vulnerable to military campaigns that could lead to temporary extensions of borders, but the nuclear zones of these respective powers remained intact. Within Andhra itself, the Muslim presence was confined primarily to the northwestern portion of the modern state's expanse.[46]

In this context of relative stability, quite different representations of Muslims surface in Andhra inscriptions. Throughout the fifteenth and early sixteenth centuries, Muslims figure mainly as mighty warriors. Victories over Muslims were lauded in the heroic titles of Hindu kings and chiefs or praised in their genealogies. Sometimes specific Muslim kings or generals are named, but more often generic labels for Muslims were used. So, for example, it was said of Devaraya I of the Vijayanagara empire in 1465 that 'even the powerful Turks were dried up in the fire of the prowess of this king'.[47] In this type of reference, one gets little sense that the Muslim is any more than a typical, if respected, foe. Inscriptional eulogies of the Tuluva kings of Vijayanagara's second dynasty list the Turk along with non-Muslim enemies conquered by the dynastic founder, such as the Chera, Chola, and Gajapati kings.[48] In other words, Muslims are depicted as respected political rivals, just like the other major Hindu powers of the peninsula.

Phillip B. Wagoner suggests that shifts in the balance of power affected the attitude of south Indian elites toward Muslims and delineates three phases on that basis. From roughly 1300 to 1420, Hindu polities were on the defensive, and an anti-Turkic polemic was widespread. During the second phase (from c. 1420 to 1565), however, greater appreciation of Turkic culture is expressed in Hindu literature. This state of affairs corresponds in time with the apex of the Vijayanagara empire. The sacking of the Vijayanagara capital by a confederacy of Muslim states in 1565 ushered in another period of defensive polemics. Yet by the time this third phase occurred, many aspects of Islamic material culture and administrative technique had been assimilated by the non-Muslim peoples of south India.[49] Inscriptional data from Andhra confirms the general validity of Wagoner's thesis that the representations of Muslims varied according to the success of Hindu polities in restraining Muslim power. The anti-Muslim rhetoric of the Vilasa grant occurred during phase one, when Andhra society was in a defensive posture. But, from the early fifteenth through mid-sixteenth centuries, there was little dramatic change in the power balance, and tensions subsided momentarily. Hence, in this second phase, we witness no demonization of the Muslim. Rather than an anti-Muslim polemic, the inscriptional sources display a tolerance of Muslim warriors and political power. Along the quiet frontier of fifteenth-century south India, the Muslim presence was accepted rather than rejected.

Frederick Jackson Turner's vision of the frontier as an uninhabited wilderness subdued by heroic individualism has long been rejected in favour of an understanding of frontiers as broad zones in which two societies encounter each other.[50] Their contact may be violent in nature, particularly during the initial stages of encroachment by members of the intruding society. But it is not uncommon for frontier societies to maintain an equilibrium for considerable periods of time, once this first violent confrontation is over. At about the same time that Hindu-Muslim relations in south India were going through a tranquil phase, the frontier between the Iberian Christian kingdom of Castile and the Muslim kingdom of Granada was stationary (1369 to 1482).[51] Faced with the practical reality of coexistence, a number of institutions specifically designed to facilitate mutual transactions were developed there, including procedures for negotiating truces and redeeming captives. Among the elite, alliances were formed that ignored differences in religion, while common people sometimes crossed the frontier and even converted to the other religion. Knowledge of each other's ways was widespread—in effect, a substantial degree of acculturation had taken place.

Since a majority of medieval south India's population continued to be non-Muslim, the two societies always overlapped wherever Muslims were politically dominant. A certain amount of cooperation and collaboration is to be expected in this setting.[52] The Muslim polities of the peninsula were dependent on Hindu officials and warriors for tax collection and maintenance of order in the countryside.[53] Poets of Andhra's vernacular language, Telugu, were generously patronized at the court of the sixteenth-century Qutb Shahi kingdom, which also issued many of its inscriptions in a bilingual format.[54] Conversely, Muslim expertise in military and administrative affairs was admired and adopted by their rival Hindu polities. The Vijayanagara army included contingents of Muslims on horseback, a tacit acknowledgment of Muslim superiority in cavalry warfare.[55] Many secular structures at the Vijayanagara capital exhibit an original Indo-Islamic style of architecture, complete with domes and arches.[56] Adaptations of Muslim dress were also featured on formal court occasions.[57] Nor did the ostensible demarcation between Hindu and Muslim prevent military and marital alliances from being formed across religious boundaries in this period of south Indian history. These centuries of contact and interaction also resulted in an influx of Persian and Arabic words into the Telugu language.[58] Many parallels can be drawn between medieval Spain and medieval south India, in terms of the prevalence of cultural adaptations and borrowing.

In one significant aspect, however, the Hindu-Muslim encounter in medieval south India differed from those of Christians and Muslims described by Charles J. Halperin.[59] Two of Halperin's case studies involve the Christian conquest of Muslims (thirteenth-century Valencia in Spain and the crusader kingdom of Jerusalem), whereas the two others are examples of Muslim intrusion into Christian regions (the absorption of Byzantine territory by Arabs, Seljuk Turks, and Ottomans; and the rule of the Mongol Golden Horde over Russia). According to Halperin, cultural synthesis and tolerance were displayed primarily when the intruders had not yet established total superiority. It was thus a function of the practical need for compromise. Cooperation violated the exclusivist thrust of Christianity and Islam, however, and so was never publicly discussed. In theory, the two groups remained implacably opposed, despite the considerable collaboration in practice. The ideology of silence concerning mutual influence and borrowing enabled medieval religious frontier societies to ignore the contradiction between theory and practice.

In contrast to the ideological negation of the other society found within Christian-Muslim frontier zones, an explicit scheme of accommodation can be found in the Hindu sources of medieval Andhra. This paradigm, which incorporated Muslim polities, appears from the early fifteenth century onward. It posits the existence of three major kings—the Ashvapati or Lord of Horses, the Gajapati or Lord of Elephants, and the Narapati or Lord of Men. Each element of the triad—horses, elephants, and men—forms a contingent in the traditional Indian army. Royal titles proclaiming a single king to be lord of the cavalry, elephant corps, and infantry are found elsewhere in India during the middle ages.[60] But late medieval south India was unique in dividing the various parts of an army and assigning each to a particular dynasty. The first of the titles to be assumed was Lord of the Elephant Corps, adopted by the Eastern Ganga kings of the Orissa-Andhra region as early as the thirteenth century.[61] The subsequent kings of this northeastern portion of the peninsula (fl. 1434–1538) used the epithet Gajapati, or Lord of Elephant Forces, so frequently that it has become their dynastic label in modern historiography. The heavily forested Orissa-Andhra coast had indeed been famous since ancient times for the excellence of its elephants. By a logical corollary, kings of northwestern India, where the best horses in the subcontinent were to be found, deserved to be called the Lord of Horses or Cavalry.[62] A dynasty without access to superior elephants or horses—as was the case in the dry interior of north India—would by default gain the epithet, Lord of Infantry.

The conception of a geo-political universe divided into three realms, each ruled by a king laying claim to superiority in one contingent of an army, is first witnessed in an Andhra inscription of 1423.[63] The most detailed treatment is found in a Telugu chronicle of the late sixteenth century, the *Rāyavācakamu*. In this work, the Lord of Men (Narapati) is the king of Vijayanagara, the Lord of Elephants (Gajapati) is the Orissan king, and the Lord of Horses (Ashvapati) is the Mughal emperor of northern India. The Mughals had replaced the Delhi Sultanate as the supreme Muslim polity in the subcontinent in the first half of the sixteenth century. Previously, the *Rāyavācakamu* tells us, the sultan of Delhi was the Lord of Horses. The text calls the Lords of Horses, Elephants, and Men the occupants of the 'Three Lion Thrones,' as opposed to other petty kings who lacked legitimacy. Not only did the Lords of Horses, Elephants, and Men possess authority as the rulers of ancient and prosperous kingdoms, but they also exemplified royal righteousness. As the text's translator, Phillip B. Wagoner, points out, the three Lion Thrones were regarded as emanations of the three main gods of Hinduism—Brahma, Vishnu, and Śiva.[64]

More commonly in Andhra sources, the Lord of the Horses designated not a North Indian Muslim dynasty, but a local Muslim polity of the peninsula. At times the title was applied to the Bahmani sultans in opposition to the Gajapati kings of Orissa and the Narapati kings of Vijayanagara.[65] Or it could refer to any of the leaders of the successor states that arose after the division of the Bahmani Sultanate. In other words, the Lord of Horses was a designation that could signify any Muslim king. The Qutb Shahs of western Andhra even appropriated the title in a Telugu inscription of 1600, in which we are informed that King Mahmud was ruling from the Lord of the Cavalry's throne at Golkonda.[66] The concept of a triad of lords must have been widely known indeed, for a Muslim polity to use it in reference to itself. Allusions to the three lords occur as late as c. 1800, when Andhra village histories were collected under the direction of Colin Mackenzie.[67] The notion of a triple division of power is also embodied in the *Pratāparudra-caritramu*, a Telugu prose history of the Kakatiya dynasty composed in the early to mid-sixteenth century.[68]

The tripartite scheme of the Lords of Horses, Elephants, and Men can be interpreted on one level as a pragmatic acceptance of the geo-political realities of the Indian peninsula during the fifteenth and sixteenth centuries. When the Bahmani Sultanate was established in 1347, the Muslim presence in the area had become firmly entrenched; it was now an inescapable fact. Yet the nature of this three-fold classification also suggests that Muslim polities were viewed as legitimate powers, ranking equally with the great Hindu dynasties of Orissa and Vijayanagara. Just as the Hindu Lords of Elephants and Men were granted divine sanction in the *Rāyavācakamu*, which described them as emanations of the gods, so too was the Muslim Lord of the Horses.[69] One Andhra inscription from the mid-sixteenth century claims that all three lords worshipped the god at Srisailam, Andhra's most renowned Śaiva temple.[70] Besides being valid in their possession of royal power, the Muslim kings were seen as an integral component of the political order. No member of this triad of lords could exist in the absence of the other two, in the same way that an army would be incomplete without the three contingents of cavalry, elephant corps, and infantry; or that the universe would be stagnant without the triple processes of creation, preservation, and destruction. Far from being alien intruders whose very existence was abhorrent to the natural order of the universe, as the early fourteenth-century Vilasa grant portrayed them, Muslims were now represented as an essential element in the socio-political world.

THE GROWTH OF TELUGU ETHNICITY

While Muslims, on the one hand, were increasingly viewed as intrinsic to the peninsula, the identities of non-Muslim groups were at the same time becoming more firmly differentiated. These identities had emerged in the pre-Muslim era with two, largely congruent, focal points: language and territory. Andhra was understood as the territory within which Telugu was spoken. The association between region and language is clearly drawn even in the eleventh century, when the term 'Andhra language' figures in reference to Telugu.[71] It was in the eleventh century that the earliest extant Telugu literature was produced, although another century elapsed before numerous works were composed.[72]

As the Telugu linguistic sphere expanded over time, the conception of Andhra's regional extent grew larger. At first the territory encompassed within the Telugu realm of Andhra was quite small. In the eleventh century, Andhra was defined as the region extending from southern Orissa down along the coast almost to the modern state's southern border. But the western boundary of Andhra was severely truncated, reaching only about halfway across the modern state.[73] This restricted notion of Andhra mirrors the paucity of Telugu inscriptions in the inland area. The expansion of Telugu inscriptions into the interior zone contiguous to the coast occurred during the heyday of the Kakatiya dynasty from the late twelfth to the early fourteenth centuries. The spread in the geographic distribution of Telugu inscriptions can be partly attributed to the increased tempo of the agricultural settlement in interior Andhra. But the dynamism of the Kakatiya polity is another contributing factor. As the sphere of Kakatiya influence enlarged, Telugu inscriptions increasingly appear in areas where other epigraphical languages (and other political elites) had previously been prominent.[74] By the time Kakatiya Prataparudra was proclaimed the lord of Andhra in early fourteenth-century inscriptions, the conceptual dimensions of the region encompassed about three-quarters of the modern state's territory.

When Turkic armies entered peninsular India, the basic contours of the current Telugu linguistic community had thus already been established. The other language communities of the peninsula had similarly emerged in forms that roughly approximate modern distributions. Each of the four regional kingdoms conquered by the Delhi Sultanate in the early fourteenth century corresponded with a separate linguistic realm: the Marathi-speaking area in the case of the Yadavas, the Telugu area of the Kakatiyas, the Kannada area of the Hoysalas, and the Tamil area for the Pandyas. Despite losing their respective political centres under Muslim attack, the nascent linguistic identities of these four communities continued to evolve in subsequent centuries.

From the fifteenth century onward, in fact, Andhra inscriptions display a heightened sense of being Telugu. Whereas earlier references occurred in isolation, Telugu identity was now frequently juxtaposed on other regional and ethnic identities. One inscription dated 1485, for instance, appends a phrase at the end to state that 'if an Orissan king, a Turkic king, a king of Karnataka, a Telugu king, or anyone who works for these kings should seize these (donated) cows, they will incur the sin of cow-killing and of Brahman-killing.'[75] Similar verses are widespread in Andhra inscriptions, the one difference being that the Muslim king is generally threatened with a more relevant curse. For example, an inscription from the early sixteenth century warns, 'if any Orissan king or Telugu king should violate this charity, they will incur the sin of killing cows on the banks of the Ganges; if any Turkic kings should violate (this charity), they will incur the sin of eating pork.'[76] Greater contact with other areas and polities of the peninsula may account for the increasing tendency to formulate Telugu identity in terms of its others.

In twentieth-century India, linguistic allegiance has been a highly charged political issue capable of mobilizing millions. Popular movements demanding homelands for particular language communities have resulted in the redrawing of many administrative boundaries to correspond with linguistic distributions. Echoing the modernist view of Benedict Anderson, scholars of colonial India have recently cast doubt on the existence of these language communities prior to the nineteenth century. Both David Washbrook and David Lelyveld believe that bounded linguistic populations arose out of the British colonial project to count, classify, and control Indian society.[77] The nineteenth-century preoccupation with language as the cementing bond of social relations and the belief that races or nations were situated in set territorial locations were the underlying impetus.

Indians gradually adopted their colonizer's view of language and incorporated it as one of the bases of a new social identity, according to Lelyveld and Washbrook.

To be sure, in the days before mass communication, the perception of shared commonalities would be far more attenuated than today, whether we are speaking of language, caste, religious, or regional affiliation. The tendency to identify one's spoken tongue as belonging to a major language recognized by linguists is certainly a new phenomenon. Moreover, the compilation of dictionaries, production of textbooks, and development of print, radio, and film media since the nineteenth century has led to considerable standardization of India's various languages. But even today, bounded linguistic populations are more of an abstraction than an observable reality. As in pre-colonial times, in modern India the dialects spoken at home are numerous, the line of demarcation between one language and another vague, and multi-lingualism widespread.

More relevant than the question of whether territorially based language communities existed in pre-colonial India is the issue of linguistic allegiance. Certainly the number of people who thought of themselves as members of a particular linguistic culture may have been quite small in the pre-colonial period. The depth of their attachment to a language may also have been relatively shallow when compared to the situation in modern India. As Sudipta Kaviraj observes:

> Earlier communities tend to be fuzzy in two ways in which no nation can afford to be. First, they have fuzzy boundaries because some collective identities are not territorially based. . . . Secondly, part of this fuzziness of social mapping would arise because traditional communities, unlike modern ones, are not enumerated.[78]

Because their boundaries were far more blurred, pre-modern communities were less likely to engage in collective action than modern ones. That is, they were not self-conscious to the same extent as in modern nationalisms, with their focused and intense allegiances.

The sharply articulated identities of modern nationalism are, thus, far from being the only forms of collective identity. It is untenable to argue that there was no sense of linguistic community in pre-colonial India just because the population involved was a limited or ill-defined one. To be fair, Lelyveld mentions the earlier histories of literary languages, while Washbrook concedes that pre-modern grammarians viewed languages as objects that could be classified.[79] But their main intention is to refute the notion of language communities as inherent natural entities by stressing the impact of nineteenth-century ideology and technology. In the process, they downplay the importance of pre-modern linguistic identities, at least at the literary level. Although peasants may not have consciously named the language they spoke, poets and scribes were indisputably aware of their linguistic heritage, as were the wealthy patrons who financed their literary production.

In pre-colonial India, as in other pre-modern societies, social identities were most strongly developed among the privileged. Smith describes the elite sense of belonging in medieval Europe as 'lateral-aristocratic' ethnicity in contrast to the 'vertical-demotic ethnicity of the modern period.[80] Medieval European ethnicity was centred in the aristocratic class, spanning geographic boundaries but staying within the strict confines of the upper social strata. Ethnicity in late medieval south India must have also been an elite phenomenon. Certainly, the social identities displayed in inscriptions pertain to the propertied class, the only people who could commission expensive records to document their religious endowments. They were no less meaningful for being elite in nature, nonetheless. A case in point is the Kakatiya dynasty's switch in epigraphic usage. While the Kakatiyas were nominally subordinate to the Western Chalukya dynasty of Karnataka, the bulk of their records was inscribed in Kannada, the language of Karnataka. Once the Kakatiyas ceased acknowledging Chalukyan overlordship, they immediately stopped issuing inscriptions in Kannada.[81] The Kakatiya shift to Telugu and Sanskrit inscriptions had a certain political significance, of course, but was also a symptom of a solidifying Telugu ethnicity.

Linguistic affiliation was a large, but not the only, component in the formation of south Indian ethnicities. Regions of residence and religion were also constituent elements reflected in the categories of Turk, Orissan, or of the Karnataka region (sometimes 'the land of the Kannada language'[82]) found in Andhra inscriptions. But, despite the growth of an Andhra identity derived at least partially from linguistic unity, the land of the Telugu speakers was politically fragmented after the fall of the Kakatiya capital, Warangal, in 1323. In the absence of a regional kingdom that was exclusively and uniquely Telugu, Andhra warriors increasingly relied on the memory of the Kakatiyas to construct a legitimizing past that provided them with both authority and a feeling of community. It is this emergence of a shared history that most clearly justifies calling the medieval Telugu sense of self an ethnic identity. And for Andhra society of later centuries, the Telugu past led straight back to the Kakatiyas.[83]

A striking illustration of the role of the Kakatiyas in Andhra historical consciousness is provided by the man known as Chittapa Khana. Although his name is a Sanskritized form of the Persian name, Shitab Khan,

Chittapa Khana is called an infidel in Muslim chronicles and was clearly not a Muslim. He owed his appointment as governor of the northern Andhra territories that had formed the core of the Kakatiya polity to Humayun Shah of the Bahmani Sultanate.[84] In 1504, Chittapa Khana cast off his allegiance to the Bahmanis and portrayed himself as an independent monarch in an inscription situated at Warangal, the former Kakatiya capital. Like Prolaya Nayaka and Vema Reddi of the fourteenth century, Chittapa Khana's antecedents are obscure. To secure royal prestige, Chittapa Khana drew an explicit linkage with the Kakatiyas of two centuries past in the statement:

> The great and prosperous king Chittapa Khana ... captured the beautiful city of Ekashilapuri [Warangal], formerly ruled by a number of virtuous kings belonging to the Kakatiya family, for the sake of worshipping the gods and Brahmans.[85]

In effect, Chittapa Khana was engaged in a form of cultural revival, for he tried to recreate the greatness of the Kakatiyas—the Golden Age of Andhra warriors—through his own acts. The purpose of the inscription is to commemorate the restoration of two divine images. One was Krishna, 'who was removed from his place by the strength of the wicked.' The other was the goddess, who 'was the font of prosperity [Lakshmi] for the throne of the Kakatiya kingdom' but 'had been removed from her place by the wicked Turks'.[86] Although it is unlikely that these images actually dated back to the Kakatiya period, that is clearly irrelevant to the symbolic meaning of Chittapa Khana's acts, which are intended to close the gap in historical time between the present and the pre-Muslim past. The inscription ends with a vision of Chittapa Khana daily worshipping the Warangal deity who was the protector of the Kakatiya dynasty.

Even in an era of relative political stability, when Muslims were widely depicted as a natural element in the south Indian socio-political universe, the symbolism of Muslims as evil enemies of the gods—and of Brahmans—could still be resonant. Chittapa Khana, in declaring himself and Warangal free from the nominal control of a Muslim polity, utilized the longstanding Brahmanical trope of the barbarian. Yet, the primary intent of Chittapa Khana's inscription is not to denigrate the Muslim *per se*, but to evoke continuity with a glorious Telugu past in order to substantiate his own claim to kingship. The pejorative characterization of Muslims in this instance is a by-product of the process of identity formation. Muslims are what Telugu warriors are *not*, but the main emphasis is on what a true Telugu warrior *is*—a spiritual descendant, so to speak, of the Kakatiya dynasty.

The shifting use of the title 'Lord of Horses' for both a north Indian Muslim polity and for one of the smaller Muslim polities of the peninsula indicates that non-Muslims did have some sense of Muslims as a distinct and unified group, regardless of their exact political affiliation. From a military perspective, of course, the various Muslim polities could indeed have been perceived as sharing a similar technology and emphasis on cavalry, justifying grouping them together in one larger category. Andhra inscriptions also use the various ethnic labels of Turk, Persian, and Arab interchangeably in reference to any given group of Muslims. The effacement of ethnic differences is further evidence that Muslims were seen as composing one common category. Conversely, the term 'Hindu' continued to occasionally appear in inscriptions in opposition to Turk.[87] But in the peninsular India of circa 1500, more relevant than any shared Hindu identity were the emerging identities based on common language and region of origin. And in the evolution of these incipient ethnicities, the construction and articulation of a common past played a significant part. Excluding the Muslim Other was one way through which Telugu ethnicity was consolidated, but the evoking of a shared history, centred on the Kakatiyas, was an equally important means.

TEMPLE DESECRATION

The balance of power between Hindu and Muslim polities in south India was abruptly shattered in 1565 when the peninsular sultanates launched a combined attack against Vijayanagara, leading to its defeat and the sacking of the capital city in Karnataka. The Vijayanagara kings of the fourth or Aravidu dynasty retrenched in southern Andhra but saw the territory under their control diminish rapidly over the next ninety years. The central portion of coastal Andhra fell to one Muslim polity—the Qutb Shahs of Golkonda/Hyderabad—in the 1580s. Successful campaigns in southern Andhra were conducted in the 1620s by another Muslim polity, that of the 'Adil Shahs of Bijapur, and again in the 1640s by the Qutb Shahi armies. The last Vijayanagara king, Sriranga III, eventually had to flee the region entirely; and by 1652 all of Andhra was under the hegemony of Muslim polities.

After 1565, therefore, we witness a second rapid expansion of frontiers, paralleling in enormity the events of the early fourteenth century. For a second time, existing political networks were shattered, and several new Telugu warrior lineages came to prominence in Andhra that were nominally subordinate to the tattered remnants of the Vijayanagara imperium. Somewhat surprisingly, Andhra inscriptions of this period are silent on the catastrophic events of 1565. Nor do they rail against the demonic Muslim enemy, unlike what we find in the fourteenth century.[88] One reason for the absence of anti-Muslim rhetoric may simply be the small quantity of inscriptions issued in Andhra after 1565.[89] This paucity of inscriptions is itself a consequence of the political instability that plagued Andhra in the decades following the Vijayanagara defeat. With anarchistic conditions prevailing, temple patronage declined abruptly and therefore few donative inscriptions were issued. Worship may have been suspended at many Hindu temples due to the loss of lands and valuables that supported regular temple services.

At several larger temple complexes with sufficient prestige and resources to survive in the long run, there are reports of disturbances in the course of continuing Muslim expansion in Andhra after 1565. From these reports and other evidence, it appears that temple desecration was on the rise during this third phase of the Hindu–Muslim encounter in Andhra. Unfortunately, it is very difficult to gauge the extent of damage wrought on Hindu temples without systemic and unbiased study of the subject, a project that has not yet been conducted.[90] My general impression, based upon inscriptions and the secondary literature, is that some Hindu sites in Andhra were demolished in the fourteenth century in the initial Turkic conquest and shortly thereafter. Most notable among these are the temples in the Kakatiya capital, Warangal.[91] However, there are few verifiable cases of Andhra temple destruction or desecration in the following period, when the balance of power was relatively stable (Wagoner's phase two from 1420 to 1565). Maharashtra underwent a similar experience—temple destruction occurred there primarily in the fourteenth century.[92]

The long lull in attacks on Hindu temples seems to have ended in the late sixteenth century.[93] The best-documented incident pertains to the popular Ahobilam temple (Kurnool district). An inscription dating from 1584 tells us that Ibrahim of the Qutb Shahi dynasty captured the Ahobilam temple with the help of the Hindu Hande chiefs in 1579 and held it for five or six years.[94] The record commemorates the recapturing of the site by a Vijayanagara subordinate who is said to have restored the temple to its past glory. The traditional account of Ahobilam additionally states that those jewels and silver or gold vessels belonging to the temple that survived a raid in 1565 were looted in the 1579 attack.[95] Local folklore reports that the main Ahobilam image was brought before Ibrahim Qutb Shah, who vomited blood and died as a result.[96]

Evidence also exists for the plundering of another major Andhra temple site, Srikurman (Visakhapatnam district). An inscription issued by a Muslim general of the Qutb Shahs in 1599 claims that he damaged the temple and constructed a mosque there.[97] The temple cannot have suffered substantial destruction, however, as this inscription remains on its walls alongside many others. Furthermore, a mere five years later, another subordinate of the Qutb Shahs—this time a Hindu chief—recorded his gift of a village to the temple.[98] Srisailam, a famous temple in the Nallamallai hills, seems to have been affected several decades later, when the territory surrounding it fell under Muslim control. Around 1625, the Hindu chief who ruled this area of Andhra's interior was defeated by 'Adil Shahi forces from Bijapur in Karnataka. Srisailam's traditional account tells us that this led to the appropriation of Brahman and monastic lands, forcing many people to leave the area and resulting in curtailment of ritual services.[99] At Ahobilam, also affected by this particular advance of Muslim forces, temple valuables were again taken away.[100]

Two salient points arise out of the reports of temple desecration at Ahobilam, Srikurman, and Srisailam. The first is that all the incidents took place in contested territory. Ahobilam was plundered once when the Qutb Shahi forces were on a campaign against Vijayanagara, and a second time when 'Adil Shahi armies were moving further into southern Andhra. The Srikurman incident occurred during a Qutb Shahi expedition into northeastern Andhra. At no time do we get reports of temples well within Muslim spheres of influence being looted or damaged, only of those situated along the lines of conflict. Temple desecration in Andhra is thus a phenomenon of the moving frontier, an activity occurring primarily in the highly charged moments of armed encounter. Richard M. Eaton believes that temple destruction by Turks and other Muslim rulers throughout India was motivated by political, far more than religious, considerations. The temples destroyed lay either in kingdoms in the process of being conquered or within the realms of rebels. Because a royal temple symbolized the king's power in Hindu political thought, destroying it signified that king's utter humiliation. The characterization of Muslims as rabid iconoclasts driven to destroy idols because of religious ideology is far from the truth, in Eaton's opinion.[101] The situation in medieval Andhra appears to support Eaton's thesis.

A second implication of the Andhra evidence is that violence to temples often only involved the appropriation of movable property rather than the actual demolishing of idols and buildings. The Andhra incidents described above, dating from the late sixteenth and early seventeenth centuries, are instances of temple desecration and not actual destruction, unlike the situation during the fourteenth century. However, the symbolic value of temple desecration was far greater than the material loss experienced and was exploited by both Hindus and Muslims. At Ahobilam, for example, the recapturing of the site in 1584 is represented as a major objective of Vijayanagara strategy, and its successful conclusion is celebrated through the conferral of temple honours. The Srikurman case, on the other hand, clearly illustrates the gap between reality and rhetoric in Muslim sources. It is ironic, indeed, that a Muslim warrior would have used a slab on which numerous endowments were inscribed to record his own attack, of which no visible evidence remains.[102]

This last example should warn us to be more cautious about taking Muslim claims at face value. The rhetoric of religious war in Indo-Turkish historical chronicles frequently served either to inflate the importance of minor military campaigns or to mask the raw political ambition of rulers.[103] And not until the sixteenth and seventeenth centuries does the image of the holy warrior (*ghāzī*) actually figure in Indo-Muslim writing, although this status was then attributed retroactively to numerous individuals of earlier centuries.[104] Tragically, the medieval Muslim rhetoric of iconoclasm is today being interpreted literally by Hindu nationalists and used as a weapon against Indian Muslims. Yet, just as anti-Muslim polemic in Hindu sources like the Vilasa grant of Prolaya Nayaka had self-serving motives, so too should the boasts of Muslim warriors at the edge of the Islamic frontier be regarded as efforts to enhance legitimacy. In any case, it is evident that much more research needs to be carried out before we can make any definitive statements about the extent to which Hindu temples were damaged or demolished by Muslim armies in medieval India.

CONCLUSION

In this essay, I have argued that the medieval Hindu-Muslim encounter should be viewed as a process occurring in a frontier zone. The intensity of contact varied dramatically over time along the south Indian frontier, from the devastation of the first armed conflict, through a period of equilibrium and mutual borrowing, to a renewed era of advancing military borders and cultural hostility. Only through understanding the changing contexts of Hindu-Muslim interaction can we account for the diversity in Hindu representations of Muslims. Images of Muslims as demon-like barbarians did occur in medieval Andhra, but primarily in the aftermath of severe military strife. Reports of temple desecration likewise surface mainly along the edges of an advancing frontier.

When times were more peaceful and the atmosphere more accepting, a conceptual scheme that incorporated Muslim polities circulated widely in Andhra. But both denigrating and tolerant representations co-existed at any given phase—medieval Andhra conceptions of the Muslim were never monolithic or uniform.

While Muslims were often cast as the Other in medieval Hindu discourse, Andhra inscriptions never placed Islam in the foreground as the basis of the Muslim's alien character. The Muslim warriors of Turkic origin who invaded and settled in peninsular India were certainly a separate ethnic group comprising their own social unit and possessing their own culture. But their Otherness included many distinct features beyond simply religion—language, costume, marriage customs, and fighting styles, to name but a few. This is not to say that the non-Muslim inhabitants of India were unaware of the particulars of Islamic beliefs and practice. Popular works by devotional poet-saints of the fifteenth and sixteenth centuries explicitly contrast numerous aspects of Hinduism and Islam, often in the setting of a religious debate.[105] But for the political elites who financed the composition of inscriptions, religious differences were of no great import. Far more significant were the military skills of the Turks and the administrative heritage of the Islamic civilization that they introduced into the peninsula.

Because the initial Andhra encounter with Islamic peoples took place in a context of confrontation, we witness a sharp delineation between Muslim and non-Muslim in discourse. In my interpretation, both sides used the language of us-versus-them to strengthen emergent identities in a fluid and constantly changing socio-political milieu. Neither the parvenu Andhra warriors of the fourteenth century nor the Turkic intruders of the Delhi Sultanate, relative newcomers to Islam, had much stature as authority figures. What better way to shore up shaky claims to legitimacy than to exploit the ancient symbols of their respective religious traditions? New Andhra leaders could draw on earlier Brahman images of the struggle against demons and the godless, while the Central Asian Turks could present their activities within the paradigm of the Islamic *jihād*. But the rhetoric of the destroyer of temples in the case of Muslim elites and of the protector of temples and Brahmans in the case of Hindu elites can be misleading in suggesting that the primary motivations for conflict were religious in nature. Instead, I believe that these representations should be understood as strategies aimed at consolidating community allegiance.

While the presence of a markedly different Turkic people undoubtedly facilitated the formation of a Hindu or non-Muslim identity, the growth of regional identities in medieval south India was more striking. Though restricted to the elite segment of the population, the medieval definition of self in terms of region was a precursor of regional loyalties in the twentieth century. Because the core elements of medieval regional identity included collective memories of the past, as well as a common language and homeland, it can be classified as an early form of ethnicity. For Andhra warriors during the late middle ages, unity was fostered through construction of a shared history in which the Kakatiya dynasty played a seminal role. By focusing too exclusively on religion as a source of difference, scholars have overlooked the significance of other attributes differentiating the medieval communities of India. And by failing to contextualize the development of Hindu and Muslim identities within the historical processes of migration and a moving frontier, a static and simplistic view of identity formation in South Asia has prevailed for too long.

The ethnic identities of elite groups in pre-modern India may differ from modern nationalisms in their restricted social range and rallying power. But too much has been made of the distinction between traditional and modern societies in this, as in many other, respects. Whether we are speaking of medieval India or modern India, the sense of community evolved through a twofold process—the distancing of the group from others whose alienness is highlighted, on the one hand, and the elaboration of a set of common social attributes, on the other. In the development of an ethnicity, earlier myths and images were often appropriated to provide an all-important illusion of continuity with ancient times. By representing themselves as extending far back in time, communities could claim to be natural entities, inherent to the social world. Although the antiquity of many ethnic groups is suspect, in terms of the continuity of actual membership, the symbols that represent the community's cohesion may indeed possess prior histories. In both pre-modern and modern societies, in other words, the imagining of the past was an ongoing creative process.

NOTES

Earlier versions of this article were presented at the 1993 Western Conference of the Association for Asian Studies meeting in Mexico City and the 1994 national meeting of the Association for Asian Studies in Boston. I am deeply indebted to Richard M. Eaton and Phillip B. Wagoner, my fellow panelists on both occasions, whose ideas have so heavily influenced my own. Their editorial assistance is also gratefully acknowledged, as is the help of Susan M. Deeds.

1. On Hindu nationalism, see Daniel Gold, 'Organized Hinduisms: From Vedic Truth to Hindu Nation', in *Fundamentalisms Observed*, Martin E. Marty and R. Scott Appleby, eds. (Chicago: University of Chicago Press, 1991), pp. 531–93; Peter van der Veer, *Religious Nationalism: Hindus and Muslims in India* (Berkeley: University of California Press, 1994).

2. Entry for the date 1688 in 'Hindu Timeline', *Hinduism Today*, December 1994.

3. For discussion of the Ayodhya situation, see Asghar Ali Engineer, ed., *Politics of Confrontation: The Babri-Masjid Ramjanmabhoomi Controversy Runs Riot* (Delhi: Ajanta Publications, 1992); Ramesh Thakur, 'Ayodhya and the Politics of India's Secularism', *Asian Survey*, 33:7 (July 1993), pp. 645–64.

4. For an older example of Hindu nationalist historiography, see R.C. Majumdar, 'Hindu-Muslim Relations', in *The Struggle for Empire*, vol. 5 of *The History and Culture of the Indian People* (Bombay: Bharatiya Vidya Bhavan, 1957), p. 498.

5. Romila Thapar, Harbans Mukhia, and Bipan Chandra, *Communalism and the Writing of Indian History* (Delhi: People's Publishing, 1969); Harbans Mukhia, 'Communalism and the Writing of Medieval Indian History: A Reappraisal', in *Perspectives on Medieval History* (New Delhi: Vikas Publishing, 1993), pp. 33–45.

6. Sandria Freitag, *Collective Action and Community: Public Arenas and the Emergence of Communalism in North India* (Berkeley: University of California Press, 1989).

7. Gyanendra Pandey, *The Construction of Communalism in Colonial North India* (Delhi: Oxford University Press, 1990).

8. C.A. Bayly, 'The Pre-History of 'Communalism'? Religious Conflict in India, 1700–1860', *Modern Asian Studies*, 19:2 (1985), p. 202.

9. Pandey, *Construction of Communalism*, p. 199.

10. *Imagined Communities: Reflections on the Origin and Spread of Nationalism*, 2nd edn. (London: Verso, 1991).

11. Anthony D. Smith, *Ethnic Origins of Nations* (Oxford: Basil Blackwell, 1986).

12. Van der Veer, *Religious Nationalism*, pp. 12–24; John D. Rogers, 'Post-Orientalism and the Interpretation of Premodern and Modern Political Identities: The Case of Sri Lanka', *Journal of Asian Studies*, 53:1 (1994), pp. 10–23; David N. Lorenzen, 'Introduction: The Historical Vicissitudes of Bhakti Religion', in *Bhakti Religion in North India: Community Identity and Political Action*, D. Lorenzen, ed. (Albany: State University of New York Press, 1994), pp. 2–13.

13. Sheldon Pollock, "Ramayana and Political Imagination in India," *Journal of Asian Studies*, 52:1 (1993), p. 264.

14. The inscriptions examined for this study, which all contain some reference to Muslims, were culled from a larger corpus of about 1,600 records issued in Andhra in this time period. The existence of another 400 inscriptions from the same era and place has been reported by the epigraphical branch of the Archaeological Survey of India, but the majority of these records are either heavily damaged or no longer available for consultation.

15. Pollock, 'Ramayana and Political Imagination', p. 282.

16. N. Venkataramanayya and M. Somasekhara Sarma, ed., 'Vilasa Grant of Prolaya Nayaka', *EI* 32: 239–68. Parts of the inscription are translated in M. Somasekhara Sarma, *A Forgotten Chapter of Andhra History* (Madras: Ananda Press, 1945), pp. 20, 35–36, 44–45.

17. The last two Sultanate expeditions into Kakatiya territory (in 1321 and 1323) were led by the man then known by the title Ulugh Khan, who became Sultan Muhammad bin Tughluq in 1325. The Khiljis had conducted several earlier campaigns against the Kakatiyas, beginning in 1303. Although this inscription indicates that there were eight Sultanate campaigns during the reign of Kakatiya Prataparudra, Muslim sources describe only five (N. Venkataramanayya, *The Early Muslim Expansion in South India* [Madras: University of Madras, 1942], pp. 23–4, 31–43, 83–5, 99–108, 115–19).

18. Author's translation from Sanskrit; Venkataramanayya and Somasekhara Sarma, 'Vilasa Grant', verse 21.

19. Author's translation from Sanskrit; 'Vilasa Grant', verse 28.

20. Aloka Parasher, *Mlecchas in Early India; A Study in Attitudes towards Foreigners* (New Delhi: Munshiram Manoharlal, 1991), pp. 121–24 and 240–43; Romila Thapar, 'The Image of the Barbarian in Early India', *Comparative Studies in Society and History*, 13:4 (1971), pp. 420–1.

21. Parasher, *Mlecchas in Early India*, pp. 45 and 213.

22. Romila Thapar, 'Imagined Religious Communities? Ancient History and the Modern Search for a Hindu Identity', *Modern Asian Studies*, 23:2 (1989), p. 224.

23. North Indian uses of these terms are frequent as well, see Ram Shankar Avasty and Amalananda Ghosh, 'References to Muhammadans in Sanskrit Inscriptions in Northern India—AD 730 to 1320', *Journal of Indian History*, 16 (1936), pp. 24–26 and 17 (1937), pp. 161–84; Pushpa Prasad, *Sanskrit Inscriptions of the Delhi Sultanate* (Delhi: Oxford University Press, 1990).

24. Smith, *Ethnic Origins of Nations*, p. 49.

25. John A. Armstrong, *Nations before Nationalism* (Chapel Hill: University of North Carolina Press, 1982), pp. 3–7. For more on boundaries between groups, see Kerwin L. Klein, 'Frontier Tales: The Narrative Construction of Cultural Borders in Twentieth-Century California', *Comparative Studies in Society and History*, 34:3 (July 1992), pp. 464–90.

26. 'Nationalism, Mauritian Style: Cultural Unity and Ethnic Diversity', *Comparative Studies in Society and History*, 36:3 (July 1994), pp. 566–67.

27. Cynthia Kepley Mahmood, 'Rethinking Indian Communalism: Culture and Counter-Culture', *Asian Survey*, 33:7 (1993), pp. 722–37; Wendy Doniger, 'Hinduism by Any Other Name', *Wilson Quarterly*, 15:3 (1991), pp. 35–41.

28. *SII* 16.4: *NDI* copper-plate 10 and Kanigiri 23; *EI* 13.1; N. Ramesan, 'The Kraku Grant of Harihara II', in *Epigraphia Andhrica*, vol. 2, N. Venkataramanayya and P.V. Parabrahma Sastry, eds. (Hyderabad: Government of Andhra Pradesh, 1974), pp. 73–87.

29. Carl W. Ernst, *Eternal Garden: Mysticism, History and Politics at a South Asian Sufi Center* (Albany: State University of New York Press, 1992), pp. 22–3.

30. Andre Wink, *Early Medieval India and the Expansion of Islam*, vol. 1, pp. 190 and 5 of *Al-Hind: The Making of the Indo-Islamic World* (Delhi: Oxford University Press, 1990).

31. Ernst, *Eternal Garden*, pp. 24–5.

32. George de Vos, 'Ethnic Pluralism: Conflict and Accommodation', in *Ethnic Identity: Cultural Continuities and Change*, George de Vos and Lola Romanucci-Ross, eds. (Palo Alto: Mayfield Publishing Company, 1975), pp. 9–18; Charles F. Keyes, 'The Dialectics of Ethnic Change', in *Ethnic Change* (Seattle: University of Washington Press, 1981), pp. 7–10.

33. Thapar, 'Imagined Religious Communities?', pp. 77–8; Pollock, 'Ramayana and Political Imagination', p. 286.

34. In this early period, the majority of Muslims in India most probably were either foreign immigrants or their descendants. They were thus marked with many distinctive non-Indian features in areas such as dress and food, in addition to their separate languages and religious beliefs. As the number of converts to Islam increased, the initial sense of ethnic separateness must have faded, explaining why ethnic referents were largely discarded in favor of the religious label Musalman in the Andhra of later centuries. Very little research has been conducted on conversion to Islam in medieval South India, unfortunately, so it is not possible to pinpoint when the trend emerged.

35. David A. Chappell, 'Ethnogenesis and Frontiers', *Journal of World History*, 4:2 (1993), pp. 267–75; Igor Kopytoff, 'The Internal African Frontier: The Making of African Political Culture', in *The African Frontier: The Reproduction of Traditional African Societies*, Igor Kopytoff, ed. (Bloomington: Indiana University Press, 1987).

36. David Harry Miller, 'Ethnogenesis and Religious Revitalization beyond the Roman Frontier: The Case of Frankish Origins', *Journal of World History*, 4:2 (1993), pp. 277–85.

37. Cynthia Talbot, 'Political Intermediaries in Kakatiya Andhra, 1175–1325', *Indian Economic and Social History Review*, 31:3 (1994), pp. 261–89.

38. J. Ramayya, ed., 'Madras Museum Plates of Vema', *EI* 8:9–24.

39. People of less elevated status typically made religious gifts to temples rather than to Brahmins in this period, and had their benefactions recorded in stone at the endowed temple. The most widespread gift was that of milk-bearing animals to provide oil for temple lamps.

40. Author's translation from Sanskrit; Venkataramanayya and Somasekhara Sarma, 'Vilasa Grant', verse 37.

41. Author's translation from Sanskrit; Ramayya, 'Madras Museum Plates', verse 12.

42. Smith, *Ethnic Origins of Nations*, pp. 58–67; Armstrong, *Nations Before Nationalism*, pp. 201–40.

43. For example, Dietrich Gerhard, 'The Frontier in Comparative View', *Comparative Studies in Society and History*, 1:3 (1959), pp. 205–29; Robert Bartlett and Angus MacKay, ed., *Medieval Frontier Societies* (Oxford: Clarendon Press, 1989); Howard Lamar and Leonard Thompson, ed., *The Frontier in History: North American and Southern Africa Compared* (New Haven & London: Yale University Press, 1981); William H. McNeill, 'The Great Frontier: Freedom and Hierarchy in Modern Times', in *The Global Condition* (Princeton: Princeton University Press, 1992), pp. 5–63.

44. *The Rise of Islam and the Bengal Frontier, 1204–1760* (Berkeley: University of California Press, 1993). An additional exception is John F. Richards, 'The Islamic Frontier in the East: Expansion into South Asia', *South Asia* n.s., 4 (October 1974), pp. 90–109.

45. Leonard Thompson and Howard Lamar, 'Comparative Frontier History', in *The Frontier in History: North American and Southern Africa Compared*, H. Lamar and L. Thompson, eds., pp. 7 and 10.

46. John F. Richards, *Mughal Administration in Golconda* (Oxford: Clarendon Press, 1975), pp. 7–8.

47. Based on translation of T.A. Gopinatha Rao, 'Srisailam Plates of Virupaksha: Saka Samvat 1388', *EI* 15:24.

48. *SII* 16.47; P.V. Parabrahma Sastry, 'The Polepalli Grant of Achyutaraya', in *Epigraphia Andhrica*, vol. 4, P.V. Parabrahma Sastry, ed. (Hyderabad: Government of Andhra Pradesh, 1975), pp. 133–40; N. Ramesan, ed., 'The Jadavalli Grant of Sadasivaraya', in *Copper Plate Inscriptions of the State Museum*, vol. 2 (Hyderabad: Government of Andhra Pradesh, 1970), pp. 21–8.

49. Phillip B. Wagoner, 'Understanding Islam at Vijayanagara' (Paper presented at the meeting of the Association for Asian Studies, Boston, April 1994).

50. Robert I. Burns, 'The Significance of the Frontier in the Middle Ages', in *Medieval Frontier Societies*, R. Bartlett and A. MacKay, eds., pp. 307–12.

51. Jose Enrique Lopez de Coca Castaner, 'Institutions on the Castilian-Granadan Frontier', in *Medieval Frontier Societies*, R. Bartlett and A. MacKay, eds., pp. 127–50; Angus McKay, 'Religion, Culture and Ideology on the Late Medieval Castilian-Granadan Frontier', pp. 217–22.

52. For more positive coverage of Hindu-Muslim relations in medieval India, see H.K. Sherwani, 'Cultural Synthesis in Medieval India', *Journal of Indian History*, 41 (1963), pp. 239–59; W.H. Siddiqi, 'Religious Tolerance as Gleaned from Medieval Inscriptions', in *Proceedings of Seminar on Medieval Inscriptions* (Aligarh: Centre of Advanced Study, Dept. of History, Aligarh Muslim University, 1974), pp. 50–8.

53. Stewart Gordon, *The Marathas, 1600–1818* (Cambridge: Cambridge University Press, 1993), pp. 41–58; Richards, *Mughal Administration in Golconda*, pp. 18–33.

54. K. Lakshmi Ranjanam, 'Language and Literature: Telugu', in *History of Medieval Deccan*, vol. 2, H.K. Sherwani and P.M. Joshi, ed. (Hyderabad: Government of Andhra Pradesh, 1974), pp. 161–3. An example of a bilingual inscription is ARIE No. 48 of 1970–71.

55. Stein, *Vijayanagara*, 29; K. Nilakanta Sastri and N. Venkataramanayya, *Further Sources of Vijayanagara History*, 3 vols. (Madras: University of Madras, 1946), vol. 1, pp. 106–8 and 267.

56. John M. Fritz, George Michell, and M.S. Nagaraja Rao, *Where Kings and Gods Meet: The Royal Centre at Vijayanagara, India* (Tucson: University of Arizona Press, 1984), pp. 122–45.

57. Phillip B. Wagoner, '"Sultan among Hindu Kings": Dress, Titles, and the Islamicization of Hindu Culture at Vijayanagara', *Journal of Asian Studies*, 55:4 (1996), pp. 851–80.

58. K. Iswara Dutt, *Inscriptional Glossary of Andhra Pradesh* (Hyderabad: A.P. Sahitya Akademi, 1967), p. cxxv; Lakshmi Ranjanam, 'Language and Literature: Telugu', p. 172.

59. 'The Ideology of Silence: Prejudice and Pragmatism on the Medieval Religious Frontier', *Comparative Studies in Society and History*, 26:3 (1984), pp. 442–66.

60. Phillip B. Wagoner, *Tidings of the King: A Translation and Ethnohistorical Analysis of the Rayavacakamu* (Honolulu: University of Hawaii Press, 1993), 178 n. 49; Prasad, *Sanskrit Inscriptions*, p. 56.

61. C.V. Ramachandra Rao, *Administration and Society in Medieval Andhra (AD 1038–1538) under the Later Eastern Gangas and the Suryavamsa Gajapatis* (Nellore: Manasa Publications, 1976), pp. 85–6.

62. I thank Thomas R. Trautmann for bringing the correlation between the geographical location of these lords and the distribution of horses and elephants to my attention. For more on elephants in ancient India, see Trautmann, 'Elephants and the Mauryas', in *India: History and Thought, Essays in Honour of A.L. Basham*, S.N. Mukherjee, ed. (Calcutta: Subarnarekha, 1982), pp. 263–6. For a discussion of the quality of horses during the medieval period, see Simon Digby, *War-Horse and Elephant in the Delhi Sultanate* (Oxford: Orient Monographs, 1971), pp. 21–31.

63. The Kaluvacheru grant of the Reddi queen Anitalli, partially published in Somasekhara Sarma, *Forgotten Chapter*, pp. 111–2. This Sanskrit inscription identifies the Lord of Elephants as the king of Utkala (a sub-region of Orissa), the Lord of Horses as the ruler of the territories in the west, and the Lord of Men as Kakatiya Prataparudra, the Andhra king. In this instance, the Lord of Horses in the west must refer to the Bahmani Sultanate, which controlled the territories to the immediate west of northern Andhra during the early fifteenth century.

64. *Tidings of the King*, pp. 60–9.

65. Andugula Venkayya's *Narapati Vijayamu*, cited in Lakshmi Ranjanam, 'Language and Literature: Telugu', p. 165.

66. *SII* 10.753.

67. T.V. Mahalingam, ed., *Summaries of the Historical Manuscripts in the Mackenzie Collection*, vol. 2 (Madras: University of Madras, 1976), pp. 36–7.

68. C.V. Ramachandra Rao, ed., *Ekamranathuni Prataparudracaritramu* (Hyderabad: Andhra Pradesh Sahitya Akademi, 1984), pp. 59–71.

69. Further expression of the idea that Muslim kings were god-like in the same manner as Hindu kings is found in an episode from the *Prataparudra Caritramu*. This story, repeated in the later *Rāyavācakamu* as well, concerns the Delhi sultan's mother, who one night viewed the sleeping bodies of her son and the captive, Kakatiya Prataparudra. The brilliant light issuing forth from their forms made her realize that both the Delhi sultan and Prataparudra were manifestations of the gods Vishnu and Shiva (Ramachandra Rao, *Prataparudracaritramu*, pp. 66–7; Wagoner, *Tidings of the King*, pp. 122–3.

70. *SII* 16.175 of 1550 AD; unfortunately, only the first few lines of the inscription survive. It was issued by Santa Bhikshavritti Ayyavaru, the head of

the Virasaiva monastery at Srisailam, who also asserts that the three lords were his disciples.

71. Iswara Dutt, *Inscriptional Glossary*, p. iii.

72. N. Venkataramanayya and M. Somasekhara Sarma, 'The Kakatiyas of Warangal', in *Early History of the Deccan*, G. Yazdani, ed. (London: Oxford University Press, 1960), p. 691.

73. K. Sundaram, *Studies in Economic and Social Conditions of Medieval Andhra* (Machilipatnam and Madras: Triveni Publishers, 1968), p. 1.

74. Prior to the Kakatiya period, most inscriptions from western Andhra were composed in Kannada (the language of the Karnataka region to the west), while inscriptions in southern Andhra were often composed either in Kannada or Tamil (the language of Tamil Nadu to the south). For details, see Cynthia Talbot, *Precolonial India in Practice: Society, Region, and Identity in Medieval India* (N.Y.: Oxford University Press, 2001), pp. 34–7.

75. Author's translation from Telugu, 11, pp. 12–15 of *SII* 4.659.

76. Author's translation from Telugu, 11, pp. 157–62 of *EI* 6.22.

77. David Washbrook, '"To Each a Language of His Own": Language, Culture, and Society in Colonial India', in *Language, History and Class*, Penelope J. Corfield, ed. (London: Blackwell, 1991), pp. 179–203; David Lelyveld, 'The Fate of Hindustani: Colonial Knowledge and the Project of a National Language', in *Orientalism and the Postcolonial Predicament*, Carol A. Breckenridge and Peter van der Veer, eds. (Philadelphia: University of Pennsylvania Press, 1993), pp. 189–214.

78. Sudipta Kaviraj, 'The Imaginary Institution of India', *Subaltern Studies VII*, Partha Chatterjee and Gyanendra Pandey, eds. (Delhi: Oxford University Press, 1992), p. 26. Kaviraj does not believe that language formed the basis for pre-modern communities in India, however. Whatever the situation might have been in the Bengali-speaking area, which was Kaviraj's case study, I believe that the medieval South Indian evidence sufficiently demonstrates the existence of elite linguistic identities there.

79. Lelyveld, 'Fate of Hindustani', 201; Washbrook, '"To Each a Language"', p. 180.

80. Smith, *Ethnic Origins of Nations*, pp. 79–84.

81. Early Kakatiya records are *HAS* 13.6, 7, 12; *IAP-K* nos. 14, 15, 19, 22, 24; *IAP-W* nos. 14, 22, 25, 29. Later Kakatiya inscriptions are *ARIE* no. 126 of 1958–59; *HAS* 13.3, 56; *IAP-W* no. 37; *SII* 4.1071, 1095, 1107; *SII* 6.212.

82. *SII* 6.796.

83. For some other historical memories of the Kakatiyas, see Talbot, 'Political Intermediaries', pp. 281–3.

84. Hirananda Sastri, *Shitab Khan of Warangal*, Hyderabad Archaeological Series No. 9 (Hyderabad: H.E.H. the Nizam's Government, 1932), pp. 3 and 10.

85. Based on the translation of Ibid., p. 23.

86. Based on the translation of Ibid., p. 24.

87. *SII* 26.622; Parabrahma Sastry, *Select Epigraphs of Andhra Pradesh*, Andhra Pradesh Archaeological Series No. 31 (Hyderabad: Government of Andhra Pradesh, n.d.), pp. 76–7.

88. However, other types of sources do engage in an anti-Muslim polemic. Notable among these are the *Rāyavācakamu* (Wagoner, *Tidings of the King*) and the village, family and temple histories (*kaifiyat*) collected by Colin Mackenzie around 1800, many of which mention anarchy and destruction in the decades after the battle of 1565 (Nilakanta Sastri and Venkataramanayya, *Further Sources*, 2:245–50).

89. In contrast to the 862 records originating in the eight decades between 1490 and 1570 AD, the eighty-year span from 1570 to 1650 AD yields only 318 inscriptions—a mere third of the earlier total.

90. At present, lists of sites where Hindu temples were destroyed and mosques or tombs (*dargah*) built in their place are being circulated by nationalist scholars. The data upon which these lists are based are not always provided, making the evidence suspect. Muslim chronicles and Perso-Arabic inscriptions are sometimes utilized, but neither of these types of sources is totally reliable. Sita Ram Goel is one scholar compiling such lists, see his 'Let the Mute Witnesses Speak', in *Hindu Temples: What Happened to Them, A Preliminary Survey*, Arun Shourie *et al*, eds. (New Delhi: Voice of India, 1990), pp. 88–181; in *Hindu Temples: What Happened to Them, Pt. 2 The Islamic Evidence* (New Delhi: Voice of India, 1991). Thanks are due to Richard M. Eaton for acquainting me with these works.

91. George Michell, 'City as Cosmogram: The Circular Plan of Warangal', *South Asian Studies*, 8 (1992), p. 12.

92. Sherwani, 'Bahmanis', p. 208.

93. Although I believe Goel's lists are greatly inflated, this statement would be true even by his reckoning. In the approximately 140 sites of temple desecration that he records for Andhra Pradesh ('Let the Mute Witnesses Speak', 88–95), the dates for the alleged incidents are given in sixty instances. Five date from the fourteenth century (phase one), six come from phase two, and nineteen date from 1565 to 1650 AD (phase three). The remaining thirty or so cases stem from the century after 1650, with a notable bunching of incidents in the late 1600s, when the Mughal empire was absorbing the former Qutb Shahi kingdom of Golkonda.

94. *SII* 16.296.

95. The Ahobilam Kaifiyat is summarized in Nilakanta Sastri and Venkataramanayya, *Further Sources of Vijayanagara History*, 3:246.

96. P. Sitapati, *Sri Ahobila Narasimha Swamy Temple* (Hyderabad: Government of Andhra Pradesh, 1982), p. 15.

97. *SII* 5.1312.

98. *SII* 10.755 and *SII* 5.1260. The same chief additionally granted a village to the famous temple at Simhacalam, also in northeastern Andhra. This leads K. Sundaram to surmise that the Simhacalam temple had been plundered at the same time as that of Srikurman (The *Simhacalam Temple* [Simhacalam, A.P.: Simhacalam Devasthanam, 1969], pp. 33 and 104).

99. P. Sitapati, *Srisailam Temple Kaifiyat*, 2 vols. (Hyderabad: Government of Andhra Pradesh, 1981), p. 13.

100. Sitapati, *Ahobila Temple*, p. 16; Nilakanta Sastri and Venkataramanayya, *Further Sources*, 3:246.

101. 'Temple Desecration and Indo-Muslim States', in Richard M. Eaton, *Essays on Islam and Indian History* (New Delhi: Oxford University Press, 2000), pp. 94–132.

102. The other inscriptions on this slab are published as *SII* 5.1289–1311.

103. Ernst, *Eternal Garden*, pp. 22–9 and 38–59.

104. Richard M. Eaton, *The Rise of Islam and the Bengal Frontier, 1204–1760* (New Delhi: Oxford University Press, 1997), pp. 72–7.

105. This is true of the North Indian poet-saints, Kabir and Guru Nanak (Lorenzen, 'Vicissitudes of Bhakti', p. 12) as well as Eknath from Maharashtra (Eleanor Zelliot, 'A Medieval Encounter between Hindu and Muslim: Eknath's Drama-Poem Hindu-Turk Samvad', included in this volume).

APPENDIX

In citing inscriptions, the following abbreviations have been used:

ARIE	*Annual Report on Indian Epigraphy* (New Delhi: Archaeological Survey of India).
EI	*Epigraphia Indica* (New Delhi: Archaeological Survey of India).
HAS 13	P. Sreenivasachar, ed., *A Corpus of Inscriptions in the Telingana Districts of H.E.H. The Nizam's Dominions*, Pt. II, Hyderabad Archaelogical Series No. 13 (Hyderabad: H.E.H The Nizam's Government, 1940).
IAP-K	P.V. Parabrahma Sastry, ed., *Inscriptions of Andhra Pradesh: Karimnagar District*, Andhra Pradesh Govt. Epigraphy Series No. 8 (Hyderabad: Government of Andhra Pradesh, n.d.).
IAP-W	N. Venkataramanayya, ed., *Inscriptions of Andhra Pradesh: Warangal District*, Andhra Pradesh Govt. Epigraphy Series No. 6 (Hyderabad: Government of Andhra Pradesh, 1974).
NDI	Alan Butterworth and V. Venugopal Chetty, eds., *A Collection of the Inscriptions on Copper-Plates and Stones in the Nellore District*, 3 vols. (1905; rpt., New Delhi: Asian Educational Services, 1990).
SII	*South Indian Inscriptions*, 26 vols. (Madras or New Delhi: Archaeological Survey of India).

PART TWO

Religion and Political Power

India's long rule by Muslims generated a range of Islamic traditions related in some way to the exercise of political power. Some were produced at political centres and were dependent upon their connection with power; others appeared at a distance from, or even in opposition to, that power.

The first two essays in this section examine Indo-Muslim traditions promulgated from the Mughal imperial centre during the reigns of Akbar and Aurangzeb, respectively. By placing the religious policies of these two emperors in their contemporary political and social contexts, the essays challenge hackneyed stereotypes that contrast the 'good' Akbar (liberal, compassionate) with the 'bad' Aurangzeb (narrow-minded, bigoted). Iqtidar Alam Khan situates Akbar's well-known religious policy of 'peace with all' (*suḥl-i kull*) in the context of that emperor's various experiments with winning political support for the empire. Thus his initial abolition of discriminatory measures such as pilgrimage or jizya taxes occurred in the 1560s, when he was endeavouring to recruit Rajput nobles into the imperial service. But upon resorting to the use of force against Rajput opponents, as he did at Chitor (1568), Akbar issued a 'proclamation of victory' (*fathnāma*) exulting in his having waged jihād against infidelity. In the 1570s, while trying to attract Indian Muslims to the imperial cause, he re-imposed the discriminatory jizya tax on non-Muslims, and even had himself declared 'King of Islam'. But when such measures failed to prevent the outbreak of a serious rebellion among his Muslim nobles in 1580–81, Akbar abandoned his 'pro-Islamic' policy for good and returned to a conciliatory posture on religious matters.

Satish Chandra follows a similarly historicist mode of reasoning in explaining Aurangzeb's religious policies. Noting that the emperor waited for twenty-two years before imposing the jizya tax on non-Muslims, Chandra looks for historical events occurring just prior to 1679, the date the tax was reimposed, that might explain this change of imperial policy. This leads him to consider the political conditions in the Deccan, which had begun to deteriorate sharply from 1676, and the emperor's perception that some striking declaration was needed to rally Sunni Muslim opinion in the face of the Marathas' alliance with the Shi'i state of Golkonda.

If some Islamic traditions like the jizya tax were products of state policy, others emerged at a spatial and/or ideological distance from Muslim centres of power, but in dialogic relationship with that power. The famous statement by the Chishti shaikh, Nizam al-Din Auliya (d. 1325)—'my room has two doors; if the sultan comes through one door, I will leave by the other'—captures the distrust of state power felt by some (but not all) Sufi shaikhs, a topic taken up in the following section of this volume. Other Muslim groups, convinced that the End of Time was at hand, went further and assumed an oppositional, and occasionally militant, stance *vis-à-vis* established authority.

In the third essay of this section, Derryl MacLean examines the movement launched by Saiyid Muhammad of Jaunpur (d. 1505), who in 1495 declared himself '*mahdi*', the figure who in classical Islamic thought was expected to appear near the last days and cleanse society in preparation for the Day of Judgement. Scholars generally regard millennial movements like his as doomed to failure, owing to their alleged hostility to state authority and their socially marginalized support base. It is true that ruling authorities in both Gujarat and Sind exiled Saiyid Muhammad when he confronted and condemned the socio-political order of his day, and that subsequent rulers executed his successors. But MacLean finds that most of Saiyid Muhammad's followers were not at all social rabble, but members of the Muslim socio-political élite. Moreover, after enduring state persecution for most of the sixteenth century, by the seventeenth century the movement had become socially and theologically accommodated to the Mughal state. The author's evidence with respect to this kind of Indian Islamic tradition thus challenges received assumptions concerning the social composition and ultimate fate of millennial movements.

5

The Nobility Under Akbar and the Development of His Religious Policy, 1560–80*

Iqtidar Alam Khan

The significant changes that were introduced in the organization of Mughal government and the accompanying shifts in Akbar's administrative and religious policies during the period 1560–80 have remained for long a favourite subject of study for a number of modern historians. The existing interpretation of these changes seems largely to run parallel to Abu'l-fazl's line of argument, which seeks to explain the growth of institutions and policies in terms of the unfolding of Akbar's personality. Abu'l-fazl often tries to ignore, or brush aside as the outcome of 'wrong advice', all those measures or decisions that appeared to him inconsistent with Akbar's policy during the last 25 years of his reign.[1] The impression created by Abu'l-fazl is reinforced by a similar tendency in Badayuni, who, from an opposite point of view, quite frequently mixes up his comments on some of Akbar's enlightened measures of the later period with the events of the earlier phase, when there was hardly any ground for him to find fault with Akbar from a doctrinal angle. Under the influence of these interpretations modern historians also tend to disregard facts that are inconsistent with Abu'l-fazl's theory of Akbar's gradual 'unveiling' of himself as 'the superman', through the introduction, one after another, of his policies based on the principles of *ṣuḥl-i-kull* and universal kingship. This has often resulted in reducing discussion of Akbar's religious policy and his relations with the Rajputs largely to speculation based on selected facts that have been highlighted by Abu'l-fazl and Badayuni. It may further be pointed out that the whole problem of the nobility under Akbar is generally sought to be understood in terms of their relations with the king, which is no doubt an important aspect to

* Reprinted from the *Journal of the Royal Asiatic Society of Great Britain and Ireland* (1968), pp. 29–36.

be considered, but not the only one. The exclusive attention given to this has served to hide from view many other equally important factors such as the pattern of racial and religious alignments within the nobility, tribal or clan ties among groups of nobles, and their relations with other sections of the people. These kinds of interactions determined to a large extent changes in the role and standing of the nobility.

In this essay an attempt is made to suggest a reappraisal of Akbar's early policies by raising certain points which tell against the accepted interpretation. The views put forward here are purely tentative and by no means based on an exhaustive analysis of the available evidence. The purpose of this appraisal will be served if it succeeds in stimulating fresh thinking about some of the well-known generalizations so often repeated in textbooks.

A significant aspect of the transformation that came about in the nature and functioning of the institutions of the Mughal empire in the sixteenth century was the evolution of a culturally unified nobility out of the multiracial and religiously heterogeneous elements brought together by Akbar. An analysis of the list of nobles who accompanied Humayun to Hindustan in 1555 shows that the nobility inherited by Akbar consisted chiefly of two racial groups',[2] the Persians and the Turanis; and of the two, the Turanis enjoyed a pre-dominant position. The nobility left behind by Humayun had thus essentially a Turani complexion. The Persian nobles with the exception of Bairam Khan, Mirza Nijat, and Mirza Hasan were simply exalted scribes who could exercise but little influence on state policies.[3] But for the promotions received by a few (hardly three or four) persons of Persian origin,[4] the composition of the nobility remained unaltered during the regime of Bairam Khan. But after Bairam Khan's fall the situation gradually changed. As is apparent from the accompanying tables, two new elements of local origin entered the imperial service between 1560 and 1575. These new elements were the Rajput chiefs and the Indian Muslims (mostly *shaikh-zādas,* the majority of whom belonged to the families living on *madad-i ma'āsh* grants or enjoying *zamīndārī* rights). At the same time, there was a marked increase in the relative strength of the Persians, especially in the higher grades.[5] The net result of this process was the gradual fading away of the Turani complexion of the nobility as well as the erosion of the Chaghatai traditions and customs of state organization,[6] thus indirectly facilitating Akbar's quest for an alternative theory of kingship in the subsequent years.

The Persian nobles seem to have improved their position in the period 1562–7 [7] mainly by earning promotion in the course of military operations during the revolt of sections of the nobility. It may be noted that except for the temporary desertion by Asaf Khan in 1565–6, none of the revolts that took place in this period were staged by the Persians, or for that matter by any other non-Turani section of the nobles.[8] Even the rebellion of the Uzbek officers led by 'Ali Quli Khan, who himself had a Persian background, was in reality the rebellion of the whole clan of the Uzbek nobles serving under Akbar. All the leading figures like 'Abd Allah Khan, Ibrahim Khan, and Sikandar Khan, were Turanis, but for 'Ali Quli Khan and his brother.[9] It is also suggestive that during the operations against the Uzbek officers—while Mun'im Khan, the most senior Chaghtai noble of the realm, endeavoured to secure a peaceful settlement—a group of senior Khurasani officers such as Khwaja Jahan, Asaf Khan, Mu'izz al-Mulk, and Mir Ghiyath al-Din appeared to be quite apathetic, if not actually hostile, towards the efforts aimed at reconciliation.[10]

There is another piece of information which sheds some light on the attitudes of the Turanis and Khurasanis during this period. Abu'l-fazl has noted that a large section of the Turani nobles participating in the operations against Mirza Sharaf al-Din and Shah Abu'l-ma'ali in 1563–4 were quite lukewarm, while Persian officers like Husain Quli Khan, Isma'il Quli Khan and others who were directing the operations, as well as other Persians serving under them, were steadfast and unsparing in their support of the royal cause.[11] On no occasion after 1567, not even in 1580–1,[12] was such undivided support of the Persian nobles available to Akbar in his struggle with the recalcitrant sections of the nobility. These facts put together indicate clearly that the trend visible in the fortunes of the Persians, from the Table for 1565–75, is not unreal or accidental, and also confirm the suggestion that the rise in their numbers in the higher grades actually took place between 1562 and 1567.

There can be no doubt that the recruitment of the Rajputs in Mughal service commenced soon after Akbar's assumption of the direction of the state. The same was perhaps the case with the shaikh-zādas. The presence of important clans of the Rajputs and the shaikh-zādas in Mughal service can be traced as far back as 1561.[13] Apparently during this period Akbar was anxious to win recruits from these sections by placating and befriending them in different ways. One of the measures for the attainment of this goal was his move to establish matrimonial relations with the Rajput chiefs. Indeed, it is possible that an attempt to establish similar relations was made with the shaikh-zādas of Delhi and Agra, though it seems to have proved abortive.[14] The abolition of the pilgrimage tax in 1562 and that of the jizya in 1564[15] were steps of a similar nature, dictated principally by the exigencies of state policy rather than consideration of religious tolerance or intellectual influences of any kind.

It is interesting to note that soon after the suppression of the Uzbek rebellion, Akbar's attitude towards the Rajputs changed radically. Now he adopted a vigorous policy to reduce them to submission by force. There was a corresponding shift in religious policy too, shown by efforts at placating orthodox Muslim sentiments. The appeal of such a policy was, apparently, directed towards the Persians, Turanis, and the newly recruited Indian Muslims, all of whom were equally bigoted in their devotion to Islam. The public manifestation of Akbar's attitude during the siege of Chitor (1568) is quite instructive in this connection. The fall of Chitor was proclaimed by him as the victory of Islam over infidels. A *fatḥnāma* issued on 9 March, 1568, conveying the news of his victory at Chitor to the officers of the Punjab, is so full of intolerant professions and sentiments and couched in such aggressive language that it could compete favourably with similar documents issued by the most orthodox of Muslim rulers of India.[16] There is some other evidence as well which reinforces the impression conveyed by this document. For example, a *farmān* of Akbar, presumably of this period, directs Qazi 'Abd al-Samad, the *muḥtasib* of Bilgram, and other officials of the town 'to prevent the Hindus of that *pargana* from practising idol-worship and take such other steps as might help in eradicating the manifestations of heresy and deviation from that pargana'.[17] The reimposition of jizya in 1575 was the logical culmination of this policy.[18] Apparently, this policy of Akbar was by and large successful in attaining the object that he had in mind: it is noteworthy that all the important Rajput chiefs, with the exception of the Kachwahas, joined Akbar's service after the fall of Chitor and not before it.[19] This would suggest that the factors that induced the Rajputs to join Mughal service were anything but their appreciation of Akbar's attitude towards non-Muslims.

It would appear from the breakdown of the total figure of nobles for 1565–75, 1580, and 1575–95 under different racial categories that Indian Muslims who entered the Mughal service in the early 1560s improved their positions, particularly during 1575–80.[20] It is significant that during the rebellion of 1580–1, Indian Muslims and Rajputs as a body sided with the king, while the Turanis, and to a lesser degree Persians as well, were divided over it.[21] This clearly shows that during the years preceding the revolt, the Indian nobles must have been specially cultivated to make them the most steadfast supporters of the central authority in a conflict about certain issues vitally affecting their position.

The emergence of the Indian Muslims as an important section of the nobility was also important insofar as it must have contributed towards creating wider support for the empire among the Muslim communities in India. Apparently, the reorganization of the Department of *Ṣadārat* during the 1570s was motivated by Akbar's desire to gain and preserve the sympathies of still further sections of the Muslim upper class in north India. Shaikh 'Abd al-Nabi, after his appointment as *Ṣadr* in 1564–5, was given wide powers, and considerable resources were placed at his disposal for the purpose of obliging 'deserving people'. According to Badayuni, 'if the bounty of all former kings of Hind were thrown into one scale and the liberality of this age into the other, yet this would preponderate.'[22] It is evident even from Badayuni's bitter denunciation of the policy of resuming excessive land from grants carrying more than 100 *bighas* of land (1575) that this measure was aimed not so much at curbing the theologians as at extending state patronage to a larger number of influential and leading Indian Muslims, without any particular distinction between 'the learned' and 'the illiterate'.[23] Similarly, Akbar's well-known order (of 1578) directing all the madad-i ma'āsh grants in a *pargana* to be concentrated in a few select villages, and making it obligatory for grantees to reside in the villages where their grants were situated, has been criticized by Badayuni for the hardships it imposed on the grantees. But as the original text of the farmān now discovered shows, the intention was to protect the grantees against *jāgīrdārs*, and due care was taken to ensure that their interests were not adversely affected.[24]

In this discussion, a reference to the much debated *maḥḍar* of 1579 will not be without interest. It is obvious that the maḥḍar reproduced by Badayuni and Nizam al-Din was the outcome of Akbar's eagerness to win recognition as the sole head of the orthodox Muslims of India, and not of the whole world.[25] This policy had little in common with the concept of 'universal kingship' that won official recognition later. In the maḥḍar the king's title as head of the orthodox Muslims (*amīr al-mu'minīn* and *bādshāh-i Islām*) rests on the sanction given by the 'ulama of the realm, while, according to the theory that developed later, kingship is recognized as a divine attribute: it is communicated by God to kings without the intermediate assistance of anyone.[26] It is therefore natural that Abu'l-fazl, an exponent of the later theory, should have thought it fit not to reproduce the text of the maḥḍar, but to treat it rather casually. He does not disclose the fact, pointedly mentioned by Badayuni, that the chief architect of the document was his own father, whose works, even when quite minor, are referred to by him in the most laudatory terms. Moreover, the summary of this document as given by him is inaccurate and tendentious. It tends to create the impression that the maḥḍar declared the king's role to be that of an arbitrator, not only between the orthodox schools of Muslim law, but also between the various religions and sects (*kesh-hā wa madhhab-hā*). There is also no reference in Abu'l-fazl's account to the titles of bādshāh-i Islām and amīr al-mu'minīn used for the king in the maḥẓar.[27] It is obvious that Abu'l Fazl found it rather embarrassing to handle the maḥḍar, which would seem to have been the final and by far the most blatant of Akbar's measures to placate and win over orthodox Muslim opinion in India. Hence the full significance of the maḥḍar can be appreciated only if it is viewed against the background of Akbar's general attitude of promoting and befriending the Indian Muslims. It was in line with a series of other measures by which Akbar strove to show that he shared the religious beliefs and sentiments of his Muslim subjects. His devotion to the tomb at Ajmer,[28] his relations with Salim Chishti,[29] his hostility towards the Mahadavis (who were so unpopular with the orthodox sections),[30] and his attempt to deliver the Friday sermon[31] make a definite pattern, and show Akbar's great anxiety to conciliate Muslim orthodoxy.

This phase in Akbar's policy ended some time around 1580. Apparently, the attempt to project Akbar's image as bādshāh-i Islām proved abortive. The revolt of 1580–1 showed that it failed to create the desired impression upon the Turani and Persian nobles who took a major part in it,[32] and who were feeling agitated over the introduction of *dāgh* (branding of horses), a new mode of revenue collection, and such other administrative reforms that affected their income and power. The dismissal of Shaikh 'Abd al-Nabi and Makhdum al-Mulk (December 1579) and the abolition of the jizya for the second time (1580),[33] in the tense political atmosphere in the east, indicate a sudden collapse of the policy pursued so vigorously during the preceding thirteen years.

The turning-point might well have come immediately after the maḥḍar. This document not only failed to strengthen Akbar's hands but was responsible for reopening a very sensitive issue as it sought to provide a theological justification of his sovereignty. It is noteworthy that a *fatwā* of *kufr* against Akbar appeared only after the signing of the maḥḍar.[34] Akbar soon realized that issuing the maḥḍar had been a mistake and decided to revoke it.

But if the policy behind the maḥḍar ended in a debacle, this very failure enabled Akbar to distance himself from a pro-Islamic policy. Subsequently, there was, more or less, a smooth unfolding of Akbar's enlightened religious policy based on his philosophy of ṣuḥl-i kull. The ground for

Table 5.1
Racial Composition of the Mughal Nobility, 1555–95

Period	*Manṣab* of Nobles	Total No.	Turanis	Persians	Indian Muslims	Rajputs and Other Hindus	Unspecified
1555		51	27 (52.9%)	16 (31.4%)	—	—	8 (15.7%)
1565–75	500 and above	96	38 (39.6%)	37 (38.5%)	9 (9.4%)	8 (8.3%)	4 (4.2%)
	All ranks	176	67 (38.1%)	48 (27.3%)	25 (14.2%)	18 (10.2%)	18 (10.2%)
1580		272	66 (24.3%)	47 (17.3%)	44 (16.2%)	43 (15.8%)	72 (26.5%)
1575–95	1,000 and above	87	32 (36.8%)	24 (27.6%)	14 (16.1%)	14 (16.1%)	3 (3.4%)
	500 and above	184	64 (34.8%)	47 (25.5%)	34 (18.5%)	30 (16.3%)	9 (4.9%)

this was partly prepared by Akbar's success in putting down the rebellion of 1580–1, and partly by the experience acquired during the twenty years preceding 1580, when the alternative had been given a full and fair trial.

Table 5.2
Racial Composition During 1565–75

Manṣab	Turanis	Persians	Indian Muslims	Rajputs and Other Hindus	Others	Total
3,000–5,000	15	15	2	4	—	36
1,000–2,500	14	17	5	3	4	43
500–900	9	5	2	1	—	17
Manṣab not known	29	11	16	10	14	80
Total	67	48	25	18	18	176

Table 5.3
Racial Composition During 1575–95, Based on the List of *Ā'īn-i Akbarī*

Mansab	Total No.	Tura-nis	Persians	Indian Muslims	Rajputs	Other Hindus	Others
5,000	15	7	6	—	2	—	—
4,500	2	—	2	—	—	—	—
4,000	6	2	2	—	2	—	—
3,500	2	—	2	—	—	—	—
3,000	11	8	3	—	—	—	—
2,500	5	2	—	2	1	—	—
2,000	17	4	3	5	3	1	1
1,500	7	2	—	3	2	—	—
1,250	1	—	—	—	1	—	—
1,000	21	7	6	4	2	—	2
900	34	13	9	8	3	—	1
800	2	1	—	1	—	—	—
700	22	12	3	3	2	1	1
600	4	1	3	—	—	—	—
500	35	5	8	8	9	1	4
Total	184	64	47	34	27	3	9

Table 5.4
Rebellion of 1580–1

	Turanis	Persians	Indian Muslims	Rajputs, Other Hindu Officials and *Zamīndārs*	Unspecified	Total
On the side of the rebellion	33	12	3	6	22	76
				All *zamīndārs* of east		
On the Imperial side	28	32	41	37	50	188
Neutral	5	3	—	—	—	8
Total	66	47	44	43	72	272

NOTES

1. A glaring example of such an atti: ıde is Abu'l-fazl's attempt to create an impression that the *maḥḍar* (1579) recognized Akbar as an arbitrator not only between the orthodox schools of Muslim jurisprudence but also between different religions and sects. It is significant that he fails to give the text of the document, which according to Badayuni was drafted by Shaikh Mubarik, and is reproduced both in the *Ṭabaqāt-i Akbarī* and *Muntakhab-ut-Tawārīkh.* Cf. *Akbar Nāma* Bibliotheca Indica, III, pp. 269–70.

2. See Table 5.1. For this analysis the list of nobles accompanying Humayun in 1555 as given by Abu'l-fazl is taken as the sample with the modification that the following six persons then known to be minor attendants or officials at Humayun's court have been excluded: Baqi Beg, *yatish begi*, Khwaja 'Abd al-Samad, Mir Saiyid Ali, Khwaja Ata Allah, *dīwān-i-khāk*, Mir Shihab Nishapuri, Khwaja Amin al-Din Mahmud. Cf. *Akbar Nāma.* Bibliotheca Indica I, p. 342.

3. See Table 5.1. Turanis were 52.9 per cent of the total. But if it is kept in mind that a number of Turani nobles, including Mun'im Beg, were left behind in Afghanistan there is every reason to believe that the actual percentage was much higher.

4. I have noticed only four such persons: Haji Muhammad Khan Sistani, Wali Beg, Shihab al-Din Ahmad Khan, and Khwaja Jahan.

5. See Table 5.1. The figure for the absolute number of nobles for the period 1565–75 is arrived at by putting together the names contained in Abu'l-fazl's lists for various campaigns and expeditions of these years. Although this figure

of 176 cannot be treated as conclusive, still, for a tentative study of this kind, it can be accepted as a reasonably good sample.

6. Commenting on Mirza Sulaiman's arrival at the court in 1575, Badayuni observes: 'At this time (the Emperor) revived the old *tora-i chaghatai*. For some time, in order to exhibit it to Mirza Sulaiman, they spread royal tables in *dīwānkhāna* and the *tawāchis* entertained the soldiers. But when the Mirza departed, all these (revived customs) departed too.' (*Muntakhab-ut-Tawārīkh*, II, 216.) The English translation (II, 220) of this passage is inaccurate and misleading.

7. See Table 5.1. Although their strength in absolute numbers fell from 31.4 per cent in 1555 to 27.3 per cent in 1565–75, this does not necessarily prove a decline in their position. This fall in percentage was more the result of the sharp rise in the total number of the nobles with the expansion of the empire. There was a corresponding fall in the absolute strength of the Turanis as well. What is more important is the fact that in the higher grades, the Iranis had come to equal the Turanis and their percentage was also considerably higher (38.5 per cent). This clearly suggests rapid promotion of the Persian nobles during the period.

8. There were six major rebellions between 1562 and 1567:

(a) Revolt by Mirza Sharf al-Din, 1562–63.
(b) Shah Abu'l-mā'ali's revolt, 1564.
(c) 'Abd Allah Khan's revolt, 1564.
(d) 'Ali Quli Khan's revolt, 1565–67.
(e) Asaf Khan's desertion, 1565–66.
(f) The revolt by the Mirzas, 1566.

9. 'Abd Allah Khan was a close relative (perhaps a stepbrother) of Babur's well-known noble, Qasim Husain Khan Uzbek (maternal grandson of Sultan Husain Mirza of Herat), and an uncle of 'Ali Quli. He served under Humayun in 1536. Cf. *Akbar Nāma*, I, 142; Gulbadan, *Humāyūn Nāma*, p. 17.

Sikandar Khan, a former servant of Mirza Kamran, remained in Mughal service from the early years of the reign of Humayun and was not one of those who joined Humayun's service in Persia. Cf. Mirza Haider Doghlat, *Tārīkh-i Rashīdī*, tr. Ross, 1895, p. 474.

Ibrahim Khan was the seniormost among the Uzbek officers. 'Ali Quli Khan treated him just like an uncle. For his biography see *Maāthir ul-Umarā*, Calcutta, I, p. 75–7. Cf. *Tārīkh-i Alfī*, MS, India Office, Ethe 12, f. 620a.

10. For the attitudes of these officers see *Akbar Nāma*, II, pp. 261–2, 268–9; *Tadhkira-i Humāyūn wa Akbar*, pp. 288, 290; *Ṭabaqāt-i Akbarī*, II, p. 187; *Tārīkh-i Alfī*, f. 620a. From a reference in Bayazid's account it appears that at the time of Asaf Khan's selection as the commander of the royal army that was sent against 'Ali Quli Khan in 1565, there arose a controversy which had racial overtones. In the heat of argument Khwaja Jahan is reported to have remarked: 'Even a single hair of Asaf Khan is more useful than the whole of the Chaghtai clan.'

11. *Akbar Nāma*, II, p. 200.

12. Table 5.4. In 1580–1, while 32 Persians supported the imperial side, 12 actually joined the rebels and 3 remained neutral.

13. See *Akbar Nāma*, II, pp. 155, 180. The most important section of the shaikh-zādas taken into service was composed of the Saiyids of Barha. They were in service as far back as 1561. The list of *Ā'īn-ī Akbarī* contains the following nine names from the Barhas: Saiyid Mahmud (No. 75), Saiyid Ahmad (No. 91). Saiyid Qasim (No. 105), Saiyid Hashim (No. 143), Saiyid Raju (No. 168), Saiyid Jamal al-Din (No. 217), Saiyid Chaju (No. 221), Saiyid Bayazid (No. 295), Saiyid Lad (No. 409). Numbers within brackets are those given by Blochmann. With the exception of the last two, all belonged to the categories of *manṣabdārs* of 500 and above.

14. *Muntakhab-ut-Tawārīkh*, II, pp. 61–2.

15. *Akbar Nāma*, II, pp. 190, 203–4.

16. See Abu'l-qasim Namakin, *Munsha'āt-i Namakīn*, Aligarh MS, ff. 26a–32a. 'As directed by the word of God', Akbar claims, 'we, as far as it is within our power, remain busy in *jihād* and owing to the kindness of the supreme Lord, who is the promoter of our victories, we have succeeded in occupying a number of forts and towns belonging to the infidels and have established Islam there. With the help of our bloodthirsty sword we have rased the signs of infidelity from their minds and have destroyed temples in those places and also all over Hindustan.'

17. *Sharā'if-i 'Uthmānī* MS, Department of History, A.M.U. Aligarh (a local history of Bilgram compiled in the 18th century, containing a large number of documents), f. 144a. The date is illegible. From certain other documents reproduced in the same book (ff. 56a and 58a) it appears that Qazi 'Abd al-Samad was alive during the years 1571–92. Obviously, there is greater likelihood of its being issued in the 1570s rather than in the 1580s or 90s, when according to the unanimous testimony of our authorities, Akbar was drifting away from orthodox Islam.

18. See *Muntakhab-ut-Tawārīkh*, II, 210. 'During the same period (983H) (the Emperor) directed Shaikh 'Abd al-Nabi and Makhdum al-Mulk to investigate and reimpose (*muqarrar sākhtand*) the jizya on Hindus. *Farmāns* to this effect were sent on all sides. But this order soon disappeared like a painting on water. Lowe's translation of the passage (II, 231) is misleading. He has dropped the word jizya.

19. This point is amply borne out by the following chronology of Akbar's relations with the Rajput chiefs:

Raja Ram Chand of Bhatta attacked		1561
Kachwahas joined service, gave daughter in marriage	Jan.–Feb.	1562
Mirtha reduced	Jan.–Feb.	1562
Raja Ram Chand sent Tan Sen		1562
Abortive expedition against Jodhpur		1563
Military measures against the Ujjaynia Chief, Gajpati of Achna	down to	1567
Chitor occupied	February	1568
Ranthambor reduced	May	1569

Kalinjar surrendered by the ruler of Bhatta	August	1569
Chandra Sen, Jodhpur, joined service	November	1570
Kalyan Mal, Bikaner, joined service, gave niece in marriage	November	1570
Har Rai joined service and gave niece in marriage	November	1570
Raja Gajpati Ujjainiya of Achna joined service		1567–73
Jai Chand of Nagarkot disgraced and expedition sent against his state	Feb.–March	1573

See *Akbar Nāma*, II, pp. 155, 182–3, 197–8, 335–40, 340–1, 358; *Muntakhab-ut-Tawārīkh*, II, pp. 49, 50, 63, 161–2, 179–80.

20. Table 5.1.

21. Table 5.4.

22. *Muntakhab-ut-Tawārīkh*, II, 71; tr., II, 70.

23. Ibid., p. 205.

24. Ibid., p. 254; *Akbar Nāma*, III, p. 240; The original *farmān* in preserved in the U.P. Record Office, Allahabad (No. 24). See Irfan Habib, *The Agrarian System of Mughal India*, p. 302n. 21.

25. *Ṭabaqāt-i-Akbarī*, II, pp. 345–6; *Muntakhab-ut-Tawārīkh,* II, p. 272. Cf. Nurul Hasan, 'The "Mahzar' of Akbar's Reign', *Journal of U.P. Historical Society*, 16 pt I, p. 126, where it is maintained that although the titles used are *Sultan-i-Adil* and *Amir ul-Muminin*, the 'intention of the signatories was clearly to call Akbar a *Khalifa*'. It may well be that the use of the word *khalīfa* was avoided because the intention was to proclaim Akbar as the head of the Muslims of India and not of the whole world. The very opening lines of the *maḥḍar* make it quite clear that it was exclusively concerned with conditions in India.

26. Abu'l-fazl, *Ā'īn-i-Akbarī*, I, ed. Sayed Ahmad Khan, 3; tr. Blockmann, I, 3.

27. *Akbar Nāma*, III, pp. 269–70.

28. Apparently Akbar's interest in Ajmer was very great between 1568 and 1579. During this period he visited Ajmer almost every year. But his veneration for Khwaja Mu'in al-Din Chishti seems to have disappeared rather abruptly after his last visit in September 1579. Next year in July he avoided going there on the occasion of the annual *'urs* and deputed his son, Daniyal, to officiate for him. While mentioning this fact Abu'l-fazl specifically states that he no longer believed in visiting tombs. See *Nafāis ul-Maāthir* MS. British Library, f. 53 a & b; Shaikh Mustafa Gujarati, *Majālis*, (Haiderabad), p. 58; *Akbar Nāma*, II, p. 276, 317; *Muntakhab-ut-Tawārīkh*, II, pp. 49, 105, 108, 124, 132, 139, 170, 172, 185, 198, 226, 272.

29. It appears that relatives of Shaikh Salim Chishti greatly benefited in terms of wealth and status by the Shaikh's close relations with Akbar. See *Muntakhab-ut-Tawārīkh*, II, p. 109.

30. See *Nafāis ul-Maāthir*, MS, British Library, ff. 62a & b. 'Ala al-Daulah, the earliest authority on Akbar's reign, quotes a proclamation issued by Akbar before setting out from Ajmer to invade Gujarat in which it was stated that the Emperor considered it necessary to subjugate Gujarat in view of the fact that a number of the Afghans in that region deviating from true Islam (*rāh-i Ḥaqq wa*

ṭarīq-i hidāyat) had accepted Mahdawiism and were tyrannizing the orthodox people (*'ulamā'-i dīn*).

According to Ghausi Shattari, Shaikh Muhammad of Nahrwala, a Bohra theologian of orthodox views, had taken a vow not to put on a turban as long as heresy was not eradicated from the Bohra community. When Akbar reached Nahrwala he promised the Shaikh that he would do his best for the suppression of the Mahdawis and he himself put the turban on the Shaikh's head. A reference to this event is made by Abdul Haq Dehlvi and also in some of the Mahdawi sources. Cf. *Gulzār-i Akbar*, MS, John Rylands Library, f. 207b; *Akhbār ul-Akhyār*, Delhi, 1322H. p. 28; Mahmud Shirani, 'Faizi-i 'Am' (A summary of a *mathnavi* written in 1141H.), *Oriental College Magazine*, 1940, p. 48.

31. *Muntakhab-ut-Tawārīkh*, II, p. 268; *Ṭabaqāt*, II, p. 344.

32. Table 5.4.

33. *Akbar Nāma*, II, p. 278; *Muntakhab-ut-Tawārīkh*, II, p. 276. Cf. *Ṭabaqāt-i-Akbarī*, II, p. 347.

34. *Muntakhab-ut-Tawārīkh*, II, p. 276.

6

Jizya and the State in India during the Seventeenth Century*

Saṭish Chandra

The reimposition of jizya by Aurangzeb in 1679 is generally regarded as a turning-point in the history of the Mughal empire in India, and as marking the culmination of the spirit of religious bigotry which, in turn, led to the alienation of the Rajputs, the Marathas, and the Hindus generally, and hastened the disintegration of the empire.[1] On the other hand, some writers have represented the step as a consequence of the growing spirit of opposition to the empire among the Hindus, leaving Aurangzeb no option but to appeal to the loyalty of the Muslims by reverting to a more specifically Muslim state.[2] In both cases, discord and hostility between the Hindus and the Muslims, and the growth of a spirit of particularism are regarded as the main factors in the reimposition of jizya. However, in order to understand the measure, it is also necessary to take into account the political and economic developments in the empire, the religious trends at the court, and, in particular, the controversy regarding the nature of the state, which had continued with some changes of form and approach since the establishment of Muslim rule in India.

The explanations advanced by a number of contemporary and near contemporary observers for the reimposition of jizya by Aurangzeb may be examined first. Muhammad Saqi Musta'id Khan, who wrote on the basis of official papers and may almost be regarded as the official historian of Aurangzeb's reign, says:

> As all the aims of the religious Emperor were directed to the spreading of the law of Islam and the overthrow of the practice of the infidels, he issued orders to the high *dīwānī* officers that from Wednesday, the 2nd April, 1679/1st Rabi' I 1090, in obedience to the Qur'anic injunction 'till they pay

* Reprinted from the *Journal of the Economic and Social History of the Orient* 12, part 3 (September 1969), pp. 322–40.

commutation money (jizya) with the hand in humility' and in agreement with the canonical traditions, jizya should be collected from the infidels (*dhimmīs*) of the capital and the provinces.[3]

Isardas (Ishwardas) and 'Ali Muhammad Khan are in broad agreement with Saqi Musta'id Khan, but emphasize the role of the 'ulama in the matter. Isardas says, 'the theologians, the learned men, and the traditionalists, in view of the regard of the Emperor, the shadow of God, for the (true) faith, represented to him that the levying of jizya was necessary and compulsory according to *sharī'a*.[4] 'Alī Muḥammad Khan says:

Since His Majesty was inclined to promote the faith and to give currency to the laws of the *sharī'a*, rejecting all things contrary to *sharī'a* in the fixing of expenses, and in all matters of state as well as in all revenue and administrative matters, at this auspicious moment, the learned men, the theologians and the saintly persons, in view of his regard for the faith, represented to the Emperor, that the levying of jizya upon the opponents of the (true) faith was compulsory according to *sharī'a*, and urged him to reimpose it in the provinces of the Empire.[5]

These statements, which run on parallel lines, may be taken to represent the official point of view. In official pronouncements, emphasis would naturally be placed on the emperor's regard for the true faith and his deference to the suggestions of the theologians, the learned men, etc. as the reason for the re-imposition of jizya. But this does not explain why it should have taken Aurangzeb, who was himself well-versed in the *sharī'a*, twenty-two years from his accession to the throne to arrive at the orthodox position regarding jizya, which was sufficiently clear and which had been repeatedly expounded by the orthodox 'ulama.[6]

The contemporary European travellers and the agents of trading companies posted in India suggest a somewhat different explanation for the measure. Thomas Roll, the president of the English factory at Surat, wrote in 1679 that jizya was being collected with great severity with the object not only of replenishing Aurangzeb's exhausted treasury, but also of forcing the poorer sections of the population to become Mohammedans.[7] Manucci, writing about a quarter of a century later, emphasized the same factors, remarking:

The death of Jaswant Singh was used by Aurangzeb as an opening to oppress the Hindus still more, since they had no longer any valiant or powerful rajah who could defend them. He imposed upon the Hindus a poll-tax, which everyone was forced to pay, more or less. ... Aurangzeb did this for two reasons: first, because by this time his treasuries had begun to shrink owing to expenditure on his campaigns; secondly to force Hindus to become Mohammedans.[8]

The argument that by imposing jizya, Aurangzeb wanted to force the non-Muslims to accept Islam, may have been sincerely believed by many of his contemporaries but is hardly tenable in the light of historical scrutiny. In particular, the Hindus had stubbornly clung to their faith despite the prevalence of Muslim rule in large parts of the country for over four hundred years.[9] During most of this period, they were required to pay jizya.[10] Aurangzeb could hardly have been sanguine enough to expect a different result from his reimposition of jizya. Though this was a regressive tax, and bore more heavily on the poor than on the rich, there is no proof of any large-scale conversions during his reign on account of this measure. Had any such developments taken place, they would have been recorded with glee by the emperor's eulogists as a triumph of his policy.[11]

As far as the purely economic motive is concerned, it is true that when Aurangzeb reviewed his finances in the thirteenth year of his reign, he found that expenses had exceeded income during the preceding twelve years. Consequently, a number of economies were effected, including 'the retrenchment of many items in the expenditure of the Emperor, the princes, and the Begums'.[12] It may also be presumed that continuous wars in the Deccan, particularly after 1676, frontier wars in the northeast, intermittent fighting with the Afghan tribesmen, and later the breach with the Rathors and Sishodias—none of which secured any large territorial gains or monetary compensation—must have strained the royal treasury. During his reign, Aurangzeb issued a number of orders forbidding a large number of customary cesses.[13] Similar orders had been issued by earlier rulers also. We are told that, despite these orders, the revenue department continued to include the income from the forbidden cesses in the *jama'dāmī* (valuation) of the *jāgīrs*.[14] It was apparently expected that the *jāgīrdārs* would make these remissions out of their sanctioned income. But only a few nobles, such as Raja Jaswant Singh, offered to do so. Others demanded compensation in lieu of the income they were required to surrender,[15] and since there was not enough money available to pay this, the remission remained a dead letter in the jāgīr. Thus, there is little basis for the argument that since Aurangzeb had abolished the cesses not sanctioned by Islam, he was justified in levying the jizya—one of the taxes specifically sanctioned by Islamic law.[16]

We do not possess any figures from the reign of Aurangzeb for the yield of jizya in the Mughal empire. According to an eighteenth-century writer, Shivdas Lakhnawi,[17] the realization (*ḥāṣil*) from jizya in all the provinces of the empire was 40 m. rupees. This figure, although it is given in the context of the (re)abolition of jizya at the instance of Raja Jai Singh following the defeat of the Saiyid brothers in 1720, may be taken to apply to the empire as a whole after the annexation of Bijapur and Golkonda. According to Jagjiwandas, the ḥāṣil of the Empire around 1708–9 was a little over 260 m.[18] From these figures, income from jizya may be reckoned at about 15 per cent of the total income. However, it may be doubted if the full amount of the jizya could be realized every year. According to the *Nīgār-nāma-yi Munshī*, another eighteenth-century work, at the outset, jizya was reckoned at rupees one hundred upon 1,00, 000 *dāms* (of the *jama'*), i.e. at the flat rate of 4 per cent in the *khāliṣa* and *jāgīr maḥāls*, the officials of the *khāliṣa* and the jāgīr-holders being left free to realize the amount from the peasants in the manner they considered fit.[19] Exemption from jizya could be asked for in the case of crop failure, and such exemptions seem to have been made fairly regularly. The towns were apparently assessed separately, and it is difficult to form even a rough estimate of the income from them. According to Khafi Khan, Mir 'Abd al-Karim, the *amīn-i-jizya*, reported in 1092/1681 that he had realized Rs. 26,000 as jizya from the city of Burhanpur during the previous year, and that in three months he had fixed Rs. 1,08,000 as the amount payable by half of the wards (*pur-jāt*) of Burhanpur.[20] From a document pertaining to the town and pargana of Badshahpur, we find that out of a total assessment of Rs. 2950, the share of the town was Rs. 2,140-10-0 or roughly 72 per cent.[21] While it is difficult to generalize on the basis of such scanty evidence, it may not be wrong to infer that the income from the towns was quite considerable. This may explain why opposition to jizya manifested itself so often in the towns, and the leading role in it was often played by traders and merchants. An additional duty of 1½ per cent was levied in lieu of jizya on all goods imported by the Christian traders, i.e. the English, French, Portuguese, and other European Companies trading with India.[22]

Thus, the yield from jizya was not a negligible sum. It should be noted, however, that the proceeds were to be lodged in a separate treasury, called the *khazāna-yi-jizya*, and were earmarked for charitable purposes.[23] That being so, jizya can be regarded as a device for relieving the pressure on the general treasury only to the extent that it could be shown that it was possible for the state to economize on the amounts disbursed from the general treasury to pay the *yaumiyadārs*, or cash stipend-holders.[24]

It follows from the above that the purely financial motive can hardly be regarded as a major factor in the reimposition of the jizya. The measure cannot be understood without taking into account the character, position, and role of the large number of stipend-holders who were dependent on the state, and the political and ideological controversies of the period regarding the nature of the state, the position of the Hindus, and the extent to which the 'ulama should determine the basic policies of the state.

The army of stipend-holders, which included theologians, recluses, widows and orphans, a section of the literati, and a large number of nondescript hangers-on, was always a problem for the medieval sultans. That the state should provide some sustenance for all able-bodied Muslims, particularly those who possessed some learning in the Holy Law, was a part of the vague egalitarian and humanitarian legacy of early Islam. As early as the time of Balban, steps had to be taken to curtail the grants and privileges of these sections. But in general, the responsibility of providing for this miscellaneous mass—one of the important ways in which the state carried out welfare work—was not denied by any ruler. Akbar tried to organize it on a new basis, setting aside villages for grants to the *a'immadārs*. But with the passage of time, the problem became serious again and had to be tackled afresh by Aurangzeb.[25]

The theologians formed a considerable group among the stipend-holders. They had a virtual monopoly of education, and exercised considerable patronage on behalf of the rulers. Their services were utilized by a number of monarchs in administration also. Though their arrogance was distasteful to many rulers, and the venality of many of the qazis brought the 'ulama into disrepute, they could scarcely be ignored by the rulers, since Islam was felt to be the only bond of unity among the diverse groups and sections of the Muslims in India. While the 'ulama were by no means a united body, the rigidity of the *sharī'a*, which had been developed in West Asia where conditions were vastly different from those obtaining in medieval India, created many political difficulties for the rulers. The extent to which a sultan in India could rule in accordance with the *sharī'a* was anxiously debated. Generally speaking, it was agreed that the state in India could not be Islamic in the true sense of the word,[26] and that many un-Islamic features, such as the appropriation of the *bait-al-māl* by the sultan for his personal use, the maintenance of great pomp and show by the sultan, the shedding of Muslim blood, etc., must be tolerated. Nevertheless, the 'ulama expected the sultans to act as the champions of Islam by suppressing *bid'at* and the open practice of things forbidden by the *sharī'a*. They also expected them to wage a constant jihād against the Hindus, to degrade and humiliate them, and not permit them to make an open display of idolatrous practices.[27] Most of the theologians considered that the payment of jizya was necessary and that it was meant to humiliate the Hindus. Some of the 'ulama went to ridiculous lengths in their advocacy of the humiliations that should be heaped upon the Hindus by the collectors of jizya.[28] For the theologians, the imposition of jizya was thus a badge of the inferior and dependent status of the Hindus, and a means of asserting the position of the Muslims as the ruling class, and thereby also the superior status of the 'ulama, the upholders of the true faith, in the state.

As political realists, the sultans and their leading nobles were not prepared to pursue policies that might create unnecessary political difficulties. The divergence between the interests of the 'ulama and the sections exercising political power must be regarded as a characteristic feature of Muslim society in medieval India. As might be expected, neither the 'ulama nor the political elements formed a united body. The debate between the two trends, the orthodox and the liberal, one of which advocated the policy of treating the Hindus as perpetual enemies, humiliating them and excluding them from all share in political power, and the other, which favoured a policy of leniency to the Hindus once they had submitted, and of trying to win over the Hindu rajas to a position of active alliance by various concessions, remained a feature of intellectual and political life in the country till the eighteenth century. The orthodox trend could call to its assistance the powerful forces of dogmatism, taking a rigid stand on the letter of the law, which took little account of the situation prevailing inside India.[29] The 'liberal' trend appealed to political expediency. Doctrinal differences, such as the controversy between the advocates of *waḥdat-al-wujūd* and those of *waḥdat-al-shuhūd*, also divided them.

The break-up of the Delhi Sultanate and the setting up of a number of provincial kingdoms resulted in the establishment of closer relations between the Muslim rulers and the indigenous Hindu 'nobility' in these areas. The settlement of Afghans in large numbers in rural areas had the same effect. The trend towards the association of Hindu zamīndārs in the service of the state at various levels was given a powerful fillip by the Lodi and Sur rulers,[30] and was adopted as a matter of policy by Akbar. These developments implied the virtual breakdown of the theory of the state painfully evolved during the Sultanate period. A further breach was made by Akbar's decision to abolish the jizya in 1564.

According to Abu'l-fazl, the emperor had to override 'the disapproval of statesmen' and 'much chatter on the part of the ignorant'. The opposition of the 'ulama, 'the stiff-necked ones of the age', seems to have been particularly vehement, but it was of no avail.

The basic arguments advanced by Abu'l-fazl in justification of the abolition of the jizya were political and ideological, though the economic aspect was not overlooked. He argued that jizya was formerly levied on account of 'the opposition of the Hindus and the greed of the rulers'.

However, due to 'the abundant goodwill and graciousness of the lord of the age', people of different religions had 'like those of one mind, bound up the waist of devotion and service, and exert themselves for the advancement of the dominion', and for this reason, a distinction had to be made between them and that old section which cherished mortal enmity. Moreover, he argues, formerly jizya was levied because of the neediness of the rulers and their assistants, but thanks to his abundant treasures, the emperor had no need of it at that time. He therefore concluded that while the benefits of jizya were 'imaginary', its imposition tended to 'promote dissensions among the subjects'[31] and was, therefore, politically harmful.

By arguing that the Hindus were as loyal to the state as the Muslims, Abu'l-fazl sought to remove the chief prop of the theological argument in favour of jizya.[32] He also stressed that the levying of jizya under these conditions was against political expediency and natural justice.

The concept that no distinction could be made between the subjects on the ground of their loyalty, combined with the underlying concept of ṣulḥ-i-kull, that all religions were roads to the one God, clearly tended to put the state as an institution above any particular religion (though not opposed to religion as such). Thus Akbar's concept of the state was strikingly modern and secularist, and cut at the root of clerical privileges. For this reason, if no other, it was unacceptable to orthodox opinion.

It is not necessary for our purposes to attempt a detailed analysis of the conflict between the forces of orthodoxy and liberalism during the seventeenth century. The orthodox elements found a mentor in Shaikh Ahmad Sirhindi, and rallied under the slogan of *waḥdat al-shuhūd*. The exact political and intellectual influence of Shaikh Ahmad Sirhindi during the seventeenth century must not be over-estimated. Nevertheless, there seems little doubt about the existence of a fairly powerful trend of orthodox opinion, both among the nobility and the 'ulama. A group in the nobility resented the breach in their monopoly of power in the state, looking upon the monarchy as a racist and religious institution.[33] They resented the logic of Akbar's policy of bringing ever wider groups of the indigenous ruling-classes into the nobility in order to strengthen the empire. In the early years of Shah Jahan's reign, the Marathas who held ranks of 5000 and above already outnumbered the Rajputs.[34] An extension of this policy was bound to adversely affect the older group in the nobility. The opposition of the orthodox 'ulama to Akbar's concept of the state was no less unrelenting, as has been already noted. The fundamental political problem before the Mughal emperors was to allay the opposition of the orthodox elements without, however, abandoning Akbar's basic policy of allying with the Rajputs and other elements of the indigenous ruling class. This is turn presupposed a policy of broad religious toleration. Jahangir avoided giving open offence to the orthodox elements, but on the whole effected little change in the situation. Shah Jahan tried to assert the fundamentally Islamic character of the state by formally proclaiming himself a defender of the faith, ordering the destruction of newly erected temples, and putting down heretical practices, such as mixed marriages of Hindus and Muslims in Bhimbar.[35] At the same time, he firmly denied the 'ulama a say in determining policies, and extended state patronage and support to all sections of the 'ulama, including the *wujūdīs* as well as the *shuhūdīs*. Shah Jahan's concept of the state was a retrogression from the concept of Akbar as expounded by Abu'l-fazl. But taking into account the entrenched power of Muslim orthodoxy, it was perhaps the only compromise possible in seventeenth-century India.[36] Like all compromises, it rested on no clear principle save political expediency and was, therefore, unstable. Once the fundamentally Islamic character of the state was granted even in theory, the arguments for basing it on the *sharī'a* became overwhelmingly strong. These ideological arguments were reinforced by the fear of a reversion to Akbar's concept of the state, if Dara succeeded to the throne.

Even though Aurangzeb refrained from raising the slogan of Islam prior to the battle of Samugarh,[37] and entered into a political alliance with the Rajputs—notably with Rana Raj Singh of Mewar and, to some extent, with Jai Singh Kachwaha of Amber[38]—his accession to the throne raised the expectations of the orthodox 'ulama. Aurangzeb revived the earlier order against the building of new temples and carried out many innovations. He also executed Dara and imprisoned Murad on the ostensible plea that they had violated the law of Islam. But it seems that at the outset he was not prepared to go beyond the framework of Shah Jahan's policies. Thus, Aurangzeb refrained from reviving jizya, though there was little doubt about its obligatory nature according to orthodox opinion. He also firmly maintained the policy of allying with the Rajputs and other elements of the indigenous ruling class, granting to Jai Singh and Jaswant Singh a higher position in imperial affairs and in the imperial hierarchy than had been accorded to any Hindu since the days of Raja Man Singh. The 'ulama were not allowed a share in shaping state policies. However, the influence of the orthodox elements gradually increased, partly through Aurangzeb's policy of using religion to counter the popular revulsion against him for imprisoning his father and for the way he treated his brothers.[39] Aurangzeb's own orthodox bent of mind, and his banning of many traditional practices and observances on the ground that they were opposed to *sharī'a*, also gave powerful encouragement to this group.

We are told by one contemporary writer that although the question of the revival of jizya engaged the emperor's attention at the commencement of his reign, he 'postponed the matter due to certain political exigencies'.[40] These political exigencies have not been described by the author, but we may assume that the need to maintain the alliance with the Rajputs was one of them. Aurangzeb may also have hoped to arrive at some accord with the Marathas. These hopes, however, faded, particularly after the failure of Bahadur Khan's negotiations with Shivaji in 1676, Shivaji's attempt to carve out a Maratha dominion in the south in alliance with Golkonda, and his virtual assumption of the mantle of being the defender of the Deccani states against the Mughals.[41] It was in these circumstances, and in order to cope with the danger of the imminent dissolution of the Deccani states, that in 1676 Aurangzeb resolved upon a policy of all out expansion of the Mughal empire towards the Deccan. He thus abandoned the policy of limited encroachments, which the Mughals had pursued since the days of Akbar, and which had been the policy of Shah Jahan in his settlement of 1636, and Aurangzeb's own policy since his accession.[42]

Thus, politically, by the year 1676, Aurangzeb had reached a parting of ways with Shah Jahan's policies. A new era of extended warfare and strenuous effort was opening up. The period from 1676 to 1678 saw vigorous operations in the Deccan. As a minimum objective, the Mughals attempted to establish for themselves a position in Bijapur and Golkonda that would enable them to detach these states from their alliance with the Marathas, safeguard against the danger of their passing under Maratha domination, and enable the Mughals to utilize the resources and territories of these countries against the Marathas. However, by 1678 the Mughals had failed to attain even these limited objectives. It appears that in the circumstances, Aurangzeb felt the need to make some striking declaration, which might rouse enthusiasm and rally Muslim opinion behind him. In the past, when faced with a critical situation, rulers had proclaimed a jihād. To the essentially conservative mind of Aurangzeb, it seemed that nothing could be more appropriate than that the new phase in the expansion of the empire should be marked by the reinstitution of jizya, signifying the reversion to a more orthodox type of state.[43] The Rajput war, too, should perhaps be seen in the context of this new aggressive mood caused by the deepening political crisis of the empire in the Deccan. Although the reimposition of jizya coincided with the outbreak of the Rathor War, it did not imply abandoning Akbar's policy of allying with the Rajputs and other elements in the indigenous ruling class. This is apparent from a number of pronouncements by Aurangzeb.[44] Recent research has established that the number of Hindus in the various echelons of the nobility did not decline, but actually increased after 1679.[45] Thus, the reimposition of jizya can hardly be taken to mark the inauguration of a more bitterly anti-Hindu policy, as had sometimes been argued.

We have suggested that the revival of jizya marked a deepening political crisis, due primarily to the deterioration of the situation in the Deccan. The Rathor War further accentuated the crisis, but was not its cause.[46] Another factor in the reimposition of jizya was the growing unemployment among the clerical elements. Even the descendents of Shaikh Mu'in al-Din Chishti, the patron saint of the Mughals, were living in poverty and deprivation.[47] By earmarking the proceeds of jizya for distribution in charity among the learned, the faqirs, the theologians, etc. and further, by providing that the new department of jizya, with its own treasury and set of *amīns*, should be staffed predominantly from these sections,[48] Aurangzeb offered a huge bribe to the orthodox clerical elements. Through clerical influence, Aurangzeb hoped to rally all sections of the Muslims behind him. However, the clerical elements took advantage of the situation for large-scale exactions and oppressions, and the amassing of private fortunes. The Imperial news-reporter wrote from Mertha that the qazi there had extorted large sums from the Hindus by way of jizya.[49] Manucci goes further and asserts that the amīns of jizya kept back half or even three-fourths of the proceeds for themselves.[50] There is some evidence, too, that the qazis sometimes used the realization of jizya as an occasion to insult and humiliate those who paid it.[51]

Aurangzeb thus tried to tread his way back to a more orthodox type of state, which had some parallels in the Sultanate period. As Khafi Khan and Ma'muri[52] state, the true purpose of the measure was 'to distinguish *dār-ul-Islām* (i.e. land where *sharī'a* ruled) from *dār-ul-ḥarb* (i.e. land of infidelity)'. But Aurangzeb did not bear in mind that India of the seventeenth century was not the same as that of the fourteenth and fifteenth centuries. The forces of mutual tolerance and integration had grown powerfully during the period, and the traditions of Akbar were strongly established. Even Aurangzeb realized that it was not possible to exclude the Hindus from the nobility and thus from wielding political and military power on behalf of the Islamic state.

The revival of jizya was thus a meaningless gesture. It was opposed by a powerful section of the nobility—including, it is said, Jahanara Begum.[53] It is significant that shortly after the death of Aurangzeb, the lead in abolishing jizya was taken by Asad Khan and Zu'l-fiqar Khan, two of the premier nobles of Aurangzeb.[54] Evidently, they represented that section of the ruling class which considered jizya politically inexpedient and also found distasteful any growth in clerical influence, or opportunity for clerical interference in political affairs.[55] It was bitterly resented by the Hindu rajas not in the service of the state.[56] The exact incidence of the jizya on each section is not easy to compute. A modern estimate is that the city labourer had to pay about one month's wage in the year as jizya.[57] But it is possible that ordinary labourers and people who only earned enough to support themselves and their families were classified as 'indigent',[58] and as such excluded from paying jizya. Again, while Aurangzeb objected strenuously to exemptions from payment of jizya,[59] such exemptions seem to have been regularly granted.[60] In 1704, jizya was remitted in the entire Deccan on account of the distress caused by the famine and war.[61]

Politically, the greatest objection to jizya was that it harassed and alienated some of the most influential sections of the Hindus, namely the urban masses, particularly the rapidly growing class of merchants, shopkeepers, financiers, etc., who occupied an increasingly important place in the social and economic life of the country.[62] These people were subjected to great harassment and oppression by the collectors of jizya, and in retaliation resorted on a number of occasions to hartal and public demonstrations.[63] Finally, jizya proved a convenient slogan to the political opponents of the empire for rallying Hindu sentiment against it.[64] Well might Prince Akbar write:

> In your Majesty's reign the ministers have no power, the nobles enjoy no trust, the soldiers are wretchedly poor, the writers are without employment, and traders are without means. The peasantry are downtrodden .... On the Hindu tribe (lit. *firqah* or community) two calamities have descended, (first) the exaction of jizya in the towns and (second) the oppression of the enemy in the country (i.e. the Marathas). When such sufferings have come down upon the heads of the people from all sides, why should they not fail to pray for or thank their rulers![65]

The experiment of Aurangzeb with jizya, if it demonstrated anything, demonstrated the practical impossibility of basing the state in India even formally on the *sharī'a*, and of maintaining a distinction between the Hindu and the Muslim subjects on that basis. Ultimately, neither the broad-based, secularist state of Akbar, nor the narrow-based state of the Sultanate period prevailed. What generally prevailed during the eighteenth and nineteenth centuries under Muslim rulers was the eclectic compromise of Shah Jahan.

NOTES

1. Jadunath Sarkar, *History of Aurangzeb* (5 vols., Calcutta, 1912–30), Vol. iii, pp. 264–5, 274, 325.

2. Zahiruddin Faruki, *Aurangzeb and His Times* (Bahraich, 1935, reprint, Delhi, 1972–80), pp. 148–51; I.H. Qureshi, *The Muslim Community in the Indo–Pakistan Sub-Continent* (The Hague, 1962), pp. 161–3.

3. Mustaid Khan, *Ma'āsir-i-'Ālamgīrī*, Bib. Ind., Calcutta, 1870–75 (trans. J.N. Sarkar, Calcutta, 1947), p. 174.

4. Isardas Nagar, *Fatūḥāt-i-'Ālamgīrī*, British Library, Add. 23,884, f. 74a.

5. Ali Muhammad Khan, *Mir'āt-i Aḥmadī*, ed. Nawab Ali (2 vols., and Supplement, Baroda, 1927–8, 1930), i, p. 269.

6. Only the followers of Abu Hanifa gave a choice between Islam, or death, or payment of jizya. According to the followers of all other orthodox schools, the only choice was between Islam and death. (*Encyclopaedia of Islam*).

7. *The English Factories in India* (New Series), 1670–84, ed. Charles Fawcett, (4 vols., Oxford, 1936–55), 3:241. The Deputy-Governor at Bombay ascribed the measure to 'this king's treasury being much exhausted by his long and chargeable wars with Sevagee, the Pattans and his Rashboots' (*O.C.*, Vol. 40, No. 4705, d. 18[?] August 1680).

8. Niccolo Manucci, *Storia do Mogor* (trans. W. Irvine, 4 vols., London 1907–8), 2:233–4, 3:288.

9. For the attachment of the Hindus to their faith, and the difficulty of converting them, see the remarks of Shaikh Nizam al-Din Auliya (Amir Hasan Ala Sijzi, *Fawā'id al-fu'ād* (Nawal Kishore Press, Lucknow, AH 1302), pp. 65, 150, 195–7.

10. It is not possible to enter here into the controversy whether jizya was distinct from *kharāj* during this period and whether the Hindus were required to pay both kharāj and jizya. It has been suggested that jizya was not distinguishable from kharāj in medieval India. (P. Hardy, s.v. Djizyah, *Encyclopaedia of Islam*). Although kharāj and jizya were sometimes treated as synonyms, a number of fourteenth-century theological tracts treat them as separate imposts. Thus, see *Fawā'īd-i-Fīruz Shāhī*, Bankipore, xiv, No. 1225, ff. 298a–300a; *Fiqh-i-Fīrūz Shāhī*, I.O. No. 2987, ff. 411b–419a. K.A. Nizami (*Some Aspects of Religion and Politics in India during the 13th Century*, Aligarh 1961, p. 315) is of the view that jizya was merged in the kharāj and treated as part of the total incidence of taxation, but is silent about the situation in the towns. Under Aurangzeb (*infra* fn. 19), at the outset jizya was realized along with kharāj in the rural areas, but was assessed as a separate tax in the towns. The situation may have been similar during the Sultanate period.

11. For the problem of conversion to Islam in medieval India, see S. Nurul Hasan, *Chishti and Suhrawardi Silsilahs in India during the 13th and 14th centuries*, Unpublished thesis, Oxford University, 1948); S.A.A. Rizvi, *Muslim Revivalist Movements in Northern India in the 16th and 17th Centuries* (Agra, 1965), pp. 15–21.

12. *Ma'āsir-i-'Ālamgīrī, loc. cit.*, p. 100.

13. Mirza Muhammad Kazim, *'Ālamgīr Nāma* (Bib. Ind., Calcutta, 1865–73), ii, pp. 392, 432–38. A number of orders issued by Aurangzeb at various periods are mentioned in *Mir'āt-i Aḥmadī*, i, pp. 259, 264, 285, 288. According to *Mir'āt*,

by the abolition of these cesses a loss of twenty-five lakhs was suffered in the *khāliṣa* lands alone (ibid., p. 249).

14. Khafi Khan, *Muntakhab al-lubāb* (Bib. Ind., Calcutta, 1869), ii, pp. 88–9.

15. *Mir'āt*, i, pp. 288–91.

16. Cf. Aziz Ahmad, *Islamic Culture in the Indian Environment* (Oxford, 1964), p. 148.

17. Shiv Das Lakhnawi, *Shāhnāma-i-Munawwar Kalām*, B.M. Or. 26, ff. 64b–65a.

18. Jagjiwan Das, quoted by I. Habib, *Agrarian System of Mughal India* (Asia, 1963), p. 409.

19. *Nigār-nāma-yi-Munshī*, Or. 1735, ff. 98a–b; *Mir'āt-i Aḥmadī*, i, p. 298; Irfan Habib, *Agrarian System of Mughal India*, p. 245. I. Habib thinks that the officials and jāgīrdārs, after paying jizya at the flat rate of 4 per cent, were to collect jizya at authorized rates from the peasants. Later, detailed registers were maintained of the assessment, realizations and disbursement from jizya (*tūmār-i-jizya*, *mujmal*, *jama'-kharch*, *roznāmchah*, *āwarjah*) and the *chaudhrīs* and the *qānūngos* were required to countersign them. (*Khulāṣatu-s Siyāq*, British Library, Add. 6588, f. 39a–b). The realizations were apparently made through the normal revenue machinery, with the help of zāmīndars, and under the supervision of amīns appointed for the purpose. For a sample of *tūmār-i-jizya* for the town and pargana of Badshahpur, see *Khulāṣat-us-Siyāq*, 39b–41b. S.R. Sharma, *The Religious Policy of the Mughal Emperors* (London: Oxford University Press, 1940), pp. 163–4 also quotes such documents from Maharashtra. Similar documents are found in the Rajasthan State Archives also.

20. Khafi Khan, *Muntakhab*, ii, p. 279, Shah Nawaz Khan, *Ma'āsir-ul-Umarā*, Bib. Ind., 3 vols., Calcutta, 1888–91 (trans. H. Beveridge, Vol. i, Calcutta, 1941, Vol. ii, trans. Beni Prasad, Calcutta, 1952), Text: iii, pp. 609–10; Tr. ii, p. 132.

21. *Khulāṣat-us-Siyāq*, ff. 39b–41. It is doubtful if the categories in which the villagers have been divided in the document can be a sufficient basis for a classification of rural society. The document refers not to a single village, but to *muwāẓi'* (villages) in the *pargana* of Badshahpur. The suspiciously low number of the assessees—only 280 out of whom 185 were taxed—suggests that either the figures are ficititious or the villages included large numbers of Muslims who were not liable for the tax. (cf. I. Habib, *Agrarian System*, pp. 119–20).

22. *Bombay L.S.*, No. 9 dt. June 3, 1680 (To Surat); *Surat Diary L.S.* 91 dt. 1 Dec. 1682 (to Hoogly), dt. 30 Nov. 1682 (to England) *et. seq.* The English entered into negotiations with the Governor, Ranmast Khan, and in 1683 sent a *wakīl* to Aurangzeb's court, but his efforts as well as the efforts of the Company failed to get the increase removed. Both Roll and Child commented on the loss of Indian esteem of Europeans, partly entailed by their 'timely submitting to this imposition.' *The English Factories* (ed. William Foster, 1670–1684), p. xxix.

23. *Jaipur Records* (Sitamau transcripts), *Waqa-i Darbar-i Ala 29 Sha'bān* yr. 24/14, Sept. 1680. See also *Mir'āt*, ii, pp. 30–1.

24. It has been argued that by providing separate funds for charitable purposes, jizya did relieve the pressure on the treasury by allowing the amounts hitherto

spent on charity to be diverted to other purposes. But it is difficult to say to what extent this could be done in practice. (cf. Faruki, *Aurangzeb*, pp. 158–61).

25. For a fuller discussion, see I. Habib, *Agrarian System*, pp. 298–316. Under Aurangzeb, the position of the grantees was strengthened, and their hereditary rights in the lands held by them were recognised, subject to some control by the state. This is another example of the considerable influence enjoyed by this section in medieval times.

26. Thus, see Ziyauddin Barani, *Tārīkh-i-Fīrūz Shāhī* (Bib. Ind., Calcutta, 1862), pp. 41–4; excerpts from *Fatāwa-i-Jahāndārī* by M. Habib in the *Political Theory of the Delhi Sultanate* (Kitab Mahal, 1961), originally published in *Medieval India Quarterly*, Aligarh, Vol. 3 (1957–58), pp. 137–8.

27. Ibid.

28. Thus, see advice of Qazi Mughis al-Din to 'Ala al-Din Khalji, Barani, *Tārīkh*, p. 290. See also Sh. Ahmad Sirhindi, *Maktūbāt-i-Imām-i-Rabbānī*, Vol. I, ed. Yar Muhammad Taliqani (Nawal Kishore Press, Lucknow), Letter No. 163.

29. K.M. Ashraf, *Life and Condition of the People of Hindustan*, reprinted from *Journal of the Royal Asiatic Society of Bengal, Letters*, Vol. I (1935), pp. 183–4.

30. Thus, Rai Saladin was granted a few parganas in *iqṭā'* in Chanderi by Mian Husain (Farmuli) during the time of Ibrahim Lodi; Jagat Singh Kachwāhā was also granted an *iqṭā'* there. In the time of Sikandar Lodi, Rai Ganesh was assigned an *iqṭā'*, comprising the parganas of Patiali, Shamsabad, Kampil and Bhogaon (Rizqullah Mushtaqi, *Wāqi'at-i-Mushtāqī*, British Library, Add. 11,633, Aligarh Univ. Rotograph, f. 63b); Nizam al-Din Ahmad, *Ṭabaqāt-i-Akbarī* (Vol. I, Lucknow, 1875, Vols. II & III, Calcutta 1936, 1940), i, p. 332; Ni'matullah, *Tārīkh-i-Khān Jahānī* (Vols. I & II, Asiatic Society of Pakistan, Dacca, 1960, 1962), i, p. 173 (I am grateful to Mr. Iqtedar Siddiqi, Department of History, Aligarh University for calling my attention to these references.). See also A.B. Pande, *First Afghan Empire* (Calcutta, 1956), p. 140 (Raj Singh Kachwaha appointed commander of Narwar fort), and H.N. Sinha, *Development of Indian Polity* (London, 1963), pp. 356–62.

31. Abu'l-fazl, *Akbarnāma* (Calcutta: Asiatic Society of Bengal, 1877–86, trans. H. Beveridge, Calcutta, 3 vols., 1902, 1912, 1939, reprint Delhi, 1972), ii, pp. 316–7.

32. For a further discussion, see S.A.A. Rizvi, *Muslim Revivalist Movements in Northern India* (Agra, 1965), pp. 258–60.

33. Abdul Qadir Badayuni, *Muntakhabu-i-Tawarikh* (3 vols., Bib. Ind., Calcutta, 1864–69), ii, p. 339; Vol. 2, trans. W.H. Lowe (Calcutta, 1898, 2nd ed. 1924), p. 350.

34. Abdul Hamid Lahauri, *Bādshāhnāma*, Bib. Ind. (3 vols., Calcutta, 1866–72), I-a, p. 328.

35. See B.P. Saksena, *History of Shah Jahan of Dihli* (Allahabad, 1958), pp. 293–94. During the campaign against the Deccani states, Shah Jahan proclaimed it his duty to suppress heresy, and warned the ruler of Golkonda against the Shī'i *khuṭba*. (Lahauri, *Bādshāhnāma*, Vol. I, Pt. II, pp. 130–33).

36. See Rizvi, *Revivalist Movements*, pp. 407–09.

37. See M. Athar Ali, *Religious Issues in the War of Succession, Proceedings, Indian History Congress* 22 (1961), pp. 253–4.

38. For the exchange of letters between Aurangzeb and Rana Raja Singh, see Shyamal Das, *Vir Vinod* (two parts in 4 vols., Udaipur, n.d.), Vol. II, pp. 415–31. Aurangzeb promised the Rana the rank of 7000, restoration of the parganas sequestered in 1656, and other favours equal to those enjoyed by his forefathers.

39. Thus, on the occasion of his second coronation, the chief qazi of the Empire had given the opinion that it was not valid to read the *khuṭba* in Aurangzeb's name since his father was alive. Aurangzeb was greatly perturbed, till Qazi 'Abd al-Wahhab came to his rescue by arguing that since Shah Jahan had become too feeble to exercise his functions, there was no legal objection to *khuṭba* being read in Aurangzeb's name. As a reward, Qazi 'Abd al-Wahhab was appointed the Chief Qazi. (*Mir'āt*, i, pp. 248).

40. *Khulāṣat-us-Siyāq*. f. 38b.

41. Sarkar, *Shivaji*, pp. 277–80. For Bahlol Khan's treaty with Shivaji, see Sarkar, *Aurangzeb*, iv, p. 243.

42. Jadunath Sarkar, *Shivaji and His Times* (4th rev. ed., Calcutta, 1948), pp. 214–16.

43. Despite the reimposition of jizya and the emphasis on the Islamic character of the state, Aurangzeb could not carry all sections of the Muslims with him in his plans of annexing the Deccani states. In 1686, Qazi Shaikh al-Islam refused to give a *fatwā* that the war against Bijapur and Golkonda was a *jihād*. He was replaced and ordered to proceed on *haj* (Abu'l-fazl Ma'muri, *Tārīkh-i Aurangzib*, Or. 1671, Aligarh Muslim University, rotograph, f. 162a), Qazi 'Abd Allah was also forbidden the court for suggesting a peace with Golkonda (Ibid., f. 173b). Other nobles such as Bahadur Khan Kokaltash, S. 'Abd Allah Khan Barha, Mu'min Khan Najm Sani, Sadiq Khan, and Prince Shah 'Alam were also opposed to the outright annexation of the Deccani states (Ibid., ff. 168b–169a, 171a–b; Khafi Khan, *Muntakhab*, ii, pp. 320–1, 330–4).

44. Thus, see Aurangzeb's reply to the letter of M. Amin Khan, rejecting his suggestion of the dismissal of a Shī'i bakhshi, *Ahkam-i Alamgiri*, Calcutta, 1912, 1925, trans. J.N. Sarkar, *Anecdotes of Aurangzib* (4th ed., Calcutta, 1949), No. 39.

45. See Athar Ali, *Mughal Nobility under Aurangzeb* (Bombay: Asia Publishing House, 1966), p. 31.

46. Abu'l-fazl Ma'mūrī (*Tārīkh*, f. 149a) says that jizya was reimposed after the suppression of the Satnamis and before Aurangzeb left for Ajmer, and that it was meant for 'the affliction of the rebellious unbelievers' (*mankūb sākhtan kuffār-i-dār-ul-ḥarb*).

47. *Waqā'i Sarkar Ajmer wa Ranthambhor*, Hyderabad, Asafia Lib., Fan-i-Tarikh 2242. Aligarh Muslim University, transcript, pp. 24, 26, 30, 32. The *sajjada-nashin* said that the number of *rozinadars* had grown ten to forty times.

48. *Ma'āsir-i-'Ālamgīrī*, p. 174, *Mir'āt Ma'āsir*, p. 297.

49. *Waqā'i 'Sarkar Ajmer*, pp. 467, 473, 508–9, 614, et. seq.

50. Manucci, *Storia*, ii, p. 415; iii, p. 291. See also Bhimsen, *Nuskhah-i Dilkusha*. British Library, Or. 23. Trans. V.G. Khobrekar, *Tarikh-i-Dilkasha* (Bombay, 1972), text, f. 139b.

51. *Akhbārāt-i Darbār-i Mualla*, 23, *Ramaẓān* Yr. 38/18 May, 1694 (A Hindu employee of the deceased *Amīr-ul-Umara* Bahramand Khan asked to pay jizya personally); Khafi Khan, *Muntakhab*, ii, pp. 27, 377 (*Amīn-i-jizya* killed). See also *Malda Diary and Consultations*, ed. W.K. Firminger, *Journal of the Asiatic Society of Bengal*, New Series (1918), pp. 97, 120; *The Diary of William Hedges Esq. (1681–87)*. (3 vols., London: Hakluyt Society, 1887–89), i, pp. 136–7. (The two latter references have been kindly provided by Dr. Irfan Habib).

52. Manucci, *loc. cit.*, ii 415, iii 291. See also Bhimsen *Nuskhah-i Dilkusha*, British Library Or. 23 (trans. V.G. Khobrekar, Bombay, 1972), f. 139b.

53. Manucci, *Storia*, iii, pp. 288–91.

54. Satish Chandra, *Parties and Politics at the Mughal Court, 1707–40* (Aligarh, 1959), p. 45. Earlier, notwithstanding the orders that jizya was not to be remitted, Asad Khan had reprimanded Sharif Khan, the *amīn-i-jizya* in the four subahs of the Deccan, for his strictness in realising jizya. (Jaipur Records, *'Arẓdāsht*, d. 15, *Jamāda* II Yr. 31/17 April, 1688).

55. See *Waqā'ī' Ajmēr*, p. 437 for the suggestion that in place of qazis, a noble from the court should be appointed in each district to collect jizya. In a sarcastic letter to Aurangzeb written in 1672, Mahabat Khan remarked that 'the Empire had become dependent on the qazi' (Royal Asiatic Society, Pers. Cat. 173, ff. 8a–11a). On another occasion when Ja'far Khan and Mahabat Khan were asked to crush Shivaji, Mahabat Khan remarked that 'an army was not necessary since the denunciation of a qazi ought to be sufficient.' (Khafi Khan, *Muntakhab*, ii, pp. 216–17).

56. *Dilkusha*, text, f. 75a, *Mir'āt*, i, p. 390; Jaipur Records, *'Arẓdāsht*, No. I, 77d, dated 29 Muharram, Yr. 38/30 Sept. 1693.

57. I. Habib, *Agrarian System*, pp. 246–7.

58. *Dhimmī nādār*. There was, however, no agreement on the definition of 'indigent', and poor (See N.P. Aghanides, *Mohammadan Theories of Finance*, New York and London, 1916, pp. 399–405). Under Aurangzeb, it was laid down that 'if a person owned no property and his income from labour (*karb*) did not exceed his and his family's necessities, jizya was not to be charged from him'. *Mir'āt*, i, pp. 260–7. According to *Khulāṣat-us-Siyāq* (f. 39b), a person who could save (only) forty *dirhams* (about ten rupees) per year after meeting all essential expenses, was poor. It is not clear whether labourers were exempted under this clause or not. Perhaps, the matter depended upon the discretion of the *amīn*.

59. Aurangzeb on one occasion censured Amanat Khan, the *diwān* of the Deccan, who, it was said, had granted *sanads* remitting jizya to more than half the Hindus. Aurangzeb remarked that he had reimposed jizya after great difficulty. (Ma'muri, *Tārīkh-i-Aurangzeb*, f. 179a, Khafi Khan, *Muntakhab*, ii, pp. 377–8).

60. Jizya could be remitted in case of crop failure (See *Nigār-nāma-yi-Munshī*, British Library, Or. 1735, ff. 180a). In 1688–89 jizya of *ṣūbah* Hyderabad was remitted for one year due to drought Isardas, *Fatūḥāt*, f. 111b).

61. *Akhbārāt* 48/36 & A245, quoted by I. Habib, *Agrarian System*, p. 246.

62. Manucci says that while journeying from one place to another, the merchants were required to carry a certificate of having paid the jizya, but 'if they chance to lose this paper, or if it be stolen, they are made to pay again, either in the same or in another province,' (*Storia*, ii, p. 415). 'But when they travel to another kingdom or province, the said passport is of no value. On their outward and their return of journey, the same amount is collected. In this way the merchants suffer from great impositions, and many of them and the bankers are ruined' (Ibid., iv, p. 177).

63. Thus, see Jaipur Records, '*Arẓdāsht* 704 d. 12 Jamāda I, Yr. 49/1 Oct., 1704 (*hartal* by shopkeepers of Ujjain in protest against jizya); *Mir'āt*, i, pp. 340–1 (opposition of *desais* and *seths* to jizya to be met firmly), Ma'mūrī, *Tārīkh-i-Aurangzib*, f. 149a–b, ibid., ii, p. 255 (protest demonstration against jizya at Delhi) and Khafi Khan, *Muntakhab*, ii, 278 (at Burhanpur with *faujdars* and *muqaddams* aiding the disturbances and the resistance).

64. See the letter of Shivaji to Aurangzeb (*Khatūt-i-Shivāji*, Royal Asiatic Society, London MS 173, Letter No. 32, trans. Sarkar, *Shivaji*, *loc. cit.*, pp. 306–9. Text also given in *Bisāt-ul-Ghanā'im*, India Office Library, 3595, ff. 52a–55a).

65. *Khaṭūt-i-Shivāji* Letter No. 15, English trans., J.N. Sarkar, *Aurangzib's Reign*, Calcutta, 1933, pp. 100–01.

7

The Sociology of Political Engagement: The Mahdawiyah and the State*

Derryl N. MacLean

In the course of the Muslim ninth century (fifteenth century AD), a number of millennial movements emerged throughout the Muslim world in anticipation of the tenth century and the impending appearance of a *mahdī* ('rightly-guided one'), a messiah-like figure who, it was widely believed, would herald the events of the end of the world at the close of the first millennium. Most of the movements were ephemeral, and we know of their existence primarily in refutations of the jurists. One, however, did exhibit considerable chronological durability and textual productivity. This movement was the Indian Mahdawiyah founded by Saiyid Muhammad Jaunpuri (847–910/1443–1505), a pious religious scholar and Chishti Sufi from Jaunpur in northern India who claimed to be the long-awaited Mahdi in 901/1495. The followers of the Indian Mahdi have survived down to the present, in varying conditions of prosperity, in Sind, Baluchistan, Gujarat, Rajasthan, and the Deccan.[1]

Little is known of Saiyid Muhammad's early life, although he clearly received a quality Chisti education at Jaunpur, the Muslim cultural centre of north India during the fifteenth century. He entered history proper on his arrival at Ahmedabad in Gujarat at the advanced age of fifty-three. Here he began to teach an activist Chishti message of absolute renunciation of the world and its representatives, and in the process attracted a number of disciples and controversy. Exiled from Ahmedabad for his views on the physical vision of God (*dīdār*), and then from Patan for his *takfīr* ('anathema') of those who desire the world, he settled at Barli, just outside

* Reprinted from *Revue des mondes musulmans et de la méditerranée*, 91–92 (2000), pp. 243–60.

Patan, where the mixed messages of his earlier years were clarified in a direct audition from God: 'You are the promised Mahdi: proclaim the manifestation of your Mahdiship, and do not fear the people' (Wali, 1947, p. 12). His public proclamation of the Mahdiship (*mahdīyat*) at Barli propelled him from those with acceptable, if radical, Sufi charisma into the more dangerous messianic realm of Mahdi charisma. His increasingly focused rejection of the political and religious status quo, coupled with mounting support among the elites, led to his expulsion from Gujarat. Saiyid Muhammad emigrated first to Sind and then, after his expulsion there, to Khurasan, where he settled at Farah (southwestern Afghanistan) and spent the last three years of his life, dying on Monday 19 Dhū a-Qa'dah 910 (23 April 1505).

In his teachings, the Mahdi laid particular stress on recreating in the last days the original primal community of the Prophet Muhammad as realized at Medina.[2] Just as Muhammad the Prophet was the seal of prophecy (*nubūwat*), so Muhammad the Mahdi was the seal of sanctity (*wilāyat*). While the Prophet had explained in perfect form the Qur'anic laws relating to *īmān* ('faith') and *islām* ('submission', i.e., actions), so the Mahdi had explained in similar perfect form the Qur'anic laws relating to *iḥsān* ('spiritual perfection'). It was the eschatological authority of the Mahdi, engendered by his wilāyat and equal in the last days to the prophetic authority of former times, that empowered the recreation of the original Medinan paradigm. This restoration necessitated the purification of historical Islām from innovations (*bida'*) subsequent to the Prophet. Rejecting especially the post-prophetic notions of juristic imitation (*taqlīd*) and Qur'anic abrogation (*naskh*), the Mahdi was able to locate textual and conceptual space to refer for social and moral directives directly back to the Qur'an and the prophetic *ḥadīth*, as re-read by the Mahdi (Badayuni, 1972, pp. 80). The Mahdawis then attempted to recreate at the end of time the original righteous community where they could concentrate their actualization of the imminent millennium. To do so, the Mahdi recovered the Qur'anic notion of *hijrah* ('emigration') as a religious duty (*farḍ*) defining the community of believers at the millennium. While emigration was from a cluster of existing physical and social ties, it was also immigration to new residential communes formed by the Mahdawis. Called *dā'iras*, or 'circles', and modelled after Sufi hospices, they consisted of an enclosed compound governed through the consensus (*ijmā'*) of its members. Within these communes, the Mahdawis practised intensive breath meditation (*pās-i anfās*) and an extended but silent liturgy (*dhikr-i khāfī*), forbade its members from earning a living (*kasb*) or receiving a sinecure, and distributed all unsought income daily and equally (*sawīyat*) to the commune members. The purpose of these arrangements was to facilitate the removal of obstacles between man and God and, through the various disciplines, achieve the direct vision of God (dīdār) thought to be a sign of the true Muslims of the last days.

This essay intends to draw attention and criticism to important issues in the secondary literature concerning the Mahdawiyah as an Islamic millennial movement: its social location and its political profile. In the first instance, modern historians of Indian Islam generally assume that the Mahdawiyah was a mass movement of popular revolt on the part of the oppressed and disenfranchised, a movement that emerged from the smaller tradition of the villages and was engendered by the chaotic conditions of the period. Thus, Mohammad Yasin characterizes the movement as 'a plebian revolt of the simple-hearted' (1974, p. 124), and K.A. Nizami refers to it as 'a crisis and a commotion in the lower strata of society' (1989, p. 51). In the second instance, the political corollary of locating the Mahdawiyah among the distressed masses is to conclude that the relationship between the movement and the state was volatile. A.S.B. Ansari, for example, compares the Mahdawi 'cult of the dagger' to the Isma'ili Assassins, relates it to their feelings of oppression, and suggests that the state authorities 'were perfectly justified' in their attempts to put down the movement by force (1963, pp. 64, 68). That is, the assumption is that the Mahdawiyah, due to its social colouring and Mahdi typology, occurred on the level of religio-political revolt against the state and elicited an equally vigorous state policy of containment.

There are several conceptual and methodological problems in this line of analysis. One can observe the unfortunate tendency to combine earlier and later Mahdawi sources, as well as those from different regions, in order to form a composite picture of something reified as the Mahdawiyah. The undeniable presence of a considerable body of later Mahdawi literature in the vernaculars, especially in the eighteenth century, cannot be introduced as evidence for a populist, mass-based movement in its sixteenth-century origins. Nor can the Mahdi's pronouncements be used as evidence for much later developments within the movement. The Mahdawis engaged in a constant re-reading of the Mahdi's texts, a process leading them into diverse positions depending on the changing context.

Further, a series of comparative and qualitative arguments from religion are introduced into the reading. General and theoretical observations about the nature of Mahdi-type movements are taken as given from classical Arabic texts, combined with a sociology from prior or subsequent Mahdi movements such as the Sudanese Mahdiyah, and then applied to the reading of the Indian Mahdawiyah on the grounds that it was after all a Mahdi movement. Moreover, there is a tendency to assume that the Mahdawiyah tenets, apart from those deemed orthodox, are demonstrably irrational and explicable due to the social location among the simple-minded villager. 'It is peculiar to Muslim masses,' observes Ansari, 'that the credulous among them are always ready to gather around such pretenders and lend them support' (1963, p. 43). The problem is compounded by the location of the modern discussion within the genre of 'disputation' (*munāẓarat*), where the analysis tends to be replaced by either refutation or affirmation, depending on religious convictions. What is perceived as irrational is simply that which is not part of a pan-Islamic tradition as reformulated during the course of the nineteenth century. Like many of the reified modern arguments concerning pre-modern Muslim India, it is unlikely to prove convincing to those who do not share the perspective.

In what follows, I intend to reattach the Mahdawiyah to its historical contexts and suggest that changing social circumstances had an impact on the relationship between the movement and the state. In short, I see two general chronological phases in the pre-modern social and political history of the movement: the first, the activist phase, extended from the death of the Mahdi through the first five Mahdawi *khulafā* ('successors') and their followers until toward the end of the sixteenth century, while the second, the quietist phase, was roughly coeval with Mughal suzerainty in the seventeenth and early eighteenth centuries. The analysis will first confront the social location and political profile of the early Mahdawiyah, for which the evidence is more complete, before drawing a series of contrasts between the two phases.

A preliminary prosopographical analysis of the onomastic data of first generation Mahdawi converts permits a profile of their geographical, social, and occupational location. As far as status hierarchy related to lineage claims is concerned, the vast majority of the Mahdawis for whom titles of descent are known, claimed elevated *ashrāf* status (82 per cent), especially *saiyid* and *ṣiddīqī.* The status is avowed equally by those with a pre-Mahdawi religious or secular vocation. Moreover, of those converts with a discernable occupation, the largest group comprised those holding positions at the court or in the military (52 per cent), the two being intertwined during this period, followed by Sufis (29 per cent) and *madrasa*-educated 'ulama (14 per cent). Only one person, the quasi-legendary intoxicated Brahman gardener, Hajji Mali, is given a service occupation ('Abd al-Rahman, 1948, pp. 65–70). None are peasants.

This preliminary collation, imperfect though it is, strongly suggests that the first generation of converts tended to be recruited from those claiming ashrāf descent, belonging to the political and religious establishment, and holding positions of influence in urban areas such as Ahmedabad, Patan, Thatta and Bayanah.[3] This was not a middling elite of minor bureaucrats and insignificant scholars. In Sind alone, the Mahdawis managed to attract the conversion, among others, of the qazis of the two largest cities, the commander-in chief (*amīr al-umarā*) of the army, and the primary spiritual guide of the Sammah sultan.[4] Equally importantly, the converted tended to come from families with a tradition of membership in the elite. Qazi Qadan, for example, was a scion of a renowned family of Bhakkari saiyids and qazis and would eventually occupy his father's post as qazi of Bhakkar (Qaniʿ, 1886, v. 3, pp. 137–8), while the Nuri brothers were Faruqi descendants of Farid Ganj-i Shakkar and inherited the family's Chishti hospice in Ahmedabad (Sulayman, n.d., v. 3, pp. 138–77). The examples are not isolated and confirm that we are concerned with members of an entrenched elite, bearing the cultural resources and expectations of such an elite, and not with upwardly mobile recent Hindustani converts to Islam.

The case of Shah Niʿmat (a first generation convert and the third Mahdawi *khalīfa*) is particularly instructive since he is at times extolled as a reformed highway robber who became a Mahdawi, with the Robin Hood-like implication that mass elements of social protest were attached to the movement. On closer examination, however, his family turns out to be Ṣiddīqī ashrāf, originally from Syria or Iraq, who had become viziers of the Gujarat sultans (Husain, 1961, pp. 218–31; Rūḥ Allāh, 1952, pp. 81–118). Shah Niʿmat himself actually succeeded to his father's office at the royal court. He did, it is true, get into trouble with the sultan over certain financial irregularities connected with his official position and later became a renegade after slaying a favourite African slave of the king. His example, however, cannot be adduced as evidence of social banditry in the normally understood sense.

I must add a cautionary note, however. The above prosopography is preliminary and naturally subject to disconfirmation as the data base expands. There are also many well-known problems with this type of analysis. For one thing, the numbers of converts about whom we cannot extract any information beyond the name is rather high (29 per cent), and this raises problems of how representative the profile is of the membership at large. Indeed, it seems likely that the analysis is primarily of the Mahdawi leadership or those important to subsequent lineages, for whom more fulsome biographical data is preserved, and it is possible that the leadership came from a different class than the majority of the followers. Moreover, the location of class and status must rely on the later *tadhkirāt* literature, which may well exaggerate the pre-conversion status of those founding lineages of pīrs of subsequent importance, although in some cases we can confirm the social location through non-Mahdawi sources.

Still, the prosopographical suggestion of the movement's social colouring is supported by lists of convert communities given in indictments of the Mahdawis. Thus, the 'ulama of Gujarat represented to Sultan Mahmud the danger posed to the state by the Mahdawi conversions of religious scholars ('ulama), nobles (*umara*), viziers, noble women (*khawātīn*), gentry (*mulūk*), soldiers (*lashkarīyān*) and Sufis (Burhan al-Din, 1959, pp. 117, 183). In Surid north India, the 'ulama's concern was with the Mahdawi recruitment of landlords (*dihqānān*), merchants (*tujjār*), and high-ranking state officials (*ḥukkām*), primarily Afghan commanders (Niʿmat Allah, 1960–2, v. 1, p. 380). The groups noted in the indictments are the same as those located by the prosopography and confirm that we are concerned with an entrenched political and religious elite and not with a peasant movement. If it had been a revolt of the proletariat or the peasantry, surely the indictments would have dwelt on what would have been a most unsavoury connection.

Finally, the idiom of expression of the earliest Mahdawi sources is that of the highly educated Indo-Muslim elite. The initial literature is written either in Arabic or a cultured court Persian with a high percentage of passages in untranslated Arabic.[5] Indeed, code-switching between Arabic and Persian is a characteristic of the early Mahdawi literature. The Arabic is not translated into Persian, nor is the Persian translated into any indigenous language. The assumption of the texts is that the audience will be highly literate in both Persian and Arabic, the languages of pan-Islamic and pan-Indian discourse.

These early Mahdawi works can be located in the high tradition of Muslim discourse that evolved in India. The themes discussed in the literature, the authorities invoked in defence of the themes, and the technical vocabulary utilized to discuss them are all familiar from other Indo-Muslim works. If anything there is a heightened concern with alphabetic and linguistic dexterity and complexity. The *kalam* ('discourses') of Miyan Ilahdad Hamid, a first generation convert, is constructed solely from undotted letters, anticipating the much later undotted *tafsīr* of Fayḍi.[6] Miyan Malik Mihri, another first generation convert, plays similar games at the end of time, registering almost every known device of Persian prosody. In one series of *ghazals*, he alternates dotted and undotted letters, then dotted and undotted words, ending in a flourish with dotted and undotted ghazals (1892, v.1, pp. 36–7).

It is clear that the quality of Mahdawi discourse was considered a crucial proof of the truth of their position. To a certain extent, early Mahdawi literature appears as a kind of Islamist discourse over the authority to interpret. Thus, one finds, for instance, a series of arguments or incidents that reduce to the superior grammar or knowledge of Mahdawi foundational texts. A fine example of this is given by the historian Badayuni in his lengthy report of the disputations of Shaikh 'Ala'i Mahdawi (d. 957/1550) at the court of Islam Shah Sur. In front of the king and the assembled nobles and scholars, the Mahdawi sharply criticized the Arabic pronunciation and grammar of a certain Mulla Jalal Bhim, focusing especially on the mulla's misreading of the ḥadīth description of the Mahdi, *ajall al-jabhah* ('broadest of brow'), as if derived from *jalāl* (the mulla's own name) and not the more proper *jalā.* 'By God', Shaikh 'Ala'i told the mulla, 'you represent yourself among the commonality as the most learned of the 'ulama, yet you cannot express yourself properly. You know nothing of the subtleties, allusions, and particulars of the sciences of ḥadīth (Badayuni, 1865–69, v. 1, pp. 401–2). The poor mulla, we are told, 'became ashamed and said not another word'. The incident is not isolated. Non-Mahdawi sources make it clear that the intellectual challenge of the Mahdawiyah was based on standard texts and interpretive conventions, and moreover, was formidable.[7] This is, of course, to be expected from their social location.

It is now possible to turn our attention to the complex relationship between the early Mahdawiyah and the state. The Mahdi himself always held a view that messianic sanctity (wilāyat) must be manifested in concrete ways, but he was unclear about what this meant in terms of the state. His personal views concerning the political implications of his Mahdiship seem to have evolved from an initial activism to a quietist stance, the dividing line being the expulsion from Sind. Those who perceive his wilāyat as unitary are thus able to locate pronouncements of the Mahdi that support either an activist or a quietist position *vis-à-vis* the non-Mahdawi Muslim state.

On the one hand, the emphasis placed by the Mahdi on the singularity of the Mahdawi righteous community, along with the constant takfīr (charging with infidelity) of opponents, could be interpreted as legitimizing compelling action against non-Mahdawi Muslims. In the Mahdi's first public pronouncement, an open letter addressed to the sultan of Gujarat, he laid down his agenda in uncompromising terms with clear political implications:

> I say by the command of God Almighty that I am the promised Mahdi of the end of time.... It is obligatory (*lāzim*) on everyone—sultans, nobles (*umarā*) officers (*khawānīn*), viziers, the wealthy, the faqirs, 'ulama, the pious and all people—to investigate, verify the truth, and accept it. If you allege that I impute slander and lies to God and disavow me, then it is incumbent on you

> to prove my lie and execute me. If you do not [and you are right], everywhere I go I will proclaim my mission to the people and lead them astray, inflicting harm on them. It is incumbent on the authorities of the time (*hākimān-i zamān*) to select one of the two options [convert or execute]. If they do not, their faces will be blackened in both the worlds.[8]

Moreover, the Mahdi referred many times to those who denied his Mahdiship as non-Muslim (*kāfir*), and once even told Shaikh Sadr al-Din, the chief qazi of Thatta, 'If God Almighty gave me the power, I would levy the jizya [poll-tax on non-Muslims] on them,' raising his sword in the air and adding, 'for them only this remains' (Wali, 1947, p. 25). Since the reference in the tradition is specifically to mullas, this seems to charge the Muslim religious elite with being non-Muslim, and implies the possibility of a jihād against those who were formally Muslim. The Mahdi's use of the inflammatory term *ḥarbī* (someone from *dār al-ḥarb*, 'the abode of war') in this incident would support the interpretation.[9]

On the other hand, the emphasis placed by the Mahdi on the inner life of his followers could be used in support of a quietist stance. The vast majority of the Mahdi traditions relate directly to personal conduct and intensified group ritual, primarily on a radical Chishti pattern. Only one of the twenty chapters of the first major compilation of the Mahdi's sayings, the *Inṣāf-nāma* of Miyan Wali, concerns jihād (1947, pp. 205–10). The remainder focus on such matters as the renunciation of the world (*tark-i dunyā*), the obligations of continual *dhikr*, the vision of God (dīdār), and the organization of the institution of hijrah to the dā'ira. Indeed, by elevating hijrah over jihād as the crucial duty of true believers at the millennium, the Mahdi could even be seen as advocating an ethic of retreat, not expansion. Although hijrah, of course, textually bears the implication of subsequent jihād, the Mahdi himself did not consistently draw this connection.

In short, the reported sayings of the Mahdi, like the ḥadith of the Prophet, are ambiguous and opaque, occasionally contradictory, and always capable of interpretation by subsequent generations. It is not surprising, then, that not long after the death of the Mahdi, his followers would disagree sharply over the stance the nascent community should adopt toward non-Mahdawis and the state. The argument and its resolution in martyrdom are usually subsumed in Mahdawi sources under the rubric *qātalū wa qutilū* ('they fought and were slain').[10] The discussion revolves around a *tafsīr* ('commentary') given by the Mahdi on Qur'an 3:195: 'For those who emigrated (*hājrū*) and were driven out of their homes and were damaged for My cause and fought and were slain (*qātalū wa qutilū*), I shall forgive their sins and admit them to gardens watered by running streams as a reward from God.'

In his tafsīr, the Mahdi began by adopting a mystical exegesis of the verse: defining 'those who emigrated' as those who reoriented their natures to the domain of higher truth (*'ālam al-ḥaqīqat*), receiving the manifestation of the quality of Lordship in proximity to God; and 'those who fought and were slain' as those who struggled with the sensual self (*nafs*) and slew it with the sword of sincerity (*ṣidq*). Expanding on the theme, however, the Mahdi ruled that while the greater, mystical jihād was with sensuality, sanction had been given by God to fight (*qātalū*) in the case of oppression (*ẓulm*), citing the important Mahdawi proof text, Qur'an 22:39–40, in support of such action.

Not long after the death of the Mahdi, Saiyid Khundmir, the second Mahdawi khalīfah, argued that the time of oppression foretold in the Qur'an and by the Mahdi had now arrived. This was due to the actions of Sultan Muzaffar II (917–32/1511–26) of Gujarat who, alarmed by the expansion of the movement, had received and begun to act on a fatwā of execution (*qatl*) of the Mahdawis, burning dā'iras, killing some members, and exiling or branding others with an iron claw. Not surprisingly, Khundmir read these developments in the light of the proof texts and decided on action: 'it has now become a general religious obligation (*farḍ-i 'ayn*) for all—men and women, slaves and freepersons—to defeat the oppressors (*ẓālimān*) so that the faithful (*mu'minān*) will be victorious' (Wali, 1947, p. 206). The battle lines have been clearly drawn: on the one side are the followers of the Mahdi, the faithful (mu'minān), while on the other are the Muslim religious and state authorities, the oppressors (*ẓālimān*). The hijrah of the faithful now leads to jihād against the oppressors, as expected by the Medinan paradigm.

A number of the senior members of the community, however, had reservations about Khundmir's interpretation, arguing that calling Muslims non-Muslim and fighting them would require the abrogation (*naskh*) of the Qur'an and the Shari'a and 'this is unlawful since the Mahdi was the clarifier of the Qur'an and not its abrogator, and the follower of the law of Muhammad and not its abrogator' (Wali, 1947, p. 207). Moreover, they continued, if this interpretation were to be accepted without limits, then it would follow that it would be lawful (*ḥalāl*) to appropriate the wives and daughters of such non-Mahdawi Muslims without benefit of marriage and confiscate their property, and this clearly would be scandalous and illegal.

Saiyid Khundmir responded quickly to this internal criticism, raising the level of rhetoric and confrontation, and eventually winning over the majority of Gujarati Mahdawis, although significant opposition remained. The examples of the foundational martyrs, 'Ali, Hasan, and Husain, were adduced: just as it was in the first generation after Muhammad the Prophet, so it would be now in the first generation after Muhammad the Mahdi. Khundmir then declared the era of the law of fighting (*ḥukm-i qātalū*), despatched Mahdawi brothers to assassinate the promulgators of the fatwā, and began to prepare for a messianic Battle of Badr (*jang-i badr-i wilāyat*) equivalent in the last days to the original prophetic Battle of Badr (Husain, 1961, p. 97). An armed conflict inevitably ensued and, after an initial victory, the Mahdawis were routed in 930/1523 and a large number martyred, including Khundmir himself. As a vivid reminder of the danger of messianic revolt, the body of Khundmir was beheaded, skinned, stuffed with straw, and paraded through Gujarat. His head, skin, and torso were then buried in three different places.

The activist view of Saiyid Khundmir would persist after his martyrdom throughout most of India, as Mahdawis attempted to locate an arena for political victory (*ghalaba-yi ṣūrat*): in Gujarat with the Puladi Afghans and Ulachis; in Sind with the Arghuns; in Rajasthan with the Jalori Afghans; and in the Deccan with the Barid Shahis and especially the Nizam Shahis.[11] It was, however, in the communes of Bayanah, an important administrative and trade centre on the route from Gujarat to Agra, that the activist expression of the Mahdawiyah reached its apex during the reign of Islam Shah Sur (952–61/1545–54). These communes, composed primarily of Afghans, were extremely forthright in their approach to the religious and political establishment. Shaikh 'Abd Allah Niyazi, who founded the first Mahdawi *dā'ira* in the region and on whose cell Akbar would later construct his *'ibādat-khāna*, is said to have been the spiritual guide (pīr) of the Niyazi Afghan faction during their revolt, touring the hill country with a band of three or four hundred fully armed men preparing a revolt (Badayuni, 1865–69, v. 1, p. 403). Shaikh 'Ala'i, his even more militant disciple, is reported by Ni'mat Allah (1960–2, v. 1, p. 380) to have surrounded himself with men 'always carrying with them swords, shields, and other instruments of war.' When eventually summoned to the king's court to account for his beliefs and actions, Shaikh 'Ala'i appeared with his companions provocatively armed and armoured, giving weight to the argument of the Shaikh al-Islam that the Mahdawis were guilty of rebellion (*khurūj*) since their creed (*da'wah*) holds that the Mahdi would be the king (*pādshāh*) of the world (Badayuni, 1865–9, v. 1, pp. 399–400). The Bayanah incident culminated in the scourging of Shaikh 'Abd Allāh and the execution of Shaikh 'Ala'i. The corpse of the latter would be torn apart by state elephants in a public spectacle, suggesting the seriousness with which the state authorities viewed the implications of a politically embedded Mahdawiyah.

In the long run, however, it was the quietist approach to living in the world that would prevail among Indian Mahdawis. The key turning-point appears to be the Mughal invasion of Gujarat in 980/1572, the cultic heart of the movement, the loss of a political base there with the defeat of the Puladis and the taming of the Jaloris, and the failure of the attempt by Shaikh Mustafa Gujarati to convince Akbar of a Mahdawi legitimization for the Mughals (MacLean, forthcoming). The last recorded attempt to locate a political arena was that of the Mahdawi commander, Jamal Khan, who raised Isma'il Nizam Shah (997–9/1588–90) to the throne of Ahmadnagar and established an aggressive but short-lived Mahdawi state (Firishtah, 1864–5, vol. 2, pp. 150–2). Thereafter, the Mahdawis would relinquish the notion of either constituting or confronting the state. There is a sociology of this second phase as well, and in what follows I would like to draw a series of contrasts between the two phases and suggest some implications by way of conclusion.

While the initial leadership of the movement tended to be recruited from the political and religious establishment, later Mahdawis did not actively recruit new membership but were more concerned with the retention of present members. In this, they were largely successful. Where conversions did occur, and they were rare, they tended to originate not from the urban Muslim elite, but from artisanal castes (*ahl-i ḥirfat*), such as weavers, cotton carders, and dyers, in the vicinity of Jalor (in south-western Rajasthan) and Palanpur (in northern Gujarat), regions dominated by an existing Mahdawi petty state ('Ali Muhammad Khan, 1930, p. 73). The Mahdawiyah did not originate among the masses and never did become a mass movement, although in the course of the second phase, it was relegated to districts along the imperial frontier where it would evolve its understanding of the millennium.

While the early Mahdawis were preoccupied with urgent apocalyptic expectations, believing that the chain of end events had been set in motion and anticipating the imminent appearance of 'Isa (Jesus), later Mahdawis responded to the inevitable cognitive dissonance caused by the failure of these events by creating a theology of the delay of the apocalypse. They argued, for instance, that the ḥadīth placing the Mahdi and 'Isa in the same eschatological time frame was a Shi'ite forgery (Qāsim, 1974, pp. 5–6), and perceived the Mahdi as ushering in the era of the last millennium and not the immediate apocalyptic events, which are transferred to 'Isā (Fazl Allah, n.d., p. 561). By doing so, the Mahdawis were able to shift their millennial expectations from the present to the future. The world would be filled with justice, as expected of the Mahdi by ḥadīth, but through divine intervention in the future and not by the collective political action of Mahdawis in the present. Until then, the just earth (*'arḍ*) referred to by the ḥadīth is that of the Mahdawi dā'ira, echoing with continual *dhikr*.

At the same time, the later Mahdawis proposed a compromise in the social realization of the millennium, dividing the members of the movement into two discrete groups: the *ahl-i tark* ('renouncers') and the *ahl-i kasb* ('providers').[12] Strict observance of the totalizing Mahdawi rituals and schedules would eventually be limited to the renouncers, based in the dā'ira and led by lineages of gate-keepers, the *pīrzādagān*, descended from first generation Mahdawis, especially the Mahdi and Saiyid Khundmir. The providers, on the other hand, received a special dispensation (*rukhṣat*) to remain in the mundane world procuring a living and financing the renouncers of the dā'ira through tithe (*'ushr*) and interest-free loans. The Mahdi's charisma was routinized not into a political dynasty but into lineages of spiritual guides who were attentive to providing for the needs and identity of the community, but realistic about the real world outside the dā'ira. The intellectual energy of these second phase pirs would be directed to enforcing community compliance to the consensus of the dā'ira, primarily through the production of creedal statements (Qasim, 1944; Shihab al-Din, 1963, pp. 98–104).

While the early Mahdawis, after a period of vacillation, generally adopted an uncompromisingly activist stance toward the establishment, the later Mahdawis tended to prefer a low profile and a quietist stance. The later community was able to practise withdrawal from the world through the renouncers, and at the same time to permit the participation of lay Mahdawis in the Mughal or Deccan political systems. The unique beliefs and rituals of the movement were relegated either to the private sphere of the dā'ira or to the public sphere of the Mahdawi-dominated district (Palanpur) or quarter (Chanchalgudah), where it was supported materially by the lay community. This process enabled the lay Mahdawis to pursue a secular career without any religious implications and, indirectly, to safeguard the autonomy and identity of the larger community.

The early Mahdawiyah, then, was a protest movement directed against the religious and political establishment by members of that establishment. To a certain extent, the social colouring of the movement dictated the response of the establishment. The state 'ulama, who bore the brunt of the initial Mahdawi condemnation—'flies buzzing around human excrement' Shaikh Mustafa called them (n.d., p. 48)—were naturally in favour of direct state action against the movement and promulgated a series of fatwās calling for their execution or banishment. Mahdawi and non-Mahdawi sources alike, however, portray the political establishment, the state, as being very reluctant to act on the authority of such fatwās, except where its constituent military and administrative elites were perceived as being in some way compromised by the movement. For Sultan Muzaffar II of Gujarat, the deciding factor for military action came when, according to Hajji al-Dabir (1970, 32), 'his creed spread and the amir and the army commanders believed in his talks.' For Islam Shah Sur, it was the alarming conversion of major Afghan governors along with their troops—men like Bahwa Khan Lohani and A'zam Humayun Sarwani—in the context of a widespread Afghan revolt that resulted in the persecution of north Indian Mahdawis (Badayuni, 1865–9, v.1, pp. 402–8; Ni'mat Allah, 1960–2, v. 1, pp. 383–5). As long as the Mahdawiyah was perceived as challenging the state through the active recruitment of an oppositional elite from within groups constituting the state, the Mahdawiyah appears to have been repressed. It was not the doctrine of the Mahdi by itself that led to the suppression of the movement, but the class location and political volatility of its supporters.

It is clear, however, that Deccani rulers and the Mughals were willing to tolerate a quietist Mahdawi presence where it did not exist in opposition to the state. During the second phase of Mahdawi development, with the Mahdawi political elite becoming minor political participants without religious colouring, the state was willing to adopt a policy of non-interference. The Afghan Mahdawi petty dynasty of Jalor, later Palanpur, is an example of this change in political profile. Initially supporting Saiyid Khundmir and opposing Akbar in his conquest of Gujarat, they would transfer their allegiance to the Mughals, marry into the royal family, and serve quietly as lower ranking *manṣabdārs* first of the Mughals, and then, when political fortunes shifted, the Marathas and the British (Gulab Miyan, 1914). When the Mahdawi spiritual guide, Saiyid Ibrahim, provided advice to his patron Mujahid Khan (1048–74/1638–63) on how to govern Palanpur, his emphasis would not be on political representation of the Mahdawiyah to the outside world but on pious actions, especially the provision of the material conditions for local Mahdawi prosperity through financial grants to the pirs (Ibrahim, n.d.).

Although opposition to the Mahdawiyah remained, the state 'ulama, previously vehemently opposed to the movement, now tended to support a benign policy. The sea change is best evidenced in the *Mubāḥathah-yi Ālamgīrī*, which records a discussion between the Mughal emperor Aurangzeb, his chief qazi Abu Sa'id, and a delegation of Mahdawis at Ahmadnagar in 1095/1683. The qazi on being questioned by the emperor after the interrogation, referred to the movement as simply a legal school (*madhhab*), not a sect or heresy, and adduced no legal provisions for subjecting its members to execution, imprisonment, or banishment.

Aurangzeb is said to have responded:

> I am pleased to know this, for they are orthodox (*mutasharri'*) in thought and deed. They conducted the interrogation with proofs from the Qur'an, the traditions, and the words of established religious scholars. They speak the *kalima* ('creed') of our Prophet, are not opposed to religious law, act in agreement with the command of God and the Prophet, and follow the orthodox community (*ahl-i sunnat wa jamā'at*). They do say that the Mahdi has come and gone, but this phrase does not require any legal penalty. Give them permission (*rukhṣat*) to depart. (Abū al-Qāsim, n.d., 9)

What is of concern here is not the accuracy of this portrayal of Mahdawi beliefs and actions, but that the chief Mughal qazi and the emperor have followed the Mahdawi lead in de-emphasizing the movement's disengagements from the Muslim mainstream. In this benign reading, they are simply Sunni Muslims who believe that the Mahdi has come and gone. That the individuals articulating this genial view are Saiyid Abu Sa'id, a descendant of Saiyid Muhammad Tahir who had been assassinated by Mahdawis in 986/1587, and Aurangzeb, who is often thought to have adopted a sternly militant and uncompromising view of deviations from orthodoxy, simply underlines the success of the rapprochment. The emphasis has shifted from confrontation to compromise. The Mughal state clearly did not perceive its legitimacy threatened by a millennial movement whose theology had turned inward and whose lay members could be manipulated like any other.

When conflict does emerge during this second phase, it tends to originate not from the pan-Indian level but from a regional or district base, from local 'ulama and petty officials, elements operating on the cusp of the imperial system. Thus, when Saiyid Raju Shahid was martyred (1056/1646) during Aurangzeb's earlier governorate of Gujarat, it was through the overly aggressive actions of the *kōtwāl* (municipal officer) in the context of local Ahmedabad politics (Gulab, 1914, 170–4). As one might expect, this type of conflict tends to increase with the dissolution of effective Mughal authority and the growth of successor states, especially those states legitimized by an appeal to an exclusive Islamist platform in a situation of increased exterior or interior threats.[13]

In conclusion, I would like to emphasize the striking Mahdawi compromise with the state during the second phase. The evidence of the Mahdawiyah will not support the view that Mahdi-based movements, due to the textual expectations of a Mahdi, differ from other millennial movements in being essentially activist and militant, committed to establishing a perfect Islamic state on earth through a jihād. Like millennial movements elsewhere, the Mahdawiyah has a complex social and political history; it was not held captive of formative texts that prefigured social· engagement. In some social contexts, as in the first phase, *hijrat* did lead to jihād, political volatility, and a clash with the state. But in other contexts, as in the second phase, it did not, but formed the basis for the Mahdawi retreat inwards and political disengagement as a movement.

NOTES

1. The Mahdawis have never been enumerated separately in the census, and thus their numbers are open to speculation. Mahdawi estimates range from 150,000 to 300,000. See Tashrifillahi, 1990, pp. 243–532, for a gazetteer of the movement.

2. The following discussion of the teachings of the Mahdi is extracted from Wali, 1947, the earliest extensive collection of the traditions of the Mahdi. For a modern view of the doctrines, see Palanpuri, 1990.

3. Naturally, the precise social composition varied from region to region, with Sind having a somewhat larger Sufi component, gentry (*mulūk*) being prominent particularly in Gujarat, and army officers with tribal connections, especially Afghans, dominating the movement in north India, Rajasthan, and the Deccan.

4. That is, Qazi Qadan, Shaikh Muhammad Uchhi, Darya Khan, and Shaikh Sadr al-Din Tattawi (Qāni, 1886, v. 3. pp. 54–5, 137–8, 216–18). Note that all four claimed saiyid descent, although that of Darya Khan was weakly supported.

5. All of the early Mahdawi proof literature is written in Arabic (see, e.g., Sajawandi, 1945), while the traditions and biographies of the Mahdi are written in Persian with a high percentage of Arabic. The *Inṣāf-nāma*, e.g., while primarily in Persian, contains entire sections in untranslated Arabic (Wali, 1947, pp. 59–63, 80–3, 146–50).

6. Faydi, Akbar's poet laureate, would have been acquainted with the Mahdawis and Ilahdad through his father, Shaikh Mubarak (a sympathizer) and Saiyid Yusuf, a Mahdawi who dedicated his biography of the Mahdi to Faydi (MacLean, forthcoming).

7. The intellectual challenge required action and explains the considerable energy expended on refutation of the Mahdawiyah by prominent contemporary scholars such as 'Ali al-Muttaqi (d. ca. 975/1567). See GAL II, 503, S II, 518, for details of manuscripts. The need to produce works of refutation disappears in the second phase.

8. The text of the letter is preserved by Miyan Saiyid Yusuf (1954, pp. 61–2), a great grandson of the Mahdi, although its existence is hinted at by earlier sources (Wali, 1947, pp. 13–14).

9. It should be noted that the original tradition (Wali, 1947, 25) contains the jizya but not the sword swinging nor the *ḥarbī* references. These are given as separate memories of the incident by Saiyid Khundmir (Ibid., 26), well known for his activist readings. A quietist reading would note that the Mahdi said *if* God granted the power, but God did not do so.

10. Unless otherwise cited, all subsequent references to the incident are from Wali (1947, 205–10). For subsequent readings of Saiyid Khundmir, see the detailed and complex discussion by Saiyid Burhan al-Din in the first volume of his *Ḥadīqat al-ḥaqā'iq*.

11. See Sulayman, *Khātam* 12 (n.d., v. 4, 356–497), for a long account of Mahdawi political connections. For a time, it seemed as if Burhan Nizam Shah (d. 961/1533) would opt for a Mahdawi legitimacy to differentiate his sultanate from his neighbours, although he would eventually opt for Shi'ism.

12. For the distinction, see the suggestion in Qasim, 1968, 12, and the outline in Mahmudi, 1968, pp. 466–8.

13. Thus Tipu Sultan would expel the Mahdawis from Srirangapatan in 1212/1797, and the Battle of Chanchalgūdah would break out in Hyderabad in 1238/1822 as the Mahdawis, Shī'ites, and Sunnis struggled to influence the Nizam (Tashrifillahi, 1990, 281–3, 293–333). The tensions in Hyderabad would remain high.

BIBLIOGRAPHY

'Abd al-Rahman, S., 1948, *Sīrat-i Imām Mahdī maw'ūd*, Hyderabad, Jam'īyat-i Mahdawīyah (written c. 950/1543).

Abu al-Qasim, M., n.d., *Mubāḥathah-yi 'Ālamgīrī*, Hyderabad, Qawmī Press (written c. 1095/1683).

'Ali Muhammad Khan, 1930, *Khātimah-yi mir'āt-i Aḥmadī*, ed. S. Nawāb 'Alī Calcutta, Baptist Machine Press (written 1175/1761).

Ansari, A.S.B., 1963, 'Saiyid Muhammad Jawnpuri and his movement (A historico-heresiological study of the Mahdiyyah in the Indo-Pakistan sub-continent)', *Islamic studies*, 2, pp. 41–74.

Badayuni, 'Abd Al-Qadir, 1865–69, *Muntakhab al-tawārīkh*, ed. M. Aḥmad 'Alī, 3 vols., Calcutta, Asiatic Society of Bengal (written 1004/1595).

——, 1972, *Najāt al-rashīd*, ed. S. Mu'īn al-Ḥaqq, Lahore, Idārah-yi Taḥqīqāt-i Pākistān (written 999/1590).

Burhan al-Din, M.S., n.d., *Ḥadīqat al-ḥaqā'iq*, Kutub-khānah-yi Saiyid Muḥammad Asad Allāh Isḥāqī (written 1058/1648).

——, 1959, *Shawāhid al-wilāyat,* Hyderabad, Jam'īyat-i Mahdawiyah (written 1052/1642).

Fadl Allah, M.S., n.d., *Intikhāb al-mawālīd*, Kutub-khānah-yi Saiyid Dā'ūd 'Ālim Pālanpūri (written 1158/1745).

Firishtah, M.Q.H., 1864–5, *Tārīkh-i Firishtah*, 2 vols., Lucknow, Nawal Kisōr (written c. 1015/1606).

Gulab Miyan, S., 1914, *Tārīkh-i Pālanpūr*, 3 vols., Delhi: Maṭba'-i Zabān.

Hajji al-Dabir, 'A.M., 1970, *Ẓafar al-wālih bi-Muẓaffar wa-ālihi*, tr. M.F. Lokhandwala, Baroda, Oriental Institute (written before 1020/1611).

Husain 'Ālim Saiyidan M.S., 1961, *Tadhkirāt al-ṣāliḥīn*, Hyderabad, Jam'īyat-i Mahdawiyah (written 1106/1694).

Ibrahim, M.S., n.d., *Naṣīhat-nāma*, Kutub-khānah-yi Saiyid Dā'ūd 'Alim Pālanpūrī (written c. 1062/1651).

Ilahdad Hamid, M., 1892, *Kalām-i Ilāhdād*, Hyderabad, Qawmī Press (written 911/1505).

Maclean, D.N., 2000, 'Real men and false men at the court of Akbar: The *Majālis* of Shaykh Mustafa Gujarati,' in David Gilmartin and Bruce B. Lawrence, eds., *Beyond Turk and Hindu: Rethinking Religious Identities in Islamicate South Asia*, Gainesville, University Press of Florida, pp. 199–215.

Mahmudi, S. Ḥusain, 1968, *Al-Mahdī al-maw'ūd*, Hyderabad, Idārah-yi Shamsīyah.

Mihri, M. Malik, 1892, *Dīwān-i Mihrī*, 2 vols., Hyderabad, Qawmī Press (written 930/1523).

Mustafa Gujarati, M.S., n.d., *Majālis*, Kutub-khānah-yi Saiyid Dā'ūd 'Ālim Pālanpūrī (written before 983/1576).

Ni'mat Allah, Khwajah, 1960–2, *Tārīkh-i Khān Jahānī wa makhzan-i Afghānī*, ed. S.M. Imām al-Dīn, 2 vols., Dacca, Asiatic Society of Pakistan (written 1021/1612).

Nizami, K.A., 1989, *Akbar and Religion*, Delhi: Idarah-i-Adabiyat-i-Delli.

Palanpuri, S. Khub Miyan, 1990, *Ḥudūd-i dā'ira-yi Mahdawiyah*, Hyderabad, Idārah-yi Tablīgh-i Mahdawiyah (written 1352/1933).

Qani' Tattawi, M. 'Ali Sher, 1886, *Tuḥfat al-kirām*, 3 vols., Lucknow, Maṭba'-i Nāṣirī (written 1181/1767).

Qasim Mujtahid, S., 1944, *Jāmi' al-uṣūl*, Hyderabad, Jam'īyat-i Mahdawiyah (written before 1043/1633).

——, 1968, *Shifā' al-mu'minīn*, Hyderabad, Jam'īyat-i Mahdawiyah (written c. 1038/1628).

——, 1974, *al-Ḥujjah*, Hyderabad, Jam'iyat-i Mahdawīyah (written c. 1032/1622).

Ruh Allah, M.S., 1952, *Panj faḍā'il*, Hyderabad, Jam'īyat-i Mahdawiyah (written 1094/1682).

Sajawandi, M. 'Abd al-Malik, 1945, *Sirāj al-abṣār*, Hyderabad, Jam'īyat-i Mahdawiyah (written 960/1552).

Shihab al-Din 'Alim, M.S., 1963, *Māhīyat al-taṣdīq*, Hyderabad: Jam'īyat-i Mahdawiyah (written 1153/1740).

Sulayman Malik, M., n.d., *Khātam-i Sulaymānī*, 4 vols., Kutub-khānah-yi Saiyid 'Abd al-Karīm Yadillāhī (written 1191/1777).

Tashrifillahi, M.S., 1990, *Muqaddimah-yi Sirāj al-abṣār*, 3rd ed., rev., Hyderabad, I'jaz Printing Press.

Wali, B.M., 1947, *Inṣāf-nāma*, Hyderabad, Shamsīyah (written before 950/1543).

Yasin, M., 1974, *A Social History of Islamic India*, 1605–1748, New Delhi, Munshiram Manoharlal.

Yusuf, M.S., 1954, *Maṭla' al-wilāyat*, Hyderabad, Jam'iyat-i Mahdawiyah (written 1016/1607).

PART THREE

History, Literature, and Law

The three kinds of Indo-Islamic traditions discussed in this section—history, romance literature, and law—encompass an enormous body of textual material spanning the entire period from the eighth to the eighteenth century.

In the first essay, which considers Indo-Muslim history-writing, Peter Hardy analyses common features of the work of five major historians of the Delhi Sultanate period. These include: a strictly court-centred perspective; a tendency for human actors to conform to ideal prototypes; a sense that the present succeeds, rather than grows out of, the past; a reluctance to interrogate evidence or the credentials of those whose testimony is received and recorded; and the assumption that all events are determined by God. Hardy explains these features partly on theological grounds, i.e., the idea that history is a component of the Islamic revelation. But he also finds an historical explanation for features such as the concentrated focus on the Indo-Muslim king—namely, that following the collapse of the Abbasid Caliphate in 1258, the Islamic world lacked a political and religious centre of gravity; consequently, for several generations after that event historians in India looked to the Delhi Sultan as the 'pivot of the fortunes of the Muslim community.' This suggests one reason why not all the features described by Hardy are found in the works of Indo-Muslim historians of later periods, such as those writing in regional sultanates or under the Mughals.

A very different genre of Indian Islamic tradition, the vernacular Sufi romance, is analysed by Aditya Behl in this section's second essay. Whereas the historians described by Hardy were virtually 'colonial' inasmuch as they still identified at some level with their ancestral homelands in Central Asia or Iran (then overrun by Mongols), the poets studied by Behl were firmly planted in India, both politically and culturally. Most of them, living after 1398 when Timur sacked Delhi and shattered the Tughluqs' unitary empire, wrote under the patronage of regional Indo-Muslim kingdoms that had become deeply invested in local cultures. Thus poets like Qutban, who lived in the Jaunpur region, eschewed both Sanskrit and Persian and elevated vernacular Hindawi to literary status. In the process, they created a new genre of literature, the vernacular Sufi romance. Though rooted in both Perso-Islamic romance poetry and classical Indian theories of aesthetics, the genre was distinct from both. In fact, Behl argues that this genre of literature represented the fusion of a transregional Islamicate world-system with local, Hindustani societies, and that its appearance marked Islam's assimilation into an Indian cultural environment.

The final essay in this section examines a type of Indo-Islamic tradition that lies at the heart of Islamic culture anywhere—namely, law, and more specifically, texts that function to apply Islamic law to particular societies. Alan Guenther's study of one such text, the *Fatāwá-i 'Ālamgīrī*, affords unusual insight into the workings of the Muslim scholarly and legal establishment, or 'ulama, during the reign of Aurangzeb. Faced with the practical business of reconciling law that is theoretically immutable with social or cultural realities that were both diverse and very mutable, jurists looked to rulings by earlier jurists for guidance. But to which jurists, and to which rulings? Contradictory judgments had inevitably appeared during the centuries since the Hanafi school of law first came to predominate in north India. To meet such problems, approximately once each century since the thirteenth, legal scholars in India compiled 'final' editions of those previous rulings they deemed to be authoritative. The compilation of the *Fatāwá-i 'Ālamgīrī* was commissioned by Aurangzeb himself, who took great personal interest in supervising the eight-year project. The emperor also used the finished text to guide his *farmāns*, or imperial decrees, although this did not prevent him from tailoring his interpretations of the text to fit particular circumstances.

The essays of both Behl and Guenther, then, explore some of the ways that an understanding of the socio-cosmic order that had originally emerged to the west of the Khyber Pass were, between the fourteenth and eighteenth centuries, accommodated to India's cultural environment.

8

Some General Characteristics Analysed*

Peter Hardy

As Sir Henry Elliot long ago pointed out in relation to Muslim historiography in India generally,[1] the five authors of the Delhi Sultanate period herein discussed—Ziya al-Din Barani, Shams al-Din Siraj 'Afif, Yahya ibn Ahmad, Amir Khusrau, and 'Isami—devote themselves to recording the action and commenting upon the deeds of 'grandees and ministers, thrones and imperial powers'. What the sultan did, where he went, what battles he fought, whom he appointed to office, who rebelled against him, and what acts of beneficence he performed, this is the stuff of these accounts. None of these historians would think of taking their meals in the kitchen as the economic and social historian is reputed to do; a festive table at court was their idea of a proper observation post for historians. Indeed, for Barani, history should concern itself only with the activities of the great in both the religious and temporal spheres. But sultans, *wazīrs*, *amīrs*, soldiers, and saints so completely fill the foreground of these works that the spectator not only cannot see the background, but is left unaware that a background exists.

For it is not merely that the fortunes of the powerful and great only are recorded, but that they are recorded in a purely personal way. Each man is treated as an 'island sole'; his actions are complete and perfect within themselves, they are possessions which are enjoyed through some individual right; as if a wealthy man owes his riches wholly to his personal qualities and not at all to the social usages, the laws, and the attitudes which ensure that he may enjoy them in peace and security. In relation to other men at least, the characters in the Muslim histories discussed are portrayed as stark individualists. By Barani and the others, in the words of Sir Henry

* Reprinted from Peter Hardy, *Historians of Medieval India: Studies in Indo-Muslim Historical Writing*, New Delhi: Munshiram Manoharlal, 1997.

Elliot, 'society is never contemplated either in its conventional usages or recognized privileges; its constituent elements or mutual relations; its established classes or popular institutions; in its private recesses or habitual intercourses.' It is true that Barani gives a long account of measures taken by 'Ala al-Din Khalji to control prices and to increase the revenue yield of his dominions. They are however described as if they were the result of the personal will and force of the sultan acting upon passive circumstances and passive people. Similarly, it is possible to detect the presence of such institutions as the *dīwān-i-wizārat*, the financial administration, from incidental references in 'Afīf, for example, but not to reconstruct its working policies and any changes in those policies. For in 'Afif the institution is depicted either as the passive recipient of orders from the sultan, or as the glass in which the qualities of Firuz Shah Tughluq are refracted.

The customary, and, so far as it goes, valid explanation of this constriction of the medieval Indo-Muslim historians' horizons to the doings of the politically great and powerful, is that they were courtiers writing in the enjoyment or in the expectation of royal patronage and that in their choice of subject matter they obeyed 'market forces'. Sultans, it may be argued, prefer to hear about other sultans, particularly if they are connected to them by family, or, as 'Isami implied in his eulogium on the role of the Turks in Islam, racial ties. It is clear that Barani, 'Afif, and the rest were not wounded in their 'professional pride' by writing about the deeds of men of the class to whom their patron, or expected patrons, belonged. Considerations of a non-economic order also had their weight in their choice of subject matter and in their biographical, personal mode of treatment.

As the 'Abbasid caliphate ceased to be the effective political power in the eastern Muslim world and, from the middle of the fourth/tenth century became a purely titular institution acting as a legitimating authority for the numerous Persian and Turkish rulers who exercised effective sovereignty, so the office of sultan came to be regarded by Muslim writers on government as the pivot of the fortunes of the Muslim community, the one institution upon which depended that political and social stability without which the Islamic revelation and the Muslim Holy Law could not be studied with a quiet mind and put into practice by the faithful.[2] The destruction in 656/1258 of the caliphate in Baghdad by the Mongol Hulagu only tended to confirm this tendency.

Al-Ghazali's *Naṣiḥat al-mulūk* (c. 499/1105–6), Wassaf's *Akhlāq al-sulṭanat* and *Naṣiḥat-i mulūk*[3] (first decade of the eighth/fourteenth century) and Barani's own *Fatāwa-yi-Jahāndārī*, all look to the sultan to assume the functions in the Muslim community previously allotted to the Caliph. It was he who should guard the *Dār al-Islām*, safeguard the Holy Law, appoint God-fearing persons to office and see that the canonical taxes, the *zakāt* and the jizya, were levied. If the historians of the Muslim community could collect, record, and publish abroad the deeds, whether good or evil according to Islamic criteria, of previous occupants of such an awesome office, they would be serving the cause of true religion.

To serve the cause of true religion, namely Islam. Therein lies one of the principal motives for Muslim historical writing. Of the historians discussed, Barani was the author most consciously interested and Yahya ibn Ahmad the least consciously interested in this purpose. But the motive was not wholly absent in any of the others, not even in Amir Khusrau and 'Isami, who did not teach any particular doctrines or principles but who contented themselves with commending virtue and reprobating vice in general. Ziya al-Din Barani praised the study of history as a component of the Islamic revelation, worthy to be set beside Qur'anic commentary, the study of ḥadīth, of *fiqh*, and of the *ṭarīqa* (way) of the mystics. It was morality teaching by examples, a means of strengthening the judgement and the moral fibre, and of detecting unorthodox belief. It should not, however, be thought that Ziya al-Din Barani was unique in these views on the usefulness of history, taking the total span of Islamic historiography into consideration. The *Raudat al-ṣafā*, a general history written in Herat in the second half of the ninth/fifteenth century by Mir Khwand, contains almost exactly the same sentiments.[4] Similar views may also be found in the *Tārīkh-i-Baihaq* by Ibn Funduq, a history of the district of Bayhaq completed in 563/1168.[5] Among later works, Zahir al-Din Mar'ashi's *Tārīkh-i-Ṭabaristān wa Rūyān wa Māzandarān* (c. 881/1476)[6] and the near contemporary Al-Sakhawī's *al-I'lān*, a defence of historiography as a suitable subject in the curriculum of religious studies, equally stress the religious and moral utility of historical writing in terms analogous to those of the *Tārīkh-i Fīrūz Shāhī*.[7] Al-Sakhawī's *al-I'lān* also quotes earlier authors as saying that he who writes about a saint will be with that saint in his rank on the Day of Resurrection and that the memory of pious men is a source of divine mercy.[8]

There would appear to be three main characteristics for which the Islamic or the didactic religious framework of Muslim historiography, as exemplified by the five writers discussed, was responsible. First, an almost exclusive concentration on the deeds of Muslims in Hindustan. For Barani, 'Afif, Yahya ibn Ahmad, and 'Isami, non-Muslims are as the furniture and properties for the stage on which the drama of the Muslim destiny and the Muslim political achievement in Hindustan is played. The

Hindus are not mentioned, for the most part, except as the passive material on which Muslims impose their will. It is the function of the Hindus to provide opportunities for the practice of Muslim virtue; they are never interesting in themselves, but only as converts, as capitation tax-payers, or as corpses. Even Amir Khusrau, who in his *Nuh Sipihr* shows considerable interest in the languages, music, and sciences of the Hindus, does so more to illustrate the interesting environment in which the Muslims in Hindustan live than to understand Hindu civilization. Even he cannot resist pointing out that Hindus live, metaphysically, in error and in ignorance of the truth. Although none of the five authors examined prefaces his account of the fortunes of Muslims in Hindustan with a brief conspectus of general Islamic history from the time of the Prophet (as do, for example, the *Ṭabaqāt-i-Nāṣirī* by Minhaj al-Siraj or the *Tārīkh-i-Muḥammadī* by Muhammad Bihamad Khani), that does not betray them as indifferent to the history of their community. For them, indeed as for Muslim historians outside India, the only significant history is the history of the Muslim community; they are historians of the *res gestae* of the politically prominent members of a group united by ties of common faith rather than historians of the whole people of the area controlled by the Delhi sultan. They are, so to speak, the first Muslim communalists in India.

The second consequence of the Indo-Muslim historians' acceptance of the Muslim world order and the determination of some of them, at least, actively to strengthen it by their writings, is that the past is observed through religious spectacles. Indeed, with the almost general acceptance of the fundamental doctrine of Ash'arite theology—the doctrine of an omnipotent and eternally active Sovereign Lord—by all the historians in question, this is unremarkable. Whatever happens is brought under the categories of Muslim thought, whether or not religion is an element in the situation. Of course, this idiom is more dominant in some of the writers discussed than in others. In the actual treatment of events it is weakest in Yahya ibn Ahmad Sihrindi and strongest in Ziya al-Din Barani. Of the problems this poses for the modern historian, they are not unlike those posed by Communist practices of discussing every issue in the terminology of dialectical materialism. But in Barani, Amir Khusrau, and 'Isami, the relations between the sultans of Delhi and their Hindu subjects, the struggle for the throne between Khusrau Khan and Ghiyath al-Din Tughluq, and the differences with his subjects of Sultan Muhammad bin Tughluq, for example, are all recorded under the guise (and of course it need not be merely a guise) of differences over religious issues, however unimpassioned or impassioned the different authors may be about them.

This draws with it the third consequence of the religious presuppositions of the Indo-Muslim historians discussed: their disinclination for facts in all their detail and in all their manifold variety. With them an ounce of religious truth weighs more than a pound of fact. Sometimes this attitude is expressed in a humble acceptance of their own ignorance—as with Yahya ibn Ahmad Sihrindi's 'God knows best' or 'God alone knows the truth'. At other times it is expressed in Ziya al-Din Barani's decision not to set down all he knew about the reign of Muhammad bin Tughluq, but only the information sufficient to enable readers with the right approach to life to understand the 'true inwardness' of that sultan's reign. Thus a writer like Ziya al-Din Barani (and he is perhaps alone among the five in this respect) in effect produced 'Whig' history in the sense defined by Professor H. Butterfield in *Whig Interpretation of History*—a significant abridgement of the past, an organization of the past upon the assumption that what matters is not the story in all its detail and complexity, but where that story is going and the message it is carrying. A passionate judgement of values is preferred to a careful investigation into the facts of the actual process of historical change, to which all parties and not merely the 'party of light', as so conceived by the historian, contribute. Barani, however, was not interested in investigating the subtle mediations by which his present came into being, or in examining the clash of opposing viewpoints about which the historian must try his hardest to be neutral lest he miss some strand in the skein. Barani wished only to attend to those facts which, in the light of his religious presuppositions, must, *a priori*, have been decisive in explaining what happened in history.

This brings the discussion to the question of how, in general, the five Indo-Muslim writers on history did explain what happened in history. All are alike in imputing to Divine Decree the final role in the determination of events. God awards victory, takes away thrones, punishes wrongdoing, and decrees that a man shall die. Moreover, for 'Afif, Yahya ibn Ahmad, Amir Khusrau, and 'Isami, the working of His Will is open and direct; it bears directly down upon the fortunes of individuals, by so to speak, individual attention. There is no question for these authors of God's intervention being indirect or mediated through social forces. He does more than build the railway, construct the engine, and provide the fuel and the staff to run the whole system. He actually ordains, at the moment of movement, every turn of the wheels, every shovelful of coal, every operation of the signals. The whole universe is His creature. It is in keeping with this metaphysic that, for example in 'Afif and 'Isami, God acts and provides the explanation for events through the unchangeable disposition with which He endows a man at the moment of his creation.

Thus, Firuz Shah Tughluq acts as he does by reason of his God-given disposition. Such a disposition is a kind of unchanging substratum in history, determining the reactions that are visible externally. Men's dispositions would not of course be omitted from any explanation of events, but the distinctive feature of those characters as depicted by the Indo-Muslim historians is that they are unchanging, they are created by God, and while they influence events and actions, events and actions do not influence them.

An important feature of the works of Barani, 'Afif, Amir Khusrau, and 'Isami is the deference paid therein to the Sufi mystics to whom they attribute a determinative role in history as men of God. Barani attributed, for example, the misfortunes of Jalal al-Din Khalji to the killing of Sidi Maula and the glories of the reign of 'Ala al-Din Khalji to the *barakāt* of Shaikh Nizam al-Din Auliya near whose grave he was buried.[9] 'Afif chose the *manāqib* form for his account of the reign of Firuz Shah Tughluq, eulogized the sultan for his respect for prominent mystics of his time (hence his general credit in Indo-Muslim literature?), and attributed the immunity of Hansi from pillage by Timur's forces to the barakāt of the saints buried in the vicinity.[10] Amir Khusrau took Shaikh Nizam al-Din Auliya as his pir, made a collection of his sayings, the *Afḍal al-fawā'id*, and eulogized him in the *Dewal Ranī Khiḍr Khān*.[11] 'Isami traces the handing down of the mantle of discipleship (*khirqa*) from the Prophet to a mystic of his own day, Zain al-Haqq, and partly ascribed the misfortunes of Delhi under Muhammad ibn Tughluq to the disgust by which he was regarded by a prominent mystic. Indeed, the key to the practically general discredit in which Muhammad ibn Tughluq is held in the literature of the medieval period, is probably to be found in his relations with the mystics and the reports that were put into circulation by them about him.[12] All the histories discussed provide, by implication, evidence that in pre-Mughal Muslim India at least, the mystic orders both set the tone of religious life and enjoyed harmonious relations with the orthodox 'ulama. The historical literature of the Sultanate period in India supports the thesis of a rapprochement in Islam between orthodoxy and mysticism immediately following the life's work of al-Ghazali.[13]

Even when historical personages appear to be acting autonomously and their own wishes and decisions appear to explain what happens, further investigation will reveal the hand of God in the background. This is particularly true of the outlook of the poets Amir Khusrau and 'Isami. Men act as other men, orthodox Muslims, would expect them to act in certain formal situations. Thus fathers feel paternal love, sons filial devotion, and guardians a sense of responsibility towards their charges. Rebels act rebelliously and unbelievers act wickedly. They all act according to rule and to rules which express a conventional Muslim expectation that the world is composed of men, some with good natures, some with evil, some born to be good fathers, good sons, good sultans, and pious believers, others to be wicked rebels and contumacious infidels. Amir Khusrau and 'Isami offer a literary dramatization of history in accordance with the ethics of orthodox Islam; they see each situation as complete in itself and history as a succession of moments, each possessing symbolical significance.

For Amir Khusrau and 'Isami, aesthetic considerations were paramount in explaining the past. They were concerned to see truth in terms of art, as imagined rather than discovered. They were more interested in telling a good story, one which would stir the emotions, than in telling what was actually done, what people actually thought, and what they actually wanted to do. They were not interested in the drama of fact but in the fact of drama. Hence, the intrusion of dreams into the narrative of the *Futūḥ al-salāṭīn* and the *Tughluq-nāma*; hence the dramatic accounts of the malevolent workings of Muhammad bin Tughluq's mind; hence the willingness to argue from consequence to sequence with the aid of a little dogma—that if, for example, a sultan, such as Muhammad bin Tughluq, failed in his enterprises it must have been because he was impious, or if the armies of Bughra Khan and Mu'izz al-Din Kayqubad did not actually come to blows in Awadh, it must have been because sentiments of paternal care and filial devotion had governed the conduct of both father and son. It should not be forgotten, too, that 'Isami explicitly said that he weighed what he had read or heard against 'first principles'.

One characteristic unites all five writers in their manner of finding, or of seeing intelligibility in history. They do not find or see it in the historical process itself. Men are puppets in a drama beyond their feeble comprehension, not so much because of its vastness and complexity, but because of its starkness and simplicity. Only God knows its meaning. For Ziya al-Din Barani in particular, the study of history was the study of God, not of man; the past is a commentary upon the Divine Purpose for men, a vehicle of Revelation. For Shams al-Din 'Afif, it is a spectacle of virtue made manifest, and for the poets, a drama of the clash of gods or devils, but hardly of men. Of the human predicament and of the fulfilment or the frustration of human purposes these Indo-Muslim writers did not intend to write except to discover a Divine Command or to point a moral.

As a corollary of this presupposition that history happened above the heads of historical men, there was an indifference to the discovery and portrayal of human personality in all its manifold individuality. Interest concentrated on how far a man conformed to an ideal prototype, not how far he diverged. Firuz Shah Tughluq, for example, was portrayed as a tailor's dummy upon which was hung the qualities of ideal rulership. Ziya al-Din Barani attempted to reduce Muhammad bin Tughluq's personality to the measurements possible for Barani's calipers and his actions to examples of obedience or disobedience to rules that Barani could understand. Furthermore, the idea of the development of a human character in response to his experiences, of deliberate self-discipline in response to a compelling moral, or personal ambition, was quite alien to the cast of thought of any of the historians treated. Events betrayed but did not mould human dispositions. The historians tended to write biography with the unique individual traits omitted, offering their readers a list of stereotyped qualities in place of an integrated personality, and a melodramatic sequence of episodes in which the hero or the villain figures, in place of a life story.[14] The *manāqib* genre, adopted by 'Afif, only reinforced this tendency.

As the five historians were not concerned to describe individual personality, so too they were not much concerned to describe change. Change they did of course record, but only unintentionally. The flatness of the narrative in Yahya bin Ahmad is due to more than humility before the facts or indifference to them; it expresses the assumption that there is little new under the sun. The names of men and sultans may change, but little else. The present succeeds the past; it is not the outcome of the past, which is, *ex hypothesi*, considered to be dissimilar to it.

It is not the main task of this essay to offer detailed explanations of these features of Islamic historiography, but a few comments may not be inappropriate. It would appear that the presuppositions underlying what the Indo-Muslim historians wrote rested upon the foundations of Ash'arite theology. For the school of al-Ash'ari, God is the absolute sovereign who creates good and evil, belief and unbelief (in Islam), allowing some men to disbelieve.[15] The world is an arena in which good and evil co-exist in mortal combat, which is never quite mortal. All human acts are by man's own acquisition, but God creates them and they are by His Will. All temporally produced things are created by God; He is the perpetually active, continually willing Sovereign of the universe.[16] There is thus no order of nature, but an endless succession of divine acts sustaining the universe.[17] As formulated by al-Baqillani, the universe is considered to be a totality of indestructible atoms or *monads*, kept in being, and kept in relationship with each other by the Will of God. They do not modify each other by interaction; all change and action in the world are produced by these monads entering into, and dropping out of, existence, and not by any change in themselves or by any modification of each other. But their existence must have a cause and their juxtaposition must have a cause: that cause is God. The Will of God creates and annihilates the monads and their qualities and thus brings about all the motion observable in the universe. A man writes with a pen on a piece of paper; God creates in his mind the will to write; at the same moment he gives him the power to write and brings about the apparent motion of the hand, the pen, and the appearance of ink on the paper. Not one of these events is the cause of the other. God has brought about the appearance of creation and motion by an appropriate willing of monads.[18]

If this was the background of metaphysical assumptions with which Indo-Muslim historians were armed (and in his *Fatāwa-yi-Jahāndārī*,[19] Barani expicitly condemns the doctrine that God does not know particulars), the absence of synthesis, of a total view of society and its interactions, should not be a matter for surprise. If society was, on the analogy of the monads, a fortutious concourse of atoms thrown together and kept together by the Will of God continuously exercised, and if the determining relationship was that between God and each individual man rather than that between men themselves, the absence of an organic sense of history as the story of a society, with that society having a character different from that which individuals themselves possess, need not cause surprise. It is possible that even today the orthodox Muslim confrontation of an omnipotent Sovereign Lord by his individual humble servants makes it difficult for Muslims to view the historical process under the categories of the workings of impersonal social forces and of the frustration of human purposes, not by God, but by the very structure of events and the weight of human and social inertia. The medieval Muslim view of history as a succession of events, of untouching moments, made significant only by their relationship to God, ill accords with presuppositions of social organism, change, and process.[20]

One last theme remains to be discussed in this historiographic study—the Indo-Muslim historian's attitude towards his material. It may be said, on the basis of the five historians examined, that Indo-Muslim writers on history were recorders first and researchers a long way after; they wrote history from authority and from authority conceived in a quasi-religious sense. Although they practised, in fact, a selection of data—Yahya ibn Ahmad, for example, grouping his material under reigns in the *Ta'rīkh-i-Mubārak Shāhī* and Ziya al-Din Barani ordering each of his reigns in the form of a parable—they did not regard their task as essentially that of selecting and marshalling significant facts in response to personal curiosity about the past. They received information; they did not put evidence to the question. They respected their predecessors; they did not presume to examine their credentials or their predilections. Historical facts were something known to someone somewhere; they were not discovered by the critical thinking of the historian himself. Thus Barani appealed to the authority of his relatives for proof of the truth of what he wrote, 'Afif to the authority of honest narrators, Amir Khusrau to what eyewitnesses told him. Thus 'Isami did not sift from tradition, and Yahya ibn Ahmad appropriated without acknowledgment the work of unnamed earlier historians. Thus Barani would not write anything that disagreed with the *Ṭabaqāt-i-Nāṣirī* for fear of confusing the latter's readers, and 'Afif offered as the only reason for preferring one account of the actions of Khwaja Jahan Ahmad Ayaz to another that what he heard at a certain gathering was true.

It will have been observed that some of the five writers were undoubtedly willing to subordinate fact to effect. Thus Barani put his own views into the mouths of his personages; and 'Isami, in his testing of his data against ' first principles and correct deduction', did not scruple to include imaginary accounts of dreams in his *Futūḥ al-salāṭīn.* However, the latter account was intended to be popular, and his readers would not be deceived. It should be noted that the influence of Persian was certainly stronger than that of Arabic historiography upon these five historians. Not for them the employment of *isnād.* The influence of the *fürstenspiegel* tradition on Barani is manifest in his *Fatāwa-yi-Jahāndārī* and is not altogether absent in his *Tārīkh-i Fīrūz Shāhī*; 'Isami himself said that his work was modelled upon Firdausi's. It should not be thought that any of these authors would have felt guilty on being charged with casualness towards historical facts. They would either, like Barani and 'Afif, have replied that what they wrote corroborated the great Revelation of Islam and therefore could not, on the highest level of truth, in the light of eternity, be false; or, like Yahya ibn Ahmad Sihrindi, have humbly placed the matter in the hands of God; or, like Amir Khusrau and 'Isami, have been incapable of understanding the charge.

NOTES

1. *Bibliographical Index to the Historians of Muhammedan India*, vol. I, *General, Histories*, Calcutta, 1849, p. xv.
2. On the various phases and specifications of this development in Persia see A.K.S. Lambton, 'Quis Custodiet Custodes: Some Reflections on the Persian Theory of Government', *Studia Islamica* 5, Paris, 1956.
3. Found in Waṣṣāf, *Tārīkh-i Waṣṣāf*, lith. Bombay, 1269/1853, pp. 484–97.
4. *The Rauzat-us-Safa*, by Muhammad ibn Khavandshah ibn Mahmud, trans. E. Rehatsek, ed. F.F. Arbuthnot, London, 1891, vol. I, pp. 25–31.

5. 'Alī ibn Zayd al-Bayhaqī (Ibn Funduq), *Tārīkh-i-Baihaq*, text, Teheran (solar), 1317/1937, pp. 7–12 *passim*.

6. ed. 'Abbās Shayagān, Teheran (solar), 1333/1954, p. 6.

7. *al-I'lān bi-l-tawbīkh li-man ẓamma ahl al-tawrikh*, trans. F. Rosenthal, in *A History of Muslim Historiography*, Leiden, 1952, pp. 205–9, 215–60 *passim*.

8. Ibid., pp. 235, 237.

9. Amir Khwurd, *Siyar al-auliyā*, lith. Delhi, 1885, p. 313.

10. Ziya al-Din Barani, *Tārīkh-i Fīrūz Shāhī*, edited as *The Tārīkh-i Feroz-shāhī of Ziaa al-Din Barni*, by Saiyid Ahmad Khan, Calcutta: Bibliotheca Indica, 1891, pp. 81–2.

11. School of Oriental and African Studies (London), Persian MS. No. 18729, pp. 15–16.

12. See Muhammad Habib, 'Shaikh Naṣīruddīn Maḥmūd Chirāgh-i-Dehli as a Great Historical Personality,' *Islamic Culture* 20, no. 2, April, 1946, pp. 138–43.

13. As expounded, for example, by Sir Hamilton Gibb in *Mohammedanism*, London, 1949, pp. 139–43.

14. See G.E. von Grünebaum, *Medieval Islam : a Study in Cultural Orientation*, 2nd ed., Chicago, 1953, pp. 221–6, 280.

15. *Abu'l Ḥasan 'Alī ibn Ismā'īl al-Ash'arī's Al-Ibānah 'an uṣūl ad-diyānah*. A translation with introduction and notes by Walter C. Klein, New Haven, 1940, pp. 50–1.

16. al-Ash'arī, *Kitāb al-luma'*, trans, R.J. McCarthy, in *The Theology of al-Ash'arī*, Beyrouth, 1953, pp. 33–6.

17. See Majid Fakhry, *Islamic Occasionalism*, London, 1958, pp. 25–48.

18. See D.B. Macdonald, *Development of Muslim Theology, Jurisprudence and Constitutional Theory*, New York, 1903, pp. 201–05.

19. Ziya al-Din Barani, *Fatāwa-yi-Jahāndārī*, India Office Library, Persian MS 1149, fol. 121a.

20. On the Ash'arite denial of potentiality in nature, see S. Van den Berg, *Averroes' Tahafut al-Tahafut*, vol. I, London, 1954, p. xxii.

9

The Magic Doe: Desire and Narrative in a Hindavi Sufi Romance, circa 1503

Aditya Behl

One of the major genres of pre-modern north Indian poetry is the Awadhi or eastern Hindavi *prema-kahānī* (literally 'love-story') composed by Muslim Sufi poets, members of the Persian-speaking courtly élite of the Delhi Sultanate, from the fourteenth century onwards. These narrative poems, called Sufi romances by modern critics, are commonly assumed to put forward 'the equation of human love and love for a divine being.'[1] Written and performed in Delhi, Jaunpur, and the eastern province of Bihar, they mark the inauguration of a new literary culture in a local language, an Indian Islamic literary tradition.[2] The Chishti Sufis, the first known composers of the Hindavi mystical romances, describe the ascetic quest of the hero towards the revelatory beauty of a heroine (or God) by linking mortification, fasting, and prayer with a female object of desire. Drawing on the local language of ascetic practice, they make their hero into a yogi, while the heroine is a beautiful Indian woman. While eroticism and asceticism have frequently been linked together in Indian religious traditions and in Sufi mysticism, the Hindavi romances are distinctive because in them the hero attains his 'divine' heroine after an arduous ascetic quest and brings her to live with a hostile wife who represents the world. The formula of the conflictual coexistence of this world and the hereafter can be read within the context of the uneasy interdependence between the Chishtis and political rulers during the Sultanate period and their conflicting claims to authority.[3]

This Indian Islamic literary tradition marks the full indigenization and assimilation of Islam into an Indian cultural landscape. Indigenization accounts for the Indian elements in Indian Islamic culture as the result of conscious and purposeful adaptations made to the local environment by agents who remained Muslim in their religious orientation, in contrast to the widespread explanation of a haphazard 'syncretism' or 'accretion' of disparate elements. These poems are distinct both from Persian and from the older classical traditions of India, an Indian Islamic creation which emphasizes its double distance from these older canons even while borrowing important ideas and conventions from them. The poets of the genre used Hindavi, a spoken local language that they elevated into a literary medium, and the earliest manuscripts of their poems are written in Persian script. Their romances express a Sufi message through a poetics derived in part from Persian, in part from Sanskrit, and in part from regional literary conventions, an indication that these poets had arrived on the cultural scene and that they were fully indigenized as Muslims.

The narrative universes of the Hindavi Sufi romances stand at the juncture of two different but interlinked directions of enquiry. On the one hand, they are part of a formulaic genre with its own logic of the transformation of desire into the savour of love (*prema-rasa*). *Rasa* itself was defined famously in Bharata's eighth-century Sanskrit aesthetic treatise, the *Nātya-Śāstra*, as the juice or flavour of a poem arising from 'the combination of the *vibhāvas* (sources of rasa), the *anubhāvas* (actions, experiential signs of rasa), and the transitory emotions (*vyabhicārībhāvas*).'[4] The aim of reading or listening is to experience the dominant rasa that animates the poem, as the *sahṛdaya* or sympathetic reader feels the emotions of the parted lovers in the poem. The Hindavi Sufi poets approach these classical ideas creatively, using Persian, Sanskrit, and regional linguistic conventions and themes to put together entertaining poems that carried a mystical charge. Their romantic fictions hold out the promise of love and enchantment, an invitation to realms of magic, marvels, and adventure.

On the other hand, they are part of a larger historical world with its own struggles and interactions. Even though the primary purpose of the poet who creates an imaginary universe may not be to represent historical events, poetic uses of narratives and motifs are linked with larger historical processes and have a history of their own. The travels of narrative motifs mark deep and long cultural interactions between peoples in the pre-modern global economy that linked Asia, the Middle East, and Europe in what Janet Abu-Lughod and others have termed a pre-modern world system.[5] In Marshall Hodgson's phrase, this was an 'Islamicate' world system, not always linked 'directly to the religion, Islam, itself, but to the social and cultural complex historically associated with Islam and the Muslims, both among Muslims themselves and even when found among non-Muslims'.[6] As Phillip Wagoner has pointed out in his innovative study of the court dress code in the south Indian kingdom of Vijayanagara, this systemic shift also entailed a cultural change. In the cultures surrounding the Indian Ocean, people adopted cultural and discursive practices from the Turkish Sultanate of Delhi and the regional Afghan kingdoms while maintaining indigenous culture as part of the useful repertoire of symbolic forms.[7] Among these forms were the composite literary and artistic genres that flourished in the Islamic sultanates and the non-Islamic polities that surrounded the littorals of the Indian Ocean.

Following the pioneering and broad-based historical work of K.N. Chaudhuri, scholars have focused on the cultures of the Indian Ocean as a group of societies linked by trade, the annual compulsion of the monsoon winds, commonalities of social and religious practice, and networks of circulation and exchange.[8] The various Sufi *silsilas* that composed Hindavi poetry in north India have to be understood against this broad historical backdrop. The Indian Sufis were fully steeped in the conventions and symbolism of the various genres of Persian poetry, both lyric (*ghazal*) and narrative (*mathnawī*). At the same time, they were fascinated by the poetics and alluring imagery of Indian poetry as they encountered it in musical and dance performances and in poetic recitation. The cultural history of sultanate India is in part the history of the enthusiastic participation of Sufis and other Muslims in the formation of the canons of Indian poetry, art, and music. The genre of the Hindavi Sufi romance should be read against this larger background of cultural appropriations, comminglings, and creative formulations. The Hindavi Sufi poets used Sanskrit rasa theory and the conventions of Persian poetry to create a mystical romantic genre centred around the various meanings of prema-rasa, the juice or essence of love. While it is important to understand their poems as aesthetic and mystical creations, the genre can nevertheless also be read for marks of historical process and as embodying a history of narrative motifs.

The Hindavi romantic ideal of desire and its transformation into Sufi love is set in a fantasy world of marvels and exotic locales, of supernatural helpers and agencies who aid the hero along his way. The poets of the Hindavi Sufi romances articulate their distinctive aesthetics of self-transformation through narrative, the unfolding of a story in a fantastic fictional universe. These narrative universes have four characteristic features. First, inspired by Persian verse narratives (mathnawīs), they relate the story of a spiritual quest that proceeds through the deferment of desire and the enticement of the hero/reader further and further on the journey of self-transformation. Second, the fictional universe is formulaic and episodic, but the poet structures these formulaic motifs using abstract characters or narrative options like the different kinds of love, or, as in the romance discussed in this essay, the relative values of asceticism and sensual pleasure. Third, they are not directly allegorical but suggestive of general Sufi values through the ordeals and experiences of the hero. Finally, the narrative motifs that the poets use reveal a history of complex interactions between, on the one hand, Persian and Arabic story-telling, and on the other, Sanskrit, Prakrit, and other narrative traditions in the Islamicate and pre-Islamic world of the Indian Ocean.

In writing the first Hindavi verse romance, the *Cāndāyan,* Maulana Da'ud adapted the Ahir folk-epic of Lorik and Canda into a distinctive Sufi story in 1379. He developed a narrative formula for representing the play of desire between God, the Sufi, and the world as an erotic relationship between a man and two women. The enterprise involved a balancing act between the military aristocracy of the Delhi Sultanate and the Sufis who produced new romantic narratives in Hindavi, using the generic conventions of Indian poetry to express a Sufi agenda. The next surviving Hindavi Sufi romance, Qutban's *Mirigāvatī* (c. 1503), recreates the formulaic pattern of the *Cāndāyan.* In reading the *Mirigāvatī*, we have to come to terms with the conventionality, the multiple origins, and the range of responses to the fantastic universes created by the Hindavi poets. In his study of formula stories as art and popular culture, literary critic John Cawelti notes that narrative genres like the American western persist 'not because they embody some particular ideology or psychological dynamic, but because they maximize a great many such dynamics.'[9] The same is true of the Hindavi *premākhyāns*, which circulated among a variety of audiences and used narrative formulae and terminology that had a wide appeal. This essay investigates Qutban's formulaic construction of the fantasy world in his tale of the love between the Prince of Candragiri ('Moon-Mountain') and the beautiful Mirigāvatī, the magic doe-woman.

Although we know very little about Qutban, he dedicated his romance to his cultivated but politically defeated patron Husain Shah Sharqi (1458–1505), ruler of the regional sultanate of Jaunpur. The world in which he lived was dominated by the intensely local struggles between Husain Shah Sharqi and the Lodi sultans of Delhi for control over Awadh and Jaunpur. Nothing of this struggle appears in Qutban's literary fantasy, which relates the story of a handsome Prince who goes on a quest for a beautiful magic doe. As we shall see, the quest for this elusive object of desire is structured through the contrasted narrative options of *yoga* and *bhoga*, asceticism and sensual pleasure. Qutban's narrative of the ascetic quest of the Prince of Candragiri draws on motifs found also in the voyages of Sindbad the Sailor. The reinscription of the Arabic genre of the marvels of India in the adventures of the hero of the *Mirigāvatī* points to an ongoing exchange of narrative motifs between Indian and Islamic traditions of story-telling. These exchanges, couched in terms of the marvels and wonders encountered by travellers, allow us to investigate the complex ways in which narratives frame cross-cultural interactions and make them represent larger ideological purposes. Multiple uses of the same set of motifs demonstrate the links of fiction with the historical processes of trade and cultural encounter. These allow us to place the heavily indigenized world of the Hindavi narratives within the Islamicate world-system that had evolved by the fifteenth century through the exchanges of gems, cloth, spices, and other merchandise through the trading networks of the Indian Ocean.

The fictional universes of the Hindavi Sufi romances, set in exotic locales like Serendib or the City of Gold (Kancanpur), are constructed out of well-known sequences of narrative motifs in the various story-telling traditions in the languages surrounding the Indian Ocean. There was always a trade in stories that went along with the mercantile, sometimes even martial, encounters among cultures in this Islamicate world-system. The Hindavi Sufi romances share in this historical moment to the degree that their own distinctive narrative formula is constructed out of a patchwork of Sanskrit, Persian, and regional motifs and conventions. The second surviving romance of the genre, Qutban's *Mirigāvatī*, was completed in 1503, probably at the court of the defeated sultan of Jaunpur, the musically talented and literate Husain Shah Sharqi. A key figure in the transmission of classical musical traditions, he was also the generous patron, despite his circumstances in exile in Bihar, who enabled many artists, poets, and musicians to ply their respective crafts. The unique narrative formula of the Hindavi Sufi romance that is created by Qutban's adoption of Da'ud's distinctive pattern more than a hundred years after 1379 has three distinctive features. First, the plot moves through the arousal and deferment of desire, drawing the reader along with the hero to a narrative, aesthetic, and erotic consummation. Second, the hero and heroine are usually presented with narrative options such as the different kinds of love: lustful, sacred, violent, and so on. They have to choose to accept or to fight with these options in order that the plot may proceed. Third, characters frequently exemplify abstract qualities such as love, wisdom, mystical absorption, and spiritual guidance.

To begin the historical placement of the Sultanate of Jaunpur at a specific moment, it will be seen that the invasion of Timur in 1398 was a fatal blow to the centralized Tughluq state that had evolved up to the end of the fourteenth century. After the eclipse of Tughluq power in the fifteenth century, the Saiyid and Lodi sultans of Delhi could not assume even a titular sovereignty over the rulers, landholders, and *iqṭā'dārs* of the different regions of northern, central, and eastern India. Pre-eminent among the sultanates of the east was the Sharqi kingdom of Jaunpur, founded in the 1390s by Malik Sarwar, a eunuch or *khwājah-sarā* in the service of Sultan Firuz Shah Tughluq. Appointed custodian of the town of Jaunpur, he played an important part in the succession disputes following Firuz Shah's death in 1388 and eventually consolidated his own position as ruler of Jaunpur. His successors through an adoptive son, Malik Mubarak, strengthened the realm and ruled the region as independent sultans till the accession in 1458 of Husain Shah Sharqi, who involved himself in a protracted and ill-fated struggle to conquer Delhi from the Lodi sultans, Bahlol (1451–89) and Sikandar (1489–1517).[10] Husain Shah Sharqi was dethroned by Bahlol Lodi's capture of Jaunpur in 1483, and fled to a small enclave in the town of Chunar in Bihar. Despite repeated campaigns against Sikandar Lodi, Bahlol's successor, Husain Shah, could not dislodge the Lodi forces from Jaunpur. He was later given Colgong or Kahalganv in Bhagalpur district in Bihar by the Bengal sultan 'Ala al-Din Husain Shah, and he had coins bearing his name issued until his death in 1505.[11]

The establishment of regional sultanates such as Malwa, Gujarat, Jaunpur, Bengal, and the Deccani states had as a necessary corollary the development of new regional cultures. As the Turks and Afghans adapted enthusiastically to the north Indian cultural landscape, they invented regional artistic and literary styles out of the Islamicate culture of the Delhi Sultanate and local languages and aesthetic media. Husain Shah Sharqi himself was a poet and a noted patron of the distinctive Sharqi style of architecture. He was also an accomplished musician, credited with the creation of Raga Jaunpuri, the various Syams, and four different versions of the morning Raga Todi in north Indian classical music.[12] Husain Shah was a key figure in the recreation and transmission of Indian music. He provided a model for other cultured rulers such as Raja Man Singh Tomar (1468–1517) of Gwalior. Raja Man Singh collected all the new melodies and techniques of singing and music-making invented at the courts of Delhi and the regional sultanates in his *Māna* ('The Curiosity of Man Singh'). Later musicians and theorists drew extensively on the *Māna Kutūhala*, which was accepted as an authoritative source on the musical theory and practice that had evolved in the courtly artistic, literary, and performative cultures of the various regional Indian sultanates that followed the more centralized Delhi Sultanate. Indeed, the tradition of singing Hindavi lyrics in the *khayāl* style (rather than the more sombre *dhrupad* style, derived from Indian temple chants) can be traced back to Husain Shah's complex and creative part in the history of Indian music.[13] Qutban, a poet attached to Husain Shah's court in exile, dedicated the *Mirigāvatī* to him in 1503. Little is known about Qutban except that he was a disciple of Shaikh Buddhan Suhrawardi, whom he mentions as his spiritual preceptor in the prologue to the *Mirigāvatī*.

The identity of Shaikh Buddhan, whose name means simply 'the eldest one', is a matter of some controversy. S.A.A. Rizvi notes that Shaikh Buddhan was 'the disciple of Shaikh Muhammad Isa Taj of Jaunpur. Although Shaikh Isa Taj was a distinguished Chishti, Shaikh Buddhan seems to have been initiated into both the Chishtiyya and Suhrawardiyya orders.'[14] S.M. Pandey has suggested that Qutban was affiliated to a Chishti Shaikh Buddhan, a 'great musician, [who] lived during the time of Husain Shah Sharqi in Barnawa in Meerut district near Delhi'.[15] Barnawa's proximity to Delhi places the town in the direct path of the invading armies of the Lodis and the Sharqis, far too dangerous a place to set up a hospice. Additionally, Shaikh Buddhan Chishti (d. 1497) is known to have had musical contests with his patron Husain Shah, who lived in Bihar rather than next to the Lodi sultans in Delhi. Shaikh Buddhan's solely Chishti affiliation, moreover, makes Qutban's discipleship with him an unlikely possibility.[16] In any case, Qutban drew on the mystical ideas common to both the Chishtis and the Suhrawardis in his romance, as well as on the generic model of the *Cāndāyan* of Maulana Da'ud.

Although no other extensive Hindavi romances by Muslim authors survive from the period, the popularity of the *Cāndāyan* in the fifteenth century is attested to by the discourses of a later Chishti shaikh, 'Abd al-Quddus Gangohi (1456–1537). According to the account given in his son Rukn al-Din Quddusi's hagiographical *Laṭā'if-i Quddūsī*, the Shaikh began a translation of *Cāndāyan* into Persian verse couplets in his youth and completed a substantial portion of it.[17] As the *Laṭā'if-i Quddūsī* asserts, a partial motivation for the translation was the absence of an account of the Prophet's ascension to heaven (*mi'rāj*) in Da'ud's text. However, the handwritten manuscript of the translation was destroyed (*faut shud*) in the military campaigns and counter-campaigns of sultans Bahlol Lodi and Husain Shah Sharqi. Perhaps as a result of this war Qutban's narrative does not open with the topos of the *nagara-varṇana*, a description of the idyllic town where the poet is sheltered in a political utopia by his princely patron. Instead, the story revolves around two contrasting narrative options, yoga and bhoga, asceticism and sensual pleasure. The Prince of Candragiri, whose name is literally 'Prince', Raj Kunvar, sees a seven-coloured magic doe while out hunting in the forest and wants to capture her. When he follows her he sees that she sinks deep into a lake and disappears. The poet describes this lake as the site of the flash of divine manifestation (*tajallī*), where Mirigavati and her band of heavenly nymphs come to play. The interplay between yoga and bhoga structures a plot in which episode after episode describes the near-death experiences of the Prince in his effort to convert into love the desire (*kāma/shauq*) which has been aroused in him by his vision of Mirigavati.

Before the transformation of desire into the rasa of love is set in motion, however, there is an Islamic prologue that contains a much more developed set of Hindavi theological terms than does the earlier *Cāndāyan.* Although the first folios of all the available manuscripts of the text seem to be damaged, the critical edition of D.F. Plukker reconstructs the first few lines, which describe an Islamic metaphysics:

> O Singular Sound, invisible Creator,
> you stay, at play, in the whole world.
> Unseen, beyond taint, you cannot be seen.
> Whoever sees you in the form of light
> forgets himself. Absolute God,
> perfected one, highest divinity,
> you do not take man's form, nor woman's.
> God does not have mother, father,
> nor kinsmen. One alone, God has
> no match or second. [M 1][18]

The terms used here for the formless, ungendered, attribute-less divinity translate Islamic theology effectively into Hindavi. The term *ekoṃkāra*, the 'Singular Sound' or Om, translates the Arabic word with which Allah began the creation of the universe. Allah said *'kun!'* ('Be!'), and creation was set into motion (*'fayakun'*). The open form of the *nūn* in *kun* points to the open-endedness of creation, an ongoing process through which *kun* or Om, the *brahma-nāda* or divine sound, resonates. Absolute divinity (*parama brahma*) on the highest plane does not take on a gendered form, and the Qur'ānic notions of Allah's absolute divinity, unity, and peerlessness are transformed by Qutban into eloquent verse about Allah not having a mother, father, or brothers (*mātā pitā bandhu nahi koī*). The moving force within this metaphysic is desire, and in the phenomenal world, God's desire is echoed in created beings who wish to return to the source of their being. The first manifestation of divine essence, impelled by desire. is in the form of light (*joti sarūpa/nūr*), suggested through the flashingly beautiful image of the heroine's body.

The first manifestation of divine essence, in the form of light, is mentioned in the fourth verse of Qutban's prologue. The poet evokes the widespread notion of the Muhammadan light (*nūr-i Muḥammadī*):

First He created the light of Muhammad,
Then, afterwards, He made everything for his sake.
For his sake, He manifested himself,
And created Śiva and Śakti in two bodies...
The one who repeats God's name in his heart,
Is liberated and gains the throne of Indra. [M 4]

Here Qutban expresses Ibn 'Arabi's major idea of the 'reality of Muhammad' (*ḥaqīqat-i Muḥammadiyya*), the first refraction of light from the divine. The world is created because Allah is a 'hidden treasure' who longs to be known, and this desire brings into existence first the 'reality' of Muhammad, then all other things in their turn. The moving force within this metaphysic is desire, and in the phenomenal world, Allah's desire is echoed in created beings who wish to return to the source of their being. Qutban goes on to approximate the creation of men and women as Śiva and Śakti, the two bodies or genders. Note that here an elaborate local mythology of godhead is being shorn of its overtly Śaiva superstructure and refitted into an Indian Islamic framework. Similarly, he makes the throne of Indra the ultimate spiritual reward for reciting the words of faith. The strategy is characteristic of the Hindavi Sufi poets, who use Indian myth, religion, and literary and social convention freely, yet with a distinctive slant. They are thus fully part of an Indian cultural landscape, indigenized yet competing with other groups to articulate their distinctive theology.

In their mystical poems, this seductive divinity is represented by the heroine's body. In Qutban's text, the heavenly nymph Mirigavati, who has seen the Prince hunting, desires him and reveals herself in the shape of a magic doe to make him desire and follow her. While on his hunt, the Prince sees far off in the distance the glimmering shade of a seven-coloured doe, and decides to follow it. The doe lures him on, but then disappears into a magic lake in the forest:

He saw in the distance a seven-coloured doe,
such as he had never seen in his life.
He said, 'That cannot possibly be a doe,
born with a skin so marvellous!
All the omaments it wears are of gold
and it walks like a beautiful woman.'
Seeing the astonishing marvel in the distance, the Prince spurred on his horse.
He thought, 'Should I kill it with an arrow? Or dismount and capture it by force?' [M 19]

The Prince dismounts and follows her on foot, thinking 'If only I could approach her! I'll die if I cannot capture the beautiful doe.' [M 20] But the doe skips away and evades him, until they are separated from the company of hunters:

> The Prince and the doe were alone in the forest.
> No third person observed them there.
> The Prince was enraptured, in love with the doe,
> his intelligence was forgotten, all sense fled his body.
> He saw a great green tree in the forest,
> with a clear pure lake flowing beneath it.
> The doe was frightened when the Prince drew near.
> She sank into the waters of the lake.
> She hid herself in the pure water,
> and would not come out again at all.
> The Prince tied his horse to the tree, disrobed, and left his clothes on the shore.
> He jumped into the pure lake quickly, hoping to find the vision he had seen. [M 21]

The elusive doe is Mirigavati, who awakens in the Prince a desire that overpowers his mind and heart and does not allow him any peace. This narrative motif echoes, of course, the famous golden hind that lured Rama away while Ravana abducted Sita, and shows how entwined the Sufi poets were with the non-Sufi local traditions, both religious and literary.

At this flash-point of desire, it is important to realize that the plot's impulse is towards consummation through a series of narrative incidents that delay the satisfaction of desire until the seeker is purified. The moment of desire is the initial arousal in the series of deferrals that are implied by the Sufi idea of ordinate love, in which each object of desire is loved for the sake of one higher to it, all the way up to God. Desire for the magic doe is an external force that seizes the lover in its cruel grip, and, characteristically, it is entwined with the widespread Sufi notion of annihilation, or *fanā*—the Prince exclaims that he will die if he does not gain the doe. When he searches for the beautiful shimmering form he has seen, however, he cannot find her. Although the Prince jumps into the lake to find her, she disappears completely, and he is left lamenting. The poet uses a visual technique reminiscent of miniature painting to depict the Prince's sense-numbing grief at losing the magic doe:

> He longed and looked only for his love.
> The Prince leant against the green tree and wept.
> He cried like a spring cloud in Bhadon
> and the world was filled with his liquid tears.
> Clouds came massing out in the sky,
> great and small, and filled the heavens.

The world was darkened by the tide of his tears.
His eyes rained constantly, never stopping,
like clouds in the season of rains.
He prayed, 'God, give me wings,
that I may fly wherever I hear she lives.' [M 23]

Playing with poetic opposites, the poet describes the Prince as burning with longing, yet bringing on a monsoon flood in the world through his tears. He sits weeping inconsolably like a spring cloud by the lake, where his companions find him under a tree that glitters like a royal canopy. The shimmering lake by which he sits is the purifier of sins and of those who drink from it, and many lush images are used to describe it: black bees hover over its white lotuses, drunk with love, and lovely fragrances pervade the atmosphere from its camphor and khus-scented water. The Prince will not return to court with them, and sits by the lake meditating on the vision he has seen.

When the company returns to court and informs the Prince's father, the entire town comes out to the forest to reason with the Prince. The Prince will not return and instead wants a boon. He asks his father the King to build him a seven-levelled red and gold palace around the shining lake. The King assents, and craftsmen, painters, architects, and goldsmiths arrive to construct the fantastic gold-encrusted palace that will encompass within its painted and sculpted form the formless absolute, which has flashed in the Prince's eyes. The palace has seven levels, with four-coloured steps on all four sides. Over them stretches a gold and red *caukhaṇḍī* or four-cornered pavilion that is painted with scenes from the *Rāmāyaṇa* and the *Mahābhārata.* Interlaced through them are depictions of the golden doe that has affected the Prince so severely. He keeps looking at the golden doe and weeping. His nurse (*dhāī*), a character standing for a Sufi pir or spiritual guide in these narratives, comes to him to ask what is wrong.

Although at first he cannot respond to his nurse because his mind and heart are concentrated on the golden doe, he describes his sorrow through the seasons of the year in an abbreviated form of the *bārah-māsā*, or 'song of the twelve months.'[19] In the dark nights of the season of rains, he cannot sleep because of the lightning flashing in his eyes, an elusive flickering of divine essence that he cannot catch. In the winter, the fire of separation (*viraha agni*) keeps him wailing with its intensity all night. The Prince's fire sears winter itself, the personification of cold, and covers the season with ashes. The cold retreats to a distance of twenty *kosas* from the Prince, and the earth becomes green again. Summer comes, and the month of Jeth, but the fire burning in the Prince's body does not subside. He burns constantly, like a smouldering ember, and sandal paste does not cool his agony. He stays on by the lakeside, ignoring all human company, oblivious to all but the desire that has him in its grip.

After a year, seven heavenly nymphs come to play in the magic lake, all of them perfect in their beauty, each like the full moon on the fourteenth night. Fairest among them is Mirigavati, and they play about in the lake like the moon and all the constellations come down to earth. Mirigavati notices that there is a new palace there, and they are all amazed because not even the shadow of a human has ever fallen on the place. The Prince is struck dumb with their beauty, losing his fair colour and turning to a blackened cinder with longing for the vision he has been granted. When he rushes forward to catch Mirigavati, the entire group of lotus-faced nymphs flies away to heaven. He lies stricken by the lakeside, with no one intelligent enough to give him what he needs to alleviate his condition, 'words full of *rasa*, a love story that would awaken him' [M 48]. His nurse or spiritual guide comes again to him, revives him with nectar (*amṛta*), and makes him sit up in her arms. For him, his nurse is like his mother, since she eases his transformation and rebirth into a life with love. To her he confides the vision that has flashed in his eyes like lightning, using the generic set-piece of the *sarāpā*, or head-to-foot, description of Mirigavati.

The Prince's vision uses the language of analogy to describe the unrepresentable divine essence in bodily form, to suggest 'what cannot be spoken' through poetic imagery:

> I saw that which cannot be spoken,
> and desire burnt my mind from within...
> The sun rose blinding in the east,
> and I could not distinguish her features.
> Lightning flashed in my eyes, and I broke all controls and restraints!
> Let me describe that beauty: the parting in her hair, her breasts, and her hands and feet. [M 49]

From the parting in Mirigavati's hair, described as a line of cranes against a dark monsoon cloud, to her cruel black-tipped breasts, and her golden limbs dusted with vermillion, love's inventory suggests in her divine form both Allah's might and majesty (*jalāl*) and His gentle grace (*jamāl*). The nurse is sympathetic to the severe physiological effects of this revelation on the Prince, and advises him on how to go about obtaining the golden doe.

She is confident that the nymphs will return to the lake for the religious observance of breaking their fast on the 'waterless' eleventh fast day of the summer month of Jeth. On that occasion, she tells him, he must steal Mirigavati's sari, and she will be in his power. Here Qutban employs a motif that occurs frequently in folk and fairy-tales, the story of the Swan Maiden who can be overpowered by robbing her of her swan coat.[20] This narrative motif, which occurs in Indian folk-tales as the seduction or wooing of a bathing girl by stealing her clothes, is found in stories from Kashmir to the south and in the Assam hills,[21] as well as in the mythology of Krishna and the bathing cowgirls. The use of formulaic sequences of action makes us insist on their completion, much like the Prince whose mind and heart have been captivated by the magic doe and who waits by the lakeside faithfully for her return. When the eleventh day of Jeth dawns, Mirigavati is drawn irresistibly to the lake in the forest. She persuades her fellow nymphs to fly there with her. They do so, and the Prince is again dazzled by the play of lights. Like Pururavas with Urvaśi, the Prince runs away with Mirigavati's sari while she is in the water. She cannot now return with her friends.

He brings her to the palace and lives with her, feasting his eyes on her beauty but unable to consummate his desire. He pleads with her, invoking the shadowy form of the doe in which she first appeared to him:

> 'On the day you showed me the shadow of the doe,
> you brought the noose of love to trap me!' [M 81]

But even though he has captured her in return and they live in the painted palace by the magic lake, they do not make love. When he reaches out his hand to touch her breasts through her necklaces, Mirigavati delays the satisfaction of his desire yet again. She invokes her aristocratic status and uses rasa to argue that violence cannot bring love's fulfillment:

> Mirigavati said, 'O Prince, control yourself!
> I will tell you something, if you will follow it!
> You are a King's son, and desire me,
> but I am of noble birth myself.
> Stop, I tell you, listen to me,
> just let my girlfriends arrive.
> Force does not count; only through *rasa*
> can you enjoy the savour of love.
> Then that will count as true love
> within this world and the hereafter.
> *Rasa* cannot be enjoyed through violence,
> it is a savour which only comes through *rasa*
> If you talk of enjoying *rasa,* I have told you gently what *rasa* means.
> Only those who are coloured with *rasa* can savour it now or hereafter.'
> [M 86]

Mirigavati's description of rasa not only stays the Prince's hand but also emphasizes the narrative necessity of the earned transformation of desire into the savour of love. Earning love can be a protracted and painful process, one that will involve much self-mortification and serve as the basis for the extension of the story through many episodes. Rasa involves the interplay of asceticism and pleasure before love is gained: the bliss that is promised by Mirigavati's revelation of herself at the magic lake needs to be earned by the Prince through asceticism before their mutual desire can be consummated.

One day the Prince's generous father, who dotes on the Prince and has given many gifts to Mirigavati as her father-in-law, sends a message to the Prince asking him to visit the royal court. Despite adverse omens, the Prince rides out, and in his absence the nurse is left to look after Mirigavati, who confuses the nurse by telling her far-fetched stories and sagas, and then sends her on an errand. Mirigavati then finds her magic sari and puts it on. When the nurse returns, she cannot see the nymph anywhere. Finally, she happens to look up and sees Mirigavati perched on a roofbeam outside the palace. Before flying off, Mirigavati tells the nurse that the Prince will have to work hard to earn what he has so far enjoyed through tricking and constraining the doe. The town over which her father rules is Kancanpur, the City of Gold, and she instructs the nurse to tell the Prince that he can find her there. Love does not work through force or violence, but through the cultivation of a sympathetic understanding among lovers, Sufis, and listeners—an understanding that can appreciate the suggestive ambiguity of reference in the poetic imagery. Rasa is the basis for a textual erotics in which the ideal reader, the Sufi practitioner, and the hero of the love-story must all transform their subjectivity to become sensitive to *prema*. The passion for meaning in the narrative dynamics of *Mirigāvati* means transforming desire, aroused by/in the poem, into the savour of prema or *'ishq*.

Here, another aspect of plot and the formulaic nature of this fantasy world comes into focus: the larger narrative design for the structure of the story entailed by the generic model of Da'ud's *Cāndāyan*. This involves the hero's accomplishment of his quest by leaving the world as a yogi and the conflict between the two wives who represent this world and the hereafter. And here Qutban does not disappoint his audience. When the Prince returns to the magic lake, he is devastated, and he and the nurse consider the future. The poet introduces asceticism as the necessary means of transformation: 'Now he worried about yoga and tantra. Pleasure ran away, hearing of the onset of ascetic rigour.'[M 105] Here Qutban brings into the foreground the contrasted narrative options of yoga and bhoga.

The Prince's period of closeness to the object of his desire is over, and now he must work his way towards the golden city, Kancanpur. He puts on a yogi's guise, with all the accoutrements of the Gorakhnath *panth*: the matted locks, the basil-bead rosary, the stick, the begging-bowl, and the deerskin on which to meditate. As the poet puts it:

> Wisdom, virtue, asceticism, prayer, and absorption only take you so far—
> when that sly crooked glance meets your eyes, you are lost! [M 108]

The Prince-turned-yogi is similarly lost in love. The object of his meditation is not yogic immortality, but the beautiful Mirigavati. He sets off singing of his pain in separation from his love, accompanying himself with his stringed *kingarī*.

On the Prince's journey of self-transformation, he goes through a series of ordeals. Qutban structures the Prince's quest by referring to particular virtues that the hero has to acquire, so that each ordeal has a specific suggestive valence. Each is designed to test the Prince in some particular Sufi virtue such as chastity, trust in God, or the power of rigorous meditation. On his travels, he first comes to a kingdom whose king is deeply moved by his song. He loses consciousness because of the power of the Prince's words, and the audience is entranced. When the king recovers, he wants to reward the singing ascetic with much wealth and a beautiful wife, but the only thing the Prince wants is news of Kancanpur. The king sends for a famous ascetic who knows the way to Kancanpur. Even though the ascetic protests that it is a difficult path, full of dark forests haunted by ghouls and man-eating demons, impassable oceans, and inaccessible roads, the Prince is not daunted. If he dies on the difficult path of asceticism, he says, he will attain spiritual perfection (*siddhi*). He has no life to lose, because prema has taken his life away. The sage is moved by compassion, and leads him to a dark seashore with a boat moored at it, which is the only way to Kancanpur.

In order to take this road, the Prince has to remember God (the Sufi *dhikr*) and rid himself of fear. Only if he proves himself absolutely fearless will he reach the farther shore. As he climbs in and begins to row, the sea's waves begin to rock the boat more and more furiously. All at once he is in the grip of a fierce whirlpool. The boat is about to sink, but the Prince concentrates his attention and prays to God to release him from the whirlpool. A huge wave rears up and washes him ashore, saving his life. On the shore he notices a great mountain, and two men come to greet him. They are bound on the same path as the Prince, but the mountain in the distance has no *ghāṭ*, or landing place at which to dock a boat. They inform him that the shore they are on is the lair of a vicious serpent that comes there daily in search of a man to eat. The Prince is afraid and begins to weep, but then remembers Mirigavati and her sorrow should he be killed. He recovers himself and begins to pray to God, and while he is doing so the serpent appears. The Prince feels happy to die for love, but by God's grace another serpent appears and begins to fight with the first one. While they are locked in combat, another great wave sweeps the two out to sea, and sweeps the Prince on his boat to the mountain. Saved from death for the second time, the Prince leaves his boat on the mountainside and heads on to Kancanpur.

On his quest he comes to a mango grove with mangoes sweet as nectar hanging from its trees and a matchless palace built within their shade. When the Prince goes up to the palace, he discovers in it a lovely young woman, as beautiful as a half-open lotus imprisoned in a lake of nectar. Here the second wife, who is characteristic of the love-triangles of the genre, is introduced. The young woman's name is Rupmini, and she tells him she is held there in captivity by an evil demon who has terrorized the town over which her father rules, allegorically named Subudhya, the 'City of Intelligence'. The demon demanded the sacrifice of the young princess, and her parents agreed in order to save the town. Rupmini is terrified that the demon will eat her up, but the Prince tells her not to worry. He promises to save her with 'a pure mind'. Suddenly the ferocious demon appears, ready to fight. He has fourteen arms and seven heads, and attacks the Prince. The Prince shoots his *cakra* or sharp-edged steel discus at him seven times, decapitating a head at each throw, and the demon falls dead. Rupmini guesses that he is no yogi and extracts the story of his love for Mirigavati from him.

The Prince tells her all and escorts her home, but refuses to marry her or to touch her in a carnal way. Rupmini's father, however, is delighted at the eligible bridegroom who seems to have appeared from heaven and offers him his daughter's hand in marriage and half his kingdom. The Prince refuses, for he is a yogi and has no desire for earthly things. He informs the king that he has given up the path of bhoga, or sensual pleasure. The king is enraged and puts him in prison, promising him release on the condition that he marry Rupmini. Against his will, he agrees, but does not consummate the marriage because he wishes to keep his love chaste and spiritual. Although Rupmini is burning with desire for him, he whiles away the nights with her in making sweet excuses and keeping himself chaste. In Subudhya, the City of Intelligence, he keeps his own mind pure, despite the temptations of the marriage bed.

The Prince has now conquered fear and lust, but still does not know the way to Kancanpur. He has a guest-house built for wandering ascetics and *sādhūs,* and asks all who pass if they know the way. A great company of ascetics comes in, bound for the banks of the Godavari river, and they inform him that Kancanpur is quite far from there. One of the band of wandering adepts advises him:

'The City of Gold is quite far from here.
Between us and that city, there lies
a deep ocean and a plaintain forest,
like a blind well with no way out.
If you walk steadily you'll gain the path, but only if you walk in truth.
If you are true, truth will be your friend, and the lions and tigers will not eat you.' [M 158]

The adept's words lay out the path for the Prince, using coded language from the esoteric yogic poetry ascribed to Gorakhnath. In his *Gorakhbānī*, the dry or 'blind well' (*andhā kuān*) refers to the place of nectar in the microcosmic subtle body,[22] while the plaintain forest (*kadalī vana*) refers to a place of ascetic mortification.

The Prince accepts his guidance by taking the adept's yogic garb. He seizes his chance to escape while on a hunt outside the bounds of the town. He abandons his horse and princely attire, and puts on the adept's clothes. He walks away from his virgin wife and into the dark forest. He wanders round and round seeking a path out of the forest, but in order to reach there, he has to acquire another spiritual value, the ability to keep to the path of truth (*ḥaqīqat/sat*). His steps falter in the dense shades of the trees, and he walks a long way, constantly meditating on his love. When he finally gives up all and trusts to God (the Sufi quality of *tavakkul*), he reaches the end of the forest and sees before him the sunlit slopes of a sunlit country.

He sees flocks of goats and sheep grazing on the grassy slopes before him, and thanks God because he has come to an inhabited land. A herdsman is grazing the flock, and he comes up and offers hospitality to the yogi. The herdsman leads him to the cave that is his home, and the Prince follows unsuspectingly. Once the Prince is inside, the herdsman rolls a huge rock across the entrance and traps him inside just as Polyphemos does to the wandering Odysseus in Homer's *Odyssey*.[23] The Prince looks around him and sees a number of other prisoners in the cave. They are all extremely fat, and cannot walk, or even crawl, because of their size. On questioning them he finds that they have all been fed a drug-like herb by the herdsman, and that has made them so fat as to incapacitate them. They warn him that the herdsman is a cannibal, and that he should not accept the drug from him if he wishes to stay alive. The Prince is distressed, but realizes that losing his life on the path of truth will gain him spiritual perfection, that the quality of sat will lead to siddhi. He concentrates on *sat,* praying and mentioning the name of truth in his Sufi *dhikr*, trusting to God to release him from the herdsman's cave.

Just then the herdsman comes in, catches one of the imprisoned men, and bangs his body against the cave floor to kill him. He roasts the man and eats him up, chewing up even the hard parts of his body. The Prince is terrified. The herdsman belches in content, and goes to sleep after his meal. The Prince puts a pointed pair of metal tongs in the fire to heat them. When the tongs are red hot, he takes them out and puts them into the herdsman's eyes, blinding him instantly. The herdsman screams in agony, but since he is blind he cannot catch the Prince. He vows revenge, however, and sits by the cave mouth to prevent the Prince's escape, like the Cyclops in the Greek epic. The deadlock continues for three days, but finally the Prince thinks of a stratagem. He kills one of the largest he-goats in the herd, skins it, and dries the skin. Then he puts it on, and, when the cannibal herdsman releases his herd for grazing, the Prince slips out among the goats and sheep. The herdsman feels the back of each animal to make sure it is not a man, but does not feel underneath. When he comes to the Prince he is suspicious, but the Prince runs out before he can stop him. He continues on his way, vowing not to trust anyone but God, and praying to God to unite him with his beloved.

The appearance of this Homeric narrative motif in a sixteenth-century Hindavi romance suggests a deep and long set of narrative interactions between the story-telling traditions of the Indian Ocean. Even though the fiction of an imaginary world can be set apart from the author's historical and social world, the narrative motifs woven into its formulaic pattern have a history of their own and reinscribe larger historical processes within the landscape of fantasy. The fantasy world of *Mirigāvatī* is part of a regional indigenous tradition with its own poetics and politics, but the region itself is part of a larger Islamicate world in which stories, people, and merchandise travel. Movements of people, in K.N. Chaudhuri's phrase, involve the 'exchange of ideas, economic systems, social usage, political institutions, and artistic traditions.'[24] While we have so far taken for granted that narrative motifs are common to many traditions and consequently have widespread appeal, they also have a history of their own and occur in unexpected places. Nowhere is the process of cultural exchange more vivid than in the accounts of the marvels and wonders found in new places by travellers. The movements of scholars, Sufis, traders, and travellers through the familiar and less familiar parts of the world known to the Arabs engendered not just travel narratives, but also geographies, nautical guides, and accounts of the marvels found in the lands and oceans stretching from India to China.

The sense of the marvellous, that which causes astonishment (*'ajab*), can be construed both as an imaginative escape from the humdrum and as a mark of cultural encounter and exchange. I have demonstrated elsewhere that the cannibalistic herdsman and the hero's encounter with him constitute a narrative sequence of events that can be traced back first to the voyages of Sindbad the Sailor in the *Arabian Nights*, then to the tales of the marvels of the India and China seas reported by the Arab sailors when they returned to the port-cities of Basra and Baghdad.[25] Further, these story-motifs can be traced back even to Sanskrit tale-collections and the story of Sanudasa, the merchant in an eighth-century Nepali Sanskrit recension of the *Kathā-Sarit-Sāgara* ('The Ocean of the Streams of Story'). The travels and appropriations of these motifs is part of the larger cultural world of the Indian Ocean, in which composite artistic and literary forms are created from elements drawn from multiple traditions.

The subsequent creation of imaginative literature seems to demonstrate what Henry James posited as a general attribute of romance: 'experience disengaged, disembroiled, disencumbered, exempt from the conditions that we normally know to attach to it and ... relieves it ... of the inconvenience of a related, a measurable state, a state subject to all our vulgar communities.'[26] In a sense, these fantasies liberated readers and listeners from the bounds of ordinary experience and allowed them to travel to faraway lands and unlikely places populated by wondrous beasts and beings. Although they were bounded by an overarching sense of a cosmic and natural order overshadowed by God, the marvels and wonders of creation stretched the limits of the imagination and of what James calls 'all our vulgar communities.'

Similarly, as the geographical accounts and cosmographies of Arab writers grew more elaborate, they ventured more into the realms of fantasy and imaginative literature. 'The taste for the fantastic was so pronounced in the medieval Arab world', writes critic and historian Robert Irwin, 'that it spawned a distinctive genre of literature, that of *aja'ib* (marvels), and books were written on the marvels of Egypt, of India and of the cosmos as a whole. Such books were hugger-mugger compilations of improbable information about the stupendous monuments of antiquity, strange coincidences, the miraculous powers of certain plants, stones, animals, and feats of magic. Many of the marvels first found in 'non-fiction' works on cosmography eventually made their way into the *Nights*. The Sindbad cycle, which is a fictional reworking of mariners' yarns about the wonders to be found in the Indian and China seas (among them the wak-wak tree with its human-headed fruit, the Old Man of the Sea and the fish as large as an island), is the most obvious example of this process'.[27] The sense of astonishment over the radically different, as well as over the stupendous and magical, is a state that comes to a person 'at the time of that person's ignorance of the *sabab* (cause) of something.'[28] Amazement is frequently accompanied by a formulaic affirmation of Allah as the supreme creator of all things found in the universe. Marvels are thus fitted into the totalizing frame of the divine will that is expressed through creation, signs of wonder that make humans aware of Allah's omnipotence.

To return to our wandering Prince, we find that his final adventure on his ascetic quest involves ingenious mechanical devices, or automata. These devices, familiar to readers of the *Kathā-Sarit-Sāgara* and the *Arabian Nights*, mark out a place of enchantment and great danger in the story of *Mirigāvatī*. The Prince arrives at a moonlit palace built by magic where he sees a wondrous sight. Four doves appear in the palace, twisting about and then turning into four beautiful women. They speak a mantra, and beds appear and walk up to them. The beds are made ready for sleep without any human hands. Another mantra is spoken, and four dancing peacocks appear. They turn into men and sit on the beds with the women, laughing and flirting and spending the night in pleasure. After four watches of the night have gone by, a runner appears to them and reports that the herdsman has been blinded. The Prince realizes that they are connected with the evil cannibal, and flees in terror. He runs as far and as fast as he can. Finally he reaches a shady tree, and sits under it considering what to do next. He has passed through five near-death experiences, and proved himself as a seeker by purifying himself of fear and lust and holding to the path of truth and trust in God.

As he sits there in puzzlement, the scene shifts to Mirigavati , who has returned to Kancanpur after her stay with the Prince. Her girlfriends flock to her to ask about her absence, and she explains her capture by the Prince and reaffirms the value of true love and the necessity of mystical annihilation:

'Only he understands the taste of love,
who can wipe himself out on the quest.
Talking doesn't give you the joy of love's savour—
only the one who gives his life can enjoy it.
Love is a high, inaccessible fortress,
only a madman tries to conquer it without sorrow!
The one who wants to play the game of love
must first stake his head, have no regard for his life.' [M 194]

Here sensual pleasure and asceticism are subordinate to the value of mystical love, which is entwined with the common Sufi notion of annihilation of self (*fanā*). And although the Prince is still not quite there, Mirigavati will test him further when he gets to Kancanpur. While he is struggling to reach his goal, Mirigavati's father passes away and she becomes Queen of Kancanpur.

Meanwhile the puzzled Prince is still seated under his shady tree. Appropriately enough, it is narrative itself which resolves his dilemma. The Prince overhears two birds talking on the branch above him. They tell a tale within a tale, of a Prince who has turned into a yogi for love of Mirigavati. The birds foretell that not many days of sorrow remain for the Prince, and he rejoices to hear the news. When they fly from the branch, he follows them, and they lead him finally to Kancanpur. It is a golden city surrounded by a paradisaical garden planted with many flowering and fragrant trees, including mango orchards irrigated by continuously running water-wheels. He asks a beautiful woman filling water at a well the name of the town, and rejoices to learn that he has reached Kancanpur, the kingdom ruled by Mirigavati.

When our travel-weary ascetic goes within the walls, he is amazed to see all the houses gilded with gold leaf and encrusted with jewels; prosperous merchants sit in the town's great market. All sins fall away at the sight of that city, says the poet, and the yogi Prince advances through the streets to the door of the royal palace. There is a throng of aristocrats at the court, as well as many cultured and learned men. Everyone clamours for admission to the royal presence, and when the Prince sees the crowd he worries that he will not gain access to the object of his desire. He takes his stringed viol (*kingarī*) and begins the song of his separation. The town is in a tumult from the power of his song, and Mirigavati hears of the accomplished yogi who has arrived. She has him summoned to her presence. He leaps up the seven steps of her palace gate. Qutban cryptically suggests that each step has a different emotional valence or allegorical significance (*bhāva*), but leaves the specifics to the reader's imagination. The Prince crosses them and enters within to find Mirigavati enthroned like the shining moon, surrounded by handmaidens who appear like the Pleiades, or like night-lotuses blooming in a lake. The yogi cannot take another step, and falls unconscious in front of the divine vision.

Mirigavati doubts that he is a yogi, and tells her handmaidens to revive him by sprinkling water on him. When he comes to, they ask him the reason for his fainting away. He tells them that he has seen a vision beyond the bounds of reason or human capacity, and adds that their ruler is responsible for his state. They scold him and tell him that a lowly wanderer like him cannot ever aspire to their Queen. He laughs and replies that in the game of love, the stakes are high:

> 'Only the one who's burnt knows this pain.
> The lamp knows, whose body is flame.
> Whoever dies burning, lives on in death,
> and only he can drink the wine of love's *rasa*.
> Rare is the one who enjoys this *rasa*.
> Whoever gets it, becomes immortal!' [M 216]

These mystically charged words convince the handmaidens that he is a spiritually perfected being, and they suspect that he is the Prince who captured her at the magic lake. They speak to the Queen on his behalf. Although she has already divined his secret, she wishes to test him further. He tells her that she has stolen his heart, just as she has stolen her eyes from the doe, her voice from the koel, her waist from the lion, and her gait from the elephant.

She knows then that he is the Prince who had stolen her sari, and although she is happy to see him she threatens to execute him for his foolish talk. But he is not afraid, and only re-emphasizes that he has already lost his life to her, that he would only be liberated by dying on the path of love. After some more coquetry, she relents, and tells him to throw off his yogic garb—his quest has been successful. She is adorned with all the twelve ornaments (*bārah abharan*) for the night of union, and the palace is made ready in grand style. There are perfumes sprinkled everywhere, and illuminations and fireworks light the night sky.

At last, the Prince and Mirigavati sit together on their nuptial bed. He tells her the story of his quest, and she is moved by the troubles he has endured for her sake. The narrative options of asceticism and sensual pleasure come together as she allows him to taste the joys she has so far withheld:

> The black bee took all her fragrance
> and drank all the nectar of the great *rasa*.
> His heart's desire and thirst were at peace.
> All the sorrows and pains of his heart fled. [M 238]

After this the couple live happily together, enjoying each other's company, and Mirigavati offers him her throne and kingdom. The Prince takes on the trappings of royalty in place of his yogic garb. Royalty has been translated into asceticism and back, gaining the spiritual and mutually fulfilling love of Mirigavati on the way. Without, donning the yogic disguise and going on his quest, no Prince or King can attain the divine heroine of the story.

It must be emphasized that the poet does not hesitate to weave smaller formulaic motifs into the larger narrative design of the plot. One day Mirigavati is called to the wedding of a friend of hers, and she leaves the Prince in her palace with the warning that he can go everywhere in the palace except for one room. In an episode strikingly reminiscent of Bluebeard's castle[29] with gender roles reversed, the Prince is unable to resist the temptation. Inside the room is a large wooden chest, within which there is a *dānava* or demon. He pleads with the Prince to set him free, promising that he will serve him faithfully. The Prince does so, but the demon once released is a fierce evil ogre (*dānava*) who carries the Prince off and dashes him into a great gulf of the sea in order to kill him. When Mirigavati returns she is distraught at the loss of her besotted lover, and does not know where the ogre can have cast him down. Now the roles of seeker and sought on this quest are reversed, suggesting the Sufi interchangeability of lover and beloved, God and man. Mirigavati sets out in search of the Prince. By a fortuitous chance, the wind acts as a messenger between the two. It finds the Prince clinging precariously to life and informs Mirigavati, who rushes to him and rescues him. In a lovely set of poetic images, the two are compared to a bee and a lotus finally coming together.

The creative and skillful weaving of story motifs from various sources into the larger narrative design suggests the openness of the formula to multiple social and artistic concerns. Formulaic sets of motifs particular to given historical contexts can be open to usages for multiple social agendae. However, formulaic fictions also set up narrative patterns that form the generic expectations of their audiences and limit the innovations possible within the form. The formula that Qutban chooses to use is Da'ud's pattern of the hero with his two wives. Accordingly, he brings the plot to a close with a resolution of the Prince's unconsummated marriage with Rupmini. In his absence, she burns with the pain of separation, and spends her time on the ramparts of her palace looking for her lost love in the distance. She sees instead a caravan of traders, and sends a tearful message in the form of a *bārah-māsā*, a song describing her suffering through the twelve months of the year, through the leader of the caravan.

The Prince is full of remorse, and with Mirigavati and one of his two sons by her, he retraces his path to his father's kingdom. They leave the other son in charge of the kingdom. Finally they are reunited with Rupmini, and the three of them return to Candragiri where the Prince's father is King. The two wives fight, as in the *Cāndāyan*, but the Prince separates them from each other. He calms them down, sleeping with both of them in turn to satisfy their jealous desire. This happy romantic resolution, however, contains an unusual twist at the end. One day, the Prince goes out hunting in the forest, and gets into a fight with a tiger. Although he wounds the tiger, the beast is enraged and kills him in its own death-agony. The Prince dies, and the whole universe is saddened by his death. The entire kingdom mourns, and both Mirigavati and Rupmini fling themselves in anguish on his funeral pyre. The three of them burn to ashes, with love consummated, desire extinguished, and the narrative options of yoga and bhoga transformed into the rasa of love.

This narrative pattern might seem to indicate a certain fixity in the formulaic plots of the premākhyāns. As we have seen, the plot moves through the deferred and interrupted drive to pleasure, through the use of narrative options, and through embodying abstract functions as characters. Even though narrative desire and the desire represented in narrative carry the reader and the hero forward, the plot is also static in that it repeats the formula of the *Cāndāyan.* Without becoming an ascetic, no Prince or King can attain the divine heroine of the story. The hero has to have two warring wives between whom he has to make peace. Within this larger narrative design, however, Qutban's plot in *Mirigāvatī* shows a great deal of inventiveness in reinterpreting the formula. In formulaic literature, 'originality is to be welcomed only in the degree that it intensifies the expected experience without fundamentally altering it.'[30] As Cawelti notes in his study of formulaic fiction,

> Since the pleasure and effectiveness of an individual formulaic work depends on its intensification of a familiar experience, the formula creates its own world with which we become familiar by repetition. We learn in this way how to experience this imaginary world without continually comparing it with our own experience.[31]

The pleasure of entering this fantastic world can be maximized by the author's use of the most widespread and conventional social and narrative forms.

However, fantasy worlds are also linked to particular historical circumstances. Qutban's romance is a product of a world in which poets attached to Sufi *silsilas* wrote entertaining romances for kings and noblemen to underscore the superiority of their religious and poetic vision. If one thinks of how the sequence of events in the narrative is related to the social order, there is no single key explanation that would allow us to posit a homology between narrative and social form. The ending of *Mirigāvatī* depicts the annihilation of all the major characters. In terms of the Sufi logic of the story, the Sufi's relation with God and with the world has been resolved in this utopian ending in which two hostile co-wives have been brought into an amicable truce. Moreover, desire has been extinguished because the narrative and human worlds are eventually folded back into the divine essence, since the Sufi seeker has mortified his body and gained union with divinity. Royalty has been translated into asceticism and back, gaining the spiritual and mutually fulfilling love of Mirigavati on the way. The imaginal world can now be folded back into non-existence, echoing the annihilation of all things except God in Sufi schemes of the world's emergence from and return to God. What is being suggested here is that, in the creative imaginations of the Hindavi Sufi poets, the social and the narrative worlds are subordinate to the mysterious ways of the absolute invisible divinity that is the anchor of Sufi cosmology.

CONCLUSION

The romance may construct a fantasy world to liberate the imagination, but we must examine the fantasy within the historical circumstances of its articulation. As critics and readers, we must realize that for many cultures fantasy does not mean the hesitation between the real world and the imaginary one. The voyages of Sindbad, for whose marvels nineteenth-century positivistic western scholars even tried to find 'real' scientific and geographical analogues,[32] are a useful indicator of the ways in which mercantile and ideological purposes can be mixed with the experience of wonder. Sindbad's voyages and the travels of the yogi Prince appear in many unlikely and unexpected places, from Homer's *Odyssey* to the nineteenth-century versions of the *Arabian Nights*, from sailors' yarns in Basra and Baghdad to the ancient Indian tales of Sanudasa the Merchant. They have a place within the larger trajectory of the Indian Ocean trade that had already been going on for centuries before the Arabs came on the scene.

Placing our reading of this text, a romance based on the ascetic quest for a magic doe, in the context of the Islamicate world-system demonstrates that the creation of a generic formula shares in the larger logic of exchange and circulation that governed cultural interactions around the Indian Ocean. No single story-telling tradition was the source of the literary tradition of the Hindavi Sufi poets. Instead, a diversity of sources of story and a richness of literary imagination is evident in the cosmopolitan, ornate poetry of the period. This means, for students of Indian Islamic traditions, that both Muslims and non-Muslims fitted into the systemic shift entailed by the creation of the Islamicate world-system that was to change forever with the arrival of the Portuguese on the Malabar coast in the last decade of the fifteenth century. Before this later shift, the cultures around the Indian Ocean produced a fascinating and dazzling variety of composite artistic and literary forms, all multiplying themselves through a rich dialogue with diverse linguistic traditions.

This factor allows the formulaic plots of the Hindavi romances to be enjoyed by many different audiences, much like the Indian cinematic extravaganzas of the present day. Like these films, the generic formula of the Hindavi Sufi romances contains a set of easily predictable conventions and motifs. Originality consists of using the formula in new ways, but the basics remain the same: the hero's quest for self-transformation impelled by an initial dream, vision, or encounter, the use of abstract characters or narrative options in the progress of true love, the entwined articulation of erotics and asceticism in the service of an ideal of mystical love, and the use of an aesthetics of rasa that is reworked from its classical sources to express a distinctive Hindavi agenda of Sufi love.

In reading this literature, we have to shift the frame of reference away from a formalist reading of narrative to illuminate instead the more encompassing realm of culture, seen as a framing system of beliefs, actions, and practices of cultural production and reception. In doing this, we move religion off centre-stage in the study of pre-modern India to excavate a deeper cultural logic common to the many groups who competed for a place in the sun during the period of the Turkish and Afghan sultanates. The societies of the period are best understood as linked families of cultural practice. For Pakistani or Indian historians to invoke a dualistic or syncretistic understanding of the past means that one is maintaining fixed lines of identity or claiming an essentialism for modern religious and national groupings that they do not warrant. Instead, we need to look for areas of similarity in the diverse cultural remains of the Sultanate period so that we can examine processes of cultural convergence and encounter. The creation of composite cultural forms follows almost an economic model based on the circulation and reciprocal acceptance of alien cultural elements in these Indian Ocean societies. These marvellous exchanges, mercantile and narrative, are not impermanent, for they have left traces and marks in the cultural, literary, and artistic genres that were created during the period. One cannot imagine these complexly creative exchanges through the study of a single literary tradition in isolation from the fertilizing cross-currents of the diverse languages that ebbed and flowed over the trade routes of the Indian Ocean.

NOTES

1. R.S. McGregor, *Hindi Literature from Its Beginnings to the Nineteenth Century* (Wiesbaden: Otto Harrassowitz, 1984), p. 64. For an excellent summary account of the genre, see ibid., pp. 26–8, 65–73, and 150–4.

2. For a detailed analysis of the aesthetics, narrative conventions, and literary culture of the Hindavi Sufi romances, of which this essay forms part of Chapter 3, see my *Shadows of Paradise: An Indian Islamic Literary Tradition, 1379–1545*, forthcoming. For an example of the genre in English verse, see Mir Sayyid Manjhan Shattari Rajgiri, *Madhumālatī: An Indian Sufi Romance*, translated by Aditya Behl and Simon Weightman with S.M. Pandey (Oxford: Oxford University Press, 2000).

3. See Simon Digby, 'The Sufi Shaikh as Source of Authority in Mediaeval India', in *Islam et Société en Asiê du Sud: Collection Puruṣārtha 9*, edited by Marc Gaborieau (Paris: École des Hautes Études en Sciences Sociales, 1986), pp. 57–77, included in this volume as ch. 11; and Aziz Ahmad, 'The Sufi and the Sultan in Pre-Mughal Muslim India', *Der Islam* 38 (1963), pp. 142–53.

4. Translated in J.L. Masson and M.V. Patwardhan, *Aesthetic Rapture: The Rasādhyāya of the Nāṭya-Sāstra* (Poona: Deccan College Postgraduate and Research Institute, 1970), Vol. I, p. 46. For a succinct and clear account of Bharata's theory, see David L. Haberman, *Acting as a Way of Salvation: A Study of Rāgānugā Bhakti Sādhana* (Oxford: Oxford University Press, 1988), pp. 13–16.

5. Janet L. Abu-Lughod, *Before European Hegemony: The World System AD 1250–1350* (New York: Oxford University Press, 1989), pp. 153–84.

6. Marshall G.S. Hodgson, *The Venture of Islam: Conscience and History in a World Civilization* (Chicago: University of Chicago Press, 1974), Vol. I, p. 59.

7. Phillip B. Wagoner, '"Sultan among Hindu Kings": Dress, Titles, and the Islamicization of Hindu Culture at Vijayanagara', *Journal of Asian Studies*, Vol. 55, no. 4 (November 1996), pp. 851–80.

8. K.N. Choudhuri, *Trade and Civilization in the Indian Ocean: An Economic History from the Rise of Islam to 1750* (Cambridge: Cambridge University Press, 1985), p. 44. See also George F. Hourani, *Arab Seafaring in the Indian Ocean in Ancient and Early Medieval Times* (Princeton: Princeton University Press, 1995), pp. 51–84, and Genevieve Bouchon and Denys Lombard, 'The Indian Ocean in the Fifteenth Century', in Ashin Das Gupta and M.N. Pearson, eds., *India and the Indian Ocean, 1500–1800* (Calcutta: Oxford University Press, 1987), pp. 46–70. For an excellent survey of seagoing trade in the period, see Simon Digby, 'The Maritime Trade of India', in Tapan Raychoudhuri and Irfan Habib, eds., *The Cambridge Economic History of India, Volume I: c. 1200–c. 1750* (Cambridge: Cambridge University Press, 1982), pp. 125–59.

9. John G. Cawelti, *Adventure, Mystery, and Romance: Formula Stories as Art and Popular Culture* (Chicago: The University of Chicago Press, 1976), p. 30.

10. For a more detailed history of the period, see M. Habib and K.A. Nizami, *A Comprehensive History of India, Volume V: The Delhi Sultanate* (*AD 1206–1526*) (Delhi: People's Publishing House, 1970), pp. 630–732. For a detailed history of the Sharqi kingdom, see M.M. Saeed, *The Sharqi Sultanate of Jaunpur: A Political and Cultural History* (Karachi: University of Karachi, 1972).

11. Saeed, *The Sharqi Sultanate of Jaunpur*, p. 111. See also S.H. Askari, 'Qutban's Mrigavat: A Unique Ms. in Persian Script', *Journal of the Bihar*

Research Society, Vol. 41, no. 4 (December 1955), pp. 457–8, *idem.*, 'Bihar Under Later Tughlaqs and Sharqis', in his *Medieval Bihar: Sultanate and Mughal Period* (Patna: Khuda Bakhsh Oriental Public Library, 1990), pp. 22–31, and D.F. Plukker, ed., *The Miragāvatī of Kutubana* (Academisch Proefschrift, University of Amsterdam, 1981), p. xviii, n. 4.

12. For details see Saeed, *The Sharqi Sultanate of Jaunpur*, pp. 111–2 and pp. 206–7, and A. Halim, 'History of the Growth and Development of North-Indian Music during Sayyid-Lodi Period', *Journal of the Asiatic Society of Pakistan*, Vol. 1, no. 1 (1956), pp. 46–64.

13. See A. Halim, 'Music and Musicians of the Court of Shāh Jahān', *Islamic Culture*, Vol. 18, no. 4 (1944), pp. 354–60, esp. pp. 355–6.

14. S.A.A. Rizvi, *A History of Sufism in India* (Delhi: Munshiram Manoharlal, 1978), Vol. I, p. 367.

15. S.M. Pandey, 'Kutuban's *Miragāvatī:* its Content and Interpretation', in R.S. McGregor, ed., *Devotional Literature in South Asia: Current Research, 1985–1988* (Cambridge: Cambridge University Press, 1992), p. 180.

16. Another possibility for Qutban's teacher has been suggested by M.M. Saeed in the person of the Mahdavi Shaikh Burhan al-Din Ansari of Kalpi (d. 1562–3). Shaikh Burhan al-Din was also a Hindavi poet and instructed Malik Muhammad Jayasi, the author of the *Padmāvat.* However, in view of Qutban's mention of Shaikh Buddhan Suhrawardi in the text, the ascription cannot stand. See Saeed, *The Sharqi Sultanate of Jaunpur*, p. 200.

17. Rukn al-Din Quddusi, *Laṭā'if-i Quddūsī* (Delhi: Mujtabā'ī Press, 1894), pp. 99–100. See also Simon Digby, "Abd al-Quddus Gangohi (1456–1537 AD): The Personality and Attitudes of a Medieval Indian Sufi', *Medieval India: A Miscellany*, vol. 3 (1975), pp. 54–56, and S.M. Pandey, 'Maulana Daud and His Contributions to the Hindi Sufi Literature', *Annali dell' Istituto Orientale di Napoli*, Vol. 38 (1978), pp. 87–8.

18. Qutban, *Mirigāvatī*, ed. D.F. Plukker (Amsterdam: Universiteit van Amsterdam Academisch Proefschrift, 1981), verse 1. I have also consulted the editions of Mataprasad Gupta (Agra: Pramāṇik Prakāśan, 1968), as well as Parameshvarilal Gupta (Varanasi: Viśvavidyālaya Prakāśan, 1967). The translated excerpts are part of my forthcoming complete annotated translation of *Mirigavati*. All further references will be incorporated into the text by verse number after the abbreviation M.

19. For examples of these, as well as a sound discussion of the meanings and literary place of the *bārah-māsā*, see Charlotte Vaudeville, *Bārahmāsā in Indian Literature: Songs of the Twelve Months in Indo-Aryan Literatures* (Delhi: Motilal Banarsidass, 1986).

20. See Stith Thompson, *Motif-Index of Folk-Literature: A Classification of Narrative Elements in Folktales, Ballads, Myths, Fables, Mediaeval Romances, Exempla, Fabliaux, Jest-Books, and Local Legends* (Copenhagen: Rosenkilde and Bagger, 1956), Vol. II, p. 34, motif D361.1.

21. See Stith Thompson and Jonas Balys, *The Oral Tales of India* (Bloomington: Indiana University Press, 1958), p. 325, motif K 1335. For an example of the use

of the motif of the magic sari to ensnare a heavenly nymph, see the Kannada folktale 'Adventures of a Disobedient Son', in A.K. Ramanujan, *Folktales from India* (New Delhi: Viking Penguin, 1991), pp. 274–85.

22. Gorakhnath, *Gorakhbānī*, ed. P.D. Barthwal (Prayag: Hindī Sāhitya Sammelan, 1979), p. 9.

23. Homer, *The Odyssey*, ed. W.B. Stanford (London: St. Martin's Press, 1959), IX. 105–566, Vol. 1, pp. 134–48.

24. K.N. Choudhuri, *Trade and Civilization in the Indian Ocean*, p. 34.

25. See my *Shadows of Paradise: An Indian Islamic Literary Tradition*, Chapter III.2.

26. Henry James, *The American* (New York: Charles Scribner's Sons, 1907), p. xvii.

27. Robert Irwin, *The Arabian Nights: A Companion* (London: Penguin Books, 1994), p. 182.

28. Raghib al-Isfahani, *al-Mufradāt fī Gharīb al-Qur'ān*, ed. M. Kailani, p. 322, cited in Roy P. Mottahedeh, '*Ajā'ib* in *The Thousand and One Nights*', in Richard G. Hovannisian and Georges Sabagh, eds., *The Thousand and One Nights in Arabic Literature and Society* (Cambridge: Cambridge University Press, 1997), p. 30.

29. For Bluebeard, see Charles Perrault, 'La Barbe Bleue', in Andrew Lang, ed., *Perrault's Popular Tales* (Oxford: Clarendon Press, 1888), pp. 23–9. For extensive parallels in European folklore, see Lang's introduction to the collection, pp. lx–lxiv. For the literary origin of the European Bluebeard in Charles Perrault's tale, see 'Bluebeard', in D.A. Leeming and M. Sader, eds., *Storytelling Encyclopedia: Historical, Cultural, and Multiethnic Approaches to Oral Traditions Around the World* (Phoenix, Arizona: Oryx Press, 1997), pp. 81–2.

30. Robert Warshow, *The Immediate Experience* (Garden City, New York: Doubleday Anchor Books, 1964), p. 85, cited in Cawelti, *Adventure, Mystery, and Romance*, p. 9.

31. Cawelti, *Adventure, Mystery, and Romance*, p. 10.

32. See R.H. Major, 'Introduction', *India in the Fifteenth Century. Being a Collection of Narratives of Voyages to India, in the Century Preceding the Portuguese Discovery of the Cape of Good Hope; from Latin, Persian, Russian, and Italian Sources, Now First Translated into English* (London: Hakluyt Society, 1857), pp. xxxi–xlv.

10

Hanafi *Fiqh* in Mughal India: The *Fatāwá-i ʻĀlamgīrī*

*Alan M. Guenther**

From the time of the earliest caliphs, Muslim scholars had been active in producing legal opinions from which the ruler could draw assistance in formulating laws. This ideal was seldom realized to the fullest extent because the ruler was reluctant to compromise his supreme authority, and the ʻulama refused to be fully assimilated into the state structure. Thus while some of the ʻulama would accept, or even at times pursue, appointments as qazis with responsibilities to make legal judgements, others preferred to retain their independence of the state and function as legal advisors. These advisors were *fuquhā* (plural of *faqīh*), men skilled in the study of jurisprudence (*fiqh*), who provided *fatwās*, or legal judgements to questions put to them by the qazis in the courts or by the populace in general.[2]

Various approaches to the sources of Islamic law, the sharīʻa, and to the role of reason in deciding matters of law led to the development of several schools of law, or *madhhabs*. The Hanafi madhhab, which came to dominate in India, had its origins in the teachings of Abu Hanifa (d. 767) and his disciples, Abu Yusaf (d. 798) and Muhammad al-Shaibani (d. 805). These early teachers of Islamic law tended to favour a living legal tradition that gave a more prominent role to reason in determining Islamic law and had a looser reliance on direct quotations from the Hadith, the growing body of traditions regarding the Prophet Muhammad that were viewed as authoritative in matters of Islamic practice.[3] Their followers, however, adopted a style similar to those of other schools in investing primary authority in the interpretations of past fuquhā, and in refusing to diverge from them.[4] Nevertheless, the sharīʻa as interpreted by all the

* Institute of Islamic Studies, McGill University.[1]

schools retained a dynamism enabling it to be adapted by the theorists and practitioners to meet the needs of the evolving Muslim communities. The rulings attributed to the founders of the school were thus expanded, with the resulting commentaries and abridgments becoming further authorities for succeeding generations.

HANAFI FIQH IN INDIA

In India, Hanafi scholars arrived along with the earliest Muslim conquerors from Central Asia.[5] *Fiqh* scholarship in the Hanafi school had been fully developed and dominated in Central Asia throughout the medieval period, resulting in numerous authoritative works, of which the *Hidāya* of 'Ali ibn Abi Bakr al-Marghinani (d. 1196) was the best known.[6] After the advent of Muslim rule in north India, Indian 'ulama, while continuing to rely on the rulings of Hanafi 'ulama in Central Asia and the Middle East, also began to produce their own collections of authoritative rulings from earlier texts, selected to address their peculiar needs. The *Fatāwá-i Ghiyāthiyya*, produced as early as the thirteenth century, was ascribed to Sultan Ghiyath al-Din Balban (r. 1265–87).[7] Other notable compendiums of Muslim law followed, each usually compiled by an individual scholar demonstrating his expertise in matters of law, and often sponsored by the reigning emperor or one of his nobles, as in the case of the influential *Fatāwá-i Tātār Khānī*, produced at the request of Khan-i 'Azam Tatar Khan, a noble during the reign of Firuz Shah Tughluq (r. 1351–88).[8] During the reign of the Mughal emperor Aurangzeb, two fatwā collections besides the *Fatāwá-i 'Ālamgīrī* were produced, one by Mu'in al-Din Muhammad bin Khwajah Mahmud al-Naqshband (d. 1674) and one by Mufti Abu'l-barakat bin Hussam al-Din Dihlawi in 1698. As the written authorities to be consulted thus increased, their aggregate sum would become somewhat unwieldy for those jurists seeking to be comprehensive in their judgements.

Throughout the period of Muslim rule in India, the relationship of the 'ulama to the ruling powers was in flux. Certain rulers, whether from motives of personal piety or political expediency, chose to patronize the 'ulama and created a favourable environment in which their scholarship could thrive, while other rulers were more eclectic in their choice of means to validate their rule, and of principles by which they governed. The 'ulama themselves were not uniform in their response to the overtures of successive rulers, some willingly accepting government patronage in return for their loyal service, especially in its legal system. Others remained at a distance and offered a critical evaluation of the government's performance against a standard derived from Islamic teachings, thus continuing the pattern set by their forebears in earlier centuries.[9] That the political ruler had a role in determining matters in Islamic law had been recognized since at least the time of the 'Abbasids.[10] But the 'ulama fiercely resisted attempts by caliphs to usurp their religious authority, as occurred in the ninth century when al-Ma'mun forced his judges to accept the doctrine of a created Qur'an.[11] When the great Mughal emperor Akbar (r. 1556–1605) similarly passed a decree that declared himself to be the final authority in matters of interpretation and application of religious law, he based it on ḥadiths (authoritative traditions) defining the position of the 'just ruler'.[12] But this decree, along with other actions that did not conform to what the 'ulama perceived to be properly Islamic, received strict censure. Perhaps the best known reformer who objected to the religious condition of Akbar's court was Shaikh Ahmad Sirhindi (d. 1624), a Naqshbandi scholar and Sufi.[13]

AURANGZEB'S ROLE IN THE FORMATION OF THE *FATĀWÁ-I 'ĀLAMGĪRĪ*

In contrast, Akbar's great-grandson, Aurangzeb (r. 1658–1707), encouraged religious learning and overtly implemented Islamic practices to demonstrate his commitment to Islam. Aurangzeb forcibly took control of the Mughal empire in 1658, overcoming the opposition of both his father, Shah Jahan (r. 1628–58), and his older brother, Dara Shukoh (d. 1659). Because Aurangzeb seized power while his father was still alive, the chief qazi refused to recite the sermon (*khuṭba*) in his name. Aurangzeb pursued the religious approval of his reign by persuading another *'ālim*, Shaikh 'Abd al-Wahhab (d. 1675), to convince the qazi that his accession was legal.[14] He continued to invoke Islamic symbols to legitimatize his power, putting forth his orthodox credentials to demonstrate the superiority of his claim to the throne over his brother.[15] Whether driven by the political necessity of a legitimate claim to the throne, or by personal devotion to an expression of Islam that closely followed the sharī'a, or a mixture of such factors, Aurangzeb's appeal to Islam won him the support of the 'ulama.[16]

During his reign, Aurangzeb did increase the role of the 'ulama and promulgated laws that overtly conformed to the dictates of the sharī'a. The Mughal historian Khafi Khan notes, 'the Emperor gave such extensive powers to the Qaḍis in the civil administration and general and detailed affairs of the state that it become a cause of jealousy and envy of the leading nobles of the Empire.'[17] Prohibition of the use of intoxicants, of extravagant pilgrimages to Hindu places of worship, and of music and dancing were decreed. The state systems of taxation were brought in line with the sharī'a, and patronage of court astrologers ceased.[18] As a result, subsequent generations of 'ulama as well as a number of modern scholars have declared Aurangzeb as a champion of orthodox Islam, citing the triumph of Sirhindi's reforms.[19] Others have challenged that view, suggesting that the records indicate that Aurangzeb's practice was more eclectic, especially later in his reign, and have argued that political considerations outweighed any commitment to religion.[20] While scholars continue to debate his motivations and how the legacy of Aurangzeb is to be portrayed, what is evident is that the 'ulama perceived his reign as one that enhanced their influence in the imperial court.

One major contribution by Aurangzeb to the promotion of the sharī'a in India was the commissioning of the manual of *fiqh* which came to be known as the *Fatāwá-i 'Ālamgīrī*. According to tradition, it was begun relatively early in his reign and completed eight years later, approximately from 1667 to 1675.[21] In some accounts, the initiation of the compilation is linked with the termination of the official written history.[22] When Mirza Kazim, author of the *'Ālamgīr-nāma*, finished and presented the history of the first ten years of Aurangzeb's reign to the emperor, the latter realized that many histories were composed in the world without requiring official patronage. And since the foundation of good government was justice, improving knowledge of the law would be a project worthier of his patronage. Other Mughal historians simply state that Aurangzeb's aim had been to make the general Muslim public act in accordance with the legal decisions of the 'ulama of the Hanafi school.[23] The problem he encountered was that rulings, as found in existing law books, were mixed up and lacked decisive authority because of contradictory decisions by past 'ulama and the weakness of supporting hadiths. The number of books to be consulted had also grown to such proportions as to make research unwieldy. The solution at which he arrived was to commission the compilation of one comprehensive collection of authoritative rulings by qualified Indian 'ulama who would make a detailed examination of all the relevant law books in the imperial library and extract the necessary rulings.[24] According to this account, Aurangzeb's ostensible purpose was not only to direct the Muslims of India to live according to the sharī'a, but also to facilitate its implementation in the courts. Experts in Islamic law served the Mughal empire as qazis or functioned as *muftis*, and in both roles needed to be thoroughly familiar with the legal rulings of previous generations.[25] Since the judicial process would be hampered by the lengthy process of consulting all relevant written authorities, such a compilation—bringing together the best sources and deciding between contradictory rulings—would be of immense value.

Other motivations for the sponsorship of the *Fatāwá-i.'Ālamgīrī* can be postulated. Aziz Ahmad, who describes the compilation as 'the theoretic crystallization of Aurangzib's theocratic principles', considers that the emperor made use of the 'ulama by setting them to work on this monumental task.[26] Aurangzeb could be seen as attempting to free himself from the independent influence of the religious leadership by sponsoring this definitive compilation of judicial decisions.[27] In a similar argument, S.A.A. Rizvi sees in the choice of the 'ulama a shift from delivering a reformist message, such as had appeared in the work of Sirhindi and 'Abd al-Haq Dihlavi under previous Mughal rulers, to a co-option of their efforts by the state.[28] In this view, the 'ulama surrendered the role of challenging the ruling powers in return for the security of government patronage. Clearly, a large number of scholars were employed in the effort, and with wages came a measure of indebtedness to the regime. However, such monetary remuneration could equally be seen as the patronage of Islamic learning rather than an attempt at its subjugation.[29] Medieval Muslim rulers and other wealthy individuals vied with each other to establish reputations of being great patrons of scholarly as well as artistic endeavours. By his patronage of a definitive work of Hanafi *fiqh*, Aurangzeb was sending a clear signal regarding his priorities. The historians of the time recorded that Rs. 200,000 of the imperial coffers were spent on the project.[30]

Beyond selecting and funding the scholars, historical accounts record that Aurangzeb participated in the project personally. Shah Wali Ullah (d. 1762) recalled an incident told by his father, Shah 'Abd al-Rahim Sahib Dihlawi (d. 1719), that suggests close involvement by the emperor.[31] Shah 'Abd al-Rahim, while examining the portion he was responsible for, encountered a problem that had been confused with an unnecessary complication. Through further research, he discovered the source of the complication to be the conflation of two different accounts by the compiler and noted his own correction in the margins. The overseer of the compilation of the *Fatāwá-i 'Ālamgiri* as a whole, Shaikh Nizam (d. 1679), had been reading a few pages of the work in progress every day to the emperor Aurangzeb, who is described as closely supervising the writing and editing of the book. On the day that the passage under question was read, Shaikh Nizam accidentally read Shah 'Abd al-Rahim's note along with the confusing text. The emperor immediately noted the confusion and challenged the scholar to explain the passage, causing an investigation that eventually led back to Shah 'Abd al-Rahim and, according to him, resulted in his dismissal. Whether these daily readings continued throughout the eight-year period of the compilation, or rather only during the final checking of the project, is not indicated. The account would nevertheless imply a keen interest and a knowledgeable evaluation of the contents of the *Fatāwá-i 'Ālamgīri* by Aurangzeb. One can estimate that such regular scrutiny of the sharī'a would have had a considerable impact on his own law-making, motivating an ongoing reform rooted in Islamic principles.

The account by Shah Wali Ullah regarding his father also illustrates the process of selection of the fuquhā for the work.[32] Shah 'Abd al-Rahim had been invited to participate in a portion of the project under the direction of Mulla Hamid Jaunpuri and was promised a fixed daily wage. Initially, Shah 'Abd al-Rahim had refused the invitation, but his mother's displeasure compelled him to relent and accept the employment. However, he continued to seek a means of escape, with the strong encouragement of his spiritual advisor. Shah 'Abd al-Rahim's only request to his advisor was that he might be released from his commitment without once again incurring his mother's wrath. When the dismissal finally came in the circumstances related above, the emperor is again portrayed as being personally involved. He is described as conducting a periodic examination of the list of all those employed in the compiling of the fatwās, issuing orders for appointment and dismissal. When the name of Shah 'Abd al-Rahim was removed by the scribes, he was offered a certain grant of land, possibly as a *suyurghal* grant, which was frequently given to retired teachers and servants of the state—a grant that he refused.[33] Besides illustrating Aurangzeb's involvement in the compilation of the *Fatāwá-i 'Ālamgīrī*, the account also hints at the division between those 'ulama who participated with the state and those who steadfastly refused to participate for religious or ideological convictions.

TEXT OF THE *FATĀWÁ-I 'ĀLAMGĪRĪ*

The *Fatāwá-i 'Ālamgīrī*, rather than being a collection of primary fatwās (i.e., answers to specific questions) as the name might imply, is a comprehensive legal text of Hanafi fiqh.[34] In this respect it is not unlike other compilations of authoritative decisions by Hanafi fuquhā, arranged systematically to provide a comprehensive reference work of Islamic law.[35] A lengthy introduction discusses the nature of fiqh and Islam in general, and provides information about the sources used and the jurists named as authorities.[36] The selected subjects and their arrangement in the *Fatāwá-i 'Ālamgīrī* deliberately follow those of the *Hidāya* of al-Marghinani, attempting to cover every topic on which a fatwā could be issued. This general division and arrangement of both the *Fatāwá-i 'Ālamgīrī* and the *Hidāya* would appear to have been adopted from such standard books of Hanafi fiqh as Muhammad al-Shaibani's *Jama'-i Saghīr*. The few changes made in the *Fatāwá-i 'Ālamgīrī* consist of combining two sections into one, renaming another section, and the addition of five new sections. Of these five, the most significant include chapters on judicial proceedings and decrees (*muḥāḍir wa al-sijillāt*), legal forms (*shurūt*), legal devices (*ḥiyal*), and rules of inheritance (*farā'iḍ*).[37] Their significance is that, unlike the fifty-seven other sections dealing with details of laws regarding religious rites, economic transactions, treatment of slaves and employees, land, etc., these appear to deal more with principles of determining and applying the laws.

For each topic dealt with, cases are given from the standard works of Hanafi fiqh. Interspersed with the cases are more abstract works showing the reasons for the judgements, unless the reason is drawn directly from the Qur'an or Hadith.[38] The source of each case is given; and where the given source quotes other sources, those are given as well. In the case where two conflicting opinions are found and one is manifestly superior, both are still cited. It is also noted whether the source cited has been quoted word for word or merely summarized. In total, at least 124 sources are cited, omitting none of the major Hanafi works.[39] In size, the *Fatāwá-i 'Ālamgīrī* is four times that of the *Hidāya*, containing a greater number of cases in each section. Therefore, while the *Hidāya* continued to be used and cited by Muslim law-makers, the *Fatāwá-i 'Ālamgīrī* had the advantage of providing a comprehensive review of all authoritative books of Hanafi fiqh, including those prepared by 'ulama writing subsequent to Marghinani. These included works produced by Indian 'ulama such as the *Fatāwá-i Ghiyāthiyya* and the *Fatāwá-i Qarākhānī* of the thirteenth century, *Fatāwá-i Tātār Khānī* of the fourteenth century, and the *Fatāwá-i Barhāniyyah* from the time of the emperor Akbar. In this manner, the *Fatāwá-i 'Ālamgīrī* becomes a register of those works of jurisprudence produced in India that had attained a level of authority that made inclusion in such a compilation essential.

Though originally written in Arabic, in keeping with the tradition of Islamic legal writing, the *Fatāwá-i 'Ālamgīrī* was soon translated into Persian. The *Mirāt al-'Ālam* records that 'Abd Allah Chalpi Rumi, a scholar from Asia Minor, was appointed along with his pupils to translate the work into Persian, though it is not clear whether it was completed since no copy seems to have survived.[40] Another tradition records that a translation into Persian was made by the order of the emperor's daughter, the Princess Zeb al-Nisa.[41] When the British administration was in the process of recording Muslim law toward the end of the eighteenth century, Arabic copies of the *Fatāwá-i 'Ālamgīrī* were found in Calcutta, as well as imperfect, incomplete copies of the Persian.[42] The Chief Qazi, Muhammad Najm al-Din Khan, seems to have completed a Persian translation in preparation for publication.[43] English translations of portions of the *Fatāwá-i 'Ālamgīrī* were made later in the middle of the nineteenth-century by Niel B.E. Baillie (d. 1883), who considered it a pity that the *Hidāya* had been adopted instead of the *Fatāwá-i 'Ālamgīrī* as the standard authority for the East India's Company's courts of civil justice. The *Fatāwá-i 'Ālamgīrī*, he argued, had the advantage of being compiled in India by the authority of an Indian Muslim ruler.[44] The work was first translated and published in Urdu in the late nineteenth century[45] by Maulana Saiyid Amir 'Ali of Lucknow (d. 1919), a distinguished 'ālim who also translated and published other works of Qur'anic commentaries, traditions, and jurisprudence.[46]

This brief overview of the text of the *Fatāwá-i 'Ālamgīrī* demonstrates that it is consistent with the tradition of *fatwā* collections. Its major divisions, referred to as *kitābs*, are almost identical to those of other key Hanafi texts. The sources used are not limited to the Qur'an and the Hadith, but embrace those recognized as the most authoritative Hanafi sources, including those of Indian origin. One should note, however, that although these later collections originated in India, their use was not limited to that region. Since they were written in Arabic, they became as important to Hanafi jurists in Central Asia and the Ottoman empire as they were in India. The *Fatāwá-i 'Ālamgīrī* likewise gained a reputation as a crucial Hanafi authority in the larger Muslim community where it was (and still is) known as *Fatāwá al-Hindiyya*.[47] Apart from the additional sources, its increased comprehensiveness—and therefore increased length as well—and its authorship by the collective effort of a wide range of 'ulama make its contribution to Hanafi *fiqh* distinctive. Its contribution to the Mughal administration of Aurangzeb will be discussed later.

COMPILERS OF THE *FATĀWÁ-I 'ĀLAMGĪRĪ*

The *Fatāwá-i 'Ālamgīrī* was compiled by a considerable number of 'ulama working together in a hierarchical arrangement.[48] The overseer was Shaikh Nizam from Burhanpur in the Khandesh region east of Gujarat. The work was divided into sections, each assigned to a chief editor who was then responsible to Shaikh Nizam for any errors in his section. Each chief editor had a group of other 'ulama who were assigned to work with him as assistants. The *Mirāt al-'Ālam* notes that one of the chief editors had ten such assistants assigned to him; if this was standard, there could have been forty to fifty 'ulama involved in preparing the *Fatāwá-i 'Ālamgīrī*.[49] The number of chief editors is often taken to be four, since four names are known to be so designated. Some historical records naming other scholars responsible for major portions of the text, however, suggest the possibility of more chief editors. The interaction of these various levels has already been described in the incident involving Shah 'Abd al-Rahim Sahib Dihlawi. The strength of this arrangement was that it combined the expertise of numerous scholars of Islamic law, many with significant experience in the legal bureaucracy of the empire. The biographical dictionaries mention certain 'ulama who, like Shah 'Abd al-Rahim, were able to solve difficult problems encountered while bringing together contradictory rulings found in the ancient sources.[50]

The compilers of the *Fatāwá-i 'Ālamgīrī* were 'ulama drawn from all over Muslim India. The historian Khafi Khan states that these authors were 'ulama from Delhi and Lahore,[51] but an examination of other historical texts shows that the collaborators were drawn from a much wider area.[52] 'Ulama from northern India, the heart of the Mughal empire, seemed to predominate. Qazi Muhammad Husain and Mulla Hamid, both chief editors, came from Jaunpur in the Allahabad province, as did assistants Muhammad Jamil Sadiqi, Qazi 'Abd al-Samad Jaunpuri, and Qazi 'Ali Akbar Sa'd Allah Khani, while another chief editor, Jalal al-Din Muhammad, came from the nearby town of Machhlishahr. From Awadh, the province north of Allahabad, came another chief editor, Shaikh Wajih al-Din Gopamau'i, and at least four other assistants: Mulla Abu'l-wa'iz Hargami, Mulla Sa'id, Qazi 'Ismat Allah Lukhnauwi, and Qazi Muhammad Ghauth. To the east, the province of Bihar produced Shaikh Raza al-Din Bhagalpuri, Qazi Ghulam Muhammad Lahori (the designation 'Lahori' referred to his later appointment to Lahore), Saiyid 'Inayat Allah Monghiri, Mulla Wa'iq Bihari, and Mulla Wajih al-Rabb. Further west, from the province of Agra came Saiyid Muhammad Qanauji, from Delhi and province, Shah 'Abd al-Rahim, Mufti Abu'l-barkat Dihlawi, and Maulana Muhammad Shafi' Sirhindi, and from Lahore, Mulla Muhammad Akram Lahori. Sindh contributed two scholars, Saiyid Nizam al-Din Thathavi and Qazi Abu'l-khair Thathavi. As has already been mentioned, the overseer of the project, Shaikh Nizam, came from Khandesh, from where he appears to have been joined by a colleague, Amir Miran 'Alama Abu'l-farh.

It is possible that these geographical designations may not indicate the origins of the collaborators since scholars travelled widely, both to study and to serve in government posts in the judiciary. Additionaly, while names of numerous scholars are associated with the *Fatāwá-i 'Ālamgīrī*, proof of their participation is difficult to obtain from available sources.[53] Such an extensive project lasting roughly eight years would have involved many scholars in some way. Later biographers would naturally accept reports of involvement if the person had been a well-known jurist. Families also would try to find a connection to the project for their ancestors. An absence of verification, however, does not necessarily imply the claim is spurious. The lack of an official list necessitates the investigation of all historical accounts, whether written or oral. The result of such diversity as the records appear to indicate is that no localized clique dominated the work with its particular interpretation of the sharī'a, and that different scholars contributed their eclectic perspectives to insure a well-balanced presentation of Hanafi fiqh.

In addition to diversity of geographical origin, the available biographical notes provide other valuable information. A number of the compilers, including two of the chief editors, Shaikh Wajih al-Din and Qazi Muhammad Husain, had been involved in the administration of Emperor Shah Jahan's regime. Shaikh Wajih al-Din had served in various capacities, including as tutor to Dara Shukoh and ultimately, as Sadr of the province of Allahabad.[54] With the ascension of Aurangzeb, he left his post to return to his home district and continue scholarly pursuits; presumably his close connection to Aurangzeb's rival, Dara Shukoh, made his release from this position desirable. However, he was soon reinstated to a position of honour as a chief editor of the *Fatāwá-i 'Ālamgīrī*. Muhammad Husain had been qazi of Jaunpur under Shah Jahan, and served as qazi of Allahabad under Aurangzeb. Both were senior scholars with extensive experience in the judiciary, making their contribution to the *Fatāwá-i 'Ālamgīrī* invaluable. Their inclusion demonstrates Aurangzeb's recognition that their scholarship and organizational abilities were more important than their rival political affiliations.

One could argue that the inclusion of associates of past political rivals is evidence of an attempt to forestall any challenges to the emperor's legitimacy, but the inclusion of close friends among the compilers of the *Fatāwá-i 'Ālamgīrī* refutes that argument.[55] The overseer, Shaikh Nizam, as well as others such as Amir Miran 'Alama Abu'l-farh and Qazi Muhammad Ghauth, had served Aurangzeb in the Deccan prior to his ascent to the throne. Saiyid Muhammad Qanauji and Mulla Abu'l-wa'iz had been teachers of Aurangzeb, and Mulla Hamid and Mulla Muhammad Akram were appointed as tutors for his sons. The inclusion of such close associates suggests that the work of compiling the *Fatāwá-i 'Ālamgīrī* was seen by Aurangzeb as an honour fit for his learned friends, rather than an exercise to keep recalcitrant 'ulama busy.

In addition to the regular salary received during the duration of the project, a number of the participants also received advanced postings in the administration or land grants as *madad-i ma'āsh*. Qazi Muhammad Husain was appointed as Iḥtisāb of the imperial court.[56] Saiyid 'Ali Akbar was appointed Qazi of Lahore and also served as Chief Qazi when Qazi 'Abd al-Wahhab fell ill.[57] Mulla Muhammad Akram eventually held the post of Chief Qazi permanently.[58] Title deeds to *madad-i ma'āsh* grants still extant directly link the grants of land to participation in the compilation of the *Fatāwá-i 'Ālamgīrī*.[59] Another ongoing legacy of some of the 'ulama was the educational institutions they established or enhanced. Shah 'Abd al-Rahim of Delhi, who has already been mentioned several times, went on to found the Madrasa-yi Rahimiyya. Mulla Fasih al-Din was a key instructor with numerous disciples in Phuwar.[60] Barbara Metcalf also notes that the patriarch of Farangi Mahal school, Mulla Qutb al-Din, and his sons had assisted in the work on the *Fatāwá-i 'Ālamgīrī*.[61] They were awarded a grant of land by Aurangzeb and were given a revenue-free tenure of land known as Farangi Mahal. While these generous gifts were consistent with Mughal patronage of religious scholars, they also once more demonstrate the importance Aurangzeb placed on the compilation of the *Fatāwá-i 'Ālamgīrī*.

THE QAZI IN THE *FATĀWÁ-I 'ĀLAMGĪRĪ*

In its section on *Ādāb al-qāḍī*, the *Fatāwá-i 'Ālamgīrī* addressed the necessary qualifications and responsibilities of a qazi from the perspective of Hanafi fiqh. Towards the end of the initial section defining terms, comes an extended discourse on the work of the qazi as a mufti, that is, a religious scholar qualified to give legal rulings.[62] In addition to a good character, he must have a knowledge of the Qur'an and the Sunna (customs of the Prophet Muhammad), as well as a capacity for *ijtihād*, or independent reasoning. If, however, the mufti is merely quoting the opinion of some authority, these qualifications are not required, as long as he is qualified as a transmitter of tradition. In issuing fatwās, or legal rulings, he must be impartial and just, without discriminating between rich and poor, powerful and weak, male and female, or young and mature. The written question is to be received with respect and studied in depth before it is answered. The answer must end with an invocation of God as the infallible One, and then preserved, since it bears the name of God. While answering, the mufti must be thoroughly familiar with the principles and methods of the imām, or 'founder', of his school. It is considered preferable if the fatwā is issued without remuneration, but people are permitted to hire the services of a mufti or fix a salary for him.

This discussion on the qualifications of a mufti provides a significant insight into the *Fatāwá-i 'Ālamgīrī*. The editors of the text held that to be a mufti one must be qualified to perform ijtihād (independent legal reasoning), citing the appropriate authorities to support that position.[63] Since these editors also believed that no one in their day was so qualified, it meant that in principle no one was qualified to be a mufti. And what were called fatwās could therefore not, in fact, be true fatwās, since there were no true muftis. Other medieval works on Islamic law written in India in the fifteenth to seventeenth centuries took a similar position on the necessity of the mufti being a qualified *mujtahid* (one who performs ijtihād).[64] But what is striking is the phrase 'in our days' used in this passage of the *Fatāwá-i 'Alamgīrī*, referring to the period of time in which the compilers were doing their work. This seems to indicate the compilers' conscious adaptation and application of traditional law to their contemporary situation. Though saturating the text with authorities from previous centuries, the editors were not merely compiling abstract legal theory. Rather, as the repeated use of this phrase in other passages of the *Fatāwá-i 'Ālamgīrī* shows, they were deliberately reflecting on their contemporary context in the light of centuries of Islamic legal decisions.

Another section of the *Ādāb al-qāḍī* contains instructions on the order of authorities to be observed in the practice of law, enabling the qazi to form an accurate judgement consistent with the practice of the Hanafi madhhab.[65] The first of these sources is necessarily the Qur'an; and a qazi must know the principles of abrogation, must be able to distinguish between clear and obscure texts, and to recognize those which are doubtful. The second major source is the Hadith (traditions of the Prophet); and the skills necessary for its correct use are to know which traditions have been superceded, to be able to distinguish between spurious and genuine traditions, and to be familiar with the science of tracing the genealogy of the traditions (*isnād*). The consensus (*ijmā'*) of the Prophet's Companions and that of the subsequent generations, the Successors, are given as the third and fourth sources. Where there is disagreement or no ruling to be found in the above sources, the qazi, if he is a qualified mujtahid, is to give a ruling consistent with established principles of jurisprudence (*usūl al-fiqh*).

Figuring prominently in the discussion of the usūl al-fiqh is the comparative weight to be given to precedents and decisions given by the three jurists considered to be the founders of the Hanafi school.[66] If the case before the qazi has not been addressed by these three, he is to look to decisions by subsequent lawyers. If there, too, he finds no assistance, he is then free to exercise his own judgement, provided he is qualified in the knowledge of fiqh. If others more qualified than he are present, namely muftis, he must follow their opinion. The consequence of this subordination of the qazi to the mufti was that muftis devoted more of their time to the necessary study of the texts and functioned as advisors to the qazis, often in an official capacity. Consonant with the purpose of the *Fatāwá-i 'Ālamgīrī* to provide a compendium of Hanafi fiqh, this description closely follows the traditional image of the role of a qazi in any Muslim society; not surprisingly, it does not introduce additional elements peculiar to the Indian context. On the other hand, the text's references to successive rulings by qualified jurists reveal the law's cumulative nature. By implication, then, repeated compilations such as the *Fatāwá-i 'Ālamgīrī* were a necessary element of Islamic law in its practice, and qualified jurists functioning as muftis and qazis were essential in maintaining the dynamism of the shari'a by applying it to concrete situations.

Though this section of the *Fatāwá-i 'Ālamgīrī* effectively conflates the roles of qazi and mufti, it is helpful to recognize their distinctions. Actually, four separate roles of the Muslim jurist can be distinguished: qazi, mufti, author-jurist, and professor.[67] While the qazi was employed by the state to judge law cases in court, the mufti prepared answers to questions regarding legal matters—questions that could come from a qazi requiring clarification on a point of law, or from any ordinary person seeking a ruling based on the shari'a. On the other hand an author-jurist, in explicating the reasoning and sources used to arrive at a decision, wrote his fatwās with considerably more detail than did a regular mufti; collected works of these fatwās became authoritative for subsequent generations. Professors taught students or disciples in all matters of fiqh.

An accomplished jurist could fill all these roles, or be limited to one or several of them. In light of the foregoing discussion of the role of the mufti and qazi in the *Fatāwá-i 'Ālamgīrī*, it is apparent that the job of a state-appointed qazi was not seen as the culmination of a successful legal career. Biographical dictionaries portray accomplished jurists as men who were active in issuing fatwās, writing texts and teaching, but not necessarily working as qazis.[68]

The link between the shari'a as legal discourse and the shari'a as a social instrument is precisely the work of the muftis in producing fatwās derived from previous works of law but addressing real questions in their contemporary circumstances.[69] Collections of fatwās initially reflected the reality to which they were addressed, with the original question addressed to the mufti followed by the answer given in reply. These were transformed into substantive law or *furū'* as the question/answer format was abstracted from the concrete situation and abridged to illustrate a general principle. Wael Hallaq, one of the leading scholars in the field of Islamic law, designates the two types of legal rulings as 'primary *fatwās*' and 'secondary *fatwās*'.[70] The *Fatāwá-i 'Ālamgīrī* is a representative of the latter, consisting of a collection of fatwās that had undergone considerable editing since appearing in their primary form, and which were arranged to delineate principles of Hanafi law. Having moved from a specific question and answer, to a collection of such rulings, to an edited form comprising substantive law, the collection now functioned as the comprehensive, authoritative source informing the qazi, or the mufti advising him, as he answered more questions, thus completing the circle. Hallaq's description of the purpose of *furū'* works aptly applies to the *Fatāwá-i 'Ālamgīrī*:

> [T]he function of *furū'* works was to provide the jurisconsults with a comprehensive coverage of substantive law. These works were expected to offer solutions for all conceivable cases so that the jurisconsult might draw on the established doctrine of his school, and to include the most recent as well as the oldest cases of law that arose in the school. This explains why *fatwās* were incorporated into these works, for they represent the oldest and most recent material that is relevant to the needs of the society as it had developed and changed by a certain point in time.[71]

THE *FATĀWÁ-I 'ĀLAMGĪRĪ* IN AURANGZEB'S JUDICIAL ADMINISTRATION

While the *Fatāwá-i 'Ālamgīrī* defined the qualifications and the role of the qazi, it left the power to appoint him in the hands of the state. Aurangzeb's administration basically followed the pattern of previous Mughal rulers, organizing its judiciary along the lines suggested by the jurists.[72] Through their system of educating and training subsequent jurists, and through their insistence that all fatwās must be in line with previous rulings of the Hanafi madhhab, the muftis were self-regulated and self-perpetuating. Patronage by the state, the community, or wealthy individuals, and income from the produce of endowed properties, provided for the material needs of the 'ulama. From this pool of scholars, then, the state would select and appoint judges to serve at all levels of the judiciary. They held their positions at the emperor's pleasure, and could be dismissed at any time by him directly or on a report of an overseeing department.[73] Aurangzeb expressed in his letters his high expectations of qazis since they had the power to imprison or execute people of God.[74] The records show, however, that some influential qazis failed to live up to that ideal.[75] The chief qazi, or *qāḍīul quḍāt*, was appointed directly by the emperor, while the judges of smaller jurisdictions were appointed on the recommendation of the *ṣadr al-ṣudūr*, the head of the chancellery.[76] Upon presentation of his credentials to the local authority, then, the qazi took up his responsibilities.

The duties of the qazi included first of all passing judgement on all civil and criminal cases that came before him in his court.[77] The chief qazi of the province was expected to perform additional functions such as supervising prisons; and later in the reign of Aurangzeb, he was entrusted with the custody of the government treasury.[78] He also served as a consultant to the governors and the emperor on legal matters, assisting them in deciding cases brought before them.[79] The *Fatāwá-i 'Ālamgīrī*, then, was written to provide the qazi and his advisors with a comprehensive compilation of Islamic law to assist them both in making legal rulings and in advising the emperor about the prescriptions of the sharī'a to aid him in his law-making.

The historical record shows that the *Fatāwá-i 'Ālamgīrī* did prove to influence the emperor's work in framing the law. As a source from which law could be derived, the *Fatāwá-i 'Ālamgīrī* provided him with the fullest expression of the sharī'a according to the Hanafi tradition. But it was only one of several sources of law utilized by Aurangzeb, which also included the *Ḍawābiṭ-i 'Ālamgīrī* and other *qānūn-i 'urfī*, or *'ādat* law.[80] The working of this plurality is illustrated in Aurangzeb's *farmān* (directive) to Muhammad Hashim in Gujarat, issued in 1669/1670 when the *Fatāwá-i 'Ālamgīrī* was nearing completion.[81] The principles of land revenue administration in the farmān clearly reflect those sections of the *Fatāwá-i 'Ālamgīrī* treating this subject. The differences between the two, however, are also significant, revealing the special needs of the empire at that time. The farmān stipulates rates of taxation in excess of those given in the *Fatāwá-i 'Ālamgīrī*, and states that, in the case of orchards, they be levied sooner.[82] Other clauses in the *Fatāwá-i 'Ālamgīrī* have been omitted or considerably altered in the farmān since they bore no relation to the reality of the Indian situation.[83]

Another farmān issued by Aurangzeb a few years later addresses the matter of punishing criminals guilty of theft, murder, counterfeiting, and the like.[84] Like the previous farmān, it also carries the influence of the *Fatāwá-i 'Ālamgīrī*, and likewise abridges or adapts it to suit specific needs. The preamble states that the emperor's overwhelming concern is that justice be expedited so that accused criminals would not be imprisoned indefinitely while awaiting trial. To conclude as one writer does that

Aurangzeb 'perceived that the penal laws of the Muslim jurists were crude and insufficient, and did not meet the requirements of the society', seems to fail to understand the interplay of the two as indicated by their similarity.[85] This interplay is a natural result of their respective roles—the *Fatāwá-i 'Ālamgīrī* was prepared by the 'ulama for the 'ulama and was intended as a compendium of Islamic law and the principles governing its derivation and application. By contrast, the farmāns were prepared by the emperor for subordinate rulers and judges, and were intended to be implemented as the laws of the empire. Committed to governing along Islamic lines, and involved as he was in the compilation of the *Fatāwá-i 'Ālamgīrī,* the emperor saw the latter as a source for his farmāns.

Aurangzeb's independence of the *Fatāwá-i 'Ālamgīrī* is further demonstrated in an incident involving the execution of captured rebels, both Muslim and Hindu.[86] The emperor had ordered the Chief Qazi to make a ruling regarding their fate. Upon receiving a decision decreeing a light punishment for the Muslims and release for the Hindus if they converted, Aurangzeb returned it with his notation, 'This decision [is] according to the Hanafi school; decide the case in some other way, that control over the kingdom may not be lost.'[87] He argued that there were four legal madhhabs from which to choose. The Qazi and the muftis returned with a new ruling that they declared was based on the *Fatāwá-i 'Ālamgīrī*—hence still within the Hanafī fiqh—but which decreed that the prisoners should be executed. This met with the emperor's approval and was implemented. This illustrates not only Aurangzeb's independence and his manipulation of the law and its theoreticians for his own ends; it also shows the availability of contradictory rulings within the larger corpus of Hanafi judicial writings, making such a reversal possible and fully legal.

CONCLUSION

The preceding examination of the *Fatāwá-i 'Ālamgīrī* and its compilation demonstrates that it played a unique role in the development of Hanafi *fiqh* in India. The work united diverse 'ulama from various regions of Muslim India in a common project of reviewing the existing collection of authorities, weighing their relative authority, deciding between contradictory rulings, and selecting the material most applicable to seventeenth-century India. The result was a comprehensive, multi-volume compendium of Islamic law. Through its regular quotation of older authorities, it provided continuity with the past. Through its inclusion of the best of recent Hanafi works, some of them written by Indian scholars, it updated the sharī'a to take the current situation into account. Being written in Arabic, it served to strengthen the role of Indian fuquhā in mainstream Hanafi thought.

It has also been emphasized that the *Fatāwá-i 'Ālamgīrī* was not a collection of fatwās issued by muftis of the time, and certainly was not a collection of fatwās issued by the Emperor Aurangzeb, as the name might suggest. Nor was it a code of law promulgated by Aurangzeb. Rather, it was a comprehensive review of Hanafi fiqh produced to aid qazis and muftis in their work of making legal rulings according to the sharī'a. The fact that it was translated into Persian soon after its compilation indicates that it quickly moved from the realm of legal speculation and theorizing to being applied by ordinary judges at all levels of administration. While not comprising a law code for the empire, the influence of the *Fatāwá-i 'Ālamgīrī* on the formation of laws, however, cannot be denied. It assisted the 'ulama in their work of advising the emperor and subordinate rulers about the dictates of Islamic law. Aurangzeb's own participation in the project doubtless influenced the laws he subsequently put into effect.

Moreover, Aurangzeb's patronage and keen interest in the project reveals his own predilection for a more sharī'a-based Islam, while his departures from a strict observance of its precepts reflects his continuing independence of it and the exigencies of the empire. As part of his patronage of the compilation of the *Fatāwá-i 'Ālamgīrī*, Aurangzeb assisted the sharī'a-minded 'ulama as well, increasing their influence as one of the groups of the imperial court to a greater level than it had been under the previous Mughal rulers. As a result, their rise to prominence during Aurangzeb's reign was more a consequence of the emperor's patronage than a cause of it. Seen in the broader sweep of Muslim history, the compilation of the *Fatāwá-i 'Ālamgīrī* and what it demonstrates of the relationship between the 'ulama and the ruler, is consistent with the pattern established in the formative period of Islamic law. With the fuller involvement of the 'ulama both in the scholarly activity of researching the texts of fiqh and in influencing state laws, it is perhaps closer to the ideal relationship desired by the 'ulama than that under the previous Mughal rulers in India.

NOTES

1. I would like to express my appreciation to Professor Sajida Alvi for her assistance and guidance in preparing this paper, and to Richard Eaton for his encouragement to complete it.

2. Muhammad Khalid Masud, et. al., 'Muftis, Fatwās, and Islamic Legal Interpretation', in *Islamic Legal Interpretation: Muftis and their Fatwās*, ed. Muhammad Khalid Masud, et. al. (Cambridge, MA: Harvard University Press, 1996), pp. 8–26.

3. Fazlur Rahman, *Islamic Methodology in History*. Publications of the Central Institute of Islamic Research (Pakistan), 2 (Karachi: Central Institute of Islamic Research, 1965), pp. 31–40. For a more detailed discussion, see Christopher Melchert, *The Formation of the Sunni Schools of Law, 9th–10th Centuries* CE., Studies in Islamic Law and Society 4 (Leiden: Brill, 1997), pp. 1–67.

4. For a description of this process, see chapter 2, 'Early *Ijtihād* and the Later Construction of Authority', in Wael B. Hallaq, *Authority, Continuity and Change in Islamic Law* (Cambridge: Cambridge University Press [forthcoming]).

5. Aziz Ahmad, 'The Role of Ulema in Indo-Muslim History', *Studia Islamica* 30 (1970), p. 2; Richard C. Foltz, *Mughal India and Central Asia* (Karachi: Oxford University Press, 1998), p. 82.

6. 'Ali ibn Abi Bakr al-Marghinani, *The Hedaya or Guide: A Commentary on the Mussulman Laws*, trans. by Charles Hamilton, 2nd ed. (1870; rpt. Lahore: Premier Book House, 1963).

7. Zafarul Islam, 'Origin and Development of Fatāwāi-Compilation in Medieval India', *Hamdard Islamicus* 20, no. 1 (1977), p. 8.

8. See ibid. pp. 9–11 for descriptions of these and other works of note in India during the medieval period.

9. K.A. Nizami presents a detailed portrait of both types of 'ulama from the thirteenth century, including a description of the various judicial and other bureaucratic functions open to them, in his *Some Aspects of Religion and Politics in India during the Thirteenth Century*, Publications of the Department of History, Aligarh Muslim University, Aligarh, no. 16 (Aligarh: Department of History, Muslim University, 1961), pp. 150–73.

10. Muhammad Qasim Zaman, *Religion and Politics under the Early 'Abbasids: The Emergence of the Proto-Sunni Elite*, Islamic History and Civilization: Studies and Texts 16 (New York: E.J. Brill, 1997), pp. 82–106.

11. Ibid., pp. 106–18.

12. Aziz Ahmad, *Studies in Islamic Culture in the Indian Environment* (Oxford: Clarendon Press, 1964), pp. 170–71.

13. Yohanan Friedmann, *Shaykh Ahmad Sirhindi: An Outline of his Thought and a Study of his Image in the Eyes of Posterity*, McGill Islamic Studies 2 (Montreal: McGill-Queen's University Press, 1971), pp. 80–2.

14. Rafat Bilgrami, 'Shaykh 'Abd al-Wahhab and his Family under 'Alamgīr', *Journal of the Pakistan Historical Society* 31, pt. 2 (Apr. 1983), pp. 100–14.

15. Aziz Ahmad, *Studies*, pp. 195–6.

16. Iftikhar Ahmad Ghauri, 'Ideological Factor in the War of Succession, 1657–1658'. *Journal of the Pakistan Historical Society* 8, pt. 2 (1960), pp. 113–5.

17. 'Khafi Khan's History of 'Alamgir,' trans. by S. Moinul Haq, *Journal of the Pakistan Historical Society* 18, pt. 1 (1970), pp. 52, 198.

18. Ibid., pp. 48–51.

19. Musta'id Khan, Muhammad Saqi, *Maāsir-i 'Ālamgir: A History of the Emperor Aurangzib-'Ālamgir (reign 1658–1707)*, trans. by Sir Jadunath Sarkar, Bibliotheca Indica (Calcutta: Royal Asiatic Society of Bengal, 1947), pp. 312, 314; Gail Minault Graham, 'Akbar and Aurangzeb—Syncretism and Separatism in Mughal India: A Re-Examination', *Muslim World* 59 (1969), pp. 122–3.

20. S.A.A. Rizvi, *Muslim Revivalist Movements in Northern India in the Sixteenth and Seventeenth Centuries* (Agra: Agra University, 1965), pp. 410–17; Satish Chandra, *Mughal Religious Policies, the Rajputs and the Deccan* (New Delhi: Vikas Publishing House, 1993), pp. 194–211; Mohammad Akram Lari Azad, *Religion and Politics in India during the Seventeenth Century* (New Delhi: Criterion Publications, 1990), pp. 212–15.

21. Maulana Mujibullah Nadvi, *Fatāvá-i 'Alamgīrī ke Mū'allifin* (Lahore: Markaz-i Taḥqīq Diyāl Singh Trust Library, 1988), pp. 18–19. A.S. Bazmee Ansari gives earlier dates: 1664–1672 in his brief article on 'al-Fatawa al-'Alamgiriyya' in *Encyclopaedia of Islam*, New Ed.

22. John Herbert Harington, *An Elementary Analysis of the Laws and Regulations Enacted by the Governor General in Council at Fort William in Bengal for the Civil Government of the British Territories under that Presidency*, Vol. 1 (Calcutta: [Honorable Company's Press], 1805–18), p. 244.

23. Musta'id Khan, *Maāsir*, p. 315.

24. Ibid. The *Mir'āt al-'Ālam* contains a very similar account; see Abul-Muzaffar, 'Aurangzeb and the Fatawa-i-Alamgiri', *Al-Islam* 1, no. 8 (1953), p. 62.

25. Rafat M. Bilgrami, *Religious and Quasi-Religious Departments of the Mughal Period (1556–1707)* (New Delhi: Munshiram Manoharlal Publishers for Centre of Advanced Study, Department of History, Aligarh Muslim University, Aligarh, 1984), p. 103.

26. Aziz Ahmad, 'Role of Ulema', p. 9. See also Gregory C. Kozlowski, *Muslim Endowments and Society in British India*, Cambridge South Asian Studies (Cambridge: Cambridge University Press, 1985), p. 105.

27. Barbara Daly Metcalf, *Islamic Revival in British India: Deoband, 1860–1900* (Princeton, NJ: Princeton University Press, 1982), p. 23.

28. Rizvi, *Muslim Revivalist Movements*, pp. 426–7.

29. Zafarul Islam, 'Origin and Development', p. 11.

30. Musta'id Khan, *Maāsir*, p. 316.

31. Shah Wali Ullah, *Anfās al-'ārifin: Walī Ullāhī Silsilah Taṣawwuf kī Ma'rikah ārā Kitāb*, trans. by Saiyid Muhammad Faruqul Qadri (Deoband: Maktabah al-Falāḥ, n.d.), pp. 74–5.

32. Ibid., p. 74.

33. For details regarding the *madad-i ma'āsh* grants, see, Bilgrami, *Religious and Quasi-Religious Departments*, pp. 59–61.

34. J. Schacht, 'On the Title of the *Fatāwā al-Ālamgīriyya*', *Iran and Islam: In Memory of the Late Vladimir Minorsky*, ed. C.E. Bosworth (Edinburgh: Edinburgh University Press, 1971), p. 475. The distinction between primary and secondary *fatwās* will be addressed later.

35. Masud, *Islamic*, pp. 14–15; Zafarul Islam, 'Origin and Development', p. 7.

36. Anwar Ahmad Qadri, 'The Fatāwā-i-'Alamgīri', *Journal of the Pakistan Historical Society* 14, pt. 3 (July 1966), pp. 188–99.

37. Harington, *Analysis*, pp. 245–55.

38. Niel B.E. Baillie, *The Moohummudan Law of Sale according to the Huneefeea Code: from the Futawa Alumgeeree, a Digest of the Whole Law, Prepared by Command of the Emperor Aurungzebe Alumgeer* (1850; rpt. Delhi: Delhi Law House, n.d.), p. vii.

39. For a list of sources, see Nadvi, *Fatāwá*, pp. 14–17.

40. Ibid., pp. 19–20, 98–100.

41. Harington, *Analysis*, p. 243. Abul-Muzaffar considers this claim to be 'astonishing' (p. 62), but makes no reference to Harington, who cites the Chief Qazi as his source.

42. Ibid.

43. Abul-Muzaffar, 'Aurangzeb', p. 62.

44. Neil B.E. Baillie, *A Digest of Moohummudan Law Compiled and Translated from Authorities in the Original Arabic with an Introduction and Explanatory Notes Containing the Doctrines of the Hunifeea Code of Jurisprudence*, rev. ed. (Lahore: Premier Book House, n.d.), p. xii. See also Baillie, *Moohummudan Law*, p. vii.

45. *Fatāwá-i Hindiyya al-ma'rūf b'l Fatāwá-i 'Ālamgīrī*, trans. Maulana Saiyid Amir 'Ali, 10 vols. (Lukhnau: Matba Naulkishōr, 1932). A recent edition has been published with a forward by Justice Maulana Mufti Muhammad Taqiy 'Asmani (Karachi: Dadul Ashā'at, 1989).

46. 'al-Saiyid Amir 'Ali al-Lukhnawi', *Nuzhat al-khawāṭir*, ed. by Saiyid 'Abd al-Hayy, pt. 8 (Hyderabad al-Dakkan: Matba'at Da'irat al-Ma'arif al-'Usmaniyya, 1931–70), pp. 75–6. He is not to be confused with Saiyid Amir 'Ali (d. 1928), the author of *The Spirit of Islam* as well as works on Islamic law, primarily in English.

47. Qadri, *Fatāwā*, p. 192.

48. Mujib Allah Nadvi, *Fatāwá*, pp. 20–2; Abul-Muzaffar, 'Aurangzeb', pp. 62–3.

49. Mujib Allah Nadvi, *Fatāwá*, p. 21.

50. Abul-Muzaffar, 'Aurangzeb', p. 82.

51. Haq, 'Khafi Khan's History', p. 192.

52. Although a complete list of compilers is not found in any source, several modern scholars have compiled composite lists. See works by Mujib Allah Nadvi and Abul-Muzaffar already cited; the preface to the 1989 edition of the *Fatāwá-i 'Ālamgīrī* by Muhammad Taqiy 'Asmani, pp. 4–5; Muhammad Ishaq Bhatti, *Barr-i Ṣaghīr-i Pāk-o-Hind meṇ 'Ilm-i fiqh* (Lahore: Idarah Saqafat

Islamiyyah, 1973), pp. 245–380; 'Fatāwá-i 'Ālamgīrī', *Urdū Dā'irah Ma'ārif-i Islāmiyyah*, v. 15 (Lahore: Danishgah-i Panjab, 1959), pp. 145–55.

53. Mujib Allah Nadvi, *Fatāwá*, pp. 94–5.
54. Abul-Muzaffar, 'Aurangzeb', p. 79.
55. Ibid., pp. 79, 100, 110, 119.
56. Mujib Allah Nadvi, p. 33.
57. Bilgrami, *Religious and Quasi-Religious Departments*, pp. 120–1.
58. Ibid., pp. 111, 122.
59. Abul-Muzaffar, 'Aurangzeb', pp. 100, 101, 111.
60. Mujib Allah Nadvi, *Fatāwá*, pp. 110–12.
61. Metcalf, *Islamic Revival*, pp. 29–30.
62. *Fatāwá-i Hindiyya*, v. 5, pp. 109–11; M. Khalid Masud has translated this portion as an appendix to his article, '*Ādāb al-mufti*: The Muslim Understanding of Values, Characteristics, and role of a *Mufti*', in *Moral Conduct and Authority: The Place of* Adab *in South Asian Islam*, ed. Barbara Daly Metcalf (Berkeley, CA: University of California Press, 1984), pp. 146–9, from which the following description is summarized.
63. Ibid., p. 146.
64. Ibid., p. 133.
65. *Fatāwá-i Hindiyya*, v. 5, pp. 112–6. J.H. Harington has translated the section *Dalā'il par 'Aml Karnē kī Tar[t]īb* in his *An Elementary Analysis*, pp. 225–33, from which the following description is summarized.
66. Harington, pp. 227–9.
67. Hallaq, *Authority*, chapter 6, 'The Jurisconsult, the Author-jurist and Legal Change'.
68. Ibid.
69. Wael B. Hallaq, 'From *Fatwās* to *Furū*: 'Growth and Change in Islamic Substantive Law', *Islamic Law and Society* 1, no. 1 (April 1994), p. 31.
70. Ibid., pp. 31–45.
71. Ibid., p. 55.
72. Bilgrami, *Religious and Quasi-Religious Departments*, pp. 103, 107.
73. M.L. Bhatia, *Administrative History of Medieval India: A Study of Muslim Jurisprudence under Aurangzeb* (New Delhi: Radha Publications, 1992), pp. 51–2.
74. Ibid., p. 53.
75. Bilgrami, *Religious and Quasi-Religious Departments*, pp. 118–20.
76. Ibid., p. 120. Bhatia, *Administrative*, pp. 82–4, 101–04.
77. Ibid., pp. 88–9, 135–63.
78. Ibid., pp. 89–92.
79. Ibid., pp. 84–8, 92–4.
80. Bhatia, *Administrative*, p. vii.
81. Zafarul Islam, *Socio-Economic Dimension of Fiqh Literature in Medieval India* (Lahore: Research Cell, Dyal Singh Trust Library, 1990), p. 70.
82. Ibid., pp. 74–5.
83. Ibid., p. 77.

84. Bhatia, *Administrative*, pp. 243–9.
85. Wahed Husain, *Administration of Justice during the Muslim Rule in India, with a History of the Origin of the Islamic Legal Institutions* (Calcutta: University of Calcutta, 1934), p. 137.
86. Jadunath Sarkar, *Anecdotes of Aurangzeb and Historical Essays*, translation of *Aḥkām-i 'Ālamgīrī* (Calcutta: M.C. Sarkar & Sons, 1912), pp. 141–2.
87. Ibid., p. 141.

PART FOUR

Sufi and Shi'i Traditions

The topic of Sufi shaikhs and their institutions, which forms the focus of the first two essays in this section, has probably elicited more scholarly attention than any other topic in Indo-Muslim studies. Several factors might explain this: the visual and social prominence of magnet-like Sufi shrines that dot the South Asian landscape, the availability of a large number of original materials on the subject, people's intrinsic fascination with charismatic figures, and prevailing fashions within academic disciplines, especially anthropology.

On the other hand, Simon Digby makes a compelling case for highlighting the historical significance of Sufi traditions in the history of South Asian Islam. In this section's first essay, Digby argues that the dominance of a single Sufi shaikh of fourteenth-century Delhi, Nizam al-Din Auliya, 'has permanently affected the historical consciousness of Muslims of the subcontinent'. Because of that dominance, moreover, the particular school or 'order' of Sufism taught by that shaikh, the Chishti, has become associated with 'the enduring Muslim presence in India.' To sustain this argument, Digby places the early history of Indian Sufism in the context of the launching of Turkish rule in north India in the years after 1192, when large numbers of Central Asian emigrés settled down in the region. For those immigrants, he argues, spiritually powerful shaikhs facilitated an 'Islamic sanctification of a new homeland.' Most importantly, Chishti shaikhs like Nizam al-Din happened to be at (or very near) the epicenter of an expanding Tughluq empire, whose propagandists were often disciples of these same shaikhs. As a result, the Indo-Islamic traditions generated by these men and their followers—especially their recorded conversations (*malfūẓāt*) and biographies (*tadhkirāt*)—came to provide a textual basis for what Digby calls 'the historical consciousness' of South Asian Muslims.

If Digby is concerned with the traditions associated with the careers of Sufi shaikhs, the essay by Richard Eaton focuses on the traditions of the shrines that grew up over the tombs of such shaikhs. Concentrating on one such shrine complex, that of Shaikh Farid al-Din Ganj-i Shakar (d. 1265) in the western Punjab, the essay explores how, in the decades and centuries after 1265, the shaikh's spiritual power (*baraka*) became institutionalized in a series of traditions such as succession rituals, gifting ceremonies, the circulation of amulets, welfare kitchens, and death-date rites. Together with imperial patronage from the Tughluqs through the Mughals, these traditions helped make the shrine one of the largest and most popular Muslim pilgrimage sites in South Asia. The essay also explores the shrine's role, played over the course of seven centuries, in gradually integrating non-Hindu Jat clans into an increasingly Islam-oriented religious culture, a change occurring simultaneously with the transition of those clans from a predominantly pastoral to agrarian life.

Although South Asia's Shi'i communities comprise a minority of the region's total Muslim population, physical proximity to Iran, since c. 1500 a Shi'i majority region, enabled fairly regular immigration of Iranian Shi'is to India. Ali Asani's essay on the Khojah Isma'ilis—a Shi'i sect centred in Sind and Gujarat—shows how two kinds of Indo-Muslim traditions have for many centuries sustained this sect's identity, though one distinct from other South Asian Muslims. One of these is their tradition of hymn-like poems, the *gināns*, which have served as vehicles for transmitting Isma'ili teachings across generations. Asani's description of this medium as '"secondary" texts generated in the vernacular [in order] to transmit the teachings of "primary" scripture—the Qur'an—to non-Arabic speaking peoples' suggests how this sect of Muslims became indigenized in the Indian environment. Serving the same end was their adaptation of a Sindi mercantile script, Khojki, for liturgical purposes, just as Sikhs did with Gurmukhi, a local Punjabi script.

The closing essay by Juan Cole shifts the focus from Isma'ili Shi'is to Shi'ism's larger, 'Twelver' sect, and also to the very public domain of Muharram rituals in late eighteenth- and early nineteenth-century Lucknow. Although the subject of Cole's study lies somewhat beyond the chronological limits of this volume, the rituals he describes were historically connected with the decline of centralized Mughal power. In fact, they recall the dynamic traced in our earlier chapter by Aditya Behl: just as the decline of the centralized Tughluqs enabled more localized Islamic traditions to flourish in provincial fifteenth-century Jaunpur, so also the decline of centralized Mughal power three centuries later shifted patronage to the provinces, where successor states far from Delhi once again promoted localized Islamic traditions. Thus, in the late eighteenth-century, the Shi'i rulers of the rapidly growing post-Mughal provincial town of Lucknow lavishly patronized public Shi'i institutions such as the ornate Great

Imambarah (1791), prompting other Lucknawi nobles vying for social prestige to build smaller such structures. These in turn helped institutionalize the public performance of specifically Shi'i traditions such as the mourning sessions and processions that take place in the month of Muharram. It is Cole's contention that these traditions—enthusiastically participated in by Shi'i and proto-Shi'i groups (including Sunnis and Hindus)—contributed to the consolidation of a Shi'i community in pre-colonial Lucknow.

11

The Sufi Shaikh as a Source of Authority in Medieval India*

Simon Digby

THE HISTORICAL BACKGROUND

The period of the greater Delhi Sultanate began with the events of AD 1192, when the upper Gangetic plain with the site of Delhi itself was permanently wrested from Hindu Rajput control by a victorious Muslim army, whose commanders and functionaries were of immigrant Central Asian background. The Muslim conquest of Sind had taken place at the hands of the Arabs in the eighth century, and Lahore and Multan had been attached to the Ghaznawid kingdom of the Afghan plateau for a century and a half. After the new breakthrough of 1192 a great military camp was established on the site of Delhi; and within a few years Muslim arms swept across the vast Gangetic plain of eastern India, destroying the great Buddhist monasteries and putting an end to the Sena dynasty of Bengal. Circumstances a few decades after the initial conquests not only gave the Delhi sultans independence; they also forced them to struggle to maintain the newly founded state without outside aid. Qutb al-Din Aibak, the slave general of the Ghorid rulers of what is now Afghanistan, became the first independent sultan of the new realm in 1206; less than two decades later Ghor, Ghazni, and the Khurasani homelands had been overwhelmed and engulfed by the Mongol confederacy of Genghis Khan, a horde of unknown invaders, seemingly invincible and as yet un-Islamicized and un-Persianized. In these Asian lands, as in Europe, they appeared to be a manifestation of the Wrath of God.

For the following 180 years the Sultanate of Delhi survived as the dominant military power of northern India. It repelled numerous and

* Reprinted from Marc Gaborieau, ed., *Islam et Société en Asie du Sud*. Paris: École des Hautes Études en Sciences Sociales (*Puruṣārtha* 9, 1986), pp. 57–77.

formidable Mongol invasions from the northwest, and it expanded by plundering and sometimes annexing the Hindu kingdoms of the south and east. This was a pan-Indian realm, which at one time or another exercised control over an expanse of the subcontinent comparable to the realms of Ashoka and of the Mughal emperors in their heyday and only exceeded by the British colonial unification. The expansion of the Delhi Sultanate was only limited by the tendency, which grew stronger with time, for the remote areas of Muslim conquest to break away and form independent sultanates, and by occasional regroupings of Hindu resistance after the shock of the initial conquest.[1] Thus, Bengal, the Deccan, and Ma'bar (the southern Coromandel coast) were lost to Delhi long before the debacle of 1398. In the north, local Rajput dynasties, not wholly subdued, tended to recover some of their power and regain lost frontier territories in moments of weakness of the Delhi Sultanate; and the southern Deccan witnessed the emergence in the late fourteenth century of the new and powerful Hindu state of Vijayanagara. The debacle of 1398 was the invasion of Amir Timur, the Tamerlane of European history, who had reorganized the Central Asian tribal confederacies and brought them to devastate the established civilized economies.

By this time the city, or perhaps one should say the cities of Delhi, which were of enormous extent, were sacked.[2] Many of their inhabitants were taken into captivity and slavery and the surviving army of the sultanate was destroyed. This event perhaps only set the seal on a rapid decline of the administration and of the capital city, which was already the scene of civil war within the gates. Through the fifteenth century we witness a different political scene. The provinces of Muslim conquest—Bengal, Jaunpur, Gujarat, Malwa, and the Deccan—developed as independent sultanates. They contended among themselves for mastery, and consolidated the cultural and administrative traditions, transported from the Persian-speaking lands of eastern Islam, which they had inherited from the Delhi Sultanate.[3]

THE ISLAMIC SANCTIFICATION OF THE NEW HOMELAND

At the close of the twelfth Christian century, when the victorious army of Islam entered its new domain, the military camp of the invaders was established near a Hindu fort of moderate dimensions, in a good strategic situation for the consolidation of power over the conquered territories; and the need for symbolic legitimation and sanctification of the Muslim presence in this still alien land was felt. Immediate plans were made and the foundations were laid for the building of a mosque and a minaret on a most ambitious scale.[4]

There were many earlier Middle Eastern Islamic precedents for the appropriation, after conquest, of non-Muslim edifices or building materials to create mosques for Muslim worship. Here in Delhi the inscription at the eastern entrance of the mosque records not only the initiation of the project by the general in command, but also the estimated building cost of the twenty-seven Hindu and Jain temples from which materials had been plundered for the new structure.[5] At the same time, the great arched screen to the prayer hall and a huge freestanding minaret (known today as the Qutb Minar) were begun. Hindu temple stonemasons and sculptors—the latter doubtless instructed to avoid un-Islamic figural representation—were employed to construct in stone a semblance of what the conquerors remembered of the brick monuments of Ghazna and Khurasan.

The mosque of Qubbat al-Islam ('The Pinnacle of Islam') was also embellished with objects that were symbols of the domination of Islam in these new territories. The great fourth-century iron column of Chandragupta, its Hindu deity lopped off above the capital, was placed beneath the central arch of the mosque screen.[6] Later, at the close of the thirteenth century, large bronze idols from the conquest of Malwa were smashed and carried back to bury before the threshold of the mosque.[7]

The re-use of carved Hindu pillars and masonry set a pattern for subsequent spoliations during the initial phases of conquest and colonization in Gujarat and the Deccan. The richness of the materials is only matched in the other great monument of the initial decades of the Delhi Sultanate, the early thirteenth century mosque at Ajmer known as the *Arhā'ī din kā jhōnprā*. There the finely carved temple columns are surmounted by cusped arches, creating an even more elegant effect.[8]

In the early decades of the thirteenth century, the Muslim outpost at Ajmer confined the Chauhans and their Rajput allies from an attempt at the reconquest of Delhi. In the subsequent historical image of the Muslim colonization, there is a polarity between the capital city and the perilous outpost. Ajmer is a town cradled in rocky hills, and down the precipitous slopes run the lines of ancient fortifications. There are great rocks and springs and lakes, and at the summit of the hill are the graves of Muslim martyrs who died in frays against the infidel.[9] These are the picturesque and sentimental adjuncts to the legend of Mu'in al-Din Chishti, called 'the Deputy of the Prophet in India',[10] the Sufi shaikh whose presence is thought to guard the welfare of Muslims throughout the Indian subcontinent.

A programme of mosque-building was not in itself sufficient to satisfy the longing for the sanctification of a land where, a single generation after the conquest, the Muslim population grew up in the shadow of the loss of the immediate homeland of their fathers. This need also inspired the provision made by the sultans, their great officers and other people of means, of stipends for those who called to prayer or otherwise officiated in the mosques that were being built, of qazis to administer Islamic law, and of 'ulama, experts in the traditional Islamic sciences.

However, such measures provided meagre spiritual fare for a community of Muslim believers that came to include a growing number of assimiles living within a political and cultural system that was novel in the environment. An easier path of devotion, of mediation and guidance in the sometimes arid landscape of mandatory Muslim beliefs and observances, seemed to be at hand in a tradition of holy men, the tradition of the Sufis, which was introduced in the evolved state to which it had developed in Khurasan and elsewhere in the lands of Islam by the time of the creation of the Delhi Sultanate. This tradition provided a channel of intercession with the deity that might procure benefits in this world or the next, and might even lead to heights of mystical experience. What it certainly provided was a local Muslim identity that bound the newly formed community to the land where they dwelt.

SUFISM AS IMPORTED INTO THE DELHI SULTANATE

In the eleventh and twelfth Christian centuries there was a vigorous Sufi tradition in Khurasan (the northeast of modern Iran together with most of modern Afghanistan). It was characterized by 'orders' (*ṭarīqa* or *silsila*) of quite recent historical development, but the strictly linear chronological development propounded by J. Spencer Trimingham, from *khānqāh* (the hospice of a Sufi shaikh or teacher) through ṭarīqa ('path', in this usage synonymous with silsila, 'chain') to *ṭā'ifa* ('group'—seldom used in this sense in Indo-Persian literature) is not found in Khurasan. The concept of the transmission of baraka (charisma) through a ṭarīqa or silsila of Sufi shaikhs is strongly held, but examples of all three of Spencer Trimingham's groupings may be found at one and the same time, and the structures are to some extent reversible or interchangeable. Moreover, claims to the inheritance of authority were not always accompanied by an identity of practice.[11]

However, patterns of the holy life and of Sufi organization were transmitted from Khurasan to the Delhi Sultanate. Among the substrata of what was transmitted were traits, which are often ignored by modern writers, describing in a pietistic tradition the activities of Sufi shaikhs of the Delhi Sultanate: an uncompromising arrogance despite professions of humility in the advancement of personal claims to spiritual eminence, and examples of the display of *jalāl*, 'splendour', but in practice the 'wrath' that led to the discomfiture, misery, and often, death of those who presumed to oppose the shaikh. Here the character of the shaikh too often approaches that of the *darwīsh* in Persian folklore, a disagreeable and terrifying figure, exercising his supernatural powers with malignance.[12]

Such traits are visible among other strands of sentiment, belief, and practice in Indo-Persian hagiographical literature; and they also recur in the non-Muslim collections of biographical narratives of later date, modelled on the Sufi *tadhkiras*, in the vernacular literatures of northern India.[13] This substratum of malignance rather than benevolence, combined with supernatural powers acquired magically by the practice of austerities, has ancient Indian parallels, but here appears to be a re-importation from a wide Central Asian milieu, partly Turkish and replete with practices described by modern writers as shamanistic, thinly disguised by some centuries of superimposed Islamic piety.

Some of the wilder, less 'orthodox' or approved practices among ecstatic Sufis, which make their appearance in the Indian conquered territories in the thirteenth century, appear ultimately to derive from the extended and culturally alloyed late Indo-Buddhist culture of Central Asia. Even if this was submerged under the apparatus of traditional Islamic learning, it was a part of the mental stock-in-trade of the Sufis, which particularly commended them not only to the immigrant Turkish soldiers of the armies of the sultanate, but also to a considerable portion of the non-Muslim population of the north Indian plains. Vaishnava *bhaktamālas*, Sikh *janamsākhīs*, and other *vitae* of non-Muslim men of religion repeat the emphasis and structure of Sufi anecdotes, particularly regarding contests of superiority, magical displays, and a general lack of charity towards opponents and doubters.[14]

THE ATTRIBUTES OF A SUFI SHAIKH

> [As the present writer has stated elsewhere], a detailed study of a medieval Sufi Shaikh will often reveal inconsistencies of attitude, character and behaviour. Acceptance of a Sufi in his lifetime as a great Shaikh depended on the recognition that he possessed, to an impressive degree, qualities which showed that he was the recipient of Divine grace. The balance of these qualities in a single Shaikh might vary, just as a winning hand at cards may be stronger in some suits than in others. Descent from the Prophet, his Companions, or other *ashrāf*; connection with a Sufi *silsila* of already established prestige; a reputation for strict orthodoxy; austerities sometimes of a more and sometimes of a less orthodox character; a mastery of Islamic doctrinal or Sufi texts, or an abundance of literary compositions; the working of miracles together with a careful avoidance of vulgar display

of them; a reputation for inaccessibility and of dislike of human society, often combined with a care for disciples and accepted hangers-on (as well as strangers and visitors); visible ecstasy, often of a Shamanistic type and often also linked to a refined sensibility to (mainly Persian) poetry and (to) music—all these qualities were held to be evidence of the especially close relations of the Shaikh with the Deity, and all contributed to his prestige and the winning of devotees.[15]

Not all of these attributes were wholly reconcilable with one another, and Sufi shaikhs were confronted with certain problems of choice in the lifestyles that they adopted.[16] An obvious division was between Sufi claimants who were described as *bā-shar*‘, whose behaviour was in conformity with Islamic law as they understood it, and those who were *bī-shar*‘, who considered themselves in some way excused from its observance.[17] This was a division that increasingly came to resemble, among the hierarchies and the devotees of Sufi cults and shrines, the division between the pure and impure Hindu castes, among Indian Muslims between the *ashrāf* (the 'noble' or perhaps we should say the respectable) and the *ajlāf* or *ardhāl* (the 'base').[18] The ashrāf are prone to a process of 'Islamization' (using this term on the analogy of M.N. Srinivas's 'Sanskritization') in which the quest or maintenance of high social status leads to a stricter conformity of belief and observance of the propositions of Muslim doctors and jurists of the 'classical period'. Such strictness can be advanced as a claim to authority on the part of a Sufi shaikh or a *silsila* of such shaikh. The last of the great Chishti shaikhs of the Delhi Sultanate advances the claims of the religious law in conjunction with his own claims to authority:

> People keep on saying that *ḥaqīqat* ('Truth', the mystical Sufi perception of God) is the Divine secret; but I Muhammad Husaini say that *sharī‘at* (the observance of Muslim law) is the Divine secret because I have also heard talk of *ḥaqīqat* from Haidaris, Qalandars, Mulḥids and Zindīqs; nay, I have even heard of it from the mouths of Jogis, of Brahmans, and of Gurus: but talk of the *sharī‘at* I have not heard from anyone's mouth than the people of true faith and belief (i.e. Sunni Muslims). From this it is evident that *sharī‘āt* is the Divine secret.[19]

Immediately after this statement the shaikh (Saiyid Muhammad Gesudaraz) put forward his own claims to authority—learning and orthodoxy in conjunction with descent from the Prophet and his own rank as a Sufi shaikh: 'There are few men who are at once a *faqīh* (jurist), a Sufi, a Sunni, and a Saiyid. All these four qualities are present in me.'[20] In addition to the symbols of authority that Saiyid Muhammad Gesudaraz claimed to have inherited from his predecessor in the Chishti order,[21] we may note another claim to authority as a shaikh, that God had preserved him to an extreme old age in order to vindicate him from an assertion that he was too young to have had authority transmitted to him at the time when he claimed that this event had occurred.[22]

Somewhat distant from orthodox Islamic belief and observance is another well-attested source of prestige. This is poetic sensibility, which extended also to the music of sung or chanted verse. The popular appeal of this characteristic during this period usually outweighed deprecations from the point of view of Islamic orthodoxy. Such sensibility was shared by all the great Chishti shaikhs of the Delhi Sultanate, although some may have possessed it in greater measure than others,[23] and we lack detailed information in the case of the founder of the lineage in India. The second shaikh of the *silsila* there, Qutb al-Din Bakhtyar Kaki, is alleged to have expired after four days of violent ecstasy at the recital of a Persian *bait* (couplet):

kushtagān-i khanjar-i taslīm-rā
har zamān az ghaib jān-i dīgar ast.
'For those slain by the dagger of belief
Every time from the Unseen there is new life.'[24]

This event is said to have occurred in 1235. Down to the twentieth century there have been attested examples of death in ecstasy at *samā*' or audition parties. In the Persian-speaking world of the medieval period, the connections between poetic sensibility and Sufism are almost inseparable. The verse of the greatest of Persian poets, Sa'di and Hafiz, as well as that of many of their predecessors, contemporaries and successors, would often have been unintelligible without some knowledge of Sufi concepts and practice. Even when the poet himself had worldly connections and employment, and did not live the life of a Sufi shaikh or whole-time disciple, he had strong claims to admission to their companionship. This was the case of Amir Khusrau (1253–1325), the greatest of the Indo-Persian poets, who was an intimate companion of Shaikh Nizam al-Din of Delhi; and of his rival Amir Hasan, author of a record of the conversations of the same shaikh.[25]

As suggested above, the hand of cards held by different Sufi shaikhs in their bids for allegiance would be stronger in some suits than others. The hagiographies composed by their followers are likely to resort to myth and invention in order to explain away potential deficiences or weak suits. The Chishti shaikhs in India were mostly unable or unwilling to travel beyond the territories of the Delhi Sultanate, although subsequent sources credited them with wider ranges of travel.[26] By the end of the thirteenth century, conditions of travel to the central lands of Islam had become easier as a result of the diminution of the ferocity of Mongol attacks and the annexation of Gujarat. Explanations might therefore be sought as to why a major shaikh like Nizam al-Din had not performed the Muslim duty of *ḥaj*, pilgrimage to the Holy Places of Mecca and Medina. An explanation current within decades of his death is that a camel used to arrive at his khānqāh on Friday eve, to transport him through the air to Mecca, where he was observed at the congregational prayers by a trustworthy witness.[27] The same story is told in another fourteenth-century source about a less reputable contemporary of Nizam al-Din, the *majdhūb* or madman Khwaja Gurg, and the identical story or close analogues are related about other Sufi figures down to the present day.[28]

BELIEF IN THE MIRACULOUS AND SUPERNATURAL

Modern writers, when they make use of the hagiographical literature of the Delhi Sultanate as historical evidence, often ignore and pass over in silence frequent mentions of the appearance of supernatural beings and narratives of the exercise of supernatural powers. In a dated and unquestionably authentic narrative of individual conversations of the great Shaikh Nizam al-Din, we find a succession of anecdotes of a preacher in a mosque who was so transported by his own eloquence that he flew away from the pulpit (*miṃbar*) to a neighbouring wall;[29] of meetings in deserted places with Khwaja Khizr, who has everlasting life;[30] and of various 'fairy people'—of the *abdāls* who physically fly above the territories that they protect from harm,[31] of a holy man circling around the vault of the chief mosque at Delhi through the night till the dawn,[32] and of the *mardān-i-ghaib*, 'men of the Unseen' who appear and disappear, and sometimes call away a mortal to join them.[33] Shaikh Nizam al-Din and his successor at Delhi, Shaikh Nasir al-Din Mahmud, shared these folk-beliefs with their followers.

A strong, often crude, belief in the miraculous pervaded all sections of society, including the learned and the powerful. *Karāmāt* ('graces', in fact miracles) were proofs to the devotees of a Sufi shaikh that he had attained to the status that they attributed to him. The shaikh's interventions in the ordinary course of nature (*kharq-i 'ādat*) extended from the trifling affairs of individuals, to whom they supplied amulets,[34] to an influence over major political events. In the opinion of their followers, they held powers for the making and unmaking of kings and kingdoms.[35]

THE TERRITORIAL WILĀYAT OF THE SHAIKH

The *Kashf al-maḥjūb* of 'Ali Hujwiri, written at Lahore before the beginning of our period, provides a theoretical basis for this large assumption of supernatural powers:

> God has saints (*awliyā*, pl. of *walī*) whom he has especially distinguished by his friendship and whom He has chosen to be the governors of His kingdom [...] He has made the saints the governors of the universe... Through the blessing of their advent the rains fall from heaven and through the purity of their lives the plants spring up from the earth and through their spiritual influence Muslims gain victories over unbelievers...[36]

Above the authority of mundane rulers there is ordained a hierarchy of those with supernatural powers, perpetually watchful over the welfare of all the regions of the world. The lowest rank of these, the *abdāls* ('substitutes') are also *walīs* ('friends [of God]'); through the Arabic trilateral root *walia*, a conceit is pursued and elaborated, identifying *walāya* or *wilāya* (Divine 'friendship') with *wilāya* (Persian *wilāyat,* 'governance'), which comes to be used for spiritual jurisdiction over a specific territory.[37]

Such claims to the *wilāyat* of a specific territory were actively and vigorously pursued by shaikhs in Khurasan in the eleventh and twelfth centuries, and the concept is very common in fourteenth-century and later Indian Sufi literature. In the Delhi Sultanate this notion of the territorial *wilāyat* of a Shaikh led, at the beginning of the fourteenth century, to the common identification of Shaikh Nizam al-Din of the Chishti *silsila* with the well-being and fortunes of the capital city of Delhi and the realm over which it held sway. In his lifetime, the question arose in people's minds whether such wilāyat was personal, or had passed away at his death. A quarter of a century after this, the poet 'Isami, writing in the new secessionist Muslim state of the Deccan, maintained that power and prosperity passed away from Delhi at Nizam al-Din's death:

> He was one of the friends of God
> Through whom the realm of Hindostan was maintained.
> First that man of wise dominion
> Set out from Delhi to another kingdom (the next world);
> After this that city and country were ruined;
> Discord prevailed in that realm.[38]

With this concept of territorial jurisdiction, it was difficult for a locally established shaikh to tolerate the presence of another shaikh of powerful charisma in his vicinity. Baha al-Din Zakariya at Multan, we are told, laid out the shoes of the Chishti Shaikh Qutb al-Din Bakhtiyar, indicating that he should set out towards Delhi.[39] Nizam al-Din mentions that his predecessor Farid al-Din considered that his own wilāyat extended a certain distance from Ajodhan towards Multan, and was replaced at that frontier by that of Shaikh Baha al-Din Zakariya. He himself could give protection to a traveller only up to that frontier.[40]

The dominance of Nizam al-Din at this place and moment of time, in Delhi at the apogee of the power of the Sultanate, has permanently affected the historical consciousness of Muslims of the subcontinent and has furthered the notion of a special position of the Chishti *silsila* in the establishment of the enduring Muslim presence in India. Yet this local pre-eminence was not achieved without struggle and rivalry, nor was it unquestioned in its day by those who put forward rival claims to authority—representatives of other Sufi lineages, upholders of Muslim law and traditional sciences, and the sultans themselves, who held material sway over the territories whose spiritual jurisdiction was assigned in popular estimation to the shaikh.

CONFLICT AND ACCOMMODATION WITHIN THE SILSILAS

The rivalry between the Suhrawardi *silsila*, with its centre of power in Multan, and the Chishtis, influential in Delhi and the lands of the new conquests, was conducted amicably, possibly because all the Chishti shaikhs in India used manuals of Sufi practice, such as the *'Awārif al-ma'ārif*, which had been compiled or transmitted in the Suhrawardi environment. By contrast, no early hagiographical work regarding the lives of the great Suhrawardi shaikhs of Multan entered the mainstream of the hagiographical tradition; and no such work is accessible to us. In consequence, we are exclusively dependent on sources which present the Chishti view of the relations that obtained between the two *silsilas*.

The Chishti sources emphasize the virtue of the rule of poverty (*faqr*) as practised by the shaikhs of the order, who did not accept land-grants which would have yielded an assured income, and distributed before nightfall the *futūḥāt* (offerings) that were presented to them. This is contrasted with the accumulation of wealth and property by Baha al-Din Zakariya and his successors at Multan.[41] Early in the thirteenth century a *khalīfa* (deputy) of Mu'in al-Din Chishti at Ajmer, Hamid al-Din Suwali of Nagaur in Rajasthan, sent epistles to Baha al-Din Zakariya criticizing his departure from the Sufi rule of faqr.[42] Yet during the same period a Suhrawardi khalīfa, also called Qazi Hamid al-Din Nagauri, was on terms of intimacy with the other Chishti khalīfa of Mu'in al-Din at Delhi, Qutb al-Din Bakhtyar Kaki, enthusiastically participating with him in *samā'* (listening to music).[43] Neither of these two shaikhs maintained a khānqāh (hospice). The considerably later sources possibly exaggerate the extent of the influence of Qutb al-Din and Qazi Hamid al-Din upon the pious Sultan Shams al-Din Iltutmish and upon the urban population of Delhi.[44]

In early thirteenth-century Delhi the principal religious conflicts of authority of which record remains, concerned the question of the lawfulness of *samā*‘, and the arraignment on an accusation of adultery of the migrant Suhrawardi khalīfa Jalal al-Din Tabrizi. The Chishti and the Suhrawardi shaikhs were on the same side, and their main opponent was the *Shaikḥ al-Islām*, Najm al-Din Kubra. Our Chishti sources record that he received appropriate retribution for his attempt to humiliate Jalal al-Din Tabrizi. The latter, sitting by the banks of a river, saw by clairvoyance the death of Najm al-Din Kubra. He invited those present to participate in funeral prayers, remarking: 'If the *Shaikh al-Islām* sent me out of Dehli, my shaikh sent him out of the world.'[45]

By the early fourteenth century, when the influence of Nizam al-Din in Delhi was at its height and he had established a considerable khānqāh there, Rukn al-Din, grandson of Baha al-Din Zakariya, came on a visit to the city from Multan. A whole section of our principal source, the *Siyar al-auliyā*', is devoted to anecdotes of the mutual courtesy and the consideration that the Chishti and the Suhrawardi shaikhs extended to one another. When Rukn al-Din was received by Nizam al-Din, he was presented with a silken purse through which the glitter of the red-gold coins could be seen, a detail that sheds a curious light on the actual practice of *faqr* and the distribution of futūḥāt at the khānqah at this period. Rukn al-Din disclaimed any intention of setting up his own khalīfa in rivalry to Nizam al-Din in the capital city, even though (or perhaps because) this was the suggestion of the reigning sultan. At the death of Nizam al-Din, Rukn al-Din himself led the funeral prayers.[46]

There is a real contrast between earlier Chishti and Suhrawardi practice in the matter of the acceptance of land-grants and the accumulation of treasure, even if the difference has been exaggerated by the Chishti sources. This difference of practice may have been dictated by the differing political conditions that prevailed at Multan, when compared to Delhi and the inner territories of the Delhi Sultanate. Multan was in an exposed position on the insecure western frontier. It was at different times under the control of the Delhi Sultans and of the Chaghatayid Mongols of Transoxania, or of provincial satraps serving both sides. To maintain the Suhrawardi khānqāh through periods of adversity required a prudent conservation of resources. This suggestion is supported by the fortress-like site of the khānqāh at Multan, on an ancient inhabited site on the crest of one of the two hills (possibly 'tells') of Multan; and by the mediatory political roles that were played by the Suhrawardi shaikhs acting on behalf of the inhabitants of Multan.[47] Similar circumstances may have dictated the abandonment in the fourteenth century of the rule against the acceptance of land-grants at the border Chishti khānqāh of Ajodhan (Pakpattan).[48]

The amicable relations that existed between the Chishtis and Suhrawardis contrast with those of which we have fragmentary record between the Chishti shaikhs in the capital city and a group of successors of the Khwarazmian Shaikh Najm al-Din Kubra (d. 1221), who later became known as the Firdausi *silsila*. As his name suggests, the Shaikh al-Islām Najm al-Din Kubra belonged to this group. In a Firdausi source he is predictably described as *mard-i buzurg ṣāḥib-i-wilāyat* ('a holy man, possessor of *wilāyat*'). The same source sharply criticizes Qutb al-Din Bakhtyar for the hold he had acquired over the population of Delhi by the display of miraculous powers.[49]

The hostility that existed between the Chishtis and the Firdausis is well illustrated by an unpleasant incident that occurred in the early fourteenth century. This is worthy of extended notice, both as an example of the attribution of not wholly beneficent supernatural powers to Sufi shaikhs, and as a demonstration of the tendency, even when there are two accounts written within the same hagiographical tradition by partizans of the same shaikhs, for a conflict either of memory or of veracity to occur.

The anecdote occurs in its simpler form in the *Siyar al-auliyā*, although this is the later of the two nearly contemporary sources:

> The writer of these words (has heard) that Shaikh Rukn al-Din, who was not too sincerely attached to (Nizam al-Din), had come outside the city and also made a residence on the banks of the river Jamuna at the limit of Kilokhri; and had set up as a Shaikh (i.e. he had set up a *khānqāh*, deliberately not called such by our source, in proximity and rivalry to that of Nizam al-Din). His sons were adolescent and his *murīds* were impertinent towards the servants of Nizam al-Din ('servants' is a polite periphrasis). Time and again, riding in a boat, they used to pass the house of the Shaikh (Nizam al-Din) in *samā*' (music) and *raqṣ* (ecstatic dancing). One day, a little after the midday prayer, in a body and performing *samā*' and *raqṣ* they passed before the house of the Shaikh in this manner. The Shaikh himself was seated on the roof of the *jamā'at-khāna* (congregational hall), and he was sitting 'occupied' (*mashghūl*), i.e. in the performance of *dhikr*. The father of the author of this account was present standing in the gathering. When they came into view of the Shaikh, in their boat and making excessive noise with their *samā*', he remarked: 'Praise be to God! It is years since (I) have drunk my heart's blood and offered my soul in this Path. Others are growing boys and say, "Who are you that we are not?" He raised his blessed hand towards them and said: 'Now go away!'
>
> The moment that the boat of Shaikh Rukn al-Din's sons arrived below their own house with all that noise, they came out of it and wished to

perform their ablutions; but as soon as they went into the water they were instantly drowned. The author (Amir Khwurd) has heard this story from his uncle [...] Saiyid Husain.[50]

The same incident is recorded in the *Khair al-majālis*, directly from the lips of Nizam al-Din's successor at Delhi, Nasir al-Din Mahmud. A new comb had been brought to him by a young Arab. He recalled how Nizam al-Din had been relating an anecdote regarding the latter's pir, Farid al-Din. A darwish (with the insolent behaviour characteristic of *qalandars*) had insistently demanded a comb from Farid al-Din. Just as Nizam al-Din was telling this story, some 'friends' (*yārān*, i.e. devotees) arrived in the shaikh's assembly and announced: 'We were present at the invitation of the Tusis; in that gathering the sons of 'Imad Firdausi were present. They said something (abusive) about the servants (polite periphrasis) of the Shaikh.'

In the continuation of the anecdote that Nizam al-Din was telling when their conduct was reported to him, the darwish finally stated that *barakat* would accrue from the gift of the comb, but Farid al-Din terminated the interview by saying: 'We have sent that *barakat* down the river (*ān barakat-rā dar āb ravān kardīm*)!' The darwish was a traveller and he came to a river near the settlement (of Ajodhan), which was fordable. He went into the river to perform his ablutions and vanished from sight.

According to Nasir al-Din Mahmud's relation, which is recorded in the *Khair al-majālis*, after Nizam al-Din had finished telling this anecdote:

> There immediately arose from the direction of Kilokhri a clamour that the sons of 'Imad Firdausi had drowned. The question was asked how they had drowned. The reply was that they had come from the *khānqāh* of the Tusis. In a boat they had passed below the *khānqāh* of the Shaikh (Nizam al-Din) and had arrived at Kilokhri. The *langar* (charitable kitchen) of Maulana 'Imad Firdausi was there. They had got out of their boat and had taken off their clothes and gone into the water to wash their bodies. One brother had begun to drown and called out to the other:
> 'Take hold of my hand!'
> He grasped his hand, but could not come up. At this time the water flowed strongly and both were drowned. The cry rose that both the *shaikhzādas* (sons of 'Imad) had been drowned in the river, until in time this news reached the Shaikh (Nizam al-Din).

It was then ascertained that these were the two sons who had abused Nizam al-Din at the celebration of the Tusis, and that the drowning had occurred just at the time when Nizam al-Din was telling the story of the darwish who had vanished (or drowned) in the river after Farid al-Din's parting remark. The compiler of the *Khair al-majālis*, Hamid Qalandar, concludes his record with 'a cheer for the miracles of miracles in miracles' of Farid al-Din and Nizam al-Din.[51]

It is obvious that both these accounts describe the same incident, and they have certain details in common. One account is an immediate record from apparently first-hand testimony, while the other purports to be the version of the compiler's uncle, who told him about an event witnessed by the compiler's father. Apart from the variation in the name of the Firdausi Shaikh ('*imād* and *rukn* both meaning 'pillar' and therefore easily confused), they have totally different accounts of how Nizam al-Din was occupied and what he said at the time of the drowning. The second anecdote from the *Khair al-majālis* is of more elaborate structure, implying Nizam al-Din's foreknowledge that the news of the misconduct of the Firdausi shaikh's sons was about to be brought to him; and it makes clear that the fate that was about to befall them would resemble that which had befallen someone who had been equally disrespectful to Nizam al-Din's own pir.

A hagiographer of the Firdausi *silsila*, writing only a few decades later, was familiar with both these sources, which he cites on other occasions. He only refers obliquely to the incident, but his statement is indicative of the hostility between the *silsilas*:

> The Shaikhs of the age were envious of (Rukn al-Din Firdausi's) upbringing and *tarīqa*. Shaikh Nizam al-Din was too pure to show malevolence, but malevolence was characteristic of his *murīds* and devotees. They were watching for calamities and accidents. If anything of temporal misfortunes befell Khwaja Rukn al-Din, they loosed their tongues and said:
> 'This calamity or this accident of Khwaja Rukn al-Din has occurred from the pronouncement (*nafas*) of Shaikh Nizam al-Din or from his heaviness of heart!'
> It is well known that all the people of Delhi were devoted to Shaikh Nizam al-Din. They all dared to wish harm to Khwaja Rukn al-Din.[52]

The Firdausis, with their enduring tradition of hostility to the Chishtis, appear to have achieved little success in the capital city of Delhi, but in the middle of the fourteenth century, their influence was established in Bihar through the activities and writings of Sharaf al-Din Ahmad bin Yahya of Maner. Paradoxically, this success may be a consequence of their failure in Delhi.

The hagiographical tradition of the Firdausis is embodied in the *tadhkira Manāqib al-asfiyā*. This was written shortly after the sack of Delhi in 1398, and in it there are signs of an enduring tradition of hostility to those in power in the capital city. The establisher of the *silsila* in eastern India had initially been the pupil of Maulana Ashraf al-Din Tawwama. Regarding him we are told that ' in the days when the country of Bengal was subject to the King of Dehli', the ruler, who is not named, had exiled Ashraf al-Din to Sunargaon, because 'from the excess of the obedience of the population (to him), the King feared that he might seize the realm.'[52] After a stay with Ashraf al-Din Tawwama at Sunargaon, Sharaf al-Din went to Delhi, where he observed the shaikh of the time with deprecation. 'If this is Shaikhhood, then I am a Shaikh!' He attended upon Nizam al-Din, who did not accept him as a disciple, but turned him away with a courteous phrase and a leaf of *tambūl* (betel). However, when he appeared before Khwaja Najib al-Din Firdausi (khalīfa of Rukn al-Din) he felt an awe (*dahshat*) which he had not felt before Nizam al-Din, and he became his *murid*.[53]

The links of the *silsila*, at the time when it spread in Bihar, with the capital city were further embittered by an incident that occurred late in the reign of Firuz Shah Tughluq (r. 1351–88) and not long before the death of Sharaf al-Din (d. 1381). Two of the shaikh's followers, Ahmad Bihari and 'Izz Kakawi, one described as mad (*dīwāna*) and both at the wilder end of the Sufi spectrum, went to Delhi, where their 'open words about the mysteries of Union' were heard by the people of Delhi, who accused them before the sultan. The sultan held an inquest (*maḥḍar*) with all the notables of the city, and the poor wretches (*miskīnān*) were put to death. 'There were many shaikhs of [the Chishti] *tarīqa*; not one of them by a defence of madness or the like of this caused them to be spared.'[54]

The (possibly spurious) *apologia* of the sultan has a sharply differing account of 'a group [...] who made *murīds* and spoke words of *kufr* (infidelity). The leader of those who had gone astray was called Ahmad Bihari, and a faction from Bihar called him God (*khudā*) ... One of his disciples said, "In Delhi God has arisen!"'[55]

When the news of the two executions reached Sharaf al-Din, we are told that he remarked (with predictable consequences) that 'it would be strange if the city should continue to flourish, where the blood of such as these had been spilt!'. These words reached the sultan, who once more called together the 'ulama and notables and was persuaded by them to despatch a farmān summoning the shaikh to Delhi. He was persuaded to rescind the order when he found that the noted Suhrawardi shaikh who was then visiting Delhi, Saiyid Jalal al-Din Bukhari ('Makhdūm-i jahānīān') had been in retreat reading the epistles (*maktūbāt*) that Sharaf al-Din had sent to him.[56]

PRECEPT AND PRACTICE AMONG SUFI SHAIKHS

In this period there was an unavoidable conflict between professed aims and necessary practice in the pursuit of the role of a great shaikh. This is visible in the hagiographical literature, and thrown into sharper relief if other evidence is taken into consideration. The Chishti shaikhs were committed to a lifestyle of personal austerities, poverty, or even deliberate indebtedness, inaccessibility, avoidance of cities, and of contact with worldly people—and especially of avoidance of contact with the rich and the powerful, and to the concealment of *karāmāt* (miraculous powers). Their charisma largely derived from the widespread conviction that they possessed these qualities, but for this charisma to be recognized they had often to proceed in exactly the opposite way. Prestige also depended on the ablility to construct, extend, and organize a khānqāh; to feed, accommodate, and attend to the material and spiritual needs of disciples and often numerous dependents; and to accommodate travellers according to Muslim precept and the expectations of hospitality. The principal means to support such necessarily extensive establishments were likely to be offerings from the wealthy and powerful, sometimes by a system of monasterial labour. Such offerings implied the accessibility of the khānqāh and of the shaikh himself, contrary to the ideal of inaccessibility and avoidance of worldly contacts.

The fond descriptions of Farid al-Din's khānqāh at Ajodhan, which passed from the record of Nizam al-Din's conversations into later hagiographical literature, embody many memorable and striking circumstantial details—the shaikh and his disciples going out to gather firewood and unappetizing fruits of the jungle, Farid's own mother eaten by a wild beast a short distance away from the road, female descendants of the Prophet washing the soiled clothes of the disciples who had walked the long way to Ajodhan, the thatched huts and the rustic fare—all the details and anecdotes in this vein suggest a remote idyll of rural simplicity and holy poverty.[57] Nevertheless the khānqāh lay on a major route between the populous cities of Delhi and Multan, along which trade and travellers constantly passed. It had a stable for the horses, and it stands, like the Suhrawardi khānqāh at Multan, in a commanding position at the height of what is probably an ancient 'tell', dominating the small walled town.[58]

According to the hagiographical tradition, in the early days after the foundation of the khānqāh, Farid al-Din was visited here by Ulugh Khan, the future Sultan Balban, who was then in command of the western marches of the Delhi Sultanate.[59] An offer of a grant of villages was rejected by Farid, but in the following century such grants appear to have been accepted from the Tughluq sultans of Delhi by his descendants.[60] Ibn Battuta remarked that the town of Ajodhan belonged to the shaikh. Himself a traveller of high social status, he commented unfavourably on the manners and arrogance of the incumbent shaikh, who was in fact a grandson of Farid.[61]

There is the same visible conflict between precept and practice in the location and organization of the khānqāh of Nizam al-Din, located in the area of southern New Delhi, today known as 'Hazrat Nizamuddin'. If, as is claimed by the hagiographic sources, the khānqāh was established on this site in order that the shaikh might reside there free from the distractions of urban life, it was also conveniently accessible from the city or denser urban areas of Delhi, a suburb to which all classes of people could throng.

Those who did resort to the khānqāh included the ill-fated royal princes, Shadi Khan and Khizr Khan, sons of Sultan 'Ala al-Din Khalji. They are stated to have built the *jamā'at-khāna*, a building that served both as communal residence hall and as a mosque. On its roof, the shaikh spent a part of his time (as mentioned in an anecdote quoted above). If it is the present building, which stylistically can hardly date from later than the early fourteenth century, this is one of the grandest of the red sandstone monuments of its period in Delhi.[62] Many court officials as well as humbler members of the urban population came to profess their devotion at the khānqāh; and it was a centre of the literary life of the capital. One has an uneasy impression that 'everyone who was anyone', despite the shaikh's professed desire for solitude, came to Nizam al-Din's khānqāh and were received with courtesies appropriate to his station in life. The exception was the reigning monarch, the sultan.

At an earlier stage in the establishment of the Chishti *silsila* in Delhi, meetings took place between Qutb al-Din Bakhtyar and the pious Sultan Iltutmish.[63] The events that had led to the execution of Sidi Muwallih, as well as the ascendancy and recognition that Nizam al-Din had achieved, necessitated a careful proclamation by the shaikh of his freedom from worldly ties and of his lack of concern with the administration of the sultanate.[64] Total avoidance of either attendance upon the sultan at his court or of the reception of the sultan at the khānqāh prevented a potentially disastrous confrontation of incompatible claims to secular and spiritual governance over the same territory:

> In every realm although there is a ruler (*amīr*),
> He is under the protection of a *faqīr*;
> Although the rulers may be at the head of the kingdom,
> The *faqīrs* are the drinkers (averters) of disaster of the kingdom.[65]

Confrontations between Nizam al-Din and the ruler were narrowly averted in the reigns of each of the three Khalji sultans (1290–1320).[66] The appparent subjection of the shaikh by Sultan Ghiyath al-Din Tughluq terminated with the death of both figures within months of one another in 1325.[67] The coercion of Sufi shaikhs by Muhammad bin Tughluq (r. 1325–51) was a part of the developing feud of the sultan with the majority of the educated and possessing classes of his capital city and realm.[68] Just as he sought to employ foreigners and 'new men' in high administrative posts, he found an external legitimation of his authority in the mandate of the 'Abbasid Caliph in Egypt. In the Sufi hagiographical tradition, Amir Khwurd explains his death, on the distant campaign of Thattha, as a consequence of his having summoned Nizam al-Din's khalīfa Nasir al-Din Mahmud from Delhi to join him, and of not having treated him as he should have done (*ka-mā ḥaqquhu*).[69] Sultan Firuz Shah Tughluq (r. 1351–88) sought the approval of a number of Sufi shaikhs;[70] and the death of Nasir al-Din Mahmud in 1356 left the capital city without any shaikh exercising a predominant authority. A composition of a follower of Nasir al-Din Mahmud in the last decade of the century reveals strong hostility to the sultan and his court.[71] In the fifteenth century, conflicts of authority between sultans and Sufi shaikhs were to recur in the Deccan and in Gujarat.[72]

THE RISE TO PRE-EMINENCE OF THE CHISHTI SHAIKHS

How is it that the Chishtis, from a relatively obscure lineage outside India, attained their position of dominance in the Delhi Sultanate, which has in turn led to their legends, their tombs, and shrines exercising so great an influence on the historical imagination of South Asian Muslims for several centuries down to the present day?

Answers to such historical questions are necessarily personal assessments, which are not susceptible to proof. The decisive factor, I suggest, is neither the abundance and variety of the qualities that contributed to the charisma of a great shaikh, nor the number of devotees in their lifetimes. The historical advantage that the Chishtis in India have possessed is rather that of ascendancy at a particular moment in the development of the capital city of a great kingdom, whose literary, cultural, and institutional traditions spread to the farthest areas of the subcontinent. At that moment the ideologues and the writers (some of whose works were transmitted to posterity) recognized a pre-eminence of charisma in a particular shaikh and embodied that opinion in their literary records.

This occurred around the first decade of the fourteenth century, when the two principal Persian poets of their time and place, Amir Khusrau and Amir Hasan, expressed allegiance to Nizam al-Din, and were joined by their younger contemporary, the historian of the Delhi Sultanate, Ziya al-Din Barani.[73] In this context the importance of Amir Hasan was not as a poet, though his poetry was esteemed and read by posterity, but as the author of a valuable and striking historical record of the conversations of Nizam al-Din.

This record, the *Fawā'id al-fu'ād*, was begun in 1308 and finished nearly fourteen years later. Like Barani's history, the *Ta'rīkh-i Fērōzshāhī*, it was evidently circulated in parts before the whole was completed.[74] It enjoyed contemporary popularity and was in demand in the capital city.

According to the historian Barani, a furore of piety was inspired in the capital city by the presence of Nizam al-Din during the reign of Sultan 'Ala al-Din Khalji. This was expressed in the performance of obligatory and supererogatory prayers and fasts, and in demands for works of Muslim learning and manuals of Sufi instruction, the *Ihyā' al-ulūm*, *Qūt al-qulūb*, *'Awārif al-ma'ārif* and others; and also for copies of Amir Hasan's *Fawā'id al-fu'ād*.[75] One may suspect that only the last work was perused with understanding and enthusiasm. A further testimony to the popularity of this work is that it inspired a whole series of fabricated *malfūẓāt* (recorded conversations) of Nizam al-Din's predecessors in the Chishti *silsila*.[76] By internal evidence and references, as well as traces of their influence on the genuine collections of malfūẓāt and tadhkiras of the second half of the fourteeenth century, these fabrications were produced in Delhi in imitation of the *Fawā'id al-fu'ād*, probably in response to the immediate popular demand which that work had created. The fabrications were filled with even more incredible anecdotes than those found in the genuine hagiographical works and with examples of even cruder popular levels of superstition. They were not generally recognized as spurious (as they so obviously are), and they were copied and lithographed until modern times. To this day, Urdu translations of them are sold at Sufi festivals and in ordinary bookshops.

The contemporary popularity of Amir Hasan's work had therefore brought into being a corpus of literature which, however trivial or worthless the contents, continued to circulate as evidence of the singular importance of the Chishti shaikhs in general and of Nizam al-Din in particular. This advantage was denied to shaikhs of rival silsilas. The literary contributions of Amir Khusrau and of Ziya al-Din Barani to the pre-eminence of Nizam al-Din were of different kinds.

Amir Khusrau has remained from his own day through subsequent centuries the most famous and widely read of the Persian poets of India. His *mathnawīs*, or longer narrative or didactic poems, following the model of those of Nizami of Ganja, usually contain a section devoted to the praise of a Sufi pir following the praise of the Prophet and preceding the poet's submission to the reigning sultan. In Amir Khusrau's case the pir is Nizam al-Din, sometimes with a mention of his predecessors Qutb al-Din and Farid al-Din.[77] Thus every reader of Amir Khusrau's mathnawīs, whether in his own day or later, was made familiar with the spiritual gifts of Nizam al-Din. No other Indian Sufi shaikh possessed a comparable panegyrist.

The allegiance of the historian Barani had a similar effect. The Delhi Sultanate was, as we have suggested, a key period in the development of Indo-Muslim culture. The historical record for a large portion of the period, from the mid-thirteenth to the mid-fourteenth century, is more dependent upon Barani's narrative than upon any other source. Even when the testimony of this somewhat devious recorder is suspect, subsequent historians whether they wrote in Persian in the sixteenth century or are writing in English at the present day, must reproduce, even when they question, Barani's assertions. In this case Barani testifies to the unique position of Nizam al-Din in the religious life of the capital and the sultanate.[78] Once again, no rival shaikh had a comparable publicist as disciple.

From the late period of his life, when Nizam al-Din had founded his hospice and was receiving the allegiance and offerings of a large body of supporters in the royal court and the city, one may project the story of the rise of the silsila backwards. Nizam al-Din had the advantage of a scholarly education before he enrolled as a disciple of Farid. He was also a *saiyid*, and he was brought up in Badaon, one of the principal subsidiary Muslim settlements of the Doab after the main conquest of 1192. He had strong claims to have inherited the mantle of Farid al-Din (d. 1265) many decades before he set up his khānqāh.[79]

Farid al-Din is a key figure in the rise of the Chishti silsila, and Nizam al-Din could not have achieved his ascendancy without his precursory activities. A detailed picture of his personality emerges from the numerous anecdotes that Nizam al-Din related about him. He was the offspring of a line of Muslim 'ālims, previously connected with the Ghaznawid and Ghorid rulers of Khurasan, but long settled in the Punjab. He had a formal Islamic education, and from adolescence displayed a mania for austerities, as well as an abundance of human and poetic sensibilities. After receiving his licence from Qutb al-Din, having acquired some reputation in the capital, and after an intervening period at Hansi, he set up his khānqāh at Ajodhan, situated, as we have seen, on a major route between Delhi and Multan.[80] Reports of the personality of the shaikh and of the ideal poverty of the hospice were carried by travellers; they served to spread and enhance the reputation of the silsila, and to emphasize its connection with the still fragile power of the Delhi Sultanate.[81] When Nizam al-Din received his leave from Farid al-Din and finally moved back from Ajodhan to Delhi, there must have been many in the metropolitan population who looked forward to a time when he might establish his own hospice.

The personalities of the predecessors of Farid al-Din are less well remembered in a mere handful of anecdotes in the *Fawā'id al-fu'ād* and the *Siyar al-auliyā*. Qutb al-Din's ecstatic sensibilities, his practice of *samā*', and his manner of death entered popular folk-memory. He was evidently held in some esteem by the pious Sultan Iltutmish, and the hostile Firdausi tradition maintains that he had an equivocal reputation for the display of *karāmāt* (abnormal powers).[82] Possibly his utterance expressing where he wished to be buried at Delhi had some part in strengthening popular faith in the connection of the silsila with the capital.[83] Subsequently the presence of his grave as a place of pilgrimage strengthened this link.[84]

The historical facts that can be established regarding Mu'in al-Din are few indeed. 'He emerges from the clouds of legend as an obscure darwish: either contemporary writers were ignorant of his existence, or they found little in it to interest them.'[85] Yet for the legend of the Chishtis, the presence of this lineal predecessor in Ajmer in the first days of the Muslim conquest was a powerful link with the destinies of the Muslim community on Indian soil.

We have noted the need of the newly established, part immigrant, part convert or *assimilé* population of the sultanate of Delhi, for a Muslim sanctification of their land. The Chishti shaikhs appealed, and their shrines continue to appeal, to Indian Muslims in search of a sanctification of their native land. All of the great Chishti shaikhs of Delhi, including Saiyid Muhammad Gesudaraz (who at one point boasted of a connection with Delhi extending back twelve generations) were of ashrāf Muslim families established in the subcontinent from the early days of the conquest of Delhi or from the earlier Muslim conquests of the Punjab.[86] Their graves stood as symbols of their presence, and they were observers of the practice of *ziyārat*—visiting the graves of the pious dead—even when, as we have noted, their deficiency in performing ḥajj to Arabia was a matter of concern for their hagiographers.[87]

FROM LIVING SHAIKHS TO TOMB-CULTS: THE GROWTH OF THE LEGEND OF MU'IN AL-DIN AT AJMER

With the decay and eclipse of the Delhi Sultanate in northern India, the power and prestige of living Chishti shaikhs came to an end, and representatives of lineages at Delhi ceased to exercise a wide charisma. Later Chishti shaikhs who sometimes resided at Delhi—'Abd al-Quddus of the Chishti Sabiri line in the early sixteenth century, Shah Kalim Allah in the revived seventeenth-century capital of Shahjahanabad, and Maulana Fakhr al-Din at Mehrauli at the end of the eighteenth century—were all incomers from distant areas.[88] At Pakpattan (Ajodhan) the numerous descendants of Shaikh Farid al-Din came to exercise leadership over the rural tribes of that area of the Punjab.[89] In the Deccan Saiyid Muhammad Gesudaraz founded a powerful Chishti wilāyat, part of the appeal of which lay in the historical connection of the immigrant Deccani Muslims, their language and culture, with the expansion and eclipse of the Delhi Sultanate. This was a second cycle of expansion followed by loss of the original homeland, like that which had overtaken the Delhi Sultanate after its foundation in the early thirteenth century.

The image of the activities of the earlier Chishti shaikhs remained potent, even when shaikhs from other silsilas, often staking their claims on different sources of prestige (one of which was that they were but newly arrived in India from the older and holier lands of Islam) established networks of influence in the subcontinent in the fifteenth and sixteenth centuries. Delhi in the early sixteenth century was thinly populated. It was considered a city of the hallowed dead, in which holy men would assemble and hold discourse on successive days of the week at different sanctified places.[90] The Lodi sultans of Delhi, although they held court at Agra, were buried in royal tombs close to the hospice of Nizam al-Din.[91] The alien conqueror Babur, when he took possession of the city in 1526, in the course of a day's sightseeing visited the tombs of two of the three great Chishti shaikhs buried there, Qutb al-Din Bakhtiyar and Nizam al-Din.[92]

Among the tombs of the early Chishti shaikhs, that of the founder of the lineage in India, Mu'in al-Din Chishti at Ajmer, had the greatest potential appeal. Although little was remembered about his activities and possibly less committed to writing during the fourteenth century, his burial-place provided an appropriate mythopoeic setting for the greatest tomb-cult of Indian Muslims. In the later fourteenth century, Amir Khwurd briefly adumbrated the development of the territorial legend of Mu'in al-Din. The Muslim presence in India itself is listed as a karāmat ('miracle', 'grace') of Mu'in al-Din. The land of Hindostan was a country, the whole of which as far as the sunrise was (full of) unbelief, idols and idol worship, and its disobedient people were polytheists who bowed down before stones and clods, beasts and cattle and their excrement. 'By the arrival of the blessed footsteps of "that Sun of the People of Belief" [...] the darkness of this land was illuminated by Islam [...]. Whoever will become a Musalman in this land, enduring to the Day of Resurrection, as well as their offspring as they are engendered who will be Musalmans; and those who will be brought from infidel territory (*dār-i ḥarb*) to the land of Islam (i.e. slaves taken from unconverted Hindu territories and converted)—until the day of Resurrection the recompenses of these are added to the lofty court (*bārgāh*) [...] (of Mu'in al-Din) [...] in obedience to him.'[93] Thus his wilāyat extends over all India. His blessed tomb was in Ajmer. 'The pure earth of the grave of this saint is medicine for the hearts of those in pain. May (they) obtain the good fortune of pilgrimage (*ziyārat*)!'[94]

The site of the grave was neglected in the period immediately after Mu'in al-Din's death, though if it was where the present tomb is located, with a massive excavated tank (reservoir) behind it, it is probably, as the legends and local traditions suggest, a Hindu site of some importance, which has been taken over by the adherents of the new cult.[95]

The practice of visiting tombs (*ziyārat*) was popular in the fourteenth century and considered commendable and efficacious by the Chishti shaikhs. Mu'in al-Din's tomb at Ajmer was visited by Sultan Muhammad bin Tughluq and at least two important Chishti khalīfas in the fourteenth century.[96] In the decline of the early fifteenth century, Ajmer passed altogether out of Muslim hands, a fact that emphasized the 'frontier' appeal of the site. In the later fifteenth century, the sultans of Malwa, apparently inspired by the legend of Mu'in al-Din, gained control of Ajmer as an outpost of their own dominions, and the shrine was re-colonized by alleged descendants of the shaikh from Malwa.[97]

The pilgrimages of the emperor Akbar on foot to Ajmer between the years 1562 and 1579 are testimony of the popular reputation of the shrine and cult;[98] and the emperor's visits doubtless added to that reputation. By the beginning of the seventeenth century Ajmer attracted, apart from visitors of distinction, large numbers of pilgrims from distant areas of India who congregated on the occasion of the '*urs* (commemoration of the date of the shaikh's death).[99] The fullest and most highly embroidered literary exposition of Mu'in al-Din's legend dates from this period, the *Siyar al-aqṭāb* of Ilahdiya Chishti. It provides a fantastic narrative of how Mu'in al-Din vanquished local material and spiritual powerholders by his magical powers, and gained possession of this sacred site—an emblem for Indian Muslims of their tenures in the subcontinent.[100] It also describes in the same style the election of the person of Mu'in al-Din and of the *topos* of Ajmer to fulfil this role among Indian Muslims:

> It is related that the Shaikh was 52 years old when he received the gifts (*tabarrukāt*) of his *pir* (and set out on his own mission). Everywhere he went he customarily lived in cemeteries, and wherever his reputation spread he tarried no longer, but secretly departed from there. After some days he came to the House of the *Ka'ba* and stayed there for some days.

Then he went to Medina the Illuminated, and performed the pilgrimage to the Holy Tomb of the Lord of the World (the Prophet Muhammad). He stayed there for a while, until one day from inside the pure and blessed Tomb a cry came: "Send for Mu'in al-Din!" The servitor of the Tomb called out the name, and from several places heard the reply:
"I am here for Thee!"
The servitor went back and stood before the door of the radiant and holy Tomb, and again the cry came forth:
"Send for Mu'in al-Din Chishti!"
The servitor came forward and told what he had been ordered, and at that moment a strange ecstasy, such as cannot be described, came over the *khwāja* (Mu'in al-Din). Weeping and crying and invoking blessings, he came to the door of the Tomb and stood there.
The voice cried:
"Enter, O Polestar (*quṭb*) of Shaikhs!"
Lost to self and intoxicated, the *khwāja* went in and was exalted by the sight of the world-adorning beauty of that Presence; and he beheld that Presence speak to him:
"Mu'in al-Din, you are the essence of my faith, yet you must go to Hindostan. There is a place called Ajmer, to which one of my sons (descendants) went for a holy war. Now he has become a martyr and the place has passed again into the hands of the infidels. By the grace of your footsteps Islam shall once more be manifest there, and the infidels punished by God's wrath."
Then the Prophet—on whom be Blessings and Peace—gave a pomegranate into the hands of the Khwāja and said:
"Look into this, so that you may see and know where you have to go!"
At his command the *khwāja* looked into the pomegranate, and he saw all that exists between the east and the west; and he looked well at Ajmer and its hills. He humbly offered prayers and sought help from that *Dargāh* ('Court') which is the envy of the heavens. Then he set out for Hindostan.[101]

From this wholly legendary recital we may note how, as a result of the historical circumstances by which the shaikhs of the Chishti silsila attained an ascendancy in the Delhi Sultanate, a devotional legend of lasting appeal has gained currency among Indian Muslims. The 'urs, or festival of the anniversary of the death of Mu'in al-Din, is today the greatest pilgrimage festival of Muslims of the Indian subcontinent, with the annual number of pilgrims in the 1970s sometimes reaching 300,000.[102]

BIBLIOGRAPHICAL NOTE

Sufi hagiographical works cited in this paper may be identified in Bruce B. Lawrence, *Notes from a Distant Flute: Sufi Literature in Pre-Mughal India*, Tehran 1978; cf. also C.A. Storey, *Persian Literature: a Bio-bibliographical*

Survey, Volume I, Pt. 2 N. Biography: (b) Saints, mystics etc., pp. 923–1066, which however lists only *tadhkiras*, and not collections of *malfūẓāt*. For the historical literature of the Dehli Sultanate, see P. Hardy, *Historians of Medieval India*, London 1960; C.A. Storey, op. cit., Volume I, Pt. 1, M. History of India: (b) Sultans of Delhi, pp. 493–516; Sir H.M. Elliot and J. Dowson, *The History of India as Told by its Own Historians: the Muhammadan Period*, 1867–1877, Vols. II and III. Secondary literature on Sufism in medieval India is listed in the "Select Bibliography" of Lawrence, op. cit., pp. 108–120. Among the more important contributions to this are the publications of Muhammad Habib, K.A. Nizami, Aziz Ahmad and S.A.A. Rizvi, though their formulations are sometimes to be accepted with caution. In this paper use is made of P.M. Currie, 'The Shrine and Cult of Mu'in al-Din', University of Oxford, 1978, since published as *The Shrine and Cult of Mu'in al-Din Chishti of Ajmer*, Delhi, 1989. Where possible, historical texts are cited in 'standard' editions (e.g. Bibliotheca Indica, Calcutta). The usually lithographic printings of Sufi hagiographical texts that are here cited are all listed by Lawrence, op. cit., with the exception of a 'critical' edition of the *Fawā'id al-fu'ad*, ed. M.L. Malik, Lahore 1966. After the first citation, modern secondary works are referred to by the brief-name of the author and place and date of publication, e.g. Digby, Aligarh 1975.

NOTES

1. A.B.M. Habibullah, *The Foundation of Muslim Rule in India*, Allahabad 1961, pp 142–60.
2. For the extent of the cities of Delhi, see J. Burton-Page in *Encyclopedia of Islam*, 2nd ed., s.v. Dihlī.
3. For a general outline of the history of this period, see M. Habib and K.A. Nizami, ed., *A Comprehensive History of India*, Vol. V, *The Delhi Sultanat* (sic) AD *1206–1526*, Delhi, 1970.
4. J.A. Page, *An Historical Memoir on the Qutb*, Delhi, Calcuttta 1926.
5. J.A. Page, op. cit., p. 29.
6. Y.D. Sharma, *Delhi and its Neighbourhood*, New Delhi 1964, pp 48–9.
7. Amir Khusrau, *Miftāḥ al-futūh*, qu. in Elliot and Dowson, *History of India*, III, p. 542.
8. Percy Brown, *Indian Architecture: the Islamic Period*, 2nd ed., Bombay (1946), pp. 12–13.
9. For a general description, see H.B. Sarda, *Ajmer: Historical and Descriptive*, Ajmer 1941.
10. Amir Khwurd, *Siyar al-auliyā*, Delhi A.H. 1302/A.D. 1885, p. 45.
11. J. Spencer Trimingham, *The Sufi Orders in Islam* (Oxford, 1971): review by S. Digby, *Bulletin of the School of Oriental and African Studies*, xxxvi, 1, 1973, pp. 136–9.
12. L. Elwell-Sutton, 'The *Darvīsh* in Persian Folklore', *Proceedings of the Twenty-sixth International Congress of Orientalists*, New Delhi, 1964, New Delhi 1968, pp. 200–03.

13. S. Digby, review of W.H. McLeod, *Guru Nanak and the Sikh Religion* (Oxford 1968) in *Indian Economic and Social History Review*, VII, 2, 1970, p. 305.
14. Digby, ibid., p. 306.
15. S. Digby, 'Abd al-Quddūs Gangōhī (1456–1537 AD): the Personality and Attitudes of a Medieval Indian Sufi', *Medieval India, a Miscellany*, III, 1975, pp. 17–18.
16. S. Digby, '*Qalandars* and Related Groups: Elements of Social Deviance in the Religious Life of the Delhi Sultanate', *Islam in Asia*, I, ed. Y. Friedmann, Jerusalem 1984, pp. 72–6.
17. M. Titus, *Islam in India and Pakistan*, 2nd ed., Calcutta 1959, p. 131.
18. M. Gaborieau, "Les ordres mystiques dans le sous-continent Indien: un point de vue ethnologique", in A. Popovic and G. Veinstein (ed.), *Les ordres mystiques de l'Islam: cheminement et situation actuelle*, Paris, E.H.E.S.S., 1986, pp. 105–34.
19. 'Abd al-'Aziz b. Sher Malik, *Ta'rīkh-i ḥabībī*, Urdu tr., Hyderabad, Deccan, n.d. [*c*. 1920], p. 36.
20. Loc. cit.
21. Muhammad Akbar Husaini, *Jawāmi' al-kalim*, Hyderabad [Deccan] Faṣlī 1356, p. 240; Muhammad 'Alī Sāmānī, *Siyar-i Muḥammadī*, Allahabad 1347/1928, pp. 17–19.
22. *Siyar-i Muḥammadī*, p. 5.
23. Bruce B. Lawrence, *Notes from a Distant Flute*, Teheran 1978, pp. 29–31.
24. Amir Hasan 'Alā Sijzī, *Fawā'id al-fu'ād*, Lahore 1966, p. 246; *Siyar al-auliyā*, p. 55.
25. The connection of the two poets with Nizam al-Din is discussed below.
26. P.M. Currie, 'The Shrine and Cult of Mu'in al-Din', maps showing places associated with Mu'in al-Din in the *Siyar al-auliyā*, *Siyar al-'ārifīn*, *Siyar al-aqṭāb* and *Hasht bahisht*, pp. 57, 69, 148, 353.
27. *Siyar al-auliyā*, pp. 143–4.
28. Muhammad Isma'il Lahauri, *Asrār al-majdhūbīn*, Digby Ms 10. fol. 4b; S. Digby, 'Anecdotes of a Provincial Sufi of the Delhi Sultanate, Khwaja Gurg of Kara', *Iran*, xxxii, 1994, p. 106. 'The Waterseller's Pilgrimage', *Lycidas* (Wolfson College, Oxford), III, 1974–5, pp. 20–1.
29. *Fawā'id al-fu'ād*, pp. 83–4.
30. Ibid., pp. 211–13. See *Siyar al-auliyā*, p. 51.
31. Ibid., pp. 3–4.
32. Ibid., p. 19.
33. Ibid., pp. 24–5; but see p. 343.
34. Ibid., p. 336.
35. S. Digby, 'The Sufi shaikh and the Sultan, A Conflict of Claims to Authority in Medieval India', *Iran*, xxviii, 1990, pp. 75–8.
36. 'Al-Hujwiri, *Kashf al-maḥjūb*, tr. R.A. Nicholson, London 1911, p. 213.
37. *Fawā'id al-fu'ād*, p. 22; Ashraf Jahangir Simnani, *Maktūbāti-Ashrafī*, British Museum MS Or. 267, fol. 109a; *Jawāmi' al-kalim*, p. 164; 'Isami, *Futūḥ al-salāṭīn*, ed. Usha, Madras 1948, pp. 455–6.

38. *Futūḥ al-salaṭin*, p. 456.
39. *Siyar al-auliyā*, p. 61; K.A. Nizami, *The Life and Times of Faridu'd-din Ganj-i-shakar*, Aligarh 1955, p. 17.
40. *Fawā'id al-fu'ād*, p. 236; Jamali, *Siyar al-'ārifin*, Delhi 1311/1893, p. 115; cf. 'Afif, *Ta'rīkh-i, Fērōzshāhī*, Calcutta 1891, p. 61.
41. K.A. Nizami, *Some Aspects of Religion and Politics in India during the Thirteenth Century*, Aligarh 1961, pp. 185–229; idem., 'Early Indo-Muslim Mystics and their Attitude towards the State', *Islamic Culture*, 22, 23, and 24 (1948–50).
42. *Siyar al-auliyā*, p. 158.
43. *Fawā'id al-fu'ād*, pp. 315, 407–8; *Siyar al-'ārifin*, p. 149.
44. *Siyar al-auliyā*, pp. 53, 54–5; Nizami 1961, p. 189; the hostile Firdausi source implies the reality of that influence, see below, note 49.
45. *Fawā'id al-fu'ād*, p. 245.
46. *Siyar al-auliyā*, pp. 135–41; 'Abd al-Haqq, *Akhbār al-akhyār*, Delhi 1309/1892, p. 65.
47. *Fawā'id al-fu'ād*, pp. 206–7; *Siyar al-auliyā*, p. 579; Sirhindi, *Ta'rīkh-i Mubārakshāhī*, Calcutta, 1931, p. 100; K.A. Nizami, 'The Suhrawardi *Silsila* and its Influence on Medieval Indian Politics', *Medieval India Quarterly*, III, 1957, pp. 109–49.
48. See below, p. 249, and notes 60, 61.
49. Shaikh Shu'aib Maneri, *Manāqib al-asfiyā*, Calcutta 1895, pp. 121–2.
50. *Siyar al-auliyā*, p. 147.
51. Hamid Qalandar, *Khair al-majālis*, Aligarh (1959), pp. 202–3.
52. *Manāqib al-asfiyā*, p. 124.
53. Ibid., pp. 131–2; cf. *Siyar al-'arifin*, p. 84.
54. *Manāqib al-asfiyā*, pp. 130, 137.
55. *Futūḥāt-i Fērōzshāhī*, ed. S. Abdur Rashid, Aligarh 1954, p. 8.
56. *Manāqib al-asfiyā*, pp. 137–8.
57. For a modern presentation with an abundance of details, see K.A. Nizami, *The Life and Times of Shaikh Faridu'd-din Ganj-i-shakar*, Aligarh 1955.
58. A.M. Stow, 'The Road between Delhi and Multan', *Journal of the Punjab Historical Society*, III, 1, 1914–15, pp. 26–37; S. Digby, 'Sufis and Travellers in the Early Delhi Sultanate: the Evidence of the *Fawā'id al-fu'ād*', in Attar Singh, ed., *Socio-cultural Impact of Islam on India*, Chandigarh (1976), pp. 171–7.
59. *Siyar al-auliyā*, pp. 79–80.
60. Barani, *Ta'rīkh-i Fērōzshāhī*, Calcutta 1862, p. 543. Richard M. Eaton, 'The Political and Religious Authority of the Shrine of Bābā Farīd', in B.D. Metcalf, ed., *Moral Conduct and Authority: the Place of Adab in South Asian Islam*, California 1984, pp. 339–40. Reproduced in this volume on pp. 263–84.
61. Ibn Battuta, *Riḥla*, Paris 1855, III, p. 135; cf. *Siyar al-auliyā*, pp. 193, 195.
62. *Siyar al-auliyā*, p. 74; cf. Zafar Hasan, *A Guide to Nizamu-d Din*, Calcutta 1922, p. 14.
63. *Siyar al-auliyā*, p. 53; *Siyar al-'ārifin*, p. 20; *Jawāmi' al-kalim*, p. 207.
64. *Siyar al-auliyā*, p. 134; for Sidi Muwallih's death, see Digby, Jerusalem 1984, pp. 67–8, and refs. there given.
65. *Futūḥ al-salāṭīn*, p. 456, referring to Nizam al-Din.

66. *Siyar al-auliyā*, pp. 132–5, 151–2; *Siyar al-'ārifīn*, p. 75.

67. *Siyar al-auliyā*, pp. 526–32; *Siyar al-'ārifīn*, pp. 88–90; *Ta'rīkh-i Fērōzshāhi*, pp. 96–7; Badayuni, *Muntakhab al-tawārīkh*, Calcutta 1868, I, p. 225.

68. *Rihla*, III, pp. 294–311; *Siyar al-auliyā*, pp. 215–8.

69. *Siyar al-auliyā*, p. 246.

70. 'Afif, *Ta'rīkh-i Fērōzshāhī*, pp. 27–9.

71. S. Digby, 'The *Tuḥfa-i naṣā'iḥ* of Yusuf Gada: an Ethical Treatise in Verse from the Late-Fourteenth Century Delhi Sultanate,' in Metcalf ed., op. cit., California 1984, pp. 107, 118–9.

72. Firishta, *Ta'rīkh*, Bombay 1831, I, pp. 633–5; ibid., Kanpur 1290/1874, pp. 328–9; Tabataba'i, *Burhān-i ma'āthir*, Hyderabad, 1355/1936, pp. 54–65; H.K. Sherwani, *The Bahmanis of the Deccan*, Hyderabad (1955), pp. 166–7; Sikandar bin Muhammad, *Mir'āt-i Sikandarī*, Baroda 1961, pp. 86–93; Sir E.C. Bayley, *The Local Muhammadan Dynasties: Gujarat*, London 1886, pp. 153–60. Cf. Digby, "Sufi Shaikh", *Iran*, xxviii, 1990, pp. 71–81. See also Aziz Ahmad, 'The Sufi and the Sultan in pre-Mughal Muslim India', *Der Islam* 38, 1–2, 1962, pp. 142–53.

73. *Siyar al-auliyā*, pp. 301–5, 308, 312–3, 346–7; Barani, *Ta'rīkh-i Fērōzshāhī*, pp. 359–60; M.W. Mirza, *The Life and Works of Amir Khusrau*, Lahore 1962, pp. 116–9; Amir Hasan Sijzi, *Dīwān*, ed. M.A. Mahvi, Hyderabad 1352/1933, intro. pp. 1–14.

74. Barani's reference (p. 346, see note 75 below) implies that it was in circulation by AD 1315. For the contemporary circulation of portions of Barani's own work, see S. Digby, 'Muhammad bin Tughluq's Last Years in Kathiavad and his Invasions of Thatha; in H. Khuhro, ed., *Sind through the Centuries*, Karachi 1981, pp. 133–4.

75. Barani, *Ta'rīkh-i Fērōzshāhī*, pp. 343–46, 360; cf. *Siyar al-auliyā*, pp. 308, 346–7, quoting from Barani's lost *Ḥasrat-nāma*.

76. M. Habib, 'Chishti Mystic Records of the Sultanate Period', *Medieval India Quarterly* I, 3, pp. 1–42.

77. Amir Khusrau, *Matla' al-anwār*, Kanpur 1302/1884, pp. 17–20; *Laylā Majnūn*, Aligarh 1917, pp. 13–14; *Shīrīn u Khusrau*, Moscow 1961, pp. 15–16; *Ā' īna-i Iskandarī*, Aligarh 1917, pp. 11–14; *Dawal Rānī Khiḍr Khān*, Aligarh 1917, pp. 15–16; *Nuh sipihr*, Calcutta 1948, p. 23–8.

78. Barani, loc. cit. (Note 75 above).

79. *Siyar al-auliyā*, pp. 99–116; M. Habib, *Ḥaḍrat Niẓām al-Dīn Auliyā*: *ḥayāt aur ta'līmāt*, Delhi 1970.

80. Nizami, Aligarh 1955, pp. 10–11, 15–16, 21–3, 36ss.

81. *Fawā'id al-fu'ād*, pp. 252–3; Digby, Chandigarh 1976, pp. 171–7.

82. See notes 44, 63 above.

83. *Fawā'id al-fu'ād*, p. 425; *Siyar al-auliyā*, p. 55.

84. *Fawā'id al-fu'ād*, pp. 132, 315; *Siyar al-auliyā*, pp. 50–1, 126, 264; *Khair al-majālis*, p. 57.

85. Currie, 'Shrine and Cult', p. 4.

86. Nizami, *Life and Timès*, pp. 10–11; *Akhbār al-akhyār*. p. 54; *Khair al-majālis*, intro. by K.A. Nizami, p. 39; *Ta'rīkh-i ḥabībī*, pp. 7–8.
87. See p. 241 and note 28, above.
88. Digby, ''Abd al-Quddus Gangohi', pp. 10, 25–7; K.A. Nizami, *Ta'rīkh-i mashā'ikh Chisht*, Delhi 1953, pp. 369–85, 460–71.
89. R.M. Eaton in Metcalf, California 1984, pp. 341–53.
90. Rizq Allah Mushtaqi, *Waqi'āt-i Mushtāqī*, British Library MS Add, 11,633, fol. 31a, British Library MS Or. 1929, fol. 31b.
91. S. Digby, 'The Tomb of Bahlūl Lōdi', *Bulletin of the School of Oriental and African Studies*, XXXVIII, 3, 1975, pp. 553–4.
92. *Bābur-nāma*, London 1905, fols, 267b–268a; tr. Beveridge, London 1921, II, p. 475.
93. *Siyar al-auliyā*, p. 47.
94. Ibid., p. 48.
95. Currie, 'Shrine and Cult', pp. 151–2; Sarda, *Ajmer* 1941, p. 90.
96. S. Digby, 'Early Pilgrimages to the Graves of Mu'īn al-Dīn and other Chishti Shaikhs', in *Islamic Society and Culture*, ed. M. Israel and N.K. Wagle, New Delhi 1983, pp. 95–100; *Siyar al-auliyā*, p. 264; *Akhbār al-akhyār*, p. 91.
97. *Akhbār al-akhyār*, p. 177; Currie, 'Shrine and Cult', p. 170.
98. A.L. Srivastava, *Akbar the Great*, Agra 1962, I, pp. 61, 246.
99. *Jahangir's India*: *the Remostratie of Francisco Pelsaert*, tr. Moreland and Geyl, Cambridge 1925, p. 70; *Travels of Peter Mundy*, London 1914, II, p. 244.
100. Ilahdia Chishti, *Siyar al-aqṭāb*, Kanpur 1889, pp. 125–31; Digby, 'Encounters with Jogis in Indian Sufi Hagiography', Seminar on Aspects of Religion in South Asia, London, January 1970, cyclostyle.
101. *Siyar al-aqṭāb*, pp. 123–4
102. Currie, 'Shrine and Cult', pp. 196–7.

12

The Political and Religious Authority of the Shrine of Baba Farid*

Richard M. Eaton

In Islam, the ultimate source of moral authority is unambiguous. As a guide to how individuals and society ought to be, the Qur'an proclaims its moral authority on the basis of its being the very Word of God, for in Islam God revealed Himself not in any historical personage, but in a Book. The moral ideal thus established by the Qur'an is at once objectively knowable, universally applicable to all peoples and times, and derived from a source external to humanity. These basic features of Islamic moral authority stand in contrast to Hindu-Buddhist ethical doctrines according to which reward and retribution operate on the self-fulfilling and self-regulating principle of *karma*, rather than on the judgement of a wholly transcendent, external god.

To Muslims literate in Arabic, the Qur'anic source of moral authority presents no problems in terms of gaining access to that authority. But what could non-literate, non-Arabic-speaking villagers or pastoralists make of such a religion? With reference to contemporary Morocco, Ernest Gellner has argued that to the unlettered Berber tribes of the Atlas, the lineages of holy men, saints, are not just interpreters of Islam for the tribesmen nor mere representatives of a world religion. 'Koranic propriety emanates from their essence, as it were,' writes Gellner. 'Islam is what they do. They *are* Islam.'[1]

Another way in which the Book was conveyed to such peoples was through the vast shrines built over the tombs of saints. In India these

* Reprinted from Barbara D. Metcalf, ed., *Moral Conduct and Authority: the Place of Adab in South Asian Islam* (Berkeley: University of California Press, 1984), pp. 333–56.

shrines displayed, theatre-style and in microcosm, the moral order of the Islamic macrocosm. Although such shrines possessed important economic, political, and social ties with the masses of villagers who frequented them, their fundamental raison d'être was religious. For it was through its rituals that a shrine made Islam accessible to non-lettered masses, providing them with vivid and concrete manifestations of the divine order, and integrating them into its ritualized drama both as participants and as sponsors. Theologically, this involved interposing the spirit of the saint, sustained and displayed through the shrine institution, between the devotee and the supreme deity of the Qur'an. For it was believed that the saint enjoyed a closer relationship with God than the common devotee could ever have, and that the saint's spiritual power (*baraka*) to intercede with God on the devotee's behalf, outlasted the saint's mortal lifetime and adhered to his burial place. The latter therefore frequently evolved into a great centre of pilgrimage for persons seeking divine aid in their personal, matrimonial, or business affairs.[2]

In the nineteenth century, reformist movements such as that expressed by Maulana Thanawi's *Bihishtī zewar* vigorously opposed the entire culture of saints and shrines, the colourful pageantry they displayed, and above all the claims that they possessed an intermediate status between Man and God. Accordingly, supporters of these reformist movements sought to replace the shrine as the source of Islamic moral authority with a reassertion of the Book as the only legitimate source. Theatre, in a word, was to be replaced by Scripture. Inasmuch as this was the case, an investigation of the formation and nature of this theatre-oriented Islam as represented by one such shrine, that of Baba Farid in Pakpattan, Punjab, would be appropriate.

The shrine of Shaikh Farid al-Din Ganj-i Shakar (d. AD 1265), known to his devotees as Baba Farid, lies on the right bank of the Punjab's most southeasterly river, the Sutlej, roughly halfway between Ferozepore and Bahawalpur. The town in which the shrine is located, known since the sixteenth century as Pakpattan, is the ancient city of Ajodhan. As the principal ferry point on the Sutlej river, this town served from ancient times as a major nexus for east-west trade between the Delhi region and Multan. Ajodhan also lay fully exposed to the brunt of Turkish migration and invasions of India from the late tenth century onward, a process that culminated in the thirteenth century when Mongol pressures forced waves of Turkish settlers into the subcontinent, many of them settling permanently in the urban centres of the Punjab, such as Lahore, Dipalpur, and Multan. Hence Baba Farid's decision to establish himself in Ajodhan was but one part of a larger process; it was the religious dimension of a very slow transformation of the Punjab's cities from a Hindu to a Turkish-Islamic orientation. Even when Baba Farid reached Ajodhan sometime in the early thirteenth century, a Jami' mosque had already been established there, a resident qazi was there administering justice according to Islamic law, and the city was politically subordinate to a Muslim governor in neighbouring Dipalpur.[3]

This is not the place to discuss the tradition of Sufism as espoused by Baba Farid, which in any case has been superbly treated in the writings of K.A. Nizami.[4] Suffice it to say that two traditions of Islamic devotionalism developed at Ajodhan during Baba Farid's lifetime. One was the tradition of mystical endeavour practised by full-time residents at Baba Farid's convent (*jamā'at-khāna*), men who had been initiated into the Chishti order, who lived a communal life of a strongly ascetic nature, and who, in short, had resolved to tread the arduous Sufi path to God. The second tradition was more popular-oriented and is the one with which the remainder of this essay is concerned. At the same time that Baba Farid instructed his elite group of initiates (*khalīfas*) in the mysteries of his order, he also handed out *ta'wīdh* or amulets to the common masses, who saw in these ta'wīdh a protection against evil, a boon for good fortune, or an agent for the cure of an illness. As is recorded in the contemporary hagiography by Amir Hasan Sijzi,

> Once when Shaikh Nizam al-Din Auliya started for Ajodhan, a neighbor, Muhammad, who had a serious ailment, requested him to bring an amulet for him from Shaikh Farid. When Nizam al-Din placed Muhammad's request before his master, the latter asked him to write a *ta'wīdh* on his behalf. Shaikh Nizam al-Din wrote the following names of God on a piece of paper and presented it before the Shaikh who touched it, read it, and gave it back to him to be handed over to Muḥammad.[5]

Huge crowds gathered daily at Baba Farid's convent to receive ta'wīdh which, as in the case cited above, normally consisted of paper on which were written the names of God or some Qur'anic verses. The tediousness of writing out these ta'wīdh, however, compelled the saint to delegate much the work to assistants. This was an aspect of Islamic devotionalism that has not changed at all from the thirteenth century to the present; even now the successors of Baba Farid and his assistants, in common with those of other shrines in the Punjab, continue to write ta'wīdh for the masses.

When the ta'wīdh passed from the shrine to the devotee, the latter, or *murīd*, would frequently offer to the shrine some kind of gift, called *futūḥ*. This would typically be in the form of sweets,[6] but could be almost anything, and even in Baba Farid's own day the gifts swelled to enormous proportions.[7] Baba Farid's giving of ta'wīdh or amulets, and the devotees' giving of futūḥ or gifts, provided the structural framework upon which the subsequent devotionalism of the shrine rested. In a religious sense the ta'wīdh-futūḥ system defined and sustained Baba Farid's intermediary status between the devotee and God, as a conduit through whose intercession with God one's wishes may be fulfilled. In a social and institutional sense, moreover, the ta'wīdh-futūḥ system required the shrine to adopt a certain degree of rational organization with respect to the distribution of material wealth. For it was Baba Farid's practice to distribute among his khalīfas and the common devotees the presents that other devotees had brought.[8] The shaikh's convent, and later his shrine, thus served as a nexus for the circulation and redistribution of a great deal of material wealth in the region.

In 1265 Baba Farid died, and with his death began the career of the vast shrine complex based on his tomb, in time encompassing a mosque, a welfare kitchen (*langar-khāna*), and a number of related buildings. By the thirteenth century, it had become commonly believed in the Muslim world that a great shaikh's spiritual power (baraka) adhered, after his death, to is familial descendants as well as to the place of his burial. Accordingly, the position of prime successor to Baba Farid, later called the '*dīwān*', fell to his son, Badr al-Din Sulaiman (1265–81).[9] The accession of Badr al-Din as the Diwan immediately set a pattern of hereditary religious leadership at the shrine. Amir Khusrau mentioned the annual *'urs* or death-date celebration on the occasion of the fiftieth anniversary of the shaikh's death and described in detail the 'urs celebration for the year 1315: the pilgrimage of pious persons to Ajodhan, the recitation of the saint's wonderful deeds, and the entertainments performed by an ensemble of darwishes.[10] The *Jawāhir al-Farīdī*, an important collection of biographies of Baba Farid's spiritual and lineal descendants compiled in 1623, records that all the major rituals of the shrine had become instituted in Badr al-Din's day. These included the tying on of the turban (*dastār bandī*) indicating formal inheritance of Baba Farid's spiritual authority; the regularizing of ecstatic singing (*qawwālī*) at the shrine; the establishing of a public kitchen (langar khāna) from which the dīwān himself would, on formal occasions, direct the distribution of food and sweets; and the tradition of the dīwān opening the southern door (*bihishtī darwāza*) of Baba Farid's tomb on the occasion of the shrine's annual 'urs celebration, allowing the masses of common devotees to pass by the shrine's *sanctum sanctorum*, ritually entering heaven.[11]

The successorship of the second dīwān, Badr al-Din's eldest son, Shaikh 'Ala al-Din Mauj Darya (1281–1334), firmly established a tradition of hereditary religious leadership associated with Baba Farid's shrine and witnessed the spectacular growth of a popular cult that focused on the shrine. We find two dimensions of this growing cult: patronage by the Delhi court and the extension of mass devotionalism into the countryside. Although Baba Farid himself assiduously avoided contact with the mundane world of the court and its ministers,[12] and although the Khalji sultans (1288–1321) do not seem to have been interested in the shrine, the whole picture changed with the advent of the Tughluq period (1321–98). It happened that in the late Khalji times the governor of Dipalpur, the future Sultan Ghiyath al-Din Tughluq, became one of the many local notables attracted to the spiritual power and piety of Diwan 'Ala al-Din Mauj Darya.[13] He accordingly made frequent visits from Dipalpur, which was the administrative capital of the central Punjab, to nearby Ajodhan to pay respects to the dīwān. On one such occasion, according to the fourteenth-century chronicler Shams-i Siraj 'Afif, the governor brought along his son and nephew, the future sultans Muhammad bin Tughluq and Firuz Tughluq, and all three were given a turban by Diwan 'Ala al-Din and told by him that each was destined to rule Hindustan.[14] Apart from rationalizing the subsequent patronage of Baba Farid's shrine by the leading Tughluq sultans, the story also weaves together the shrine's dastār bandī ceremony with succession to the royal throne in Delhi, effectively merging the symbols of the shrine and of the royal court.

Although hagiographic traditions refer to 'Ala al-Din's immense piety and his refusal to consort with royalty,[15] the renowned world traveller Ibn Battuta, certainly an impartial authority in this matter, wrote that Sultan Muhammad bin Tughluq had bestowed the city of Ajodhan on the shrine.[16] This seems to be the earliest reference to the court's alienation of local revenues in favour of the shrine's support. Court patronage, however, was also expressed in other ways. The hagiographic tradition has it that Muhammad bin Tughluq, who was also a disciple of Diwan 'Ala al-Din,[17] expressed his desire to build a magnificent tomb for the dīwān, but the latter refused the offer, saying that if a tomb were built at all, this could be done only after his death.[18] Accordingly, soon after 'Ala al-Din's death in 1335, Sultan Muhammad commissioned two engineers to construct what proved to be one of the finest examples of Tughluq architecture in the subcontinent.[19] It is also the most imposing structure in the entire shrine complex, dwarfing by far Baba Farid's own tomb.

Once begun, the Tughluq court's patronage of the shrine continued to grow as 'Ala al-Din's successors proved more pliable to the court's will. In fact, his son and successor, Diwan Mu'izz al-Din, was even called to Delhi by Muhammad bin Tughluq, placed in government service, and sent to Gujarat as deputy governor.[20] The dīwān's brother, meanwhile, was appointed to the ofice of Shaikh al-Islam of India.[21] Never were the affairs of the shrine more firmly welded to court interests. The shrine's leaders were now under Delhi's control, and the shrine became even more dependent economically upon court patronage. In Mu'izz al-Din's brief successorship (1335–38), Muhammad bin Tughluq granted an endowment or *mu'āf* in support of the shrine's public kitchen.[22] And Barani recorded that Sultan Firuz Tughluq (1351–88) not only repaired the tomb of Baba Farid, but granted robes of honour to his descendants and confirmed them in possession of their villages and lands.[23]

There was, however, a second and even more significant dimension of the shrine's institutionalization process, also clearly evident in the early fourteenth century. This was its growing popularity among the rural masses and its recognition even beyond the frontiers of India. In 1334, toward the end of 'Ala al-Din's fifty-four-year term as dīwān, Ibn Battuta visited the shrine and later recalled, 'We reached the city of Ajodhan, a small city belonging to the pious Shaikh Farid-ud-din of Badaun [sic] whom at Alexandria the holy and pious Shaikh Burhan-ud-din al-'Araj had foretold that I would meet'.[24] The man whom the famous traveller actually met was not Baba Farid, of course, but his grandson, Diwān 'Ala al-Din Mauj Darya. Nevertheless, the passage shows that Baba Farid, the saint, was now clearly identified with the physical shrine complex, and that his (its) fame had spread as far as Egypt.

It was also at about this time that small memorial shrines to Baba Farid began appearing, scattered throughout the countryside of the central Punjab, and that the baraka or spiritual power and authority of Baba Farid became physically established over the land in much the same way that political/administrative authority was. As for the memorial shrines, what is significant is that they were built not by the Tughluq sultans as were the main structures of the Ajodhan complex, but by the common people themselves. Amir Khwurd, a contemporary of 'Ala al-Din Mauj Darya, recorded that the dīwān had become so well known that 'in the countryside around Ajodhan, Dipalpur, and in the hills toward Kashmir, the people out of love and belief have built structures and tombs in the name of his shrine [i.e., the shrine of Baba Farid] and they go to these village for alms and devotions'.[25]

The appearance of these shrines shows that a certain tract of the Punjab had become identified with Baba Farid's *wilāya*, or spiritual kingdom, which to his devotees was perceived as having specific geographic boundaries that bordered the *wilāyas* of other saints. Thus we read in an early-sixteenth-century hagiography that Baba Farid's spiritual power protected a certain 'Abd Allah Rumi from highway robbers as he travelled southwest from Ajodhan to Multan, for the saint had told the traveller that from here [Ajodhan] to such-and-such a village is in my charge, and from such-and-such a reservoir is the frontier of Shaikh Baha al-Din Zakariya [beyond which] is in his charge.[26] This passage clearly demonstrates how closely the notion of spiritual sovereignty could parallel, in spatial terms, that of political sovereignty, and represents one of several ways in which the shrine of Baba Farid fused religious and political categories of authority.

Who were the rural folk who frequented the main shrine in Ajodhan and also the memorial shrines in the surrounding countryside? It is well known that in the mid-thirteenth century, Balban, in order to build a defensive bulwark against Mongol incursions, pursued the policy of strengthening and populating certain cities in the Punjab with large garrisons of Turkish elements.[27] The effect of these measures was to augment considerably the pattern of Muslim settlement in the urban centres of the Punjab, including not only the soldiers but also thousands of refugees fleeing before the advancing Mongols—artisans, merchants, petty officials, and the like. Although Ajodhan was not one of these garrisoned cities, the large size of its Jami‘ mosque, originally constructed before Baba Farid's arrival and now part of the shrine complex,[28] attests to the presence of a substantial Muslim population at that time.

Behind and beyond these urban centres of the western Punjab, all of which were economically based on intensive cultivation of food crops along the flood plains of the rivers, lay a vast tract of sparsely populated land, the *barr* country between the five rivers. This area, though possessing excellent natural soils for agriculture, was but little cultivated owing to the very scanty rainfall that has always characterized the western Punjab. The *barr* country could and did, however, support an ecological system less demanding of the land than peasant agriculture. This was a type of pastoral nomadism based primarily on the herding of goats and camels.[29] Unlike the nomadism of Baluchistan or Afghanistan, where pastoral tribes move between plains in the wet winter season and the mountains in the dry season, the pastoralists of the western Punjab 'moved only down to the riverain [sic] in the hot dry months and returned to the *barr* and *thāl* after rains, never leaving the Punjab plains and covering at the most a distance of less than one hundred miles'.[30] This pattern placed the peoples of the *barr* country in a symbiotic relationship with the settled peoples of the riverine area. The pastoralists needed access to the rivers for their herds, which placed them in a position of potential conflict with the riverine peoples, but they were nevertheless dependent upon the agrarian-based urban centres for trade. Moreover, and this is an important theme to which I shall return shortly, they were also dependent upon the riverine peoples for providing the rituals and belief structures that made up their religious system.

The pastoralists to which I refer were primarily Jat groups that had been moving up from Sind into the Multan area between the seventh and eleventh centuries. The seventh-century Chinese traveller Hsuan Tsang wrote of river groups in Sind who 'give themselves exclusively to tending cattle and from this derive their livelihood,' 'have no masters,' and possess 'an unfeeling temper' and a 'hasty disposition.'[31] The eighth-century *Chach–nāma* styled these groups 'Jats,' located them in the wastes of the Indus valley in Sind, and noted an absence of social hierarchy among them.[32] This evidence all points to the conclusion that these Jat pastoralists, before their entry into the Punjab, had not yet been integrated into Hindu society. Indeed, there is evidence that in the eighth century, when Arabs replaced Brahmans as rulers of Sind, the new rulers merely continued the earlier practice of requiring the Jats to associate themselves with dogs—unclean to Muslims as well as to Hindus—and in this way to affirm their lowly status.[33]

In the eleventh century, Jats were fighting Mahmud of Ghazni in the Multan region, though their social standing was still miserably low at that time, as al-Biruni referred to them as 'cattle-owners, low Sudra people'.[34] By the time of Baba Farid, however, in the 1260s, we find the first mention of Jats occupying the Punjab proper, specifically the Bet Jullundur and Bari doabs—i.e., the Sutlej-Beas *barr* and the Beas-Ravi *barr*.[35] In describing the success of Balban's governor of Lahore and Dipalpur in resisting the Mongols, the historian Barani referred to the governor's campaigns against the 'Jats, the Khokhars, the Bhattis, the Minas, the Mandahars, and other similar tribes'.[36] In 1519 and again in 1525, Babur described Jat pastoralist groups in the Sind Sagar *doab* and Sialkot regions, giving us good descriptions of Jat relations with the dominant Rajput groups in the former region.[37] The northward movement of Jat clans and their settlement in the grazing tracts of the Punjab is thus well supported by contemporary evidence.

By the end of the sixteenth century, the Jats had multiplied prodigiously and spread throughout the Punjab, as is vividly reflected in the *Ā'in-i Akbari's* statistics for the Lahore and Multan *ṣūbas*, compiled about 1595. For each *pargana*, Abu'l-fazl listed the dominant *zamīndār* caste, together with its assessed revenue. If the number of zamīndārs listed by Abu'l-fazl as 'Jat' is added to that of other named castes listed as Jat by the British ethnographers Ibbetson and Rose,[38] it appears that of the total 186 Punjabi *parganas* whose dominant *zamīndārs* are known, fully 82, or nearly half, were controlled by Jat groups.[39] Only in the extreme western Punjab, in

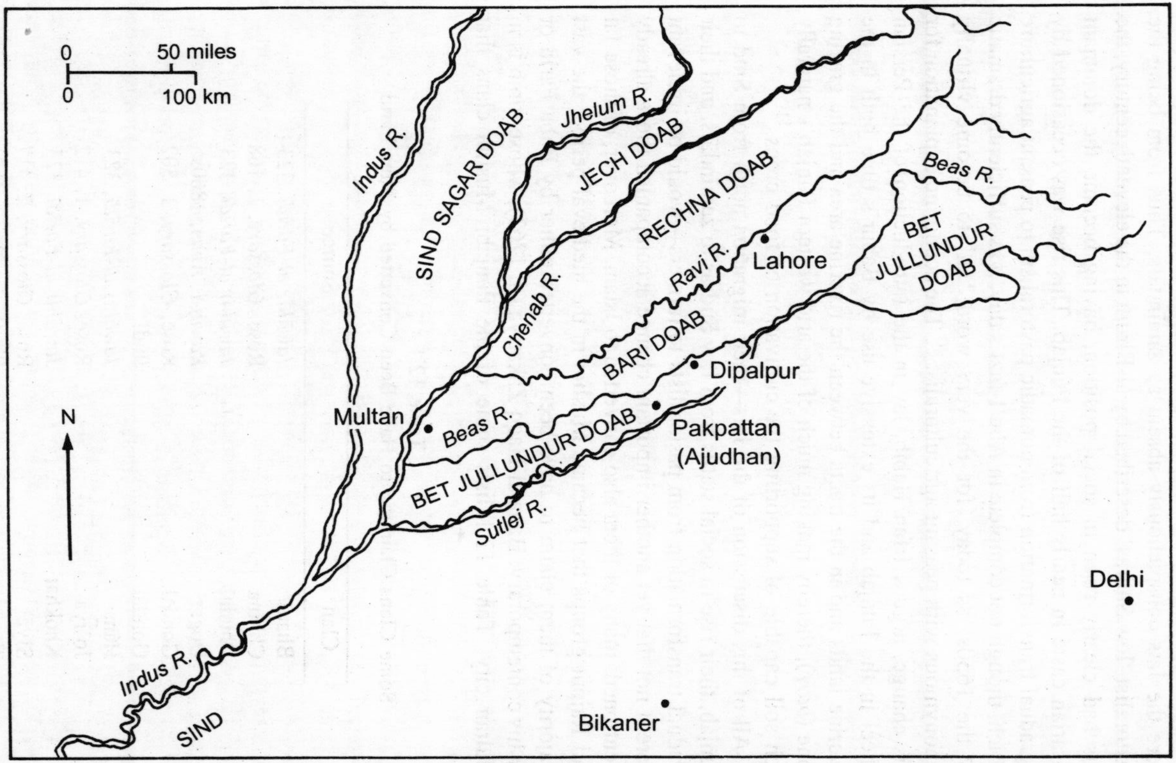

Map of Punjab circa 1605

the Sind Sagar doab, where the Janjua Rajputs and Ghakkars dominated, were the Jats conspicuously absent as zamīndārs. Thus from being the pastoralist 'low Sudras' described by al-Biruni in the eleventh century, the Jats had clearly risen in social position, having become the dominant agrarian caste in nearly half of the Punjab. This rise was occasioned by a gradual transformation from nomadic pastoralism to peasant agriculture which, though not complete in Abu'l-fazl's day, was sufficiently dramatic by the 1650s, as today, for the very word 'Jat' to become virtually synonymous with peasant agriculturalist.[40] The economic explanation for this change, argues Irfan Habib, lay in the introduction of the Persian wheel in the Punjab and its extensive use by Babur's time both in the riverine lands and in the tracts between the riverine area and the grazing zone (*barr*), thereby making much of the arid western Punjab's naturally rich soil capable of supporting the cultivation of food crops.[41]

All of this discussion of the Jats—their migration north from Sind to Punjab, their rise in social status from low Sudras to zamīndārs, and their gradual transformation from pastoralists to farmers—would be irrelevant were it not that yet another important change accompanied those already mentioned: many of them also converted to Islam. Moreover, of those Jat and Rajput groups that became Muslim in the medieval period, the vast majority of them claim to have been converted either by Baba Farid or by his contemporary, Baha al-Haqq Zakariya (d. 1263), whose tomb is in Multan city. Table 12.1 lists some of the Punjabi Muslim clans that

Table 12.1
Some Clans Claiming to Have Been Converted by Baba Farid

Clan	Source
Bhattī	*Jawāhir al-Farīdī*, 323
Chhīna	Rose, *Glossary*, 1, 168
Dhudhī	*Jawāhir al-Farīdī*, 323
Dogar	*Rawāj-i 'Āmm*, 1860s
Gondal	Rose, *Glossary*, 1, 302
Gondāl	Ibid.
Hāns	*Jawāhir al-Farīdī*, 323
Jo'iya	Rose, *Glossary*, 1, 412
Khokhar	*Jawāhir al-Farīdī*, 323
Siyāl	Rose, *Glossary*, 2, 417
Tīwāna	Sir 'Umar Ḥayāt Khān
Wattū	Rose, *Glossary*, 2, 491
Kharral	Oral tradition
Arā'in	Oral tradition

traditionally claim Baba Farid as the agent of their conversion. But as Mohammad Habib notes, converting non-Muslims was not a function of the early shaikhs of the Chishti order, Baba Farid included;[42] and the earliest primary sources on Baba Farid make no mention of his having converted anyone. Indeed, it is probable that many if not most of these clans, in the course of their northward migrations up the rivers of the Punjab, had not yet reached the Ajodhan area during Baba Farid's lifetime.

On the other hand, we need not, because of these hagiographic and chronological problems, dismiss outright the claims of the clans. If one were to hypothesize that the agent of the clans' conversion, instead of Baba Farid himself, was the shrine of Baba Farid as a highly complex religious and social institution, a number of problems fade away. Baba Farid resided in Ajodhan only sixteen or twenty-four years,[43] which is a very short time span for the many eponymous clan founders or *māliks* who claimed to have met him actually to have been there. The shrine, on the other hand, has been there all along, sustaining the powerful baraka of the saint through its line of dīwāns. The identification of the shrine with the spirit of Baba Farid has been so thorough, in fact, that by the sixteenth century, the very name of the city containing the shrine, Ajodhan, became known as Pakpattan ('the holy ferry'), in honour of Baba Farid's memory. Under these circumstances it would hardly be surprising that the clans, in reconstructing the story of their own conversion to Islam, should recall the name of the saint himself and not that of any particular dīwān.

Moreover, throughout the period when Jat groups moved up the riverine region and on to the barr country, there were several non-religious ways in which the shrine patronized the clans and thus integrated them into its wide orbit of social and political influence, paving the way for the Jats' gradual integration into its ritual and religious structure. In Clifford Geertz's terms, the shrine provided the tribes with a tiny 'theater-state' of their own;[44] that is, it displayed through the ceremonies and celebrations that marked its liturgical calendar, the pageantry of both the court of God and the court of Delhi, albeit on a microcosmic scale. The shrine thus gave clan leaders and their followers not only access to Islam, but the honour of participating in the reflected splendor of the Sultanate or Mughal courts without actually being directly subservient to the authorities in Delhi.

As an intermediary institution in both a religious and a political sense, the shrine of Baba Farid was itself patronized by Delhi. We have seen how, since the third *dīwān*, the Delhi court lavished the revenues of towns and villages in support of the shrine and its attendants. No major ruler passed by the area without showing deference to its spiritual power. For instance, in October 1398 Timur, amidst his plundering of northern India, took the time to visit the shrine.[45] Likewise, Akbar, in March 1571, opened his sixteenth regnal year in Pakpattan, where he implored strength at Baba Farid's shrine.[46] And in 1629 Shah Jahan issue a farmān indicating precisely what his and his predecessors' policy was *vis-à-vis* the shrine:

> The sacred town of Pak Pattan with all its dependencies is by old agreement held in grant from the preceding emperors for the 'Langar' expenses of the shrine of the revered saint Baba Shekh Fureed Shukur Gunj by Shekh Mohammad, Sujjadah Nahseen of the shrine, a descendant of the Baba, and the proceeds thereof are applied to his own maintenance and to that of the Durveshes and Khadims attached thereto, as well as to the feed of Travellers and the repair and adornment of the building. Continue the whole 'Muhal' [i.e., *pargana*] in endowment to the shrine.[47]

In return for this royal patronage, the dīwāns of Pakpattan performed several functions for the Mughal government. Above all, on certain tracts of land they received the government's share of all crops on which revenue was levied in kind, whereas the tax on cash crops such as cotton, indigo, or tobacco had to be paid in cash and went straight to revenue officials without passing the dīwān.[48] It was therefore in the dīwān's interest as a *de facto chaudhrī*, first, that agriculture be expanded at the expense of pastoralism, for the dīwān derived no cattle tax from the *barr* clans, and secondly, that food crops be sown instead of cash crops. Although there is no corroborating evidence to this effect, these circumstances suggest that the *dīwāns* might have been promoters of peasant agriculture, and might explain the *Jawāhir al-Farīdī's* seeming approval of peasant agriculture as a way of life for the shrine's dependent clans.[49]

As the Delhi court patronized the shrine, so also the shrine patronized the agricultural clans, in some ways even mimicking the symbols of the larger court. For example the very word for 'shrine' used in the subcontinent, '*dargāh*', is also the word for a royal court. More significantly, the special title of Baba Farid's chief successor, a personage who at other shrines was designated simply *sajjāda nishīn* ('one who sits on the prayer carpet'), at Pakpattan was and is '*dīwān*', a term taken directly from the lexicon of Indo-Islamic royal courts, and possibly alluding to the man's revenue-collecting function mentioned above. Similarly, the *dastār bandī* ceremony, tying on a turban symbolically bestowing legitimate authority on someone, has obvious parallels with a coronation ceremony. Thus in the hagiographic literature reconstructing the story of Baba Farid's sending off the Siyal chief to settle and populate the Chenab-Ravi area, he gave the chief a frock and a turban,[50] thus combining a specifically Sufi symbol of authority (the frock) with a symbol conferring authority in both courtly and Sufi contexts (the turban).

The clans' attachments to the shrine were far more than merely symbolic, however. The darwishes and *khādims* (i.e., 'servants') mentioned in Shah Jahan's farmān as receiving royal support, comprised the many hundreds of lineal descendants of Baba Farid living in the Pakpattan region.[51] So numerous were these descendants that they literally formed a separate zamīndār caste in the area, the 'Chishti' caste, possessing both economic privileges and ritual status *vis-à-vis* the local clans. An 1897 British Assessment Report for this area described the Chishtis as 'a semi-religious Mussalman tribe' having 'considerable local influence,' who 'are not working agriculturalists, but depend for cultivation entirely on tenants'.[52] It is probable that the Chishtis enjoyed the same sort of proprietary rights in relation to their tenant clients from a very early date.

More interesting is the well-documented fact that the clans swore allegiance not to Baba Farid but to his family—i.e., the Chishti caste of Pakpattan. Our early-seventeenth-century source, the *Jawāhir al-Farīdī*, states the matter quite clearly: 'The Khokhars, Bhattis, Dhudhis, and Hāns are found in the environs of Pakpattan, and all the clans take *bai'a* with this family and have become *murīds*.'[53] Elsewhere the same source mentions that 'these clans serve the *progeny* of Baba Farid'.[54] Now, *bai'a* means a compact of allegiance, which in early Sufism meant spiritual allegiance only, but which among the unlettered Jat clans carried political as well as ethical obligations. In fact, one passage of the *Jawāhir al-Farīdī* suggests that even military obligations were involved in the taking of *bai'a*:

> And in these environs [Pakpattan] the Khokhars, Dhudhis, Jo'iyas, Bhattis, Wattus, and other groups who became Muslim from the time of Baba Farid, until now are busy in prayer and fasting [i.e., they conform to the outward observances of Muslim law]. For they are the possessors of dignity in the environs of Pakpattan. They can place ten thousand cavalry and foot soldiers in his [Baba Farid's] service, and have complete faith in Baba Farid and his descendants, and are their *murīds*.[55]

The above account having been written during Jahangir's reign, when the Mughals enjoyed effective authority in the Punjab, we do not hear that the dīwān's Jat murīds were actually called upon to do battle in service of the shrine. In the mid-eighteenth century, however, Mughal decline had allowed various local powers to assert their independence and to expand their holdings at their neighbours' expense. Thus in 1757 Diwan 'Abd as-Subhan (1752–66) gathered an army of his Jat murīds, attacked the raja of Bikaner, and thereby expanded the shrine's territorial holdings for the first time to the east of the Sutlej.[56] Then, however, he had to face the expanding Sikh power to the north, in particular the Nakkai *mithl* headed by Hira Singh. Supported mainly by his Wattu murīds,[57] the dīwān successfully repelled a Sikh attack on Pakpattan around 1776 in which Hira Singh was killed, and then pursued the retreating Sikhs with four thousand cavalry, killing a great number of them.[58] In 1810 the shrine's extensive holdings were seized by Ranjit Singh, and the dīwāns of Pakpattan, their brief period of political independence now at an end, reverted to their former status of political intermediaries.[59]

What bound the clans to the shrine even more powerfully than economic or political ties were the ties of kinship and intermarriage established between dependent Jat and Rajput groups and the dīwān's family. The significant point here is that the latter groups gave their daughters to the dīwāns and their immediate family, whereas Chishti daughters were evidently kept within the caste. In traditional Indian kinship terms, client-patron relations among castes are often structured by the direction of bridegiving, the bride-giving groups normally being clients of the bride-receiving group. In fact, the kinship relations of the dīwān and the clans immediately call to mind those of the Mughal court and its subordinate Rajput clans, except that in the case of the dīwāns religious as well as political patronage was involved.

The *Jawāhir al-Farīdī* not only lists the clans that, as of 1623, had entered into a bride-giving relationship with the dīwān and his family, but even names the groom and the bride's father in such alliances. Accordingly, we find that of the thirteen marriage alliances between the Khokhars and the shrine, seven of the Khokhar brides were daughters of clan māliks, or chiefs. And on the other side of the contract, we find that of these same thirteen alliances, three brides went to the dīwāns themselves and six went to sons of various dīwāns. The earliest instance of this Khokhar-dīwān connection was that of a Khokhar bride given to a son of Dīwān Ahmad Shah, who was dīwān of the shrine from 1452 to 1474.[60] Similar data exist for other groups, namely the Bhattis, Hans, and Dhudhis. Of five exchanges involving the Bhattis, two brides were daughters of Bhatti chiefs and three grooms were sons of dīwāns, the earliest alliance dating back to the late 1400s.[61] Of four alliances mentioned between the dīwān's family and the Hans and Dhudhi tribes, one involved a chief's daughter and two others involved granddaughters, and on the other side one alliance involved a dīwān and the other three, sons of dīwāns.[62]

Paralleling these economic, political, and kinship ties between the shrine and its neighbouring clans, the latter gradually became integrated into the shrine's ritual functionings, to the point that they eventually came to define themselves in religious terms the same way the shrine so defined itself—in Muslim terms. As argued above, it seems reasonable to discount the clans' claims that their eponymous founder or some other early migrant from Sind or Rajasthan actually met Baba Farid and was converted to Islam by his suasion. The evidence presented below further indicates that at no time, whether in Baba Farid's day or later, were the tribal *murīds* of the shrine converted to Islam en bloc. On the contrary, the conversion process seems to have been remarkably slow.

In his discussion of conversion to Islam in Iran, Richard Bulliet has suggested an objective index for measuring the overall rate of change from any given religion toward Islam in a specified region—namely, the frequency with which Muslim given names were bestowed on males. Observing that 'the naming of children is an act of free choice such as most individuals do not often have in their lifetime,' Bulliet notes that in selecting names,

> one overriding motivation in many instances is the specific desire either to display group membership in a name, or to conceal group membership. Unless there is some peculiar reason for doing so, parents are generally loath to burden their children with names that will cause them to be ostracized. In other words, naming for many parents is an act that reflects, usually unconsciously, their view of the society around them at that particular point in time.[63]

According to both the shrine's hagiographic accounts[64] and the earliest known history of the clan,[65] the Siyals of Jhang District were introduced to Islam by Baba Farid himself, who converted Ray Siyal, the clan's founder. After this event, according to these accounts, all Siyals presumably were Muslim. A very different picture emerges, however, if—as I have done in Table 12.2—one applies Bulliet's methodology to the fourteen genealogical charts of prominent Siyal families given in the *Tārīkh-i Jhang Siyāl.* These charts record twenty generations of leading Siyals from Ray Siyal to the time of the book's composition in 1862. Knowing, as we do, the dates of the Siyal chiefs in the ninth and seventeenth generations, we can estimate the approximate date of each generation by using the rule-of-thumb of three generations per century. This would place Ray Siyal's life in the early thirteenth century, not far, in fact, from Baba Farid's lifetime.

As Table 12.2 indicates, however, all masculine given names through the sixth generation remained Punjabi secular names; it was only in the early fifteenth century that specifically Muslim names began appearing at all. Gradually, between then and the early seventeenth century, the incidence of Muslim given names edged up from 10.24 per cent of the total to 39.21 per cent, not achieving parity with Punjabi secular names until about the middle of that century. It was not until the early eighteenth century that Muslim names became clearly preponderant (81.81 per cent).

Table 12.2
Changes in Names of Males of the Siyal Clan, circa 1217 to 1862

Generation	Year	Total names recorded	Number of Punjabi secular names	Number of Muslim names	Per cent of Muslim names to total
1	ca. 1217	1	1	0	0
2	ca. 1250	3	3	0	0
3	ca. 1283	13	13	0	0
4	ca. 1316	11	11	0	0
5	ca. 1349	9	9	0	0
6	ca. 1382	15	15	0	0
7	ca. 1415	39	35	4	10.25
8	ca. 1448	27	20	7	25.19
9	Mal Khān (d. 1481)	51	45	6	11.76
10	ca. 1514	51	38	13	25.49
11	ca. 1547	53	41	13	24.52
12	ca. 1580	61	42	18	29.50
13	ca. 1613	51	31	20	39.21
14	ca. 1646	34	15	19	55.88
15	ca. 1679	12	5	7	58.33
16	ca. 1712	22	4	18	81.81
17	Walīdād Khān (d. 1749–50)	12	3	9	75.00
18	ca. 1782	8	3	5	62.00
19	ca. 1815	10	0	10	100.00
20	1862	8	0	8	100.00

Source: Maulawi Nur Muhammad, *Tārīkh-i Jhang Siyāl* (Meerut, 1862), pp. 15–28.

After that time, our data become skewed because of the shrinking data base, but nonetheless indicate a total disappearance of Punjabi secular names by the early nineteenth century. The whole conversion process thus involved a period from the sixth to the nineteenth generation, or from the late fourteenth to the early nineteenth centuries.

If these data on the Siyals are at all indicative of the conversion pattern for the other clans that had taken *bai'a* with Baba Farid's shrine, or for that matter with any other shrine, then we may conclude that religious conversion among Punjabi clans was very slow indeed—not only slow, but probably unconscious as well. This was, after all, a period long before either British census officials or zealous reformers began urging Indians to place themselves into sharply differentiated religious categories. Accordingly, murīds of Baba Farid's shrine probably saw themselves less in terms of adherents of the Book and more in terms of clients and sponsors of a theatre-shrine that displayed the wondrous baraka of its saint through its pageantry, festivals, and ceremonies. As Miles Irving wrote in 1911,

> To the ordinary Montgomery cattle-thief who comes once a year to Pakpattan to obtain remission for the enormities of the past twelve months, Baba Farid is the mediator by whose merits he obtains forgiveness, assurance of which he obtains through the presence in the flesh of the descendant of the saint.[66]

Contemptible as this form of Islam may have been to nineteenth- and twentieth-century reformers, the shrine in the medieval period had managed gradually to give the clans an identity which, in their own estimation at least, was Islamic. In both the Sultanate and Mughal periods a long tradition of economic, political, and social patronage by the dīwāns had absorbed into the shrine's orbit of ritual influence groups which, as former pastoralists who had only recently achieved a settled way of life, had not formerly been integrated into anything approaching urban culture. It was the shrine's historical function to incorporate local systems of culture into a larger cultural system, to connect rustic clans politically with Delhi and religiously with Islam. This process, however, did not involve for newly incorporated groups a change from a Hindu to a Muslim identity, for at the time of the clans' first contact with Baba Farid's shrine these groups had not yet become integrated into the Hindu ritual or social structure. Although the precise nature of the Jats' pre-Muslim religion is as yet unclear, they seem to have had a deep-rooted tradition of social egalitarianism. Hence their rise in status from low Sudras to agrarian zamīndārs could more easily find ideological/ritual expression in Islam than within the highly stratified Hindu social system via the process of 'Sanskritization'.[67]

CONCLUSION

Although I have argued that the shrine of Baba Farid integrated local systems of culture into a larger one, the shrine nonetheless remained a local manifestation of that larger culture. The Chishti brotherhood of Sufis, of which Baba Farid was himself one of the most renowned spokesmen, was historically the first great order of Sufis in the Indo-Muslim capital of Delhi. This meant that the tombs of these Sufis—e.g., that of Mu'in al-Din Chishti at Ajmer, that of Nizam al-Din Auliya at Delhi, and that of Baba Farid at Pakpattan—became the first Muslim holy places *within* India. As such, they assumed immense importance, for it meant that South Asian Muslims were no longer compelled to look exclusively to the Middle East for spiritual inspiration.[68] Shrines like that of Baba Farid made a universal culture system available to local groups, enabling such groups to transcend their local microcosms.

In carrying out this role there evolved a distinctive code of conduct, or *adab*, of the shrines, just as medieval Indo-Muslim culture had evolved an equally distinctive adab of the court, i.e., a highly elaborated code of etiquette and pageantry that both dazzled and integrated into its structure the subjects of the kingdom. At Pakpattan this *adab* comprised the whole set of rituals and symbols that became institutionalized almost immediately after Baba Farid's death and that served progressively to assimilate various groups into its social and religious structure. Consider, for example, the symbolic power of the turban. Precisely because the shrine of Baba Farid assimilated people religiously as well as politically and socially, the tying of the turban (dastār bandī) possessed a great symbolic repertoire: it defined relations of kinship between the shrine and subordinate clans, it symbolically conferred legitimacy on actual rulers in Delhi, and it conferred spiritual discipleship at the shrine itself. Another aspect of the shrine's adab was its carefully defined formula for achieving religious transcendence, namely, the practice of passing through its Gate of Paradise (bihishtī darwāza), enabling all who did so to ritually enter paradise.

Yet the adab of the shrine, like that of the court of Delhi, also established and sustained a hierarchic principle: in descending rank there was the dīwān, the dīwān's family, the khalīfas and shrine functionaries, the Chishti caste, the clan leaders, and the common Jat agriculturalists. Even while integrating diverse peoples into a common religious culture, the shrine's highly elaborated code of conduct sorted, arranged, and held such peoples in a graded hierarchy that has persisted for centuries.

NOTES

1. Ernest Gellner, *Saints of the Atlas* (Chicago, 1969), p. 149. The emphasis is Gellner's.

2. The remarks of a British officer concerning the mediating role of Punjabi saints in 1911 are equally true of medieval shrines: 'The general idea of our riverain folk seems to be that the Deity is a busy person, and that his hall of audience is of limited capacity. Only a certain proportion of mankind can hope to attain to the presence of God; but when certain individuals have got there, they may have opportunities of representing the wishes and desires of other members

of the human race. Thus, all human beings require an intervener between them and God.' Major Aubrey O'Brien, 'The Mohammedan Saints of the Western Punjab,' *Journal of the Royal Anthropological Institute* 41 (1911): 511.

3. Shaikh Jamali Kamboh Dihlawi, comp., *Siyar al-'ārifīn* (Delhi, 1893), pp. 33–4.

4. See his *The Life and Times of Shaikh Farid-ud Din Ganj-i-Shakar* (Delhi, 1973) and his *Tārīkh i mashāikh i Chisht* (Islamabad, n.d.).

5. Amir Hasan Sijzi, comp., *Fawāid al-fu'ād* (Lucknow, 1884), p. 62. Cited in Nizami, *Life and Times*. p. 52n.

6. Ibid., p. 127. Cited in Nizami, *Life and Times*, p. 53.

7. Ibid., pp. 124–5, 41. Cited in Nizami, *Life and Times*, p. 54.

8. Mir Khwurd Kirmani, comp., *Siyar al-auliyā* (Delhi, 1885), p. 131.

9. It is noteworthy that although every *dīwān* of the shrine down to the present has been the eldest son of his predecessor, Baba Farid's own first and second sons were passed over in favour of Badr al-Din, who was the third son. Moreover, he was the only successor not to have received the office from his fathcr and predecessor, as he was given the office directly by the Chishti elders in Chisht, western Afghanistan. *Siyar al-auliyā*, p. 188.

10. Amir Khusrau, *Rāha al-muḥibbīn*, Urdu edition (Lahore, 1957), pp. 63–4. Cited in M. Abdullah Chaghatai, 'Pakpattan and Shaikh Farid', *Iqbal Review* 9 (1968): 131.

11. 'Ali Asghar Chishti, comp., *Jawāhir al-Farīdī* (Lahore, 1883–84), pp. 298–300.

12. Ziya al-Din Barani records that Baba Farid warned a certain Sufi, who was then leaving Ajodhan for Delhi, in the following words: 'I give thee a bit of advice, which it would be well for thee to observe. Have nothing to do with maliks and amirs, and beware of their intimacy as dangerous; no *darwesh* ever kept up such intimacy, but in the end found it disastrous.' *Tarīkh-i Fīrūz Shāhī,* abridged trans. in H.M. Elliot and Dowson, *History of India as Told by Its Own Historians* (Allahābad, 1964), 3:144.

13. Ahmad Nabi Khan, 'The Mausoleum of Shaikh 'Ala al-Din at Pakpattan (Punjab): Significant Example of the Tuqluq Style of Architecture', *East and West* 24, nos. 3–4 (Sept.–Dec. 1974): 324–5.

14. Shams-i Siraj 'Afīf, *Tārīkh-i Fīroz Shāhi*, ed. Mauavi Vilayat Husain (Calcutta: Asiatic Society of Bengal, 1891), pp. 27–8.

15. As Amir Khurd recorded, 'In no way would he go anywhere except to the door of the Jāmi' mosque, and if kings would come, he would not budge from his place.' *Siyar al-auliyā*, p. 194.

16. Ibn Battuta, *Rehla of Ibn Batuta*, trans. and ed. Mahdi Husain (Baroda, 1953), p. 20.

17. *Siyar al-auliyā*, p. 196.

18. *Jawāhir al-farīdī*, pp. 307–08.

19. Ibid. *Siyar al-auliyā*, p. 196. For a discussion of the architectural aspects of the magnificent tomb of 'Ala al-Din Mauj Darya, see Ahmad Nabi Khan, 'The Mausoleum of Shaikh 'Ala al-Dīn.' The date of construction of the tomb comes

from an inscription on the tomb itself——Safar, 737, which corresponds to Sept./ Oct., AD 1336.

20. *Siyar al-auliyā*, p. 196. See also Barani, *Tārīkh-i Fīrūz Shāhī* (Calcutta, 1862), pp. 347–8, 518.

21. *Siyar al-auliyā*, p. 196.

22. *Jawāhir al-Farīdī*, p. 308.

23. Barani, *Tārīkh-i Fīrūz Shāhī* (Calcutta, 1862), p. 543. Cited in H.A. Rose, ed., *Glossary of the Tribes and Castes of the Punjab* (Patiala, 1970), 1:495.

24. Ibn Battuta, *Rehla*, p. 20.

25. *Siyar al-auliyā*, p. 193.

26. *Siyar al-'ārifīn*, p. 115.

27. Barani, *Tārīkh-i Fīrūz Shāhī*, in Elliot and Dowson, *History of India*, 3:107, 109. See also Briggs, *Rise of the Mahommedan Power*, 1:143–5. Garrisoned cities included Lahore, Multan, Sirhind, Bhatinda, and Dipalpur.

28. Chaghatai, 'Pakpattan and Shaikh Farid', pp. 134–5.

29. For an excellent discussion of the ecology of the western Punjab, see chapter 1 of Emily Hodges' dissertation, in progress (University of California, Berkeley, Department of History).

30. Ibid., p. 22.

31. Cited in Irfan Habib, 'Jatts of Punjab and Sind,' in Harbans Singh and N.G. Barrier, eds., *Punjab Past and Present: Essays in Honour of Dr. Ganda Singh* (Patiala, 1976), p. 94.

32. See ibid.

33. Y. Friedmann, 'A Contribution to the Early History of Islam in India', in Myrian Rosen-Ayalon, ed., *Studies in Memory of Gaston Wiet* (Jerusalem, 1977), p. 332.

34. Edward Sachau, ed., *Alberuni's India* (New Delhi, 1964), 1:401.

35. See map of Punjab, circa 1605. In our period the Beas River did not, as it does now, end at the point where it joins the Sutlej. Rather, after joining the Sutlej above Ferozepur it again split off from it in a southwesterly direction until it joined the Chenab below Multan. In the 1790s the old Beas bed below Ferozepur dried up, so that what had formerly been two *doabs* below Ferozepur, the Bet Jullundur and the Bari, now became one, the Bari Doab between the Sutlej and the Ravi. See Herbert Wilhelmy, 'The Shifting River: Studies in the History of the Indus Valley,' *Universitas* 10, no. 1 (1968): 53–68.

36. Barani, *Tārīkh-i Fīrūz Shāhī*, in Elliot and Dowson, *History of India as Told by Its Own Historians* 3:109.

37. John Leyden and William Erskine, trans., *Memoirs of Zehir-ed-Din Muhammad Babur* (London, 1921), 2:93–5, 102, 163–4.

38. See Rose, ed., *Glossary of the Tribes and Castes*, vols. 2 and 3.

39. From Abu'l-fazl 'Allami, *Ā'īn-i Akbarī*, trans. H.S. Jarrett, 2nd ed. (Calcutta, 1949), 2:320–35 passim.

40. *Dabistān-i madhāhib* (Calcutta, 1809), p. 276. The author of this work wrote that in Punjabi 'Jat' meant 'villager' (*dihistānī, rūstā'ī*).

41. Habib, 'Jatts', p. 98. See also idem., 'Presidential Address', *Indian History Congress Proceedings* (1969), pp. 153–4. In describing the Persian wheel as an

ingenious irrigation device, which he had apparently never seen before, Babur specifically mentioned the Bet Jullundur and Bari Doabs ('Lahore, Dipalpur, Sirhind, and the neighbouring, districts'), where it was prevalent; *Memoirs of... Babur*, vol. 2, pp. 296–7. In 1832 Captain Wade, who led the earliest English expedition down the Sutlej valley, noted the remains of an extensive irrigation system based on the Persian wheel. See F. Mackeson, 'Journal of Captain Wade', *Journal of the Asiatic Society of Bengal*, 6 (1837): 181, 187–8, 194.

42. Mohammad Habib, 'Shaikh Nasirrudin Mahmud Chiragh-i Delhi as a Great Historical Personality', *Islamic Culture* (April 1946):140.

43. *Siyar al-auliyā*, p. 63.

44. Clifford Geertz, *Islam Observed: Religious Development in Morocco and Indonesia* (Chicago, 1971), p. 38.

45. Emperor Timur, *Malfūẓāt-i Tīmūrī*, abridged trans. in Elliot and Dowson, eds., *History of India*, 3: 421. Like any other of Baba Farid's millions of devotees, Timur implored the saint's intercession with God for the attainment of worldly concerns—in his case, victory in battle. With or without Baba Farid's help, Timur's prayers were certainly answered.

46. Abu'l-fazl 'Allami, *Akbarnāma*, trans. H. Beveridge. (Delhi, n.d.), 2: 525–6.

47. West Pakistan Board of Revenue, Lahore. File 131/6/24/24.

48. *Punjab District Gazetteers*, vol. 18-A. *Montgomery District, 1933* (Lahore, 1935), p. 38.

49. In enumerating the shrine's *murīd* clans, the *Jawāhir al-Farīdī* records: 'so these clans—Adhank, Valank, and Sipan—are all farmers in Pakpattan, and are descendants of the aforesaid Makh, and are commonly known as Bughutis, Daks, and Sapan. The Baritis are originally Jats.... They live in Pakpattan and practice agriculture. Then there are the Jakh, whose descendants are called Jhakarwalis. The Dikan, Dahkan, Sipan, Baritis and Bughutis are all farmers.' *Jawāhir al-Farīdī*, p. 397.

50. Ibid., p. 324.

51. It was on account of this vast proliferation of descendants that even in the seventeenth century Baba Farid himself was called 'the Second Adam'. G.A. Storey, *Persian Literature, a Bio-bibliographical Survey* (London, 1927–71), 2:986.

52. Patrick J., Fagan, *Assessment Report for Pakpattan Tahsil* (Lahore, 1896), p. 50.

53. *Jawāhir al-Farīdī*, p. 323.

54. Ibid., p. 396. Emphasis added.

55. Ibid., pp. 397–8.

56. *Montgomery District Gazetteer* (1933), p. 38.

57. Ibid., p. 35.

58. Syad Muhammad Latif, *History of the Panjab* (Lahore, n.d.), p. 312.

59. To be sure, it was under much worse terms than under the Mughals. Ranjit Singh allowed the dīwān and his retainers only Rs. 1,000 a year for their maintenance, derived from the town duties of Pakpattan, in addition to a fourth

share of four small villages nearby. *Journal of the Asiatic Society of Bengal* 6 (1837): 193.

60. *Jawāhir al-Farīdī*, pp. 323–4
61. Ibid., p. 324.
62. Ibid.
63. Richard W. Bulliet, 'Conversion to Islam and the Emergence of Muslim Society in Iran', in N. Levtzion, ed., *Conversion to Islam* (New York, 1979), p. 43.
64. *Jawāhir al-Farīdī*, pp. 324, 397.
65. Maulawi Nūr Muḥammad, *Tārīkh-i Jhang Siyāl* (Meerut, 1862), pp. 4–7.
66. Miles Irving, 'The Shrine of Baba Farid Shakarganj at Pakpattan', *Journal of the Panjab Historical Society* 1 (1911–2): 73. It was, of course, Irving's imperial administrative viewpoint that caused him to judge most clans of the *barr* country as 'cattle-thieves' and their actions as 'enormities'.
67. In fact, it is just this dynamic, as Irfan Habib has suggested, that lay behind the attraction of other Jat tribes, in another part of the Punjab, to the equally egalitarian creed of Sikhism. See Habib, 'Jatts', pp. 99–100.
68. We find, for example, early hagiographic manuals declaring that a certain number of pilgrimages to certain Sufi shrines in India would be equivalent in moral value to a single pilgrimage to Mecca.

13
Creating Tradition Through Devotional Songs and Communal Script: The Khojah Isma'ilis of South Asia*

Ali S. Asani

I

Among the Muslim communities of South Asia, the Khojahs[1] constitute a distinctive minority on the basis of both numbers as well as their religious history and beliefs. Believed originally to be members of the Hindu Lohana caste, the vast majority of them today identify themselves as Shi'i Muslims of the Nizari Isma'ili persuasion. They regard the Aga Khan to be their religious and spiritual leader, *ḥāḍir Imām* ('present Imam') or *Imām-i zamān* ('Imam of the time'). According to their belief, the Imam, by virtue of his direct descent from the Prophet Muhmmad's daughter Fatima (d. 633) and son-in-law 'Ali (d. 661), is endowed with special knowledge (*'ilm*) to interpret the Qur'an and provide authoritative guidance on all matters, religious and otherwise. At present, they believe that Aga Khan IV is the forty-ninth Imam in direct succession from the first Imam, 'Ali. It is their belief in the infallible guidance and authority of the Aga Khan as ḥadir Imām that sets the Khojah Isma'ilis apart from the majority of Muslims. On account of this tenet of their faith they are referred to by other Muslims as 'Aga Khanis', often in a perjorative sense.

During the course of their history, the Khojah Isma'ilis, like their fellow Isma'ilis in other parts of the world, have been conspicuous for

* Reprinted from Ali S. Asani, 'The Isma'ili *Ginān*s: Reflections on Authority and Authorship', in Farhad Daftary, ed., *Mediaeval Ismaili History and Thought* (Cambridge: Cambridge University Press, 1996), pp. 265–80, and idem., 'The Khojki Script: a Legacy of Ismaili Islam in the Indo-Pakistan Subcontinent', *Journal of the American Oriental Society* 107, No. 3 (1987), pp. 439–49.

stressing the esoteric dimension of their faith over the exoteric. Their religious vocabulary includes terms like *pīr*, *murshid*, *murīd*, *dhikr* (*zikr*), *jamā'at-khāna*, *ṭarīqa*, which resonate with the Sufi tradition, but set them apart from formulations of Islam that emphasize orthopraxy or legalistic norms.[2] In their understanding of Islam as well as some of their religious practices, the Khojahs have also been strongly influenced by their Indian cultural ancestry. For example, until recently, they understood the Shi'i Muslim concept of the Imam through a reformist interpretation of the concept of the *avatāra* from Vaishnava Hinduism.[3] Specifically, they identified the Shi'i Imam 'Ali with the long-awaited tenth avatāra of the Hindu deity Vishnu, and the religion of Islam as the completion of Vaishnava Hinduism, just as in the Near Eastern context Islam was represented as the culmination of Judaism and Christianity. Through such formulations, members of this community could and did consider themselves simultaneously as true Hindus and true Muslims. Not surprisingly, neither the orthodox Muslim nor Hindu would claim him as a co-religionist.[4]

Communities like the Khojahs, which do not conveniently fit into preconceived spaces, have always been problematic to categorize. The historian Bernald Lewis declared them as 'Hindus under a light Muslim veneer'.[5] The late Aziz Ahmad, scholar of several works on Islam in South Asia, grouped them along with other 'syncretic' sects of indeterminate identity, declaring that their chief interest is as 'curiosities of mushroom religious growth',[6] which until recently added 'color to the bizarre pageantry of India'.[7] The ordinary Hindus and Muslims, he further remarks, looked on such communities as 'spiritual freaks'.[8] Not surprisingly, as questions of religious identity became increasingly important in nineteenth- and twentieth-century India, groups perceived as inhabiting the halfway house between Islam and Hinduism came under heavy attack.[9] On the one hand, Muslim reformist groups, such as the Faraizis and Wahhabis, assaulted a range of practices among Muslims which they considered as borrowings from Hinduism and therefore, in their opinion, un-Islamic.[10] Hindu revivalist groups joined the battle on the other side, producing aggressive propaganda aimed at re-absorbing these 'half-baked' adherents of Islam into their ancestral Hindu tradition.[11]

In the early nineteenth century, the Khojahs participated in several identities simultaneously. Their religious life was 'a unique blend of Hindu and Muslim, as well as Shi'i and Sunni customs and beliefs'.[12] At the same time, they clearly saw themselves and were perceived by others as a caste closely associated with trade. In fact, tradition claims that the title '*khojah*', meaning 'lord, master', was bestowed on converts to Islam by the fifteenth-century preacher-saint Pir Sadr al-Din. The title, it is further claimed, was a replacement for the original Hindu Lohana title '*thakur*' or '*thakkar*', also meaning 'lord, master', the intent being to bestow some sort of caste status on the new converts who lived in a milieu in which caste was fundamental to defining social status and societal relationships.[13] We have evidence from Bombay (Mumbai), a major centre of Khojah settlement, that the *jamā'at* or community had regular meetings to which adult males were summoned by a crier who went through the streets.[14] At such gatherings, which, in fact, one Khojah described as being identical to the meetings held by various Hindu castes, all kinds of disputes, including those related to marriages, were presented for arbitration. In cases of violation of caste norms, members could vote on excommunication. There were also special caste dinners for which the caste, as a corporate body, owned its own cooking utensils.[15]

In many social customs, the Khojahs followed traditional Indian or Hindu norms, marriages being accompanied by a host of rituals and ceremonies dictated by local custom.[16] Widow re-marriage, as in the case of Hindu castes, was a strict taboo.[17] In personal law, including matters of inheritance, which was limited only to males, the community was, according to one scholar, 'caught within the meshes of Hindu customary law'.[18]

Notwithstanding the above, the Khojahs were of course Muslims; the association of trading communities with Islam was not uncommon in the history of Islamic civilization. But what kind of Muslims? Their version of Islam integrated multiple and supposedly 'contradictory' strands. On the one hand, there was a Sunni *mullā* at the *masjid*, or mosque, at their cemetery in Bombay who conducted the funeral ceremonies, while a Sunni qazi, or judge, presided over the official Islamic *nikāh* ceremony at Khojah weddings.[19] However, the Khojahs were clearly not Sunni, for they displayed deep reverence towards 'Ali, the first Shi'i Imam, and participated in all the traditional Shi'i rituals commemorating the martyrdom of Husain and other Imams in the month of Muharram. Indeed, those who could afford the expense, would have the bodies of their dead shipped from Bombay for burial to Karbela in Iraq near the shrine of Imam Husain, the greatest of the Shi'i martyrs.[20] Unlike most other Shi'i groups, however, the Khojahs did not believe in the hidden Imam, for they had living Imams. They venerated the Isma'ili Imams in Iran as their leaders, regularly sending tributes to them. They also went to see them as part of a pilgrimage rite considered more significant than going to Mecca.[21]

In terms of their prayers, they recited the traditional *namāz/ṣalāt* only during the two *'Īds*; otherwise they had their own ritual prayer in the Gujarati language, containing a sprinkling of Arabic and Persian phrases, which they recited three times a day.[22] Other rituals they practised, such as the *ghaṭ pāṭ*, resembled the prayer ritual of the Shaktipanthi Hindu Lohanas.[23] They also recited hymn-like poems called *gināns* during religious ceremonies.

II

Among the literary genres associated with the Ismai'li tradition, the gināns of the Khojah communities of South Asia are unique. Composed in several Indic languages and dialects, these hymn-like poems have been strongly influenced by north Indian traditions of folk poetry and piety.[24] They thus represent a distinctive regional strand within a larger corpus of Isma'ili literature that is mostly in Arabic and Persian. Not surprisingly, the gināns are markedly different in their style and ethos from the more scholarly Arabic and Persian Isma'ili treatises that have usually attracted the attention of researchers.

The apparently 'syncretistic' manner in which the gināns employ Indian or Hindu mythological and theological concepts to present religious ideas has raised questions about their 'Islamic' character.[25] For example, Aziz Ahmad felt that the gināns possessed a 'literary personality' that is 'un-Islamic', presumably on account of their vernacular and 'syncretistic' characteristics.[26] Such judgements have, in turn, provoked debate within the community concerning the validity of using externals of culture such as language and idiom as yardsticks for measuring Islamic identity.[27] Ironically, in earlier times, when the religious identity of the Khojah community was the subject of intense dispute, the courts of colonial British India drew on evidence from these very hymns to determine that the Khojah were indeed Muslims of the Nizari Isma'ili persuasion.[28]

For historians of religion, the gināns are of particular interest for the prominent role they play in the religious life of Ismai'li Khojah communities in the Indian subcontinent and elsewhere.[29] Like many genres of Indian devotional poetry, they are intended to be sung in designated ragas or melodies. The singing of gināns constitutes a prominent item during prayer meetings held every morning and evening in the jamā'at khānas (halls of congregation). As Tazim Kassam points out, to sing a ginān in the context of the Khojah religious practice is to pray. The singing of gināns constitutes ritualized worship, a phenomenon generally characteristic of the Indian religious landscape.[30] Participation in ginān singing, especially in a large congregation, can have a powerful emotional and sensual impact on individuals, even those who may not fully understand the meanings and significance of the words they sing. During a particularly melodious ginān recitation, it is not uncommon to observe individuals being moved sometimes to the point of tears. An oft-repeated story within the community concerns the penitence and redemption of Isma'il Ganji, a not exactly pious Isma'ili of Junagadh, after he was reduced to tears one evening while he was sitting in the jamā'at khāna listening to the recitation of a ginān.[31]

Beyond their role in worship, the ginān s permeate communal and individual life in many ways. At a communal level, functions or meetings, be they religious or secular, frequently begin with a short Qur'an recitation followed by one from the ginān s. Verses from the ginān s are often cited as proof-texts during sermons, religious discussions, and in religious education materials. Certain ginān s have even been interpreted as predicting modern scientific and political developments such as the atom bomb or the rise of Communism.[32] Occasionally, for both entertainment and religious edification, special concerts or *ginān maḥfil/mushā'ira* are organized, during which professional and amateur singers recite ginān s to musical accompaniment.[33] Again, outside the context of formal worship or liturgy, community institutions responsible for religious education may sponsor ginān competitions in which participants are judged on their ability to sing and properly enunciate ginān texts. Such competitions are a popular method among religious educators to encourage the learning of ginān s among young students and adults.

At a personal and family level, too, ginān s are used in many different contexts: individual verses can be quoted as proverbs; verses can be recited in homes to bring *baraka*, spiritual and material blessing; housewives, in a usage that stresses the links between the ginān s and the folk tradition, often recite them while working or as lullabies; audio-cassettes with ginān s sung by popular singers or recordings of ginān maḥfils can be found in many an Isma'ili home and even in automobiles!

As I have discussed in a previous article,[34] the ginān s enjoy a scriptural status in the Khojah Isma'ili community, for they are commonly perceived as being 'holy' or 'sacred'. Some members of the community declare them to be a 'divine literary corpus',[35] a viewpoint to which not all could comfortably subscribe. The ginān s have been described as 'an unbounded and immeasurable sea of knowledge, a unique storehouse of wisdom, and guidelines for everyday life.'[36] They contain instruction on a broad range of themes, including the religious obligations of the believer, ethics and morals, eschatology, the mystical life, and the spiritual quest of the soul. Indeed their function as vehicles for imparting religious teachings and precepts is reflected in the very name, which is derived from the Sanskrit word *jñāna*, meaning 'knowledge' or 'sacred wisdom'.

In the community's traditional self-image, the gināns originated in mediaeval times, approximately around the eleventh or twelfth centuries, when they were first composed by Iranian preacher-saints, called *pīrs*. The pīrs were sent to north India by Isma'ili Imams from Iran on missions to convert Hindus to Isma'ili Islam and to provide spiritual guidance for the newly-created convert communities. These preacher-saints, tradition asserts, in order to overcome cultural and linguistic barriers facing potential converts, composed gināns to explain the gist of the Qur'an and Isma'ili Islam to Indian populations in their native languages and idioms. According to one community publication, these poetic compositions provided the faithful with an understanding of the 'true meaning' of the Qur'an as well as the true meaning of religion.[37] Another explains that they are living commentaries on the Qur'an,[38] serving to penetrate its 'inner (*bāṭin*) signification'.[39] The gināns are, in effect, 'secondary' texts generated in the vernacular to transmit the teachings of 'primary' scripture—the Qur'an—to non-Arabic speaking peoples.[40]

The authority of the gināns and the veneration accorded to them is largely due to their being perceived as substantiations of the truth of faith as taught by the pirs. For those who revere them, the gināns are sacred since they were uttered by the pīrs. These preachers were no ordinary missionaries and evangelists; in the community's understanding, they were spiritually enlightened individuals whose religious and spiritual authority the Isma'ili Imams had formally endorsed by bestowing on them the title of pīr.[41] The gināns extol the virtues of love for and unquestioning obedience to the pīr and his teachings, for he is the true guide (*sat guru*) who can guide the faithful on the path to salvation.[42] Since the Imams resided in Iran, the pīrs became tangible symbols of the Imams' authority in South Asia with total control over the community and its members. W. Ivanow describes their theological position as being the 'link between God and man, really the "door", *bāb*, of the Imam, without whose guidance and instruction all efforts of the individual may remain futile and useless'.[43] Not surprisingly, the pīrs stand out in the tradition's history as figures of dominating importance, next only to the Imam.[44] In fact, in many contexts the gināns do not always distinguish between the pīr and the Imam, both being merged in doublets such as *gur-nar* and *pīr-shāh*, meaning 'guide and lord'.[45]

The most vexing question confronting scholars of the gināns concerns their provenance and authorship. As is the case with many of the poet-saints of mediaeval India, we possess remarkably little accurate historical information about the reputed authors of the gināns and their activities. What we do have, however, are hagiographic and legendary accounts, some of which are incorporated in the gināns themselves. Notwithstanding the admirable attempts made by Azim Nanji to analyse this 'mythic' material, the historical personalities of the pīrs remain 'dim and obscure'.[46] In the case of many pīrs, we do not possess even basic biographic information such as birth and death dates. In fact, doubts have been cast on the historical existence of Pir Satgur Nur, the pīr claimed in traditional accounts to have been the first to be sent to India as early as the tenth or eleventh century.[47] According to Azim Nanji, this pīr remains at best a symbolic and archetypal figure.[48] We are on only slightly firmer ground with his successors, Pir Shams, Sadr al-Din, and Hasan Kabir al-Din. In addition to a host of problems associated with their biographies, there is much confusion about the exact identities of the first two.[49] A fourth figure, Imam Shah (d. 1513), about whom we possess somewhat more reliable information, was allegedly the founder of a 'schismatic' movement that resulted in the formation of the Imam-Shahi subsect.[50] Consequently, the Isma'ili Khojah tradition only accords him the status of '*sayyid*', a rank inferior to that of pīr. To these four personalities, who reportedly lived between the twelfth and fifteenth centuries, are attributed the vast majority of gināns.

The gināns contain very little evidence to corroborate religious claims that they were composed during the historical period traditionally associated with these early pīrs. On the contrary, the linguistic and grammatical features of the gināns, as well as their idioms and style, point to later origins. W. Ivanow, though afraid of offending the sentiments of his Isma'ili friends, declares that in his opinion gināns attributed to a certain pīr seem to be more *about* him than *by* him and that there was no doubt about their being composed much later.[51] Christopher Shackle and Zawahir Moir, in their recent study, remark:

> No realistic discussion of the *gināns* is possible without first facing the realization that they are, at least in their present form, of quite recent origin. The linguistic evidence, which reveals a notable lack of discernibly archaic features, is itself a quite sufficient demonstration of the truth of this assertion.[52]

They go on to state quite confidently that many, perhaps most, of those gināns that are attributed to the early pīrs are in fact compositions from a later period in the community's history, the so-called 'age of the *sayyids*', which extend from 1500 to 1850 AD.[53] A growing number of studies on works ascribed to individual pīrs arrive at similar conclusions concerning authorship. Tazim Kassam's analysis of the *Brahma Prakasha*, a work attributed to Pir Shams, points to a much later date of composition than that of the period identified with the pīr.[54]

My own study of the *Būjh Nirañjan*, attributed to Pir Sadr al-Din, demonstrates with a massive array of evidence that this ginān was not composed by him but rather by an anonymous individual affiliated with the Qadiri Sufi order.[55] Similarly, evidence from Pyarali Keshwani's study of the ginān *Sī Ḥarfī* suggests a possible Sufi origin for that work as well.[56] Clearly, we are treading here on delicate ground where the results of scholarly research are in open conflict with the truth claims of religious tradition.

The situation becomes even more complex when one discovers in manuscripts and printed texts that the same gināns are attributed to two or more authors. The *Sī Ḥarfī*, for example, has been variously attributed to Ahmad Shah, Nur Muhammad Shah, and Imam Shah.[57] Then again the ginān *Allah ek khasam subuka* has two pīrs as authors, Pir Sadr al-Din and Pir Hasan Kabir al-Din, raising the possibility of either a joint authorship or perhaps one pīr (Hasan Kabir al-Din) transmitting the work of an earlier predecessor (Sadr al-Din).[58] A few gināns have as their authors individuals whose names are associated with Hindu mythological figures such as Sahadeva, the youngest of the five Pandava brothers, and Harishchandra, a king known for his legendary generosity.[59] In several compositions the author's name simply consists of an honorific title, such as *sat gur brahmā* (the divine guide), or *bār gur* (the guide of the twelve), or a compound of terms like Pīr Satgur Nur, 'the True Guide of Light'. The identity of authors is further obscured by the occurrence of similar sounding names such as Pir Indra Imam al-Din, Imam Din, and Saiyid Imam Shah. Tradition believes these names to refer to the same individual, but the poetic style of verses suggest that we may in fact be dealing with three different persons. Finally, there are a few anonymous gināns, not attributed to any particular pīr. The obvious example in this category is the ever popular *Kalām-i Mawlā*, claimed to be an anonymous translation into Hindustani of an Arabic or Persian work allegedly written by the first Shi'i Imam, 'Ali bin Abi Talib (d. 661).[60]

What are we to make of this terribly confused state of affairs? The tradition's claims of authorship of gināns by pīrs rest on the fact that in almost every composition there occurs a *bhaṇitā*, or 'signature-verse'. This verse, which normally occurs towards the end of the ginān, customarily contains the name of a pīr. When the pīr's name is mentioned during recitation, members of the congregation demonstrate their respect and devotion to his spiritual authority by bowing their heads slightly and touching with their forefinger the lips and/or the bridge of the nose and the forehead in a bipartite or tripartite gesture.

The bhaṇitā is not a poetic feature unique to the ginān̄s. It is in fact an essential element of many genres of South Asian religious poetry including the *pada*, the most popular form of devotional verse in north India. As in the ginān̄s, the bhaṇitā containing the name of the poet occurs in the last one or two verses of mediaeval devotional poems as an oral signature. And as is also the case with the ginān̄s, these signatures have been generally interpreted as indications of authorship.

In a ground-breaking study on the role of the bhaṇitā in north Indian devotional poetry, John Hawley convincingly demonstrates that this verse signifies authorship in other ways than simply 'writer', as we commonly use the term.[61] Citing definitions of the word 'author' from the *Oxford English Dictionary*—'a person on whose authority a statement is made', and 'a person who has authority over others'—he argues that the occurrence of a poet's name in a poem points in the direction of authority rather than strictly authorship.[62] For example, in the hymns of the *Guru Granth Sahib*, the sacred scripture of the Sikhs, one hears only the name of Guru Nanak, the first *guru* of the community, even in verses known to have been composed by other gurus. Guru Nanak's name clearly serves as a symbol of authority rather than personal identity. When the gurus after him composed poetry, they did so in his name, invoking his authority.[63]

In support of his contention, Hawley analyzes the bhaṇitā in the poetry attributed to prominent poet-saints of the North Indian *bhaktī* tradition such as Ravidas, Surdas, and Mirabai. In every case, he shows the many ways in which the authority of the poet in the signature-verse is more significant than the actual fact of composition:

> In devotional Hindi poetry, to give an author's name is not so much to denote who said what, as to indicate the proper force of an utterance and the context in which it is to be appreciated. The author's name is no mere footnote. It anchors a poem to life, a personality, even a divinity that gives the poem its proper weight and tone; and it connects to a network of associations that makes the poem not just a fleeting flash of truth—not just new and lovely—but something that has been heard before and respected, something familiar and beloved.[64]

The bhaṇitā serves as a means of 'anchoring' the poem by invoking a poet-saint's authority. In this connection, Hawley also points out that the bhaṇitā may also be called *chāp*, 'stamp or seal', a term that indicates its function authoritatively; that what has been said is true and bears listening to.[65] It functions, in a way, as an authoritative seal of approval for the poem.

Several of Hawley's other observations are relevant to our discussion on authorship of the ginān̄s. A cursory examination of signature-verses in the gināns shows that the name of the relevant pīr is invariably associated with verbs that mean to speak, to say, to utter, to instruct, or to teach. It is on account of phrases such as 'pīr so-and-so says' that those who revere these hymns and use them in worship, as well as those who study them, have assumed that these signatures signify the simple fact of a ginān's authorship. Significantly, a substantial proportion of bhaṇitās in Hindi devotional poetry, too, either explicitly contain the verb 'to say', or some variant of it, or imply it in context. But this should not mislead us. In order to better understand this apparently confusing situation, we need to first examine the relationship of the poetic signature to the rest of the verse and, second, the relationship of the bhaṇitā itself to the rest of the poem.

We observe in the diction surrounding the bhaṇitās of the gināns that there is frequently a break in syntax between the name mentioned in the signature and the remainder of the verse. A similar situation exists in Hindi devotional poetry, where this 'grammatical hiatus' in the bhaṇitā transfers the responsibility for forming the grammatical connection between signature and verse to the listener.[66] Since verbs of actual 'authoring' rarely occur in the bhaṇitās of the gināns or any other mediaeval Indian devotional verse, the interpretation of these verses is fraught with ambiguity. This ambiguity is further compounded by the telegraphic style of poetry so greatly favoured by poets in the tradition. In this regard, Hawley remarks that the 'relation between the signature and the line of which it is a part can be an intricate matter indeed—not at all so simple as the linear "Surdas says" or "Ravidas says" would suggest'.[67]

As regards the relationship of the bhaṇitā to the entire poem, we can usually notice a subtle change in the direction of the poem when the poet's signature is revealed. The purpose of this shift, Hawley suggests in the examples of poetry he examines, is to convey not only 'authorship' but also to highlight authority.[68] Such a reorientation is characteristic of many gināns where it is marked by dramatic changes in the narrative perspective of the bhaṇitā, frequently from the first or third person.[69] Sometimes there will be a prayer or petition:

> Pīr Sadruddin says: 'O Master, it is to You that we owe all that we have eaten. If You are merciful, the soul will be delivered.'[70]
>
> Pīr Indra Imamuddin, with hope on his lips, has entreatingly said: 'Master, forgive the sins of your community!'[71]

But often the verse will consist of a command, an injunction, or a proverbial religious truth addressed to the listener:

> Pīr Tajuddin says: 'Magnify the Lord! Only true believers will be rewarded, O brother.'[72]

> 'O brother', Pīr Imam Shah has said, 'Listen, O brother believers. Let those who would wake remain awake, for the Light has been revealed.'[73]
>
> 'Assemble, O congregations, and perform your devotions', says Pīr Sadruddin.[74]
>
> Pīr Sadruddin has said: 'If anyone would make his mind understand, then what comes of washing clothes? Discovery comes through cleansing the heart.'[75]

The point to note here is that the bhaṇitā, whether it contains an intercessory petition, a command, or a statement of religious truth, invokes in some manner the authority of the pīr.

If we now re-evaluate and re-examine the signature-verses of the gināns as being invocations of authority, then some of the confusion on the 'authorship' issue begins to dissipate: the disproportionately large number of compositions attributed to the three or four pīrs who, in the community's self-image, played a central or seminal role in the development of the tradition; the inconsistencies of style in works supposedly written by the same author; and the anachronisms of content. All of these points can now be better comprehended. Considering the bhaṇitā from this perspective makes it possible to understand that disciples of individual pīrs, like those of the bhakti poet-saints, could compose poems in the names of their spiritual guides as a way of expressing their spiritual affiliation, as well as their devotion and veneration to their mentors.[76] Furthermore, the pīrs' names served to 'anchor' the poems giving them validity and weight, confirming that the teachings contained within them were in conformity with those preached by the great masters. Significantly, the gināns themselves contain some supporting evidence. An obvious example occurs in a popular ginān, *Ae raḥem raḥemān*, by the only known female composer, Saiyida Imam Begum (d. 1866?). In the bhaṇitā of this composition, Imam Begum invokes the name of her pīr, Hasan Shah, to validate her teachings, since she herself was not regarded as a pīr.[77] Similarly, the ginān *Murbandhjo achoro* contains a reference to the effect that it is being recorded by Vimras, a disciple of Pir Shams. Elsewhere, the pīr asks the same disciple to recite gināns to new converts presumably in his name.[78] In several other cases, some verses specifically indicate that gināns attributed to Pīr Shams were uttered by his devotees.[79]

That the name of the pīr in the bhaṇitā was conceived as a way of 'anchoring' a composition to the Isma'ili pīr tradition is also illustrated by the case of the *Būjh Nirañjan*. In my study of this text, I have shown that textual and linguistic evidence overwhelmingly indicates that this ginān was composed outside the Khojah tradition, specifically in the Qadiri Sufi order.[80] As a mystical poem, outlining the various stages and experiences on the spiritual path, its general tenor has a strong affinity to Isma'ili mystical ideas. Historically, Isma'ili and Sufi relationships, in the Iranian and Indian contexts, have been so intimate that there even developed a style of discourse in Persian that Ivanow has appropriately termed 'Sufico-Ismaili', since works composed in it could be interpreted within both the Sufi and the Isma'ili perspectives.[81] Keeping in mind both the close Sufi-Isma'ili links and the 'authorizing' role of the bhaṇitā, we may suggest that the name of Pir Sadr al-Din, perhaps the most important personality in the Khojah pīr tradition, was added to the *Būjh Nirañjan* not as a way of establishing 'authorship', but as a way of validating its teachings and stating that they were in consonance with the pīr's precepts. It is significant that the signature-verse, which is rather unusual in its phraseology, says: 'Know the path of Pir Sadr al-Din, which is eternally accepted.' The verse makes no claim of the pīr writing the poem; it simply endorses his path and thus his authority.[82] His name serves as a 'stamp of approval', making the work legitimate for his disciples. With it, Isma'ili audiences could interpret the mysticism and esotericism of the *Būjh Nirañjan* within a meaningful Isma'ili context. To view the insertion of the pīr's name as an act of plagiarism or forgery is to miss the point. As Hawley points out, 'the meaning of authorship in devotional India is not what we have come to expect in Europe and America since the Renaissance'.[83]

One more issue pertains to the subject of the origins and authorship of ginān s. Khojah tradition itself, as well as scholars who have studied the ginān s, concur that these religious poems began as oral literature and for a considerable period in their history were transmitted orally before being recorded in writing in Khojki, a script peculiar to the community.[84] Though at present very few ginān manuscripts date earlier than the eighteenth century (the earliest recorded manuscript dates to 1736)[85], A. Nanji postulates that the tradition of written transcription may have begun around the sixteenth century.[86] While no scholar to date has examined the corpus of ginān s from the perspective of its oral origins, we have little reason to doubt this theory, especially when we bear in mind parallel traditions of religious literatures in South Asia, such as the *sant*, the *bhakti*, and the Sufi ones. Shackle and Moir consider a long period of oral transmission very plausible in light of the fact that some older members of the community today can still recite a repertoire of two hundred or more ginān s by heart.[87] Nanji, citing evidence concerning the bardic role of the Bhatias of Sind, a caste from which many Khojahs seem to have originated, speculates that the teachings of the pīrs may have been put to music and sung for adherents by professional bards.[88] My own examination of the role of ginān̄s in the community's religious life indicates that even today, notwithstanding the existence of printed texts, the ginān̄s function primarily as scripture in their oral/aural dimensions.[89]

If the ginān̄s did indeed originate as oral literature and were orally transmitted in their early history, then, from this perspective too, we need to re-evaluate the way in which we have been approaching the issue of their authorship. My late colleague Albert Lord argued that it is a myth to assume that in the oral tradition there are fixed texts that are transmitted unchanged from one generation to another, through an analysis of which one can trace 'original authors'.[90] Songs that are transmitted orally are both synchronically and historically 'fluid' in the sense that performers may change outward forms such as wording, which they consider 'inessential'. Only the basic idea or combination of ideas forming the core of the song remains fairly stable. In other words, Lord observes that:

> His [the singer's] idea of stability, to which he is deeply devoted, does not include wording, which to him has never been fixed, nor the inessential parts of the story. He builds his performance on the stable skeleton of narratives.[91]

Consequently, in the oral tradition, concepts such as 'author' and 'original' have no meaning at all, or they may have a meaning quite different from the one usually assigned to them.[92] The fluidity of the song makes it virtually impossible to retrace the song through the generations of singers to the moment when the first singer performed it; each performance is in a sense an original.[93] It is only with the onset of the written tradition that the 'correct' text is fixed, sounding the death knell for the oral tradition process; singers become reproducers rather than recreators.[94]

Albert Lord's remarks may explain the tremendous variations in ginān texts as they are recorded in manuscripts and the 'great latitude' that seems to have existed in the rendering of the originals.[95] But more importantly, they serve as words of caution for societies permeated by the written tradition, societies that feel that for every text there must be an 'original' that can be scientifically attributed to a certain author. If, during part of their history, the ginān̄s did indeed exist as an oral tradition before they were reduced to writing, then by searching for evidence of 'original authors' in them, we may be asking questions that are illogical and inappropriate. 'Once we know the facts of oral composition', Albert Lord writes, 'we must cease trying to find an original of any traditional song'.[96]

This essay suggests the need for new approaches to the issue of the authorship of the ginān̄s. It argues on several grounds for the need to redefine the manner in which 'authorship' as it applies to these religious poems has been usually viewed. Although the implications of its arguments may seem to challenge traditional religious claims, the essay does not deny that the central core of the ginān literary tradition may have in fact been originally initiated by the pīrs. Its intent is only to point out that, on account of factors intrinsic to the very nature of these poems, the search for evidence within the gināns themselves to resolve questions of their 'authorship' (as we normally understand this term), will be a frustrating exercise that will only leave us dissatisfied. The application of conventional canons of textual criticism involving the tracing of transmission lines to an ideal archetype or autograph is futile and inappropriate. Between the actual composition of the gināns and their first reduction to a written form lie several generations of singers, reciters, and devoted redactors who have left their impress on most of these poems.[97] The more interesting and fruitful questions we need to ask about the gināns concern their 'relational, contextual or functional' qualities.[98] By this we mean the interaction of these religious poems with the people who memorize, recite, and listen to them. In the final analysis, texts are 'sacred' only when a religious community can discover within them religious meaning, inspiration, and truth.[99]

III

Khojki (or Khojaki) is the name of the script used by the Nizari Isma'ilis of the Indian subcontinent to record their religious literature. Originating in Sind, the southern province of modern Pakistan, and commonly used to transcribe several languages including Sindhi, Gujarati, Hindustani, and Persian, the script was in active use within this particular Isma'ili community from at least the sixteenth century, if not earlier, until about the late 1960s.[100] The name 'Khojki' is most likely derived from the word 'khojah'. According to Isma'ili tradition, the fifteenth century *dā'ī* (preacher, missionary) Pir Sadr al-Din, who bestowed this title on new Indian converts to Isma'ili Islam, was also responsible for inventing the Khojki script.[101]

Archaeological excavations at Banbhore, the eighth-century Muslim settlement in lower Sind, however, have uncovered a 'proto-Nagari' script with characters remarkably similar to those found in modern Khojki.[102] This script, clearly the prototype of Khojki, has been identified as Lohanaki or Lari, the script of the Hindu Lohana community.[103] As it happens, the Lohana community was one of the communities among whom Pir Sadr al-Din (c. 1350–1400) was most active. Thus while the Isma'ili tradition that he invented Khojki is clearly inaccurate—in any case, scripts evolve slowly because they are necessarily cultural and not individual products—the pīr may indeed have played a role in its elaboration, as we shall see below. That is speculative, however. What is not speculative is that Khojki is a refined and polished form of Lohanaki.[104]

Khojki was one of the many scripts prevalent in Sind over a period of several centuries.[105] As early as the ninth and tenth centuries, various Arab geographers and travellers referred to the fact that the inhabitants of Sind had many different scripts for writing their language.[106] Ibn al-Nadim (d. 995) reports that approximately 200 scripts were employed in the region.[107] Al-Biruni (d. 1048) provides more specific information about three of these scripts: a script called '*Malwārī*' predominated in southern Sind, the '*Ardhā-Nāgarī*' in some other parts, and the '*Saindhava*' in the ancient city of Bahmanwa or al-Mansura.[108] We can also be reasonably certain that after the Arab conquests of the eighth century, among this multitude of scripts, one or more forms of the Arabic script were also current.

Through a substantial portion of its history, there had been little incentive for the development of a single uniform script for the Sindhi language, principally because it was used only as a spoken language or for popular folk literature that was oral in character. Thus, during the long period of Muslim rule, Persian, and not Sindhi, was the favoured language in official administrative and literary circles. As a consequence, the use of multiple scripts for Sindhi prevailed well into the nineteenth century. In a paper on Sindhi alphabets presented at the July 1857 meeting of the Royal Asiatic Society (Bombay branch), Ernst Trumpp, the German Orientalist and author of a distinguished Sindhi grammar, noted the use of various alphabets, Muslims preferring Arabic characters loaded 'with a confusing heap of dots', while Hindus employed a medley of alphabets known by the name of *Banyan*.[109] The English adventurer Richard Burton also remarks that the 'characters in which the Sindhi tongue is written are very numerous', and among the various alphabets in use he mentions 'that used by the Khwajah tribe' presumably referring to Khojki.[110] George Stack, in his *Grammar of the Sindhi Language*, published in 1849, tabulates thirteen script systems, including Khojki, which were in use for transcribing Sindhi. His Table reveals that the scripts used in Sind varied from one geographical region to another and that different religious and caste groups favoured distinctive script styles.[111]

Khojki and most of the scripts used for writing Sindhi belong to the group of Indian scripts that have been classified by Grierson under the heading 'Landa' or 'clipped' alphabets.[112] They were employed especially by the Hindus of Sind and Punjab for the purpose of commerce. In fact, in Sind, Landa was called *Baniyān* or *Wāṇiko*, indicating its use primarily as a mercantile and commercial script.[113] The Landa group, in turn, is related to the larger family of alphabets commonly employed by the subcontinent's mercantile classes, showing particularly close affinity to two members of this family, Tankri (Takari), a crude script system used in its many varieties by uneducated shopkeepers and the like in the lower ranges of the Himalayas and the Punjab hills, and Mahajani (Marwari), the character originating in Marwar and popularized among trading classes all over north India by the Marwar traders.[114] Another noteworthy parallel to the Landa group of Punjab and Sind exists in Gujarat, where a variety of Gujarati character, known as *vāṇiāī* (from *vāṇio*, 'shopkeeper') or *ṣarrāfī* (from *ṣarrāf*, 'banker') or also *bōḍīā* (from *bōḍī*, 'clipped' or 'shorn'), is used exclusively by merchants and bankers.[115]

The mercantile origin of this extensive family of alphabets, to which Khojki and its Landa analogues belong, may explain why the entire family was not well suited for literary purposes. Mercantile scripts have limited, specialized purposes; consequently they tend to be crude by literary standards. Often being a kind of shorthand, these scripts are not only imperfectly supplied with vowel signs but frequently omit the few vowels that they do possess, making them quite illegible or, even worse, liable to being misread.[116] Indeed, the omission of all vowels, except when initial, was the norm in ordinary mercantile correspondences.[117] Not surprisingly, there are numerous stories about the misreading of these mercantile scripts, the most popular being one of a Marwari merchant who went to Delhi; his agent wrote home: *Bābū Ajmer gayō baṛī bahī bhej dīje*, 'The Babu has gone to Ajmer, send the big ledger'; but the letter was read *Bābū aj margayō, baṛī bahū bhej dīje*, 'The Babu died today, send the chief wife (to perform his obsequies)!'[118] Evidently, the inconvenience of the omission of vowel marks or *mātrās* is not much felt in the limited scope of mercantile written communications such as *hunḍīs* (bills of exchange), in which almost identical sentences or phrases are constantly repeated.

A poorly developed vowel system, the chief characteristic of Indian mercantile alphabets, constitutes the major deficiency of the Landa scripts, many of which have no signs for initial vowels.[119] The Landa scripts are further handicapped by consonants that are far from being clear and that vary greatly from place to place. In most of them a single letter could often represent a number of different sounds. Indeed, in a few cases some consonants seem to have been represented merely by ciphers, combinations of numbers and fractional parts.[120] Remarking on the capriciousness of Landa, Grierson observes that 'it is seldom legible to anyone except the original writer and not always to him'.[121] In this regard he also quotes a Sindhi proverb: '*Wāṇikā akhar ḅuṭā, sukā paṛhan-khān chuṭā*'; which means that the Waniko [i.e., Landa] letters are vowelless; [as soon as the ink is] dry, they are released from reading [i.e., are illegible].[122] Burton comments that these alphabets are so useless that 'a trader is scarcely able to read his own accounts, unless assisted by a tenacious memory'.[123] Even Trumpp, who fiercely opposed the universal adoption of the Perso-Arabic writing system for transcribing Sindhi on the grounds that the alphabet was 'foreign', confessed that an emendation of the native Landa system would be more useless by far than that of the Perso-Arabic character.[124]

Among this hodge-podge of commercial scripts—scribbling, we could truly say in many cases—a small number, including Khojki, actually developed into vehicles of literary expression. Although for some scripts such as Khudawadi in Sind, Dogri in Jammu, and Chamiali in Chamba, this evolution took place as a result of official governmental initiative and encouragement in the late eighteenth and early nineteenth centuries, for Khojki the advance came about much earlier owing to (as we shall presently see) the script's affiliation with a minority religious community.

Expression in written literature, as in music, requires an instrument, and instruments require technical development. In Khojki, two technical developments made a new range of expression possible. First was a system of medial vowel marks called *lākanā*. In the region of Sind, Khojki was the only Landa script to have sustained and perhaps even developed the use of this medial vowel system.[125] It was this distinguishing characteristic of Khojki that made the script suitable for its extensive use in recording a considerable corpus of Isma'ili religious literature, in particular the genre of the ginān.[126] Incidentally, it is possible that the dā'ī Pir Sadr al-Din, whom the tradition credits with the invention of the script, may have been responsible rather for introducing the lākanā and possibly other refinements to Khojki.[127]

The second improvement in the Khojki script concerns its capacity to retain the individuality of contiguous words written on the same line. In mercantile scripts it is not only the omission of vowels that is responsible for the propensity to misread and misinterpret, but it is also the non-separation of words from each other.[128] Because writing in mercantile scripts is, as a rule, continuous, adjacent words are often joined erroneously leading to alterations in the meanings of sentences. The 'mess', as Bendrey has termed it, is thus due to the arbitrary reconstruction of a group of letters by the readers.[129] This peculiarity, when combined with the absence of medial vowels, can be particularly fatal. As we have seen above, a phrase such as *Bābū Ajmer gayō*, 'The Babu has gone to Ajmer', could quite innocently be read as *Bābū aj margayō*, 'The Babu has died today.'

To prevent such misrenderings, Khojki adopted a surprisingly simple solution: the use of colon-like punctuations to demarcate the ends of individual words.

Notwithstanding these technical refinements, the Khojki script never evolved into an entirely satisfactory script. The question therefore immediately arises: Why was it adopted for recording religious literature when more sophisticated and developed scripts such as Devanagari or the Perso-Arabic were available? The answer lies perhaps in the strong desire among religious groups in medieval India, both Hindu and Muslim, to make religious literature more accessible to the masses. The move away from the use of classical languages such as Sanskrit, Arabic and Persian; the corresponding blooming of the regional languages as vehicles of religious literature; the use of symbols and imagery taken from daily village life—all these are only a few examples of this trend. Certainly in its form, style, and imagery, the major genre of Khojah Isma'ili religious literature (the ginān literature) exhibits the same concern. Consequently, in the case of the Khojah Isma'ili tradition, the adoption of the Khojki script, a 'local' script, was most likely part of the attempt to make religious literature more accessible by recording it in a script with which the local population had the greatest familiarity. That the adoption of a 'local' script for preserving religious literature may have been customary with various groups in medieval India is further evident from the Sikh adoption of Gurmukhi as an 'official' script for its religious literature. Like Khojki, Gurmukhi is a Landa script of Punjab that was improved and polished by the borrowing of vowel signs and the refining of existing Landa characters.[130]

As a vehicle of Sikh religious literature, Gurmukhi contributed to the consolidation of the Sikh religion, becoming particularly important in the eighteenth and nineteenth centuries when the Sikhs exercised political hegemony over Punjab and Kashmir. S.S. Gandhi points out that the adoption of the Gurmukhi script was of great significance, for the Sikhs could develop their culture only by adopting a script that was their own, and which was suited to their language. Furthermore, he observes, the popularization of Gurmukhi was a 'well-calculated' move designed to make its readers, that is converts to the Sikh religion, part with 'Hindu compositions written in [Devanagari] Sanskrit.'[131] The adoption of a common script to strengthen ethnic and linguistic ties was by no means confined to primarily religious groups. The political and cultural ascendancy of the Marathas, the major rivals to Sikh power in late Mughal India, was also marked by the selection of a single, uniform script for the Marathi language. This script, the Modi script, was purportedly invented by the secretary to the great Maharashtrian hero, Shivaji.[132]

We may therefore surmise that much more was involved in the selection of the Khojki script than access to religious literature. The script, by providing an exclusive means of written expression commonly shared by Isma'ilis living in three regions (Sind, Punjab, and Gujarat), was influential in the development of cohesion and self-identity within a widely scattered and linguistically diverse religious community. No doubt the script facilitated the flow and the transmission of religious literature, especially the gināns, from one area to another.[133] Use of the script may have also served to confine religious literature within the community—this precaution being necessary to avoid persecution from outsiders not in agreement with the community's doctrines and practices.[134] In this respect, Khojki may have served the same purpose as the secret languages, such as the so-called *balabailān* language, utilized by Muslim mystics to hide their more esoteric thoughts from the common people.[135]

One final parallel between Khojki and Gurmukhi deserves notice. Just as the Isma'ili tradition associates its script with Pir Sadr al-Din, a charismatic religious personality who is believed to have played a significant role in consolidating the young community and to whom are attributed an overwhelming number of gināns,[136] so also the Sikh tradition associates Gurmukhi with the second Guru, Guru Angad (1538–52). According to Sikh tradition, Guru Angad was responsible for improving the Gurmukhi script when he found that the Sikh hymns written in the original Landa form were liable to be misread. This is why the alphabet is called Gurmukhi, for it came forth from 'the mouth of the Guru.'[137]

NOTES

1. The term 'Khojah' is used in this essay to refer to Nizari Isma'ilis originating in Sind, Punjab, or Gujarat who hold Aga Khan IV to be their religious leader or Imam. Believed to be a popularization of the Persian word *Khwaja*, meaning lord or master, the title *Khojah* was bestowed on Hindu converts to Isma'ili Islam in mediaeval times. Between the mid-nineteenth and early twentieth centuries, various secessionist movements within the larger community resulted in the formation of small Sunni and Ithna'ashari (Twelver) Shi'i Khojah groups as well.

See W. Ivanow, 'Khodja', *Shorter Encyclopedia of Islam*, pp. 256–7, and W. Madelung, 'Khodja', *Encyclopedia of Islam* (2nd ed.), Vol. 5, pp. 25–7.

2. Ali S. Asani, *The Būjh Nirañjan: An Isma'ili Mystical Poem* (Cambridge, MA., 1991), p. 38–41; Azim Nanji, *The Nizārī Ismā'īlī Tradition in the Indo-Pakistan Subcontinent* (Delmar, N.Y., 1978), pp. 126–7.

3. Ibid., pp. 110–20.

4. Ali S. Asani, 'The Khojahs of Indo-Pakistan: The Quest for an Islamic Identity', in *Journal of the Institute of Muslim Minority Affairs* 8 (1987), p. 34.

5. G.E. von Grunebaum, ed., *Unity and Variety in Muslim Civilization* (Chicago, 1955), p. 8.

6. Aziz Ahmad, *Studies in Islamic Culture in the Indian Environment* (Oxford, 1964), p. 156.

7. Ibid., p. 162.

8. Ibid., p. 163.

9. Asani, 'The Khojahs of Indo-Pakistan: The Quest for an Islamic Identity', pp. 31–2.

10. Annemarie Schimmel, *Islam in the Indian Subcontinent* (Leiden-Koln, 1980), pp. 179–80.

11. M. Mujeeb, *The Indian Muslims* (London, 1967), p. 527.

12. J.C. Masselos, 'The Khojas of Bombay: The Defining of Formal Membership Criteria during the Nineteenth Century', in *Caste and Social Stratification among Muslims*, ed. I. Ahmad (Delhi, 1973), p. 6.

13. Bombay Government, *The Gazetteer of the Bombay Presidency* (Bombay, 1899), p. 39.

14. Masselos, 'The Khojas of Bombay', p. 4.

15. Ibid., p. 6, and Hatim Amiji', 'Some Notes on Religious Dissent in Nineteenth-Century East Africa', in *African Historical Studies* 4 (1971), pp. 607–8.

16. Bombay Government, *The Gazetteer of the Bombay Presidency*, p. 45.

17. S.T. Lokhandwalla, 'Islamic Law and Ismā'īlī Communities (Khojas and Bohras)', in *India and Contemporary Islam*, ed. S.T. Lokhandwalla (Simla, 1971), pp. 385–6.

18. Hamid Ali, 'Customary and Statutory Laws of the Muslims in India', in *Indian Culture* 11, (1937), p. 355.

19. Masselos, 'The Khojas of Bombay, p. 7.

20. R.E. Enthoven, 'Khojahs', in *Tribes and Castes of Bombay* 2 (Bombay, 1922), pp. 229–30.

21. Joseph Arnould, *Judgement of the Hon'ble Sir Joseph Arnould in the Kojah Case Otherwise Known as the Aga Khan Case* (Bombay, 1867), p. 15; and J.N. Hollister, *The Shi'a of India* (London, 1953), pp. 390–2.

22. Mujtaba Ali, *The Origins of the Khojahs and their Religious Life Today* (Bonn, 1936), pp. 63–7.

23. Bombay Government, *The Gazetteer of the Bombay Presidency*, pp. 48–9.

24. For a brief summary of the principal features of the gināns see Ali S. Asani, 'The Ginān Literature of the Ismailis of Indo-Pakistan: Its Origins, Characteristics and Themes', in *Devotion Divine: Bhakti Traditions from the Regions of India*, ed. D. Eck and F. Mallison (Gröningen-Paris, 1991), p. 1–18, and Christopher Shackle and Zawahir Moir, *Ismaili Hymns from South Asia: An Introduction to the Gināns* (London, 1992).

25. The most dramatic instance of this controversial 'mixing' of traditions occurs in gināns, such as the 'classic' *Dasa Avatāra*, which through a process of mythopoesis, seek to create an ostensible correspondence between the Vaishnava

Hindu concept of avatāra and the Isma'ili concept of the Imam. The tenth avatāra of the Hindu diety Vishnu, renamed in the ginān tradition as Nakalanki, 'the stainless one', was identified with 'Ali, the first Imam. Other basic Hindu deities were redirected to significant Islamic personalities: Brahma, for example, was identified with the Prophet Muhammad, while the Prophet's daughter, Fatima, was identified with Sakti and Sarasvati. See Azim Nanji, *The Nizārī Ismā'īlī Tradition*, pp. 110–200.

26. Aziz Ahmad, *An Intellectual History of Islam in India* (Edinburgh, 1969), p. 126. As a reaction to such perceptions, recent editions of gināns published by the Isma'ili community have purged terms that could be perceived as 'non-Islamic' or 'Hinduistic', replacing them with those considered more in consonance with the Islamic tradition.

27. One angry tract on this subject asks: 'Do we think that Islam can be preached and understood only through the medium of Arabic and Persian languages, and the same teaching presented in any other [Indic] language should be regarded as a Hindu element?' See 'Observations and Comments on our Modern *Ginānic* Literature'. Paper presented by His Highness the Aga Khan Shia Imami, Ismailia Association for Canada, at the Ismailia Association International Review Meeting, Nairobi, Kenya, 1980, p. 30.

28. See, for example, the famous Khojah Case of 1866, presided over by the Bombay High Court Judge Sir Joseph Arnould, described in Asaf A.A. Fyzee, *Cases in the Muhammadan Law of India and Pakistan* (London, 1965), pp. 504–49. Evidence from the gināns was also presented before Justice Russell of the Bombay High Court in the Hajji Bibi Case of 1908.

29. Due to a combination of social, economic, and political factors, the Khoja community has, since the early twentieth century, established itself in East Africa, Southeast Asia, Western Europe, and North America.

30. Tazim R. Kassam, *Songs of Wisdom and Circles of Dance: Hymns of the Satpanth Isma'ili Muslim Saint, Pir Shams* (Albany, 1995), p. 3.

31. *The Great Ismaili Heroes* (Karachi, 1973), pp. 98–9.

32. To cite one example of this trend, a lecture at a communal function in Toronto on 29 January 1982 was entitled, '*Gināns*: Prophesies and Science in *Gināns*'. The use of scriptures as 'scientific proof-texts' is a common phenomenon in the history of religions.

33. In deference to the reluctance among many Muslims to permit the use of musical instruments in explicitly religious contexts, such concerts are not usually held within the premises of *jamā'at-khānas*.

34. Ali S. Asani, 'The Ismaili *Gināns* as Devotional Literature', in *Devotional Literature in South Asia*, ed. R.S. McGregor (Cambridge, 1992), pp. 101–12.

35. His Highness the Aga Khan Shia Imami, Ismailia Association for Canada, 'A Suggestive Guide to the Islamic Interpretation and Refutation of the Hindu Elements in our Holy *Gināns*', Paper presented at the Ismailia Association's International Conference, Nairobi, Kenya, 1979, p. 11.

36. Comments made during a speech by a prominent preacher in Pakistan. See 'The Ismaili Tariqah Board: Two Special Evenings', *Ismaili Mirror* (August, 1987), p. 33.

37. Aga Khan, 'Observations and Comments', p. 26.

38. Idem., 'A Suggestive Guide', p. 20.

39. Ibid., p. 10.

40. Viewed from this perspective, the 'mediating' role of the gināns has its parallels with other works of Islamic literature in the vernacular, such as Mawlana Jalal al-Din Rumi's *Mathnawi* (popularly called 'the Qur'an in Persian') or the Sindhi poet Shah 'Abd al-Latif's *Risālo*, the collection of mystical poetry so sacred to Sindhi-speaking Muslims.

41. '*Pīrs* are appointed by the Imam of the Time, and only such persons can claim to call themselves *Pīrs*. The son, brother or a relative of a *Pīr* cannot on his own accord become a *Pīr* [through inheritance], unless he has been so designated by the Imam of the Time.' See *Collection of Gināns Composed by the Great Ismaili Saint Pīr Sadruddin* (Bombay, 1952), foreword, p. 3.

42. Shackle and Moir, *Ismaili Hymns*, p. 21.

43. W. Ivanow, 'Satpanth', in *Collectanea*, Vol. I, ed. W. Ivanow (Leiden, 1948), p. 31.

44. Aziz Esmail, 'Satpanth Ismailism and Modern Changes within it, with Special Reference to East Africa' (Ph.D. thesis, University of Edinburgh, 1971), p. 14.

45. Shackle and Moir, *Ismaili Hymns*, p. 22.

46. Nanji, *Nazārī Ismā'īlī Tradition*, p. 69.

47. Shackle and Moir, *Ismaili Hymns*, p. 7.

48. Nanji, *Nizārī Ismā'īlī Tradition*, p. 61.

49. See ibid., pp. 50–83, and Kassam, 'Songs of Wisdom and Circles of Dance: an Anthology of Hymns by the Satpanth Ismā'īlī Saint, Pir Shams' (Ph.D. thesis: McGill University, 1992), ch. 5: Pir Shams: Problems of Historical Identity, pp. 143–205.

50. See W. Ivanow, 'The Sect of Imam Shah in Gujrat', *Journal of the Bombay Branch, Royal Asiatic Society*, NS, 12 (1936), pp. 19–70.

51. Ivanow, 'Satpanth', p. 41.

52. Shackle and Moir, *Ismaili Hymns*, p. 15.

53. Ibid., p. 8.

54. T.R. Kassam, 'Syncretism on the Model of Figure–Ground: A Study of Pir Shams' Brahma Prakasa, in *Hermeneutical Paths to the Sacred Worlds of India*, ed. Katherine K. Young (Atlanta, 1994), pp. 231–4l, as quoted in her thesis 'Songs of Wisdom', p. 9.

55. Ali S. Asani, *The Būjh Nirañjan*.

56. Keshwani, 'Sī Harfī: A Ginānic Treatise, Text and Context' (unpublished paper); see especially ch. 2: The Authorship of *Sī Harfī*.

57. Ibid., pp. 105–06.

58. See the text in *Sau ginānjī ćopaḍi ćogaḍievārī* (Bombay, 1903), pp. 48–50.

59. Tradition claims that these Hindu mythological names are epithets of the great Pir Sadr al-Din. See Shackle and Moir, *Ismaili Hymns*, pp. 154, 191.

60. See *Kalame Maula* (8th edn., Bombay, 1963).

61. John S. Hawley, 'Author and Authority in the *Bhakti* Poetry of North India', *Journal of Asian Studies* 47 (1988), pp. 269–90.
62. Ibid., p. 270.
63. Ibid., p. 273.
64. Ibid., p. 287.
65. Ibid., pp. 285–6.
66. Ibid., p. 278.
67. Ibid.
68. Ibid., pp. 282–5.
69. Shackle and Moir, too, remark on the directness of speech that characterizes the signature-verses of ginān̄s, where it is a regular commonplace; see their *Ismaili Hymns*, p. 27.
70. Ibid., ginān number 32.
71. Ibid., ginān number 11.
72. Ibid., ginān number 8.
73. Ibid., ginān number 16.
74. Ibid., ginān number 30.
75. Ibid., ginān number 12.
76. A similar situation is found in the poetry of Maulana Jalal al-Din Rumi (d. 672/1273), the greatest mystical poet of the Persian language, who uses the name of his mentor, Shams-i Tabriz as his own poetic name or *nom de plume*.
77. See *Sau ginānjī ćopadī ćālu ginān āgal na ćhāpāelā bhāg trījo* (1st edn., Bombay, 1903), p. 108.
78. Nanji, *Nizārī Ismā'īlī Tradition*, p. 13.
79. See ginān̄s number 13, verse 8, and number 37, verse 12, in Shackle and Moir, *Ismaili Hymns*, pp. 86, 132; and ginān number 68, verses 11–12, in Kassam, 'Songs of Wisdom', p. 319. Dr. Kassam translates the word 'ginān' here as 'wisdom'.
80. See Asani, *Būjh Nirañjan*, ch. 1, pp. 19–46.
81. W. Ivanow, *Ismaili Literature: A Bibliographical Survey* (Tehran, 1963), pp. 10ff., 130–131, and idem., 'Sufism and Ismailism: The Chiragh-Nama', *Revue Iranienne d'Anthropologie* 3 (1959), pp. 13–17. See also Azim Nanji's comments: 'The Nizārī *da'wa*, when it entered the Subcontinent, already carried within its repertoire a strain of mysticism rooted in Ismā'īlism but tinged with the Sufic terminology of the time, in his *Nizārī Ismā'īlī Tradition*, p. 126.
82. For detailed contextual analysis of this *bhaṇitā* see Asani, *Bujh Nirañjan*, pp. 24–5.
83. Hawley, 'Author and Authority', p. 287.
84. For a fuller description of this script see Ali S. Asani, 'The Khojki Script: A Legacy of Isma'ili Islam in the Indo-Pakistan Subcontinent', *Journal of the American Oriental Society* 107 (1987), pp. 439–49.
85. See Zawahir Noorally [Moir], *Catalogue of Khojki Manuscripts in the Collection of the Ismaili Association for Pakistan* (Unpublished, Karachi, 1971), Ms. 25. See also Ali S. Asani, *The Harvard Collection of Ismaili Literature in Indic Literatures: A Descriptive Catalog and Finding Aid* (Boston, 1992).

86. Nanji, *Nizārī Ismā'īlī Tradition*, p. 12. A Gujarati history of the community, *Khoja Vrttant* by S. Nanjiani (Ahmadabad, 1892), pp. 240–50, also notes that Pir Dadu (d. 1593) was supposedly instructed by the Imam to collect the teachings of the earlier pīrs and produce a written record.

87. Shackle and Moir, *Ismaili Hymns*, p. 15.

88. Nanji, *Nizārī Ismā'īlī Tradition*, p. 13.

89. Asani, 'The Ismaili *Gināns* as Devotional Literature', pp. 104–06.

90. Albert Lord, *Singer of Tales* (Cambridge, Mass., 1968), p. 9.

91. Ibid., p. 99.

92. Ibid., p. 101.

93. Ibid., p. 100.

94. Ibid., p. 137.

95. Ivanow, 'Satpanth', p. 41.

96. Lord, *Singer of Tales*, p. 100.

97. I am aware that this statement may appear puzzling to some readers in light of my previous work on the *Būjh Nirañjan*, in which I do consider questions of its provenance. That ginān, however, represents a rather unusual case for which there exists a written attestation from independent sources. The presence of a reasonably developed manuscript tradition justifies my approach in this particular case. At present, the only other work in the ginān tradition for which we have a manuscript existing outside the community is the *Sī Harfi*. See Keshwani, *Sī Harfi*, ch. 2.

98. I borrow this term from William A. Graham's study of sacred texts, *Beyond the Written Word: Oral Aspects of Scriptures in the History of Religion* (Cambridge, 1987).

99. As testimony to the strength of communal authority, we note here that popular compositions attributed to individuals who technically did not have the 'official' status of *pīr*, namely the so-called 'unauthorized' pīrs', are nevertheless accepted as part of the ginān literature. Examples of 'unauthorized' pīrs include Imam Shah (d. 1513) and his son Nur Muhammad Shah (d. ca. 1534), the pivotal figures of a sixteenth century schismatic group, the Imam-Shahis, and the so-called Saiyids who disseminated religious teaching within the Isma'ili communities in the eighteenth century. For all intents and purposes, most members of the community do not differentiate in status between these 'unofficial' gināns and those by 'authorized' pīrs. Audience appeal is clearly more important than considerations of religious history.

100. G. Allana believes that the Isma'ilis in Sind and Kutch began using the Khojki script in the latter half of the reign of the Sumra dynasty (1051–1351). G. Allana, *Sindhī Suratkhati* (Hyderabad, Pakistan, 1964), p. 4.

101. A. Nanji, *The Nizārī Ismā'īlī*, pp. 9, 74.

102. F.A. Khan, *Banbhore: a Preliminary Report on the Recent Archaeological Excavations* (Karachi: Dept. of Archaeology and Museums, 1976), p. 16. See especially figures 2 and 3.

103. G. Allana, *Sindhī Ṣuratkhatī*, 1969 edition, p. 20.

104. Ibid., p. 24.

105. Although the earliest extant Khojki manuscript dates to 1736, there is considerable evidence that the tradition of writing in the script goes back much earlier. See Nanji, *Nizari Isma'ili Tradition*, pp. 9–11, and Z. Noorally, *Catalogue of Khojki Manuscripts in the Collection of the Ismailia Association for Pakistan* (in manuscript form, Karachi, 1971).

106. Allana, *Sindhī*, pp. 16–19.

107. Ibn al-Nadim, *Al-Fihrist* (Cairo, 1348/1929), pp. 27–8.

108. Abu Raihan al-Biruni, *Kitāb al-Hind*, Eng. trans. E.C. Sachau, *Alberuni's India*, ed. with intro. and notes by A.T. Embree (New York, 1971), p. 173.

109. 'Abstract of the Society's Proceedings', *Journal of the Bombay Branch of the Royal Asiatic Society* 5 (1857), p. 685.

110. R. Burton, *Sindh and the Races that Inhabit the Valley of the Indus*, repr. (Karachi, 1973), pp. 152–3.

111. G. Stack, *A Grammar of the Sindhi Language* (Bombay, 1849), pp. 3–8.

112. G. Grierson, *Linguistic Survey of India* (Calcutta, 1903–28), Vol. VIII, Part I, p. 247.

113. Ibid., p. 14.

114. Grierson suggests that Landa, Tankri, and Mahajani are in fact descendants of one original alphabet that was current over the whole of northwestern India. 'On the Modern Indo-Aryan Alphabets of North-Western India', *Journal of the Royal Asiatic Society*, 1904, p. 67.

115. D. Diringer, *The Alphabet, A Key to the History of Mankind*, 2 vols., 3rd edn. (New York, 1968), Vol. 1, p. 290.

116. J. Prinsep, 'Note on *A Grammer of the Sindhi Language Dedicated to the Rt. Honorable Sir Robert Grant, Governor of Bombay by W.H. Whalen Esq.*', *Journal of the Asiatic Society of Bengal* 6 (1837), p. 352.

117. Grierson, *Linguistic Survey*, Vol. IX, Part II, p. 338.

118. Ibid., p. 19, n. 1.

119. Diringer, *Alphabet*, p. 295.

120. Prinsep, 'Note', p. 352.

121. Grierson, *Linguistic Survey*, Vol. VIII, Part I, p. 247.

122. Ibid., p. 14. In the same note he relates a story according to which a merchant wrote to his son to send 'the small account book with the cover', (*nanḍhī wahī puṭhe sūdhī*). The son read this as *nanḍhī wahū puṭ sūdhī*; 'send the youngest daughter-in-law with (her) son!'

123. Burton, *Sindh*, p. 153.

124. E. Trumpp, *Grammar of the Sindhi Language* (Leipzig, 1872), p. 6.

125. Stack, *Grammar*, p. 2, note. Stack remarks that while he had been informed that the medial vowel marks were also used with other Sindhi scripts, he had not been able to locate any corroborative examples.

126. In addition to gināns, Khojki manuscripts record *farmāns* (commands, guidances given by the Imam or religious/spiritual leader of the Nizari Isma'ilis), religious stories, popular Hindu *bhajans* (devotional songs), as well as an assortment of *ghazals* and *kafis*. For a detailed description of the contents of Khojki manuscripts, see Ali S. Asani, *Harvard Collection*.

127. Allana, *Sindhī*, p. 24. See also Nabi Bakhsh Khan Baloch. *Sindhị Bolī jī mukhtaṣar tārīkh* (Hyderabad, Pakistan, 1962), pp. 114–15.
128. Diringer, *Alphabet*, p. 291.
129. Ibid.
130. See Ali S. Asani, 'The Nizari Isma'ili *ginān* Literature: Its Structure and Love Symbolism' (A.B. honours thesis, Harvard College, 1977).
131. S.S. Gandhi, *History of the Sikh Gurus* (New Dẹlhi, 1978), pp. 174–5, quoting Gokal Chand Narang.
132. B.A. Gupte, 'The Modi Character', *Indian Antiquary* 34 (1905), p. 28.
133. A recent research trip to the subcontinent revealed a tradition among the Nizari Isma'ilis which holds that there used to be a group of professional scribes, '*Akhunds*', who would travel from one village to another for the purpose of transcribing 'fresh' copies of deteriorating manuscripts (*copḍās*) or making available texts of *gināns* not available previously in the area. Some tenuous evidence of this practice is provided by manuscripts in the same hand and found in diverse places, but further research needs to be carried out to determine the authenticity of this tradition. Interview with Abdul Hussain Alibhai Nanji, Hyderabad, Pakistan, January 1982.
134. Nanji, *Nizari Isma'ili Tradition*, p. 9.
135. See Ignaz Goldziher, 'Linguistisches aus der Literatur der muhammadanischen Mystik', *Zeitschrift der Deutschen Morgenlandischen Gesellschaft* 26 (1872), p. 765, and Alessandro Bausani, 'About a Curious Mystical Language', *East and West* 4, no. 4 (1958).
136. Nanji, *Nizari Isma'ili Tradition*, p. 9.
137. Grierson, *Linguistic Survey*, Vol. IX, Part I, p. 624. See W. Owen Cole and P.S. Sambhi, *The Sikhs: Their Religious Beliefs and Practices* (London, Boston, 1978), p. 19.

14

Popular Shīʻism*

J.R.I. Cole

An understanding of the Awadh Shiʻis' social origins explains why scattered Shiʻi lineages existed to support the Nishapuri nawabs and to benefit from their rule. But it does not explain how these Shiʻi or proto-Shiʻi groupings developed into a community. In the Mughal period, and especially under Aurangzeb, Shiʻis had no public rituals separate from Sunnis that could serve as the matrix of community formation. Religious identity and social networks within a genuine religious community could only grow up around a set of uniting public rituals. Under the patronage of the nawabs and their Shiʻi courtiers and notables, such public rituals developed in Awadh.[1]

The Shiʻis of nawabi Awadh created a distinctive set of practices and rituals. Many new believers in the Imams entered the fold in this period, making their own contributions. Their rituals changed over time, shrines grew up, and lay believers of various classes and both sexes practised their faith in their own ways, sometimes in opposition to the strictures of the growing corps of scripturalist ʻulama. Large numbers of Sunnis and Hindus were drawn into participation in the mourning rites for the martyred Imam Husain, bringing their own influence to bear. Yet popular Shiʻi practices most often resulted from the cultural dynamism and creativity of ordinary labourers, artisans, and shopkeepers, themselves partisans of ʻAli, rather than deriving from 'corruption' by Hinduism. As Bryan Turner argues, popular religion involves a specialization of religious services for different lay markets.[2]

The rites of popular Shiʻism in early-nineteenth-century Awadh had two conflicting effects. On the one hand, widespread urban participation in

* Reprinted from J.R.I. Cole, *Roots of North Indian Shiʻism in Iran and Iraq: Religion and State in Awadh, 1722–1859* (Berkeley: University of California Press, 1988), pp. 92–119.

Muharram rituals helped integrate, through a central ritual, the nawabi cities' diverse and growing populations. Lucknow's patron saint became the Imam Husain. On the other hand, the divisive nature of some Shi'i practices, especially cursing the caliphs honoured by Sunnis and forbidding Hindu celebrations during Muharram, encouraged the growth of an incipient communalism.

THE NAWABI TRANSFORMATION OF LUCKNOW

Under the nawabs, Lucknow became the Realm of the Shi'a (*Dār al-Shi'a*). There, artisans and labourers who newly adopted the faith of the Twelvers inventively honoured the Imams. The nawabs' administrative and architectural transformation of the city formed a crucial prerequisite for this development. Nawab Asaf al-Daulah (1775–97) moved the Shi'i nawabi court from Faizabad to Lucknow in 1775. Already more than a small town then—indeed, a major textile-producing centre—it had often served as the region's administrative capital.[3] Nevertheless, the 1775 move marked the beginning of a new era.

When the nawabs lived primarily in Delhi they could change the provincial capital according to their perception of military and security needs.[4] From the last quarter of the eighteenth century, however, they found themselves increasingly boxed in by the British. Unchanging territorial boundaries after 1801 and a stabilization of revenue collection within them brought into existence a fixed capital wherein the service elite congregated. For several decades Faizabad, with its begams, large landholders, and tax-farmers, continued to compete with Lucknow. But the capital soon grew so large that it constituted the only true metropolis in Awadh and one of the great cities of the subcontinent.

The huge expenditures by the notables based in the capital supported tens of thousands of artisans and attracted merchants "of large property" from all over India.[5] The substantial textile and horse trade between Kashmir and Bengal passed through Lucknow, and the town increased rapidly in extent and population. In 1799 William Tennant put the city's population at half a million (probably an exaggeration) and marvelled at the wide-ranging architectural works undertaken under Asaf al-Daulah. 'There are,' he wrote, 'perhaps no buildings in Britain equally brilliant in external appearance as the palaces of Lucknow.'[6] But he also remarked on the city's great poverty, filth, and vice, and on the large number of idle workers and artisans.

Asaf al-Daulah implemented an extensive building program, tearing down old buildings to landscape spacious gardens in the Persian style. Indeed, the city grew so fast in the 1770s and 1780s that Azfari found it 'unbalanced' (*nā-mawzūn*). The building program was given added impetus by the drought years of 1784–5, when, even in Awadh, no rain fell for an entire year. The areas to the west were even more badly hit, causing a great influx of refugees into Lucknow. Labourers and peasants suffered terribly, many being sold as slaves, and the price of wheat in the capital went up to an astronomical nine or ten sers to the rupee. Saiyid 'Abbas Ardistani's grandfather could remember the drought and told him that people were reduced to eating animal dung.[7]

Asaf al-Daulah, Hasan Riza Khan, and Tikait Ray, in response to this crisis, initiated construction projects on an almost pharaonic scale as a means of absorbing the influx of labourers thrown off the land and of avoiding urban food riots. In 1785 several large works began, including a market, Tikaitganj; a huge gate, the Rumi Darvaza; and the Great Imambarah. Thousands of workers laboured day and night on these projects for several years. Tradition has it that even men of respectable family worked incognito at night to earn food. The nawab-vizier spent a million rupees a year on buildings, and his many projects fueled a spiraling inflation rate as construction materials and food soared in price.[8]

Lucknow's population may have increased in the period 1775–1800 from two hundred to three hundred thousand.[9] In about 1805 Shirwani estimated that the city had 100,000 dwellings, 30,000 shops, 2,000 taverns, and 1,000 mosques.[10] The expansion was spurred not only by government-sponsored employment and markets and the famine but also by a spurt in the growth of the textile trade with Calcutta. The resulting influx of uprooted Muslim and Hindu labourers and artisans into the city created new social networks and cultural traditions. Because of the pervasive influence of the Shi'i ruling class in the capital, they often adopted some Imami practices even where they retained a formal adherence to Sunnism or Hinduism. Urban immigrants held Shi'i-style mourning sessions for the Imam Husain, and Muharram processions, organizing them on a neighbourhood basis.

THE INSTITUTION OF THE IMAMBARAH

The need for a physical site where the partisans of Imam 'Ali could publicly mourn his martyred son, Husain, brought into being the Great Imambarah and smaller similar structures. Nawab Safdar Jang raised a building for this purpose in Delhi, though the term *imāmbāṛah* (Urdu for house of the Imam) had not then come widely into use. During Shuja' al-Dawlah's reign Aqa Baqir Khan constructed an imambarah in Lucknow for his nephew, a high Mughal official, and the edifice served as a model for the Husainabad imambarah almost a century later. The north Indian imambarah of the eighteenth century may have been influenced by the Iranian *Ḥusainiyyah*, or *takiyyah*, and by the south Indian *'ashūr-khāna*.[11]

The court invited architects to submit designs for the Great Imambarah, the winner being the Delhi architect Kifayat Allah. Because neither the Mughal emperor nor the nawab-vizier controlled Rajasthan any longer, the sort of marble used in the facade of the Persianate Taj Mahal proved unobtainable, and Kifayat Allah was forced to have his engineers fall back on more native Indian techniques. They used clay bricks and stone, with ingenious mud moulding that allowed the architect to achieve an immense, unsupported ceiling 'more durable ... than our most scientific Gothic vaulting.'[12] Mashhadi estimated the cost of the building at half a million rupees, but the Iranian traveller Shushtari put the Imambarah and mosque complex with its lavish decorations at a million rupees.[13]

Isfahani also attested to the huge expenditures made by the nawabi court on the Imambarah and its ornamentation.[14] He said that even after the building's completion in 1791 (AH 1205) the nawab spent four or five hundred thousand rupees on its decoration annually. Hundreds of gold and silver replicas of the Imam Husain's tomb in Karbala were placed in the edifice as offerings to the Imam, along with innumerable glass chandeliers and candelabra. These offerings left no room for spectators and mourners to sit in the main hall. George Valentia wrote that the Imambarah was stunningly illuminated with candles during the month of Muharram, and that in various parts of the building believers said prayers. He remarked that 'every evening all unbelievers and followers of Omar, Othman, and Abu Bakr were anathematised, to the edification of the Hindoos, who, on this occasion, crowded there in great numbers.'[15]

Asaf al-Daulah's courtiers emulated his construction program in their own areas, so that in every neighbourhood they put up new mansions, imambarahs, and mosques.[16] Hasan Riza Khan built an imambarah and a mosque, and as soon as his mosque was ready, he transferred Friday prayers there from his palace. Later they were held in the large mosque Asaf al-Daulah constructed next to the Great Imambarah.[17] Most of Lucknow's Shi'i grandees, the likes of Afarin 'Ali Khan, Tahsin 'Ali Khan, Ramazan 'Ali Khan, and Tajammul Husain Khan, built imambarahs in this period, as did many Sunnis and Hindus. In the early 1800s some 2,000 large imambarahs, and 6,000 smaller *ta'ziya-khānas* embellished Lucknow.[18] The eminent Shi'i cleric Saiyid Dildar 'Ali Nasirabadi constructed an imambarah in the early 1790s, which became a major centre of religious culture and a burial site for many Shi'i 'ulama.[19] For the notable class, imambarahs performed many functions. They served as places for ritual mourning and worship, as literary salons, as personal monuments, and as family cemeteries. Increasingly, the endowment (*waqf*) of such buildings became a secure means of passing on wealth to future generations, since they could not then be sold and any income associated with them could be assigned to descendants as remuneration for supervision.[20] This institution also provided employment to subaltern 'ulama, who served as caretakers and read Qur'an verses for the deceased.

Notables spent much less on such buildings than did the nawab and his immediate circle, however. For instance, Mirza Jangali had a monthly allowance of Rs. 3,000 from his brother, Nawab Sa'adat 'Ali Khan. He bought a piece of land in Patna toward the end of his life for Rs. 3,000 and built a mosque and an imambarah on it. He appointed Rs. 50 per month for a manager, a caretaker, and the expenses of Qur'an readings and prayers. When the Mirza died he was buried on the grounds of this complex. Later nawabs continued the pension to his descendants, including the money for the upkeep of the imambarah and the mosque, but the British cut it off because of the family's involvement in the 1857–8 rebellion.[21] In contrast to Iran, such endowments rarely came under the supervision of the high 'ulama. In the case just cited the deceased's own sons supervised the endowment.

The elegiac poetry that dominated the religious culture of the imambarahs gave more public exposure to poets and reciters than to the staid 'ulama. Asaf al-Daulah's court attracted numerous poets and reciters of elegies (*marthīyyah-khwāns*), who came to hold an important place in public life. Mirza Muhammad Riza, a friend of Hasan Riza Khan's and the greatest reader of elegies in his day, used to chant from the Qur'an at the commemorations of Nawab Shuja' al-Dawlah's passing held by his widow in Faizabad.[22] Elegy reciters, such as Mulla Muhammad Shushtari and Shah Husain Vilayat, came to Lucknow from Iran, and found appreciation at the nawab's court. Asaf al-Daula appointed Shushtari, a poet and *rauḍa-khwān* with some clerical training, to recite elegies in the Great Imambarah. An expert in music (an art forbidden by the legalistic 'ulama), he had a beautiful voice, which could melt peoples' hearts.[23]

Poets, such as Mirza Rafi' al-Din Sawda and Mir Taqi Mir began making their way to Lucknow from fading Delhi, where they often turned their talents to religious elegiac, or marthiyyah, poetry. Some, such as Miyan Sikandar, Gada, Miskin, and Afsurdah, began specializing in the marthiyyah. In the late eighteenth century, poets replaced the four-line form of the Urdu elegy, favoured in the Deccan, with a more reflective six lines, beginning a transition to the almost epic feel of the mid-nineteenth-century elegies of Imam Husain.[24]

The poetry had both a literary and a ritual purpose. As ritual, reciters read it at mourning sessions as a means of making present the eternal, sacred time of 'Ashura, when the Prince of Martyrs redeemed Muslims with his blood. The rhythmic character of poetry lent itself to this task better than prose, the mourners working the rhythms into their flagellations. The symbolic appeal of Husain for the Shi'is of Awadh, who felt themselves to be in exile from Arabia or Iran, is well demonstrated by one of Mir's verses. Imam Husain stands facing his bloodthirsty foes after the loss of most of his supporting troops, holding his infant son, 'Ali Asghar. He addresses the Syrians, saying:

I now swear to you an oath
  that I shall restore my honor.
I shall go elsewhere, having left this Arab
  army; I shall make India my abode.[25]

Even Sunni scholars, such as Maulawi Mubin Farangi-Mahalli (d. 1810), made contributions to devotional literature mourning the Imam Husain. Shi'i 'ulama worked the events of Karbala into their sermons, and produced studies of the tragedy based on Arabic oral reports from the Imams.[26]

The development of the imambarah as an architectural form under the patronage of the nawabi court and courtiers provided a crucial meeting place for Shi'is. The Shi'i community, previously scattered and reticent, could now come out in public to commemorate the death of its Imams. Although the notable classes met in salons in any case, Shi'i tradespeople and labourers might otherwise have had no place to make one another's acquaintance. The imambarahs and smaller buildings, as well as the homes of believers, became centres of new Shi'i social networks and places where displaced Sunnis and Hindus could adopt Shi'ism.

THE SHRINE TO THE STANDARD OF HAZRAT 'ABBAS

Popular religion in northern India often centred on the tombs of holy men, and Shi'is no doubt yearned for a like institution within their own branch of Islam. In the late eighteenth century such a shrine grew up. One Mirza Faqir Beg returned to Lucknow with a relic from the shrine city of Karbala in Mamluk Iraq during the reign of Asaf al-Daulah (1775–97). He said that a dream helped him unearth the metal crest that had surmounted the banner of 'Abbas, the Imam Husain's half-brother, at the battle of Karbala. He kept the crest at his home in Rustamnagar, where people began bringing offerings (sing. *nadhr*) and giving them into his care. The building at first consisted of four bare walls, an unadorned roof, and a small courtyard.[27] The site's growing popularity attracted Nawab Asaf al-Daulah's attention, and he built a dome for the dervish's house, rendering it a proper shrine.[28] The place became popular for the little people in search of healing, sons, and spiritual blessings, and flower and sweets merchants began doing a booming trade in front of the gate. Brigands and ruffians also began gathering in that part of the town, attracted by the new wealth the shrine brought to Rustamnagar.[29]

A turning point came when Nawab Sa'adat 'Ali Khan fell seriously ill, in about 1801, making a vow to construct a splendid new building for the standard, should he recover. Restored to health in 1803, he took out a magnificent procession with his courtiers to the shrine of 'Abbas, distributing money along the way to the thronging multitudes lining the streets. At the shrine he said a prayer of thanksgiving, then ordered that a new edifice, with an impressive gilded dome, be raised on the site. He established a fund to cover the shrine's expenses, and people began gathering there regularly on Thursday evenings.

As members of the notable class gradually appropriated the shrine to themselves, it became necessary to provide more security. The nawab stationed patrolling police in the vicinity, with a *dārōghah* over them, who cleared out the ruffians.[30] Mrs. Ali reported that during Muharram 'by the condescending permission of the Sovereign, both the rich and the poor are with equal favour admitted', implying that during other months, access for the poor was more restricted.[31] Ever more precious offerings were kept at the shrine, including a collection of fifty-two priceless jewels. A woman's quarter was added so that females of the notable class could pray in private.[32] Notable-class women took out processions to the shrine, with great pomp and parade, after giving birth to a male child and after his circumcision. Female relatives and friends, as well as domestics and eunuchs, accompanied them, with the men riding behind and helping guard the sanctuary while the women were inside. Similar processions were taken out by both men and women of the upper classes on their recovery from illness or their preservation from possible danger.

After Mirza Faqir Beg's death, his son Fath 'Ali succeeded him as caretaker of the shrine, which in the 1820s yielded great amounts of cash and clothes, some of which the guardian of the shrine distributed to the poor in charity if he was 'a good man'.[33] Finally, the shrine was integrated into the mourning rites of Muharram in Lucknow, a process discussed below. A Sufi Shi'i, whom the 'ulama would have excoriated as a heretic, founded the shrine of 'Abbas, a purely folk phenomenon. It remained under the supervision of the founding family. Some 'ulama cast doubts on the authenticity of the crest of 'Abbas's standard, which the shrine allegedly housed, and this may indicate their own frustration at having so popular a religious phenomenon outside their control.[34] This expression of skepticism had no discernible effect upon the great numbers frequenting the shrine. The notable class made a more successful attempt to assert control over the spiritual resource, and by their patronage they gradually made it and its environs so wealthy that the area had to be strictly policed. The notable class partially restricted the access of the common people, whose creation the shrine had been, so that their ladies might safely visit it.

The shrine was only one manifestation of popular love for the family of the Prophet and belief in the efficacy of supplicating its members. In the event of sickness or loss of property, Shi'is called upon the particular Imam whose characteristics made him suited to deal with the problem. On Fridays, believers wrote supplications to the Twelfth Imam, who they thought to rule the world from a supernatural sanctuary until his millennial advent, folding them up and placing them in the Gomti River, certain that they would reach the Imam Mahdi.[35]

Some Shi'is drew pictures of the Messenger of God and the Imams, based on what they knew of their virtues and appearance, and set them up as household shrines, to which they performed visitation (*ziyārat*). When informed of this practice, Saiyid Dildar 'Ali ruled that drawing living things large enough to have a shadow was strictly forbidden in Islam, and that the 'visitation' of such images had no meaning.[36]

Another indication of popular beliefs diverging from the mujtahids' orthodoxy was the widespread existence of millenarian expectations among Awadh's Shi'is. Mrs. Ali reported that many north Indian Shi'is believed that the Twelfth Imam would return in AH 1260 (AD 1844), and that 'When the four quarters of the globe contain Christian inhabitants, and when the Christians approach the confines of the Kaabah, then may men look for that Emaum who is to come'. The Imam, they believed, would be accompanied by Jesus Christ, and together they would purge the world of wickedness so that 'all men shall be of one mind and one faith'.[37]

The Shi'is of north India keenly felt that they were encompassed by Christian power, which had effectively penetrated their quarter of the globe. The insecurity and cognitive dissonance produced by the extension of East India Company rule were involved in the sentiments expressed to Mrs. Ali that the old world order was about to be rolled up in 1844. Such millenarian expectations devalued existing institutions, posing a threat to Establishment figures like the mujtahids.

Household shrines to images of the Imams, and the shrine of 'Abbas's standard, made the sacred, manifested for Shi'is in the Imams, present to the ordinary folk of Lucknow. Yet the sacred, like material goods, became the object of a struggle for control by various social groups. As the shrine to 'Abbas's standard drew multitudes, including neighborhood toughs running protection rackets, its prestige caused the court and notables to invest it with wealth and with their own aspirations. This patronage in turn made it necessary for the state and the notables to assert control over the shrine through police and restricted access for the public, who had created the shrine by their hopes. In times of large-scale public ritual performances, the notables allowed greater access to the shrine. At the same time, scripturalist 'ulama attempted to discourage such practices as keeping household shrines to the Imams, with their decentralizing implications for religious authority, and beliefs like millenarianism that undermined faith in the Establishment. Nevertheless, the popular classes in Awadh appropriated the Imams for their own devotion.

OBSERVANCE OF MUHARRAM

The story of the martyrdom of Imam Husain and his family, and the ritual observances Shi'is developed to commemorate it, proved central to the formation of a Shi'i community in Awadh. This central story, called by Michael Fischer the 'Karbala paradigm', communicated profound existential truths about justice and injustice, life and death.[38] The distinctive manner in which Awadh Shi'is, as well as Sunnis and Hindus, responded to the mourning month of Muharram merits investigation in its own right. But their response is all the more important in that it had implications for communal relations.

Extravagance marked the observance of the month of ritual mourning, Muharram, during the Asaf al-Daulah period. In 1784, the nawab beat himself so violently on the tenth of that month that he bled profusely, falling seriously ill after accompanying representations of the Imam's tomb to the river, into which they were thrown at the end of the day. The nawab's officers followed his example in demonstrating particular munificence during the mourning session. Khwaja 'Ain al-Din, the tax-farmer of Bareli as of 1779, used, 'every year, after the 10th of Muharram, to scramble his household furniture, and refuse no one who asked him for a present.'[39]

Sa'adat 'Ali, Asaf al-Daulah's British-imposed successor, set a rather more restrained tone. Because of his territorial, and hence financial, losses to the British, he pursued greater economy, melting down several of his predecessor's gold ornaments for bullion and spending far less on Muharram ceremonies. Although the scale of expenditure for the ceremonies never again matched that of Asaf al-Daulah's days, it remained far from inconsiderable. Emma Roberts, expecting a 'fast of the most mournful kind', remarked with surprise that it was accompanied by so much pomp and splendour that strangers are at some loss to distinguish it from festivals of pure rejoicing.'[40] Believers manifested the impulse of generosity in many ways. To commemorate the thirst Imam Husain and his companions felt when denied water by their tormentors, Muslims in Lucknow distributed rose water. Some ladies gave out milk in the streets, and often people erected stands beside their houses where passersby could quench their thirst.[41]

In the early 1800s, only the high notables had their own imambarahs whereas the middle notables held mourning ceremonies in their large homes.[42] In the 1820s, when Mrs. Ali lived in the capital, many more of the wealthy had built imambarahs. They erected them on the public, male (*mardāna*) side of the house, designing them as square buildings with cupola tops. Their size depended on the wealth of the builder, and they often served also as family mausoleums. Guests sat on a calico covering overlaying a cotton carpet on the floor of the imambarah. Its walls boasted many mirrors, intended to multiply the candles and reflect the brilliance of the chandeliers, and the notables competed in decorating their imambarahs with great splendour.

Two ritual props graced the room, a stairway-like pulpit (*mimbar*) and a replica of the tomb (*zarīḥ* or *ta'ziya*) of the Imam Husain in Karbala, both facing Mecca. The pulpit, constructed of silver, ivory, ebony, or other fine materials, often matched the cenotaph. The reciter of elegies sometimes sat, and sometimes stood, on the steps of a pulpit covered with gold cloth or broad cloth (green, if owned by a Saiyid). On each side of the cenotaph were ranged banners of silk, or with gold or silver embroidery and fringes, hanging from staffs topped by crests with outspread hands whose five fingers represented the 'five pure souls': Muhammad, Fatimah, 'Ali, Hasan, and Husain. At the base of the cenotaph the host arranged objects that might have been used by the Imam, such as a fine sword and belt, set with precious stones, a shield, bow and arrows, or a turban.[43]

Believers fashioned the cenotaphs from all sorts of materials, from pure silver, to paper and bamboo, depending on the wealth of the owner. Different styles of cenotaphs developed in Lucknow, Delhi, Calcutta, and Hyderabad.[44] In the Great Imambarah stood fourteen tombs of pure silver, one for each of the Twelve Imams, the Prophet, and Fatimah.[45] The tomb replicas designed for an imambarah or a private residence were often made of ivory, ebony, sandalwood, or cedar. Mrs. Ali saw some wrought in silver filigree, and admired one the nawab had made in England of green glass with brass mouldings. The inexpensive cenotaphs, made in the bazaar from bamboo and coloured materials, ran from two to two hundred rupees in price. The labouring and lower middle classes set these up in their homes during Muharram and carried them in street processions.[46]

The imambarahs of the notables inspired wonder in the artisans and labourers who visited them in the early evening before the services began. However, notables did not allow the popular-class pilgrims to remain during the mourning sessions in the imambarahs, to which they invited only their friends and relatives and their servants.[47] The imambarahs made statements not only of piety but of wealth, power, and status. They constituted an interface between the wealthy and the poor who honoured Husain. But they also served to demarcate social lines, since the participatory mourning sessions held in them were very exclusive affairs.

The upper-class form of mourning spread from Lucknow into the rural provinces through the influence of the prestigious nawabi court at Lucknow. The nawabs of Farrukhabad became Shi'is in the late eighteenth century. In Awadh, the great landholder Imam 'Ali Khan of Bhatwamau (d. 1815) was the first Sunni *ta'alluqdār* to become a Shi'i and begin mourning practices in his provincial seat of power.[48] Some Shaikhzada leaders in Lucknow had converted to Shi'ism under Safdar Jang, maintaining marital links with the Sunni rural magnates. Muhammad Imam Khan (d. 1760s) of the large Mahmudabad estate in Sitapur married a Shi'i Shaikhzada woman. One of their sons, Muhammad Mazhar 'Ali Khan (d. 1790s), under the dual influence of his mother and the Lucknow court, converted to Shi'ism, inheriting the smaller portion of the estate in Belehra, Bara Banki. Although his conversion gave him an entree into the ruling circles in Lucknow, he faced a great deal of hostility from his father and other relatives.

The larger Mahmudabad portion of the estate remained under the control of Mazhar 'Ali Khan's Sunni brother, Ikram 'Ali Khan (d. ca. 1775). One of Ikram's sons, Musahib 'Ali Khan, ruled the Mahmudabad estate 1805–19, ruthlessly building up his holdings to a huge 232 villages and establishing good relations with the Awadh court by supporting it against rebels. Although he remained a Sunni, he initiated mourning rites for the Imam Husain in a building inside the fort at Sitapur. He had no male issue, and in 1836 his widow adopted a son of the Shi'i Belehra branch of the family, Raja Nawwab 'Ali Khan, who had lived long in Lucknow and become close to Nasir al-Din Haidar's court. From his accession, Mahmudabad, one of the largest rural estates in Awadh, was Shi'i-ruled.[49] Even the Sunni Raja of Nanpara kept Shi'i 'ulama, many of them from Kashmir, at his provincial seat to read elegies for the Imam Husain.[50]

The accounts of European travellers make it very clear that the poor as well as the wealthy commemorated Muharram. Even in villages, Shi'is during that month marked their homes with the spread-hand symbol.[51]

Although notable Mughals and Saiyids may have been most prominent in promoting Shi'i practices, many of the *popolino*, the little people of Awadh's urban centres, enthusiastically embraced the cult of the Imam Husain during Muharram. Roberts wrote that 'every person who has a small sum to spare subscribes, with others of the same means, to purchase the necessary articles for the purpose.'[52] The public processions in the streets, where mourners displayed bamboo cenotaphs, banners, and parasols, were easier for the popular classes to participate in, as they did not require ownership of a large room. Persons of all classes took out processions for the Martyr, filling the streets, some effusing pomp and splendour, and 'others content with a very humble display'.[53]

Since the lower-middle-class mourners could not afford to build a separate imambarah, they decorated the best room in their dwelling as a substitute. The banners about the cenotaph in these humble homes were of coarse materials, tinsel or dyed muslin, with cheap metal staffs. Where mirrors proved too expensive, they resorted to oil-burning lamps of various shapes, brightly painted and decorated with cut paper.[54]

Oil for the lamps came dear to people on the edge of subsistence, and many families of lower-middle-class means scrimped and saved all year so that they could put on an extravagant show for the Imam (and for their neighbourhood).[55] Such zeal denoted not only piety but something of the same striving for status through lavish expenditure that characterized Awadh's magnates. In this practice, as in the extravagant expenses associated with weddings, the artisan and laboring classes attempted to usurp status by emulating the lifestyle of the notables, an emulation financially ruinous for classes more often exploited than exploiting. Only through collectivism, pooling their resources to share in the paraphernalia of Muharram, could many labourers participate in the commemorations at all.

THE MOURNING SESSION

Two central rituals for Shi'is dominated Muharram: the mourning session (*majlis*), held in an imambarah or a private dwelling, and the procession. The procession, by far the more ancient of these rituals, originated at least by the time of the Shi'i Buyid dynasty in early-tenth-century Iraq. The stylized mourning session developed during the Safavid period in Iran, though gatherings to mourn the martyred Husain had more ancient antecedents.[56] In Awadh in the early nineteenth century, notables held mourning sessions in their imambarah twice a day during the first ten days of Muharram. The evening sessions, with their dazzling lighting derived from myriads of candles, mirrors, and chandeliers, were the best attended.

Rauzah-Khwani (mourning session). Courtesy of the British Library.

The host and his male relatives sat on the carpeted floor near the cenotaph, the guests crowding in wherever they found room. The host hired a *maulawī* to read that day's passage from a Persian prose text that described the sufferings of the Imam Husain and his supporters and family in their struggle against the Umayyads. Among the Persian-educated notable class in Awadh, such readings could be extremely effective, particularly if the maulawī wept and groaned with great sincerity from his *miṃbar*.[57]

Since this role only required some Persian education, the maulawī could be one of the subaltern 'ulama or even relatively untrained in specialized religious sciences. High 'ulama often held their own sessions, where they tied their recitations of the martyr's sufferings more closely to Arabic oral reports from the Imams, a style known a *ḥadīth-khwānī*. One of his students described Saiyid Muhammad Nasirabadi, then Lucknow's chief mujtahid, reciting oral reports from the Imams with translation:

> I found him on the tenth of Muharram in the mourning session mentioning the calamities that befell the Martyr at Karbala, weeping violently, as was his audience. Then he descended from the miṃbar, barefoot, bareheaded, tears streaming from his ruddy cheeks. This was always his wont on such days. He thereafter went home and people gathered there.[58]

After the Persian reading, called the 'ten sessions' (*dah majlis*) because the works read from had ten chapters (one for each of the first ten days of Muharram), came an intermission during which servants handed around sweetened rose water to the gathering of mourners. Devout Shi'is in the 1820s refrained from chewing betel leaves during Muharram, so servants passed about an assortment of spices on small silver trays. The highest ranking members of the assembly smoked water pipes during the intermission, though the rest of the guests, of even slightly lower rank, dared not join them.[59]

After the refreshments, specialized reciters chanted elegiac poetry in Urdu. Even the illiterate could understand this part of the session, which must have formed the core of popular mourning sessions. Some of the verses had refrains, and the whole assembly often joined in.[60] In the early nineteenth century, some reciters of such poetry employed a vocal technique that approximated singing. Readers presented verse works commemorating the martyrdom of the Imam Husain in various rhetorical styles. The 'ulama favoured the straightforward reading of the poetry (*taḥt al-lafẓ-khwānī*), similar to that practised by poets in secular poetry readings. Another style, antedating in India the rise of Shi'i culture in Awadh, involved the chanting (*sūz-khwānī*) of elegies. In Asaf al-Daulah's time Haidari Khan, a great singer, further innovated in this field, teaching Saiyid Mir 'Ali, a highly respected performer at the court of Sa'adat 'Ali Khan. In such performances the musical modes (*rāginīs*) could be emphasized or played down, according to taste. Women, artisans and labourers, whether Shi'i, Sunni, or Hindu, greatly loved the more musical styles. At the time of Ghazi al-Din Haidar (1814–27) people came from all over Awadh to Lucknow during Muharram in hopes of hearing the courtesan Lady Haidar sing elegiac lyrics mourning the Imam.[61] Women commonly sang *marthiyyahs* in public, though the 'ulama condemned such mixed meetings.

Some of the more strict, legal-minded Shi'is questioned Saiyid Dildar 'Ali Nasirabadi about the singing of elegiac poetry. He replied that listening to elegiac verses for the Imam Husain, weeping for him, and mourning him all have great rewards. If read with a sorrowful and pained voice, they presented no difficulty at all. But he disapproved of chanting *marthiyyahs* with remodulation (Persian *tarjī'*, Urdu *kaṭkar*) as being too close to music, promising that anyone who avoided listening to such performances would be spiritually rewarded.[62]

After the mourning verses the entire congregation rose and enumerated the legitimate successors after the Prophet Muhammad according to Shi'is, the Twelve Imams, asking blessings upon them individually. Then they repeated the names of the early caliphs, whom Shi'is regard as usurpers, pronouncing imprecations on them. These two rituals consisted of taking an oath of allegiance (*tawallā*) to the Imams and pronouncing imprecations (*tabarra'*) on the caliphal usurpers.[63] The mourning session concluded with a frenzied period of self-flagellation called the obsequy (*ma'tam*). Even Shi'i notables practised it, Mrs. Ali reporting of upper-class ceremonies:

> I have even witnessed blood issuing from the breast of sturdy men, who beat themselves simultaneously as they ejaculated the names 'Hasan' 'Hosein'! for ten minutes, and occasionally during a longer period, in that part of the service called Mortem.[64]

Again, the 'ulama disapproved of flagellation. Mrs. Ali wrote that 'Maulvees, Moollahs, and devoutly religious persons never joined in beating their breasts, although they were present in the audience while others thus violently expressed their grief. The 'ulama carried on their own mourning practices for longer than most believers in the 1820s, for a full forty days. They apparently did not participate in the mourning processions.[65] Saiyid Muhammad Nasirabadi, asked about self-flagellation in the 1820s or 1830s, replied that wailing and beating one's chest over the calamities that befell the family of the Prophet was permissible only if one lost control of one's self.[66]

Women also commemorated Muharram, though only a few princesses and wealthy courtesans had their own imambarahs. Almost all the hostesses made their best room in the ladies' quarters into a temporary imambarah, allowing only females in. Mrs. Ali thought the grief of women during the first ten days of Muharram greater than that of men, such that pious women would neglect their private sorrow during that period. In Hyderabad, Shi'i women beat their breasts in self-flagellation, just as did men.[67] In Lucknow, women gave up betel leaves, the wearing of jewellery, and bright (especially red) clothes, instead loosening their hair and garbing themselves in dark colours. Some even mortified themselves by wearing their mourning clothes in torrid, sultry Lucknow for ten solid days. Mrs. Ali's serving-maid went the entire time without drinking water during the day. Every evening the ladies gathered about the cenotaph they had set up, with female friends, slaves, and servants surrounding the hostess.[68]

As elsewhere in the Shi'i world, educated women presided at these distaff sessions.[69] In Awadh they derived for the most part from indigent Saiyid families that lacked the dowry to attract a high-status Saiyid groom but refused to accept one from a less prestigious caste, in accordance with the hypergamy (marrying up but not down) widespread among Indian Muslims. They often served as Qur'an teachers for the daughters of notable families. Hostesses hired them for the first ten days of Muharram, presenting them in remuneration not only with a fee but with fine gifts as well. They read both the Ten Sessions in Persian and the elegiac poetry in Urdu.[70]

The mourning sessions held in homes during Muharram and during other months of the Shi'i sacred calendar provided crucial opportunities for the development of social networks among Shi'is, whether male or female, notable or commoner. Mourners went from session to session, spreading news and giving Shi'is of one neighbourhood or village a sense of unity with their coreligionists elsewhere. Lucknow became a place where Shi'is from all over Awadh could meet at Muharram and thus overcome their sense of being isolated minority communities through congregation in the Realm of the Shi'a. The sessions reflected in their social composition the class and status of the host, with tradespeople excluded from notable gatherings. But within social classes and neighbourhoods, the sessions did much to foster a sense of community identity.

PROCESSIONS

The mourning sessions held in homes or imambarahs, although public, largely reflected kin and friendship ties in their composition. The truly civic rites, the processions, brought together in the streets persons from all over each major city, as well as many visitors from nearby villages. With the development of processions, Shi'ism came into its own as a religion in Awadh. No longer the furtive creed of isolated Saiyid communities in the service towns, it blossomed as the court's favoured rite, central to the ritual life of cities like Lucknow and Faizabad.

Particular activities marked each of the ten days of Muharram. At the end of the preceding month, Zu'l-hijja, middle- and working-class men brought that year's bamboo cenotaphs home from the bazaar with great ceremony. Notable families with permanent cenotaphs prepared a room or an imambarah to receive guests for the mourning sessions. The first day of Muharram witnessed, not activity, but an eerie quiet as shops closed and families began mourning at home.

On the second day, the public marvelled at the imambarahs of magnates and visited the cenotaphs of friends. The devout saw such visitation as a ritual obligation substituting for the expensive pilgrimage to Karbala itself.[71] From this day multitudes crowded the streets and alleys, most on foot, but with some notables on horseback or in palanquins, making social rounds, visiting cenotaphs, and participating in the twice-daily mourning sessions. On the third day of Muharram women sent sweet dishes to friends and relatives, as well as to poor families, in remembrance of the Imam's passing, just as they would have on the third day after a loved one's death. They repeated this on the seventh and fortieth days after the first of Muharram.[72]

On the fifth of Muharram believers took out processions throughout Lucknow to Rustamnagar, where they had their standards blessed at the shrine of ʿAbbas. Mrs. Ali witnessed a notable's entourage undertaking the trip. At the head of the procession walked a guard of soldiers around four elephants, which carried men and silk-and-gold banners. In the train of the elephants came a band playing Indian instruments, as well as trumpets. Next in order came a mourner holding a black pole from which two swords hung on a reversed bow. Behind him walked the owner of the banners, accompanied by reciters of verse elegies and a large number of friends. The verses chosen for the procession particularly concerned the sufferings of ʿAbbas. Thereafter came a horse, representing Husain's steed, Duldul, a fine white Arabian. His legs were stained with red, and arrows appeared to be stuck in various parts of his body. A turban rode on the tragically empty saddle. Friends of the family, servants, and private foot-soldiers brought up the rear.[73]

Thousands of other, less affluent mourners also headed for the shrine with their banners. They entered it by a flight of steps from the courtyard. A shrine attendant took the banner of each person through the right entrance and touched it against the crest of ʿAbbas's own staff. Each mourner moved on after his banner touched quickly to the sacred crest. Mrs. Ali estimated that shrine attendants consecrated forty or fifty thousand banners in a single day.[74] Whatever the number, the ritual demonstrates a rather high level of organization and corporate cooperation for a pre-modern South Asian city, given that neighbourhoods of all religions and classes apparently took part.[75]

The next big day, the seventh of Muharram, commemorated the battlefield wedding of Qasim, the Imam Husain's doomed nephew, to the Imam's daughter. In Awadh, mourners remembered the wedding through the staging of premarital processions and formalities. Notables took out processions to the imambarah of a social superior, reproducing the pattern of hypergamy as practised by Indian Muslims. At the imambarah the mourners reposited a model of Qasim's tomb. After the completion of prenuptial ceremonies for Qasim and his bride, notables distributed money to the poor, just as they would have at a real wedding. Middle- and labouring-class people also commemorated the ill-starred wedding, but did so at home rather than with costly processions.[76] Elsewhere in India mourners introduced variations on this ritual. In Hyderabad to the south, a man sometimes impersonated Qasim and was prepared for burial at the imambarah. On the seventh of Muharram in that city, mourners painted a representation of the Imam's horse made of wood and decorated it with jewels.[77]

The climax of the mourning period came on the tenth day, the anniversary of the Imam Husain's own martyrdom. Participants rose in the early hours of the morning and began preparing for the procession, women sometimes lighting candles at the cenotaph before dawn and making requests. At dawn the mourners set out for a symbolic burial ground on the outskirts of the city, called a Karbala. In Safavid Iran, the labouring classes participated in street processions; the wealthy favoured the mourning sessions inside.[78] In Awadh, however, many notables joined the street processions with great fervour. The wealthy put together a military funeral parade, with elephants, bands, a bearer of the sword staff, banners, and a caparisoned and bloodstained Duldul with a royal umbrella above his head. Friends and family of the owner, elegy chanters, incense bearers, and the owner of the cenotaph display himself walked behind, often barefoot and with heads exposed to the sun. Next came the cenotaph of Husain surrounded by banners and covered by a canopy supported by silver poles, in the style of a Muslim funeral, then the cenotaph of Qasim and the wedding paraphernalia. Several elephants brought up the rear, from which servants threw money to the poor, who crowded behind the processions of the grandees. These not only sought money and blessed bread from the train of the notable's parade, but conducted their own humble processions in its wake, with their coarsely made cenotaphs held high. They thereby also sought security, since the wealthy had a guard of matchlock-men in case of trouble from brigands or Shi'i-Sunni violence.[79]

From time to time the procession halted, sometimes as often as every five minutes. Then the notables listened to the elegies being chanted, or mourners flagellated themselves to the accompaniment of drums. Although the labouring-class mourners could not compete with the splendid pageants of the notables, they could nevertheless gain divine rewards and social status among their peers through extreme breast-beating. In north Indian cities at this time, tens of thousands of people assembled in the streets. The processions often arrived after nightfall at their Karbalas, four or five miles distant, where mourners ritually interred the cenotaphs and performed the whole ceremony of a funeral. Tempers ran high on this day of collective grief, and Sunni-Shi'i riots sometimes broke out among Awadh's habitually armed men.

On their return home the rich distributed food, money, and clothes to the poor. The horse Duldul and his expensive attire was donated to a poor Saiyid family.[80] In the 1820s the mourning ceremonies were effectively over on the tenth of Muharram. On the third day after, men began shaving their beards again, women threw off their mourning vestments, bathed, and put on jewellery. The populace began chewing betel leaves once more. Only a few very devout persons continued to mourn for forty days.[81]

Shi'i 'ulama took a critical attitude toward some of the Muharram practices, incidentally reinforcing their own status as purists. In 1808 the Iranian immigrant scholar Aqa Ahmad Bihbahani endeavoured to convince notables in Faizabad to give up the practice of beating drums to the accompaniment of their breast-beating.[82] A believer in Lucknow asked chief Shi'i cleric Saiyid Dildar 'Ali Nasirabadi whether it was proper to employ drums and symbolic horses and camels on the tenth of Muharram. He replied that drums were a heretical innovation, but that using camels to evoke the caravan of the doomed Imam's family for the purpose of rendering hearts tender presented no difficulties.[83] In later years camels draped in black were brought during the month of Muharram to the Nasirabadis' imambarah itself.[84] Some later Shi'i 'ulama condoned other folk practices. Maulavi Abu'l-Hasan Kashmiri wrote in defence of even the use of drums in mourning the Imam.[85]

Werner Ende has discussed how some Arab 'ulama in the modern period defended flagellation, suggesting that they felt it to be in their interest, pecuniary or otherwise, to encourage mass participation in Muharram rites.[86] Since the Awadh 'ulama in the early nineteenth century received their patronage from the semi-feudal notables rather than from the bazaar, they could afford in general to take a much more elitist approach. Even then, they often had to come to terms with the folk practices of the notables; Saiyid Muhammad's ruling allowed flagellation if the mourner forgot himself, providing a convenient out to those who wished to practice it. The 'ulama's exclusion of music, including drums, from Muharram practices derived from their greater scripturalism, but it had the effect of further differentiating them as a status group from their notable patrons.

In Iran, very late in the eighteenth century, a new practice associated with mourning the Imam grew up—the passion play (*ta'ziya*). From representational acts in the tenth-of-Muharram processions, wherein mourners portrayed Husain and his enemies, a tradition emerged of folk theatre centred in a fixed playhouse. In Awadh, no such indigenous development occurred during the period under discussion. Shi'i notables there did sponsor Hindu style plays about Krishna, and perhaps these performances preempted the development of alternative theatrical traditions. Accounts by travellers in Bengal and Bihar reveal a higher level of play-acting and representing during Muharram than existed in Awadh.[87] 'Ulama in Awadh gave rulings against the use of tableaux or religious paintings as backdrops during mourning sessions.[88]

The processions of Muharram filled the streets of Awadh's cities with flagellating mourners. The frenzied multitudes that so impressed Western travellers with their zeal hid, in their numbers and the seeming chaos of the crowded streets, an underlying organization. Procession marchers grouped themselves by neighbourhood, by patron, by status group. The degree of organization that must have been necessary to consecrate thousands of standards at the shrine to the standard of 'Abbas bespeaks a vast increase in Lucknow's cohesion and a sophistication in Shi'i and non-Shi'i Muharram networks.

NON-SHI'I PARTICIPATION IN MUHARRAM

The culture of Awadh, a pre-industrial society, demonstrated syncretic tendencies. Cultural mediators, such as Sufi pīrs, drawing their clientele from both Muslim and Hindu, transmitted symbols from one group to another. Muharram rites in Awadh began to serve the same mediating function for some groups. Boundaries between religious communities existed, and riots occurred between Hindu and Muslim or Sunni and Shi'i. But to a greater extent in the early nineteenth than in the early twentieth century, cultural mediators linked popular-class groups.[89]

Sunni Muslims in Awadh in the eighteenth and nineteenth centuries also held mourning sessions, but frowned on the breast-beating and ritual cursing of the Shi'is. Sunnis likewise participated in Muharram processions, but in various ways differentiated themselves from Shi'is. For instance, although the latter held up five fingers to symbolize the Prophet's immediate family, the Sunnis would hold up three fingers, for the first three caliphs.[90] For Awadh's Sunnis, 'Ali and his sons were the rightful successors of the caliphs, not their victims. Although Sunni-Shi'i violence frequently broke out on this occasion, it derived from a different conception of the caliphs, rather than from any sympathy for the Umayyad enemies of Husain. After the 1820s some Sunnis began to speak well of the Umayyads, probably as a reaction against the Shi'i atmosphere of Awadh. Only in the first decade of the twentieth century did the two communites become so estranged that even Sunnis who mourned Husain began taking their model cenotaphs to different burial fields than the Shi'is for interment.[91]

The vast Hindu majority often also took part in the mourning for Imam Husain, incorporating his cult into their ritual calendar as yet one more divinity in the pantheon. The Iranian traveller Shushtari saw Hindus commemorating Muharram all over north India in the late eighteenth century. He wrote that in Delhi, wealthy Hindus with not the least trace of Islam about them went to great trouble to construct imambarahs. They fasted during Muharram, recited elegies for the Imam in Hindi, Urdu, and Persian, pelted each other with stones in mortification, and fed the poor. They constructed replicas of the Imam's cenotaph, bowed to them, and supplicated them for favours. After the tenth of Muharram they threw the cenotaphs in the river or buried them. Shushtari found some of the Hindu approaches to fasting and self-mortification during Muharram quite strange, maintaining that Indian Muslims copied them.[92]

The Kayastha scribal caste in particular adopted Muslim customs, owing to their long association with Muslim rulers as secretaries and revenue-department civil servants. Many Kayastha notables built their own imambarahs.[93] But Hindu popular-class participation in Muharram processions and attendance at public mourning sessions, such as those at the Great Imambarah, cut across caste lines. Emma Roberts wrote,

> Hindoos ... are frequently seen to vie with the disciples of Ali in their demonstrations of grief for the slaughter of his two martyred sons: and in the splendour of the pageant displayed at the anniversary of their fate. A very large proportion of Hindoos go into mourning during the ten days of Mohurrum, clothing themselves in green garments, and assuming the guise of fakeers.[94]

Fanny Parkes's Hindu cook spent forty rupees on a bamboo cenotoph for the Imam, performed all the Muharram rites, and then resumed his Hinduism when he had interred his cenotaph with funeral offerings of rice, corn, flowers, and cups of water.[95] In the Hindu-ruled provinces of central and southern India, as well, Hindus celebrated Muharram with processions and illuminations. Strict, scripturalist Brahmans often opposed this practice, but even some of them mourned Husain. In Sunni-ruled Hyderabad, riots would sometimes break out between Hindus and Muslims during Muharram, and the Hindus participating in the mourning rites would actually take the Muslim side against their co-religionists.[96]

Hindus therefore not only widely participated in the Muharram rites but helped influence their shape in India by introducing practices that even high-caste Muslims adopted. Garcin de Tassy pointed out that Muharram, like the festival for the Goddess of Death, Durga, lasts ten days. On the tenth day of Durga *pūjā* Hindus cast a figurine of the goddess into the river, parallelling the Shi'i custom of often casting the Imam's cenotaph into the river on the tenth day of Muharram. The Muslims made the same offering to the Imam that Hindus proffered their sacred figures.[97] Since high-caste Shi'is and Hindus considered each other ritually impure and unbelievers, popular-class syncretism of this sort sometimes posed problems for strict Shi'is. Someone asked the chief mujtahids in the early 1830s whether an unbeliever could properly give an offering in cash or kind to the Imams and distribute cooked food to poor believers during Muharram. The mujtahid replied that the most cautious course was for them to bring such food only if the host of the mourning session asked them to do so (*aḥvaṭ ast kih bar ṭibq-i guftah-i mālik ārand*).[98]

Widespread, though not universal, Sunni and Hindu participation made Muharram rites trans-communal. Sunnis in Awadh genuinely loved and supported Husain, and the tears they shed for the Prophet's grandson helped soften hardline Shi'i attitudes toward them. Hindus commemorated Muharram as well, adopting Husain as a god of death, his bloodstained horse and his severed head lifted aloft on Umayyad staves presenting no less terrible an aspect than Kali Durga with her necklace of skulls. Syncretism and cultural intermediaries, such as readers of elegiac poetry, helped create a Shi'i-tinged traditional culture in a society where, among the popular classes, religious communal identity was still weak, or at least not exclusivist in tone.

CONCLUSION

Muharram rituals constituted a complex of practices carried out on a mass scale. These rituals were highly ambiguous, both in regard to vertical stratification among religious communities and in regard to horizontal stratification within the Shi'i grouping. Some of these practices, bearing an ecumenical aspect, were joined in by many Sunnis and Hindus. Others helped spread Shi'i ideals among the masses and promoted social networks among believers not only within city quarters, but between city dwellers and visitors from *qaṣabas* in the hinterland. More than anything else, the practice of cursing the caliphs helped erect communal barriers between Shi'is and others, and the violence it provoked helped reinforce internal Shi'i solidarity. Yet that solidarity did not completely obscure the social distinctions separating notables and commoners.

The Muharram commemorations, including the 'pilgrimages' to the cenotaphs and the focus on death, demonstrate the coexistence of structure and anti-structure. On the one hand, social distinctions temporarily broke down into liminality and a generalized feeling of levelled community (*communitas*), which the late Victor Turner found typical of such rites.[99] The notables of both sexes demeaned themselves in bereavement for the Imam, men walking barefoot and bareheaded under Lucknow's harsh sun, and highborn ladies wearing the same sweaty clothes for ten days in a climate that called for frequent baths.

The mourning processions and the notables' distribution of largesse created a sense of solidarity among social classes. But in important ways mourners intensified structure, emphasizing distinctions of class and status in the exclusivity of the mourning sessions at imambarahs and in the primacy of notable pageants during the Muharram processions. Indeed, the processions constituted a microcosm of Awadh's prebendal hierarchical social structure. Muharram was a prime opportunity for the display of wealth and various sorts of expenditure that contributed to the expression of high status. Moreover, at the same time that the ceremonies drew together the participants from various classes and religious communities, they often sparked communal violence because some Sunnis and Hindus objected so strongly to them.

The mourners of Husain in the bazaar or in the large villages worked their own genius on Muharram rites, such that they often created ritual forms later usurped by the notables, including veneration at the shrine of 'Abbas. Although the notables excluded the popular classes from the services at their private imambarahs, and forced them to march behind their elephants in the procession, the popular classes in many ways led the way in venerating the Martyrs, expressing their grief in everyday ways that helped make the Imam and his family real to them. For they were, after all, the experts in what it meant to be oppressed.

The Shi'i notable class, whose distribution of gifts and cash during processions helped ensure the participation of the poor, promoted the extensive mourning rites for Husain. Fenced in by the East India Company, the notables had little opportunity to invest in territorial expansion, expressing their culture and prestige through religious architecture and patronage instead. In addition, informal labouring-class associations shared expenses and promoted the rites. In some places Sufi faqirs organized the ceremonies, during which they received offerings.[100]

People used the story rhetorically and allegorically as well as ritually. Some notable-class Shi'is depicted the encroaching British as the evil Yazid in the 1857–8 rebellion. Among labouring-class devotees of the Imam, the tax collectors and police of the Shi'i government itself may have been seen at times as the real Yazid. Moreover, where Muslim villagers were a small minority surrounded by unbelievers, the Umayyad armies attacking Husain came to be portrayed as Hindus.[101]

The artisans, labourers, and peasants depended on the largesse of the Shi'i rulers, and this link of dependency encouraged the little people to share with the rulers in their religious practices. In this way a general Shi'i community came into being, still loosely organized, but enjoying new and wide-ranging social networks built around the sacred calendar of Imami mourning sessions and processions. In the early nineteenth century, this calendar was also shared by many Sunnis and some Hindus. Yet some Awadh government policies helped make Muharram rites, at times, divisive of religious communities. When the early stages of political mobilization began late in the nineteenth century, Muharram processions and violence began serving a new purpose in creating communal identities, which grew into political ones in the twentieth century.[102]

NOTES

1. My conception of a growing community identity that could lead to communalism derives from Sandria Freitag, *Collective Action and Community: Public Arenas and the Emergence of Communalism in North India* (Berkeley: University of California Press, 1989). Clearly, however, here I am discussing a much earlier phase, which might be called community formation.

2. Bryan S. Turner, *For Weber* (Boston: Routledge & Kegan Paul, 1981), p. 126.

3. See Rosie Llewelyn-Jones, 'The City of Lucknow before 1856', in K. Ballhatchet and J. Harrison, eds., *The City in South Asia, Pre-Modern and Modern* (London: Curzon Press, 1980), pp. 91–8; and H.K. Naqvi, *Urban Centres and Industries in Upper India,* 1556–1803 (Bombay: Asia Publishing House, 1968), p. 139.

4. C.A. Bayly, *Rulers, Townsmen, and Bazaars* (Cambridge: Cambridge University Press, 1983), pp. 115–17.

5. Viscount George Valentia, *Voyages and Travels to India*, 4 vols. (London: F.C. and J. Rivington, 1811), 1:120.

6. Reverend William Tennant, *Indian Recreations*, 3 vols. (London: Longman, Hurst, Rees, and Orme, 1804), 2:405.

7. 'Ali Bakht Azfari, *Vāqi'at-i Azfarī*, ed. T. Chandrasekharan (Madras: Nuri Press, 1957), p. 96; see In'am 'Ali, 'Awṣāf al-Āsaf', Farsi Tarikh, MS 25, foll. 63a–65a, Mawlana Azad Lib., Aligarh Muslim University, Aligarh, and Murtaza Bilgrami, *Ḥadīqat al-aqālīm* (Lucknow: Naval Kishor, 1879), p. 155; Saiyid 'Abbas Ardistani, 'Al-ḥiṣn al-matīn fī ahwāl al-wuzarā' wa's-salāṭīn', 2 vols., Arabic MSS 235a–b, 1:94, National Archives of India, New Delhi; see also H.R. Nevill, ed., *Lucknow District Gazetteer* (Allahabad: Government Press, 1904), p. 30.

8. Abu Talib Isfahani, *Tafḍīḥ al-ghāfilīn*, trans. W. Hoey (Lucknow: Pustak Kendra, repr. 1971), pp. 72–3.

9. Llewelyn-Jones, 'The City of Lucknow before 1856', p. 104

10. Zain al-'Abidin Shirwani, *Bustān as-siyāhah* (Tehran: n.p., 1897), p. 523.

11. K.A. Nizami, 'Imām-baṛa', *Encyclopedia of Islam* (2nd edn.), S. Agha Mihdi Lakhnavi, *Tārīkh-i Lakhna'u* (Karachi: Jam'iyyat-i Khuddām-i 'Azā, 1976), pp. 152–3.

12. James Ferguson et al., *History of Indian and Eastern Architecture*, 2 vols. (London: John Murray, 1910), 2:328–29.

13. For the building of the Imambarah, see 'Abd al-Latif Shushtari, 'Tuḥfat al-'ālam', Add. 23, 533, British Lib. fol. 194a (the figure mentioned is 2 crores, but an Iranian crore equals half a million, or five lakhs); Murtaza Bilgrami, *Ḥadīqat*, p. 155; Kamal al-Din Haidar Husaini Mashhadi, *Savāniḥāt-i Salāṭīn-i Avadh* (Lucknow: Naval Kishor, 1896), p. 112; Nevill, ed., *Lucknow District Gazetteer*, pp. 30, 203.

14. Isfahani, *Tafḍīḥ al-ghāfilīn*, Hoey trans., pp. 73ff.

15. Valentia, *Voyages and Travels*, 1:122–3.

16. Isfahani, *Tafḍīḥ al-ghāfilīn*, Hoey trans., p. 72.

17. Mihdi Lakhnawi, *Tārīkh-i Lakhna'u*, p. 49.

18. See, e.g. ibid.; pp. 49–50 77, 127, 182–3, 192–3; and Zain al-'Ābidin Shirwani, *Riyāḍ as-siyāḥah*, 3 vols. (Moscow: Shu'bah-'i Adabiyyāt-i Khāvar, 1974), 3:1053.

19. Mihdi Lakhnawi, *Tārīkh-i Lakhna'u*, pp. 154–5; M.H. Zaidi, 'Eine Einführung zu der Muharram-Feierlichkeiten von Lucknow zur Zeit der Avadh Dynastie, 1722–1856', *Zeitschrift der Deutschen Morgänlandische Gesellschaft* Supp. 3 (1977): 639.

20. Cf. Saiyid Dildar 'Ali Nasirabadi, 'Najāt as-sā'ilin', Fiqh Shi'ah, Persian MS 256, fol. 7a, Nasiriyyah Library, Lucknow. This is a collection of legal rulings by Lucknow's first chief mujtahid, made in the first decade of the nineteenth century.

21. Farzand 'Ali Khan to Chief Commissioner, Oudh, 7.9.60, Board of Revenue, Lucknow, File 2607, Uttar Pradesh State Archives, Lucknow.

22. Muhammad Faizbakhsh, *Tārīkh-i farahbakhsh*, trans. William Hoey, *Memoirs of Delhi and Faizabad*, 2 vols. (Allahabad: Government Press, 1888–89), 2:112.

23. Shushtari, 'Tuḥfat al-'ālam', foll. 197b–198a; Azfari, *Vāqi'at*, pp. 104–5.

24. See Muhammad Sadiq, *A History of Urdu Literature* (London: Oxford University Press, 1964), ch. 9; Ralph Russell and Khurshidul Islam, *Three*

Mughal Poets: Mir, Sauda, Mir Hasan (Cambridge: Harvard Univ. Press, 1968); 'Abd al-Halim Sharar, *Guzashtah Lakhna'u: mashriqī tamaddun kā ākhirī namūnah* (Lucknow: Nasim Book Depot, 1974), pp. 100–01; trans. E.S. Harcourt and Fakhir Hussain as *Lucknow: The Last Phase of an Oriental Culture* (Boulder, Colo.: Westview Press, 1976), p. 84. Cf. Zahra Eqbal, 'Elegy in the Qajar Period', in Peter J. Chelkowski, ed., *Ta'ziyeh: Ritual and Drama in Iran* (New York: New York University Press, 1979).

25. Mir Taqi Mir, *Kulliyāt-i Mīr*, ed. S. Ihtisham Husain, 2 vols. (Allahabad: Ram Narain Lal Beni Madhu, 1972), 2:259:

> Yeh kartā hūṅ maiṅ tum sē paymān ab
> keh nāmūs apnā uthā'ūṅ gā sab
> kis-sū aur ja'ūṅ ga chhoṛā 'Arab
> Jaysh Hind apnā karūṅ gā maqām.

For Mir's *marthiyyahs*, see Safdar Ah, *Mīr aur Mīriyyāt* (Bombay: 'Alavī Book Depot, 1971), pp. 342–6

26. Saiyid Agha Ashhar Lakhnawi, *Tadhkirat adh-dhākirīn* (Jhansi: Shams Press, 1942), p. 26; the death of one of his sons prompted Saiyid Dildar 'Ali to produce one such Karbala ḥadīth study; see his 'Ithārat al-aḥzān', Arabic MS H.L. 2292, Khudabakhsh Oriental Public Library, Patna.

27. Ghulam 'Ali Naqavi, *Imād as-sa'ādat* (Lucknow: Naval Kishor, 1897), p. 172.

28. Mihdi Lakhnavi, *Tārīkh-i Lakhna'u*, pp. 116–7.

29. Naqavi, *'Imād*, p. 172.

30. Ibid.; Ardistani, 'Al-ḥiṣn al-matīn, 1:56–7.

31. Mrs. Meer Hasan Ali, *Observations on the Mussulmans of India* (London: Oxford University Press, 1917), p. 36.

32. Mihdi Lakhnawi, *Tārīkh-i Lakhna'u*, p. 116.

33. Ali, *Observations*, pp. 34–5; Naqavi, *'Imād*, p. 172; Emma Roberts, *Scenes and Characteristics of Hindostan*, 3 vols. (London: Wm. H. Allen and Co., 1835), 2:180.

34. Mihdi Lakhnawi, *Tārīkh-i Lakhna'u*, p. 116.

35. Ali, *Observations*, pp. 91, 156.

36. Nasirabadi, 'Najāt as-sā'ilīn', fol. 21b.

37. Ali, *Observations*, p. 76.

38. Fischer defines a paradigm as having three elements: (1) a story that could include every-day problems, history, and cosmology, (2) a background contrast (e.g., Sunnism), and (3) ritual, or physical drama; see Michael M.J. Fischer, *Iran: From Religious Dispute to Revolution* (Cambridge: Harvard University Press, 1980), pp. 13–27.

39. Harcharan Das, 'Chahār gulzār-i shujā'ī', British Lib., Or. 1732, foll. 254a–b; Isfahānī, *Tafḍīḥ al-ghāfilīn*, Hoey trans., p. 35.

40. The quote is from Roberts, *Scenes and Characteristics*, 2:178–9; see also Valentia, *Voyages and Travels*, 1:121.

41. Ali, *Observations*, p. 13.

42. Valentia, *Voyages and Travels*, 1:121.

43. Ali, *Observations*, pp. 19–21.

44. Syed Husain Ali Jaffri, 'Muharram Ceremonies in India', in Chelkowski, ed., *Ta'ziyeh*, pp. 222–3.

45. 'Abd al-Vahhab Qazwini, 'Siyāḥat-nāmah-'i mamālik-i Hindūstān', p. 220, Persian MS in the library of Professor Amin Banani, UCLA, Los Angeles.

46. Ali, *Observations*, p. 18; cf. Ja'far Sharīf, *Islam in India, or the Qānūn-i-Islām*, trans. G.A. Herklots (London: Oxford University Press, repr. 1921), p. 164.

47. Ibid., p. 27.

48. Muhammad Imam 'Ali Khan, *Āsār-i yādgār* (Lucknow: Taṣvīr-i 'Ālām Press, 1902), pp. 47–8.

49. 'Ali Hasan, 'Maḥmūdābād kī tārīkh', 5 vols., Urdu MS in the library of the Raja of Mahmudabad, Lucknow, 1:38–82; interview with the Maharajkumar of Mahmudabad, 17 June 1982, Lucknow.

50. Interview with the Raja of Nanpara, April 1982, Lucknow.

51. Ali, *Observations*, p. 20 note.

52. Roberts, *Scenes and Characteristics*, 2:181–2.

53. Ibid.

54. Ali, *Observations*, p. 21.

55. Ibid., p. 28.

56. For mourning sessions, see Mahmoud Ayoub, *Redemptive Suffering in Islam: A Study of Devotional Aspects of 'Ashura' in Twelver Shi'ism* (The Hague: Mouton, 1978), pp. 158ff.; Jean Calmard, 'Le Patronage des Ta'ziyeh: Elements pour une étude globale', in Chelkowski, ed., *Ta'ziyeh*, pp. 121–3, and Peter J. Chelkowski, 'Ta'ziyeh: Indigenous Avant-Garde Theatre of Iran', in ibid., pp. 3–4.

57. Ali, *Observations*, p. 22.

58. Muhammad Mihdi Lakhnawi Kashmiri, *Nujūm as-samā': takmilah*, 2 vols. (Qumm: Maktabat-i Baṣīratī, 1397/1977), 1:245.

59. Ali, *Observations*, p. 23; cf. Sharar, *Guzashta Lakhna'u*, p. 358, Eng. trans., p. 216.

60. Ali, *Observations*, p. 23; Roberts, *Scenes*, 2:192.

61. Sharar, *Guzashtah Lakhna'u*, pp. 211–17, trans., pp. 139, 147–50 and notes.

62. Nasirabadi, 'Najāt as-sā'ilīn', fol. 22a.

63. Ali, *Observations*, p. 23; Sharar, *Guzashtah Lakhna'u*, p. 105, Eng. trans., p. 86.

64. Ali, *Observations*, pp. 22–3.

65. Ibid., p. 30.

66. Musharraf 'Ali Lakhnawi, ed., *Bayāḍ-i masā'il*, 3 vols. (Lucknow: n.p., 1251/1835–36), 3:37.

67. Sharīf, *Qānūn-i-Islām*, Herklot trans., p. 159.

68. Ali, *Observations*, pp. 23–9, cf. Sharar, *Guzashtah Lakhna'u*, p. 289, Eng. trans., pp. 182–3.

69. Compare Elizabeth Warnock Fernea, *Guests of the Sheikh: An Ethnography of an Iraqi Village* (Garden City, NY: Doubleday Anchor Books, 1969), pp. 107–15, 196–7; and Robert Fernea and Elizabeth W. Fernea, 'Variation in Religious Observance among Islamic Women', in N.R. Keddie, ed., *Scholars, Saints and Sufis* (Berkeley and Los Angeles: Univ. of California Press, 1978), pp. 385–401.

70. Ali, *Observations*, p. 29.

71. For the significance of visitation to Karbala for Shi'is, see Ayoub, *Redemptive Suffering*, pp. 180–96.

72. Ali, *Observations*, pp. 17–18, 32, 57.

73. Ibid., pp. 36–8.

74. Ibid., pp. 34, 36.

75. Cf. Bayly, *Rulers, Townsmen and Bazaars*, ch. 4.

76. Ali, *Observations*, pp. 42–6.

77. Sharif, *Qānūn-i Islām*, Herklot trans., pp. 161, 166; for Muharram in Hyderabad, see Ghulam Husain, 'Khān-i Zamān', *Gulzār-i Āṣafiyyah* (Hyderabad: Saiyid Rustam 'Ali, 1260/1844), pp. 560ff.

78. See Samuel R. Peterson, 'The Ta'ziyeh and Related Arts', in Chelkowski, ed., *Ta'ziyeh*, pp. 67–8.

79. Ali, *Observations*, pp. 46–9.

80. Ibid., pp. 50–3; Roberts, *Scenes and Characteristics*, 2:194; Fanny Parkes, *Wanderings of a Pilgrim in Search of the Picturesque*, 2 vols. (London: Pelham Richardson, 1850), 1:298.

81. Ali, *Observations*, pp. 56–7.

82. Aqa Ahmad Bihbahani, 'Mir'at al-aḥwāl-i jahān-namā', Buhar Coll., Persian MS 96, fol. 194b, National Library, Calcutta.

83. Nasirabadi, 'Najāt as-sā'ilīn', fol. 25a.

84. Sharar, *Guzashtah Lakhna'u*, p. 359; Eng. trans., p. 216.

85. Nauganawi, *Tadhkirah*, p. 54.

86. Werner Ende, 'The Flagellations of Muḥarram and the Shi'ite 'Ulama', *Der Islam* 55 (1978): 19–36.

87. Tennant, *Recreations*, 1:218–19, 184; Roberts, *Scenes*, 2:180–1.

88. Musharraf 'Ali Lakhnai, ed., *Bayāḍ-i masā'il*, 3:13. Sharar, *Guzashtah Lakhna'u*, p. 360, Eng. trans., pp. 216–17 and note 539, says that in the late nineteenth century Maulawi Mihdi Husain introduced painted curtains into the mourning session. The women of his household even staged dramas similar to Iran's *ta'ziyahs*. But these late innovations, a fad, had no lasting effect in northern India. In the Urdu, Sharar blames the development of drama on the laxness of the Nasirabadis themselves, which for some reason does not appear in the English text.

89. For pre-industrial Hindu-Muslim cultural mediation and syncretism in Bengal, see Asim Roy, *The Islamic Syncretistic Tradition in Bengal* (Princeton: Princeton University Press, 1983), ch. 2.

90. Roberts, *Scenes*, 2:192–3; Sharif, *Qānūn*, trans. Herklots, p. 159.

91. For the twentieth-century development of Muharram in Lucknow, see Sarojini Ganju, "The Muslims of Lucknow 1919–1939', in Ballhatchet and Harrison, ed., *The City in South Asia*, p. 290; Imtiaz Ahmad, 'The Shia-Sunni Dispute in Lucknow, 1905–1980', in M. Israel and N.K. Wagle eds., *Islamic Society and Culture: Essays in Honor of Professor Aziz Ahmad* (Delhi: Manohar, 1984), pp. 335–50; Keith Hjortshoj, 'Kerbala in Context: A Study of Mohurram in Lucknow, India' (Ph.D. diss., Cornell University, 1977); Sandria Freitag, *Collective Action*, ch. 7.

92. Shushtari, 'Tuḥfatal-'ālam', foll. 199a–b.

93. Cf. K. Leonard, *The Social History of an Indian Caste: The Kayasths of Hyderabad* (Berkeley and Los Angeles: Univ. of California Press, 1978), pp. 81–2, 103–04; for Kayasthas in northern India, see W. Crooke, *The Tribes and Castes of the North-Western Provinces and Oudh*, 4 vols. (Calcutta: Office of the Sup't of the Government Printing, 1896), 3:184–216.

94. Roberts, *Scenes*, 2:186.

95. Parkes, *Wanderings*, 1:296.

96. Roberts, *Scenes*, 2:186; W.H. Sleeman, *A Journey through the Kingdom of Oude in 1849–1850*, 2 vols. (London: Richard Bentley, 1858), 1:276; Sharif, *Qānūn-i-Islām*, Herklots trans., pp 166–7.

97. M. Garcin de Tassy, *Mémoire sur des particularités de la religion musulmane dans l'Inde* (Paris: l'Imprimerie Royale, 1831), pp. 11–12, 30, 38–41.

98. Musharraf 'Ali Lakhnawi, ed., *Bayāḍ-i masā'il*, 3:97.

99. Victor Turner, *Process, Performance and Pilgrimage: A Study in Comparative Symbology* (New Delhi: Concept Publishing Company, 1979), ch. 4: 'Death and the Dead in the Pilgrimage Process', and *The Ritual Process: Structure and Anti-Structure* (Ithaca, N.Y.: Cornell Univ. Press, repr. 1977), pp. 94–130.

100. Marc Gaborieau, *Minorités musulmanes dans le royaume hindou de Nepal* (Nanterre: Laboratoire d'Ethnologie, 1977), pp. 121–2, 182–3.

101. Ibid., p. 121.

102. See, especially, Freitag, *Collective Action*.

PART FIVE

Islam in the Regions

A broad geo-cultural axis stretches along the spine of South Asia from Lahore to Delhi to Hyderabad, with extensions running from Delhi east to Patna and southwest to Ahmedabad. Forged by ancient trade and migration corridors, this axis had linked South Asia with the Iranian plateau for centuries before Muslim Turks appeared in India. But over the past millennium, cultural currents flowing along these corridors greatly accelerated, creating alongside them a set of related traits that have persisted down to the present: Persian or Persianized styles of architecture, music, art, technology, dress, and cuisine; and a history of the Persian language used for administrative purposes, followed by forms of spoken Urdu. It is hardly surprising that, in addition to these non-religious 'Persianate' cultural traits, Islamic traditions found along this axis also shared much in common.

In regions lying beyond these heavily used migration corridors, however, Persian influence left somewhat less of an imprint both on Islamic traditions and on local cultures generally. It is to these 'outlying' regions, and the Islamic traditions that evolved in them, that this volume's last section is addressed. We look first at pre-colonial Kashmir and eastern Bengal. Although these two areas ultimately emerged as Muslim-majority regions, neither one experienced substantial numbers of Persianized immigrants in the late medieval or early modern periods. In both, moreover, a cultural gulf separated Brahmans from indigenous peasant cultivators, or from groups consolidating themselves into a peasantry. As a result, Islamic traditions in these regions appear to have penetrated local societies by creatively building on and reshaping Sanskritic linguistic and religious cultures that were already 'on the ground', however thinly.

In the section's first essay, Mohammad Ishaq Khan rejects the notion that immigrant Sufis from Iran or Central Asia simply came to Kashmir and 'spread' Islam. Instead, he focuses on the role of indigenous ascetics—the Rishis—who assimilated Islamic ideas to their renunciatory way of life, and whose poetry and shrines found a way into the devotional lives of peasant cultivators. Facilitating this movement were class tensions between Brahmans and peasants that were expressed in the anti-Brahman poetry of the fourteenth-century Śaiva yogini, Lalla, whom later Kashmiri poets elevated to the status of the 'Second Rabi'a' (though there is no evidence that she was Muslim). Also facilitating the movement were the Islamic traditions established by poets like Shaikh Nur al-Din (d. 1442), who transformed the Rishi tradition into a Sufi order. Of special interest is this poet's lexical creativity, for Nur al-Din not only employed words in current use, but, notes Khan, 'he contrived them in such a way as to recast their definitions, with the purpose of anchoring Kashmiri society in the wider system of Islam.'

This is precisely the angle of approach followed by Tony Stewart in his analysis of Bengali Islamic traditions and their appearance in early modern eastern Bengal. Modern scholars tend to view certain genres of pre-modern Bengali literature as corruptions of 'properly' Islamic or Hindu traditions—or as containing a confused 'hodge-podge' of disparate elements—on the grounds that they fail to fit neatly into ideal, essentialized categories. But Stewart finds in these same literary traditions 'historical witnesses to the earliest attempts to think Islamic thoughts' in the Bengali language. Texts such as the sample he translates here are acts of 'cultural translation', he argues, inasmuch as their authors endeavoured to understand an entire conceptual world, and not just single terms or phrases, in terms of another such world, and to find equivalences between the two. Analysis of this sort of literature is therefore crucial for our understanding of how Islamic culture grew in areas that, like pre-modern Bengal, lay beyond South Asia's Persianized axis.

In our final essay, Vasudha Narayanan considers the case of Tamilnadu, whose indigenous Muslims trace their historical connections with Islam to that region's ancient maritime connections with Arabia, and not to north India. The essay explores how one of the oldest and most hallowed of Islamic literary genres, the biography of the Prophet, was conveyed to Tamil-speakers by the seventeenth-century poet, Umaru. Just as Ali Raja used the linguistic and religious universe of Bengal to sow Islamic ideas in that region's cultural universe, so also Umaru in his *Cīṛāppurāṇam* used local vocabulary, images, and literary conventions to 'translate' the life of the Arabian Prophet into a Tamil cultural universe. Among other things, the poet conflated Arabia's physical landscape with that of lush and tropical Tamilnadu, and the Prophet's Mecca with a classical Tamil city. The result was both to link Tamil Muslims with a wider Islamic world and to incorporate the Prophet and the Arab culture of his day into a specifically Tamil world. In a brief coda, Narayanan discusses the historical antecedents to recent developments respecting the collective identity of Tamil Muslims.

15

The Impact of Islam on Kashmir in the Sultanate Period (1320–1586)*

Mohammad Ishaq Khan

Some six centuries preceding the foundation of the Sultanate in Kashmir in 1320, a gradual process of peaceful penetration by Muslim traders and adventurers had already begun in the Valley. According to Kalhana, Vajraditya, the son and successor of Raja Lalitaditya (AD 724–61) 'sold many men to mlecchas, and introduced into the country practices which befitted the mlecchas.'[1] Harsha (1089–1101) is said to have recruited Turkish soldiers and even introduced, under Muslim influence, some refinements in dress and ornaments.[2] Again, in the reign of Bhiksacara (1120–1), Muslim soldiers were employed and deputed to attack Sussala in Lohara.[3] By the end of the thirteenth century, it would appear that there was a colony of Muslims in Kashmir.[4] This is evidenced by Marco Polo who writes that the inhabitants of the Valley did not kill animals; instead, they sought the services of the 'Saracens' who lived among them as butchers.[5]

Marco Polo evidently refers to the Turks (the 'Turuskas' of Kalhana),[6] whose services were sought by the rulers of Kashmir not merely as soldiers, but sometimes even as artists.[7] Thus Islam did not make its way into Kashmir by 'forcible conquest,' but, as Stein observes, 'by gradual conversion, for which the influx of foreign adventurers both from the South and from Central Asia had prepared the ground.'[8]

During the Sultanate period (1320–1586), a stream of immigrants from Central Asia and Persia seems to have flowed to the Valley, due to reasons varying according to time and place. To begin with, the establishment of the Muslim Sultanate caused a number of devout Sufis from these regions to emigrate to Kashmir along with their followers, principally for the

* Reprinted from *The Indian Economic and Social History Review* 23, no. 2 (1986), pp. 187–205.

purpose of spreading their faith in a society facing challenges of immense magnitude. Zulju's invasion[9] of Kashmir in 1320 and the ravages caused by the invaders for eight months;[10] the famine that stalked the Valley after the Mongol withdrawal;[11] Rinchana's conversion to Islam[12] along with his tribe[13] and his assumption of power as the first Muslim sultan of Kashmir;[14] the defeat of Kota Rani's forces at the hands of Shah Mir[15] and the latter's foundation of a new ruling dynasty[16]—all of these started a process which ultimately undermined the very bases of a caste-oriented social order, manifested, above all, in the bold protest of Lal Ded, a Śaiva mystic of the fourteenth century, against the supremacy of the Brahman priests and the social inequalities of her age.

Kashmir thus offered a fertile ground for the zealous Sufi missionaries like Saiyid Sharaf al-Din,[17] Mir Saiyid 'Ali Hamadani,[18] his son, Mir Saiyid Muhammad Hamadani,[19] and a number of their disciples to preach the doctrines of Islam.[20] Before embarking on his journey to Kashmir,[21] Mir Saiyid 'Ali deputed two of his cousins, Saiyid Taj al-Din and Saiyid Husain, to the Valley to explore the possibility of Islamizing its inhabitants.[22] It would appear that the subsequent missionary activities of Saiyid 'Ali, his son, and their followers in the Valley need to be studied not only in the context of their missionary zeal to spread the true message of Islam but also in the context of their deep concern for the enforcement of the Islamic law in a land where the norms of the sharī'a were violated by the new converts;[23] thus, their aim was not only to reconvert, but to consolidate the foothold already gained.

Not only saint missionaries, but artisans, too, seem to have come to Kashmir from Herat, Merv, Samarqand, and Bukhara. Notwithstanding the importance of these regions as hubs of a rich civilization, Kashmir offered to the artisans living there, as well as in the neighbouring areas, the prospect of improving their fortunes. Indeed, they found a sympathetic patron of their talents and skills in Sultan Zain al-'Abidin (1420–70), who is famous not only for introducing new arts in the Valley, but also for bringing about the revival of such ancient crafts of Kashmir that had either disappeared or declined. Thus, Mirza Haidar, who ruled Kashmir during the decade 1540–50, writes:

> In Kạshmir one meets with all those arts and crafts which are, in most cities, uncommon. In the whole of Mawara al-nahr, except Samarqand and Bukhara, these are nowhere to be met with, while in Kashmir they are abundant. This is all due to Sultan Zain al-'Abidin.[24]

The excellence of Kashmiri crafts, which evoked the admiration of a keen observer like the Mirza (who possessed first-hand knowledge of

Central Asian society), shows that the skill of the Kashmiri craftsmen must have improved not merely because of royal patronage, but also because the artisans learnt new techniques consequent to their interaction with the immigrants.[25] We know, for example, that Zain al-'Abidin sent two craftsmen to Samarqand at government expense to receive training in the art of paper-making[26] and book-binding, who, after their return home, imparted the knowledge of their skill to the Kashmiris.[27] But it would also be necessary to know how, besides paper-making and book-binding, arts—such as wood-carving, gold and silver leaf-making, *papier-mâché*, shawl and carpet-weaving, etc.—became so popular as to elicit the unqualified praise of all foreign observers in subsequent periods of Kashmiri history.[28] Interestingly enough, whenever Zain al-'Abidin learnt of the arrival of an artist from Iraq, Khurasan, or Turkistan in his kingdom, he would induce him to impart the technical aspects of his craft to Kashmiri artisans. Sometimes, the sultan would even go to the extent of not granting the craftsman permission to leave the Valley until he had fully trained the local talent.[29] Srivara writes of the various amenities provided by the sultan to craftsmen so that they would settle in Kashmir. As a contemporary Sanskrit chronicler exclaims: 'Who did not seek to please the monarch, and what artists, possessed of great designs in art, did not come from distant countries like bees, to the monarch who was almost like the Kalpa tree?'[30]

Timur's conquests in Central Asia and Persia seem to have caused many to flee to the comparative safety of the lands beyond the Indus, while others may have been attracted by the accounts of travellers and compatriots of the Valley.[31] Not least of all, as a result of the patronage extended to men of letters by Sultan Sikandar (1398–1413), as also by his illustrious son Zain al-'Abidin, Kashmir undoubtedly became an El Dorado for them. Among the notable men who settled in the Valley during Sikandar's reign were Saiyid Hasan Shirazi, who was made Qazi of Kashmir by virtue of his past experience as Qazi in Shiraz, Saiyid Jalal al-Din, a Sufi from Bukhara who came along with his disciples, Baba Haji Adham and his student Baba Hasan, the logician from Balkh, Saiyid Muhammad from Khwarazm, and Saiyid Ahmed, a prolific writer from Isfahan.[32] Further, the emigration of scholars like Saiyid Muhammad Rumi, Saiyid Ahmad Rumi, Qazi Saiyid 'Ali Shirazi, Saiyid Muhammad Luristani, and Saiyid Muhammad Sistani[33] to Kashmir in the reign of Zain al-'Abidin, are further examples worth quoting to illustrate how Kashmir became a magnet, attracting even those foreigners who were well-settled in their ancestral lands.

Finally, a persistent flow of foreigners to Kashmir seems also to have been maintained by such politically ambitious groups as the Baihaqi

Saiyids, who dabbled in the political affairs of the sultanate.[34] They came to Kashmir during the reign of Sultan Sikandar and soon entered into matrimonial alliances with the royal family.[35]

In view of the foregoing discussion, it is no surprise that our Sanskrit and Persian sources are rich in information regarding the influx of foreigners into Kashmir. The 'Yavanas' or foreigners of Jonaraja[36] comprised not only the 'ulama, *fuḍalā*, and *quḍāt* (who have been described as Saiyids[37] or *sādāt* in Persian chronicles), but also men of other professions. In fact, the chroniclers seem to have used the title Saiyid as a generic name for all foreigners from Iraq, Madina, Khurasan, Mawara al-nahr, Khwarazm, Balkh, and Ghazna, among other places.[38]

The early Muslim immigrants in the Valley exercised considerable influence on the social and cultural life of the local inhabitants of Kashmir, who were mostly Hindus and Buddhists. 'As the wind destroys the trees, and locusts the *shali* crop, so did the Yavanas destroy the usages of Kashmira'[39] writes the conservative Brahman chronicler Jonaraja, adding that 'the kingdom of Kashmira was polluted by the evil practices of the mleccha'.[40] Similarly, Pandit Srivara looked askance at the abolition of existent practices and their replacement by new ones, and even attributes the misfortunes of the Kashmiris of his days to the changes in the manners and customs that set in after the establishment of the Muslim Sultanate.[41] But, in spite of these fulminations, Kashmiri society, exposed as it was to foreign ideas and practices, began to assimilate them with the passage of time. Thus Srivara writes about the adoption of Muslim manners and dress, and the consumption of beef by Hindus under the influence of immigrant settlers.[42] He also looks with disgust at Hindus adopting 'unholy practices', and at their growing laxity in the performance of prescribed ceremonies, on account of the intrusion of Islamic ideas.[43]

The denunciations and protests of these two Brahman chroniclers of the Sultanate should not be brushed aside as mere conservatism on their part. In fact, their writings reveal the innermost tensions felt by the caste-conscious group of Brahmans and their reaction to the onslaught of alien forces. In other words, the grave concern for the preservation of Brahman identity becomes a dominant note in the Sanskrit historiography of the early medieval period in Kashmir. How the community of Brahmans succeeded in maintaining its identity is a question worthy of consideration, but would lead us beyond the scope of the present essay.[44] It is enough to say that in order to find a place in the new social and administrative set-up, the Brahmans adapted themselves to the study of Persian[45] and sought work as officials, translators, and clerks in the government.[46] As time went on, the Kashmiri Pandits, as the Brahmans came to be known later, began once again to arrogate to themselves a higher position in the social order. This sense of exalted status was manifested, for example, in the Pandit's contempt for manual labour, which continued into more recent times.[47]

Two factors proved to be essential instruments of social transition. In the first place, the spread of Islamic teachings and the resultant spirit of revolt manifested by Lalla,[48] a Hindu yogini, against the social and spiritual pretensions of the Brahmans, set in motion new forces, rejecting the latter's cherished idea that social status was determined by caste.[49] An important development in this direction was the revival of the ascetic, but nonetheless humanistic, traditions and practices of the ancient Rishis of Kashmir. The value system of humanism, as advocated by Shaikh Nur al-Din (d. 1442), the founder of the Rishi order of Sufis in Kashmir, implied not merely other– but also this-worldliness,[50] co-existence with men of other religions and culture,[51] and a deep commitment to the sanctity of human life and its artistic manifestation on earth.[52] Like Lalla, Nur al-Din criticized forms of social behaviour that led to the exploitation and suffering of other human beings.[53] An important consequence of the philosophy propounded by these two great sages of medieval Kashmir was the flowering of the idea of the dignity and the fundamental equality of man, so trenchantly espoused in their teachings. No wonder, therefore, that the caste-ridden 'Hindu' society was rent asunder. In the changed situation, the status of the Brahman was not dependent on the notion of his superior birth, but on skill, hard work, and ingenuity. This explains the fact that now he had no other alternative but to regard employment with the state as the sole catalyst of upward mobility and improvement.

Thus, the pursuit of secular occupations by the Brahmans produced a more mobile and less rigidly stratified society, as well as a new social order in which the distinctions of the old world gave way to a unified class of Kashmiri Hindus, who, by means hitherto unknown or unthought of, raised themselves to comparative affluence and independence.[54] This led, in turn, to the formation of certain sub-divisions amongst the Brahmans themselves. Those Pandits who took to the study of scriptures and the performance of priestly duties were named the *bhasha bhatta* or, more simply, the *gur*. The Pandits who continued to study the scriptures but gave up priestly duties came to be known as the *jotishis*. A vast majority of the Pandits who followed secular occupations were designated as *kār-kuns*. In fact, the kār-kuns formed the main prop of various ruling dynasties in Kashmir throughout the course of its history, till the emergence of national consciousness in the 1930s.[55]

The intrusion of the Muslim immigrants proved to be an important factor in social transition, given that it brought fresh ideas, a new language, and particularly a new religion into Kashmir. It is important to note, however, that Islam did not spread in Kashmir simply as a result of the missionary activities of the Sufis from Central Asia and Persia.[56] Our refutation of the popular view is based on the fact that the pious missionaries and a host of their disciples, who are credited with having converted thousands of people to Islam, were actually separated from the people by the barriers of language. During the Sultanate period, Persian was introduced as the official language for the first time, during the reign of Sultan Zain al-'Abidin.[57] Prior to this, Sanskrit had continued to be the court language, for nearly a century after the foundation of the Sultanate. It is extremely doubtful whether Persian was, in fact, the lingua franca of the people of Kashmir in the fourteenth century, when proselytization is said to have taken place on a large scale. This is borne out not only by the Sanskrit inscriptions on the tomb-stones belonging to the Sultanate period,[58] but also by Lalla's popular verses in Sanskritized Kashmiri, which nowhere bear the influence of Persian.[59] For that matter, even Shaikh Nur al-Din's early verses are Sanskritized, though at a later stage of his life Persian and Arabic influences become evident.

It is, in fact, open to question whether the more intellectual version of Islam, when propounded by a Sufi scholar like Saiyid 'Ali Hamadani, could have been understood by the common man. What needs to be explained, then, is how an essentially esoteric mystical tradition of the Sufis from Central Asia and Persia filtered down to the masses in an appealing and comprehensible form.

In this essay, I have studied the history of Islam in Kashmir from a new angle.[60] The crux of our argument is that the 'Islamization'[61] of Kashmir never took place in a strictly religious sense during the period under discussion. As a matter of fact, the 'Little Tradition'[62] of the masses continued to be challenged by the 'orthodoxy' now as before. Our use of the term 'Islamization' in the context of medieval Kashmir has a social rather than a theological content; it is thus a development taking place *within* a particular social order which was, to use the phraseology of Alfred Weber, caught 'in the unified movement of a general and gradual progress'.[63] In European religious history, such a development was closely associated with conditions of social conflict and protest; so too the 'Islamization' in Kashmir was grounded in some major changes in social structure, and expressed in opposition to the decadent Brahmanic order, its agents, and its doctrines. This study, therefore, mainly focuses on the social roles of two prominent indigenous mystics—Lalla and Nur al-Din—rather than on the glorified activities of the Sufis from Persia and Central Asia, who stood for the strict enforcement of Islamic law in

Kashmir.[64] Notwithstanding the mystical dimensions of their speculative philosophy, Lalla Ded and Shaikh Nur al-Din Rishi appear to us as the outspoken representatives of peasant society. Given the rural character of the movement, I have approached the subject from the standpoint suggested by Robert Redfield. A brief summary of his views would suffice here to make the discussion meaningful.

Redfield's central assumption is that the culture of a peasant society is not autonomous, but an aspect or dimension of a civilization of which it is a part. Since a peasant society is a half-society, peasant culture is a half-culture. It can be fully understood only in relation to the civilization in which it is contained. In order to make intelligible the compound nature of peasant culture, Redfield introduces two important concepts—the Great Tradition and the Little Tradition. In any civilization there is a Great Tradition of the reflective few, and a Little Tradition of the unreflective many. The societal dimensions of these two traditions are the great community and little community. Thus the Great Tradition is the culture of the great community of priests, theologians, and literary men who may not even have seen the village. These two traditions are not mutually exclusive, but interdependent, two currents of thought and action, distinguishable, yet even flowing into and out of each other. Thus Redfield assumes that any peasant culture is compounded of empirically and conceptually separable Great and Little Traditions.[65]

Viewed in the context of Redfield's definition, the Little Tradition of Kashmiri peasant society seems to have linked itself with the Great Tradition of Islam through Lalla and Nur al-Din, who established channels of communication between the two traditions and set up standards of mutual reference and influence. It is important to remember that the orthodox Sufis from Central Asia and Persia, who had come to develop the Great Tradition in Kashmir, found it, in the course of time, represented by the Rishis, who carried forward elements of an indigenous culture into a much higher level of intellectual and speculative thought. Such a development was not liked by them from the orthodox point of view.[66] It is beyond the scope of this essay to dwell on these attitudes; here we shall confine our study to the significance of the roles of Lalla and Nur al-Din, whose verses of 'dissent' and 'protest' gradually created a sense of awareness in the common man against social and religious discrimination.

Although Lalla's mystical verses are marked by the denunciation of the exploitative nature of the Brahmans, the Sanskrit chroniclers[67] of the Sultanate period have maintained an intriguing silence about her. Birbal Kachru,[68] who completed his narrative in the Sikh period (1819–46), was the first Pandit chronicler to refer to her. One clear inference to be drawn from the silence of the *ahl-i qalam* ('men of the pen')[69] regarding Lalla is that she must have been considered a renegade by high caste Brahmans. This explains why Lalla's greatest eulogists have been Muslim hagiographers[70] and Persian chroniclers,[71] so much so that she has been called Rabi'a Thani[72] the Second Rabi'a. She was, according to Baba Da'ud Mishkati, a *majnūn-i 'aqīla*, absorbed in the love of God, but wise and sage.[73] It seems that Lalla proved to be a greater force than the Sufi missionaries in converting the bulk of Hindus in Kashmir to the monotheistic faith of Islam. Lalla did not preach Islam, but her *vaakh*,[74] which was not in conflict with the ontological teachings of the Sufis,[75] served the cause of Islam in Kashmir. While Saiyid 'Ali Hamadani's works[76] dealt more exclusively with mysticism proper and were generally intended for use by the author's fellow Sufis, Lalla, on the other hand, propagated the fundamental Sufi idea of divine unity in simple language, which had a deep and direct appeal to the common man. For her, true devotion did not imply various rituals and practices evolved by the Brahmans, but it meant seeking God within oneself, and also in the routine of daily life:

Śiva abides in all that is, everywhere;
Then do not discriminate between a Hindu and a Musalman.
If thou art wise, know thyself;
That is true knowledge of the Lord.[77]

Lalla's approach to religion, based on mysticism, was fundamentally humanistic and individualistic. By rejecting formal and organized religion, which was based on the supreme authority of the Brahman, she helped the common man accept the Sufi ideas of equality and the brotherhood of man:

I renounced fraud, untruth, deceit;
I taught my mind to see the One in all my fellow-men,
How [can] I then discriminate between man and man,
And not accept the food offered to me by brother man.[78]

The worship of idols was vehemently criticized by Lalla:

The idol is but stone,
The temple is but stone,
From top to bottom, all is stone.[79]

It is significant that Lalla was well aware of the success of her role in contemporary society:

Whatever I uttered with my tongue,
became a mantra.[80]

The oral value of Lalla's verses and their profound impact on Kashmiri society is amply illustrated by the fact that the founder of the Rishi order of the Sufis in Kashmir, though a devout Muslim, accepted Lalla as his spiritual preceptor. Thus, Shaikh Nur al-Din remarks:

That Lalla of Padmanpore[81]
Who had drunk the fill of divine nectar,
She was undoubtedly an avatar of ours.
O God, grant me the same spiritual power.[82]

Little wonder, therefore, that Islam (as represented by the Rishis of Kashmir) bears the dominant influence of Lalla.[83] The latter's poetry became a major vehicle for influencing the illiterate masses (particularly in rural society), who have had and still have an incredibly retentive memory for verse. It is of some significance that it was the Rishis, above all, who preserved the heritage of Lalla. Unfortunately, most modern writers on Shaikh Nur al-Din[84] have been at pains to emphasize interpolation in his poetry, without really understanding the context in which the verses of Lalla and Nur al-Din are similar. In fact, the language that the shaikh spoke was not an individual inheritance, but a social acquisition from the environment in which he grew up. Lalla's and Nur al-Din's poetry came to be the daily bread of many Kashmiris of the period, who formed their *Weltanschauung* in accordance with the picture presented to them by their two spiritual teachers. The importance of mystic poetry and literature to an average Kashmiri is evident even today to an observer of contemporary society in the Valley.

Some important questions are bound to arise when we consider the evidence regarding the elevation of Lalla to Rabi'a, 'Arifa, Maryam-i-Makani, etc., in mystic literature. Did she accept Islam? What was Lalla's position in her contemporary society?

Though it is not possible to examine these questions in great detail here, it may be pointed out that Lalla was disowned not only in her own times, but for a greater part of Kashmiri history, by the Hindu elite on account of her hostility to the Brahman creed, and that the admirable attempts of some Pandit scholars in recent times to resuscitate Lalla are, therefore, paradoxical.[85] True, Lalla's poetry nowhere gives any proof of her having embraced Islam, but the evidence of some later sources regarding her close association with Saiyid Husain Simnani[86] should not be simply dismissed as a figment of the imagination of medieval writers. This evidence suggests that Lalla did not live in a historical vacuum, isolated from the lower strata of society of the time and, more importantly, from the succeeding generations of her people.[87] It is reasonable to assume that the focal point of her supposed meeting with the Sufis, and the living tradition of calling her Lal Ded, Lal Mouj (Lalla, the Mother) by Kashmiri Muslims, particularly by the rural folk, must contain a kernel of truth about her association with Islam. In any case, such evidence indicates the important place occupied by Lalla in the lives of various strata of the Kashmiri people, as well as her role in the formation of a regional culture. Such a culture drew its essential vitality from a conflict, a division, a torment, and struggle created in the individual psyche by the challenges posed to the social order by Lalla and the Sufi missionaries.

In view of the foregoing discussion, it would also be wrong to assume that the process of 'Islamization' in Kashmir is solely attributable to the arrival of Saiyid 'Ali Hamadani[88] and his disciples in Kashmir. The fact is that even after their 'conversion' to Islam, the converts did not part with their old habits and customs, nor do they seem to have totally severed connections with their relatives. It would be more reasonable to suggest that the close contact of the new converts with their kith and kin must have accelerated the process of acculturation.[89] What is of significance is that even after their 'conversion' to Islam, Muslims would visit temples every morning.[90] There is a reference to Muslims' worshipping idols even during the time of Baba Da'ud Khaki (1521–85).[91] It is also of interest to note that Sultan Qutb al-Din once performed a Hindu *yagna* and distributed large gifts among the Brahmans.[92] Some other ancient festivals of the Hindus also continued to be observed by the Muslims in the Sultanate period.[93]

The foregoing argument implies that the ongoing process of Islamic acculturation, which is testified to by various Persian sources, should not be regarded as 'conversion' to Islam in the strict sense of the word. True, pious missionaries (like Saiyid 'Ali Hamadani and Saiyid Mir Muhammad Hamadani) exercised considerable influence in the city of Srinagar and a few towns, but even they did not remain oblivious to their limited success in converting the masses to Islam. It has escaped the notice of historians that Saiyid 'Ali Hamadani was aware of the fact that it was beyond the people of his time to grasp the message of Islam as contained in his works. That he was also conscious of the partial success of his mission is attested to by his prophetic remarks that his worth would be recognized by the seekers of truth only a hundred years after his death.[94]

It is remarkable that only a few years after the death of Saiyid 'Ali Hamadani, the upholders of his mission became the Rishis of Kashmir. Saiyid 'Ali's son, Mir Saiyid Muhammad Hamadani, who came to Kashmir in the reign of Sultan Sikandar, showered praise on Nur al-Din Rishi Kashmiri (as he calls him) for his piety, spirituality, abstinence, and other mystical attainments.[95] While Mir Saiyid 'Ali and Mir Saiyid Muhammad left Kashmir for good after doing a good deal of missionary work, it was mainly through a variety of mystical songs (composed by Shaikh Nur al-Din) that commoners were introduced to Islam in Kashmir. The Shaikh made no conscious effort to convert people to Islam but, even so, was able to bring some prominent non-Muslims within the fold.[96] What is worth noting is that it was the Rishi ascetics, and not the 'ulama or even the learned Sufis, who became the model of holiness for the rural masses. True, Nur al-Din, at a later stage in his life, laid emphasis on following the path of Muhammad (*Sunna*), but it cannot be denied that the extreme asceticism of a large number of his disciples, who were spread in every nook and corner of the Valley, added a new dimension to the historical development of Islam in Kashmir.

It is certain that the followers of Shaikh Nur al-Din, as also the Rishis of the later period, were more influenced by the early life of their spiritual master, which was marked by extreme ascetism, self-mortification, long fasts, sexual abstinence, and seclusion.[97] It is significant that prominent disciples of Nur al-Din chose the top of mountains and other such places located in awesome sites of nature, connected with the traditional science of sacred geography, as their abode of worship. There were hardly any rural areas without a site of pilgrimage and a Rishi saint to whom the people did not turn to in their moments of trial and thankfulness.[98] Even springs became the object of veneration as a result of their association with the Rishi saints.[99] In fact, the folk literature of the Rishis is replete with examples of the saints' belief in the sacredness of springs. Consequently, the contrast in the common mind between Islam and Hinduism or Buddhism weakened, thereby paving the way for the acceptance of the values of an alien system. This process of Islamic acculturation of the mass of Kashmiri people also seems to have been accelerated by other factors, which we shall now elaborate.

First, Nur al-Din seems to have visited almost every part of the Valley to spread his message of divine love and human brotherhood in the popular dialect.[100] There are a number of villages[101] in Kashmir that still preserve the tradition of his visit or sojourn[102] in one form or the other. It was, indeed, easier for the common man to understand the esoteric spirit of Islam—submission, dependence on God, obedience, contemplation, repentance, endeavour, dedication, altruism, and a fulfilment of the duties of fellowship[103]—through Nur al-Din's popular mystical verses, than through the scholarly works of the Sufi missionaries. The scholarly version of Islam, given in the Persian language by a Sufi at a gathering, was beyond the ken of the common man with his average intelligence. It seems that the poverty and humility of the Rishis and, by all accounts, their very presence had a magnetic influence[104] that was far more important than the mere knowledge of the 'ulama or the learned Sufis. They made the presence of the divinity become more perceptible and closer to the poor. No less an observer than Abu'l-fazl writes of the 2,000-odd Rishis of his time in glowing terms:

> .... the most respectable class in this country (Kashmir) is that of the Rishis who, notwithstanding their need of freedom from the bonds of tradition and custom, are the true worshippers of God. They do not loose the tongue of calumny against those not of their faith, nor beg, nor importune. They employ themselves in planting trees, and are generally a source of benefit to the people.[105]

Baba Nasib,[106] a seventeenth-century hagiographer, sums up the impact of the Rishi movement in a long poem. A few lines are worth quoting here:

Roshanā-i sham'-i dīn az Rīshīān ast
Rahnamā-i rāh-i-yaqīn az Rīshīān ast
Dilnawāz-i mardum-i ahl-i niyāz
Az ṣafā-i bāṭin-i dil-i Rīshīān ast
Khūsh sarāy khuld-i īn Kashmīr-rā
Khūsh rawāj az daulat-i īn Rīshīān ast
Nūr afshān chūn iram az har ṭaraf
Gushā-i har āstān Rīshīān ast

The candle of religion is lit by the Rishis;
They are the pioneers of the path of belief.
The heart-warming quality of humble souls
Emanates from the inner purity of hearts of the Rishis.
This vale of Kashmir that you call a paradise
Owes a lot of its charm to the traditions set in vogue by the Rishis.

Secondly, the social behaviour of the Rishis was more in consonance with the local practices than those of scholars, jurists, or Sufi missionaries. They did not marry, abstained from eating meat, and subsisted on dry bread or wild vegetables from the forest. When Mir Muhammad Hamadani asked about the reason for not eating meat, Shaikh Nur al-Din retorted that his religion did not permit killing since it was against cruelty.[107] There is evidence to show that some Rishis would occasionally eat ashes as a substitute for food. Such a practice was not favourably viewed by Da'ud Mishakati, though himself a Rishi, from the 'orthodoxy' point of view.[108] It is also important to note that some of the Rishis dressed like yogis.[109] We would, therefore, be justified in assuming that the pious missionaries from Central Asia and Persia provided only a belief structure, which was respected and accommodated within the broad framework of their traditional religious concepts by the Hindus and Buddhists of Kashmir.

Last, but not least, the process of Islamic acculturation was accelerated not only by Nur al-Din's use of rich vocabulary from the Qur'an but, more significantly, from the traditional sources of the Hindus—the *Vedas* and the *Upanishads*.[110] In his songs, the Shaikh introduced and used many words in current use; however, he contrived them in such a way as to recast their definitions, with the purpose of anchoring Kashmiri society in the wider system of Islam. His effort was, indeed, in the spirit of apologetics, but the fact remains that the variety of his songs, drawing inspiration from the local milieu, led to the growth of syncretic ideas in the Islam of Kashmir. That Nur al-Din wielded greater influence than the Sufis from Persia and Central Asia is shown by the fact that Rishi folk literature remained in many ways the most significant medium of instruction in the values of Kashmiri society; it has had a deeper impact than mosques, *madrasas*, and *maktabs*, where formal teaching was carried on. The reason why Kashmir has always had weak foundations in theology may be explained mainly in terms of the popularity of the mystic poetry of Nur al-Din among the rural masses.[111] In fact, the indelible influence of Nur al-Din on village life is shown by the fact that as late as the close of the nineteenth century, 'every cultivator in Kashmir set apart a small share of his rice crop as an offering to his shrine at Chrar-i-Shariff'.[112]

It follows that Kashmiri Muslim society, as it emerged in the Sultanate and subsequent periods of history, bears the deep imprint of the Rishi movement. The shrines of the Rishis were and still are pilgrimage centres for a great majority of the people in the Valley. Vegetarianism, which continues to be practised on the eve of anniversaries ('urs) of Rishi saints, is typical of how Kashmiri Muslims have been incorporating many old rituals and traditions into orthodox religious practices. Festivals of village saints have no orthodox sanction, but villagers choose between various classical meanings for their festivals. Even the most Islamic of the local festivals have obviously taken on elements of ritual that arose not out of the Great Tradition but out of local peasant life.[113] Thus, the practice of distributing cooked rice coloured with turmeric (*tahar*)[114] as a thanksgiving to God or a saint, or to avoid an apprehended calamity, still exists among a considerable proportion of the Muslim population in the Valley. This practice is undoubtedly of very ancient origin, since it is also common among the Kashmiri Pandits. Other examples are the ceremonies performed before planting and harvesting rice, to ensure a rich yield. Paradoxically, the sacrifice of an animal, preferably a sheep, is vowed at the shrines of Nur al-Din, Baba Rishi, and some other prominent Rishi shrines for the fulfilment of a wish. There are many more examples that illustrate the absorption and assimilation of a number of local traditions by Islam in Kashmir. Among the rituals that have inspired ecstasy to the highest degree are sincere supplications that are recited loudly with folded hands[115] before and after congregational prayers; this despite the scathing criticism of the *ahl-i ḥadīth*.[116]

The distinctive features of Islam in Kashmir, as summarized in the foregoing, can become still more intelligible when viewed against the background of the emergence of the concept of a regional identity and consciousness, characterizing the Sultanate period in Kashmir.[117] Islam did not totally destroy ancient Kashmiri culture, but steered it out of the narrow waters of Brahmanism into the broad sea of humanism. Consequently, some of the essential ingredients of the culture of the ancient Rishis were revitalized and made meaningful and creative in the new environment. The Rishi movement ushered in a period of cultural renaissance in the valley. The vast bulk of Rishi literature and the profound influence of their philosophy on the Kashmiri mind bear witness to this fact.

The rapid success of the Rishi movement also suggests that the decadent Brahmanic order had failed to create sufficiently strong institutions based on a sound religious philosophy, which could have worked as an effective bulwark against the forces of Islamic acculturation. Thus, the Rishi movement was, in the ultimate analysis, the culmination of mounting disagreement, disaffection, tension, and conflict, generated in the course of time by a particular social order itself. It should be remembered, however, that the movement, while disrupting an existing social order, still resulted in a society more securely (though differently) integrated. In other words, looked at from a sufficiently long historical perspective, the Rishis had the function of reintegrating society by crystallizing, symbolizing, and reinforcing common values and norms.[118]

In conclusion, then, despite the emergence of the distinct ideologies and identities of the Kashmiri Muslims and Kashmiri Pandits in the Sultanate period, the Kashmir region proved to be the historical locus of the genesis and development of a unique form of society, in response to a particular set of circumstances, consequent to the advent of Islam in the Valley. The creation of a new society was perceived to be distinctly Kashmiri, by both contemporary and later observers, which the modern historian might explain in terms of Frederick Jackson Turner's thesis that a 'region' is not merely a geographical expression, but rather, the arena of a unique social experiment.[119] The ethos of the Kashmiri region is best reflected in the folk literature of the Rishis, which represents an important aspect of Islamic civilization in a distinct regional setting, a shared community of meanings that define the central values of the people of Kashmir and constitute the governing spirit of their culture. The following verses, attributed to both Lalla Ded and Shaikh Nur al-Din, are worth quoting in this context:

We are the progeny of the same parents,
Then why should we differ.
Let Hindus and Muslims (together) adore God alone.[120]
We came to this world like partners,
We ought to share our joys and sorrows together.[121]

NOTES

Author's note: The manuscripts and publications of the Research and Publication Department, Jammu and Kashmir government, and those of the Cultural Academy, Srinagar, have been abbreviated as R.P.D. and C.A.P. respectively. Further, Kalhana's and Jonaraja's *Rajatarangini* are cited, one edited by Aurel Stein and the other by J.C. Dutt. These are referred to as *Rajatarangini* (Stein) & *Rajatarangini* (Dutt), respectively.

1. Kalhana, *Rajatarangini*, English trans. by Aurel Stein, repr. (Delhi, 1979), Book 4, No. 379.
2. Ibid., Book 7, No. 1149; ibid., Book 1, Introduction, p. 112.
3. Ibid., Book 8, Nos. 885–6.
4. In all probability, the earliest Muslim settlers in Kashmir must have inhabited the present locality of Malchmar which, undoubtedly, is one of the oldest sites in the city of Srinagar. While 'malch' is a derivative of *mleccha*, the term is used for foreigners in olden times. 'Mar' denotes 'place' in Kashmiri. While writing about the importance of the study of English place-names, A.L. Rowse very rightly observes: 'So much of the documentation of our early history has perished: the place-names themselves are the most reliable documents that remain.' See Rowse, *The Use of History* (London, 1963), p. 188
5. *The Travels of Marco Polo*, ed. and trans. by Ronald Lathan (Penguin Books, 1958), p. 79.
6. See *Rajatarangini* (Stein), Book 7, No. 1149; Book 8, Nos. 885, 886, 919, 923.
7. When King Kalasa (1063–89) 'wished to put a gilt parasol over the Kalasesa [temple of Śiva], there came to him an artist from the Turuska country', Ibid., Book 7, No. 528.
8. Ibid., Book 1, p. 130.
9. For details of the Mongol chief's invasion, see Mohibbul Hasan, *Kashmir under the Sultans*, 2nd edn. (Srinagar, 1974), pp. 34–6.
10. Ibid., p. 35.
11. Ibid., p. 36.
12. Rinchana was the son of a Ladakhi chief, Lha-chen-dnyos-grub (Lhachen dNgos-grub), who ruled Ladakh from 1290 to 1320. The unfavourable political

circumstances prevailing in Ladakh following his father's death drove him to Kashmir along with his followers. The political instability in the Valley, caused by the Mongol invasion, afforded him an opportunity to occupy the throne of Kashmir by the end of 1320. His rise to power and subsequent conversion to Islam at the hands of Saiyid Sharaf al-Din, a Sufi of the Suhrawardi order, must have caused a good deal of concern to the Brahman priests. It is probably for this reason that Jonaraja remarks that Rinchana wanted to become a Śaiva, but that the Brahman Devasavmi refused to initiate him into Hinduism. *Rajatarangini*, English trans. by J.C. Dutt (Calcutta, 1835), p. 21.

13. After Rinchana, his brother-in-law, Ramacandra, also accepted Islam. Although sources are silent about the fate of his devoted Ladakhi followers, it is not unlikely that they too, like Ramacandra, followed the example of their chief. It was partly due to their support that Rinchana was able to rule, though not without trouble, for a brief period of about three years.

14. Mohibbul Hasan, *Kashmir*, p. 36.

15. Ibid., p. 44.

16. Shah Mir ascended the throne under the title of Sultan Shams al-Din in 1339. His dynasty ruled Kashmir for over two hundred years.

17. Saiyid Sharaf al-Din, popularly known as Bulbul Shah, was probably the first Sufi to visit Kashmir in the reign of Suhadeva (1301–20). He came from Turkistan and was a disciple of Shah Ni'mat Allah Farsi, who belonged to the Suhrawardi order. See Mohibbul Hasan, *Kashmir*, p. 235.

18. Popularly known as Shah-i-Hamadan in Kashmir, he came to the Valley in the reign of Sultan Qutb al-Din (1373–89) from Persia. Ibid.

19. Mir Saiyid Muhammad Hamadani is reported to have made a number of converts to Islam in the reign of Sultan Sikandar (1389–1413). R.K. Parmu, *A History of Muslim Rule in Kashmir* (Delhi, 1969), p. 118.

20. A.Q. Rafiqi, *Sufism in Kashmir* (Delhi, n.d.), p. 34.

21. Saiyid 'Ali, it is said, considered travel to be the best education. See 'Abd al-Wahab, *Fathat-i-Kubrawiyya*, R.P.D. No. 17, f. 155.

22. Ibid. f. 69b; Saiyid 'Ali, *Tarikh-i-Kashmir*, R.P.D. No. 739, f. la; Muhammad A'zam Didamari, *Tarikh-i-Azami* (ed., Lahore, 1885–6), pp. 35, 38.

23. See, for instance, *Rajatarangini* (Dutt), p. 53; Saiyid 'Ali, *Tarikh*, f. 25; *Fathat-i-Kubrawiyya*, f. 147a.

24. *Tarikh-i-Rashidi*, trans. by E.D. Ross (London, 1895), p. 34.

25. According to Mohibbul Hasan, the weaver's brush and loom were probably introduced for the first time into Kashmir during Zain al-'Abidin's reign. See Mohibbul Hasan, *Kashmir*, p. 92.

26. For the history of paper-making in Kashmir, see M. Ishaq Khan, *History of Srinagar, 1846–1947, A Study in Socio-Cultural Change* (Srinagar, 1978), pp. 70–2.

27. *Baharistan-i-Shahi* (anonymous) R.P.D. No. 691: f. 47a-b; Hasan bin Ali, *Tarikh-i-Hasan*, Bodleian Library, Oxford, MS 315, Microfilm in R.P.D., f. 120a; Haidar Malik Chadura, *Tarikh-i-Kashmir*, R.P.D. No. 27, f. 120a.

28. M. Ishaq Khan, *History*, 1978, pp. 44, 47, 48, 55, 70–2.

29. *Baharistan-i-Shahi*, f. 47a; Hasan bin Ali, *Tarikh-i-Hasan*, f. 120; Haidar Malik, *Tarikh-i-Kashmir*, f. 120a.

30. Srivara, *Jaina-Rajatarangini*, trans. by J.C. Dutt (Calcutta, 1835), p. 151.

31. For the earliest Arab notices of Kashmir, see S.M. Iqbal, 'The Advent of Islam in Kashmir', *Research Biannual*, Vol. 1, No. 1, R.P.D. (1976), p. 46.

32. *Baharistan-i-Shahi*, f. 34b.

33. Ibid., ff. 48–56a.

34. Mohibbul Hasan, *Kashmir*, pp. 107, 108, 162n, 220.

35. Ibid, p. 286n.

36. Srikanth Kaul ed., *Rajatarangini of Jonaraja* (Hoshiarpur, 1967), stanzas 571, 573, 576.

37. For the arrival of different groups of Saiyids in Kashmir, see Ibid.; Saiyid 'Ali, *Tarikh-i-Kashmir*, ff. 9a–11a; *Baharistan-i-Shahi*, R.P.D. No. 691, ff. 10a–b, 12b, 13a–b.

38. See, for example, *Baharistan-i-Shahi*, ff. 15a–16b; Saiyid Ali, *Tarikh-i-Kashmir*, ff. 10b–12b, 28. Interestingly enough, Ibn Battuta tells us that the Indians address the Arabs as Saiyid. See *Rehla*, trans. by Mahdi Husain (Baroda, 1953), p. 128.

39. *Rajatarangini* (Dutt), p. 57.

40. Ibid., p. 59

41. Srivara, *Jaina-Rajatarangini* (Dutt), p. 67.

42. Ibid., pp. 236, 319.

43. Ibid., p. 320.

44. This question has been discussed at some length in M. Ishaq Khan, *Perspectives on Kashmir: Historical Dimensions* (Srinagar, 1983).

45. So popular was Persian with the Pandits, that they composed hymns and prayers to their deities in the Persian language rather than in Sanskrit. See M. Ishaq Khan, 'Persian Influences in Kashmir in the Sultanate Period', *Islamic Culture* (Jan. 1977), pp. 1–9.

46. It is interesting to note that appointment to government service was accepted as a Pandit's traditional occupation for census purposes. See *Census of India*, Vol. 24, Jammu and Kashmir State, Part 2, Jammu, by Ram, Anant, Hiran and Raina, 1933; also *Imperial Gazetteer of India*, Provincial Series of Jammu and Kashmir (Calcutta, 1909), p. 39.

47. Huxley, visiting Kashmir in the 1920s, remarks: 'The Kashmiri Pandit has a more than Spanish objection to manual labour.' Quoted in T.N. Madan, *Family and Kinship* (Bombay, 1965), p. 25.

48. Whereas the Hindus call her Lalleshwari, among Muslims she is popularly known as Lal Ded and Lalla Arifa. Though she was a Śaiva preacher of the fourteenth century seeking to remove the manifold abuses that had crept into the socio-religious life of Kashmir, Lalla seems to have gained immense popularity among the masses for her revolt against Brahman supremacy.

49. That the caste system existed among the Hindus of Kashmir before the advent of Islam in the Valley is testified by the reference to *Varnashrama*, *Chaturavarna*, and *Sudra* women in Jonaraja's *Rajatarangini* (Bombay, 1896),

Stanzas 922, 924, 1080. Srivara also refers to low caste men. See *Jaina-Rajatarangini*, 1, St. 39, quoted in N.K. Zutshi, *Sultan Zain al-'Abidin of Kashmir* (Lucknow, 1976), p. 174. His observation regarding the adoption of 'blamable practices' by men belonging to the four castes is sufficient proof of the disintegration of the caste system under the influence of Islam.

50. *Kuliyat-i-Shaikh-ul Alam*, 1, C.A.P. (1979), pp. 16, 26, 33, 50, 54, 56; 2, pp. 51–7.

51. Ibid., 2, pp. 14, 24, 26, 28, 31, 33, 35–40.

52. Ibid., 1, pp. 26, 33, 35, 50; 2, 82–5.

53. Ibid., 1, pp. 78, 117–20; 2, 51–7; also B.N. Parimoo, *Unity in Diversity*, C.A.P. (1984), pp. 169ff.

54. M. Ishaq Khan, *Perspectives*, pp. 3–5, 131–2.

55. Ibid.

56. For a contrary view, see Mohibbul Hasan, *Kashmir*, p. 235; see also A.Q. Rafiqi, *Sufism in Kashmir*, pp. 212–13.

57. Mohibbul Hasan, *Kashmir*, p. 255.

58. Graves bearing bilingual inscriptions in Sanskrit and Persian are still extant in Srinagar. It is, indeed, interesting to note that Stein refers to a sale-deed executed as late as 1682, and written in both Sanskrit and Persian. *Journal of the Royal Asiatic Society* (1900), pp. 187sqq.

59. One or two verses attributed to Lalla do bear the influence of Persian, but it would be unhistorical to make out a case purely on the basis of such verses.

60. Most modern writers (Mohibbul Hasan, G.M.D. Sufi, R.K. Parmu, and A.Q. Rafiqi) on Kashmir stress the role of the Sufis from Persia and Central Asia in the spread of Islam in the Valley. Although Rafiqi belittles the missionary role of Saiyid 'Ali (*Sufism*, pp. 38–9, 84, 85), he finally concludes: 'The Islamization of Kashmir had started before the arrival of Saiyid Ali Hamadani and his followers. The advent of the Saiyid accelerated the process.' Ibid., p. 212. That Rafiqi exaggerates the missionary role of the other Sufis is borne out by his statement that their interest 'in the welfare of the people in general must have also helped them to attract non-Muslims to their Khanqahs, providing them with an opportunity to convert the non-Muslims to Islam'. Ibid.

61. Viewed from the 'orthodox' point, Islamization is a recent phenomenon in the religious history of Kashmiri Muslims, considering the fact that the religious organisations like the *Jamat-i Islami* and the *Ali-i-Hadith* urge them to give up 'Hindu' practices, such as the worship of shrines or relics, and ceremonies and rituals associated with the anniversaries of local saints.

62. Robert Redfield, *Peasant Society and Culture* (Chicago, 1956), p. 72.

63. Cited in F. Braudel, *On History* (London, 1980), p. 193.

64. Saiyid Ali undoubtedly stood for the strict enforcement of Islamic law in Kashmir. See *Baharistan-i-Shahi*, p. 25a; Haidar Malik, *Tarikh-i-Kashmir*, f. 93a; Hasan bin Ali, *Tarikh-i-Hasan*, ff. 109b–110a.

65. Redfield, *Peasant Society*, p. 72.

66. *Asrar-ul-Abrar*, f. 236a–b.

67. Among them must be mentioned Jonaraja, Srivara, Prahyabhatta, and Suka. For the historical importance of their works, see M. Ishaq Khan 'Sources

of the History of Kashmir: Medieval Period', in S.P. Sen ed., *Sources of the History of India* (Calcutta, 1979).

68. He speaks of her as 'a saintly, chaste and pure-of-heart woman from the community of Hindus (who) had stepped up on the dais of Divine manifestation'. *Majmu-ul-Tawarikh*, R.P.D. No. 14, f. 99b.

69. The Kashmiri Pandits were very proud of their literary traditions and, therefore, styled themselves as the *Ahl-i-Qalam*.

70. The earliest recorded mention of Lalla is found in Baba 'Ali Raina's *Tazkirat-ul-Arifin*, written in 1587.

71. The first Persian chronicler to take notice of Lalla was Muhammad A'zam Diddamari, who wrote his *Tarikh-i-Kashmir*, also known as *Waqiat-i-Kashmir*, in 1747.

72. Baba 'Ali Raina, *Tazkirat*, f. 37b; see also Pir Hasan Shah, *Asrar-ul-Akhyar*, Urdu trans. under the title *Tazkira-i-Auliya-i-Kashmir* (Srinagar, 1960), p. 449.

73. *Asrar-ul-Abrar*, f. 51b.

74. Lalla's verse quatrains are generally known as 'vaakh'. For a detailed discussion on Lalla's vaakh, see Kaul, *Rajatarangini of Jonaraja*, pp. 27ff.

75. Mir Saiyid 'Ali Hamadani was a staunch advocate of *Wahadat-ul-wujud*, or the doctrine of ontological monism, which has remained the sheet-anchor of the mystic orders in Kashmir. See M. Ishaq Khan, 'Islam in Kashmir: An Historical Analysis of Some of its Distinctive Features', in Christian W. Troll ed., *Islam in India* (New Delhi, Vikas, 1985), Vol. 2.

76. Mir Saiyid 'Ali was a prolific writer. But the *Aurad-i-Fathiyya* is his only compilation which has had popular appeal. It is still recited aloud with much fervour in the mosques and shrines of Kashmir. See, for further details, Ibid.

77. Jai Lal Kaul, *Lala Ded* (New Delhi, Sahitya Academy, 1973), p. 107.

78. Ibid.

79. Ibid., p. 16.

80. Ibid., p. 59.

81. The ancient name of Pampore, situated on the right bank of the Jhelum River, about eight miles southeast of Srinagar. The place is famous for saffron cultivation.

82. *Kuliyat-i-Shaikh-ul-Alam*, 1, p. 10.

83. Rafiqi rightly points out that it was Lalla 'who influenced a section of Kashmiri Muslim saints, the Rishis, through Nur al-Din'. *Sufism in Kashmir*, p. 145.

84. See, for examples, ibid., p. 149.

85. Kaul, *Lala Ded*; B.N. Parmu, *The Ascent of Self: A Reinterpretation of the Mystical Poetry of Lalla Ded* (Delhi, 1979).

86. *Tazkirat-ul-Arifin*, f. 41a–b.

87. Pir Hasan Shah, a nineteenth century chronicler, remarks: 'The Hindus say that she was one of them. The Muslims claim that she belongs to them. The truth is that she is among the chosen of God.' *Tarikh-i-Hasan*, 2, 1985, R.P.D.P., p. 113.

88. M. Ishaq Khan, op. cit., pp. 87 *passim*.
89. Ibid.
90. *Fathat-i-Kubrawiyya*, f. 147a; see also *Tarikh-i-Saiyid Ali*, p. 8.
91. *Asrar-ul-Abrar*, f. 276a.
92. Jonaraja, *Rajatarangini* (Dutt), p. 53.
93. Srivara, *Jaina-Rajatarangini* (Dutt), p. 142; *Tuzuk-i-Jahangiri*, trans. by Alexander Rogers and Henry Beveridge (Delhi, 1968), Vol. 2, pp. 167–8; Suka, *Rajatarangini* (Dutt), (Calcutta, 1835), p. 393.
94. Jaffar Badakshi, *Khulasat-ul-Manaqib*, R.P.D., No. 658, f. 20b.
95. See *Khat-i-Irshad* of Mir Saiyid Muhammad Hamadani, reproduced in original Arabic script in *Bruj-i-Nur*, C.A.P., Srinagar, pp. 81–4.
96. Bhum Sidh, Ziya Singh, and Idi Raina came to be known as Bam al-Din, Zain al-Din and Latif al-Din, respectively, after their conversion to Islam. Their ascetic practices and miraculous powers have been described at great length in the hagiographical and historical literature of the medieval period.
97. Based on my paper, 'The Concept of Holiness in Shaikh Nur al-Din's Poetry', presented at the Colloqium on 'The Concept of Holiness in Christianity and Islam', held at the Pontifical Institute of Islamic Studies in Rome in May 1985.
98. Walter Lawrence, *The Valley of Kashmir* (repr. Srinagar, 1967), pp. 287–90.
99. While leading a trekking party of the students of Kashmir University to Kounsarnag (about 90 kilometers from Srinagar) in 1976, I was warned by the local people not to partake of meat near Mahinag, a spring situated midway between Kounsarnag and Kongwattan. The sacred spring carries with it the legend of a Rishi saint. The veneration in which some other springs are still held by Kashmiri Muslims in rural areas shows a semi-animistic pattern in their social life.
100. In one of his verses, the shaikh refers to his extensive travels in the Valley. See *Kuliyat-i-Shaikh-ul-Alam*, 1, p. 64.
101. Muhammad Ahsan has identified some of the places visited by the shaikh in 'Shaikh-ul-Alam say Mansub Aham Maqamat', *Shiraza*, C.A.P., Vol. 17 (1978), pp. 61–3.
102. An album of some important places visited by the shaikh, published by the Jammu and Kashmir Cultural Academy, testifies to the historicity of his social role. See *Muraqqa-i-Aladar* C.A.P., not dated.
103. See M. Ishaq Khan, 'Concept of Holiness'.
104. This is reflected in the praises showered on the Rishis in the hagiological and folk literature.
105. Abu'l-fazl, *Ain-i-Akbari*, trans. H.S. Jarrett (Calcutta, 1868–94), Vol. 2, p. 354; see also *Tuzuk-i-Jahangiri* (Rogers and Beveridge), Vol. 2, pp. 149–50; A.A. Razi, *Haft Iqlim*, ed. by E.D. Ross *et al.* (Calcutta, Bib. Ind., 1939), f. 156a.
106. See *Rishinama*, ff. 12a–b.
107. *Asrar-ul-Abrar*, f. 236a–b.
108. Ibid., f. 72.

109. A.Q. Rafiqi, *Sufism in Kashmir*, p. 208.
110. Moti Lal Saqi, 'Kalam-i-Shaikh Aur Vedant', *Shiraze*, Vol. 17, No. 3.3 (1978), pp. 50–4, 60.
111. In one of the folk songs, even the stars in the sky are said to have derived light from Nur al-Din. Cited in M. Ishaq Khan, 'Concept of Holiness', May 1985.
112. Lawrence, *Valley*, p. 289.
113. The social significance of these festivals is discussed at length in M. Ishaq Khan, *Kashmir's Transition to Islam: the Role of Muslim Rishis* (New Delhi: Manohar, 1994).
114. For *tahar*, see also M. Ishaq Khan, *History of Kashmir*, 1978, p. 102.
115. M. Ishaq Khan, 'Islam in Kashmir', 1985, *passim*.
116. For a history of the *ahl-i ḥadīth* movement in Kashmir, see M. Ishaq Khan, *History of Kashmir*, 1978, pp. 107–9.
117. See M. Ishaq Khan, *Perspectives*, 1983, p. 2.
118. M. Ishaq Khan, *History of Kashmir*, 1978, pp. 118–22.
119. For Alan Bogue's discussion on this point, see 'Social Theory and the Pioneer', *Agricultural History*, Vol. 34, No. 1 (1960), p. 21.
120. M. Amim Kamil ed., *Nurnama* (Srinagar, 1966), Poem 12, p. 42.
121. Ibid., Poem 96, p. 91; see also Poem 217, p. 156.

16

In Search of Equivalence: Conceiving the Muslim–Hindu Encounter Through Translation Theory*

Tony K. Stewart

From the sixteenth century to the early colonial period, the region of Bengal was notable for its vibrant religious activity, which was often closely allied to political and military fortune, economic expansion, and the opening of new lands for cultivation. As population grew, the delta region became the site of numerous encounters of religious communities, not so much in the sense of active proselytizing or efforts to lay claim to a land in the name of religion, but in the considerably more casual process of individuals and groups from different backgrounds meeting as they moved into previously unsettled territories and tried to preserve something of their religion. This is especially important to remember in the study of Islam in Bengal, because of an often naive assumption that Bengal was innately 'Hindu' and then gradually converted to Islam, when, in fact, only portions of western Bengal and the periphery around the delta were initially Hindu in orientation, while much of the remaining territory was unsettled, or only sparsely settled.

This frontier territory—much of which constitutes Bangladesh and southern parts of West Bengal today—was domesticated by practitioners of one or the other tradition on a more ad hoc basis. Those areas east of the Ganga tended to yield more readily to Muslim development, because of certain explicit restrictions on Brahman settlement and the more general fact that much of that land was insufficiently domesticated for Hindu habitation of a kind favoured elsewhere. Many of the small

* Reprinted from *History of Religions* 40, no. 3 (February 2001), pp. 260–87.[1]

communities that carved their niches in the un- or partially settled land were often remote and isolated, only eventually linking to larger metropolitan trading and political networks that we assume today to be the norm in the region that is now so heavily populated. In these outposts it comes as no surprise that religious power—the ability for individuals to negotiate and impose a meaningful moral order on an often wild, unruly physical and cultural landscape—was not automatically an issue of theology or doctrinal purity, and even less so an issue of religious practice. The evidence suggests that what was deemed right was what was powerful (and vice versa), and what was religiously powerful in these regions was simply what worked to help people endure. Regardless of their background, nearly everyone in this pre-colonial period acknowledged certain forms of local and regional power, and because of this, apposite religious structures (for example, the ascetic Hindu *sannyāsī* and the Sufi pīr) operated with a kind of exchange equivalence.[2] Doctrine seems often to have had little bearing in these situations, but that in no way should imply that doctrine was not present; it was simply used and understood differently than is the academic norm today.

If we approach the development of religious belief and practice in Bengal as a function of the local, assuming that in this environment improvisation was central to survival—as it would have to be in an area without the strong institutions of more organized religion—then we must reconceive the nature of the religious encounter that characterizes the region in this pre- and early colonial period. The reason is straightforward enough: old academic models for articulating this encounter label it conflict, in which case there is little left to say except that one succeeded and the other did not; or label it as syncretism, which produces something new and different from either original part. Seldom do we see any analysis that articulates how two or more traditions in this region might encounter one another without this ontological shift in the makeup of the tradition; the change is most often understood as syncretism.

Syncretism is predicated on the assumption that pre-existing and discrete doctrinal or ritual systems are mysteriously combined to form some unnatural admixture. But the myriad forms of the concept of syncretism (when used as an interpretive, rather than strictly descriptive, category) become highly problematic in nearly all of their applications because they nearly uniformly read into past history the very institutional (ritual, theological, social) structures that are not yet present in any enduring way. This to say that the constituent parts brought together to create this syncretistic entity are historical back formations of a kind that could only be made once the tradition was successfully rooted. And precisely because the end-product is conceived as the unholy alliance of religious entities that should be kept apart in an ideal world—again because the constituent parts are idealized, essentialized, and completely stripped of their historical grounding—the focus is on the result, rather than the process, and that product is routinely described in negative terms. Until very recently, this has been the case with nearly all of the studies of Islam in the Bengali environment.[3] Ultimately, this kind of theorizing constructs models that have little or no relation to what actually happens in the course of practice, except as an arbitrary measure of deviation from some presupposed norm, a measure that is rhetorically effective for religiously committed reformers, but is highly problematic for historians.

The extensive literatures of pre-colonial Bengal, however, suggest a very different kind of religious experience, an experience that did not produce unviable end-products as syncretists would argue, but established enduring frameworks of religious organization and interpretation that eventually grounded the traditions as we understand them today in their regional forms. These encounters emphasized the local, the creative efforts of individuals trying to make sense of an environment that did not always cooperate. The textual evidence of early Bengali Islam, which must be considered potentially idiosyncratic, individualistic, and highly localized, points to very pragmatic applications of doctrine to practice, from the ragged and incomplete to very sophisticated creations. These texts portray the struggle of individuals and their groups—various persuasions of Sufis, but also Sunnis and Shi'is—to understand Vaishnavas, Śaivas, and other Hindus, but never in terms of the gross categories of Hindu and Muslim, which are the stock and trade of syncretistic formulations. These early Bengali Islamic texts document the way authors attempted to make their understanding 'fit' with those they encountered, and that process of understanding became an extended act of 'translation'.

Translation in this context defines a way that religious practitioners seek 'equivalence' among their counterparts. As will become apparent, it is this act of translation that offers an alternative interpretive strategy for conceptualizing the way these various Sufi communities formulated their understanding of the contours of power in Bengal. Because of the local nature of this religious expression, power that was translated could be effective for everyone, regardless of persuasion; by extension, we might argue that only those constructions that were translated were truly effective, and in that dynamic process of translation comes the creative application of doctrine to real life. The results of the encounter of traditions can best be appraised in the process of this interaction, and not in the static, instantiated end-product that is often falsely understood to result.

But before examining how the processes of translation can provide a model for reconceptualizing the issue, it is necessary to understand first why the concept of syncretism fails in most cases as a viable interpretive category to explain the encounter of Islam with the various Hindu traditions of Bengal. Importantly, both arguments hinge on common but complex issues of language and category formation that are shared by nearly all religious writers of the time and region.

LANGUAGE AND CATEGORY FORMATION IN THE BENGALI MIDDLE PERIOD

In the pre-modern, pre-colonial literature of Bengal, it is not uncommon to find overtly religious texts using common technical vocabularies that today we routinely identify as significant markers of sectarian affiliation. From our early twenty-first century perspective, this language allows us to categorize the orientation of these texts as Muslim or Hindu, and those categories themselves are deemed transparent and generally unambiguous to the contemporary reader. Yet many texts from the older period do not lend themselves to such easy marking, not only in the common Bengali folk genres such as *pāñcālī* and *pālā gān*, but in romance and semi-epics, and even certain overtly religious speculations and instructional manuals. Among the latter, it is Sufi literature that is perhaps most difficult to interpret because of the mixture of technical and non-technical terms from sometimes unexpected sources. Other less overtly religious genres have adopted similar lexical strategies, so the analysis of the Sufi approaches should yield insights into the full range of forms.

Many of today's scholastically oriented, as well as many of the general educated populace, judge these texts by holding them to a standard of value that equates a purity of language to a purity of religious intention. Therefore, these Sufi and related texts are all-too-frequently deemed so problematic that they are not seriously examined as documents of a Bengali Islam. For many modern interpreters of South Asian Islam, a text is often assumed to be unworthy of study when the technical vocabulary for key theological concepts suggests anything other than a consistent use of a strict and unambiguous Islamic vocabulary that is derived from Urdu or Persian (and ultimately from Arabic). A text that mixes Islamic vocabularies with others, especially those apparently Hindu, can be acknowledged in only a limited way, if at all, and is more often simply avoided as a perhaps well-intentioned, but somehow confused, or at least confusing, and therefore a potentially dangerous, work. The effect of this approach is to divert the gaze from an important formative dimension of the history of Bengal. This negative result is further exacerbated when the depiction of Islamic life found in some of these texts appears to overlap with other religious traditions—again especially various modalities of Hindu religion—or when its praise extends to specific religious figures, mythical or historical, who are promoted or shared across these boundaries (e.g., Satya Pir). More problematic yet, is the espousal of opposing sectarian ethical or religious systems of value that appear at least on the surface to be transparently the same in their working effect (e.g., *adab* and *dharma*). In today's highly charged political climate, where language and religion and politics are often aligned to define mutually exclusive identities, the reason for this response is actually rather unambiguous: for most contemporary interpreters, whether in Bangladesh, India, Pakistan, or the West, the concept of religious encounter—which this shared vocabulary and shared experience imply—is almost automatically understood in terms of ideological 'contest', if not conflict. Such an understanding pits two opposing groups in eternal enmity, these rigid, monolithic constructs playing a very important role in nearly all theories of their interaction. Historically, however, this has not always been the case.

Because of the nature of this commonly held pre-supposition about the exclusive nature of religions and religious experience, the contemporary interpreter is generally blind to the fact that this attitude is itself the result of historical processes that have conflated religious orientations with political identities in the colonial and post-colonial periods. Since the reform movements of the late eighteenth and nineteenth centuries, starting with the Wahhabis, but eventually including others of different religious persuasions, a general and very unreflective assumption in the intellectual (and certainly the political) community of Bengal has gradually taken hold: people routinely assume that when an author uses a specialized vocabulary to talk of religious matters, that author is making a political statement about his religious intentions.[4] Since the mid-nineteenth century, it has become increasingly difficult to declare a religious preference without declaring a political proclivity, if not a clearly demarcated identity, because of the various state-imposed institutions that have historically conflated the two. This was especially precipitated in the effects of the first census taken in 1872 and then translated into other state apparatuses, such as domestic law and parliamentary representation, which guaranteed separation of religions as a standard for public polity.[5] An overt religious declaration or the equally obvious choice of technical language to speak of significant issues is now generally assumed to signify a political orientation that reveals the author's 'real' or underlying intention in writing a religious work.

But today the possibility of ever precisely determining 'authorial intent' is moot, with most modern analysts arguing that no matter what an author claims, the reader can never really know, or in the extreme, the author cannot know, fully what he is about, thereby making any estimate of intention little more than informed speculation. Speculation such as this often reflects more the concerns of the interpreter and his world. In its worst case, it can produce an outright epistemological impasse for analysis.[6] While this debate about intentionality generally focuses on fiction, it has important ramifications for other forms of writing, especially where religious values are articulated. So whenever a religious text uses a mixed language that seems to confuse 'proper' religious ideals—ideals that are determined in advance by these nineteenth- and twentieth-century standards of purity and exclusion—the pre-colonial author is judged to be either confused or just ignorant. Alternatively, his work can comfortably be ignored in a way that allows the text to be manipulated toward the ends of the interpreter. Either way, the text seems to disappear from public view as an independent document with any historical or intrinsic value.

In his pioneering Bengali literary histories, Muhammad Enamul Haq (Beng. Muhammad Enamul Hak) catalogued Muslim writers from this early period, classifying their works into genres such as *śarā-śarāyit* (legal and moral codes), *kāhinī* ('historical tales'), *sṛṣṭitattva* (cosmogony), *darśana* (theology and philosophy), *sūphītattva* (Sufi metaphysics), *premopākhyāna* (romance literature), *marsīyā* (lamentations), *itihāsika-kāvya* (historical poetry), *rūpaka* (rhetoric), *padāvalī* (lyric poetry), and a miscellaneous category for leftovers.[7] He did much the same for Sufi literature in his *Baṅge sūphī prabhāva.*[8] It is significant that in those early works, an entire class of religious literature was simply eliminated, texts that were to his eyes a hodge-podge of Sufi, Vaishnava, Natha, general *tāntrika*, and other religious ideas, both mainstream and not. It is easy to speculate that these texts were omitted precisely because in their language they failed to fit the exclusive categories he had constructed. Not surprisingly, their apparent hybridity was problematic for those construing religious or ideological purity as a litmus test for inclusion in a 'proper' literature, and just as problematic for a 'national' literature as well, both impulses applying to the Pakistan in which he wrote.[9]

Among those omitted texts, and therefore worthy of additional scrutiny, were two books called *Āgama* and *Jñānasāgara* by one Ali Raja, one of which will retain our attention for detailed analysis.[10] These books, often paired as two parts to a single book, present a sophisticated and systematic theology, grounded in an extensive cosmology that serves to justify the yogic mode of Sufi practice. The contemporary literary historian Ahmad

Shariph considers Ali Raja, whose precise dates are uncertain, to be one of the most significant thinkers of the eighteenth century, with a metaphysical acumen equal to the great Vaishnava scholar, Kṛṣṇadāsa Kavirāja, or the Muslim scholar Haji Muhammad.[11] Ali Raja (alt. Rājā, Rejā, Riḍā), who also wrote under the alias of Oyahed Kanu Phakir, was a Sufi from the village of Ośa Khāin, Anoyara District, in (Chittagong), whose family still claims a tract of land there. He had for his *murshid* and initiating *dikṣāguru* the famous Śāh Keyamuddin, and in that association he wrote extensively: in addition to the two above-mentioned works, a book of meditations put to music titled *Dhyānamālā*, and the speculative *Sirājkulupa*. He was also a poet of some stature, with no fewer than 47 of his *padas* surviving, all of which are on the theme of Radha and Krishna's love.[12] His sons were also authors of some note.[13]

All of this suggests that Ali Raja was a fairly prominent member of the Islamic literati around the prosperous region of Chittagong, who left a significant literary and religious legacy—yet Muhammad Enamul Haq's original classification scheme could find no comfortable place for his metaphysical works. It was only much later that Haq reluctantly recognized Ali Raja and others like him in his English *A History of Sufi-ism in Bengal*, where, as an obvious afterthought, he tacks on two short chapters at the end of his book to create a new category called 'Muslim Yoga Literature'. This reflects a more discrete and somewhat more neutral acknowledgement of its 'hybrid' or 'admixed' character noted previously by Abdul Karim, who had published Ali Raja's *Jñānasāgara* nearly a half century earlier.[14] By creating a separate category of syncretistic labels for this literature, Haq and his followers have operated on the assumption that these authors were engaged in an intellectual and religious activity that was somehow fundamentally different from what other 'mainstream' authors did; that writers like Ali Raja were trying to create a new religious identity or praxis that was perhaps ingenious, but ultimately confused. With this assumption hinging on Ali Raja's use of an explicitly non-Muslim vocabulary, the literary gaze is turned to works of perceived greater value. But if we begin with a different proposition about his use of this non-Islamic vocabulary, assuming that it was a search for equivalence, or an attempt to articulate sophisticated ideas of their own by using the locally available lexicon with its limiting conceptual structure, these texts suddenly come alive as examples of Islamic expansion in an entirely new mode, a linguistic and cultural appropriation, not an Islamic dissipation.

Before attempting to classify by genre the texts of Ali Raja and others like him, and automatically implying in that classification a value judgement, we might fruitfully start one step earlier in the hermeneutic process by asking ourselves about the availability and limits of language in the historical time and place of these texts. It becomes clear that no unambiguously Islamic idiom existed in Bengali during that time, or at least it was only beginning to emerge by the end of the period. Such specific Islamic technical vocabulary would not prevail until sometime later, largely with the development of institutional infrastructures, and even that language—in spite of attempts by certain factions to identify a 'Musalmani' Bengali—has never been, nor could it be, completely 'pure' in ideational terms. The reason it cannot be pure in exclusively Islamic terms is that the Bengali language itself has its roots in Sanskrit, which has been the bearer of a traditional culture that operates according to assumptions common to the religious traditions of the Hindus, and of course Jains, Sikhs, early Buddhists, and others. It has been well documented that religions and languages share many features as formal, open-ended, semiotic systems, regardless of how that structural similitude is construed.

For our purposes, one of the most relevant points of convergence is the ability of both language and religion to capture, preserve, and reify basic cultural values, to structure experience according to shared conceptual elements. Language of course is not religion, but the two rely heavily on each other in this process of articulating what is of value. Language itself structures the conceptual world of any culture to the point where certain thoughts cannot be entertained in a given language, and those structures that prevail in a language will reflect what is significant to its host culture.[15] Importantly, religion is often the most pronounced articulator and repository of those key structures of meaning and value, and in its use of texts—whether oral or written—language becomes the medium of religious experience. Any analysis should, then, account for the ways that Bengali Muslims chose to use this Bengali language that has from its inception been imbued with a religious or ideational sensibility that is other than Islamic.

The problem was not simply that these authors were attempting to use the Bengali language to express ideas that were not in the Bengali language's original conceptual structure, for many of the key concepts that control an Islamic cosmology and theology were in fact present (and this, as will become apparent, is vitally important to our strategy of interpretation). Precisely because these concepts were present—even though the terms frequently carried or at least implied additional conceptual entailments alien to Islam as an extension of the term's semantic field—Bengali offered a potentially malleable medium for the message of Islam. This is to say that the ideas were not so alien that they could not be expressed in the extant vocabulary of the sixteenth, seventeenth, and eighteenth centuries. Importantly, that Bengali should be so used is paramount to the Islamic conception of its own message, for Islam claims for itself a transnational and universal status. Muslim practitioners argue that the sublime object of their religious world is transportable across all national and cultural boundaries, and that its tenets can be conveyed in any language (in spite of the caveat that the Holy Qur'an can only be in Arabic). Had this not been so, Islam would have remained exclusively limited to Semitic language speakers in a tightly confined geographic area; yet Islam has been a vibrant force in South Asia for well over a thousand years, and in Bengal for a good portion of that. Given the developing nature of the language during the pre-modern period, coupled with the proposition that the language itself structures the very ideas being conveyed, we might not unreasonably ask how a Muslim author can use Bengali successfully to convey his religious sensibility, without compromising his commitments or inadvertently changing Islam itself. To answer this question may be the first step in determining what constitutes a distinctively Bengali Islam, as opposed to the more usual strategy of measuring Islam in Bengal against some essentialized ideal. The few extant Sufi texts are among the most extensive Islamic Bengali documents of the formative period, capturing the struggle of these early practitioners as they tried to articulate a Muslim vision in the local vernacular, a language that bore the weight of centuries of Hindu adaptation.

THE PROBLEM OF SYNCRETISM

The language of the texts composed by the likes of Ali Raja, especially the technical vocabulary, appears to our contemporary sensibility to be largely Hindu, perhaps most obviously in the yogic terminology. But that appearance only disguises to our modern eyes what were thoroughly Islamic conceptions. Most interpreters characterize this language as somehow 'hybrid' in character. Hybridity is only one version of the larger interpretive strategy that hinges on the concept of 'syncretism'. The model of syncretism is never simply applied to the language itself, but—and this is one of its biggest flaws—operates on the assumption that the language transparently and faithfully reflects the traditions behind the language, and not just their conceptual structures. The analysis, therefore, almost imperceptibly shifts from language to tradition, naively extrapolating the form of religion from its limited expression in texts. As it has been used in the history of religions, this model of syncretism assumes that two distinct entities—in these examples, 'Islam' and 'Hinduism', as if those were somehow truly monolithic entities—were brought together to form a new construction that shared parts of both, but could be classified as neither.[16]

This concept of syncretism is ultimately faulty as an interpretive model, for two closely related reasons, which have been hinted above. First, syncretism assumes at the outset its own conclusions, in a curious form of the logical fallacy of *petitio principii*, by articulating the inappropriate alliance of two things that are in their essential form mutually exclusive and distinct from each other. For example, early Bengali Sufism and yogic meditation in ecstatic practice do not 'naturally' belong together just because they have been defined as such. Second, the unstated object of the model of syncretism is its end-product, pointing to the creation of some kind of static 'entity' that, by virtue of its violation of exclusive categories, is inherently unstable. This model, which conveniently sidesteps any attempt to understand the process by which these seemingly disparate or disjunctive religious beliefs and practices interact, is forever damned to project unseemly (i.e. 'impure') entities that cannot reproduce themselves (i.e., are not viable), if in fact they are anything more than the product of the scholastic imagination in the first place. It is the way this end-product is articulated that reveals the problem most vividly, because any resort to interpretive models of syncretism appears on the surface to produce neutral descriptions that are never direct or precise: they are always metaphoric and value-laden. And the metaphoric constructs not only free the interpretor from examining syncretism itself, but generally reveal their almost universally negative implications. The metaphors, which only hint at underlying processes, imply that the resulting form is unnatural, and therefore unstable, if not doomed to eventual destruction.

There are four basic categories of metaphor that control these images, each of which demonstrates how the underlying notion of invalidity is disguised but omnipresent: [1] influence and borrowing; [2] the overlay or 'cultural veneer' [3] alchemy; and [4] organic or biological reproduction.[17]

Borrowing and Influence

Often not even understood as a form of syncretism, the economically-derived metaphor of 'borrowing' suggests that members of one group (here Sufis, in Bengal especially the Chishti and Naqshbandi) are not sufficiently creative or independent to think for themselves and must take prefabricated ideas or rituals from somewhere else (here Hindu, largely Vaishnava theology, or from yoga in modalities of meditative practice) to articulate its truths. Of course, with his limited understanding the borrower inevitably uses them improperly, that is, *not* as they were 'meant to be used'. Similarly, the astrologically based metaphor of 'influence', originally emanations from the stars and planets, is understood to exert mysterious unseen forces, often articulated through sophisticated hydraulic metaphors, causing someone or some group to be persuaded without fully understanding why. The explanation then suggests that volition was absent in the decision-making process, which thinly disguises the borrowing metaphor, making one group dependent, passively receptive, and therefore of less value than the source. For example, the Sufi poets of this early age could only imagine their religious path in already well-developed yogic terms.

'Cultural Veneer' or Overlay

Another common metaphor of syncretism is that of 'cultural veneer', an overlay of one alien culture on another, which in our examples is inevitably an imported Islam overlaid onto a Bengal that is assumed to be Hindu. While giving the appearance of accounting for historical change, since Ḥindus were assumed to be there first, the resulting amalgam describes no process, but a static condition, an end result. The entailment of the metaphor, however, is decidedly pointed with respect to an obviously anticipated result, for veneers are generally thin layers of fragile ornamental wood or other material bonded to a foundation that is coarse and sturdy. Subject to delamination, the veneer is easily damaged or destroyed, that is, it is impermanent, while the permanent base continues to function as it always had, perpetrating a not-so-subtle political commentary by the choice of metaphor. Occasionally this approach is articulated as the 'false mask', with many of the same entailments.

Alchemy

Alchemy is arguably the most popular metaphor of syncretism, one that secondarily shares in the hydraulic metaphor of influence, while maintaining a chemical basis of interaction and reaction. The combinations that can be forged in the alchemical crucible produce either permanent change or reversible temporary conditions. Understood as bad or quack science, the irreversible combination of fluids or the dissolution of a compound results in a solution created in a process that is construed as dangerous. Such daring processes create new entities that often have little or no use, and can in fact be fatal to those who come into contact with them, as religious reformers are quick to point out. The more common alchemical model of syncretism, however, is the 'mixture', a colloidal suspension of two ultimately irreconcilable liquids that will inevitably separate, or the admixture of solids that with little effort will disintegrate. In both versions of this more commonly conceived mixture of religious beliefs and practices, the parts retain their unique identities, implying that their essences are unchanged and their concoction little more than a momentary juxtaposition.

Biological Model

The biological is arguably the most persuasive model of syncretism: two or more contributing 'parents' produce through miscegenation an offspring that cannot be classed with either parent (even Manu invokes this image to explain the multitude of *varṇa* designations); equally often the offpsring is a 'bastard' of unacknowledged provenance, e.g., the mother was raped by some unknown assailant. The potentially inflammatory nature of this kind of metaphor lends itself to an obvious polemic. When the offspring's characteristics are identifiable to a parent, the 'mixture' metaphor is subsequently invoked, and those features understood to be dominant—that is, its 'real' characteristics—come through. If the product is blended in such a way that dominant features from both parents are incorporated, it is a hybrid (plant) or half-breed (animal), again classifiable with neither source. But the negative entailment of the hybrid metaphor is that these offspring do not reproduce because they are sterile, or if they manage to reproduce, they do not 'breed true', that is, most will disaggregate in one or two generations.

None of these models of syncretism adequately characterizes the process by which the religious practitioner actually encounters the other and addresses it, leaving those processes to the imagination invoked by the metaphor itself, while focusing its analysis on the ostensible end-product, itself a metaphoric creation. And, of equal import, each of the models of religious syncretism carries in its metaphor the implicit expectation of failure, falsity, or impermanence, a decidedly negative valuation in every case. The only possible exception is the occasional good alchemical solution or the rare hybrid that does manage to reproduce. On the whole, the models presuppose essentialized, dehistoricized, monolithic entities that interact in ways that cannot be described directly, but only metaphorically. The conclusion is that they are unnatural and inappropriate, not only in their original category formation, but also in the entailments of the metaphors themselves. Further, the evidence that is marshalled to make the arguments for syncretism is largely linguistic, punctuated by the occasional physical monument or record of ritual, but predicated on the all-too-easy assumption that the language of these texts transparently and directly reflects experience and practice. This assumption uncritically, although not necessarily intentionally, extends the original Whorfian hypothesis (i.e., that language reflects categories of meaning) to the instantiation and reification of religious traditions that are at best idealized constructions of the material. The reader can see in the passage below how seductive and easy it is to apply these models, which should in itself give pause. So to offer an alternative that does not naively assume that the language of the text is a literal replica of religious belief or practice, we must return to the initial language through which we understand these early Bengali Sufis and other Islamic practitioners and theologians. I would like to propose a different interpretive strategy that would refocus the question onto the active dimension of these texts, their authors, and their consumers, to account for their 'process of production', rather than describe the static end-product of this complex and challenging cultural and religious interaction.

In contrast to the model of syncretism that proposes to describe the new amalgam created by these Sufi texts, I would propose that we can reconstruct a process by which the pre-modern Sufi or other Muslim writer, working within the constraints of a Bengali language whose extant technical vocabulary was conditioned largely by Hindu ideational constructs, attempted to imagine an Islamic ideal in a new literary environment. These texts become, then, historical witnesses to the earliest attempts to think Islamic thoughts in the local language, which is to construct new thoughts for Bengali, ideas that had never previously been explicitly expressed, as shown by a lack of explicit vocabulary to support them. In order to express their ways of imagining the world, we must assume that these Muslim authors did not 'borrow' terms but, in a more intellectually astute process, sought the closest 'terms of equivalence' in order to approximate the ideas they wanted to express. Put another way—and here the direction of this method should become clear—these early Bengali Islamic authors 'translated' their concepts into the closest locally available terminology as a step toward articulating a different kind of religious orientation. But as we shall see, terminology is not just words, but entire conceptual worlds, metaphoric worlds. If we assume that the authors were fully cognizant of what they were doing, i.e., they were not confusing Islam and various traditions of Hinduism, then we can see that while appearing to write in their own language (Bengali), they were in effect *translating* into that language ideas and concepts that were at least somewhat alien to it. Eventually, a technical terminology derived from

Persian and Arabic would take its place in the Bengali of the Muslim author—a vocabulary that would prove formidable in size and effect.[18] In the earliest stages of this process, which date to the sixteenth to eighteenth centuries, that particular technical terminology was not a common or widely agreed-upon part of the Bengali language, so the texts from this period illustrate the initial experiments of these innovative and adventurous authors. In short, translation itself can become the model for interpreting these texts, for different styles of translation imply, if not explicitly dictate, systematic decisions regarding the act of translating. That is, translation theory can illustrate the complexity of the process. What follows is an all-too-brief outline of the proposed approach, based on an extended close reading of single passage of an eighteenth-century Bengali Sufi text.

'TRANSLATION THEORY' AS HERMENEUTIC MODEL

All translation is a search for equivalence, but the kind of equivalence sought is dictated by the nature of the concept being translated from the source language (SL), and the desired result in the target or receiving language (TL). In our examples, however, the language appears at first glance to be just Bengali, but in this pre-modern period, it is the special relationship of Bengali to its 'parent' languages, especially Sanskrit, that makes this 'translation' possible. In this pre-colonial period, when a Bengali author wished to speak technically about matters of religion, economics, medicine, or any specialized branch of knowledge, he tapped Sanskrit for its rich and precise vocabulary, often appropriating words and phrases *in toto* without modification. This special diglossia, which was marked by the learned who were frequently multilingual and could shift easily from Bengali to Sanskrit—or more often, who used a highly Sanskritized Bengali in complex acts of 'code-switching'—gradually enriched the Bengali language to the point where it could express ideas that previously had only been possible in Sanskrit itself.[19] The process was quickened by the numerous translations of Sanskrit epics and other works that had been commissioned by various royal patrons during the fifteenth through eighteenth centuries, translations such as the *Mahābhārata* and *Rāmāyaṇa*, the stories of the *Bhāgavata* and other *Purāṇas*.

When the first authors of distinctly Islamic texts began to write in the vernacular—something that apparently was considered unnecessary at first, since the language of the courts was generally Persian, considered a more appropriate vehicle for the lofty ideas of Islamic scholarship—most of the Bengali technical terminology and its concommitant conceptual structures were of Sanskrit origin. Problematic was the fact that the conceptual structure these Sufi authors were seeking to translate derived ostensibly from Arabic, actually primarily through Persian, but decidedly not Bengali. Interestingly, Bengali speakers in general, and especially Bengali Muslims, resisted the domination of the higher languages of the Muslim élite, unlike vernacular speakers in other regions that underwent the Islamization process.[20] This is borne out today by the role of language played in the independence of Bangladesh in 1971 and how that functioned as a unifier of diverse peoples. Consequently, after several centuries of active use of Bengali by Muslim authors, the situation is different for the users of the language, for Bengali enjoys what Bakhtin would call a polyphonic relation to the languages of its high culture (Sanskrit, Arabic, Persian, and even Urdu).[21] Before that level of adaptation could occur, however, the initial move was to seek appropriate, albeit apparently not altogether comfortable, terms of equivalence.

Relying on contemporary translation studies, we can isolate a number of often radically different formal approaches to this search for equivalence that can account for many, if not all, of the incredible linguistic manipulations found in these early religious texts, such as Ali Raja's. Religious encounter seen as translation, however, is not just an act of utterance followed by the emotional, political, and ideological conflict of conversion. Ultimately, it reveals a movement of *accommodation* by the receiving or target language and the culture it represents, which when sufficiently pursued, eventually becomes an act of *appropriation*, the target language incorporating fully the new terms and concepts that result from this encounter. This process is patently different from syncretism. The act of incorporating what is alien ultimately changes its host—and here is where we can trace some of the processes of religious change, the making of a Bengali Islam. For example, the Muslim pīr and his teaching are not just accepted as legitimate expressions of Bengali religiosity; when appropriated into the language and culture, the image of the pīr has actually had an effect on analogous, that is, 'equivalent', theological and institutional structures of Hindus by modifying their images of the holy man. This process is especially obvious in the Vaishnava case, where the power of the pīr was more readily recognized because of strong theological affinities, among other factors. The initial act of this Muslim encounter with a Hindu religious figure leads the authors to search for some kind of parallel or analogue in an effort to find an equivalent term or concept. For example, *sannyāsī*, *vairāgī*, etc., signify the original term's common features as found in 'pīr', a strong match in the semantic fields of the term and its gloss.

But as the terms of equivalence are actively used, the target language concept—in this example, the Hindu holy man—slowly yields to a dialectic of differentiation with the alien concept, in this example, the pīr. Gradually, the alien term and its concept are incorporated as similar to, but uniquely distinct from, its analogue, so that today 'pīr' and 'sannyāsī' are both recognized as Bengali words with related but distinct meanings. When the 'translation' is successful, the new term becomes a part of the target culture's extended religious vocabulary, and carries with it, or at least points to, another conceptual world. Yet this process of seeking equivalence invariably leaves out some of the original idea, while introducing new ideas into the equation. Ortegay Gasset captured something of the paradox inherent in the effort to express the thoughts of one language and its culture in those of another:[22]

> Two apparently contradictory laws are involved in all uttering. One says, 'Every utterance is deficient'—it says less than it wishes to say. The other law, the opposite, declares, 'Every utterance is exuberant'—it conveys more than it plans and includes not a few things we should wish left silent.

Like languages, when religious traditions encounter one another, they translate, and when they do, they inevitably observe this paradoxical rule of discursive transformation. This is a creative and improvisational act, which enriches and strengthens both participants; but this dialectic is uneven, and it does not automatically or predictably lead to a strange new creation, but augments the existing entities, enriching all.

To impose some logical order on our analysis of these varying processes, we will briefly sample four different strategies of increasing complexity that are in evidence in Ali Raja's text and others like it, although it would be easy to multiply the numbers: [1] formal literal equivalence, [2] refracted equivalence, [3] dynamic equivalence, and [4] metaphoric equivalence.[23] Let us turn, then, to Ali Raja, to look at a snippet of the *Āgama* text that deals with cosmogony.[24]

THE FOUNDATION OF CREATION: THE METAPHYSICS OF LIGHT (NUR-TATTVA)

> In the beginningless space, the prime mover and creator (*karatā*) alone existed. The Stainless One (*nirañjana*) was a creamy essence in the thick of the enveloping universe of bleak inertia (*tama guṇa*). When the one called Stainless rent the interior of that orb, he transformed into the Lord Iśvara. Forms (*ākāra*) began to differentiate within that universe and the unitary formless (*nirākāra*) metamorphosed into seventy-one forms. When the formless (*nirākāra*) assumed form, the Stainless (*nirañjana*) took the

name of Vishnu. The blazing effulgence (*ujjvala*) of the formless (*nirākāra*) quickened the formed (*ākāra*); and the darkness enveloped the blazing light with its dazzling colors: white (*sattva*), black (*tamaḥ*) and reddish-orange (*rajaḥ*) were latent and undifferentiated. No one could distinguish among the three qualities (*guṇa*) what was pleasing.

When the unsegmented universe was segmented into parts, consciousness (*cetana*) drifted in the primal waters. Emotional Being (*bhāva*) inferred its own existence within those primal waters. As it laboured to unite (*yoga*) with the Lord, it experienced the essence of love (*prema rasa*). No part (*kalā*) can be under the control of passionate love in a form that is unsegmented. In the absence of syzygies (*yugala*, "paired opposites") the intellect (*manas*) cannot discern name [and form]. Unable to distinguish pairs, neither action nor naming can occur. Without the conjunction [of opposites], neither speech nor love is possible. When the Stainless (*nirañjana*) conceived a love for an opposing lover, consciousness (*cetana*) permeated the realm of the unmanifest (*nirākāra*). The Prime Mover (*karatā*) was concealed within the realm of creation, and through his independent immaculate power parted the waters and cleansed the darkness. From that which was without form (*nirākāra*), the formed (*ākāra*) was born as the initial sonic-form 'a'. The formless (*nirākāra*) generated the sonic-form 'u' (*ukāra*) through the sonic-form 'a'. From the union of the sonic-forms 'a' and 'u', the sonic-form 'm' (*makāra*) was born. Its power (*śakti*) was realized as [the qualities] *sattva*, *rajaḥ*, and (*tamaḥ*). The sonic-form 'm' (*makāra*) pulled himself from the waters.

Looking at himself [reflected] in the waters, he was smitten (*mohita*) with the love of a devotee (*bhakta*). As he gazed at the reflection of his own initial image (*nija ākāra*), he gained consciousness of himself, yet he remained absorbed, undifferentiated from the sonic form 'a' (*ākāra*) and the sonic form 'u' (*ukāra*). For aeons they remained coiled together as a single form, the universe of the sonic-form 'm' (*makāra*) within the sonic-form 'u' (*ukāra*) within the sonic-form 'a' (*ākāra*). The sonic-form 'm' (*makāra*) grew fiercely hot within the sonic-forms 'a' (*ākāra*) and 'u' (*ukāra*). From the unified one came the two, a paired coupled [like] the archer with his bow properly strung. The unifying single name of the triple world remained hidden, the sonic-form 'm' (*makāra*) and the sonic-form 'u' (*ukāra*) together preserving the unifying essence. The Imperishable Syllable (*akṣara*) remained in solitude within the triple forms. It was from this single Imperishable Syllable (*akṣara*) that the triple world arose.

While others more knowledgeable of the niceties of the explicit and implied cosmological systems in this not altogether transparent text may not agree with every line of my translation, there are some unmistakably distinct acts of Ali Raja's translation that we can identify, and which will in the final analysis show him to be using this vocabulary for his own very distinct Islamic objectives.

Formal Literary Equivalence

While serving as a logical starting point, 'formal literary equivalence' in practice was seldom sought in the early Bengali Muslim writings, because formal equivalence operates on the naive assumption that each idea or concept can be literally translated from the source language (SL) into the target language (TL) without addition or subtraction of meaning. In the West, this formalism has grounded nearly all classical theories and confounded more than a few interpreters over the last two millennia. But perfect one-to-one correspondences seldom existed in the materials that early Bengali Muslim writers sought to describe. This is tacitly acknowledged by its absence; on this simplistic level, perfect equivalence makes translation invisible, which is only possible for very simple, non-technical concepts. In practice, this literalism in matters of religious import functions more as an ideal generally held by the unreflective, by those who do not translate at all, or by those who wish to make a point that deliberately runs roughshod over subtlety and nuance. For example, in the Vaishnava figure Krishna Chaitanya's argument with a pīr, wherein he equates the *Bhāgavata Purāṇa* and the Qur'ān, the point is of course conversion.[25] Beyond that basic semantic level, literal equivalence loses much of its practical value because it works only for the simplest terms or for the broadest generalizations. Take, for instance, such limited concepts as recitation of the name *ḍhikr* and *japa*; but even here supposed equivalence requires immediate clarification, which is to admit its failure. While noting that this strategy is useful for setting a base line in our analysis, there is little evidence within these works that the semantic fields of religiously significant terms were ever conceived to be identical, transparent, or literally equal to their adopted equivalents. Our examples would be limited here to very general mythic constructs such as the primal waters, the chaos before order, the darkness that pervades prior to creation, all of which are vague enough to require little or no reflection until they are later manipulated. Most of the equivalences, however, are more realistically seen as 'approximations of equivalence', which leads to the more common conception of translation that today is called, among other things, 'refraction'.

Refraction and Mirroring

'Refraction theory' suggests that literalness ought not to be the main concern when locating approximations—a strategy that was historically useful for establishing equivalent grounds of meaning between Muslims and Hindus. To describe refraction, André LeFevere coined the expression 'mirroring', for a translation reflects the original idea, but refracts it in the process; that is, it does not capture the identical semantic field, but approximates it, often with distortions, the latter being key.[26] With this approach, central religious or other concepts can be established as analogues. For instance, a Hindu notion of god, Vishnu-Narayana, is held to be the equivalent of Allah, especially through the shared concept of 'stainlessness' or *nirañjana*, as Ali Raja uses the term throughout the first paragraph. This concept, explictly denoting one of Vishnu's features, resonates strongly with the equivalent characteristics of God that are enumerated in dhikr. This kind of refraction works best in those areas where obvious and overt similarities of character or action can be aligned. In this way an author can compare in general terms an institution such as the Hindu *tola* with the Islamic madrasa, or a *guruparamparā* with a Sufi *silsila*, with a certain confidence that he will not be misunderstood as equating the two; they are roughly similar in function or form, but they are not the same. Refraction theory reaches its limit of usefulness, or is prone to confusing the reader, when it reaches the point where the communities place different values on these apparently equivalent practices or expressions, especially in their specific and technical functions. To handle this differentiation, the authors turn to a more complex strategy of establishing 'functional analogs' that bear strong resemblance to the translation theories of Eugene Nida, which emphasize the term's or phrase's context.

Dynamic Equivalence

Nida, who rejects the 'literal' and 'refraction' approaches as logically formal theories that describe impractical ideals, offers an alternative in his theory of 'dynamic equivalence'.[27] Dynamic equivalence not only accounts for overlapping semantic domains, but gives priority to cultural context, which can begin to account for the different values ascribed to equivalent terms. The emphasis shifts away from the precise content and contours of the idea being translated, toward that idea as it is used in its social context, its role and function within the target language and culture, which then allows for a kind of creative latitude in seeking equivalence. Ali Raja in this short passage utilizes a *sāṃkhya*-derived terminology to describe the basic dualism that is inherent in all Islamic cosmogonic portrayals, in which the world depends on the opposition of paired elements, the syzygies (yugala), necessary for discrimination and cognition to arise. Yet, by invoking the classical *sāṃkhya darsana* or philosophical system, he instantly finds himself embroiled in its implications, especially notable here in the generation of the three guṇas: the elements of sattva, rajaḥ, and tamaḥ. While I can find nothing in the Islamic cosmogonies that corresponds directly to this concept, these are the mechanisms by which the 'unfolding' of creation takes place, a prominent Pancaratra cosmogonic concept that bears strong resemblance to the mitosis that characterizes Islamic cosmogonies, especially some of the more elaborate among Isma'ilis and others. The point is that according to Nida's suggestion, the distinctive Bengali vocabulary for creation, which is nearly universally grounded in the terminology of sāṃkhya, is the best vehicle to translate the idea of duality, even if exact matches cannot be made and the concommitant concepts blur other distinctions. Put another way, we can say that the translation is dynamic to context. There are numerous such examples from the literatures of this period that by comparison can clarify the range of the dynamic translation even further.

Vaishnavas, for instance, talk of the descent of god or avatāra,[28] figures who descend to guide the wayward back to the path of proper conduct (dharma), and as such these figures can easily be conceived as the 'dynamic equivalent' of the Islamic concept of 'prophet', or *nabī*. For the obvious reason that only Allah can be divine, a Muslim author would clearly deny as heresy that dimension of the semantic domain that designates 'divinity' for the Vaishnava term avatāra. But because prophethood functions in an Islamic environment in a way analogous to that of the avatāra, i.e., to guide people to the proper religious path, the terms could be established as parallel or equivalent. So, in response to the popular and underlying notion of 'inspired guidance', which can be found in both nabī and avatāra, authors such as Saiyid Sultan could adopt the term avatāra to describe the Prophet Muhammad, as he did with some regularity in his monumental work *Nabī Vaṃśa.*[29]

To suggest that Saiyid Sultan understood nabī and avatāra to be identical, or that this represented a shift in basic Islamic theology (a shift that would inevitably be considered a degradation and heresy), or to propose that he was constructing some kind of new hybrid or syncretistic religious modality, is utterly to misread his text, for it is clear that he did none of these. Rather, he articulated this function of inspired guidance in terms common to a Bengali-speaking world; that is, he 'dynamically translated' the idea in context. But the effect of this dynamic translation was not unidirectional, because while Saiyid Sultan may have been simply seeking a Hindu functional analogue for nabī, in choosing avatāra, he actually expanded the semantic domain of the concept of avatāra itself. In the *Nabī Vaṃśa*, Śiva and Hari and other figures become nabīs or prophets, as much as Muhammad becomes an avatāra (although their functions were differentiated). And with this exchange, the two terms become paired in the pre-modern period as twinned concepts, not identical, but sharing in that common core of meaning in specific local contexts. At the same time, Saiyid Sultan provided sectarian Vaishnavas, Śaivas, and Śaktas with a different reading of their own traditions in a way that makes them more palatable to a broader audience, and in so doing he permanently altered the conception of avatāra itself to include this somewhat expanded meaning.[30] Elsewhere, the semantic trajectories of the two terms diverge in opposing ways. Yet when Saiyid Sultan equated nabī and avatāra, or Ali Raja translated his basic dualism into sāṃkhya-derived terms, there were implications that were not always spelled out, but which pointed to a much more complex process of translating entire conceptual worlds. It is not clear just how far Saiyid Sultan was prepared to go in this direction because most of his efforts to seek equivalence in the Bengali of his day were limited to refracted and dynamic choices, but others such as Ali Raja did take the process further.

Shared Metaphoric Worlds and the Domain of the Intersemiotic

Linguistic activity that embraces more than equivalent concepts to include larger structures to negotiate the exigencies of the world, moves us into more complex acts of appropriation and assimilation that are required to transcend the purely interlingual. Roman Jakobson refers to this as the highest level of complexity, the category of the intersemiotic.[31] On the intersemiotic level of translation we find an interchange and interpolation of ideas among mythologies, between rituals that are (to a certain extent) mutually observed, and even in the fixing of translational equivalents among the parts of extended theological systems. At this stage, which is the most vexing type of translation—a cultural translation—an entire conceptual world is understood in terms of another, not just in its single terms or phrases. Because these worlds are not identical, yet admit to being understood in terms of direct or implied comparison, they are extended, complex metaphorical constructs, which can be conceived as 'shared' or 'emergent' metaphorical worlds (and we might even argue that to call it translation is itself a metaphoric leap). Linguistically, the impulse behind this analysis is what Gideon Toury has called 'polysystem theory', which attempts to extend the processes of translation to the cultural, intersemiotic level, wherein different features of culture participate in increasingly complicated, often disjunctive, systems of discourse.[32] This theory assumes that no single mode of discourse or cultural construct can account for the varieties of lived experiences or types of exchanges within which people routinely operate, and that people comfortably shift from system to system, often without reflection, depending on the situation. The system in operation is context-dependent; the domains of meaning are not limited to exclusively verbal significations; and their application is necessarily imprecise, if not inconsistent. Translation, then, will shift from purely linguistic to symbolic and other forms of cultural expression in ways that are not naively arithmetic. Different modes of translation will embody greater and lesser degrees of conformity in the same complex act, so that depending on what is being emphasized, the various dimensions of cultural expression will be more or less translated into their equivalents. If, in our examples, each expression of religiosity attempted by these pre-colonial authors is understood to participate in a range of semiotic systems, then its translation will likewise reflect these multiple referents as well. A theological term could conceivably imply, then, certain ritual actions, cosmological expectations, political allegiances, and so forth, in an ever spiralling complication as one attempts to account for the encounter of one religious culture with another through a shared language and its metaphoric and symbolic systems.

It must be remembered, however, that what is sought is not the precise equation of the parts of one symbolic or semiotic system with another in clear one-to-one matches. Rather, this overt use of an apparently alien terminology and conceptual system is an attempt to establish the basis for a common conceptual underpinning so that the matching systems and their parts are demonstrated to be coherently conceived, or at least rectifiable—hence the possibility of equivalence—while almost certain to remain inconsistent in their particulars.[33] Equivalence in this mode suggests that two conceptual worlds are seen to address similar problems in similar ways, without ever proposing that they are identical; to express one in terms of the other—the quintessential metaphoric step—remains an act of translation, not an assertion of identity or some mysterious change of allegiance on the part of the author. This might help explain how Ali Raja's attempt to articulate the cosmogony in the opening passage of the '*nur tattva*' of his *Āgama* text, can appear to appropriate wholesale a generic Hindu cosmogonic act of differentiation through the sacred syllable '*auṃ*'. When we see how he seeks to locate some measure of symbolic equivalence through comparing parallel cosmological constructs—a move that would allow him to express a Muslim truth in a language and conceptual structure that is at least nominally Hindu—the text suddenly illuminates a very different cultural and religious process. In its application, this process of translating on a higher conceptual plane can be understood as an extension of the previously noted processes, which have upped the ante of complexity. And there is in this passage an important hermeneutic move that makes clear that Ali Raja is looking for equivalence, not voicing preference for a Hindu creation scheme.

In general but precise terms, Ali Raja asserts from the first phrase of this passage the unity of the creator before creation, while noting the ineffable connection between this unity and the dualism necessary for all existent things to interact with the divine, the dualism necessary for a relationship of love to exist. This position of *tawhid* (*tauḥīd*)—which becomes clear in the passage in the second paragraph beginning with the phrase 'The Prime Mover (*kartā*) was concealed within the creation'—is wholly consistent with any mainstream Islamic theology. Yet this same ineffable connection resonates strongly with the mainstream theology of the Vaishnavas of Bengal and their emphasis on *acintya bhedābheda*—a simultaneous distinction and non-distinction between the ultimate and the created world that is cognitively unresolvable, a mystery. It is no accident, then, that he chose the already-noted use of the term nirañjana, here connecting Vishnu with Allah.[34] It is the treatment of the processes of creation through the aural power of auṃ that suggests Ali Raja's attempt to establish an analogy with common Islamic cosmogonies. In the next few lines of the text, which redescribe the process of differentiation through which the formless becomes formed, as he noted initially in the opening paragraph, the world unfolds through sonic mitosis: it is the 'a' (ākāra) that produces 'u' (ukāra), and together they generate the 'm' (makāra). Importantly, the latter two are somehow mysteriously contained with the original ākāra and are not just discrete linear unfoldings from it.

At this juncture, Ali Raja portrays the process so that it mimics a generic Islamic cosmogony, enabling direct parallels to be drawn between a number of different Sufi, and even Shi'i and Sunni, cosmogonies. The sonic transformation of creation begins with God, Allah, as represented by the character from which all characters flow, *alif*, the number one, the uncreated who creates; from that is then generated *mīm*, Muhammad, and through him eventually all of creation. Alif and the akāra, mīm and the makāra—these are the two points of action in the creation of the world, the vowel and the consonant as the progenitors of speech and the world. The ambiguous ukāra, which at first glance appears to have no immediate direct analog between alif and mīm, is not superfluous, nor is it simply glossed over. In Ali Raja's conceptual world (as noted later in this same text), creation does not move directly from Allah to Muhammad, but is mediated through an intermediate formless-form, the *nūr muḥammadī*, the nur tattva, which separates and connects the world from God, the worldly

Prophet Muhammad from his creator; it is the Muhammad of guiding light. Yet the relationship of nur to Muhammad and that of those two to Allah is vague and mysterious, yet hierarchically progressive as the individual parts of auṃ. It is Ali Raja's treatment of the ukāra that reveals his hand and makes clear his choice of symbolic homologies.

Neither the fact that Ali Raja does not spell out that connection, nor the fact that his handling of the problematic ukāra is imprecise, should be taken as a sign of an abortive attempt to fuse theologies. Rather, it is this apparent imprecision, especially in the vagueness with which the ukāra and makāra are generated from the ākara, that alerts us to his attempt to find an analogous structure within which to translate the mystery of Sufi cosmogony. Had the auṃ been presented as a progression of discrete steps followed by the all-important silence with which it symbolically closes in the traditional Hindu cosmogonies of the *Upanishads*, Ali Raja might be understood to have attempted some synthesis or even to have adopted a Hindu perspective. But his manipulation of the parts of auṃ so that they mimic and parallel the relationship of the creation through *alif* and *mīm* suggests a search for equivalence, a translation of a fundamental but complex concept into the target culture's conceptual lexicon. And precisely because it is a search for equivalence—not an assertion of positive identity—the parts must remain vague, analogous, or at best homologous.

The use of one conceptual structure to express another suggests the coming together of metaphoric worlds that operates according to a logic of both metonymic and synechdochal displacements. Accordingly, parts can be exchanged and substituted in ways that allow one cultural system (the equivalent of a source language) to interact with, and be understood by, another (the equivalent of a target language). We might conceptualize this search for equivalence taking place on the level of a cultural meta-language, a kind of conceptual hyperglossia that allows these critically important figures to speak in a conceptual idiom that brings different cultures together while acknowledging and even justifying their own independent conceptual—and in this case religious—worlds. In our last example, it is an Islamic theology that uses and appropriates a Hindu cosmology to its own purposes, explaining the 'real' meaning of the sacred syllable auṃ to an audience that might not have otherwise seen the connection, an act that is substantially apart from syncretism. At the same time it demonstrates that the truth of God's creation has been observed by Hindus, even if they did not fully comprehend it. The result is a thoroughly Islamic view of the world in a text that uses an ostensibly Hindu terminology to express it.

CONCLUSION

In conclusion, we argue that the search for equivalence in the encounter of religions—when understood through the translation models we have characterized as literal, refractive, dynamic, and metaphoric—is an attempt to be understood, to make oneself understood in a language not always one's own. It does not necessarily reflect religious capitulation, theological ignorance, or serve as the sign of a weak religious identity. A hermeneutic strategy that acknowledges the unusual linguistic and cultural confluence found in the Bengali-speaking world clearly will help to explain how so many cultural productions could appear on the surface to violate or be inconsistent with contemporary notions of the pristine ideal standards of religious exclusion, when in fact they project a coherence of conception. The texts that reveal these actors attempting to locate commensurate analogues within the language tradition capture a unique historical 'moment' in the process of cultural and religious encounter, as each tradition explores the other and tries to make itself understood. Once the translation process can be shown to have moved from the simplistic modes of seeking equivalence to the complex realms of conceptual sharing that we have designated as metaphoric in nature, the analysis must, of necessity, shift.

This current analysis seeks to describe the nature of the discourse within which new (and old) ideas are expressed through translation. Therefore, the focus has deliberately shifted away from the ontological nature of the conceptual entity that is produced—the falsely ascribed new religious idea or end-product that results from all models of syncretism—to an analysis of the conditions, both creative and constraining, within which that production, that experimentation, is possible, that is, to the way such encounter can take place. It is a shift from preoccupation with the final form to a greater understanding of the process of its creation, dramatically altering our estimation of the result of this process. From this point, any number of plausible and useful strategies may be adopted to further explain and refine this discursive activity. Looking at these texts through the model of translation should, if applied rigorously, demonstrate a different kind of social and religious interaction among the diverse populations of Bengal, not just among different groups of Hindus and Muslims. And it may well point to previously unaccounted factors that have contributed to that perspective on the world that appears to be so uniquely Bengali, an element of identity that is perhaps Bengali first, and sectarian second.

NOTES

1. A number of people have contributed to the argument of this paper since it was first proposed during the NEH Summer Seminar, titled 'Hindu and Muslim: Rethinking Religious Boundaries in South Asia' (University of North Carolina-Chapel Hill, summer 1995), which I co-directed with Carl Ernst. The paper was subsequently delivered in nascent form as the Lyman-Coleman Lectures at Lafayette College, in a seminar on religious encounter at the College of Charleston, in a seminar on pre-modern Bengali Islam at Emory University, in a religious studies seminar at the University of North Carolina-Greensboro, and finally at the Triangle South Asia Consortium's colloquium. I would like especially to thank David Gilmartin of North Carolina State University, Carl W. Ernst of the University of North Carolina-Chapel Hill, Bruce B. Lawrence of Duke University, Robin C. Rinehart of Lafayette College, Richard Eaton of the University of Arizona, Charles Orzech of the University of North Carolina-Greensboro, Natalie Dorhmann of North Carolina State University, and Charles Kurzman of the University of North Carolina-Chapel Hill, all of whom contributed substantially.

2. For more on this phenomenon, see Tony K. Stewart, 'Alternate Structures of Authority: Satya Pīr on the Frontiers of Bengal' in *Beyond Turk and Hindu: Rethinking Religious Identities in Islamicate South Asia*, edited by David Gilmartin and Bruce B. Lawrence (Gainsville: University of Florida, 2000), pp. 21–54.

3. The most sophisticated use of the problematic concept of syncretism for Bengali religion can be found in the important book by Asim Roy, *Islamic Syncretistic Tradition in Bengal* (Princeton: Princeton University Press, 1983). It was Dick Eaton's study that marked the shift away from models of syncretism to more historically nuanced and historically contextualized studies; see Richard M. Eaton, *The Rise of Islam and the Bengal Frontier, 1204–1760* (Berkeley: University of California Press, 1993).

4. The impulse to try to ignore centuries of historical change within Islam itself, and to eliminate the inevitable subtle shifts that take place when a universal religion moves into another arena—in this case, a Perso-Arabic Islam taking root in Bengal—motivates a classical fundamentalist effort to 'purify' Islam of perceived foreign accretions and to try to re-create the experience of an archaic, pristine Islam as conceived by its original founding members. The implications should be obvious.

5. See Kenneth W. Jones, 'Religious Identity and the Indian Census' in *The Census in British India: New Perspectives*, edited by N. Gerald Barrier (Delhi: Manohar, 1981), pp. 73–101; and Bernard S. Cohn, 'The Census, Social Structure and Objectification in South Asia' in *An Anthropologist among the Historians and Other Essays* (Delhi: Oxford University Press, 1990), pp. 224–54.

6. The most commonly cited individuals responsible for this shift in perspective include Barthes, Derrida, and Bakhtin. But more immediately germane is reception aesthetics, starting with that initiated by Hans Robert Jauss at the University of Konstanz, and its follow-on in reader-response criticism. The latter diverges specifically from the initial inquiries of the phenomenology of reading (e.g., Georges Poulet), and while refining certain propositions of deconstruction,

has greatly enhanced our understanding of the role the reader plays in creating the text. The text, of course, becomes a variable entity based on what the reader brings to it and how he or she understands it. There is an obvious debt here to basic hermeneutic theory, but of more specific reader-response interest is the approach adopted by Wolfgang Iser, *The Implied Reader* (Baltimore: Johns Hopkins University Press, 1974); idem., *The Act of Reading: A Theory of Aesthetic Response* (Baltimore: Johns Hopkins University Press, 1978); Peter J. Rabinowitz, *Before Reading: Narrative Conventions and the Politics of Interpretation* (Ithaca: Cornell University Press, 1987); see also the very useful anthology, Jane P. Tompkins, ed., *Reader-Response Criticism: From Formalism to Post-Structuralism* (Baltimore: Johns Hopkins University Press, 1980).

7. Muhammad Enāmul Hak, *Muslim bāṃlā sāhitya*, reprinted in *Muhammad enāmul hak racanavalī*, edited by Mansur Musā, Vol. 1 (Ḍhākā: Bāṃlā Ekādemī, 1398 BS), for summary see pp. 375–9.

8. Idem., *Baṅge sūphī prabhāva*, reprinted in ibid.

9. After Bangladesh's independence, Muhammad Enāmul Hak expanded his doctoral dissertation in English under the title *A History of Sufi-ism in Bengal* (Dacca: Asiatic Society of Bengal, 1975) and significantly appended two new chapters that included this unique literature. It is not unreasonable to imagine that he was signalling the nature of the new Bangladeshi democracy that was more inclusive than its Pakistani counterpart.

10. These texts can be found in the anthology of pre-modern Sufi texts compiled and edited by Ahmad Sharif. See Ahmad Śaripha, ed. and comp., *Bāṅlāra sūphī sāhitya: ālocanā o nayakhāni grantha sambalita* (Dhaka: Bangla Academy, 1375 BS [1969]). Abdul Karim first publicized the works of Ali Raja, and it is from the introduction to his published edition of the *Jñānasāgara* that all biographical information has been gleaned by subsequent scholars. See Abdul Karim Sāhityaviśārada, ed., *Jñānasāgara of Ali Raja*, Sahitya Parisad Granthavali no. 59 (Calcutta: Bangiya Sahitya Parasat Mandir, 1324 BS). This entire publication has been reprinted in Ahmad Śaripha, *Bāṅlāra sūphī sāhitya*, pp. 400–532.

11. Ibid., 311ff.

12. Yatīndramohana Bhaṭṭācārya, *Bāṃlāra vaiṣṇava-bhāvāpanna musalamāna kavira padamañjuṣā* (Calcutta: Calcutta University Press, 1984), pp. 43–57. Ali Raja's surviving collected output of Rādhā-Kṛṣṇa lyrics by Muslim authors is greater than all others, save two.

13. Abdul Karim provides a genealogical chart on the second page of his introduction, giving his grandfather as Mohammad Ākbar, his father as Mohammad Śāhi, his son by his first wife as Erśād Ullā Miyā, his son by his second wife as Ephāj Ullā Miyā, and another son called Sarphat Ullā Miyā. The lineage today is traced through the first son.

14. '... *hindu musalmānī bhāvera saṃmiśreṇa*'; see Abdul Karim, *Jñānasāgara*, *bhūmika*, 1.

15. The first to argue this now widely-accepted position was perhaps Benjamin Lee Whorf, *Language, Thought, and Reality*, edited by John B. Carroll (Cambridge, MA: MIT Press, 1956) and Edward Sapir, *Culture, Language, and Personality* (Berkeley: University of California Press, 1949); see also idem., *Language: An*

Introduction to the Study of Speech (New York and London: Harcourt Brace Jovanovich, 1949), esp., chs. 7–11. There are of course cognitive science specialists who challenge this view, starting with the initial formulations of Chomsky and then pushing the implications of his propositions about the predetermined nature of grammatical deep structures; see Noam Chomsky, *Aspects of the Theory of Syntax* (Cambridge, MA: M.I.T. Press, 1965).

16. Since the first modern use of the term (1615 AD), 'syncretism' has described 'misguided' attempts at reunion of the Protestant and Catholic churches, and its earliest use was to compare the 'mixed' religions of the Hellenistic and Roman eras to 'pure' Christianity. See the *Oxford English Dictionary*, 1971 compact edition, for early use.

17. For the more detailed study of this problem, which is here only summarized, see Tony K. Stewart and Carl W. Ernst, 'Syncretism', in Margaret Mills and Peter J. Claus, eds., *Encyclopedia of South Asian Folklore* (Garland: forthcoming). The analysis itself is much indebted to the understanding of the metaphors of every day speech developed by Lakoff and Johnson; see George Lakoff and Mark Johnson, *Metaphors We Live By* (Chicago: University of Chicago Press, 1980).

18. One need only consult any of the several dictionaries of 'foreign words' in Bengali to see the extent of this vocabulary, e.g., *Dictionary of Foreign Words in Bengali*, compiled by Gobindlal Bonnerjee Kaviratna, revised by Jitendriya Bonnerjee (Calcutta: University of Calcutta, 1968).

19. Sheldon Pollock has recently argued that the use of Sanskrit in the various regions often functioned as a hyperglossia (rather than diglossia), because Sanskrit cut across regional boundaries in ways that made it and its claims universal, but also because in this transcending mode, Sanskrit was the ideal vehicle for expressing what was 'really real', the most important ideas (in contrast to the vernaculars, which were used for the mundane). See Sheldon Pollock, 'The Sanskrit Cosmopolis, 300–1300: Transculturation, Vernacularization, and the Question of Ideology', in *Ideology and Status of Sanskrit: Contributions to the History of the Sanskrit Language*, edited by Jan E.M. Houben (Leiden: E.J. Brill, 1996), pp. 197–247; and idem., 'Indian in the Vernacular Millennium: Literary Culture and Polity, 1000–1500', in Shmuel Eisenstadt and Wolfgang Schluchter, eds., 'Early Modernities', *Daedalus* 127, no. 3 (1998): 41–74.

20. See Eaton, *The Rise of Islam and the Bengal Frontier*, esp. pp. 291–7.

21. Bakhtin characterizes monoglossia as the use of a single uniform language, diglossia as the complex interaction of a language and its parent, and heteroglossia as the interaction of two or more contributing parents, but which are in conflict with each other. He resorts to polyphony to describe the conflict-free use of multiple parent contributors. While analytically useful, the practical distinction between heteroglossia and polyphony seems somewhat strained, if not artificial, in this context. See Mikhail Bakhtin, *The Dialogic Imagination*, edited by Michael Holquist, and translated by Caryl Emerson and Michael Holquist, Slavic Series no. 1 (Austin: University of Texas Press, 1981); and for Bakhtin's position relative to members of his school, see Pam Morris, ed., *The Bakhtin Reader: Selected Writings of Bakhtin, Medvedev, Voloshinov* (London: Edwin Arnold, 1994).

22. José Ortegay Gasset, *Man and People*, translated by Willard R. Trask (New York: Norton, 1957), quoted in A.L. Becker, *Beyond Translation: Essays toward a Modern Philology* (Ann Arbor: University of Michigan Press, 1995), p. 5.

23. It should be noted that to use different styles of translation (explained by the underlying translation theories) as a way of conceiving the encounter of religious traditions, or to better understand the apparent encounter, is to use 'translation' as a metaphor in its most general sense indicating the expression of one thing in terms of another. This is fundamentally different from the metaphoric basis of the concept of syncretism itself, and therefore not subject to the same critique. The reason is simple: translation is an identifiable, analysable act, a concrete process that seeks to express one set of concepts in another language with a potentially different conceptual structure. Syncretism is itself a metaphor, no matter how it is construed, and generally with no identifiable process to be uncovered; indeed, the classic metaphors of syncretism serve to cover over what is not understood about the process they ostensibly seek to describe, all too often making syncretism a pseudo-explanation. To deploy translation as a model of religious encounter (i.e., to use it metaphorically) is really to use it on the metadiscursive level, not the primary level as it is used by the constructions of syncretism.

24. Ali Raja, *Āgama* in Ahmad Saripha, ed. and comp., *Bāṅlāra sūphī sāhitya*, p. 323ff. It should be noted that in the sample passage that follows, when speaking directly of the letters that compose the *bīja mantra* '*auṃ*' I have translated *akṣara/ākāra* as 'syllable' or 'sonic form'—rather than the more common gloss of 'letter'—in order to convey the aural quality of this cosmogonic act; in other places *ākāra* is translated simply as 'form'.

25. Kṛṣṇadāsa Kavirāja, *Caitanya Caritāmṛta*, ed. with the commentary *Gaurakṛpataraṅgiṇī ṭīkā* by Rādhāgovinda Nātha, 4th edn., 6 vols. (Calcutta: Sādhanā Prakāśanī, 1369 BS), 2.18.175–203.

26. André Lefevere, 'Mother Courage's Cucumbers: Text, Systems and Refraction in a Theory of Literature', *Modern Language Studies* 12, no. 4 (1982): 3–19, and his monograph, *Translating Poetry: Seven Strategies and a Blueprint* (Assen and Amsterdam: Van Gorcum, 1975); see also idem., 'Theory and Practice: Process and Product', *Modern Poetry in Translation*, 41–2 (March 1981–2): 19–27; idem., 'Literary Theory and Translated Literature', *Dispositio* 7, nos. 19–21 (1982): 3–22. In a related vein, see also J.C. Catford, *A Linguistic Theory of Translation* (London: Oxford University Press, 1965), especially the chapters on formal correspondence and transference.

27. Eugene Nida, *Towards a Science of Translating* (Leiden: E.J. Brill, 1964); see also E. Nida and C. Taber, *The Theory and Practice of Translation* (Leiden: E.J. Brill, 1969).

28. *Avatāra* is usually misleadingly translated into English as 'incarnation', but in the Hindu conception there is no '*flesh*' (*carn-*) involved, making the translation an example of 'refraction'.

29. Saiyid Sultan, *Nabī Vaṃśa* in *Rasul Carita,* edited by Ahmad Sariph, 2 vols. (Ḍhākā: Bāṃlā Ekāḍemī, 1385 BS).

30. According to Nida, this reading would in fact have to be a more complete reading on the assumption that dynamic translation is possible in the religious context because the material being translated has at its deepest level an 'invariant core' that will always manage to transfer across the language barriers in spite of the surface dissimilarities. This idea of the invariant core stems from his assertion that religious texts (which in his endeavors were limited to Christianity, especially the Bible) were inspired or revelatory, and therefore were immune to the conceptual vagaries of different languages (defying the assertions of Whorf and Sapir). This was further justified for Nida, however, by a deliberate misreading of Noam Chomsky's ideas of linguistic 'deep structures', which were avowedly not universal, even though Nida chose to read them that way. For an incisive critique of Nida's approach and misuse of Chomsky, see Edwin Gentzler, *Contemporary Translation Theories* (London and New York: Routledge, 1993), pp. 43–73.

31. Roman Jakobson argues that translation is 'intralingual' within different parts or dialects of the same language, 'interlingual' between different languages, and finally, 'intersemiotic' between different cultural signification systems; see Roman Jakobson, 'On Linguistic Aspects of Translation' in *On Translation*, edited by R.A. Brower (Cambridge, MA: Harvard University Press, 1959), pp. 232–9.

32. Gideon Toury, *In Search of a Theory of Translation* (Tel Aviv: The Porter Institute for Poetics and Semiotics, 1980); for the implications of such an approach, see the interesting essays in Pramod Talgeri and S.B. Verma, eds., *Literature in Translation: From Cultural Transference to Metonymic Displacement* (London: Sangam, 1988). See also Gentzler's critique of polysystem theory in *Contemporary Translation Theories*, pp. 105–43. A slightly different approach that seeks to quantify discretely the complex levels of translation that account for the rich cultural context can be found in the 'variational' model as described by Lance Hewson and Jacky Martin in *Redefining Translation: the Variational Approach* (London: Routledge, 1991). In this model, the highest level of intersemiotic translation involves the isolation of multifaceted 'homologons' that lead to more tightly controlled paraphrastic constructions. This seems to be a promising model for translators to conceptualize what they do, but less useful descriptively in conceptualizing the problem as I have described the encounter of religious traditions.

33. I am here following the lead of Lakoff and Johnson, who argue in their work on metaphor in every speech that the mechanics of this process can be envisioned as seeking the 'coherence' of conceptons without worrying about the consistency of the details of the expression, image, or symbol being manipulated.

34. For a summary of the *acintya bhedābheda* theory as it was adapted by the Gauḍīya Vaiṣṇavas, see Rādhāgovinda Nātha, *Gauḍīya vaiṣṇava darśana*, 5 vols. (Calcutta: Prācyavāṇī Mandira, 1363–66 BS), 1:137–43 for a brief introduction, then vols. 1–3 passim. For an English summary, see Edward C. Dimock, Jr., 'Doctrine and Practice among the Vaiṣṇavas of Bengal' in *Krishna: Myths, Rites and Attitudes*, edited by Milton Singer (Hawaii: East-West Center Press, 1966), pp. 41–63.

17

Religious Vocabulary and Regional Identity: A Study of the Tamil *Cirāppurāṇam* ('Life of the Prophet')*

Vasudha Narayanan

India is our motherland,
Islam is our way of life,
Only Tamil is our language.[1]

We emphatically say that we who live in the South are the oldest Muslims in India. We take pride in that.[2]

INTRODUCTION

Of the 2.5 million Muslims in Tamilnadu, about 1.7 million are said to be Tamil speaking.[3] This population prides itself in being descendants of people who converted to Islam while the Prophet was alive, and in thus being the oldest among the Muslim communities of India. Yet, while their spoken and written Tamil contains many Arabic and Persian loan words, it is also closely aligned with standard Tamil and borrows from Sanskrit as well, for most Tamil Muslims see themselves as participating in Tamil literary history. Muslim men and women have been among the most eminent scholars in interpreting the ninth-century Tamil *Rāmāyaṇa* composed by Kampan (known as *Iramāvatāram* or the *Kampa Rāmāyaṇam*). M.M. Ismail, the former Chief Justice of the Madras High Court and author of some forty books on the Tamil *Rāmāyaṇa*, remarked with justifiable pride

* Reprinted from David Gilmartin and Bruce B. Lawrence, eds., *Beyond Turk and Hindu: Rethinking Religious Identities in Islamicate South Asia* (Gainesville: University Press of Florida, 2000), pp. 74–97.

that in every generation there is at least one Muslim who is an authority on the Tamil *Rāmāyaṇa*.[4] Muslims also participate in the festival of Kampan, an annual celebration devoted to the scholarship on this poet.[5]

Tamil Hindus have not paid the same scholarly attention to Islamic literature in Tamil. Instead, they have encountered the Islamic tradition more on the level of myth and ritual, incorporating some Muslim saints and teachers into their pantheon, making pilgrimages to their tombs, or weaving stories of Muslim devotees into the legends of Hindu gods. For instance, Lord Ranganatha, the manifestation of Vishnu in Srirangam, has a Muslim consort, for whom there is a special shrine in the temple complex. This pattern is repeated in several other Vaishanava shrines. Performers of classical south Indian 'Carnatic' music also incorporated what were perceived to be Muslim melodies into the traditional *rāga* structure of classical south Indian music, which shows significant Persian influence.[6]

But the interactions that have shaped the distinctive character of Tamil Muslim identities have only just begun to be studied.[7] Tamil Muslim authors have expressed their understanding of Islam through a variety of literary genres that have defined both their Islamic and their Tamil identities. This essay will begin to address this complex process of identity construction by examining one important seventeenth-century text, the *Cīṟāppurāṇam*, or 'Life of the Prophet.' It will highlight the importance of literary vocabulary, literary images, and literary conventions in shaping cultural values and expectations shared by Muslims and Hindus, even in a work that aimed at underscoring the distinctive claims of Muslims to participate in a religion of foreign origins.

THE ORIGINS OF MUSLIMS IN TAMILNADU

Many Tamil Muslims claim descent from seafarers who had encountered Islam and converted to the new religion.[8] Muslims in some areas of Tamilnadu have the last name Marakkayar, which derives from the Tamil *marakkalam*, 'ship' (*marakkāyar* means 'sailors'). Although the word may possibly derive from the Arabic *markab* ('ship'), the name 'Marakkayar' attests to the Muslims' belief that their ancestors were sailors. Significantly, the Marakkayars believe that their ancestors were either Arabs who had come directly from the Middle East, or Tamil people who had accepted Islam after contact with Arab traders during the Prophet's lifetime or within a few years of the Prophet's death, but not after the conquest of north India by Muslim Turks. Command of Tamil literature and language are thus marks of their claims to an early origin that brings them close to the time of the Prophet.

Citing reports of Muslim settlements in Kanyakumari district dating from the seventh century AD, the Tamil folklorist and literary scholar K.P.S. Hamid has argued that Tamil Muslims are the oldest Muslims in India. These earliest Muslims called themselves Lappai, Marakkayar, Malumikal, and Nayinar. For Hamid, the arrival of Islam in India was thus only one part in the larger narrative of merchants who, 'with the companionship of the southeast winds and the northwest winds', took the religion to Lanka, Malaysia, Indonesia, and China. As proof, he refers to a small mosque in Tirucchirapalli (formerly Uraiyur), the capital of the Chola empire, noting that the mosque resembles Jain and Buddhist places of worship and has an Arabic inscription dating its construction to 738 AD (116 AH).[9]

UMARU PULAVAR AND HIS BIOGRAPHY OF THE PROPHET

Muslims in Tamilnadu have composed hundreds of works in the last thousand years, not all of which deal with Islam. The earliest, composed between the twelfth and the fourteenth centuries, is the *Palcantamālai* ('The Garland of Many Metric Verses'), which seems to focus on inner love, in the classical Tamil genre of *akam* poetry.[10] But this is only the first in a long line of works by Tamil Muslims. Over the centuries, Muslims in Tamilnadu have studied both secular works and Hindu religious poetry in Tamil and skillfully utilized traditional Tamil literary conventions in their religious writings. Works on Islamic themes written by Tamil authors include several *kāppiyam* (Skt: *kāvya*, epic poems), of which the *Cīrāppurāṇam*, the biography of the Prophet Muhammad analysed in this essay, is the best known. They also include descriptions of holy places like Nagore, and hundreds of devotional poems—some addressed to a goddess, others written in a mystical Sufi genre—about the Prophet Muhammad, the Prophet's grandsons, other prophets, the early caliphs, and many Muslim saints. Finally, Arabic genres have been adapted to Tamil, such as the *kissa*; in this genre, notable examples include works on Joseph and on Ali and Zaytun.

The most famous work on Islam in Tamil is the *Cīrāppurāṇam* ('Life of the Prophet') of Umaru Pulavar (Omar the Poet, d. 1703), who lived in Kilkarai, the site of many recent Tamil Islamic conferences.[11] Although Umaru's date of birth is disputed (1642 and 1665 are both claimed), there is no disagreement about his date of death, 28 July 1703.[12] Almost all that we know of his life, however, is derived from oral tradition. From this we learn that he was born in Ettayapuram,[13] the son of a dealer in spices and perfumes, and that he was a descendant of Arab merchants who had settled down in Tamilnadu.[14] Umaru's literary brilliance so impressed Cītakkāṭi (1650–1715), a Muslim philanthropist and financial advisor to the ruler of Ramnad, that he asked the poet to compose a work on the life of the Prophet.[15] Umaru then went to a respected teacher, Lappai Ali Hajjiyar, to learn about the Prophet's life from Arabic and Persian sources.[16] But because he came in Hindu dress, Umaru was not accepted by the teacher.[17] The Prophet then appeared in the dreams of both men, directing Umaru to Lappai's brother in Parankipettai.[18] According to this account, then, either Lappai Ali Hajjiyar or his brother was the poet's teacher; but in another tradition, Umaru received his ability to sing through the grace of Shahul Hamid (Nakur Cakul Amitu Antavar), the famous saint buried in Nagore.

The first public reading of the *Cīṛāppurāṇam*, according to some versions, took place after the death of Citakkati under another patron, Abdul Kasim Marakkayar, who is praised twenty-two times in the *Cīṛāppurāṇam* itself.[19] One oral tradition narrates that this patron's wife was so entranced by the poem when she heard the section on the birth (avatāra) of the Prophet that she did not pay attention to feeding her nursing child. The child then died, possibly choking to death, but the mother, entranced by the power of the poetry and not wanting to interrupt the flow of the recitation, held the dead child in her arms quietly until the poem was recited to the end.[20]

The title of Umaru Pulavar's *Cīṛāppurāṇam* is indicative of the blending of languages that emerges in its text. *Cīṛā* is the Tamil form of the Arabic *sīrah*, meaning biography, specifically a biography of the Prophet. And *purāṇa* (Tamil: '*Purāṇam*') is a Hindu literary genre that includes pious accounts of the salvific deeds of a divine being, sometimes seen as an incarnation of the supreme deity, and containing long poetic accounts of this person's wondrous qualities. Sanskrit Purāṇas deal with the creation and evolution of the world, the genealogy of the gods or divine beings, time spans in world 'history', and the history of royal families, while famous biographical purāṇas in Tamil focus on Skanda (Murukan) as well as on Śaiva saints. Calling the life of the Prophet Muhammad a purāṇa, therefore, predisposes one to have certain ideas of the central figure in the text. The combination of a foreign (here Arabic) word with a Sanskrit one in the title hints at what is to follow: the presentation of a 'foreign' religion in a language and in terms predominantly used by Hindus. The

Cīṛāppurāṇam thus incorporates Tamil literary conventions and customs and the Tamil landscape into its account of the lives of the Prophet and his family. Moreover, the author shows exquisite knowledge of earlier Hindu devotional literature in Tamil. He seems to be particularly well-versed with the ninth-century Tamil version of the Hindu epic, the *Rāmāyaṇa* composed by Kampan, as well as with the tenth-century *Cīvika Cintāmaṇi* ('Jivaka, the Wish-fulfilling Gem'), a work composed by a Jain monk that treats the love life and conquests of a fictitious hero, Jivakan.

The *Cīṛāppurāṇam* is 5,028 verses in length and is divided into three cantos—the Birth Canto ('Vilātattuk Kāṇṭam', 24 chapters, 1240 verses), the Canto of Prophethood ('Nupuvat Kāṇṭam', 21 chapters, 1105 verses), and the Canto of the Hijra ('Kicurattu Kāṇṭam', 92 chapters, 2683 verses). The work opens with salutations to God and the Prophet Muhammad, its first verse describing God as *tiruvinnun tiruvāi* ('being the *tiru* of Tiru'). Like the Sanskrit 'Śrī', *tiru* means 'auspicious', 'fortune', 'wealth', or 'sacred.' In Vaishnava literature, both Sanskrit and Tamil, one finds words strikingly similar to Umaru Pulavar's beginning words *tiruvinnun tiruvāi.* For example, the ninth-century poet Tirumankai Alvar referred to Vishnu in the town of Terazhundur as 'becoming the *tiru* of even Tiru'.[21]

The *Cīṛāppurāṇam* thus begins with auspicious words in the Tamil language. Umaru then venerates Muhammad:

> He, the Handsome one who appeared
> as the light of the *four Vedas*,
> which showed the path in the world.
> Those who keep the words of this leader
> ever in the centre of their mouths
> will be celebrated by poets
> and praised by all.
> They will know the Truth
> so that doubts are slashed
> and one's ears are appeased.
> Thoughts that give rise to evil deeds
> will go away.[22]

The commentator then expounds on the four *Vedas*: the Taurat (Torah) was given to Muca (Moses); the Capur, a special text, was given to Tavoot (David); the Iñjil (Gospel) was given to Isa (Jesus); and the Purukan (Furqan, or Qur'an) was given to Muhammad.[23] Moreover, the words that one is to keep constantly on one's tongue, the Islamic credo ('La illah illallah...') are called the *mula mantra*, or primary mantra. In such verses, the framing vocabulary is shaped by Indian religious traditions, while the exegesis is clearly Judeo-Islamic in character.

In the opening chapter of the *Cīṛāppurāṇam*, after eight verses praising the Lord and Muhammad, the poet pays his respects to the first four Caliphs, the *walī* Mukiteen (Muhyi al-Din 'Abd al-Qadir al-Jilani, 1078–1166) of Baghdad, and to his teacher Catakkatulla Appa. He reverentially places their feet on himself. The chapter concludes with a similar note of humility, as the poet expresses his unworthiness to compose this work. Beginning a work with praise of gurus and a confession of unworthiness is typical of the *stotra* (panegyric) genre in south Indian Vaishnava works in Sanskrit, such as those of Yamuna and Kurattalvan (eleventh century), and Vedanta Deśika (thirteenth century). Writes Umaru:

Like a little ant, grown weak from hunger,
exhaling its breath
in front of the squalls and gales that churn
the seven seas and storm the mountains
as though their very nature were to change, I compose my poem
in front of the exalted Tamil poets.
Line by line,
I see nothing but fault
in all that I compose.
Step by step,
the exalted poets of yore
have obtained knowledge.
To compose in front of them
is to measure the noise that comes
when I snap my fingers
with the sound of rolling thunder.[24]

We see here how Umaru gets our attention with original, simple, and unpretentious similes. In other verses of the first chapter, Umaru Pulavar pays reverence to or refers to the twin feet of the exalted teachers, references typical of Hindu devotional literature in which a poet reveres the sacred feet of his teacher or his deity.

THE TAMIL LANDSCAPE IN ARABIA: LITERARY CONVENTIONS FROM CANKAM POETRY

Like the Tamil epic poets Kampan and Tirutakkatevar, Umaru Pulavar gives extensive descriptions of the country and the city where the Prophet is to 'descend' (avatāra). This is followed by a list of the ancestors of Muhammad. Never having travelled to Arabia, Umaru gives a description of Tamilnadu transposed to Arabia. In this method, too, he has a predecessor. Kampan, the author of the Tamil *Rāmāyaṇa*, transposes the Tamil landscape to Ayodhya in north India, as when descriptions of the Kaveri river are transferred to the river Sarayu.

A standard feature of classical Tamil poetry, especially the *puram* verses—'outer' poems, which typically deal with chivalry, praise of kings, and war—was description of the wonders of a king's land. In the Tamil verses of classical (Cankam) poetry, we find roaring cascades of water, which indicate prosperity in a part of India where drought was all too common, fertile and well irrigated fields, lush fields of paddy and sugar-cane, blossoming lotuses, and bees sucking nectar from flowers redolent with honey. The waterfalls and rivers carry precious gems fallen from the jewels worn by people who bathe in them, indicating that the king's land is filled with rich people. This is also seen in a description of Lord Murukan's domain in the fifth-century (?) poem *Tirumurukarruppatai*, which speaks of cascades of falling water and hills abounding in groves with ripening fruits.[25] Cities are also described in considerable detail in Cankam literature, where we meet prosperous seaports, terraces looming like mountains, and tall palaces rising to the sky. For cities are centres of culture where bards and courtesans flourish.

In classical Cankam literature, the wealth of a nation rests on its ability to produce food, which in turn depends on rainfall. Following this tradition, Umaru Pulavar speaks of the white clouds drinking up the sea water, becoming dark and heading for land—in this case, Arabia. The clouds cover the mountains and storms rage; the storms abate, but the heavy rains continue, flooding the land. It becomes chilly. Feeling the cold and forgetting the enmity between them, a host of animals gather in one place—elephants, deer, lions, squirrels, tigers, bisons, giant lizards, monkeys, lions, spotted deer, ant-eaters, lemurs, bears, wild dogs, buffaloes, porcupines, humped bulls. Trees fall because of the high winds. Flocks of birds fly, frightened, and floods of water spill down the slopes of the mountains into the plains. The flooding streams approach the houses of the gypsy women (with wide eyes and red lips) who live on the foothills; torrents of water crash over the emerald mountains, knocking down banana and wood-apple trees. The floods sweep away gems from the mountains just as a courtesan embraces a king and sweeps away his gold, gems, and priceless pearls.[26]

Kampan, the author of the *Rāmāyaṇam*, uses the same analogy:

> Like a courtesan embracing her lover,
> his head, his body, his feet, as if in desire
> all for a minute [and fleeing with his ornaments],
> the floods embrace the peak, the slopes, the foothills,
> and sweep away everything.[27]

Compare this with these verses from the *Cīṟāppurāṇam*:

Like a courtesan embracing the mountain-like king,
giving him pleasure, and sweeping away
gold which gives us prosperity,
precious gems, pearls and all splendid things,
and flees the frontiers,
the floods flow, carrying with them all riches.[28]

This is, of course, part of the wealthy, fortune-filled land that is being described. The waters rush like an elephant. The streams, when they slow down, look like lovely girls—their white froth like white garments worn by maidens, the dark silt resembles dark hair, the fish appear like the eyes of a girl, the water bubbles seem to be like breasts, and the whirlpools circle in the shape of the navel.

These descriptions and analogies are generally necessary in Tamil poetry to prove one's mettle as a poet. Like a Vaishya merchant, the streams carry sandalwood, ivory, pearls and gems.[29] Again, listen to Kampan:

Carrying the pearls, gold, peacock feathers,
beautiful white ivory from an elephant, aromatic *akil* wood,
sandalwood, matchless in fragrance,
the floods looked like the *vaniya* merchants.[30]

And Umaru:

Carrying the fallen sandalwood, branches from the dark
akil tree,
pearls from the broken elephant's horn, white ivory,
more precious than these, red rubies, radiant in three ways,
carrying these all towards the sea,
the stream, laden [with] rich bamboo, looked like a *vaniya*
merchant.[31]

The river flows through the mountainous (*kuriñci*) land, presumably of Arabia, across the desert (a recognized category in the landscapes of Tamil poems), and into the forests. Reaching cultivated land (*marutam*), it fills the lakes, ponds, and tanks. The streams break through the lakes and approach farming lands. They sweep through the sugarcane plantations, slushing up the ponds where the fragrant lotus flowers bloom. The water is then contained and used for irrigation. The single body of water—held in many tanks, ponds, lakes, and areas where lotus blossoms bloom—is compared by Umaru to life (Tamil: *uyir*), which appears in hundreds of millions of beings, recalling the Advaitin notion that a single soul (*ātman*) appears in many forms and bodies, seeming to be many. While Umaru does not elaborate on his analogy, it is striking that he seems at home with these Vedantic ideas.[32]

Where did all these descriptions come from? Classical Tamil poetry composed in the early Christian era, and treating romantic or heroic themes, refers to five basic situations, each corresponding to five landscape settings (*tiṇai*), birds, flowers, times, gods, etc. The five basic psychological situations for *akam* or 'inner poems' are love-making, waiting anxiously for a beloved, separation, patient waiting of a wife, and anger at a lover's real or imagined infidelity. These correspond to mountainous (kuriñci), seaside (*neytal*), arid (*pālai*), pastoral (*mullai*), and agricultural (*marutam*) landscapes.[33] Although Umaru's descriptions closely resemble those found in the first two chapters of Kampan's *Rāmāyaṇam*, each poet has his own inimitable style. Reading both is like listening to the same rāga played by two maestros.

After describing the mountainous regions, Umaru Pulavar speaks of the wealth of the cultivated land and the beauty of its women. In a striking verse, he describes the farmers' worship of the sun and the earth before they sow the seeds in the field.

Wearing jewels, quaffing toddy,
    worshipping the sun with their hands, and then
    worshiping the god of their clan, milling in crowds,
Those who labour in the fields gather and praise Earth.
Their right hands shake the sprouting seeds
    and scatter them thick on the ground.
They fall like golden rain on earth.[34]

Modern Muslim commentators interpret this verse in two ways. Justice M.M. Ismail merely says that the poet is conversant with the farming practices of south India and then projects them on to Arabia. However, in his detailed exegesis of the *Cīṛāppurāṇam*, Kavi (poet) Ka. Mu. Sherip (Sherif) takes a more literal view of Umaru Pulavar's descriptions. The sort of physical landscape described in the *Cīṛāppurāṇam*, he argues, can actually be found in Yemen; similarly, the planting practices mentioned by Umaru may well have existed in Arabia before the time of the Prophet.[35]

In classical Tamil poetry, a flourishing land is filled with voluptuous and bejewelled women who participate in the sowing of the seeds and walk through the well-tilled, fertile fields. And so, too, writes Umaru:

With twin eyes made red by drinking palm-toddy,
with slender bamboo-like shoulders heaving,
the women walk with drunken steps,

swaying softly like a swan.
Their feet tread the well-tilled land.
Mud splashes on their breasts,
which soar like the tusks
of a lusty elephant.
Their breasts, speckled with slush,
look like the tender buds of lotus flowers
swarming with tiny bees.[36]

There are half a dozen verses like this, describing women's teeth, their coral-like lips, their virtuous demeanour, etc. While these descriptions may seem somewhat startling in a work that purports to narrate the life of the Prophet, the phrases and general tone of the verses are almost standard fare in any self-respecting Tamil poem.

Umaru Pulavar also follows the conventions of Tamil poetry in describing the city of Mecca. Tirutakkatevar, the author of the Jain epic poem *Civika Cintāmaṇi*, and Kampan described towns and urban culture with great poetic skill and in considerable detail, as in the case, for example, of Kampan's description of Mithila, Sita's home city. Following this tradition, Umaru Pulavar describes the city of Mecca, beginning with a number of Tamil/Hindu cosmological details:

The isle of the woodapple
is the eye for the seven lands.
The fair land of Arabia
is most precious to behold.
It is like priceless life
that lives within the senses.
I shall now expound in brief
on the great city of Mecca.
The expansive lakes,
filled with radiant conches,
brimming with pearls,
seem like a moat with waves.
Many kinds of lotus blossoms,
filled with lustrous gems,
ring the town.
The prosperous fort appears like
a lotus flower with golden petals.
Wealth and luxurious fortune
ever increase in this prosperous town...
The city of Mecca appears
like the gem on the sacred head
of the King of Serpents [Adi Sesa].[37]

The city resounds with the activities and noises of busy urban life—chariots, horses running swiftly, elephants trumpeting like thunder, such that even the sea is afraid of making noise.

This is the standard city of Tamil poetry. Almost every literary convention in the description of the prosperous city is included in Umaru Pulavar's portrait of Mecca. Occasionally, too, the poet refers to Hindu deities. For example, Lakshmi, the goddess of good fortune, reigns victorious at the portals of the house of Abu Talib.[38] But allusions like this—e.g., references to the path of Manu, the generosity of Surabhi, the wish-fulfilling cow, etc.—recall a 'By Jove' uttered by a Christian: no attempt is made to incorporate Hindu deities within the world view of Islam, either positively or negatively. On the other hand, by using established tropes of classical literature, Umaru manages to incorporate the Prophet into a Tamil world that is shared by both Muslims and Hindus.[39]

THE CHAPTER ON FATIMA'S WEDDING

Umaru Pulavar uses other Tamil literary conventions with equal skill. The long chapter on the wedding of 'Ali to the Prophet Muhammad's daughter, Fatima (*Pāttimā tirumaṇap paṭalam*), contains a beautiful description of 'Ali's procession through the city of Medina, paralleling Kampan's description of Rama's procession through Mithila in his *Rāmāyaṇam*. Here is Kampan's description of the women of Mithila rushing to get a glimpse of Rama:

> Women, their hair adorned
> with flowers soaked [with honey],
> swiftly thronged around.
> Not seeing their hair that loosened and cascaded down,
> Not heeding their waist-belts that broke loose,
> Not pulling up the flower-soft clothes that slip away,
> Not pausing to rest their tired waists,
> they closed in [on Rama].
> Coming close they cried, 'Make way, make way'.
> Women who lend splendour to the city
> swarmed around him like bees tasting honey.[40]

Similarly, the young women of Medina, wearing bejeweled anklets and waist-belts like Tamil women, overflow from balconies trying to catch a glimpse of 'Ali, the handsome bridegroom. And when they see him, they are filled with longing and wonder: Is all this charm and beauty to be monopolized by just one woman? Writes Umaru:

Their hair, adorned by flowers
fragrant and fresh, dripping honey,
spilled out from their constraints.
Like many moons flowering on the ocean,
young maidens thronged around.[41]

Umaru's descriptions of their breasts and hair suggest an erotic mood, appropriate for a wedding; indeed, the very sight of 'Ali fills the young women of Medina with longing and makes them pale from lovesickness. This, too, is found in Tamil literary conventions, as in the pallor a woman experiences when she is parted from her lover or husband.

Finally, one notes that in all these descriptions Umaru, who comes from and lives on the seashore, lavishly deploys metaphors pertaining to the sea:

Eyes like darting fish,
necks exulting like conches,
teeth like white pearls, smile
through parted lips,
which flash like corals.
With golden skins growing pale with longing,
flowers loosened like shining foam,
A sea of women swarms thick
without any gap between them.[42]

Apart from literary conventions, the poem utilizes many words found in Hindu literature in Tamil. In Tamil texts written in the first five centuries of the Christian era, the *Vedas* and the *Upanishads* were called *maṛai*, which means 'hidden, that which is a secret, a mystery'. And Umaru, too, uses this term, as well as the 'Veda', to refer to the Qur'an. Another synonym for the *Veda* is *śruti*, Sanskrit for 'that which is heard.' We can certainly see how apt is Umaru's use of the word 'śruti' in reference to the Qur'an, which was heard by Muhammad. Similarly, the deity who revealed the Qur'an to Muhammad—'Allah' in the Arabic text—is called by Umaru '*Śrutiyōṉ*', or 'he of the Śruti.'

What did these words mean for the Hindus writing in Tamil? Several philosophers, especially those from the Nyaya ("Logic") and Mimamsaka school, had already discussed the term 'Veda' in some detail, while Vedanta teachers including Ramanuja, the most important Śrivaishnava teacher, had clearly discussed the transhuman nature of the Sanskrit *Vedas* in commentaries on the *Vedānta Sutras*. All schools of thought agreed on the transcendental aspect of the *Vedas* and their authoritative nature, though they differed on what was meant by the transhuman (*apauruṣeya*) nature of their composition. The followers of the Nyaya school believed that God was their author; and since God was perfect, the *Vedas* were infallible. The Mimamsakas, on the other hand, starting from at least the second century BC, maintained that the *Vedas* were eternal and authorless.[43] The Vedic seers (*ṛṣi*) saw the *mantras* and transmitted them; they did not compose them. Referring to the Qur'an as the *Veda*, therefore, includes at least some of these meanings as understood in Hindu writings.

Other theologically loaded words are found in the *Cīṛāppurāṇam*. For instance, the birth of the Prophet is referred to as an avatāra ('descent': '*Vilāttattu kāṇṭam, Napi avatāra paṭalam*'), the term used in Hindu theology to refer to the incarnations of Vishnu, who descended into this world 'to save the good and destroy evil' (*Bhagavad Gīta* 4: 8). In Tamil literature, too, the term is not generally found in reference to the birth of human beings. Its use for the Prophet Muhammad, therefore, exalts him above the human level. The Prophet is also called the '*tiru tūtar*', 'sacred messenger', from the Sanskrit *dhūta* ('messenger'). While the word is used in both secular and sacred language, in Hindu religious literature it is Krishna who, during the Mahabharata war, is associated with the word *dhūta* and is frequently called 'Pandava dhuta', or 'the messenger of the Pandavas'. Muhammad's mother is called the abode of dharma, another term frequently found in the *Cīṛāppurāṇam*. The use of this religious vocabulary thus helped to shape a distinctive Tamil appreciation of Islamic theology. While not implying any sort of self-conscious accommodation to Hindu ideas, this vocabulary provided the conceptual framework within which much of the Prophet's life was explained and understood.

None of this means, of course, that such writings provided a charter for Muslim and Hindu participation in common ritual practices. To the contrary, at least on the level of popular practice, it was more common for Hindus, in spite of their general lack of interest in Islamic literature, to incorporate Muslim holy men into their devotional exercises than the reverse. As Susan Bayly has demonstrated, Muslim saints and their shrines came to be important sites in the Tamil sacred landscape, frequented by Hindus and Muslims alike.[44]

The significance of a work such as the *Cīṛāppurāṇam* lies in a different direction; it illustrates how the generic conventions of Tamil literary production have defined a framework for Muslim participation in the Tamil religious world. This was the case even though the focus of devotion was a figure who lived in a foreign land, the Prophet Muhammad. On the one hand, as a sīrah, or life of the Prophet, the *Cīṛāppurāṇam* linked Tamil Muslims to a world of devotion to the Prophet whose boundaries were far wider than either Tamil vocabulary or Tamilnadu. On the other hand, the poet Umaru's claims to recognition depended on his skill in manipulating a Tamil devotional idiom defined by the text's claim to be a generic *purāṇam*. The conventions and vocabulary of the text thus rooted devotion to the Prophet in a Tamil conceptual world—a world shared by both Hindus and Muslims—and in this way helped construct a framework for identities that were simultaneously Muslim and Tamil.

MODERN IMPLICATIONS: THE TESTIMONY OF TAMIL SONGS WRITTEN BY MUSLIMS

Analysis of the *Cīṟāppurāṇam* provides historical perspective on the more recent claims by many Tamil Muslims to superior status *as Muslims* because of the antiquity of their connections to Tamilnadu. Like their early links to Arabia, familiarity with Tamil literary conventions provides evidence of their comparative antiquity as an Indian Muslim community. Tamil Muslims had, of course, long adapted Arabic and Persian forms of literature to Tamil genres, and they showed reverence to Muslim saints from other parts of India and the Middle East. At the same time, they did not identify strongly with Muslims in the rest of India, whether in Kerala, Hyderabad, or the north, whose place in Muslim India was not of comparable antiquity. Nor did the trauma of Partition seem to affect the deep south of India.

Yet the logic of this position has been challenged by the rise of Hindu nationalism. The belligerent stance taken by some Hindu nationalists in the 1980s and 1990s has called into question the self-perceptions of Tamil Muslims and prompted a growing sense of insecurity among them. Their anger, sorrow, and bewilderment—as well as their increasing identification with Muslims from other parts of India—have now surfaced in public in new Tamil Muslim songs sold in pre-recorded audio cassettes. Packaged along with standard songs glorifying Muhammad and Mecca are songs that are very patriotic, some filled with distress, others with rage. These cassettes go under titles such as 'Makkanakar Mānapi' (Great Prophet of Mecca), 'Makkāvai Nōkki' (Looking towards Mecca), or 'Paḷḷivācalil kūṭuvōm' (Let us gather at the gates of the mosque). The lyrics of two songs from 'Makkanakar Mānapi' suggest the new frameworks for identity:[45]

Song 1
India is our motherland,
Islam is our way of life,
Tamil is our language...
Who is it who said we are enemies?
Our forefathers worked and fought for freedom,
Muslims fought to get rid of the nation's sorrow.

Song 2
I swear on the earth,
I swear on the heavens,
I swear on the mother who bore me,
I swear on God who created [all].
We will not lose our faith as long as we are alive,
We will not weaken in resolve as long as we are alive.
Leaving the Land of India, forgetting its glory,
We will not flee in fear,
We will not flee in fear of anyone.

This is the land where Muslim kings ruled
for eight hundred years.
Say, does anyone have this pride [of rulership]
other than us?
We have never betrayed this country.
Muslims have served this land without end.
Our crowd rose first to seek freedom.
That is why blood began to flow in Kerala.
Will my heart forget the sacrifice of the Mappilas?
We will make countless sacrifices again for the country.
Think of the sacrifice of Bahadur Shah, who ruled Delhi
when enemies gave him his son's head on a platter.
There is no one equal to us in devotion (*bhakti*)
to the country.
He was born as the brave son of Haidar, Mysore's king...
Tipu gave his life in war.
He tried hard to free his mother country,
He bore endless grief in the British prisons.

Two strategies are visible from these verses. One is an alignment with Muslims from all over India, and not just the south (though the southern emphasis is evident in the references to the Mappilas and Tipu). Second, the verses remind the listeners of the sacrifices made by Muslims all over India during the Independence movement. Since the simplistic war cry of the aggressive Hindu is to tell the Muslim to go to Pakistan, the Tamil Muslim songs emphasize that India is their home. This patriotism is woven with songs on the Islamic faith.

The songs suggest a new aggressiveness and hardening of religious boundaries, as Hindus and Muslims compete for the right to speak for the nation. Yet they also suggest the ways in which popular literary or musical genres continue to define a common identification with Tamil language, even as they shape new conceptions of difference. Although far removed from the shared generic literary conventions that defined the *Cīṟāppurāṇam*, the language of these songs projects another type of shared generic convention—a devotionalism, now linked to country, that is rooted in a long heritage of devotional poetry shared by both Hindus and Muslims. Indeed, it is telling that many of the audio cassettes on which these songs appear were categorized by the stores that sell them, along with songs in praise of the Prophet, as simply 'Muslim devotional (*bhakti*) songs'.

NOTES

All translations in this essay are mine, except when otherwise noted. Tamil words are transliterated according to the style accepted by the Tamil Lexicon.

1. Song from a Tamil cassette, '*Makkanakar Mānapi*', see note 45.
2. K.P.S. Hamitu (Hamid), 'Tennakattil Islāttiṉ tonmai', *Islāmiyat Tamil Aṟāycci Māṉāṭu* (Research Conference on Islamic Tamil) (Tiruccirapalli: Islāmiyat Tamiḻ Ilakkayat Kaḻakam, 1973), 1: 50–1.
3. *Statistical Abstract: India 1990* (Central Statistical Organisation, Ministry of Planning, Government of India), p. 33; see also *Muslim India* 2, no. 1 (January 1984), p. 18, quoted by Syed Shahabuddin and Theodore P. Wright, Jr., 'India: Muslim Minority Politics and Society', in John L. Esposito ed., *Islam in Asia* (New York: Oxford University Press, 1987), p. 167. According to Shahabuddin and Wright, the total number of Muslims in Tamilnadu in 1981 was 2.5 million.
4. Interview with Justice M.M. Ismail, July 1993.
5. Looking through the programs on the debates and discussions in the Festival of Kampan held between 1991 and 1993, one finds names like Parveen Sultana, Abdul Khader, Abdul Karim, etc. among the participants.
6. In music, the terms 'Muslim' and 'Hindu' *rāgas* are misnomers; we may more accurately speak of Indian and Persian forms of music. Because geographic origin was often associated with religious affiliation (the word for Muslim in Tamil is *tulukka*, from 'Turk'), music from Persia was characterized as Islamic. Also, it has occasionally been claimed, though not yet demonstrated, that Sufi writings in Tamil influenced Tamil Siddha poetry.
7. Paula Richman discusses possible reasons for the neglect of Islamic Tamil literature in the appendix of 'Veneration of the Prophet Muhammad in an Islamic *Pillaitamil*', *Journal of the American Oriental Society* 113, no. 1 (1993), pp. 57–74. The encounter between Hindus, Christians, and Muslims in Tamilnadu and Kerala has been discussed in Susan Bayly, *Saints, Goddesses and Kings* (Cambridge: Cambridge University Press, 1989). See also David Shulman, 'Muslim Popular Literature in Tamil: the Tamimančari Malai', in Yohanan Friedmann, ed., *Islam in Asia* (Jerusalem: Magnes Press, 1984), 1: 174–207.
8. Interview with Justice M.M. Ismail, July 1993. See also Mattison Mines, *The Warrior Merchants: Textiles, Trade, and Territory in South India* (Cambridge: Cambridge University Press, 1984), and Bayly, *Saints, Goddesses and Kings*.
9. K.P.S. Hamitu (Hamid), 'Tennakattil Islāttiṉ tonmai', p. 51.
10. Ma. Mu. Uvais (Uwise), *Islām Valartta Tamil*, pp. 16–17, quoting Vaiyapuri Pillai, *Tamil Ilakkiya Vaṟalāru-14ān nūṟṟāṇṭu* (Chennai [Madras]: Ulakat Tamiḻāṟāycci niruvanam, 1984), p. 335.

11. On the maritime importance of Kilkarai, and its being home to many prominent Muslims, see Bayly, *Saints, Goddesses and Kings*, pp. 81–5.

12. Ma. Mu. Uvais (Uwise), 'Cīṛāppurāṇamum Umarappulavarum', in M. Ceyyitu Muhammatu 'Hasan', ed., *Cīṛāppurāṇam* (Chennai [Madras]: Maraikkayar Patipakkam, 1987), p. v.

13. K. Zvelebil, *Lexicon of Tamil Literature* (Leiden: E.J. Brill, 1995), p. 721.

14. Uvais (Uwise), 'Cīṛāppurāṇamum', p. v. His father's name was probably Sheikh Muhammad 'Ali, which was changed to Ceku (Sheikh) Mutali, this being a respectful suffix added to the names of Hindu devotees. It is noteworthy that Umaru's father's name was transformed in this way. Others say his name was Mappilai Mukammatu Nayinar.

15. For a discussion of Cītakkāṭi, whose real name was 'Abd al-Qadir, see V. Narayana Rao, David Shulman, and Sanjay Subrahmanyam, 'On the Periphery: State Formation and Deformation', in *Symbols of Substance: Court and State in Nayaka Period Tamilnadu* (New Delhi: Oxford University Press, 1992), pp. 292–304.

16. Zvelebil, *Lexicon*, 721. Uwais (Uwise), 'Cīṛāppurāṇamum', p. viii, gives the teacher's name as Catakkatulla Appa, as does Umaru himself.

17. Zvelebil, *Lexicon*, p. 721.

18. Uvais (Uwise), 'Cīṛāppurāṇamum', p. viii.

19. Ibid., p. xii.

20. Zvelebil, *Lexicon*, p. 722.

21. *Tiruvukkum tiruvākiya; Periya Tirumoli* 7.7.1. Interestingly enough, this town was the birthplace of Kampa<u>n</u>, who wrote the Tamil *Rāmāyaṇa*. It is striking that Umaru Pulavar, of course knowledgeable about the Tamil *Rāmāyaṇa*, begins his poem with the very words used to describe the deity of the place where Kampa<u>n</u> was born.

22. *Cīṛāppurāṇam*, 'Vilātattuk Kāṇṭam, Kaṭavuḷ Vā<u>l</u>ttu Paṭalam' (The Chapter on Praising the Lord), verse 6.

23. *Cīṛāppurāṇam*, 'Vilātattuk Kāṇṭam', part 1, ed. with commentary by Kalaimāmaṇi Kavi Ka. Mu. Sherip (Sharif), commentary on verse 6, p. 17.

24. *Cīṛāppurāṇam* 'Vilātattuk Kāṇṭam, Kaṭavul Vāltu Paṭalam' (The Chapter on Praising the Lord), verse 19.

25. Translated by R. Balakrishna Mudaliyar, *The Golden Anthology of Ancient Tamil Literature*, 3 vols. (Tirunelveli and Madras: The South Indian Saiva Siddhanta Works Publishing Society, Tinnevelly, 1959–60), 2:20.

26. *Cīṛāppurāṇam*, 'Vilātattuk Kāṇṭam, Nāṭṭu Paṭalam' (The Chapter on the Countryside), verses 2–9.

27. Kampa<u>n</u>, *Śrī Kamparāmāyaṇam, pālakāṇṭam*. Vol. 1, ed. Vai. Mu. KōpālaKirush<u>n</u>amācāryar (Chennai, 1964), 'Bāla Kāṇṭam, Āṛruppaṭalam', verse 6.

28. *Cīṛāppurāṇam*, 'Vilātattuk Kāṇṭam, Nāṭṭu Paṭalam' (The Chapter on the Countryside), verse 9.

29. *Cīṛāppurāṇam*, 'Vilātattuk Kāṇṭam, Nāṭṭu Paṭalam', verses 12–17.

30. Kampa<u>n</u>, *Rāmāyaṇam*, Bāla Kāṇṭam, Āṛruppaṭalam, verse 7.

31. *Cīṛāppurāṇam*, 'Vilātattuk Kāṇṭam, Nāṭṭu Paṭalam' (The Chapter on the Countryside), verse 12.

32. Ibid., verses 12–17.

33. To these five situations of love two more are added: *peruntiṇai* and *kaikkilai*, which have no corresponding landscape. *Peruntiṇai* indicates mismatched love, and *kaikkilai* unrequited love. For discussions of the landscapes, see A.K. Ramanujan, trans., *The Interior Landscape: Love Poems from a Classical Tamil Anthology* (Bloomington: Indiana University Press, 1967), pp. 104–12; K. Zvelebil, *Tamil Literature* (Leiden: Brill, 1975), pp. 98–9; idem., *Smile of Murugan* (Leiden: Brill, 1973), pp. 85–110.

34. *Cīṛāppurāṇam*, 'Vilātattuk Kāṇṭam, Nāṭṭu Paṭalam' (The Chapter on the Countryside), verse 26.

35. *Cīṛāppurāṇam*, 'Vilātattuk Kāṇṭam', Part 1, p. 80.

36. Literally, 'covered with six-legged beetles.' *Cīṛāppurāṇam*, 'Vilātattuk Kāṇṭam, Nāṭṭu Paṭalam', verse 30.

37. *Cīṛāppurāṇam*, 'Vilātattuk Kāṇṭam, Nakara paṭalam' (The Chapter on the City), verses 1–3.

38. *Cīṛāppurāṇam*, 'Vilātattuk Kāṇṭam, Pukairā Kāṇṭam Paṭalam', verse 2.

39. The pattern may be compared and contrasted with the incorporation of Krishna in Bengali Muslim literature, described by Asim Roy, *The Islamic Syncretistic Tradition in Bengal* (Princeton: Princeton University Press, 1983).

40. Kampan̲, *Rāmāyaṇam*, 'Bāla Kāṇṭam, Ulāviyar Paṭalam', verses 1–2.

41. *Cīṛāppurāṇam*, 'Kicurattu Kāṇṭam, Pāttima Tirumaṇappaṭalam' (The Chapter on Fatima's Wedding), verse 132.

42. Ibid., verse 134.

43. Jaimini composed the sutras in the second century BC, and Sabara commented on them around the second century AD. On the views of Jaimini, see Francis X. Clooney, *Thinking Ritually: Rediscovering the Purva Mimamsa of Jaimini*. De Nobili Research Series, vol. 17 (Vienna: De Nobili Research Library, Institute for Indology at the University of Vienna, 1990).

44. For a discussion of *dargāhs* in Tamilnadu, see Bayly, *Saints, Goddesses, and Kings*, chapters 3 and 4.

45. Music by Pallavi-Prakash, composed and sung by Mukavai A. Cini Mukammatu. Thirumaal Audio, produced by Mamar Khadhar, 48 Mannady Street, Madras 600 091.

Bibliography

A. PRIMARY SOURCES

Note: The sources cited below are representative, and not inclusive, of the large body of original materials on the subject.

Ahmad, Qeyamuddin. *Corpus of Arabic and Persian Inscriptions in Bihar.* Patna: K.P. Jayaswal Research Institute, 1973.

Alvi, Sajida. *Advice on the Art of Governance: an Indo-Islamic Mirror for Princes: Mauizah-i Jahangiri of Muhammad Baqir Najm-i Sani* [d. 1637]. Albany: SUNY, 1989.

Baillie, Neil B.E. *Digest of Moohummadan Law.* 2 vols. 1865, repr. Lahore: Premier Book House, 1958.

Digby, Simon. *Sufis and Soldiers in Awrangzeb's Deccan.* Delhi: Oxford University Press, 2000.

Elias, Jamal, tr. *Death before Dying: the Sufi Poems of Sultan Bahu* [d. 1691]. Berkeley: Univ. of California, 1998.

Goswamy, B.N. and J.S. Grewal. *The Mughal and Sikh Rulers and the Vaishnavas of Pindori: A Historical Interpretation of 52 Persian Documents.* Simla: Indian Institute of Advanced Studies, 1969.

——. *The Mughals and the Jogis of Jakhbar: Some Madad-i-maash and other Documents.* Simla: Indian Institute of Advanced Studies, 1967.

Habib, Muhammad, tr. *The Political Theory of the Delhi Sultanate, including a Translation of Ziauddin Barani's Fatawa-i Jahandari, ca. 1358–9 AD.* Allahabad: Kitab Mahal, 1960.

Hermansen, Marcia. *The Conclusive Argument from God: Shah Waliullah of Delhi's Hujjat Allah al-Baligha.* Leiden: Brill, 1996.

Hujwiri [d. ca. 1072]. *Kashf al-mahjub: the Oldest Persian Treatise on Sufism*, tr. R.A. Nicholson. London: Luzac, 1936.

Ibn Battuta [d. 1377]. *The Rehla of Ibn Battuta.* Tr. Mahdi Husain. Baroda: Oriental Institute, 1953.

Jayasi, Malik Muhammad [fl. 1540]. *Padmavat*. Tr. A.G. Shirreff. Calcutta: Royal Asiatic Society of Bengal, 1944.

Karim, Abdul. *Corpus of the Muslim Coins of Bengal, down to AD 1538*. Dacca: Asiatic Society of Pakistan, 1960.

Lawrence, Bruce B. *Morals for the Heart: Conversations of Shaykh Nizam ad-din Awliya, recorded by Amir Hasan Sijzi*. New York: Paulist Press, 1992.

Maneri, Sharafuddin Ahmad [d. 1381]. *The Hundred Letters of Sharafuddin Maneri*. Tr. Paul Jackson. New York: Paulist Press, 1980.

Manjhan [fl. 1545], *Madhumalati: an Indian Sufi Romance*. Tr. Aditya Behl and Simon Weightman, with S.M. Pandey. Oxford: Oxford University Press, 2000.

Prasad, Pushpa. *Sanskrit Incriptions of Delhi Sultanate, 1191–1526*. Delhi: Centre of Advanced Study of History, Aligarh Muslim University, 1990.

Rahman, Fazlur. *Selected Letters of Shaikh Ahmad Sirhindi* [d. 1624]. Lahore: Iqbal Academy, 1968.

Shamsud-Din Ahmed, ed. and trans. *Inscriptions of Bengal*. Vol. 4. Rajshahi: Varendra Research Museum, 1960.

Sharif, Ja'far. *Islam in India, or Qanun-i Islam: the Customs of the Musalmans of India*. Tr. G.A. Herklots. London: Oxford University Press, 1921.

Thackston, Wheeler. *Babur-nama: Memoirs of Babur, Prince and Emperor*. Washington, DC: Freer Gallery, 1996.

Varis Shah [fl. 1766]. *The Adventures of Hir and Ranjha*. Tr. Charles F. Usborne. London: P. Owen, 1973.

Wright, H. Nelson. *The Coinage and Metrology of the Sultans of Delhi*. New Delhi: Oriental Books Reprint, 1974.

B. SECONDARY SOURCES

Ahmad, Aziz. *Studies in Islamic Culture in the Indian Environment*. Lahore: Oxford University Press, 1964.

——. *An Intellectual History of Islam in India*. Edinburgh: Edinburgh University Press, 1969.

Ansari, Muhammad Abdul Haqq. *Sufism and Shari'ah: a Study of Shaykh Ahmad Sirhindi's Effort to Reform Sufism*. Leicester: Islamic Foundation, 1986.

Askari, S.H. *Amir Khusrau as a Historian*. Patna: Khuda Bakhsh Oriental Public Library, 1980.

——. *Islam and Muslims in Medieval Bihar*. Patna: Khuda Bakhsh Oriental Public Library, 1989.

Askari, S.H. *Medieval Bihar: Sultanate and Mughal Period*. Patna: Khuda Bakhsh Oriental Public Library, 1990.

Bal jon, J.M. S. *Religion and Thought of Shah Wali Allah Dihlawi, 1703–1762*. Leiden: Brill, 1986.

Bayly, Susan. *Saints, Goddesses, Kings: Muslims and Christians in South Indian Society, 1700–1900*. New York: Cambridge University Press, 1989.

Bhatia, M.L. *Administrative History of Medieval India (A Study of Muslim Jurisprudence under Aurangzeb)*. New Delhi: Radha Publications, 1992.

Bilgrami, Rafat. *Religious and Quasi-Religious Departments of the Mughal Period, 1556–1707*. New Delhi: Munshiram Manoharlal, 1984.

Brittlebank, Kate. *Tipu Sultan's Search for Legitimacy: Islam and Kingship in a Hindu Domain*. Delhi: Oxford University Press, 1997.

Bruijn, Thomas de. *The Ruby Hidden in the Dust: a Study of the Poetics of Malik Muhammad Jayasi's Padmavat*. Leiden: Rijksuniversitaet Proefschrift, 1996.

Buckler, F.W. *Legitimacy and Symbols: the South Asian Writings of F.W. Buckler*. Ann Arbor: Center for South and Southeast Asian Studies, University of Michigan, 1985.

Buehler, Arthur. *Sufi Heirs of the Prophet: the Indian Naqshbandiyya and the Rise of the Mediating Sufi Shaykh*. Columbia: University of South Carolina, 1998.

Cashin, David. *The Ocean of Love: Middle Bengali Sufi Literature and the Fakirs of Bengal*. Stockholm: Association of Oriental Studies, 1995.

Chandra, Satish. *Mughal Religious Policies, the Rajputs and the Deccan*. New Delhi: Vikas Publishing House, 1994.

Chattopadhyaya, B. *Representing the Other? Sanskrit Sources and the Muslims (Eighth to Fourteenth Century)*. New Delhi: Manohar, 1998.

Cole, Juan. *Roots of North Indian Shi'ism in Iran and Iraq: Religion and State in Awadh, 1722–1858*. Delhi: Oxford University Press, 1989.

Currie, P.M. *The Shrine and Cult of Mu'in al-Din Chishti of Ajmer*. Delhi: Oxford University Press, 1989.

Dale, Stephen F. *Islamic Society on the South Asian Frontier: the Mappilas of Malabar, 1498–1922*. New York: Oxford University Press, 1980.

Dallapiccola, A.L., ed., *Islam in Indian Regions, 1000–1750*. 2 vols., Heidelberg: University of Heidelberg, 1992.

Eaton, Richard M. *The Rise of Islam and the Bengal Frontier, 1204–1760*. Berkeley: University of California, 1993.

——. *Sufis of Bijapur: Social Roles of Sufis in Medieval India*. Princeton: Princeton University Press, 1978.

Ernst, Carl. *Eternal Garden: Mysticism, History, and Politics at a South Asian Sufi Center*. Albany: SUNY, 1992.

Foltz, Richard C. *Mughal India and Central Asia*. New York: Oxford University Press, 1998.

Friedmann, Yohanan. *Shaykh Ahmad Sirhindi: an Outline of his Thought and a Study of his Image in the Eyes of Posterity*. Montreal: McGill-Queen's University Press, 1971.

Gaborieau, Marc, Alexandre Popovic, and Thierry Zarcone, eds., *Naqshbandis: Historical Development and Present Situation of a Muslim Mystical Order*. Istanbul: Editions Isis, 1990.

Gilmartin, David and Bruce B. Lawrence, eds., *Beyond Turk and Hindu: Rethinking Religious Identities in Islamicate South Asia*. Gainesville: University Press of Florida, 2000.

Grube, Ernst J. *A Mirror for Princes from India: Illustrated Versions of the Kalilah wa Dimnah, Anvar-i Suhayli, Iyar-i Danish, and Humayun Nameh*. Bombay: Marg, 1991.

Haar, J.G.T. ter. *Follower and Heir of the Prophet: Shaykh Ahmad Sirhindi (1564–1624) as Mystic*. Leiden: Het Oosters Instituut, 1992.

Habib, Irfan, ed., *Akbar and his India*. Delhi: Oxford University Press, 1997.

Hadi, Nabi, *Dictionary of Indo-Persian Literature*. New Delhi: Abhinav, 1995.

Hardy, Peter. *Historians of Medieval India: Studies in Indo-Muslim Historical Writing*. London: Luzac, 1966.

Hasrat, Bikrama Jit. *Dara Shikuh: Life and Works*. Calcutta: Visvabharati, 1953.

Hodgson, Marshall G.S. *The Venture of Islam*. 3 vols. Chicago: University of Chicago Press, 1974.

Hollister, John Norman. *The Shi'a of India*, London: Luzac, 1953.

Husaini, Syeda Bilqis Fatema. *A Critical Study of Indo-Persian Literature during the Sayyid and Lodi Period, 1414–1526*. New Delhi: Syeda Bilqis Fatema Husaini, 1988.

Ikram, S.M. *Muslim Civilization in India*. New York: Columbia University Press, 1964.

Ishaq Khan, Md. *Kashmir's Transition to Islam: the Role of Muslim Rishis, Fifteenth to Eighteenth Century*. New Delhi: Manohar, 1994.

Jackson, Paul. *The Way of a Sufi: Sharafuddin Maneri*. Delhi: Idarah-i Adabiyat-i Delli, 1987.

Jackson, Peter. *The Delhi Sultanate: a Political and Military History*. Cambridge: Cambridge University Press, 1999.

Jones, Dalu. *A Mirror for Princes: the Mughals and the Medici*. Bombay: Marg, 1987.

Khan, A.D. *History of the Sadarat in Medieval India*. vol. 1: Pre-Mughal Period. Delhi: Idarah-i Adabiyat-i Delli, 1988.

Lawrence, Bruce B. *Notes from a Distant Flute: The Extant Literature of Pre-Mughal Sufism*. Tehran: Imperial Iranian Academy of Philosophy, 1978.

MacLean, Derryl N. *Religion and Society in Arab Sind*. Leiden: Brill, 1989.

Matthews, D.J. and C. Shackle. *An Anthology of Classical Urdu Love Lyrics*. London: Oxford University Press, 1972.

Matthews, D.J., C. Shackle, and Shahrukh Husain, *Urdu Literature*. London: Urdu Markaz, 1985.

McGregor, R.S. *Hindi Literature from its Beginnings to the Nineteenth Century*. Wiesbaden: Harrassowitz, 1984.

Metcalf, Barbara D., ed. *Moral Conduct and Authority: the Place of Adab in South Asian Islam*. Berkeley: University of California Press, 1984.

Moosvi, Shireen. *Episodes in the Life of Akbar: Contemporary Records and Reminiscences*. New Delhi: National Book Trust, 1994.

Morgan, David and Francis Robinson, eds., *The Legacy of the Timurids*. Delhi: Oxford University Press, forthcoming.

Mujeeb, M. *The Indian Muslims*. London: Allen & Unwin, 1967.

Mukhia, Harbans. *Historians and Historiography during the Reign of Akbar*. New Delhi: Vikas Publishing House, 1976.

Nanji, Azim. *The Nizari Ismaili Tradition in Hind and Sind*. Delmar, New York: Caravan Books, 1978.

Nizami, K.A. *Akbar and Religion*. Delhi: Idarah-i Adabiyat-i Delli, 1989.

——. *The Life and Times of Shaikh Farid-ud-din Ganj-i-Shakar*. Delhi: Idarah-i-Adabiyat-i Delli, 1955.

——. *The Life and Times of Shaikh Nasir-ud-din Chiragh-i-Delli*. Delhi: Idarah-i-Adabiyat-i Delli, 1991.

——. *Some Aspects of Religion and Politics in India during the Thirteenth Century*. Aligarh: Aligarh Muslim University, 1961.

——. *Studies in Medieval Indian History and Culture*. Allahabad: Kitab Mahal, 1966.

Pritchett, Frances, *The Romance Tradition in Urdu: Adventures from the Dastan of Amir Hamzah*. New York: Columbia University Press, 1991.

Qureshi, I.H. *The Muslim Community of the Indo-Pakistan Subcontinent (610–1947)*. Hague: Mouton, 1962.

——. *Ulema in Politics: a Study Relating to the Political Activities of the Ulema in the South-Asian Subcontinent from 1556 to 1947*. 2nd edn., Delhi: Renaissance Publishing House, 1985.

Qureshi, Regula Burckhardt. *Sufi Music of India and Pakistan: Sound, Context and Meaning in Qawwali*. New York: Cambridge University Press, 1986.

Rizvi, S.A.A. *A History of Sufism in India*. 2 vols. New Delhi : Munshiram Manoharlal, 1978.

——. *Muslim Revivalist Movements in Northern India in the Sixteenth and Seventeenth Centuries*. New Delhi: Munshiram Manoharlal, 1965.

——. *Religious and Intellectual History of the Muslims in Akbar's Reign, with Specific Reference to Abul Fazl, 1556–1605*. New Delhi: Munshiram Manoharlal, 1975.

——. *Shah Wali Allah and his Times: a Study of Eighteenth Century Islam, Politics, and Society in India*. Canberra: Marifat Publications, 1980.

——. *A Socio-Intellectual History of the Isna 'Ashari Shi'is of India*. New Delhi: Munshiram Manoharlal, 1986.

Roy, Asim. *Islamic Syncretistic Tradition in Bengal*. Princeton: Princeton University Press, 1983.

Russell, Ralph & Khurshidul Islam. *Three Mughal Poets: Mir, Sauda, Mir Hasan*. Delhi: Oxford University Press, 1969.

Shackle, Christopher, and Zawahir Moir. *Ismaili Hymns from South Asia: an Introduction to the Ginans*. London: SOAS, 1992.

Schimmel, A. *Classical Urdu Literature from the Beginning to Iqbal*. Wiesbaden: Harrossowitz, 1975.

——. *Islam in the Indian Subcontinent*. Leiden: Brill, 1980.

——. *Islamic Literatures of India*. Wiesbaden: Harrassowitz, 1973.

——. *Pain and Grace: a Study of Two Mystical Writers of Eighteenth Century Muslim India*. Leiden: Brill, 1976.

Sharma, Sri Ram. *The Religious Policy of the Mughal Emperors*. 3rd edn., New Delhi: Munshiram Manoharlal, 1988.

Siddiqi, Iqtidar Husain. *Islamic Heritage in South Asian Subcontinent*. Jaipur: Publication Scheme, 1998.

Siddiqi, M.H. *The Growth of Indo-Persian Literature in Gujarat*. Baroda: University of Baroda, 1985.

Titus, Murray. *Indian Islam: a Religious History of Islam in India*. London: Oxford University Press, 1930.

Troll, Christian, ed. *Muslim Shrines in India: their Character, History and Significance*. Delhi: Oxford University Press, 1989.

Vaudeville, Charlotte. *A Weaver Named Kabir*. Delhi: Oxford University Press, 1993.

Wade, Bonnie. *Khyal: Creativity within North India's Classical Music Tradition*. New York: Cambridge University Press, 1994.

Wink, Andre. *al-Hind: the Making of the Indo-Islamic World*, Vol. 1, *Early Medieval India and the Expansion of Islam, 7th–11th Centuries*. Leiden: Brill, 1990.

——. *al-Hind: the Making of the Indo-Islamic World*, Vol. 2, *The Slave Kings and the Islamic Conquest, 11th–13th Centuries*. Leiden: Brill, 1997.

Index

jamā'at-khana (Sufi hospice), 250, 265. *See also* khānqāh
Jamal Khan (Mahdawi commander), 160
Jami' mosque, in Ajodhan, 265, 269
Jan-i Janan, Mirza Mazhar (Sufi shaikh), 58–60
Jaswant Singh (noble under Aurangzeb), 140
Jat (community), 270, 272:
pre-Muslim religion, 279
relationship with Rajputs, 270, 276
rise from low-caste sudras to zamindars, 270, 272, 279
struggle with Mahmud of Ghazni, 270
Jaunpur, 183:
captured by Bahlol Lodi, 185
Hindavi love story from, 180, 183
Islamic tradition in, 232
Muslim conquest of, 235
Sultanate of, 184
Jaunpuri, Saiyid Muhammad (founder of Indian Mahdawiyah), 119, 150, 151
Jayanaka (*Prithvīrāja Vijaya*), 42
Jews, Qur'an on, 51
jihād ('religious striving,' moral or political), 118, 157, 164:
against Hindus, 137
Jinnah, M.A. (leader of Pakistan movement), 12
jizya (tax on non-Muslims), 134, 143, 145n, 171:
abolition of, 118, 119, 122, 125, 130, 133, 138–9, 142
and reimposition of, 118, 123, 141, 142
economic motive for, 135–6
exemption from, 136
objections to, 143
and the state, 133–43
Jonaraja (Kashmiri chronicler), 345

Kabir (mystical poet), 65
Kachru, Birbal (Kashmiri chronicler), 348
Kakatiya (dynasty in Andhra), 91–2, 99, 102, 103, 109:
collapse of, 85, 87, 92, 111n
greatness of, 103
inscriptions of, 102
Kalhana (Kashmiri chronicler), 342
Kalim Allah, Shah (Sufi shaikh), 255
Kampan (author of Tamil *Rāmāyan*), 393, 394, 397–400, 402, 403
karamat ('miracle'), 241
Karbala, 316, 319, 327
karma, principle of, 75, 76, 263
Kashmir: arts and crafts in, 343–4
growth of Muslim population in, 16, 20, 21, 346
impact of Islam on, in Sultanate period, 342–56
influx of foreigners to, 342, 344–5
Islam's absorption of local traditions in, 21, 354–5
Kashmiri, Maulavi Abu'l-Hasan (Shi'i cleric), 329
Kashmiri Pandits, 345–6, 355, 360n
Kathā-Sarit-Sāgara, Nepali Sanskrit recension of, 198, 199
Kayastha castes, adopting Muslim customs, 331
Kazim, Mirza (*'Ālamgīr-nāma*), 212
Keyamuddin, Sah (teacher of Ali Raja), 369
Khafi Khan (*Muntakhab al-lubāb*), 136, 142, 211, 217
Khaki, Baba Da'ud (Sufi shaikh), 351
khalīfa ('successor'), 131n
Khalji (dynasty of Delhi sultans), 15, 38, 267:
'Ala al-Din, Sultan, 42, 45, 170, 174, 250, 252:
legend of, 43, 46
Jalal al-Din, Sultan (sultan of Delhi), 38, 174
Qutb al-Din Mubarak, Sultan, 39, 253, 254:
performance of Hindu *yagna* by, 351

Notes on Contributors

Aziz Ahmad (1913–78) was Professor of Islamic Studies at the University of Toronto.

Yohanan Friedmann is Max Scholessinger Professor of Islamic Studies at the Hebrew University, Jerusalem.

Eleanor Zelliot retired as Laird Bell Professor of History at Carleton College, Northfield, Minnesota.

Cythia Talbot is Associate Professor in the Department of History at the University of Texas, Austin.

Iqtidar Alam Khan retired as Professor of History at Aligarh Muslim University.

Satish Chandra is Secretary-General of the Society for Indian Ocean Studies.

Derryl N. Maclean is Associate Professor in the Department of History at Simon Fraser University, Canada.

Peter Hardy retired as Professor of History at the School of Oriental and African Studies, University of London.

Aditya Behl is Associate Professor in the Department of South Asia Studies at the University of Pennsylvania.

Alan M. Guenther is Research Fellow at the Institute of Islamic Studies, McGill University, Canada.

Simon Digby is an authority on medieval Indian history and Sufism in South Asia. During the course of a long career, he has worked for the Department of Eastern Art in the Ashmolean Museum, Oxford, and has also served as Honorary Librarian of the Royal Asiatic Society, London.

Richard M. Eaton is Professor of History at the University of Arizona, Tucson.

Ali S. Asani is Professor of the Practice of Indo-Muslim Languages and Culture at Harvard University.

J.R.I. Cole is Professor of History at the University of Michigan.

Mohammad Ishaq Khan is Professor of History at Kashmir University, Srinagar.

Tony K. Stewart is Associate Professor of South Asia Religions at North Carolina State University.

Vasudha Narayanan is Professor of Religion at the University of Florida.